The Routledge Social Science Handbook of AI

The Routledge Social Science Handbook of AI is a landmark volume providing students and teachers with a comprehensive and accessible guide to the major topics and trends of research in the social sciences of artificial intelligence (AI), as well as surveying how the digital revolution – from supercomputers and social media to advanced automation and robotics – is transforming society, culture, politics and economy.

The *Handbook* provides representative coverage of the full range of social science engagements with the AI revolution, from employment and jobs to education and new digital skills to automated technologies of military warfare and the future of ethics. The reference work is introduced by editor Anthony Elliott, who addresses the question of the relationship of social sciences to artificial intelligence, and who surveys various convergences and divergences between contemporary social theory and the digital revolution.

The *Handbook* is exceptionally wide-ranging in span, covering topics all the way from AI technologies in everyday life to single-purpose robots throughout home and work life, and from the mainstreaming of human–machine interfaces to the latest advances in AI, such as the ability to mimic (and improve on) many aspects of human brain function.

A unique integration of social science on the one hand and new technologies of artificial intelligence on the other, this *Handbook* and offers readers new ways of understanding the rise of AI and its associated global transformations. Written in a clear and direct style, the *Handbook* will appeal to a wide undergraduate audience.

Anthony Elliott is Dean of External Engagement at the University of South Australia, where he is Research Professor of Sociology and Executive Director of the Jean Monnet Centre of Excellence and Network. He is Super-Global Professor of Sociology (Visiting) at Keio University, Japan; Fellow of the Academy of Social Sciences in the UK; Fellow of the Academy of the Social Sciences in Australia; and, Senior Member of King's College, Cambridge. He is the General Editor of the Routledge *Key Ideas* book series and the author and editor of over 40 books, including most recently *The Culture of AI: Everyday Life and the Digital Revolution* (Routledge, 2019), *Reinvention, 2nd edition* (Routledge, 2021) and *Making Sense of AI: Our Algorithmic World* (Polity, 2021).

The Routledge Social Science Handbook of AI

Edited by Anthony Elliott

LONDON AND NEW YORK

First published 2022
by Routledge
2 Park Square, Milton Park, Abingdon, Oxon OX14 4RN

and by Routledge
605 Third Avenue, New York, NY 10158

Routledge is an imprint of the Taylor & Francis Group, an informa business

© 2022 selection and editorial matter, Anthony Elliott; individual chapters, the contributors

The right of Anthony Elliott to be identified as the author of the editorial material, and of the authors for their individual chapters, has been asserted in accordance with sections 77 and 78 of the Copyright, Designs and Patents Act 1988.

All rights reserved. No part of this book may be reprinted or reproduced or utilised in any form or by any electronic, mechanical, or other means, now known or hereafter invented, including photocopying and recording, or in any information storage or retrieval system, without permission in writing from the publishers.

Trademark notice: Product or corporate names may be trademarks or registered trademarks, and are used only for identification and explanation without intent to infringe.

British Library Cataloguing-in-Publication Data
A catalogue record for this book is available from the British Library

Library of Congress Cataloging-in-Publication Data
A catalog record for this book has been requested

ISBN: 978-0-367-18825-2 (hbk)
ISBN: 978-1-032-02256-7 (pbk)
ISBN: 978-0-429-19853-3 (ebk)

Typeset in Bembo
by Apex CoVantage, LLC

Contents

List of figures — viii
List of tables — ix
List of contributors — x
Acknowledgements — xvi
Foreword: The World in 2062, by Toby Walsh — xvii

PART I
Social science approaches to artificial intelligence — 1

1 The complex systems of AI: recent trajectories of social theory — 3
   Anthony Elliott

2 Geographies of AI — 17
   Thomas Birtchnell

3 Artificial intelligence and psychology — 30
   J. Michael Innes and Ben W. Morrison

4 AI in the age of technoscience: on the rise of data-driven AI and its epistem-ontological foundations — 58
   Jutta Weber and Bianca Prietl

5 Work, employment and unemployment after AI — 74
   Ross Boyd

6 Affects after AI: sociological perspectives on artificial companionship — 91
   Michaela Pfadenhauer and Tobias Lehmann

7 Anthropology, AI and robotics — 107
   Joffrey Becker

Contents

  8 Ethics of artificial intelligence   122
       Vincent C. Müller

  9 Human–machine interaction and design methods   138
       Naoko Abe

PART II
Fields of artificial intelligence in social science research   155

10 Management and organisation in the age of AI   157
     Roman Batko

11 Ambivalent places of politics: the social construction
     of certainties in automated mobilities and artificial intelligence   172
     Sven Kesselring and Carolin Schönewolf

12 Smart environments   188
     Maja De Neergaard and Malene Freudendal-Pedersen

13 Models of law and regulation for AI   199
     Nicolas Petit and Jerome De Cooman

14 Artificial intelligence and cyber-security   222
     Matteo E. Bonfanti, Myriam Dunn Cavelty, and Andreas Wenger

15 Lethal autonomous weapons systems   237
     Frank Sauer

16 AI and worldviews in the age of computational power   251
     Massimo Durante

17 Technogenarians: ageing and robotic care   266
     Eric L. Hsu

18 Big data and data analytics   281
     Jo Bates

19 AI, culture industries and entertainment   295
     Sam Han

20 AI, robotics, medicine and health sciences   313
     Norina Gasteiger and Elizabeth Broadbent

21 AI, smart borders and migration 339
    Louis Everuss

Index *357*

Figures

11.1	Character poles of the vehicles	180
20.1	Paro the companion robot	320
20.2	Image showing the triage and video consultation functions on Babylon's GP at Hand app	324
20.3	iRobi, a telehealth robot for COPD patients with RPM abilities	326
20.4	Bomy, a social home-based service robot that provides reminders and delivers games	327
20.5	End-effector (left) and generic full-hand exoskeleton (right)	328
20.6	Virtual human, Baby X, learning animals	333

Tables

11.1	Overview of the film material	175
13.1	Description of law and regulation model	200
13.2	Typology and examples of externalities	210

Contributors

Naoko Abe is a sociologist, specializing in social interaction and motion analysis, with a research focus in robotics. She obtained a PhD in sociology from Ecole des Hautes Etudes en Sciences Sociales (EHESS) in Paris and a teaching certificate of Kinetography Laban from the Paris Conservatory. In 2015, Naoko Abe was a postdoctoral fellow on a humanoid robotics team at the Laboratory for Analysis and Architecture of Systems (LAAS-CNRS) in France. Since 2018, she has been a research fellow and led the research theme 'Robotics and Society' at the Sydney Institute for Robotics and Intelligent Systems at the University of Sydney.

Jo Bates is Senior Lecturer in Information Politics and Policy at the Information School, University of Sheffield, UK. Her research interests are in the field of critical data studies and include the socio-material drivers and frictions in data flows particularly in the domain of meteorological and climate data, data practitioners including the affective aspects of data science practice and critical pedagogy for data science curricula, labour conditions of data labellers in crowd-work infrastructures, and issues of discrimination and bias in algorithmic outputs such as search engines.

Roman Batko is Professor in Management Science at the Jagiellonian University, Krakow, and Military Academy of Land Forces, Wroclaw, Poland. He is a member of the Culture and Media Management Committee of the Polish Academy of Arts and Sciences. He specializes in process management, quality management, project management, audits and evaluation systems, as well as innovation management, digital strategies and automation. He conducts research on issues related to the organizations of the future, such as robotization, cyborgization, new forms of communication and changes in the labor market, focusing on the radically changing position of a human in technological networks.

Joffrey Becker obtained a doctorate in ethnology and social anthropology at EHESS and is a research affiliate at the Laboratoire d'Anthropologie Sociale – Collège de France. His work is devoted to the study of the relationships between humans and machines by paying a particular attention to the new ontological, relational and social dynamics associated to the design and the interaction with so-called intelligent systems. Joffrey Becker is the author of about 15 scientific articles, book chapters and conference papers. His book *Humanoïdes* was published in 2015 by the Presses Universitaires de Paris Ouest.

Thomas Birtchnell is a senior lecturer at the University of Wollongong. His publications include *A New Industrial Future? 3D Printing and the Reconfiguring of Production, Distribution, and Consumption* (with J Urry, Routledge, 2016), *3D Printing for Development in the Global South:*

The 3D4D Challenge (with W Hoyle, Palgrave Macmillan, 2014) and *Indovation: Innovation and a Global Knowledge Economy in India* (Palgrave Macmillan, 2013), and the edited books *Elite Mobilities* (Routledge, 2013, with Javier Caletrío) and *Cargomobilities: Moving Materials in a Global Age* (Routledge, 2014, with Satya Savitzky and John Urry).

Matteo E. Bonfanti is Senior Researcher at the Center for Security Studies. His research activities focus on the governance implications generated by the development and adoption of new technical, technological and organizational solutions to enhance cyber-security, policing and intelligence cooperation, as well as crisis management.

Ross Boyd is a researcher based in the Hawke EU Jean Monnet Centre of Excellence at the University of South Australia. His research interests include human–machine interaction, economic sociology, social theory (including theorizing as an everyday practice) and the sociologies of hope, literature and education. In recent publications he has written on algorithmic accountability, the transformative impacts of AI on the economy, work and employment, and automated mobilities. In collaboration with Robert J. Holton, he is developing a critical social theoretical approach to intelligent social machines.

Elizabeth Broadbent is a professor in health psychology in the School of Medicine at the University of Auckland, New Zealand. She has an honours degree in electrical and electronic engineering, and MSc and PhD degrees in health psychology. Her research interests include psychoneuroimmunology, illness perceptions, embodied cognition and the use of robotics and digital humans in healthcare. Elizabeth is a vice chair of the multidisciplinary CARES robotics group at the University of Auckland.

Jerome De Cooman works as a research and teaching assistant in European Competition Law and EU Law, Big Data and Artificial Intelligence Applications at the University of Liege. He is also a junior researcher in the Liege Competition and Innovation Institute (LCII). He holds a master of laws from the University of Liege and a master of management sciences from HEC-School of Management (University of Liege). His research focuses on regulation, artificial intelligence and the interactions between legal science and technology.

Maja De Neergaard is Assistant Professor at the Department of the Built Environment, Aalborg University, Denmark. Her research is broadly situated within urban studies with interests, including urban and rural transformations, housing and inhabitation practices, and the digitalization of cities and everyday life. One of the projects she is currently engaged addresses the critical implications of urban digitalization on affordable housing and social diversity. The empirical work is focused on three contemporary cases of smart housing development in Toronto, Stockholm and Copenhagen, and the contextual backdrop involves a historic treatment of modernist planning ideals in the Nordic context.

Myriam Dunn Cavelty is Deputy Head of Research and Teaching at the Center for Security Studies (CSS), ETH Zurich. Her research centers on cyber-security and its implications for international relations and security.

Massimo Durante is Professor in Philosophy of Law and Legal Informatics at the Department of Law, University of Turin. He holds a PhD in Philosophy of Law, Department of Law, University of Turin, and a PhD in Moral Philosophy, Faculty of Philosophy, Paris IV Sorbonne. He is vice coordinator of the Joint International Doctoral Degree in "Law, Science, and Technology" and Faculty Fellow of the *Nexa Center for Internet & Society* at the Polytechnics of Turin. His main interests are law and technology, information ethics, digital governance, privacy and data protection law, and AI and law.

Anthony Elliott is Dean of External Engagement at the University of South Australia, where he is Research Professor of Sociology and Executive Director of the Jean Monnet Centre of Excellence and Network. He is Super-Global Professor of Sociology (Visiting) at Keio University, Japan; Fellow of the Academy of Social Sciences in the UK; Fellow of the Academy of the Social Sciences in Australia; and, Senior Member of King's College, Cambridge. He is the General Editor of the Routledge Key Ideas Series and the author and editor of over 40 books, including most recently *The Culture of AI: The Digital Revolution and Everyday Life* (Routledge, 2019), *Reinvention* (Routledge, 2E, 2021) and *Making Sense of AI: Our Algorithmic World* (Polity, 2022).

Louis Everuss is a research associate and coordinator at the Hawke EU Jean Monnet Centre of Excellence, University of South Australia. Dr Everuss' primary research interests are located in the sociological study of mobilities, sovereignty, migration, globalization and climate change. His work has examined how systems of mobility are incorporated into representations of sovereign outsiders, and how public opinions of climate change are impacted by national context. His work has been published in *Political Geography* the *Journal of Sociology*, *Applied Mobilities* and *Borderlands*.

Malene Freudendal-Pedersen is Professor in Urban Planning at Aalborg University, Denmark. She has an interdisciplinary background linking sociology, geography, urban planning and the sociology of technology. Her research has been strongly inspired by the mobilities turn and focuses on the interrelation between spatial and digital mobilities and its impacts on everyday life communities, societies and cities. She has been co-organizing the international Cosmobilities Network linking mobilities researchers in Europe and beyond. She is the Co-Founder and Co-Editor of the Routledge journal *Applied Mobilities* as well as the Co-Founder and Co-Editor of the book series *Networked Urban Mobilities*, also at Routledge.

Norina Gasteiger is a digital health enthusiast, with a particular interest in the evaluation and implementation of innovative digital health technologies. She has previously conducted research using robots, patient portals, social media and mobile apps. Norina holds a master's degree in public health from the University of Auckland and frequently collaborates with the multidisciplinary Centre for Automation and Robotic Engineering Science (CARES) group. She is currently pursuing her PhD in health informatics at the University of Manchester.

Sam Han is an interdisciplinary social scientist, working primarily in the areas of social, cultural and critical theory, and new media and religion (as well as their various overlaps and nodal points). He is currently Senior Lecturer of Anthropology and Sociology and Deputy Director of the Korea Research Centre of Western Australia at the University of Western Australia. He is the author of several books, including *(Inter)Facing Death: Life in Global Uncertainty* (Routledge, 2020), *Technologies of Religion: Spheres of the Sacred in a Post-Secular Modernity* (Routledge, 2016) and *Digital Culture and Religion in Asia* (Routledge, 2015; with Kamaludeen Mohamed Nasir).

Eric L. Hsu is a lecturer in the Justice & Society Academic Unit at the University of South Australia, where he also leads a research platform on 'Mobilities, Migrations & Cultural Identities' at the Hawke EU Jean Monnet Centre of Excellence. Dr Hsu specializes in the sociology of sleep and the social theory of time; his research also extends into the sociology of robotic technologies. He is the editor of two works that have been published by Routledge, *Sleep: Critical Concepts in Sociology* (2017) and *the Consequences of Global Disasters* (2016). More information can be found on his website, www.ericlhsu.com.

J. Michael Innes is a social psychologist with experience in the study of social influence, performance in group settings and generally in the field of political behaviour and cognition, including the influence of economic belief systems on attitudes to climate change. He has held grants for the study of the role of mood and emotion in attitude change, social influence in virtual realities and the effects of television advertising on children's belief systems and behaviour. He has held academic and management positions at universities in the United Kingdom and the United States as well as in Australia, where he is currently affiliated with the University of South Australia. His current interests involve an examination of the effects of the development of artificial intelligence systems on the education, training and employment of professional psychologists.

Sven Kesselring, Dr Phil, is a German sociologist and professor in 'sustainable mobilities' at Nuertingen-Geislingen University (HfWU), Germany. He is the founder of the international research network Cosmobilities (www.cosmobilities.net) and was vice president of the International Association for the History of Transport, Traffic and Mobility (t2m). In 2017 he was a research fellow in residence at the Centre for Interdisciplinary Research (ZiF) at Bielefeld University, Germany. He is a co-editor of the journal 'Applied Mobilities', the *Networked Urban Mobilities* book series (Routledge) and *Studies in Mobility and Transportation Research* (Springer VS). Sven Kesselring studied sociology, political science and social psychology and holds a PhD in sociology from Ludwig Maximilian University of Munich and a doctoral degree (habilitation) from the Technical University of Munich. His research focuses on mobilities theory, sustainability, socio-technological change, new mobility concepts, corporate mobilities regimes, aeromobilities and future research.

Tobias Lehmann, MA, studied sociology and science and technology studies. Currently, he is a research assistant at the Department for Social Studies of Science and Technology at the Technical University of Berlin.

Ben W. Morrison is a senior lecturer and organizational psychologist from the Department of Psychology at Macquarie University, Australia. Ben teaches in the University's organizational psychology program and is a member of the Centre for Elite Performance, Expertise and Training. His work focuses on psychology in the workplace, including areas relating to expertise development and the implementation of advanced technology systems. Ben is currently working on research projects relating to the skilled detection of cyber-security threats, the impact of artificial intelligence on professions, and the barriers to effective and safe use of intelligent decision support systems at work.

Vincent C. Müller is Professor for Philosophy of Technology at the Technical University of Eindhoven (TU/e) – as well as University Fellow at the University of Leeds, Turing Fellow at the Alan Turing Institute, London, President of the European Society for Cognitive Systems and Chair of the euRobotics topics group on 'ethical, legal and socio-economic issues'. He was Professor at Anatolia College/ACT (Thessaloniki), Stanley J. Seeger Fellow at Princeton University and James Martin Research Fellow at the University of Oxford. He studied philosophy with cognitive science, linguistics and history at the universities of Marburg, Hamburg, London and Oxford. www.sophia.de.

Nicolas Petit is Professor of Competition Law at the European University Institute in Florence (joint appointment between the Department of Law and at the Robert Schuman Centre for Advanced Studies). He is also invited Professor at the College of Europe in Bruges. Nicolas has held professorships at the EDHEC Business School and at the University of South Australia in Adelaide. He has been a visiting researcher at Harvard Law School and a visiting fellow at Stanford University Hoover Institution. From 2017 to 2020 he was a member of the European Commission High Level Expert Group on Artificial Intelligence. Nicolas Petit's scholarly work focuses on antitrust, regulation, law, science and technology.

Michaela Pfadenhauer is Full Professor of Sociology at the University of Vienna and Vice Dean for Research and Infrastructure at the Faculty of Social Sciences. Her recent fields of research include sociology of knowledge and culture, especially communicative knowledge cultures; the interrelation of media and cultural change; smart solutions for the enhancement of knowledge exchange between professions, for cultural integration and inclusion. She is a board member of the Research Network 07 Sociology of Culture of the European Sociological Association and a member of the Council of the German Sociological Association as well as co-editor of the Routledge Book Series *Communication, Knowledge & Society*.

Bianca Prietl is a sociologist and STS scholar who works as an assistant professor for societal consequences of digitalization at Johannes Kepler University Linz, Austria. Her research is interested in the various relations of knowledge, technology and power. She has worked on how the engineering subject is gendered on the level of knowledge (cf. 'Technology Change = Gender Change?', in: *Engineering Studies* 2017). Lately, she has turned to how digital data technologies are used for producing knowledge and making decisions, asking how these modes of knowledge production relate to social relations of inequality (cf. 'Big Data: Inequality by Design?', in: *Proceedings of the Weizenbaum Conference* 2019).

Frank Sauer is a senior research fellow at Bundeswehr University in Munich. He is the author of 'Atomic Anxiety: Deterrence, Taboo, and the Non-Use of U.S. Nuclear Weapons'. In addition to nuclear issues, Frank has done research on terrorism, robotics, and cyber-security and emerging technologies, especially the military application of artificial intelligence (AI). Frank is a member of the International Committee for Robot Arms Control (ICRAC). He also serves on the International Panel on the Regulation of Autonomous Weapons (iPRAW) and the Expert Commission on the responsible use of technologies in the European 'Future Combat Air System'.

Carolin Schönewolf, Dr rer. soc., is a German sociologist located in Munich, Germany. She studied sociology and gender studies at the Technical University of Darmstadt and Ludwig Maximilian University of Munich. She received her PhD from the Munich Center for Technology in Society (MCTS) at the Technical University of Munich. Her research integrates science and technology studies, mobilities studies and sociology of science. The aim of her research is to promote a critical and responsible approach to technology futures and their socio-technical embeddings. In order to transfer these findings into practice, she is currently working in the strategy department of a German automobile manufacturer.

Toby Walsh is a Laureate Fellow and Scientia Professor of AI at the University of New South Wales and Data61, and adjunct professor at QUT. He was named by the Australian newspaper as one of the "rock stars" of Australia's digital revolution. Professor Walsh is a strong advocate for limits to ensure AI is used to improve our lives. He has been a leading voice in the discussion about autonomous weapons (aka "killer robots"), speaking at the UN in New York and Geneva on the topic. He is a Fellow of the Australia Academy of Science and recipient of the NSW Premier's Prize for Excellence in Engineering and ICT. He appears regularly on TV and radio, and has authored two books on AI for a general audience, the most recent entitled "2062: The World that AI Made".

Jutta Weber is a STS scholar and professor for media sociology at the University of Paderborn, Germany. Her research focuses on computational technoscience culture(s) asking how and for whom the non-human actors work. She has been visiting professor at Uppsala (S), Vienna (A) and Twente (NL). Some publications include: 'Technosecurity Cultures' in *Science as Culture*, ed. with Katrin Kämpf; 'Tracking and Targeting: Sociotechnologies of (In)security' in *Science, Technology & Human Values*, ed. with Karolina Follis and Lucy Suchman; and 'Keep Adding. Kill Lists, Drone Warfare and the Politics of Databases' in *Environment and Planning D. Society and Space*; see also www.juttaweber.eu.

Andreas Wenger is Professor of International and Swiss Security Policy at ETH Zurich and Director of the Center for Security Studies (CSS). The focus of his main research interests lies on security and strategic studies, the history of international relations and Swiss security politics.

Acknowledgements

This project was supported by the Australian Research Council grants "Industry 4.0 ecosystems: a comparative analysis of work-life transformation" (DP180101816) and "Enhanced Humans, Robotics and the Future of Work" (DP160100979). The book is also an outcome from my recent European Commission Erasmus+ grants "Discourses on European Union I4.0 Innovation" (611183-EPP-1-2019-1-AU-EPPJMO-PROJECT) and Jean Monnet Network "Cooperative, Connected and Automated Mobility" (599662-EPP-1-2018-1-AU-EPPJMO-NETWORK). A number of people have contributed, either directly or indirectly, to the development of this handbook for publication. Special thanks to Gerhard Boomgaarden for commissioning the work, and to Rebecca Brennan and Mihaela Diana Ciobotea at Routledge for seeing this work through the long process of writing and production. The book would simply not exist if not for the extraordinary one-man efforts of Ross Boyd, whose dedication to the project and endless patience in working with contributors appears to know no limit. Louis Everuss, Eric L. Hsu, J. Michael Innes and Bob Holton at the Jean Monnet Centre of Excellence and Network at the University of South Australia made valuable contributions throughout. Warm thanks to Lauren Palmer at the Australian Council of Learned Academies and to Chris Hatherly at the Academy of the Social Sciences in Australia. I owe a particular debt of gratitude to the following colleagues and friends: Tony Giddens, Nigel Thrift, Massimo Durante, Vincent C. Müller, Toby Walsh, Sven Kesselring, Ralf Blomqvist, Ingrid Biese, John Cash, Bo-Magnus Salenius, Rina Yamamoto, Masataka Katagiri, Roman Batko, Atsushi Sawai, Jean Elliott, Keith Elliott, Nick Stevenson, Kriss McKie, Fiore Inglese, Carmel Meiklejon, Thomas Birtchnell, Helga Nowotny, Oliver Toth, Carolyn Toth, Caoimhe Elliott, Oscar Elliott and Niamh Elliott. Finally, and most significantly, my greatest thanks, as ever, is to Nicola Geraghty.

Anthony Elliott,
Adelaide 2020

Foreword: The World in 2062, by Toby Walsh

For most of the last 30 years, no one has cared much about what I do. This is because I've spent over three decades at universities around the world trying to build artificial intelligence (AI), writing computer programs to do a variety of tasks that humans need some intelligence to do. In the last decade AI research like this has escaped from its academic beginnings and is finding its way into our everyday lives.

We are still a long way from matching human intelligence. It is hard to know how long it may take. At present, we can only build narrow AI programs that do very limited tasks. And this narrow AI tends to be brittle and unpredictable. Unlike human intelligence, AI programs today break easily, often in very unexpected and strange ways.

Expert predictions about when AI will match, or perhaps even exceed, human intelligence vary widely. A minority of experts say it will never happen, identifying one or more characteristics that they predict we will not be able to replicate in silicon. But most AI researchers, myself included, think it might take between 50 and 100 years before machines match humans.[1] However, long before the next century, we will see many aspects of our lives transformed by narrow AI. Indeed, we are already seeing some of these changes. The impact of the COVID-19 pandemic is only likely to speed up the adoption of narrow AI.

We can perhaps learn a little from history. The first industrial revolution saw a change from hand production to machines driven by steam and water power. Manufacturing shifted into factories which became a significant component of many national economies. The prosperity generated by such mechanized production supported both a significant increase in population and in the quality of the lives of that population.

The most important changes were perhaps not technological but societal. Alongside the large transformation in the nature of work, there were major structural changes in society to support this. These changes included the introduction of universal education, affordable health care, pensions, unions, labour laws and much more.

We are going through a similar change in what is sometimes called the fourth industrial revolution. This is a revolution driven by technologies like AI that will again transform the nature of work. And, once more, the most significant changes are likely not to be technological but societal. We must think then about the structural changes necessary not just to weather this transformation but to prosper. This handbook is therefore a very welcome addition to the important conversation we must have in navigating these liminal times. While technologists like myself can inform the conversation as to the possible capabilities and the likely limitations of the coming AI systems, the conversation needs to be much broader.

Foreword

When we consider an incident like that surrounding Cambridge Analytica, there are many troubling issues to address. There is, of course, the immediate issue of privacy. Many people had personal information taken without their consent. But perhaps more troubling was the use to which this personal information was put. This personal information was used to micro-target social media adverts in what appears to have been a successful attempt to manipulate the vote. This then is a conversation for ethicists, political scientists, behavioural psychologists and anthropologists, to mention just a few areas of expertise needed to inform the conversation. It is not just a conversation for technologists.

When we consider a topic like lethal autonomous weapons, there are again many troubling issues we must address. There is, of course, the problematic issue of accountability. When someone is wrongly killed by lethal autonomous weapons who, or even what, is responsible? But perhaps more concerning are the ethics of handing over the decision as to who lives and who dies to a machine. Are we prepared to live in a world where we hand over such choices to a machine, and what sort of world does it become if we do? These are again conversations for military experts, ethicists, social scientists, and the general public as much as it is for technologists.

There are many other important conversations we need to have: about the future of work, privacy, power, diversity and inclusion, laws, norms, health, ageing, culture and the future of entertainment to name just a few of the topics covered in this handbook. These conversations need to move out of Silicon Valley and into the social sciences, and from there into broader debate. Technologies like AI can help us build a better future. But we need to choose wisely how we build that future.

Note

1 *2062: The World that AI Made*. Toby Walsh, Black Inc. 2018.

Part I
Social science approaches to artificial intelligence

1
The complex systems of AI
Recent trajectories of social theory

Anthony Elliott

One of the principal aims of *The Routledge Social Science Handbook of Artificial Intelligence* is to provide students and teachers with a comprehensive and accessible guide to the major topics and trends of research in the social sciences of artificial intelligence (AI), as well as to survey how the digital revolution – from supercomputers and social media to advanced automation and robotics – is transforming society, culture, politics and economy. A unique integration of social science on the one hand and new technologies of artificial intelligence on the other, this handbook offers readers new ways of understanding the rise of AI and its associated global transformations. Another aim of the *Handbook* is to address the very wide array of phenomenon associated with the digital revolution, providing the most up-to-date coverage of developments in AI, machine learning (ML), robotics and supercomputing. Topics addressed where AI currently transforms or, in the future, promises to transform social, economic, cultural and political processes include:

- AI within discrete apps, embedded within operating systems, and operating systems based on AI.
- Single-purpose robots throughout home and work life.
- Bigger, faster, superdata analytics: 'Colossal data' (bigger big data) which will necessarily involve new data curation and analysis approaches that enable more patterns from an ever diversifying range of data.
- Low-power computational hardware, including neuromorphic computers that are more suited to some applications of AI than traditional computers.
- Miniaturized quantum encryption devices, which will underpin the security and trust that will be required before new technologies are widely applied. This particularly applies to applications with high-consequence failure modes (such as implants with direct access to the brain).
- Advances in ML.
- Advances in battery technology: enables stand-alone and mobile intelligence in a wide range of applications.
- Advances in machine cognition systems

- Mainstreaming of human–machine interfaces. This would enable a host of new applications, the easiest to imagine being those using new brain-machine interfaces.
- Massively parallel computational architectures and quantum computing.
- Advances in generalized robotics, such as multipurpose labourer robots.
- Advances in AI, such as the ability to mimic (and improve on) many aspects of human brain function.

The *Handbook* provides representative coverage of the full range of social science engagements within the AI revolution, from employment and jobs to education and new digital skills to automated technologies of military warfare and the future of ethics. A principal aim of the work is to help cross C.P. Snow's 'great divide' – in this instance, that between technical specialists and social scientists on the topic of AI.

A globalizing world of AI

As the great wave of digital technology breaks across the world, artificial intelligence creeps increasingly into the very fabric of our lives. From personal virtual assistants and chatbots to self-driving vehicles and telerobotics, AI is now threaded into large tracts of everyday life. It is reshaping society and the economy. Klaus Schwab, founder of the World Economic Forum, has said that today's AI revolution is 'unlike anything humankind has experienced before'. AI is not so much an advancement of technology but rather the metamorphosis of all technology. This is what makes it so revolutionary. Politics change dramatically as a consequence of AI. Not only must governments confront head-on the fallout from mass replacement of traditional jobs with AI, algorithms and automation, they must ensure that all citizens are adaptable and digitally literate. It will be fundamental to almost all areas of policy development.

Recent technological breakthroughs have resulted in advanced AI transforming manufacturing, the service industry and business platforms, impacting significantly on most jobs including many professions seemingly immune from digital disruption. Research in the US, UK, Japan and Australia, including both academic reviews and government inquiries, estimates that approximately 40% to 50% of existing jobs are at risk from AI technology and automation in the next 15 to 20 years. Other researchers point to a trend of increasing job polarization accompanying automation. At the same time, it has been estimated that AI could contribute approximately $16 trillion to the global economy by 2030.

Given the intricate interconnections between employment and self-identity, it is easy enough to see why more and more people are troubled by AI. Artificial intelligence is, in short, quickly changing the global economy and, fundamentally, everyday life and the self. Smart algorithms run large tracts of enterprise, executing trades, controlling new additive manufacturing, billing clients, automating customer services, navigating aviation flight paths and guiding surgical care. While there is a public fascination with chatbots and self-driving cars, however, very few people understand how AI actually functions and is changing the world in front of their very eyes. Or maybe this is the issue: AI, like electricity, is *invisible*. It is a general-purpose technology that works its magic behind the scenes. The contours and consequences of AI remain elusive to us – we can't see them in action, but we still somehow experience the impact. Like other general-purpose technologies, such as the internal combustion engine, telephony and the silicon chip, AI is becoming ubiquitous. It is everywhere and nowhere at once, both omnipresent and unnoticed.

Whilst there is a lack of agreement among researchers about how to characterize the main defining elements of AI and its related technologies,[1] there is some measure of agreement in the area of public policy and governance. The UK government's 2017 'Industrial Strategy White Paper', for example, defines AI as 'technologies with the ability to perform tasks that would otherwise require human intelligence, such as visual perception, speech recognition, and language translation'.[2] It is perhaps useful to begin with such a definition, one geared to state-promoted AI, if only because such an account is clearly quite narrow, and leaves unaddressed some of the most important deep drivers of AI. It is crucially important, for instance, to underscore the intricate interconnections between AI and ML. A key condition of AI, one not captured by the UK government's white paper, is the capacity to learn from, and adapt to, new information or stimuli. Among the deep drivers of AI are technological advances in the networked communications of self-learning and relative autonomy of intelligent machines. These new systems of self-learning, adaptation and self-governance have helped to reconstitute not only the debate over what AI actually is, but have also impacted the relationship between artificial and organic intelligence.

While AI generates increasing systems of interconnected self-learning, it does not automatically spawn a common set of human reactions or values in terms of those engaging with such technologies. The relation between AI and its technologies, including particularly people's experiences of or views on AI, is a complicated one. As a first approximation we can define AI, and its related offshoot ML, as encompassing any computational system that can sense its relevant context and react intelligently to data. Machines might be said to become 'intelligent', thus warranting the badge 'AI', when certain degrees of self-learning, self-awareness and sentience are realized. Intelligent machines act not only with expertise but also with ongoing degrees of reflexivity. The relation between AI and self-learning is considered to operate at a high level when intelligent machines can cope with the element of surprise. After all, many ML algorithms can easily be duped. Broadly speaking, AI can be said to refer to any computational system which can sense its environment, think, learn and react in response (and cope with surprises) to such data-sensing.[3] AI-related technologies may include both robots and purely digital systems that employ learning methods such as Deep learning, neural networks, pattern recognition (including machine vision and cognition), reinforcement learning, and machine decision-making. Let us take a closer look at some of these approaches and technologies.

Machine learning

Machine learning is one of the most important advancements of contemporary AI technologies, where computers execute tasks through processes of 'learning' or 'information gathering' that draw from (but are not reducible to) human intelligence and human decision making. 'Machine learning', writes Toby Walsh,

> is an important part of computers that think. It tackles the *bottleneck problem*, the problem of pouring into a machine all the knowledge we have developed over thousands of years. Programming all that knowledge ourselves, fact by fact, would be slow and painful. But we don't need to do this, as computers can simply learn it for themselves.[4]

Through analysis of massive volumes of data, ML algorithms can autonomously improve their learning over time. ML relies on algorithms ranging from basic decision trees through to artificial neural networks that classify information by mimicking the structure of the human brain. The rise of neural networks, a kind of ML loosely modelled on the structure of the human brain, consisting of deeply layered processing nodes, has been especially significant in the spread and efficacy of AI. So too, deep leaning – a more recent spin-off of neural networks – which deploys multiple layers of AI to solve complex problems has underpinned much of the explosion of interest from businesses, media, the finance sector and large-scale corporations. The essential scientific aspiration here has focused on replicating general intelligence, which for the most part has been understood largely in terms of reason, cognition and perception, as well as planning, learning and natural language processing.

Natural language processing

Natural language processing (NLP) is a fundamental aspect of AI and encompasses all AI technologies related to the analysis, interpretation and generation (of text- and speech-based) natural language. NLP has prominent applications including machine translation (such as Google Translate), dialogue systems (including Google's Assistant, Apple's Siri and Amazon's Alexa) and automatic question answering (for example, IBM's Project Debater). NLP has matured rapidly over the past 10 to 15 years as a result of the unprecedented amount of language being produced, shared and recorded in electronic and spoken forms.

The social impacts of NLP as conjoined to AI technologies have been massive, and the likely trajectory of development is set to skyrocket. From Amazon's Alexa to Google's Home, people are busy talking to intelligent machines as never before. It is estimated that more than 60% of Internet traffic is now generated by machine-to-machine, and person-to-machine, communication. IT advisory firm Gartner has predicted that by the mid-2020s the average person will be having more conversations with chatbots and robots powered by NLP than with their partner. These claims may seem the stuff of science fiction, but they spell significant change as regards society, culture and politics. I have previously looked at these developments in some detail, focusing on the likely impacts to social interaction and transformations in communication and talk. My argument was that digital devices deploying NLP programs and AI technology are plainly quite divergent from the ordinary conversations of people. Machine talk occurs as part of pre-programmed sequences built up through machine learning. As a result, machine talk – to date at any rate – can usually only respond to conversational contingencies in quite minor ways. Digital devices might be programmed to convey an impression of 'immediate talk' geared to the needs of the user, but the production of machine talk is, in fact, drawn from an enormous database of code, scripted utterances and network conversation. For example, most chatbots and virtual personal assistants consist of programmed 'appropriate replies' to even the most obscure conversations. This is underscored by Brian Christian's argument that machine language is a kind of *conversational puree*, a recorded echo of billions of human conversations. But even this is now under challenge as a result of technological breakthroughs in AI and NLP: for example, Google's Duplex. Chatbots, softbots, and virtual personal assistants have become increasingly integral to our daily lives and our identities, even if we are not always aware of their role. If talking to chatbots and virtual personal assistants becomes the new normal, we should be aware of the ways they could change how we talk to each other and how we relate to ourselves. One thing is certain. AI is having a profound impact on experiences of the self, what identity means, and of how selfhood intersects with others (both human and non-human) in the wider world.

NLP advances and breakthroughs over the past decade have been achieved with specific tasks and datasets, which are driven largely by big data. However, NLP is only ever as good as the dataset underpinning it. If not appropriately trained and ethically assessed, NLP models can accentuate bias in underlying datasets, resulting in systems that work to the advantage of some users over others. Significantly, NLP is currently unable to distinguish between data or language that is irrelevant and socially or culturally damaging. These are matters of significant social and political importance.

Robotics

Robotics has been characterized as the intelligent connection of perception to action in engineered systems. Robotics include not only human-like robots but any kind of technological system that uses sensors such as cameras, thermal imagers or tactile and sound sensors to collect data about the operational environment and construct an automated response-world of actions.

The scaling up of robotics today is hugely significant throughout much of the world. Industrial robots transforming manufacturing – from packaging and testing to assembling minute electronics – is the fastest growing source of robotic technologies. From the early 1960s when one of the first industrial robots was operationalized in a candy factory in Ontario through to the 2010s where new technologies facilitated robots working hand-in-hand with workers, there has been a growing expansion in robotics and the number of published patents on robotics technology. The number of industrial robots in the US jumped from 200 in 1970 to 5,500 in 1981 to 90,000 in 2001.[5] In 2015, the number of industrial robots sold worldwide was nearly 250,000; industrial robotics is an industry which annually enjoys global growth of approximately 10%. Automotive and electronics have been the major industry sectors for robotics use, but many other sectors are increasingly adopting robotics and technological automation. Robotics coupled with converging mobile technologies are especially transforming industry in Asia, which has dominated the ramp-up of robotics use, and with China being the primary contributor. But demand for greater productivity, mass customization, miniaturization and shorter product life cycles has also driven growth for robotics worldwide, especially in Japan, Germany, Korea and the US.

Complexity, complex digital systems and AI

AI does not exist in a vacuum. AI technologies are always intricately interwoven with social systems, as well as other technological systems. Human action (its unfolding and flows), as well as the production and reproduction of social practices, takes place today in the context of complex, powerful technological and social systems that stretch across time and space. The systematic properties of technology and society, specifically their ordering features, give a certain degree of 'solidity' to social practices which are self-organizing, adaptive and evolving. From this angle, technical and social systems are by definition emergent, dynamic and open. Yet such systems are never 'solid' in the sense that they are stable or unchanging. Complex technological and social systems, including the conditions of systems reproduction, are characterized by unpredictability, non-linearity and reversal. The ordering and reordering of systems, structures and networks, as developed in complexity theory, is highly dynamic, processual and unpredictable; the impact of positive and negative feedback loops shifts systems away from states of equilibrium.[6] Drawing from advances in complexity theory, historical sociology and social theory, my contention is that a grounded, theoretically informed account of the digitization of technological and social systems must be based on seven sets of considerations.[7] These considerations are vital to grasping the complex systems of AI. These complex, overlapping connections between technological systems and digital life can be analyzed and critiqued from the sociological considerations I now detail.

First, there is the sheer scale of systems of digitization, of technological automation and of social relations threaded through artificial intelligence – all being key global enablers of the digital data economy. Over 4.5 billion people – more than half the world's population – are online, and digital interactions increasingly impact upon even those who find themselves with limited digital resources.[8] Complex computerized systems of digitization make possible (and are increasingly interwoven with) the production and performance of social life – of business, leisure, consumerism, travel, governance and so on. These systems – of computing databases, codes of software, WiFi, Bluetooth, RFID, GPS and other technologies – make possible our everyday networked interactions, from search engine enquiries to online shopping to social media. These systems facilitate predictable and relatively routine pathways of digitization which underpin smartphone social interactions, online banking, music streaming, status updates, blogs, vlogs and related actions of searching, retrieval and tagging spawned by the Internet. Systems of digitization enable repetition. In the contemporary world of digital life, these systems include social media, CCTV, credit cards, laptops, tablets, wearable computers, uniform resource locators (URLs), smartphones, email, SMS, satellites, computer algorithms, location tagging and so on. The contemporary flourishing of complex, interdependent systems of digitization are the 'flow architectures' that increasingly order and reorder social relations, production, consumption, communications, travel and transport, and surveillance around the world.[9]

Second, AI is not a 'new technology' which simply transcends, or renders redundant, previous technologies. The complex, adaptive digital systems of AI should not be viewed as simply products of the contemporary but, in part, depend upon technological systems which have developed at earlier historical periods. 'Many old technologies', writes John Urry, 'do not simply disappear but survive through path-dependent relationships, combining with the "new" in a reconfigured and unpredicted cluster. An interesting example of this has been the enduring importance of the "technology" of paper even within "high-tech" offices'.[10] Thus, the development and exploitation of digital technologies is interwoven in complex ways with multiple pre-digital technological systems. Another way of putting this is to say that our wireless world is interdependent on a range of wired technologies. Many of the wired technologies – the wires, cables and connections of pre-digital systems – which intersect with digital technologies of WiFi, Bluetooth and RFID date from the 1830s, 1840s and 1850s. There occurred in this historical period an astonishing range of experiments with systems of electrical energy for the purposes of communication. Systems dating from that period based upon the communication potential of electricity include electromagnetic telegraphy (which was trialled in England, Germany and the US in the 1830s), the first viable telegraph line between Washington and Baltimore (constructed by Morse in 1843 with funds from the US Congress), the successful laying of early submarine cables across the English Channel and between England and Ireland in 1851–2 (with a transatlantic cable successfully laid the following decade), and the discovery of the electric voice-operated telephone (demonstrated in 1854 by Antonio Mecucci in New York, although it was some decades later that Alexander Graham Bell conceived the idea for the telephone as a communication system).[11] Subsequent to this period, the twentieth century witnessed a vast array of technological systems emerge and develop. Broadcasting systems – radio from the 1920s, television from the 1940s – were pervasive and hugely consequential for social transformations associated with mass communications. In the 1960s, the launching of the world's first geo-stationary communications satellites spelt the arrival of near-instantaneous communication on a global level. Around this time, other technological systems – from personal computing to mobile telephony – underwent early development, too. The interlinked, tangled dynamics of these 'systems', of which most people are largely unaware as they go about their everyday social activities, is of key importance. Individuals will not know, or entertain awareness of, the conditions, scale or impact of such complex systems since these different technologies fuse and enrich each other.

Third, we need to recognize the global reach of AI as embedded in complex adaptive systems. Whilst the emergence of complex communication networks coincided with the advent of industrialization, it was only in the late twentieth century and early twenty-first century that digital communication technologies and networks were systematically established on a global scale. In this connection, the exceptional significance of various technological transitions that occurred between 1989 and 2007 should be underscored. While digital technologies have progressively developed across time, 1989 was a key time in the constitution of digital life. For this was the year that Tim Berners-Lee invented the World Wide Web through the technological innovations of URL, HTML and HTTP. (The Web did not become readily accessible to people, however, until 1994.) The year 1989 is also significant because Soviet communism collapsed. According to Manuel Castells, this occurred because of Russia's failure to develop new information technologies.[12] Also in this year, global financial markets were increasingly integrated through instantaneous communications and online real-time trading. In addition, mobile telephony was launched, initially through Nokia and Vodafone, through the breakthroughs of the global system for mobile communications (GSM). In 1991, the first GSM phone call was made with a Nokia device through the Finnish network Radilinja.

As the computing technology–inspired 1990s turned into the social media–driven 2000s, the sheer technological brilliance of digitization seemed all the more striking. This next decade ushered in a range of platforms, apps and devices, and along with that the digital transformation of society. In 2001, iTunes and Wikipedia commenced operation. There were also new commercialized forms of social media. LinkedIn was rolled out in 2003, Facebook in 2004, YouTube and Flickr in 2005, and Twitter in 2006. The point, seemingly, was less to apply the digital to everyday life and more to secure one's social niche within the field of the digital. In 2007, smartphones arrived on the market. This was followed by the introduction of tablets in 2010. With the arrival of the 2010s, and such additional platforms as Instagram, Spotify, Google+ and Uber, culture and society was coming to mean status updates, SMS, posts, blogs, tagging, GPS and virtual reality. Digital technologies were transforming social life.

Fourth, there is the sheer ubiquity of AI. I am referring here to various complex, interdependent digital systems which are today everywhere transferring, coding, sorting and resorting digital information (more or less) instantaneously across global networks. With systems of digitization and technological automation, information processing becomes the pervasive architecture of our densely networked environments. As society becomes informationalized as never before, digitization emerges as the operating backcloth against which everything is coded, tagged, scanned and located. Complex automated systems of digital technology emerge as the 'surround' to both everyday life and modern institutions. These technological systems seem to usher in worlds – informational, digital, virtual – that are generalized; that is, these technologies are increasingly diffused throughout contemporary systems of activity and take on the appearance of a functionality which is 'wall-to-wall'. Today's independent informational systems of digitization are, to invoke Adam Greenfield, both 'everywhere and everyware'.[13] From GPS to RFID tagging, and from augmented reality to the Internet of Things, these various interdependent systems are the architectural surround or operational backcloth through which airport doors automatically open, credit card transactions are enabled, SMS is enacted and big data is accessed. As Greenfield contends, this increasingly pervasive digital surround scoops up 'all of the power of a densely networked environment, but refining its perceptible signs until they disappear into the things we do everyday'.[14]

To invoke the possibility of disappearance in this context, as Greenfield does, is to raise the question of the hidden and the invisible as concerns systems of digitalization. Digital life inaugurates a transformation in the nature of invisibility – operationalized through supercomputers, big data and artificial intelligence – and the changing relation between the visible, the hidden and the power. My argument is that the rise of systems of digital technology in the late twentieth and early twenty-first centuries has created a new form of invisibility which is linked to the characteristics of software code, computer algorithms and AI protocols and to its modes of information processing. The invisibility created by digital technologies is that of a protocological infrastructure which orders and reorders the many connectivities, calculations, authorizations, registrations, taggings, uploads, downloads and transmissions infusing everyday life. Codes, algorithms and protocols are the invisible surround which facilitates our communications with others and our sharing with others of personal data through the array of devices and apps and wearable technologies and self-tracking tools that monitor, measure and record people's personal data. The development of WiFi, Bluetooth, RFID and other novel technologies of artificial intelligence has thus created a new form of sociality, based on a distinctive kind of invisibility, which touches on and tracks identities and bodies and constitutes and reorders our social interactions through ubiquitous contactless technologies. But the digital field is, of course, much more extensive in scope, enabling also smart objects (or, anti-wearables) and other digital data-gathering technologies. Many objects and environments have been rendered 'smart' through embedded sensors, interactive visualizations and digital dashboards – again, with an invisible protological infrastructure and the kinds of social relations spawned by it, touching upon the operations of shopping centres, airports, road toll systems, schools and many more.

Fifth, these systems which are ordering and reordering digital life are becoming more complex and increasingly complicated. This growing complexity has powered the rise of ubiquitous computing and AI, and has been underpinned by exponential rates of technological and associated social transformations. 'Moore's Law' has been the guiding maxim of innovation since the mid-1960s, and refers to the so-called doubling of computing power every two years. Computing power is based on the number of transistors in an integrated circuit; and against the backdrop of ever-shrinking computer circuits, engineers have been able to fit exponentially more onto microchips. This has made computers more complex, powerful and cheaper: it is estimated that a smartphone, for example, possesses the computer power previously only available in large mainframe computers. More recently, reports from various technology companies – such as Samsung and Intel – have suggested that beyond 2021 it may not be feasible to shrink transistors any smaller.[15] The limits to technological miniaturization have thus propelled a debate on whether Moore's Law has reached an end point;[16] some analysts argue that quantum computing will provide the new route forward for the continued expansion of computing processing power. And many people believe that ubiquitous computing and AI, when viewed in the context of convergence with nanotechnology, biotechnology and information science, will continue to propel exponential rates of technological complexity, socio-economic innovation and social transformation. Certainly the ubiquity of digital technology, and especially complexity in AI and robotics, involves multimodal informational traffic flows, which in turn substantially depends on technical specialization and complex expert systems.

Sixth, AI technologies go all the way down into the very fabric of lived experience and the textures of human subjectivity, personal life and cultural identities. Complex adaptive digital systems and technological infrastructures are not just 'out there' processes or happenings but are condensed in social relationships and the fabric of peoples' lives. That is to say, complex digital systems generate new forms of social relations as well as reshape processes of self-formation and personal identity. Complex computerized systems, for example, 'bend' social relations towards the short-term, the fragmentary and the episodic – based upon computational interplays of connection and disconnection. 'Life on the screen' (to invoke Sherry Turkle) appears to unfold faster and faster in the early decades of the twenty-first century, as people 'life-splice' the threads of professional, business, family and leisure zones together – using multiple devices across diverse digital platforms. Digital technologies are intricately interwoven with the trend towards DIY, individualized life strategies, where people are busy using devices, apps and bots to schedule and reschedule their everyday lives and experiment with digital life. Systems of digital technology increasingly wrap the self in experiences of 'instantaneous time', and the individualized work of constituting and reinventing digital identities is built out of instantaneous computer clicks of 'search', 'cut-and-paste', 'erase', 'delete' and 'cancel'.

Web-based digital technologies play a constitutive role in social relations today, facilitating digitally downloadable and transferable files containing apps and bots which power the smart-devices that people use 'on the move'. Over 100 billion apps have been downloaded from the Apple App Store alone since 2008,[17] and over 75% of all smartphone users deploy some kind of messaging app – from Facebook Messenger to WeChat to Viber. The instantaneous, just-in-time culture of apps has been a primary conduit through which the great bulk of people in the rich North now communicate, work and socialize. The arrival of the 2020s, however, promises a wholesale shift of social relations into even more accelerated Web-based digital technologies, and specifically the rise of mobile chatbots. This is part of a growing shift to conversational computing, where language is the new user interface which people use for calling upon their digital assistants for booking a hotel room or ordering a pizza. There is already a large online source network of efficient and intelligent bots available for download, and the spread of mobile chatbots looks set to reshape social relationships – both now and into the future.

Seventh, the technological changes stimulated by the advent of complex digital systems involve processes of transformation of surveillance and power quite distinct from anything occurring previously. The expansion of surveillance capabilities is a central medium of the control of social activities – especially the control over the *spacing and timing* of human activities – arising from the deployment of digital technologies to watch, observe, record, track and trace human subjects. From one angle, complex digital systems might be said to have ushered into existence a digital observatory of greatly increased surveillance, somewhat akin to George Orwell's account of Big Brother and Newspeak. Ubiquitous CCTV in public spaces, data-mining software, RFID chips in passports and identity cards, automated software systems governing transport and the speed of vehicles, and the migration of biometric security into various organizational settings: a whole variety of convergent developments has unfolded dramatically extending the scope of digital surveillance. It is evident that the digital monitoring of the citizens' activities and the observing of the online and smartphone interactions of individuals has been undertaken by a growing number of corporations and state agencies. Since former CIA whistle-blower Edward Snowden released documents in 2013 revealing the numerous global surveillance programs run by the National Security Agency with the cooperation of telecommunication giants and various governments, the issue of digital surveillance has moved centre-stage in world politics and, for many critics, has become associated with the production and governance of citizens in the age of neoliberalism. Led by digital technology, the rise of various 'watching technologies' (from CCTV to telerobotics) indicates the arrival of always-on, 24/7 electronic surveillance and a radical extension of the surveillance of subject populations in the political sphere by the modern state.

Critics of digital surveillance tend to be heavily influenced by the late French historian Michel Foucault's notion of panoptic surveillance.[18] Foucault famously identified Jeremy Bentham's panopticon as the prototype of disciplinary power in modernity, and argued that prisons, asylums, schools and factories were designed so that those in positions of power could watch and monitor individuals from a central point of observation. Foucault's panopticon metaphor emphasized the gaze in the sense of surveillance, especially in the form of the continued observation (as in the instance of guards keeping watch upon prisoners or teachers observing a classroom of pupils). These characteristics of disciplinary power have been extended and deepened through digitized surveillance. For example, prisoners can now be kept under 24-hour electronic surveillance. The dispersal of digital technologies of watching are especially consequential for the internalization of surveillance and the more repressive features of disciplinary power. Indeed, some critics understand the digital age as a kind of lifting of the panopticon gaze to the second power, such that digitized surveillance is ever-present and complete.[19]

There can be little doubt that digital forms of surveillance have transformed power relations in contemporary societies, and much more radical developments are likely to result from the next wave of technological innovation. But it is mistaken, I argue, to see digital surveillance as maximizing disciplinary power of the kind described by Foucault. Certainly, some digital systems of surveillance depend upon authoritative forms of monitoring and control, and, in that sense, can be likened to many of the instances of direct supervision discussed by Foucault. But this is not the only aspect of surveillance which comes to the fore in conditions of digital life. Today, surveillance is often indirect and based upon the collection, ordering and control of information. Characteristic of digital interactions such as social media platforms is that there is no centralized location from which individuals are observed; there is instead a distribution of digital interaction across a range of sites and operationalized through a variety of networks. This suggests that the routine use of digital technologies can also be understood in less threatening or menacing ways. Many people now wear self-tracking devices such as Fitbit and Nike's Fuelband, designed to monitor the state of their bodies and provide information on bodily functions such as heart rate, pulse, calories burned and body temperature. New developments in telemedicine make possible the 24/7 monitoring of elderly and vulnerable people; patients who participate in self-care practices through digital monitoring systems are supported by doctors and other healthcare professionals who also access and monitor the health data of patients. Advances in telerobotic technologies within medicine and surgery have been dramatic in recent years, allowing patients in rural and remote areas to access specialist procedures in microsurgery, orthopaedic surgery and minimally invasive surgery in ways not previously possible. Many of the social changes happening to power relations in this technological context cannot be understood as only disciplinary or simply repressive; they also contribute to novel practices of self-care, new forms of selfhood and identity, and the extension of social reflexivity.

Digitized surveillance might perhaps be better characterized as distributed monitoring, a sea of interconnected digital activities ranging from self-tracking to auto-activated information gathering. Central to this idea of distributed informational monitoring, assembled across many platforms and networks, is the notion of 'sousveillance', which refers to people watching each other at a distance through digital technologies.[20] In this digitalization of life, people become part of environments which are sentient and smart, and such digital systems promote increasingly swarming behaviour. Whilst it is acknowledged that professional and personal information is routinely gathered by state agencies through the deployment of digital surveillance technologies, the important point from this perspective is that increasingly indirect forms of surveillance operate 'from below' – as people use digital technologies to click 'like', 'favourite' and 'retweet'. From this angle, people 'watching each other' on social media platforms – Facebook, YouTube, Twitter, Instagram – become caught up in wider processes of surveillance which are at once self-regulating and self-mobilizing.[21]

It follows that another attribute of information monitoring across platforms and networks is that of surveillance at a distance, where data is fluid, decentred, transferred and routinely shared with third parties. As data-mining fast becomes the DNA of the platform economy, one inadvertent, unplanned side effect of the ubiquity of AI has been that complex systems of recording, measuring and assessing the personal information of citizens have become fodder to the business of politics, elections and voting. The 2018 scandal over British political consulting firm, Cambridge Analytica, which harvested data from millions of Facebook profiles to influence voter behaviour in the 2016 US presidential election, is a single example.[22] The data mined by Cambridge Analytica had been contracted through Cambridge University psychologist Aleksandr Kogan; Facebook had previously authorized Kogan to pull data from its online profiles through an app he had developed – *thisismydigitallife* – ostensibly for academic purposes. The app was, essentially, a personality quiz for Facebook users. Before undertaking the quiz, however, users of the app needed to give consent for access to their Facebook profiles as well as the profiles of their Facebook friends. More than 270,000 Facebook users took the quiz, which ultimately resulted in Kogan gaining access to over 87 million Facebook profiles – 30 million of which contained enough information to be matched with other data trails. Cambridge Analytica had invested approximately US$7 million on harvesting this data undertaken by Kogan. Christopher Wylie, a Cambridge Analytica data scientist who became the key whistle-blower on this scandal, commented that this data had been used to construct elaborate psychographic profiles of individual voters. Many commentators argued this it was the data which enabled the Trump campaign to win the electoral college vote while losing the popular vote by three million votes.[23]

The trend towards 'behavioural micro-targeting' of individual behaviour (consumer choices, political affiliations, personal preferences) to 'nudge' or 'steer' election outcomes is part and parcel of the 'dark side' of surveillance in the age of AI. Some critics have argued that there is indeed an emerging system of ubiquitous mass surveillance which is central to the functioning of corporations and governments in contemporary societies. Digital technologies of observation, monitoring, tracking and surveillance of the public and private lives of people function across digital platforms from social networking (Facebook, Snapchat, Instagram) to mobile payment (PayPal, Apple Pay, Google Wallet) to Internet search engines (Google, Yahoo, Bing). Companies use technologies of surveillance to track Web locations, record consumer spending patterns, store emails, manipulate social networking activities and the resulting patterns linked through smart algorithms. 'Facebook', writes Zeynep Tufekci, 'is a giant "surveillance machine"'. The business of surveillance, from the data broker industry to personalized advertising, involves the mining of vast digital data, and the personal information of citizens is routinely bought and sold without the knowledge of the individuals concerned. The result includes major threats to human freedom and privacy, as corporate surveillance over the private and public lives of citizens develops unchecked.

Surveillance is not only a profound structural problem in the digital age; it has been directly marshalled by governments around the world to manipulate and control citizens. Bruce Schneier, in *Data and Goliath*, contends that the ability of governments to peer into our collective personal lives is historically greater than it has ever been:

> Governments around the world are surveilling their citizens, and breaking into computers both domestically and internationally. They want to spy on everyone to find terrorists and criminals, and – depending on the government – political activists, dissidents, environmental activists, consumer advocates, and freethinkers.[24]

Central in many of these surveillance processes is how the state security world deploys data-gathering programs of extraordinary scale, range and depth. For example, the US Prism surveillance operation mines data from Google, Facebook, Verizon, Yahoo and other key Internet companies to track foreign nationals. Similarly, the UK's Government Communications Headquarters (GCHQ) draws data from all Internet and social networking traffic entering Europe to anticipate and prevent cyberattacks, government hacks and terrorist plots. What Louise Amoore terms 'digitized dissection', the disaggregation of a person's data trail into various degrees of security risk, is of key importance to the new surveillance technologies.[25] Such data dissection occurs not only within state borders but also on a global plane. As Schneier concludes, there is today 'a global surveillance network where all countries collude to surveil everyone on the entire planet'.[26] Whilst the advantages to world security of the digital revolution have been considerable, there are clearly many costs stemming from unchecked disciplinary surveillance on citizens. Real dangers include disturbing effects on free speech and freedom of expression, loss of liberty and erosion of democracy.

The Routledge Social Science Handbook of AI

The *Handbook* sets out to provide a reasonably comprehensive account of artificial intelligence – its history, development, deepening, cultures, innovations and technologies – and its relation to the social sciences. The first section of the book examines the ways that social science theory, methods and approaches have responded to, and engaged with, AI. There is an opening detailed discussion of AI from the standpoint of the key concerns of social science, and especially contemporary social theory, by Anthony Elliott. Thomas Birtchnell traces the conditions and consequences of space, place and geography in the discourse of AI. J. Michael Innes and Ben W. Morrison lay out the path of development in the discipline of psychology for encounters with AI, giving insight into the latent conventions and occluded codes that structure psychological life, and indeed the profession of psychology itself, in conditions of advanced AI. Jutta Weber and Bianca Prietl turn to address the discourse of technoscience – the magical terrain of what might be termed 'the technological fix' – in the wider frame of machine learning and predictive analytics. Ross Boyd addresses one of the most central debates in the AI and society canon – namely, how automated intelligent machines are transforming the world of work. Michaela Pfadenhauer and Tobias Lehmann turn to consider the effects of AI, highlighting the complex ways in which personhood and passion are reshaped in the aftermath of the AI revolution. Joffrey Becker discusses AI in the field of anthropology. The sphere of ethics in the wake of AI is analyzed with great insight and sophistication by Vincent Mueller. Finally, Naoko Abe considers developments in design thinking, with a fascinating discussion of human–machine interfaces and the reworking of design and the aesthetic domain in the contemporary era.

The second section of the book shifts focus to address diverse fields of artificial intelligence in social science research. Roman Batko outlines the contributions and consequences of AI to the fields of business and enterprise, focusing on transformations of economy and organization as a result of the digital revolution. Transformations of mobility are centre stage in Sven Kesselring and Carolin Schoenewolf's encounter with AI. Maja De Neergaard and Malene Freudendal-Pedersen look at the interconnections between digitalization and smart cities. Nicolas Petit and Jerome De Cooman turn to consider new developments in law and the legal profession, considering the massive impacts of automation in the legal domain. Matteo E. Bonfanti, Myriam Dunn Cavelty and Andreas Wenger address the vital area of cybersecurity. Frank Sauer writes about some of the most perplexing issues to do with developments in lethal autonomous weapons systems, outlining the ever-increasing connections between AI and the techno-militarization of war. Massimo Durante details his impressive theory of computational power in the age of AI, focusing on how contemporary representations of the world are increasingly recast in the image of machine intelligence. The interconnections between AI, robotics and aged care is the central theme of Eric L. Hsu's discussion of technogenerians. Jo Bates looks at the world of big data, situating the datafication of the world in the context of critical data studies. Entertainment is also reconfigured powerfully as a result of the intrusion of AI into the culture industries, as Sam Han discusses in some detail. Norina Gasteiger and Elizabeth

Broadbent look at the complex relations between AI, healthcare and medicine, with a strong focus on the radical transformations that new digital technologies offer to patient care and well-being. In the final chapter, Louis Everuss provides a superb overview of how AI reshapes migration (both freely chosen and enforced), giving rise to a world of smart borders.

Notes

1. In a review of the first 50 years of AI research, for example, Hamid Ekbia identified eight major science and engineering approaches to AI, each centred on very different characterisations of what 'intelligence' is. See Hamid Ekbia, "Fifty Years of Research in Artificial Intelligence", *Annual Review of Information Science and Technology*, Vol. 44, Issue 1, 2010, pp. 201–247; See also Anthony Elliott, *Making Sense of AI: Our Algorithmic World* (Cambridge: Polity Press, 2021).
2. Department for Business, "Energy and Industrial Strategy, Industrial Strategy: Building a Britain Fit for the Future", November 2017, p. 37, www.gov.uk/government/uploads/system/uploads/attachment_data/file/664563/industrial-strategy-white-paper-web-ready-version.pdf.
3. PwC 2017. Sizing the prize: PwC's Global Artificial Intelligence Study, www.pwc.com/gx/en/issues/data-and-analytics/publications/artificial-intelligence-study.html.
4. Toby Walsh, *2062: The World that AI Made* (Melbourne: La Trobe University Press, 2018), p. 15.
5. R. Ayres and S. Miller, *The Impacts of Industrial Robots* (Pittsburgh: Carnegie Mellon Robotics Institute, 1981), p. 3; V. Sujan and M. Meggiolaro, *Mobile Robots: New Research* (New York: Nova Science Publishers, 2005), p. 42.
6. See John Urry, *Global Complexity* (Cambridge: Polity Press, 2003).
7. These seven considerations are set out in more detail in my earlier work on AI, and I draw directly from this research in what follows here. See Anthony Elliott, *The Culture of AI: Everyday Life and the Digital Revolution* (London and New York: Routledge, 2019), especially Chapter 1.
8. See "Digital Skills Crisis", House of Commons Science and Technology Committee, UK Parliament, Second Report of Session 2016–17, https://publications.parliament.uk/pa/cm201617/cmselect/cmsctech/270/270.pdf.
9. Karin Knorr Cetina, "From Pipes to Scopes: The Flow Architecture of Financial Markets", *Distinktion*, Vol. 7, 2003, pp. 7–23.
10. John Urry, *What is the Future?* (Cambridge: Polity Press, 2016).
11. John B. Thompson, *The Media and Modernity: A Social Theory of the Media* (Stanford: Stanford University Press, 1995), p. 153.
12. Manuel Castells, *The Collapse of Soviet Communism: A View from the Information Society* (Los Angeles: Figueroa Press, 2003).
13. Adam Greenfield, *Everyware: The Dawning Age of Ubiquitous Computing* (Berkeley: New Riders, 2006).
14. Ibid., p. 26.
15. Semiconductor Transistor Association, "International Technology Roadmap for Semiconductors", 2015, www.semiconductors.org/main/2015_international_technology_roadmap_for_semiconductors_itrs/ (Viewed 31 August 2016).
16. There are numerous works which express a sceptical view about the quickening pace of technological advances. Bob Seidensticker's work, *FutureHype*, offers one such sceptical account, but there are of course others. Bob Seidensticker, *FutureHype: the Myths of Technological Change* (San Francisco: Berrett-Koehler Publishers, 2006).
17. www.theverge.com/2015/6/8/8739611/apple-wwdc-2015-stats-update.
18. Numerous authors writing on the theme of surveillance in society, such as Christian Fuchs, have been highly influenced by the work of Michel Foucault. However, it should be noted that there have been numerous calls to recognize the limits of Foucault's theories, especially on the theme of panopticism. See for example Kevin Haggerty, "Tear Down the Walls: On Demolishing the Panopticon", in *Theorising Surveillance: The Panopticon and Beyond*, edited by D. Lyon (Uffculme, Devon: Willan Publishing, 2006), pp. 23–45.
19. See David Lyon, *Surveillance Studies* (Cambridge: Polity Press, 2007).
20. See Rob Kitchin, *The Data Revolution* (New York: SAGE Publications, 2014).
21. For further discussion see Christian Fuchs, "New Media, Web 2.0 and Surveillance", *Sociology Compass*, Vol. 5, Issue 2, 2011, pp. 134–147; See also Samantha Adams, "Post-Panoptic Surveillance Through Healthcare Rating Sites", *Information, Communication and Society*, Vol. 16, Issue 2, 2013.

22 Cambridge Analytica had been established in 2013 as a subsidiary of Strategic Communications Laboratories, an entity which was partly owned by Robert Mercer – an American hedge-fund manager who has strongly backed various conservative political causes. Steve Bannon, then publisher of the alt-right Breitbart News and subsequent advisor to Donald Trump, was vice president of Cambridge Analytica. See Matthew Rosenberg, Nicholas Confessore, and Carole Cardwalladr, "How Trump Consultants Exploited the Facebook Data of Millions", *New York Times*, 17 March 2018, www.nytimes.com/2018/03/17/us/politics/cambridge-analytica-trump-campaign.html.
23 In a UK TV investigative report, Cambridge Analytica's then CEO, Alexander Nix – who was subsequently suspended by the company – boasted to an undercover reporter about the 2016 Trump campaign: "We did all the research, all the data, all the analytics, all the targeting, we ran all the digital campaign, the television campaign, and our data informed all the strategy. See ABC News (2018) Cambridge Analytica bosses claimed they invented 'Crooked Hillary' campaign, won Donald Trump the presidency, 21 Mar 2018, www.abc.net.au/news/2018-03-21/cambridge-analytica-claimed-it-secured-donald-trump-presidentia/9570690.
24 Bruce Schneier, *Data and Goliath: The Hidden Battles to Collect Your Data and Control Your World* (New York: Norton, 2015), p. 7.
25 Louise Amoore, "Algorithmic War: Everyday Geographies of the War on Terror", *Antipode*, 41, 2009, pp. 49–69.
26 Schneier, *Data and Goliath*, p. 91.

2
Geographies of AI

Thomas Birtchnell

1 Introduction

The year is 2043 and getting out of bed today is a struggle for Mari. Late gig working has taken its toll.

"Sirino, start the kettle boiling."

Mari's voice projects out to the intangible artificially intelligent personal assistant (AI-PA), and then, "please", softly, with slight embarrassment. Staring at the ceiling Mari hesitates from reaching for the digital glasses at the bedside, but then weakens and slips them on. Instantly Mari's eyes scroll down the list of emails that have arrived overnight on the left of her vison, a calendar scrolls a daily itinerary on the right.

"Kettle is boiled for you, Mari. Would you like me to check your itinerary today? You have a meeting with a boss of one of your regular gigs. A breach has been detected at the border and they need a consultant human to take a look."

Those dockland AI security guards are hopeless. Just clockwork tin soldiers.

"OK Mari?"

Sirino enquires in a non-gendered, non-ageist and accent-neutral, mostly dulcet, tone of voice the way Mari likes it: suitable for a 'woke' (as the primary care-giving parent, who Mari refuses to call 'mother' – despite the arguments – disparagingly puts it using this strange, antiquated word) citizen of the world like 'they' [singular, gender-neutral, third-person pronoun, as Mari had typed into the computer] are.

Mari knows the AI's concerned sounds are a fabrication created by the software algorithm set for sensitivity but goes along with it anyway, since Mari had been the one to select the personality for the AI-PA to be 'bookish homebody' – an add-on that cost a little bit more than the standard defaults.

"Car is ready and waiting outside, Mari. You need a shower first; you smell a bit . . . human. And I don't even have a nose. The car will wait for you; I'll just reprogram its computer for the delay. The AI-driver won't mind."

Mari ponders, as the AI-housekeeper of the smart-shower finds the perfect temperature and pressure through aggregating past selections and ambient body temperature, whether a different, less humorous, personality for Sirino might be a suitable punishment for the jibe.

But they say that people who swap out their AI-PA's personalities too much need to be mindful of what this says about their own personalities.

Thomas Birtchnell

A bold statement header in a 2016 article in the journal *Nature*'s title says it all: 'a world where everyone has a robot: why 2040 could blow your mind' (Butler, 2016: 398). Enablers for this mind-blowing transition are growing exponentially in computing power; 'really' big data; escalating communication speeds; talking devices; biology booms including DNA sequencing, cloning and manipulation; 3D printing disrupting traditional manufacturing techniques; and physical robots becoming ubiquitous for military, industrial, commercial and personal uses. In this attention-grabbing piece, a series of experts give their projections for 2040, ranging from the anticipated 'Cambrian explosion' in robotics of Gill Pratt from the Toyota Research Institute to the 'first phase of true personal, assistive robots in the home' of Head of the Stanford Artificial Intelligence Laboratory Fei-Fei Li. Yet, missing from this list of engineers, geneticists, computer scientists and roboticists is the viewpoint of a social scientist. Robots and artificial intelligence (AI) are not exactly the same, but a similar group of innovations underpin both of these trends, and to say that robots are physical and AI is virtual overlooks the areas they have in common.

Here, geography offers a method to provide certitude to how AI and robotics (these two areas are treated as synonymic in this chapter) might manifest in societies. In this handbook entry, I aim to illustrate how space and place matter when considering the impacts of AI on societies. The fictional vignette at the beginning of the chapter illustrates how foresight involves taking what is important in the present and exploring limits and extremes (Birtchnell and Urry, 2013). Certainly there are many technological pitfalls and uncertainties that unhinge efforts to gauge what is ahead with clarity; however, social science offers a suite of social theories to inform foresight in a scientifically credible way (Geels and Smit, 2000).

One inference made in the vignette is that AI will be able to hold conversations with humans. Anyone who struggles with the voice recognition of Apple's 'virtual assistant' Siri will know that this remains tantalizingly out of reach (Wajcman, 2017). Despite Siri having a good range of jokes to share, it is not able to answer the most straightforward of questions about itself. If Siri did answer questions, it might be asked: what is its gender? Age? Cultural background? Does it need to have any of these 'trappings' to relate to and with the human 'us'? Geographical queries further compound this problem: where does Siri live? Does it understand what it is like to have a human body? What would it do, and where would it go, if it did have a physical body in 'our' world? Such inquiry begs the question: can AI ever truly understand 'us' and be understood by 'us', without a body or culture, or gender, or sense of place we recognize?

AI is emerging as a fruitful topic in the social sciences: as 'good to think with', particularly from a critical perspective. Human geographers are leading the charge in this regard. Since the conception of the idea that computers could match, or beat, the human intellect, the philosophy of the mind has undertaken extensive cogitations seeking to foresee the ethical ramifications on humans. A pressing question is: what dangers lie ahead in a world of thinking objects?

A major hurdle for AI is that it continues to lack one of the most obvious and fundamental human traits: 'common sense' (Mitchell, 2009). Common sense is understood as sound judgement in practical matters. Humans develop this at a very young age and are tied to human sensory systems and their interaction with the laws of physics. It is this feature, common sense, which presents the most challenges for the release of AI into human societies.

AI appears to defy conventional labour borders, as its proliferation in the Kenyan outsourcing centres where humans manually error-correct Google's self-driving cars demonstrates (also see Wahome and Graham, 2020). It has manifested in industries thought immune, as its application in audio post-production shows (Birtchnell and Elliott, 2018), and it has been startlingly successful in some areas, such as journalism, and overwhelmingly ineffective in others, such as driverless cars. Human geography offers a suite of complementary optics for scholarly engagement with AI. Four areas represent the limits of this handbook entry.

Firstly, the social theory of 'mobility justice' lends transport geography a method to scrutinize how inegalitarian aspects of the automobility system could be exacerbated by the inclusion of AI into transport modes, notably, driverless vehicles. Can they be trusted to drive humans? Secondly, the issue of common sense becomes far more profound for the use of military AI in conflict situations where common sense arises as a crucial, intuitive skill to detect the difference between a bystander and a combatant. How do they judge friend from foe? Thirdly, the evolution of cities to become 'smarter' through a range of sensors, robotics, algorithms embedded in infrastructures and data analytics is presenting an interesting perspective for urban geographers. If 'smart cities' become the norm, how are citizens' lives then potentially augmented or disrupted when lapses of common sense in AI is exploited by humans? Fourthly, this lack of common sense opens up AI systems to all sorts of human exploitation as companies who deploy them utilize strategies such as digital 'outsourcing' – that is, hiring labourers in other countries, invariably the global South, where salaries are lower and labour legislations are more lax – to compensate for AI's errors, indecisions or inefficiencies through implementing humans as a 'backup' or fail-safe. Recent research in economic geography sheds light on this important area of inquiry in geographical theory building. How will AI make work more and not less fair for humans?

The road ahead for AI appears – as with most technological innovations – to be surprising, unpredictable and a challenge to foresee. This is not to say scholars are not trying to imagine how futures with AI will unfold. There are a surprising number of reports available from government departments, think tanks, intragovernmental organizations and other notable silos of expertise. Yet, despite a voluminous amount of guidance on how AI will emerge, much of this lacks specificity and context. Here, geographical expertise applies.

Perhaps the most momentous pending innovation pertinent to AI is quantum computing as this appears to be the avenue by which progress towards sentient machines will be made. As Q-Bits grow in number and power, new possibilities emerge for computing to process tasks in parallel, with little to no latency, although error-checking continues to remain a potent threat to this technology. The link between AI and quantum computing is as of now opaque; however, social scientists in geography are engaging with the ramifications of this fruitful new area of inquiry. Already, geographers have engaged with quantum computing and sought to surmise its implications for space and place.

2 Understanding AI

The notion of a thinking object able to undertake human labour unquestionably spans back to at least the sixteenth century. In Jewish legend the Rabbi of Prague creates a humanoid from clay, the golem, by inscribing on his forehead the Hebrew word *emet*, or 'truth', in effect creating a slave able to replace human labour, a 'dream' for AI that continues to this day (Musa Giuliano, 2020). Many of the metaphors for AI arose from the time of mechanical manipulation. For example, an automaton is a collection of nineteenth-century French automata – acrobats, clowns and musicians – but is now widely used for AI functions. And the term 'Mechanical Turk', which is the name for an online crowdsourcing marketplace platform, came from an eighteenth-century fake chess-playing machine.

According to the Organisation for Economic Co-operation and Development (OECD; 2019: 21), four elements compose the current vision of AI: autonomous vehicles and robotics, natural language processing, computer vision, and language and learning. These developments map onto a range of milestones historically unfolding from the fanciful imaginings of AI in science fiction literature and art in the early twentieth century to the British mathematician Alan

Thomas Birtchnell

Turing's famous eponymous test that articulates how a computational machine might trick a human into believing it was human.

These milestones cluster around the late twentieth century: the Navlab autonomous car built by Carnegie Mellon in 1986, Dragon Systems' speech recognition software in 1997 and the defeat of chess grandmaster Garry Kasparov by supercomputer IBM's Deep Blue in the same year. The expansion of the Internet globally and the exponential growth of processor power in domestic computers and industrial servers means that so-called big data and data analytics alongside algorithmic 'machine learning' have reinforced a version of AI that is reaching consumer markets, in most cases through online services. In the next sections, I consider how geography provides insights on these four iterations of AI.

3 Claims, developments and contributions for AI in geography

In this handbook entry, I examine four aspects of AI in geography, in particular in relation to common sense, or lack of it. The first is transport geography and the burgeoning literature on automation of traffic processes and modes of travel. An overt focus in scholarship is driverless vehicles, in part to recognize the media perception of this innovation as critical for future transportation. The second area is social and cultural geography with AI attracting debate due to its use in the early twentieth century in conflict. The notion of automated warfare is a nightmare scenario for many people; however, geographers also draw attention to the human interactions and social impact of managing AI and automated systems in theatres of war. Thirdly, this section considers urban geography and the motivations for the smart city concept. These interface with AI through the proliferation of sensors across the city's infrastructure and the use of a range of digital platforms for governance and planning. The gamification of planning processes is flagged as a core area of inquiry for AI. Finally, I consider the surprising spread of AI in labour and the input economic geography is giving to analyses of outsourcing and exploitation in the global South.

3.1 AI in transport geography

> The car pulls up outside Mari's apartment entrance. Shuffling inside, the cleanliness of the seats is noteworthy. Sitting on the front left passenger seat is a smart wallet someone has left behind.
> "Sirino, can you scan the wallet's code and declare it's lost?"
> The vehicle gradually slides into traffic, entering the AI-only lane, other cars gliding aside to make room with barely a moment's hesitation.
> "The AI-driver tells me that the owner has already traced it and has made arrangements to retrieve it from the vehicle once you disembark".
> The car suddenly lurches to the right and an alarm sounds.
> "What happened?" Mari shouts.
> A jalopy Tesla from the 2010s veers past with a human sitting in the driver seat.
> "The human driver does not have AI enabled and is in the wrong lane," says Sirino, the voice temporarily corrupting due to the urgency of the response.
> "They're driving manually? That's madness. They must be a neo-Luddite!" Mari exclaims.

The study of the spatial distribution and effects of transport modalities and infrastructure, and the movement of people and goods through transport systems (Castree et al., 2013), is a chief focus of transport geography. In this sub-field of geography, AI has many implications for increasing the efficiency of traffic flows for private vehicles, enabling sophisticated inventory-keeping for bulk volume freight; and reducing uncertainties from what is known as the 'last mile' for deliveries within dense urban settlements. In the media there are predictions of a widespread transition to driverless vehicles in the near future (Cugurullo et al., 2020).

AI could change how far humans are willing to travel, particularly given the disruptions to commuting that ubiquitous homeworking has resulted in due to the coronavirus pandemic that began in 2020 (Perrine et al., 2020). AI does not necessarily lead to the removal of humans from the act of motoring per se, as multiple futures are plausible. There is advanced traffic management where AI operates behind the scenes to collect and analyze data that reduce congestion and accidents; cooperative systems, where AI assists people to drive more efficiently, safely and logically via mapping, real-time information and cruise control; and full-blown autonomous vehicles where humans do not drive (Pel et al., 2020). Beyond these structural issues are the ways that humans interact with autonomous mobility. Here, the useful term 'socio-mobility' emerges to address how communities of humans will respond to AI in transport (Kassens-Noor et al., 2020). Errors that are made by humans *and* AI during critical moments demand social inquiry that articulates how driver-bodies interact in terms of habits, routines and social practices (Bissell et al., 2020).

Imagine an autonomous vehicle, or 'driverless car', approaching a snow-person in the middle of the road (Mitchell, 2019). It would be common sense for the AI to perceive an obstacle and come to a rapid halt, placing the passengers in more danger than if it had decided to simply plough through the snow as a human would most likely choose to do, knowing that snow-people are not obstructions for cars and that humans do not have carrots for noses. AI has no way of knowing whether the snow-person is alive or not. In order to critique the notion that autonomous vehicles are soon to emerge as alternatives for human motorists, I flag the current theory of 'mobility justice' in transport geography and the mobilities sub-discipline as vital for this issue.

The framework of 'mobility justice' offers an optic to critically appraise (Sheller, 2018). The introduction of AI into transportation has pressing implications for geography given that the main obstacle to the success of this innovation appears to be its coordination with other, human, road users and the spatial nuances that arise out in the 'wild'. The present driving regime is hardly logical: speed limits are only partially adhered to in many countries, usually in proximity to speed cameras or police, and all sorts of behavioural nuances apply between drivers with a fine-grain sensitivity to responsiveness, confidence and decision-making. It is surprising, then, that sociological analyses are overshadowed by technical ones in scholarly literature (Yeo and Lin, 2020).

Human geographical inquiry foregrounds the extant ethical issues with driverless vehicles that engineering and computer science neglects. Social science analysis of how the most vulnerable and disadvantaged are affected by the widespread use of automobiles argues that driverless vehicles will compound many of the problems associated with the 'automobility' culture. Cities built around automobiles privileges this private transport mode over others and while driverless vehicles might reduce traffic congestion and collisions between vehicles it is not clear that they will reduce fatalities with pedestrians, cyclists or marginal users of streets, such as mobility scooters (Birtchnell et al., 2018).

3.2 AI in social and cultural geography

Mari enters the meeting hub, checking in with the AI-concierge via the facial and retina scanners, and sanitizing her hands accordingly. The inside of the digital spectacles light up with a call icon photo and the earpiece rings concurrently with the microphone lowering from the frame arm.

> *"Hi, boss. Running late?"*
>
> *"Mari – I've changed meeting rooms, the AI-PA stuffed up, I'm down the hall".*
>
> *Mari spins around and turns a corner. As she enters the meeting room a vast display bristles with lights and videos from an aerial drone balloon over the city. Ronin turns and points to one of the images showing cargo containers stacked high.*
>
> *"We have a breach here in the docklands at imports. Can you spend some time investigating in the afternoon? Take an AI-border control officer and have a sniff about for anything wrong. You'll need an AI-security team with you. Take over the drone control."*

The use of AI in conflict is the most disturbing manifestation of this technology. In the 2000s human geographers led an early exploratory inquiry into the use of AI in warfare, notably in the proliferation of so-called drones, or un-[hu]manned aerial vehicles (UAVs), above the skies of the Middle East during the US-led conflicts in that region. In this vein of research, questions around AI disturb the notion that machines are able to comprehend the complexities of societies, even when options appear limited: combatant or non-combatant. Rather than distancing humans from the battlefield, as in a videogame, military AI and drones enable an assemblage that immerses them into the moment, yet sets them physically apart; hence UAV operators also suffer post-traumatic stress disorder (Gregory, 2011). Just as with driverless vehicles, it is in this space between machine and human error that social science has the most to contribute.

The lack of common sense in this context has deadly consequences for humans on both sides of conflict. Indeed, it is non-combatants, so-called collateral damage, who stand to suffer most from AI in warfare: children, the elderly and those who suffer disadvantages in comparison to other humans in their social or physical setting. Instead, AI uses 'estimation algorithms' (known in the US military as 'bugsplat') to judge the efficacy of a target, thereby quantifying ethical decision-making (Emery, 2020). Social and cultural geographical theories of ethics in warfare are an important area for AI in geography.

As automation enters the public realm it will invariably be tied to systems of control as imagined in futures that involve a 'digital panopticon' – alarmingly similar to responses to the COVID-19 virus pandemic as societies locked down and aimed to contact trace vast swathes of the citizenry (Urry, 2008). In the next section this fine line between AI's use by the military in peace time will be examined further.

3.3 AI in urban geography

> *As Mari leaves the meeting hub her digital eyeglasses light up with bouncing animations and characters belonging to a painfully addictive location-based game that is all the rage. Fantastical creatures interact with the street's furniture and buildings, giving the illusion that they are really there, one even appearing to write something on the wall – a clue for extra points. With a few gestures the digital creatures are captured and points arrive in Mari's eyepiece.*
>
> *"Turn it off Sirino; I thought I requested you cap my gaming for the day? I'm so addicted to this game it's affecting my sleep."*
>
> *"I thought you wouldn't want to miss the latest campaign the mayor is launching this afternoon so I ignored your request. Double points and the chance to capture a super-rare one. You just need to fill out the survey on your last car trip and its free to play."*
>
> *"Go on then, log me in for five minutes. Gee, you know me better than I know myself!"*
>
> *Mari walks down the street, arms waving, as creatures roll and climb in bizarre ways on the walls and street lights. Another person, similarly gesticulating, smiles knowingly as they pass. Another gamer.*

The far greater surveillance necessary for managing the physical distancing and quarantine of citizens in a post-COVID-19 world is intimating a shift towards AI in urban pandemic control (Chen et al., 2020). Urban citizens are 'meeting' AI through prosaic interactions with the digital platforms that compose the 'smart city' and trace people's movements and social networks overtly and covertly (Macrorie et al., 2019). One example is through location-based gaming, Pokémon Go being a chief example, wherein AI populates public spaces and orients citizens towards the profit-making strategies of global corporations in tune with the smart city (Birchnell et al., 2020). These confrontations are not always geared towards profit-making and the market. Some digital platforms offer access to urban democracy and collective intelligence. These technopolitical digital platforms will feasibly recruit AI in order for citizens to participate more effectively with governance mechanisms at municipal levels or indeed protest against undemocratic decision-making (Smith and Martín, 2020).

For instance, with the gamification of municipal services citizens might react in the same fashion as computer gamers who routinely break the rules or exploit oversights in software design. In an urban, real-world setting this could have catastrophic results (Macrorie et al., 2019). It is not just contact tracing for viruses that is instigating a shift in how AI operates in cities. The sterilization of public space and compulsory distancing between people is creating a demand for robots and AI in airports, hospitals, hotels, restaurants, transportation systems, recreation and scenic areas and many other spaces within cities. As Zeng and colleagues (2020) describe, there are robots and AI routine and non-routine tasks and even in entertainment, teaching, comfort and assistance. Here AI is becoming just another infrastructure in the smart city that enables urban dwellers to abide by the limitations placed on them from the responses to the risk of COVID-19. Beyond logistics, disinfection and information provision robots and AI could alter how tourism happens (Xu and Jin, 2019), disrupting public life in ways similar to Pokémon Go and other digital platforms in gaming.

3.4 AI in economic geography

> *Entering the store Mari heads to the aisle where the fridges are kept. A droid ahead appears to be holding a conversation with itself as it jerks backwards and forwards against the stack of items.*
>
> *"The language is Swahili," notes Sirino. "It's troubleshooting via the carer in Africa as something has gone wrong."*
>
> *Mari reflects on the disaster last year where an insurgent overseas took over an AI-shelf-stacker and tried to attack the shoppers before stopping traffic in the centre of the city. They'd done some amazing hack apparently provided full access to mobility. Thankfully, the kill switch could be activated before anyone got hurt, but the incident on the news had seriously affected the media image of shop droids. But, no young person wants to stack shelves these days, so they were still everywhere.*
>
> *"We might come back later, just in case," said Mari to Sirino.*

A missing element in depictions of the 'rise of the robots' is the continuing and necessary role of humans in precariously digitized labour titled 'microwork' (Anwar and Graham, 2020). There is an intriguing linkage between the gig economy and AI development. There are three forms of microwork in which humans support AI, what Tubaro and colleagues term 'the trainer, the verifier and the imitator' (2020). In the first instance humans lay the foundations for AI to take the reins in the future through data generation and annotation. Humans calculate, create content, analyse images and video, and moderate language and media.

In the second instance is the verifier. Examples of this are surrogate humans who operate AI-enabled robots from very great distances in a new form of outsourcing that is akin to drone operation but in commercial and even residential settings. Here humans step in once AI has operated in the 'wild' to produce appraisal data from an operational algorithm in order to create improvements, troubleshoot client issues, or make processes more efficient.

In the third instance is the imitator. Here, chatbots are often cited as examples, where AI might be operational for a few stages of interactions with clients, but when something is misunderstood, or too difficult, for the AI to interpret a human takes their place without the human interacting with the AI realizing a change has occurred.

Invariably, humans that train, verify and imitate AI are located elsewhere, such as in countries where wages are lower and employment conditions less stable than in the global North. Critical research is being conducted by Mark Graham from the Oxford Internet Institute on the digital divide in Africa (2015). In Kenya, young workers are being recruited to manually analyze visual data from AI applications for errors; in short, performing the kind of humdrum labour that AI was meant to replace.

4 Future developments: quantum geography and AI?

The release and success of the 2017 *Quantum Physics for Babies* book looks set to herald a whole new generation to probe the mysteries of the future of computing. The discovery of the Higgs boson by a multi-billion-dollar facility in Geneva, CERN, delivers on the promise of this multinational collaboration to find the 'god particle'. Quantum mechanics has been the purview of some of the most famous scientists in history, including Albert Einstein and Stephen Hawking. Despite a century of activity, the foundations of quantum mechanics continue to be ineffable to experts and laypeople alike. Throughout the twentieth century physicists rarely spoke of what the foundations of quantum mechanics might mean for the world at the human scale, a taboo known as the 'Copenhagen interpretation'. Drawing on the ideas of Danish physicist Niels Bohr, the interpretation held that Newtonian (or Classical) mechanics govern the world of the big while quantum mechanics governs the world of the small. The relationship, while complementary mathematically, cannot be explained philosophically, or so it goes.

The reason the Copenhagen interpretation has held sway for so long is that quantum effects are strange and defy description through analogy or metaphor. Quantum effects, such as non-locality, superposition, entanglement and quantum tunnelling, are counter-intuitive, illogical and unsettling despite making mathematical sense. Since the mathematics of quantum mechanics provides some of the most accurate predictions of any scientific theory, physicists have instead resigned themselves to 'shut up and calculate' instead of delving into the philosophy of the quantum world.

Why does this latest debate in the foundations of quantum mechanics affect human geography and AI? Surely it has no relevance for the scale at which human experiences of space or place operate? In fact, the indeterminacy in where the boundary lies between classical and quantum laws is momentous for human geography and its own foundations in the laws of physics. 'What ever happened to quantum geography' asks human geographer Thomas S. J. Smith in the title of his paper (2016). A chief reason for the dearth of interest in the discipline is that, dissimilar to other genres of science, quantum mechanics is not – citing Claude Levi Strauss's famous phrase (Garber, 2012: 96) – as 'good to think with' for social scientists as it might first appear to be. Yet, as AI emerges as a social phenomenon, efforts towards trying to understand the nuances in this new field of technology are growing in appreciation in human geography.

Another area of interest for geographers interested in AI is the progress being made in quantum computing and the implications for machine learning and, more broadly, the algorithms resulting from exponential processing power. Alongside the discovery of a new force of nature in 2014 (the Higgs field and boson), the commercialization of the first fully functioning qubit (a 'quantum bit') with error rates nearing those of conventional computers intimates a new era for big data unhindered by linear task processing, meaning that quantum computers appear to be able to process an unprecedented range of tasks simultaneously.

The cloud and big data analytics is inspiring new perspectives in human geographical scholarship and this will increase with quantum computers (see Amoore, 2016). The boundary politics for human geographers considering AI that arise at this particular quantum scale of inquiry (which was until recently the sole domain of physicists, engineers, mathematicians and philosophers) is critical here when contemplating the future of AI. Can geographers ever engage fruitfully with AI if quantum mechanics becomes the new frontier of knowledge?

While it is not possible to fathom yet what quantum computers in AI *will* do for human geographers, it is certainly possible to informatively hypothesize about potential applications based on the specific quantum phenomena they drawn on: superposition, entanglement and quantum tunnelling. While a review of these ideas are beyond the scope of this handbook entry, consensus amongst particle physicists deems that the geography of the quantum world occurs at a scale largely irrelevant to the reality of human experience.

We humans, and the observable world around us, are made of atoms and molecules contained within the periodic table of elements that constitute matter. A key point of contention is the counter-intuitive interpretations of the mathematical tools that quantum mechanics afford to physicists, which defy description and grounding in everyday reality, and raise thorny issues about the true nature of reality and consciousness. As historian of quantum mechanics Adam Becker summarizes,

> The problem is that it is just not clear what quantum physics is telling us about the world around us; the connection between the theory, though it is phenomenally successful, and the world we are in is just not obvious.
>
> *(2019: 2)*

At what scale the boundary lies between quantum and classical laws of physics is one of the most confounding conundrums, if, that is, there is indeed such a border between worlds.

The quantum world is a regular fixture of everyday life in the second decade of the twenty-first century in the media speculation about the future directions of AI. The problem is, in some ways, more serious for philosophers and, by extension, human geographers, who generally cannot 'shut up and compute' and yet require a bedrock of scientific consensus about the laws of physics for their own research programmes. From this perspective, social scientists' forays into the foundations of quantum mechanics are at best unwelcome amongst the physics community. The work of Karen Barad has been influential in bringing quantum theory into human geography, although this functions as a metaphor drawn from quantum mechanics into social theory and is not specific about how phenomena observed at the quantum level scale up to the human-lived world (Sharp, 2018; Country et al., 2016; Smith and Reid, 2018).

Given this groundswell of interest in the quantum world in human geography it is no wonder that commentators on AI are inquiring about what progress at this scale means for their scholarly understandings of space, time and the laws of physics that underpin their social theories. Indeed, there have already been numerous scoping exercises of whether quantum mechanics disputes, alters or even improves human geographers' social theories.

After Smith:

> In the face of some of the most successful, yet perplexing, physical theories we are yet to develop, it is remarkable that quantum geography and its possible implications in post-classical re-engagement with our world have failed to surface even as a tangential topic for consideration.
>
> *(2016: 6)*

Despite the challenge of interpretation of foundational ideas, efforts to engage with quantum mechanics have been evident in human geography. It is not lost on commentators that attempts to gauge the quantum world represent a logical progression for human geography's inspiration on, and influence by, scientific inquiry.

'Social' science naturally looks to agree with the foundations of all science, particularly laws governing motion, thermodynamics, gravity and time. A chief reason that quantum mechanics is not simply the next frontier for social scientists' 'physics envy', as Doreen Massey put it, is that its core theories unsettle conventions about scientific measurement and observation.

Implications span far beyond sub-atomic particles to humans themselves. Problematization of the definition of what it is to be 'human' through empirical forays into the non- and post-human is now a linchpin of progress for the discipline of human geography, taking scholars into fields ranging across the geological and biological sciences. Geographical rumination of quantum mechanics arises from the turns of knowledge beyond the human geography corpus into non-human and material interactions, which are expanding the horizon of research into new disciplinary territories. The quantum world represents the farthest reaches of this endeavour, being apparently fundamental. At one end of the scale, microscopic organic matter now falls within the remit of human geography with studies of viruses and bacteria. At the other end is the cosmos and time across geological eras.

A subset of inquiry in human geography has sought to probe deeper into the fundamental constituents of experience and the spaces and places that might exist at what are, to we humans, very small scales indeed, many orders of magnitude below that of our everyday sensory experiences; that is, the world we hear, see, touch and smell. Unfortunately, forays into the human geography of the sub-atomic world encounter an invisible border that prohibits inquiry, a line in the sand beyond which human geographers are imagined as being unable to tread or to contribute to intellectually.

A handful of early pioneers in quantum geography and the social sciences more broadly who are seeking to cross this disciplinary line and critique the barriers to progress they have met, notably in controversies over scholarly measurement and observation, are part and parcel of the debate about who has authority in analyzing AI from a social science perspective (see Wendt, 2018). Resolving these boundary politics has implications for the relationship of human geography to the sister discipline of physical geography and politics around the bounding of its ontological remit.

Five shifts in progress have opened up inquiry into 'quantum geography' in the last decade that are pertinent to the debate around how AI could gain 'common sense'. Firstly, is the emergence of *quantum computing* and interest in the social and spatial implications of this innovation. If quantum computers enter public use, human geographers are bound to engage in using them.

Secondly, is the budding discipline of *quantum biology* and the claim by some scientists that quantum mechanics does in fact apply at scales far larger than the sub-atomic world: in animal, plant, bacterial and molecular interactions. Here the human world could plausibly be affected by such advances in knowledge.

Thirdly, is the notion that quantum mechanics has ramifications for the understanding of *consciousness*. The efforts amongst management, well-being, spirituality and philosophical commentators to establish heuristics drawing on recent sub-atomic discoveries has implications, too, for how AI manifests.

Fourthly, is the *lay and media interest* in large-scale endeavours in particle and cosmological physics. Partly due to interests in how taxpayers and governments fund major civil undertakings, such as the Large Hardon Collider at CERN in Switzerland and its quest to detect the Higgs boson or the collection by satellite of the all-sky map of the cosmic microwave background radiation, the media are conflating AI and quantum computing as linked phenomena.

Finally, is the *discourse* by popular scientists that breaks the taboo over discussing the foundation of quantum mechanics within particle physics and presents disciplinary debates to a non-scientific lay audience, devoid of complex mathematics and jargon, and honest about politics, histories, controversies and interpretations in the field. Although human geographers have no call to claim purview over the scale of sub-atomic particles, they are certainly able to scrutinize the scale at which quantum computers will apply in AI applications, even when not couched in terms of mathematics or quantitative analysis.

Quantum computers are gaining the support of governments and corporations. Justin Trudeau, the Prime Minister of Canada, impressed an audience in 2016 with his foreknowledge of how quantum bits of information work. And Silicon Valley, the home of the personal computer, now features many start-ups in quantum computing alongside notable corporations such as Google, Intel and IBM. So what this means is that human geographers with a scholarly interest in AI will at some point in the future need to engage with debates about the interpretation of quantum measurement and the foundations of quantum physics.

5 Conclusion

There is a common misnomer that scholarship and commentary on AI should only be the preserve of computer scientists, engineers or those who technical expertise places them in direct contact with the technology. Such an observation is not only misleading, it is dangerous, as this handbook entry has shown in the contexts of mobility, conflict, cities and work. Geographical insights afford a critically informed assessment of much of the hype to be found in the public press. The overarching focus in this handbook chapter has been the issue of common sense as an oversight in projections of the momentousness of AI as it enters societies for more fully. As quantum computing grows in power and reach, and uncertainties around error correction are broached, this profound hurdle could be overcome through emulating the neurons of the brain inside machines. Yet, it is just as likely that AI will never surmount the human capacity to muster common sense. Geography unveils this core feature of human experience because it is through interactions with objects and people *in space* that common sense becomes so utterly crucial to everyday life.

References

Amoore, L. 2016. Cloud geographies: Computing, data, sovereignty. *Progress in Human Geography*, 42, 4–24.

Anwar, M. A. & Graham, M. 2020. Digital labour at economic margins: African workers and the global information economy. *Review of African Political Economy*, 47, 95–105.

Becker, A. 2019. *What is Real? The Unfinished Quest for the Meaning of Quantum Physics*. Boston, Basic Books.

Birtchnell, T. & Elliott, A. 2018. Automating the black art: Creative places for artificial intelligence in audio mastering. *Geoforum*, 96, 77–86.

Birtchnell, T., Harada, T. & Waitt, G. 2018. On the verge of change: Maverick innovation with mobility scooters. *Environmental Innovation and Societal Transitions*, 27, 118–128.

Birtchnell, T., Mcguirk, P., Moore, C. & Vettoretto, L. 2020. Pay to play? Subverting the digital economy of pokémon go in the smart city. *Digital Geography and Society*, 1, Article number 100004.

Birtchnell, T. & Urry, J. 2013. 3D, SF and the future. *Futures*, 50, 25–34.

Bissell, D., Birtchnell, T., Elliott, A. & Hsu, E. L. 2020. Autonomous automobilities: The social impacts of driverless vehicles. *Current Sociology*, 68, 116–134.

Butler, D. 2016. Tomorrow's World. *Nature*, 530.

Castree, N., Rogers, A. & Kitchin, R. 2013. *A Dictionary of Human Geography*. Oxford: Oxford University Press.

Chen, B., Marvin, S. & While, A. 2020. Containing COVID-19 in China: AI and the robotic restructuring of future cities. *Dialogues in Human Geography*, 10, 238–241.

Country, B., Wright, S., Suchet-Pearson, S., Lloyd, K., Burarrwanga, L., Ganambarr, R., Ganambarr-Stubbs, M., Ganambarr, B., Maymuru, D. & Sweeney, J. 2016. Co-becoming Bawaka: Towards a relational understanding of place/space. *Progress in Human Geography*, 40, 455–475.

Cugurullo, F., Acheampong, R. A., Gueriau, M. & Dusparic, I. 2020. The transition to autonomous cars, the redesign of cities and the future of urban sustainability. *Urban Geography*, 1–27.

Emery, J. R. 2020. Probabilities towards death: Bugsplat, algorithmic assassinations, and ethical due care. *Critical Military Studies*, 1–19.

Garber, M. 2012. *Loaded Words*. New York: Fordham University Press.

Geels, F. W. & Smit, W. A. 2000. Failed technology futures: Pitfalls and lessons from a historical survey. *Futures*, 32, 867–885.

Graham, M. 2015. Contradictory connectivity: Spatial imaginaries and technomediated positionalities in Kenya's outsourcing sector. *Environment and Planning A: Economy and Space*, 47, 867–883.

Gregory, D. 2011. From a view to a kill: Drones and late modern war. *Theory, Culture & Society*, 28, 188–215.

Kassens-Noor, E., Dake, D., Decaminada, T., Kotval-K, Z., Qu, T., Wilson, M. & Pentland, B. 2020. Sociomobility of the 21st century: Autonomous vehicles, planning, and the future city. *Transport Policy*, 99, 329–335.

Macrorie, R., Marvin, S. & While, A. 2019. Robotics and automation in the city: A research agenda. *Urban Geography*, 1–21.

Mitchell, M. 2009. *Complexity: A Guided Tour*. Cary: Oxford University Press, Incorporated.

Mitchell, M. 2019. How do you teach a car that a snowman won't walk across the road? *Aeon Newsletter*. Aeon Media Group Ltd, Melbourne.

Musa Giuliano, R. 2020. Echoes of myth and magic in the language of artificial intelligence. *AI & Society*, 35, 1009–1024.

OECD 2019. *Artificial Intelligence in Society*. Paris: OECD Publishing.

Pel, B., Raven, R. & Van Est, R. 2020. Transitions governance with a sense of direction: Synchronization challenges in the case of the dutch 'driverless car' transition. *Technological Forecasting and Social Change*, 160, 120244.

Perrine, K. A., Kockelman, K. M. & Huang, Y. 2020. Anticipating long-distance travel shifts due to self-driving vehicles. *Journal of Transport Geography*, 82, 102547.

Sharp, D. 2018. Difference as practice: Diffracting geography and the area studies turn. *Progress in Human Geography*, 43(5), 835–852.

Sheller, M. 2018. *Mobility Justice: The Politics of Movement in an Age of Extremes*. London: Verso Books.

Smith, A. & Martín, P. P. 2020. Going beyond the smart city? Implementing technopolitical platforms for urban democracy in madrid and Barcelona. *Journal of Urban Technology*, 1–20.

Smith, T. S. J. 2016. What ever happened to quantum geography? Toward a new qualified naturalism. *Geoforum*, 71, 5–8.

Smith, T. S. J. & Reid, L. 2018. Which 'being' in wellbeing? Ontology, wellness and the geographies of happiness. *Progress in Human Geography*, 42, 807–829.

Tubaro, P., Casilli, A. A. & Coville, M. 2020. The trainer, the verifier, the imitator: Three ways in which human platform workers support artificial intelligence. *Big Data & Society*, 7. DOI: 10.1177/2053951720919776.

Urry, J. 2008. Climate change, travel and complex futures. *The British Journal of Sociology*, 59, 261–279.

Wahome, M. & Graham, M. 2020. Spatially shaped imaginaries of the digital economy. *Information, Communication & Society*, 23, 1123–1138.

Wajcman, J. 2017. Automation: Is it really different this time? *The British Journal of Sociology*, 68, 119–127.

Wendt, A. 2018. The mind – Body problem and social science: Motivating a quantum social theory. *Journal for the Theory of Social Behaviour*, 48, 188–204.

Xu, J. & Jin, C. 2019. Exploring spatiotemporal heterogeneity in online travel searches: A local spatial model approach. *Geografisk Tidsskrift-Danish Journal of Geography*, 119, 146–162.

Yeo, S. J. I. & Lin, W. 2020. Autonomous vehicles, human agency and the potential of urban life. *Geography Compass*, 14, e12531.

Zeng, Z., Chen, P.-J. & Lew, A. A. 2020. From high-touch to high-tech: COVID-19 drives robotics adoption. *Tourism Geographies*, 22, 724–734.

3

Artificial intelligence and psychology

J. Michael Innes and Ben W. Morrison

In this chapter we shall explore relationships between the science and profession of psychology and the development of artificial intelligence (AI) and robotic systems. By artificial intelligence we mean the human study and design of systems that sense the environment, take actions to increase the success of planned outcomes and, in turn, further influence their environment. This process may involve processes of perceiving, learning, planning and reasoning, and the aggregation of knowledge. We define psychology as the scientific study of behaviour and the mind (consciousness) to explore the role of the physical and social environment and of the genetic and experiential features of the agent in the prediction of behaviour. This includes the study of humans and other living creatures. We recognize that there is a long history of study of the behaviour of living creatures based upon the humanities and the arts, especially philosophy, so we shall extend our analyses to include evidence and criticism from realms other than the use of the scientific method.

We shall consider the relationship in three parts. First, we shall briefly examine the role of psychology in the development of AI systems and theories. There is a long and intimate history of such a relationship, exemplified in the arts and the social sciences as well as in computer science and engineering. Humans have been intrigued by the possibility of creating artificial beings, going back to the times of ancient Greece. Coming closer to the present day, the study and explication of the meaning of artificial life for the creatures created and for the human creators and witnesses, from the example of Mary Shelley's (1831/2004) *Frankenstein or The New Prometheus* to the very recent novel *Frankissstein* by Winterson (2019), demonstrate the longevity of this curiosity. This is especially shown in the literature of science fiction, from the robot stories of Isaac Asimov to the depiction of artificial intelligence systems in films such as *Ex Machina* (Garland, dir. 2015) and *Prometheus* (Scott, dir. 2012). We shall look at the reciprocal role that psychology played in the development of AI and the ways in which AI influenced the manner in which the discipline of psychology developed in the mid to late 20th century. We shall not undertake a detailed history of the development of AI systems and the role that psychology played. These have been set out in many texts on AI (e.g., Russell, 2019). We shall summarize the developments leading to the modern representation of AI, which can be related in turn to the impact on contemporary systems of psychology and their application.

Second, we shall examine the role that psychology has played in the understanding of the ways in which humans interact with contemporary AI systems, to influence the behaviour of the systems and, in turn, to be influenced by them. We shall include in this section the study of the methods that have developed in psychology, which may enable humans better to understand and predict how AI systems evolve and how they may use the data from the environment which contributes to the development of the systems.

Finally, we shall look at the role that AI already plays and may play in the future in the development of the profession of psychology. Other chapters in this handbook examine the impact of AI systems on general employment and the economics of society. Psychology as a practical discipline occupies important roles in the modern economy, especially in mental health systems and in the organization and productivity of the workforce. Hence, it has an impact upon the health of the economy generally. We shall look at the narrower impact that AI may play in the way in which psychology executes those roles.

Psychology and the development of AI

The modern development of AI can be traced to Norbert Weiner in his book *Cybernetics* (1948), to Alan Turing's *Computing Machinery and Intelligence* (1950), and the seminal work by Von Neumann (1958). Turing argued that humans use symbols in thinking and calculation, as do computers, and so established the relationship between the machine and the human. The specific term "artificial intelligence" was first used in a workshop held in 1956 at Dartmouth College in the US state of New Hampshire, organized by John McCarthy, Marvin Minsky and Claude Shannon. This workshop is acknowledged as the beginning of the modern era of AI. The close relationship between the development of AI and the modern development of psychology is exemplified in the later assertion (Miller, 2003) that the rise of the modern paradigm of psychology, named as the "cognitive revolution", was established by a conference held in Cambridge, Massachusetts, on the 11 September 1956, some four weeks after the AI workshop in neighbouring New Hampshire.

AI and the psychological paradigms of behaviourism and cognition

The use of the term AI requires examination. It implies a comparison with "real" or "natural" intelligence, associated in turn with human beings. Within the study of human behaviour, however, there remain extensive differences in the understanding of the term "intelligence". Over one hundred years after the seminal paper by Spearman (1904) in which he claimed to discover the g factor of general intelligence whereby all mental abilities, including problem solving, spatial orientation, general knowledge, non-verbal association and may other functions, were positively correlated and related to a central factor, psychologists can still write papers entitled "What is IQ?" (Kovacs & Conway, 2019). There are as many as twenty-seven different definitions of the term, as Malabou (2019) points out. Intelligence is measured in many different ways, all of which to some degree require the actor to respond to some form of problem or puzzle, presented verbally, spatially or pictorially, to produce a solution or to access information gained through social experience. The behaviour that results is measured in a variety of ways, from a verbal or written response or the speed of reaction to the question. The very concept of the "intelligence quotient" (IQ) is debated. What was seen as an established empirical fact at one point in time, namely the rise in IQ over several decades (the "Flynn" effect, 2009) is now, merely a decade later, being reversed. We witness, for example, the thesis that people in the Victorian era were significantly more intelligent than people in the present era because of a measurable decline in speed of simple reaction time between 1889 and 2004 (Woodley, te Nijenhuis, & Murphy, 2013). Clearly, if an index as basic as the speed of reaction to an external event can be considered as a valid measure of the ability to solve problems, there are controversies in the field regarding the processes which result in intelligent behaviour. We cannot create a definitive artificial form of "intelligence" if we have not decided what is the "natural" form of the entity. We must examine what it is that has been *operationalized* as AI over the last several decades. The development of AI is in fact having an impact upon the conception of intelligence within the discipline of psychology. The development of models comprising structural and functional systems which can be separately measured neurologically and modeled mechanically can give a clearer picture of why intelligence can be related to speed of processing (Schubert, Nunez, Hagemann, & Vandekerckhove, 2018). As in most fields of science, development occurs because of methodological, including measurement, advances (Greenwald, 2012) and there seems to be no exception with developments in neuroscience and measurement theory in psychology.

The impact of AI spreads even further. Human decision making has been shown to be improved by factors other than intelligence (deBruin, Parker, & Fischoff, 2020) and thereby appears to be a quality which would be retained by humans rather than machines, for example motivational processes, emotions and experience. However, other work shows that human factors, such as the effort expended in a task, which affects attention and thus performance, can be modeled by machines and demonstrated to affect the performance even of human infants (c.f. Shenhav et al., 2017; Kaldy & Blaser, 2020).

In this we must take account of the somewhat tortuous relationship between the development of psychology as a discipline and the development of AI. Prior to the creation of the cognitive revolution referred to by Miller, the dominant paradigm within psychology, certainly within the US, was behaviourism. This amalgam of methodology and epistemology argued that it was not possible to observe the internal mental processes which might be associated with the actions of other people and organisms. It was necessary to create a science which was dependent only on the observation of behaviour and to relate those actions to reliable and correlated environmental stimuli. This radical form of scientific endeavour is associated most strongly with the work of B. F. Skinner (1938, 1953). The movement dated from 1914 and the apogee occurred around the early 1950s (e.g., Estes, 1954), after which several methodological and epistemological critiques appeared to demonstrate the dead end into which the discipline had progressed (e.g., Wann, 1964). At this time, the cognitive revolution emerged to supplant the proposed death of behaviourism. Cognition, the awareness of consciousness and the analysis of processes of the mind that could be related to behaviour, mediating the relationship between environmental cues and action, was claimed to throw light upon the ability to initiate action as well as respond to stimuli. This sat well with the idea, with the development of computers, that the manipulation of symbols was an essential part of human behaviour which could be compared to the work of a computer.

There is an interesting irony here, however, which resonates especially today with contemporary developments in AI. Turing in his work on computing machinery proposed a test, the well-known Turing Test (Turing, 1950), to establish whether a machine could be compared to a human and to measure the degree to which the machine was inferior or superior to the human. In the test, a human actor poses a question to a human and to a machine. The human and the machine type out answers to the question and the human judge decides which answer was from the human and which from the machine. If the judge cannot decide which is which, then the machine passes the test that it is equivalent to a human. While the thinking behind this "imitation game" relies on an inference of some symbolic manipulation by both the human and the machine, the test itself is dependent upon a behaviourist methodology. It requires the presentation of a stimulus and the observation of behaviour, with an inference about the organism/machine presumably responsible for that outcome. The Turing Test provides only the same evidence that humans use every day in interaction with other humans, namely that we attribute consciousness to other humans; we seem less prepared to make that analogical leap when interacting with a machine (Davies, 2018). Skinner (1969) himself proposed, on the basis of the methods used in the comparison, that "The real question is not whether machines think, but whether people do". Within the discipline of social psychology it was possible to derive an explanation of how a person can infer, during an interaction with another person, an explanation of why that person performed an act, based upon the context in which that person made an utterance (Bem, 1965, 1966). This inference could then be generalized to allow a person to infer from their own utterance what private belief they held. While controversial at the time (Jones, Linder, Kiesler, Zanna, & Brehm, 1968), the explanation came to be accepted as a valid means to infer personal beliefs as well as the beliefs of others. A form of a Turing Test to ascertain one's own thinking!

The Turing Test is inherently biased. First, it is dependent upon a common web of circumstances and assumptions within which the problem may be posed and the answer judged. What may be perceived to be a sensible answer in one culture may not be deemed to be so in another. Second, it is a demonstration that a machine can equal the capacity of a human. Human intelligence is taken as the ultimate comparison. We need to ask, however, what is the level of the human capacity against which the machine is being compared. In an interesting account of a modern version of the Turing Test, the Loebner Prize competition, Christian (2011) provides the example of the decision by a group of human judges that a particular answer had to come from a machine because "no human could know that much", when in fact the answer came from a human, an expert in the language, literature and history of Shakespeare. In making judgements of equivalence or superiority, not only must the machine and the human have capability, the judge or judges proposing the question and judging the answer must have equal or superior capacity and knowledge to recognize the quality of the answer.

The discipline of psychology has encountered similar problems in its past. Psychology as a discipline has long been accused of being ethnocentric, generalizing from European/North American cultures, assuming their universality and underestimating the intellectual and other capacities of people from other cultural traditions. The adoption of the behaviourist paradigm, however, did allow the benefit of the experimental investigation of animals as agents, whether these be planarian worms, cockroaches, rats or primates. Without language, it was impossible to ask questions and to infer consciousness. What had to be done was to assemble environmental problems for the animals to solve. The question is, however, whether the human experimenters were of sufficient intelligence or insight to create problems that the animals found worthy of solving. This matter has been addressed more recently in the work of Franz DeWall (2016), which summarizes this enigma in the title of his book, *Are We Smart Enough to Know How Smart Animals Are?* and also in Safina (2020), *Becoming Wild*, which is essentially about animal culture, not about how alike it is to human culture. Increasingly, we see animals as much more able and "intelligent" than they were thought to be in the early and mid-part of the 20th century. Humans have become smarter in posing interesting and relevant questions with which the animals engage. In the parallel process of enquiring about the capacity of a machine, we have to ensure that the human investigators are smart enough to evaluate the quality of the answer that the machine provides.

There has always been controversy over the status of the Turing Test. What it actually means for a machine to have "passed" the test has been the subject of debate. Harnad (1991), for example, proposed a "total" Turing Test, with an assembly of linguistic and social skills included as appropriate criteria to be passed. This has led to the pursuit of building human life-like robots (androids). However, to the present day there has not been success in building a robot that passes such an extreme test. The existence of the so-called uncanny valley (e.g., MacDorman & Ishiguro, 2006) posits that a robot will be accepted as more and more human-like as the technology develops to simulate appearance, language and non-verbal behaviour, such as the synchronization of lip movements with speech, until a point in development is reached when slight imperfections are detected as artificial and the behaviour of the robot is seen as uncanny or eerie and, therefore, identified as artificial. At some further point in development, however, there will be an increasing level of attribution of humanity to the android system. Interestingly, Corti and Gillespie (2015) have created a system, based on what they call "echoborgs" in which the interface between the AI system and the human interrogator is another human being who shadows (repeats verbatim the responses generated by the artificial system). This interface resulted in a large proportion of responders unable to detect that the human being with whom they were interacting was in fact entirely the conduit for the activity of a robot. What Corti and Gillespie are proposing, therefore, is that given a "real" human, interrogators in this form of the Turing Test will overlook many slight imperfections of behaviour (which exist due to the technical limitations of the shadowing technology) and judge the person to be "human". This is contrary to the cultural depiction of android behaviour and what is a common device in story-telling, where there is a common belief that people have an ability to detect something that does not quite "fit". In the horror theme, for example in Stephan King's *Pet Sematary*, the cat and the wife are identified as abnormal when they reappear. In *Invasion of the Body Snatchers* (1978, dir. Kaufman) the owner of a laundry asks the advice of the central character, a public health inspector, about his wife because "that's not my wife" even though in every behavioural and physical aspect she looks like his wife. The man simply knew to the contrary, unlike events in a laboratory in the London School of Economics. The context of the interaction, the history of the relationship and expectations of the interactor all play a part in recognition. The role of the experiment as a method to explore these relationships is crucial and will be examined later in the chapter.

Generalized versus narrow AI

At this point it is important to refer to the distinction between the conception of generalized AI, also known as the strong version, and the narrow, or weak version. The generalized version is probably what the general public think about when confronted with the concept of AI; the idea of intelligent, sentient creatures with self-awareness and consciousness, as usually presented in science fiction and other literary and multimedia forms. For example, the film *The Terminator* (1984, dir. Cameron) represented the "Skynet" going "self-aware" on August 29, 1997, and the computer HAL in *2011: A Space Odyssey* ((1968, dir. Kubrick) attempted to eliminate the human crew members. What we will cover in the remainder of this chapter does not fit into this concept. There is no evidence to date that consciousness has arisen in the machines that have been created. The question of whether this is possible is still moot. Arguments have been proposed that consciousness will arise from increasing complexity of the organization of systems (e.g., Goff, 2019). Others emphatically argue (e.g., Koch, 2019) that consciousness will never arise in machines. In our consideration of the development of AI and its impact upon society, however, we do not need to reach this level. The effect of machines on how humans live and interact in society can be examined with the narrow or weak version where the machines are programmed by humans to carry out specific and highly expert skills without the need for them to reflect on what they are doing and what may be the ultimate "meaning of life".

The development of AI

The early development of AI after the Dartmouth workshop was based upon the demonstration that computers were capable of many different processes equivalent to human intelligence. The process of *searching* for solutions, for example, using the idea of developing a "search tree" whereby a series of actions are performed to change an initial state to achieve a goal state. The failure or success of each action generates a search tree until finally the goal is achieved.

A further goal of AI was to allow computers to interact using natural language. This appeared to have been achieved when Winograd (1972) developed "Blocks World" with a system to physically arrange objects using instructions from the user. However, the use of natural language did not generalize from the artificial world of blocks. It allowed interaction in a simulated world, not the real world.

Early enthusiasm for the development of AI, the so-called Golden Age rapidly declined in the middle of the 1970s (although the development of search programs did lead to the famous example of a computer defeating the world champion of chess, Garry Kasparov, as late as 1996). A fresh development of AI occurred late in the 1970s with the development of "expert systems" dependent upon the accumulation of knowledge, which allowed the machines to avoid dead ends in search routines, to build upon earlier experience. These expert systems were successful in constrained systems, and they could outperform humans in certain circumstances. For example, MYCIN was an expert system designed to aid humans in the identification of blood disease. It dealt with questions for which there was no certain answer, accumulating decreases in uncertainty through asking more questions. It was, however, limited to knowledge in a very constrained environment.

The modern era of AI, with which we shall be concerned in the remainder of this chapter, is mainly concerned with a technology of "machine learning". Machine-learning systems are presented with a series of examples of the things/objects/concepts that they are trying to learn. This allies the machines with the earlier concepts of human psychology in learning theory. How can the machine/organism learn to recognize that object or concept? The idea of "reinforcement" presents the system with feedback that a decision was incorrect or correct, to increase the probability of making the correct decision in the future. This is the idea of contingencies of reinforcement, so doggedly pursued by Skinner in his program of radical behaviourism and the demonstration that complex sequences of behaviour could be explained by the identification of exposure to varied structures of consequences (Ferster & Skinner, 1957). The processes of contemporary AI systems, based upon principles of learning and the contingent reinforcement of particular outcomes, are based on behaviouristic views of operation. Sejnowski (2018) notes the explicit reference to the work of Skinner (e.g., 1953) and the dismissal of the importance of Chomsky (1971), earlier championed as an example of the power of cognitive processes to predict behaviour.

Machines, given basic principles, are exposed to a large number of stimuli and on multiple occasions and develop outcomes that both exceed human capacity and provide no insight into how they arrived at the outcomes. A particularly relevant example comes from the study of the chess-playing program "AlphaZero" (Sadler & Regan, 2019). The program, which learns to play chess given only the rules of the game and guided by reinforcement-based learning, has astounded many observers by demonstrating human-like tactics in playing the game. For instance, the program plays sacrifices and employs very unusual moves, with a dynamism more typically associated with grandmasters than knowledge-based programs. One of the authors, Sadler, a chess master, describes Alpha Zero as playing like a "human on fire". Further, the program has contributed to the development of the game itself, giving grandmasters new insights into novel strategies and even being compared to the romantic games of the late 19th and early 20th century. Thus, the emergent system has developed beyond the initial program.

The development of such systems appears to enable the systems to go beyond the limits of knowledge-based systems as suggested by, for example, Rasskin-Gutman (2009). Sejnowski (2018) and Rahwan et al. (2019) give extensive accounts of machine behaviour in their recent reviews. The success of machine learning depends upon the opportunity to present vast numbers of examples to the systems; the idea of "Big Data" and the availability of large amounts of computing power, also available through the huge strides of computer engineering.

The development of reinforcement-based, "deep" learning systems is highly developed mathematically and involves the analysis of sequences of acts which are contingent not only upon the external reinforcers, but also on the continually altered states of the operator (human or machine) which have been affected by prior reinforcers, Markov Decision Processes (MDPs) (c.f., Graesser & King, 2020). The systems also take into account another feature of the operator within the system, namely the difference between the external totally observable influences (by an external, wholly knowledgeable observer) and the partially observable (PO) process available to the operator itself within the system (POMDPs). This is a mathematically formulated image of a person by system interaction in psychological research that has driven experimental research for decades. We shall look at this formulation later in the chapter.

Complexity, opacity and bias of the algorithms and whether they can be trusted

A feature which emerges from such developments in narrow AI is that the outcomes of the programs are surprising to the people who created them. This is the notion of "explainable artificial intelligence" (XAI), that in understanding the outcomes of the AI systems there needs to be a means whereby humans can excise and examine the processes which lead to the outcomes. Bridle (2018) suggests that the "fourth law of robotics", an extension of the famous three laws of robotics formulated by Isaac Asimov, should be that the robot must be open to examination by a human. The systems need to be transparent and open and, therefore, open to explanation to allow human trust in the operation of the automated systems to evolve. For instance, the uptake of algorithm-generated advice has been widely found to be determined by its relative degree of transparency in formulating a response (Dietvorst, Simmons, & Massey, 2015; Edwards & Veale, 2017; Sinha & Swearingen, 2002; Yaniv & Kleinberger, 2000; Yeomans, Shah, Mullainathan, & Kleinberg, 2019). Indeed, Yeomans et al. (2019) found that in a task where humans would be expected to outperform artificial systems (predicting which jokes people find funny), such systems still outperformed humans. Aversion to the system was observed partly due to users' belief that they understood the human process better (Yeomans et al., 2019), even though the output was seemingly sophisticated. The authors posited that in order to encourage adoption, algorithms must not only be accurate but also understood.

The underlying paradigm of AI, however, essentially goes back to the past to reconstruct in robots a radical behaviourist paradigm of psychology, back before the "cognitive revolution" of the 1950s. We are literally going back to the past while inventing the future. The systems are opaque: very much the "black box" used to describe the processes of the mind in psychology. If they are hidden, then the question can be asked: are there methodologies which can be used to infer what is occurring?

We distinguish different senses of the term "opaque", following Burrell (2016). We use the term in the sense of an emergent characteristic of machine learning and not something built into the systems deliberately to keep a system secret. Neither is it a form of technical illiteracy. We are following a suggestion by Seaver (2017) to adopt an anthropological method, an ethnography of systems.

This raises an analogy with the developments of behaviourism in psychology in the 1940s and 1950s when there was debate about "intervening variables" and "hypothetical constructs" which theorists such as Clark L. Hull (1943) were developing (MacCorquodale & Meehl, 1948). It renders the possibility that the experimental methods used then may be reconsidered and used to interrogate the workings of the robotic mind. It is not too far a stretch to suggest that we, as investigators of the complexities of the robotic mind, should pay attention to the attempts by ethologists to understand the animal mind (DeWall, 2016). It may be that we are better able to understand biologically based systems, derived from evolutionary pasts (cf. Campbell, 1994; Scerri, 2016), but we need to remember that the minds of robots capture the thoughts and insights of human beings, hence an understanding of human insights may enable insights into the robot. The work of Campbell (1963) in his exposition of the nature of human dispositions, invoking the notion of the human homunculus, an idea which emulates the concept of the artificial person or robot simulating or representing behaviour and consciousness, deserves a re-evaluation in the present era. Robots acquire "behavioural dispositions" and should be examined in that light just as are humans, about whom the investigator knows much less about the environment and history of the acquisition than in the case of the machine or robot. The work of Yeomans et al. (2019) referred to previously suggests, however, that humans, in the context of interacting with a robot, apply different levels of proof in making a decision. We shall need to return to this issue later.

We should remember, also, that complex human behaviour, upon observation, may appear to be opaque to understanding but that comprehension may be achieved by the use of experiments which enable the complex interaction of variables to be disentangled (cf. Ferster & Skinner, 1957). As Bem (1965, 1966) demonstrated, such experimental procedures can be conducted by the person upon themselves in order to ascertain their states of belief based upon their actions which may be executed within conscious awareness. The complex algorithms of AI systems are created by humans. Opening them to scrutiny, therefore, may be fruitfully achieved by experimental methods augmented by human understanding of human thought processes achieved not by self-reflection but by previous work with other non-humans, namely animals. If the programs, written by humans, operationalize the thought processes and the biases of those humans, it would be advantageous to explore the cognitive belief systems and socio-economic ideologies which are present.

There is clear evidence that the algorithms developed encapsulate the beliefs of the programmers (e.g., Broad, 2018; Muller, 2018; O'Neil, 2016; Russell, 2019; Smith, 2019). The exploration of the intrinsic and subtle biases of human experts, which are based upon "common-sense" knowledge and socio-political beliefs, using technologies from the social sciences, including social psychology, could clarify where the programs "come from". We have known for years about the intrinsic biases of human "experts" (e.g., Innes & Fraser, 1971; Kahneman, 2011) and, furthermore, about the opacity of human decision making processes to conscious awareness (Guerin & Innes, 1981; Nisbett & Wilson, 1977; Newell & Shanks, 2014). The same technical "opacity" can be revealed, however, through experimental investigation and the relationship between the behaviour and the causal environmental factors demonstrated. There is a central role for psychology and the use of psychological methodology in opening up the processes embedded in the development of AI systems.

We note here the suggestion by Miller (2019) that the ability to explain algorithmic processes may be facilitated by recourse to social scientific research into the ways in which it is possible to question people to elucidate their explanations for their own behaviour and the behaviour of others. This is essentially an extension of the Turing Test to demonstrate the ways in which an experimental understanding of social behaviour can be used to establish the humanity of the agent. Miller's review does not account for the failure of people to introspect and reveal the processes whereby cognitions arise into consciousness, but his can be explored by experimental means (Nisbett & Wilson, 1977).

It should also be noted that there are explicit constraints upon the conduct of experiments with human beings, based upon ethical issues. These constraints especially involve issues of surveillance and privacy, which preclude the use of methods that are unobtrusive. These matters affected social psychological experimentation in the 1970s and thereafter. The use of unobtrusive methods was developed to show significant findings in social relationships (e.g., Webb, Campbell, Schwartz, & Sechrest, 1966) when they were restricted. With robots and learning machines, however, the ethical constraints should be significantly less, so there is an opportunity for ingenuity in the use of observational and manipulative techniques to explore the cause and effect relationships governing robotic behaviour.

Psychology and living with AI

The rapid development of artificial intelligence (AI) brings with it increasing deployment of robots into places where human beings have previously been the sole or principal occupant. Interaction with robotic systems in the office, factory, home, schools, laboratories and hospitals will become ubiquitous (Walsh, 2018). Clearly, we expect that humans will interact and cooperate with these systems. There are many studies which are relevant, including those which explicitly refer to theories and methods in disciplines other than robotic studies (e.g., Young, Hawkins, Sharlin, & Igarajhi, 2009).

This interaction goes beyond traditional human-computer interaction, whereby humans are aided by the efficiency of the processing systems of the computer. The interaction will take the form of physical and mental interaction with a responsive "other", which will add to the outcome of the interaction over and above the capacity of humans in the system. Indeed, the robot may make significantly different inputs, changing the direction of the course of the interaction. The quality of such interaction, however, will depend upon the ability of humans to adjust to interaction with non-human artefacts, and the ability of designers to manipulate the robot to behave in a manner that will be acceptable to the human.

The modern issue of machine-human interaction goes beyond merely the age-old relationship between humans and their tools, designed to improve their control of material and space. Robotic systems engage a new sense of relationship with the human; how does the human being represent the robot? It is not merely an attitude to the robot, a sense of liking or disliking the machine with an influence on behaviour. The representation of the robot represents more a collective sense of relationship, a relationship of a human being shared with other human beings' sense of what the robot is and what it means. We can consult the work of Moscovici (Farr & Moscovici, 1984), a social psychologist who was interested in how humans conceive of broad concepts of other objects and persons in directing their behaviour towards them. While not entirely separate from attitudes and beliefs, social representations entail a broad cultural shift in behaviour (Augoustinos & Innes, 1990) which is essentially based upon an understanding of the role of common sense in how the public come to make sense of social forms and entities (Markova, 2014). Conception of how a robot is represented enables concepts of fear and liking, apprehension, hope and trust, and suspicion can be constructed and studied. The robot as a representation becomes embodied in the broader representation of humanity and how the distinctions between the two may be understood.

Commentators point out that the design of the artificial systems starts as a human endeavour, embedding within them human values, biases, preconceptions and intentions (Broad, 2018). The initial interaction of the human with such systems, therefore, involves the interaction of a human with another human, mediated by the embodiment in the robot. However, the evolution of the system, as we have seen, will eventually result in an emergent organism/machine participating in the process. The question arises: how can we explore the nature of such emergent and developing interactions so that they may be beneficial and productive and continue to be acceptable to the human participant? The nature of the participants may also require methodologists to formulate new procedures to enable understanding of the processes that emerge and lead to positive and negative outcomes of the interactions.

The AlphaGo program provides evidence of how changes may emerge in interaction with humans. But the rules of chess are transparent, simple and can be defined in a program relatively easily. Social interaction, on the other hand, has no clear rules and depends heavily on very subtle cues and responses. Therefore, in the study of social interaction between robots and humans the question arises: how do designers acquire information about social interaction that enables them to program the relevant cues and responses to enable the interactions to develop?

We may see here the "intrusion" of concepts of "common sense" into an understanding of scientific and engineering change on several levels. There is the common sense of the public coming to understand what robots represent, essential to the acceptance of AI into business, commerce and education. There is a need to understand the common sense, or tacit knowledge (which Collins & Evans, 2007 would term "ubiquitous tacit knowledge"), of the experts who design the systems. This tacit knowledge is in addition to the explicit, technical knowledge which is used in the design and implementation of the systems, and the engineers may be unaware of the influence that this may play in the design process. There are many who conceive of the role of common sense as fundamental to all knowledge systems (Campbell, 1975; Markova, 2014). Finally, there is the common sense of those who design the experiments to explore the factors which affect the interactions of robots with humans and cause the outcomes in order to provide the data that is entered into the algorithms which guide the machines.

Data quality and the development of functioning AI systems

The use of experiments in studies of human-robot interaction

The exploration of human-robot interaction (HRI), and the manipulation of factors that may affect the quality of interaction, have been advanced via the use of experimental methods. For present purposes, we define such experiments as a simulated interaction between a human being and a robot with the controlled manipulation of factors that are theoretically linked to the quality and value of the interaction. HRI researchers measure outcomes by the extent to which the interaction brings benefits, including the satisfaction of the human being resulting from the interaction, together with possible unintended and/or negative consequences. Experimentation may also entail the control of participants to the interactions, through the random allocation of participants to experimental conditions (i.e., the randomized controlled experiment). However, this is not a necessary requirement, with the possibility of manipulation of variables in less controlled field conditions where there is an inability or non-desirability to allocate participants at random.

We view the experiment as a psychological form of ethnography. This position may seem unusual, in that anthropologists characteristically perceive psychologists as being naively scientistic and lacking in insight. We maintain it as the use of a method that is actually artful in its social psychological form (Wilson, Aronson, & Carlsmith, 2010) and therefore designed to reveal the subtleties of behaviour. A true social psychological experimenter may be more related to an ethnographer practicing the art of "thick description" of the anthropologist (Geertz, 1973) than may at first appear. The concept of "practice" and its subtleties is also recognized in the physical and health sciences (e.g., Grinnell, 2009).

The use of experiments to explore HRI does not take place in a vacuum. HRI researchers can learn a great deal from the experiences of researchers in other fields of inquiry. The use of experiments has a long history in the field of experimental social psychology. Many texts describe the need for careful design and the subtle creation and control of variables in artificial conditions in order to establish valid outcomes (e.g., Wilson et al., 2010). The goal for social psychological researchers has been the creation of social features hypothetically likened to promote or inhibit social behaviour in interactional settings and observing and measuring outcomes in controlled conditions. This goal shares many attributes with the goals of HRI researchers.

The creation of the laboratory experiment can be equated to an art form; experience and tacit, intuitive expertise is required to be able to create the settings in which humans may relate to others. More specifically, we may liken it to a form of drama where human participants are exposed to social events to which they may not have been previously exposed. The choice of independent variables to be manipulated is usually dependent upon theory and the choice of dependent measures is also associated with purposively selected techniques. The relevance of these issues, and their bases upon both an intuitive understanding of the subtleties and complexities of human behaviour and the relevant theoretically important variables, has several implications for understanding experimental results.

At the most fundamental level, the design of experiments with human participants requires the structuring of interactions and the selection of variables based upon a tacit, and therefore often intuitive, understanding of human behaviour. An experimenter "knows" what it is to be human and therefore can create social settings that fit in with the expectations of participants of what is expected in a social interaction (c.f. Collins, 2019, for an extensive analysis of this concept for an understanding of social behaviour). Interaction with a robot, however, may involve a lack of understanding of what the robot understands in the setting. While a human being, at least initially, programs the robot's behaviour, the human will influence what the robot is likely to do. With continued association in an interaction, features of interaction may emerge that are not predicted from the initial program, as has occurred with the development of AlphaZero. Therefore, there may be the emergence of novel expectations and a failure to meet expectations on the part of the human participant, which the experimenter must assess and understand. The uncertainty of the initial behaviour programmed into the interaction only adds to the complexities of the interaction that will emerge.

At another level, the role of tacit knowledge in researchers' decisions to study certain phenomena and how to study them has long been considered in the literature on the sociology and the philosophy of science (Collins, 2018, 2010; Collins & Evans, 2007; Polanyi, 1958). An understanding of these fundamental processes in the conduct of scientific research is a pre-requisite in the design of HRI research studies. We can return to our comments upon the possible biases inherent in the Turing Test to demonstrate the intrinsic and tacit features of any question-and-answer session which affects the direction and outcome of a human and a robot interaction.

The quality of data entered into the systems and learning from experimental social psychology: artefacts in the design of experiments

Researchers in the field of experimental social psychology have explored the factors, which, inherent to the creation of an experimental situation, threaten the validity of the relationship between the manipulated variable and the observed outcomes. Experimentation in the social and behavioural sciences is not the same as experimentation in the physical sciences. Human interactors bring to the setting expectations, actions, and beliefs that affect it. They are not passive objects; they are actors and agents (McAdams, 2015).

Fundamental to an understanding of the significant constraints on the interpretability of experiments is the fact that the experiment is, itself, an example of a human interaction. In human social interactions, participants bring to the situation expectations, intentions, and biases, which affect the outcomes of the interaction. This is part and parcel of human interaction and its complexity. There is a process of exchange between the participants, with change in one party followed by change and accommodation in the other. In the experiment, the actors bring to the setting biases and expectations formed in previous social encounters, which are extrinsic to any of the formal, theoretical factors that the experimenter is attempting to observe and measure.

The challenge to the experimenter is to attempt to minimize the effects of these background factors and explicate the link between the manipulated variable and the observed outcome of the interaction. In addition, experimentation requires the creation of artefacts that simulate the "real" conditions of the world, and these artefacts may introduce into the experimental setting biases that affect outcomes in ways incommensurate with the original hypotheses.

Consideration of the influence of such methodological factors has been associated with many prominent figures in the field, in particular Donald Campbell and his co-workers (c.f. Shadish, Cook, & Campbell, 2002). We have already considered Campbell's (1975) views of the role of common sense, extra-scientific ideas and concepts, in the development of thinking about interaction with robotic systems. A particularly cogent exposition of the importance of viewing the intrinsic validity of experimental investigations within the broader context of the philosophy of science and psychology can be found in Campbell (1994). Campbell's critical point is that experimental artefacts may affect not only the internal validity (the existence of a cause-and-effect relationship between variables) and external validity (the degree to which the results of one experiment may generalize to another) of an experiment, but critically, its construct validity (the degree to which the variables being studied have meaning in themselves, without additional and extraneous meanings).

A large array of factors have been identified as potential artefacts that influence the outcome of experimental studies outside of the theoretically manipulated factors tested in the experiment. Demand characteristics (Orne, 1969) represent a noteworthy example of an experimental artefact. Here, the creation of a formal experimental interaction sets up expectations in the participants about what are acceptable and expected ways to behave. Participants know that they are being observed, and perhaps judged, and therefore will monitor their own behaviour to suit what they see as the appropriate rules in the setting. These implicit judgements of the participants may not align with the expectations of the experimenter. Associated with this factor is evaluation apprehension in an experiment, where the goal is that above all other aspects of the experiment there is an attempt to assess the degree to which the participant behaves in a valued, honest, or socially appropriate manner. Also, if the participant has volunteered for participation, then the motivation to volunteer may bring with it additional behavioural characteristics and dispositions, which will result in different outcomes had the person not been a volunteer.

Even the act of assessment of behaviour, in the form of a preliminary test of beliefs, attitudes, or expectations, has been shown to influence the later trajectory of behaviour over time by raising expectations about the objective of the experiment.

In addition to the factors introduced to an experimental setting by the use of human beings as participants and the interpretations which they bring to the encounter, the experiment brings with it an additional factor, namely the meta-factor of the experimenter being a participant, albeit one who is playing a different role, with different rules of engagement compared to the naïve participants. The experimenter is, at one level, an additional stimulus in the experimental setting (e.g. Brewer, 2012; Friedman, 1967; Miller, 1972; Rosenzweig, 1933) and that stimulus may have effects outside of any effect of the theoretical variables being explored. The participants may also have beliefs and expectations about the experimenters and their roles, including some suspicion about what is being done and why.

There are also biases that result from the expectation of the experimenter. The experiment is primarily conducted test a theory. While the aim of the experiment in formal philosophical terms is to falsify the theory, experimenters are usually trying to demonstrate that there exists a causal link between a manipulated variable and a behavioural outcome. These artefacts can combine to have complex effects upon the behaviour of participants, as experiments demonstrating the interaction of pre-tests and characteristics of volunteers have demonstrated. While not all studies have demonstrated biases resulting from experimenter effects (Barber & Silver, 1968), there are simply too many replications for any impartial observers to remain unconvinced (Rosenthal, 1976).

A related factor may also be relevant to the development of systems of HRI. The experimenter may also have beliefs and expectations about the expected outcomes of the study based upon extra-scientific beliefs and attitudes, which lie outside of the formal, scientific activity of designing and conducting the experiment. Such intentions may influence, perhaps unconsciously and unintentionally, the ways in which the experiment is conducted and the outcomes created (e.g., Innes & Fraser, 1971; MacCoun, 1998; Sherwood & Nataupsky, 1968). The influence of socio-political biases on the outcomes of social psychological research has recently become prominent in the field of social psychology (Crawford & Jussim, 2018; Duarte et al., 2015; Inbar & Lammers, 2012; Pastore, 1949) and these factors will increasingly need to be considered in any future research.

It is pertinent to note here that the role of experiments in human-robot interaction and a need to understand the limitations of that methodology from the point of view of psychological research is being reflected in another area of psychological research and methodology, namely in the technology of psychological measurement (Jacobucci & Grimm, 2020) where a failure to note measurement errors leads to a prevention of accurate modeling of relationships between variables.

The decline of interest in artefacts of design

The 1960s and the 1970s saw the development of methodology to understand the biasing influences of these variables. Later years, however, witnessed the demise of concerns about the influence of artefacts. Various developments in the field of social psychology led researchers to think that the demands of the setting or the biases of the experimenter were being implicitly controlled in the methodology adopted. These included the move away from the creation of behavioural encounters between participants and the substitution of hypothetical interactions in paper-and-pencil questionnaires or use of computer-based automatized interactions between participants and simulated interactors.

Recent papers have demonstrated the demise of interest in the effects of experimenters' and generalized expectancies on interactions (Klein et al., 2012) and in the inevitable intrusion of such factors inherent in the artificial creation of social interactions in laboratory settings (Bless & Burger, 2016). However, we suggest that the threats to the validity of experiments have not gone away. They have merely been forgotten or ignored.

Artefacts may vary in presence and magnitude from laboratory to laboratory, and the manipulation of variables, dependent upon the ability of the investigators to use their tacit understanding of social behaviour, may vary due to the ability of the experimenter. We asked the question: is the experimental study of such interactions in HRI failing to take account of the artefacts discussed here? (Innes & Morrison, 2020). An examination of a substantial sample of recent papers published in three high-profile research outlets found no explicit reference in the methods section to the physical presence of an experimenter or observer during the behavioural sequences and/or to the use of recording devices, which were not concealed from participants. Further, no mention was made of the potential impact of overt observation on participants' behaviour.

There was also clear evidence that in most instances the coding of data a human operator was performing the coding and interpreting the results (in some instances, without formal coding procedures or checks for inter-rater reliability, e.g., Levin, Harriott, Paul, Zhang, & Adams, 2013). In no case was there any indication that procedures were adopted to blind the observer to the condition from which the data were being extracted, so the possibility of bias, intentional or otherwise, cannot be eliminated. Some studies (e.g., Li, Ju, & Reeves, 2017) explicitly raised issues which would stimulate in respondents characteristics concerning normative expectations, without any design features built into the experiments to assess such demands.

Many of the studies adopted a *Wizard of Oz* technique (i.e., whereby participants interact with an interface without knowing that the responses are generated by a concealed human operator rather than a machine) in studying participant response to a robot. In most cases, the robot was controlled by an experimenter who possessed knowledge of the study's aims and hypotheses. However, we did not find any substantial discussion of how such a technique may threaten the validity of the results. In such instances where deception was used, some studies have used post-experimental questionnaires, which may alert participants to the use of deception (e.g., "Did you believe the robot was acting autonomously"). We should note the work, previously referred to by Yeomans et al. (2019) where humour which was generated by a machine and which was objectively superior to that espoused by humans was not in fact so judged by human observers. The context of the experiment, interacting with computers, may have generated demand characteristics which induced an enhanced sense of criticism in the judges.

It is worth considering, in the work referred to previously by Corti and Gillespie (2015) on "echoborgs", that their interrogators' apparent failure to attribute the human shadowing behaviour to a computer may be an artefact created by demand characteristics or experimenter bias. If a participant is introduced to a human interactor in a laboratory in a department of social psychology, one may be more likely to presume that that person is human than if the interaction takes place in a computer science laboratory. Corti and Gillespie (2015) do refer to the "higher expectations" (p. 13) that interactors have in certain forms of interactions than in others, clearly imputing the role that demand characteristics may play in the design and the execution of human-robot interactions. Those who are concerned with the development of algorithms using deep reinforcement learning and building into their structure terms for POMDPs, considered earlier, need to be aware of these additional features of experiments which generate the data that may be used to test the efficacy of the systems. We may term these features as "artefacts" which suggests that they are "nuisance" variables. They are in fact subtle, enduring and omnipresent factors in human, and also potentially in human-robot, interactions. Researchers at this present time need to take note of Orne's (1962) prescient statement that "The experimental situation is one which takes place within the context of an explicit agreement of knowledge to participate in a *special form of social interaction* known as 'taking part in an experiment'" (p. 777, italics added). Humans do. Robots may not do so, but may they be programmed to do so through the implicit design of their systems?

All the papers in the corpus examined revealed the same failures to take account of potential bias in the manipulation of variables and in the measurement of outcomes. This leads us to consider what may the effect of such biases in the understanding or interaction with aliens, namely robots. At the most fundamental level, artefacts and associated tacit and intuitive (perhaps unconscious) influences upon the design of experiments, can bias the data derived from experiments which will, in turn, lead to biases in the theories and programs which are built into the robots that will emerge in the interactions with humans in the workplace of the future. Algorithm bias can result from the creation of variables in experimental studies that create variables with poor construct validity, as well as from the biases that may exist in the beliefs and actions of the creators of the algorithms (Clegg, 2017; Muller, 2018; O'Neil, 2016).

The emerging and developing interactions, in turn, will change, and if the biases are not understood in the initial data, then they are unlikely to be detected and understood subsequently. As the algorithms change, the more the interactions arising from them will change. The discipline of experimental social psychology has demonstrated that human social behaviour can only be understood incompletely through the avenue of experiments, even with extensive knowledge about threats to validity. It is unlikely that the understanding of HRI will advance if there is an ignorance of these threats. Innes and Morrison (2020) make specific recommendations to improve design practices based upon social psychological research.

The impact of AI on the profession of psychology

In this section we set out three steps of an argument to address possible future trends in the employment of psychologists. We first examine the state of the profession of psychology and helping professions in the light of developments in AI. Second, we will determine the degree to which such developments may have an impact upon what is delivered as psychological services in the immediate to medium-term future and, finally, we will examine the prospects for employment as a psychological/helping professional within the same time frame.

We shall deal with the possible consequences of developments of the *weak* version of AI, where developments in machine learning and the ubiquity of large computing capabilities and large data sources have enabled developments in what can be programmed into automated services. The implications of these developments in the short term are enormous and can be viewed in optimistic or pessimistic terms. Clegg (2017) presents a positive view and the recent work of Bootle (2019) constructs a balanced view of the economic benefits of AI.

As earlier stated, we are not commenting on the generalized version of AI that envisages the development of consciousness and self-awareness. Such developments would render entirely obsolete everything that we consider here. Neither are we dealing with the impact of quantum computing, or the relationship between psychology and quantum cognition, the outcomes of which may be enormous (cf. Busemeyer & Wang, 2015; Orrell, 2018) nor with the impact of virtual reality systems upon the practice of psychology (Bailenson, 2018). We deal with the consequences of the narrow version of AI; developments in machine learning and the ubiquity of large computing capabilities and data sources that have enabled enormous advances in automation (cf. Clegg, 2017; Rahwan et al., 2019; Sejnowski, 2018, for contemporary accounts).

There is a crucial point to be made here. Adoption of the *weak* version means that we can see to what degree *simulation* of human capacities can be represented by robots with an impact upon human behaviour. We do not have to *replicate* the human processes, which is an implication of the *strong* version. We may or may not be a long way from the latter version. We are already living through the former.

Implications for employment; the employment of psychologists

The impact of technology upon employment has been debated over centuries. AI has accelerated the intensity of the debate: whether there will be decline or increase in overall employment, and upon which forms of employment the impact of AI will be greatest (e.g., Acemoglu & Restrepo, 2019; see Elliott, 2019; Walsh et al., 2019; Boyd & Holton, 2018, for reviews). Here we address the implications of AI upon the employment of professionals in the health and helping sectors. These jobs have been portrayed as immune to developments in automation and they are seen as last bastions against the encroachment of automation (cf., Frey & Osborne, 2013; Reese, 2018; Susskind, 2020; Susskind & Susskind, 2015).

Frey and Osborne (2013), for example, portrayed an evolution of automatic systems which would increase the probabilities of replacing human workers. They produced algorithms which calculated how likely it was for various "bottlenecks" to the capabilities of automated systems to impinge on human jobs. They identified these bottlenecks as perception and fine-task manipulation, creative intelligence (originality and ability to innovate), and social intelligence (caring for others, ability to negotiate and to persuade). In 2019, Frey clarified the argument presented in Frey and Osborne (2013). He predicted the *probability* that particular jobs *can be replaced* by AI, not the *likelihood* that depends upon other socially contextual matters. Our position is similar to Frey's. We do not argue that the impact of AI upon professional employment is inevitable. We argue, however, that analysis of the reality of the job specifications which does not rely upon a superficial view can provide a superior understanding of any effects of AI on job replacement. This qualitative analysis of a job, rather than a stereotypically based, quantitative analysis, such as that of Frey and Osborne, can sharpen our understanding of the consequences of AI.

Kay and King (2020) have recently repeated the opinion that a profession like psychology is akin to economics and cannot be replaced by algorithmic systems. Our point is that so much of the day-to-day activity of a psychologist has already been replaced by algorithmic systems which are mediated by humans. The humans may be removed and completely replaced by machines. We consider later in the chapter the possibility that other models of psychological practice may be adopted which will render the profession less susceptible to replacement and therefore more akin to the vision of Frey and of Kay and King that the profession is relatively immune from a takeover.

Psychology is often regarded as a profession with a "calling" (e.g., Seligman, 2018). This is the fulfilment of a person's dream to be able to help other people deal with complex problems by using a plethora of social skills of extremely high order which, by some further complex process, are partly learned but also at least partially innate. The reality in the profession and in the education establishments, however, does not meet those expectations. Frey and Osborne (2013) appear ignorant of what a psychologist actually does "in the room" and Reese, valiantly defending the romantic notion of the caring psychologist, falls into the same trap. (We use the term "romantic" here as meaning an idealized or sentimental view of reality, remote from experience [*OED*], c.f. Herman, 1995.) The Susskinds are more realistic in their evaluation. Developments in training and execution of psychological technology have already changed the landscape of practice.

The representation of psychology and the helping professions

The job of being a psychologist is that of being an *expert* in the analysis and understanding of the causes and consequences of human behaviour. Training to be an expert has been traditionally regarded as a process of socialization into the practices of an expert group; it is a social process of training and service, often with close relationships between the expert trainer and the novices. We return again to the crucial distinction by Collins (2019) between *explicit knowledge*, the shared and conscious skills that are necessary for doing the job (written down in text books and portrayed in lectures) and *tacit knowledge*, the deep understanding of the practices acquired through social immersion in the groups who possess it (Collins & Evans, 2007). Collins also distinguishes between "ubiquitous" tacit knowledge, that which comes from being socialized within the general community, and "contributory" tacit knowledge which is developed through immersion in the laboratory or within the scientific paradigm. Becoming a psychologist is not only learning the theories and the methods of the job through explicit tuition. Expertise is based upon immersion with psychologists and practising the skills again and again.

A consequence of the emergence of mass higher education, however, with increasing numbers in tertiary institutions and the difficulty of providing immersion training in skill development, has been the development of lists of skills which are seen as required for performance; *attempting to make the tacit explicit*. These are listed under various rubrics, including "inherent characteristics" and "graduate attributes". For psychologists and counsellors, these include being a good communicator, curious, creative, compassionate, non-judgemental, motivated, able to see patterns and empathic (e.g., Cranney et al., 2009).

These characteristics, however, are essentially *personal attributes*, matters which are essential to the *character of the person* and which the person may bring to the setting in which they are to be trained and to the job. They can be separated from *skills*, attributes of the job of being a psychologist that can be taught. The argument can be made that the skills of a psychologist are based upon the personal attributes of the person who is already adept to learn the skills; good psychologists are born and not made. But the training regimen within the helping professions, in the time of mass higher education, can be seen as the inculcation of explicit skills to enable the person to perform as an expert, without the necessity of acquiring the deep skills. While character may not be easily simulated, skills are relatively easier to copy. The modern "standards" for psychological training encompass this thinking where completion of training is based upon a model of competency where the candidate meets a minimum standard.

These tasks are based on the "evidence-based" training of a professional helper. Evidence-based practice is the idea that practices are based upon scientifically established evidence, invariably quantified data from observations and experiments conducted in controlled conditions. There is a belief that "science" is objectively separate from "pseudo-science" (Lilienfeld, Lynn, Lohr, & Tavris, 2015) even though within science more generally there are clear examples where the former and the latter cannot be discriminated. There are extensive treatments of the differentiation of science from non-science that render clear distinctions as simplistic. A reading of Galison (1997) and Brewer (2012) shows how complex are the issues; the scientific method is not system of inquiry which can be mechanically applied to all situations. It depends, as all "expert" systems depend, upon contextual, situationally dependent knowledge and an awareness of minor influences which can have significant effects upon the outcomes.

The adoption of a simplistic position, however, enables a curtailment of the range of skills and practices that are required in training; particular practices are believed to be insufficiently "evidence-based" and therefore need not be included in the training regimes. An example within psychology and counselling, is the rejection of therapies based upon psychodynamic

(Freudian) principles, even though there is copious evidence for their efficacy (e.g., Shedler, 2010; Tracey, Wampold, Lichtenberg, & Goodyear, 2014; Wampold & Imel, 2015; Westen & Bradley, 2005; Woolfolk, 2015). The argument is that some "evidence" is better than others (Lilienfeld, Ritschel, Lynn, Cautin, & Latzman, 2014). In fact, it can be shown that the evidence base for the adoption of "cognitive behaviour therapy" (CBT) as the overwhelmingly superior model for the treatment of a wide range of psychological disorders is itself greatly exaggerated (Leichseuring & Steinert, 2017). The continuing debate within psychology and in allied health more generally about the problematic nature of what constitutes evidence (e.g., Jureidini & McHenry, 2020) and how broadly psychologists should be trained (e.g., Newnes, 2011) shows that the issues are not solved, but psychology as a profession progresses as though they have been.

The job of the psychologist and of the helping professional

The job specifications for a professional psychologist cite four tasks, whatever may be the area of specialization. These are:

Assessment: the observation of the client (a person or an organization) and measurement of traits and characteristics to identify the state of the client. This is done by a variety of methods, including systematic behavioural observation, psychometric testing and structured interview.

Formulation: analysis of the data and the development of hypotheses to account for causal relationships between observations and the behavioural and social outcomes that were the primary reason for the client contacting the professional.

Intervention: design of an intervention to change the causal relationships between the measures which are seen as problematic and allow other behaviours and states to occur which will render the issues less problematic.

Evaluation: measurement of the states after the intervention to ascertain whether change has occurred or not and whether the changes are beneficial or detrimental.

These tasks are central to the training of a professional helper, training based upon evidence derived from the scientific disciplines of psychology, economics (for the organizational psychologist), criminology (for the forensic psychologist), neuroscience, physiology, sociology (in the sense of the development of social systems) and cognitive science. Economists Autor, Levy, and Murnane (2003) make the similar point in looking at jobs as bundles of skills rather than as a totality. Central to the specification is the concept of *evidence-based practice*, the idea that practices must be based upon evidence, invariably quantified data from observations and experiments conducted in controlled conditions. Our earlier consideration of the application of the scientific method, however, precludes the uncritical application of a quantitative approach bereft of a qualitative understanding of setting and context.

The explicit specification of skills enables the automation of skills

The increasingly specified form of these task characteristics, with more and more evidence and based upon narrow definitions of what is reliable and valid, leads, however, to the following:

Assessment: Paul Meehl (1954) more than sixty years ago demonstrated that statistical aggregation of assessment was virtually always superior to aggregation by the clinician.

This demonstration has been successively supported by researchers. The development of computer-aided tests has increasingly supplanted the provision of assessment by clinicians. Computers can deliver test items and score and monitor test-taking behaviour superior to anything that a psychologist can do in the room with a client. Item–response analysis technology enables a test to be tailored to the client within real time. The development of virtual reality technology extends this even further (e.g., Bailenson, 2018). Computer-based monitoring, including the monitoring of physiological responses in a client, may assess emotional changes in the client, superior to judgements made by clinicians. Interpretation of test results can be generated from machine algorithms based upon protocols of interpretation originating from "objectively" validated experts.

Formulation: the tacit knowledge traditionally regarded as necessary in the development of hypotheses of cause and effect can be seen not to be the result of cognitive inability of the clinician but to be the result of training in uncontrolled environments wherein there are uncertain relationships between cues and decisions. Clinicians demonstrate low performance in diagnosis and prediction (e.g., Shanteau & Weiss, 2014). These uncertain relationships can be identified and the clinician trained to make more and more predictable links (Kahneman & Klein, 2009). But machines can also learn to generalize to previously unseen cases and generate "probably almost correct" (PAC) responses to novel patterns, superior to the human operator. The argument is clear. Given particular assumptions, intuition need not be something mysterious. It can be educated and the AI system can be more reliable than the human. Machines can detect these relationships and learn from them more quickly and reliably than can humans (Morrison, Innes, & Morrison, 2017; Sadler & Regan, 2019). Machines can also generalize to previously unseen cases and generate PAC responses to novel patterns, superior to the human operator. Given these assumptions, intuition, a form of automatic generation of an expert response, need not be something mysterious. It can be educated.

The work of Tetlock (2005) is often cited to show that experts' judgements cannot be trusted. This work, however, on the contrary, demonstrates the conditions under which experts are demonstrably able to predict correctly and when not. The automation of intuition can thus be conceived. The recent advent of AlphaGo©, a program able to master the complex "Go" board game, has signalled a turning point in the design of *intuitive* robots. These machines are able to visualize the likely outcomes for an array of different options, calculate probabilities regarding their success, and use knowledge previously learned from training and play. Elements of these functions are aligned to popular notions of human expertise and intuition (e.g., the recognition of familiar cases); however, others contrast substantially (e.g., the deliberation between options). Ultimately, these machines are challenging our understanding of human expertise and intuition, as well as our previous desires to model it (cf. Morrison et al., 2017).

Intervention: the base of evidence used to demonstrate the efficacy of a narrow range of intervention enables the choice of a small number of therapies to be formulaically treated and clinicians to be trained intensively. Specific components of therapy can be identified and introduced at specific points in the therapeutic process which can be constrained and presented within limited time frames. The dominance of CBT is testimony to the prevalence of this methodology and its effects in the clinical profession. The relationship between the therapist and the client (the therapeutic alliance, cf. Wampold & Imel, 2015) previously regarded as vital, can be downplayed as less robust than the main effect of the therapeutic technique itself (Lilienfeld et al., 2014). Some go as far as to proclaim that the alliance is the result of good therapeutic outcomes and not the cause (Kazdin, 2008; Kazdin & Blasé, 2011). Therefore, training in the establishment of this alliance is seen as unnecessary. The development of a "mechanistic scientific approach" in psychopathology and the development of computational psychiatry already allows the replacement of a clinical intervention with a mechanistic one (Sharp & Eldar, 2019; Thomas & Sharp, 2019)

Evaluation: the assessment of the benefits or otherwise of the intervention can be addressed in the same manner as the prior assessment. Evaluation can be computer based, linking the pre-measures to post-measures and the data then actuarially examined. This eliminates the biases which have been identified to be present when clinicians make judgements (cf. Lilienthal et al., 2014) and the dominant literature on the prevalence of unconscious biases in thinking and judgement (e.g. Kahneman, 2011) can be used to argue for the need to use explicit and conscious processes for evaluation, which can therefore be implemented in automatic cognitive systems. The literature on the other side of the coin is relatively ignored (Newell & Shanks, 2014) and the argument that the bases of both conscious and intuitive thought are essentially the same (Kruglanski & Gigerenzer, 2011) is not addressed.

A missing ingredient?

A factor which should be emphasized at this point relates to the central argument used by those who argue that psychologists are not at risk of replacement, namely that psychologists require the attribute of *empathy* in order to act as psychologists (e.g. Reese, 2018). This is where romance affects the perception of the profession of psychology. Without empathy there can be no alliance in therapy and therefore no ability to influence and help the client.

Empathy is described as the ability to "put yourself in their (the client's) shoes", being caring, understanding and empowering. It is argued that without this capacity one cannot function as an effective psychologist; it is at the centre of the intensive marketing campaign launched by the *Australian Psychological Society* in 2017, and has even formed the basis for recent virtual-reality-driven educational interventions for trainee mental health practitioners (e.g., Formosa, Morrison, Hill, and Stone, 2018). One can reflect on the extent to which empathy exists to a significant degree in all professionals.

But we do not need to ponder the issue of there being individual differences in empathy. Some people are simply kinder than others. The question is whether empathy and kindness are necessary. There is confusion in the use of the term. Batson (2011), for example identifies nine different meanings for the term "empathy". It can be used to mean "compassion", feeling for others and sharing their joy or grief; it is felt *emotion*. It can also mean a sense of cognitive understanding; felt *cognition*. Cognitive understanding can be used to solve problems, but the induction of the emotional component can lead to bias and misunderstanding (cf. Bloom, 2016). *We make the argument that without emotional empathy the trained psychologist is better able to analyze and thereby help a person.* The argument can be developed further. A machine can be programmed to use cognitive questioning better than a human. Neural nets are already more accurate in detecting facial expressions than humans. AI is already in development to reflect on its own practice and retrain itself to deal with client responses. We do not need a kind psychologist. We need an insightful one. The degree to which the discipline of psychology has accepted the possibility of substituting behavioural indices of "empathy" for more deep-seated characteristics can be readily seen in ability-based measures of emotional intelligence which focus on recognizing emotions in others. The emphasis is on the ability of a client in a psychological relationship to *perceive* that the psychologist cares rather than actually empathizes. This can be conveyed through such behaviours as nodding the head or saying "mm-hmm" in response to a patient's comments. A robot could be programmed to send such cues. Does the work of Corti suggest that such simulation will not be accepted by the client, only that it must emanate from a human?

There are four points in the development of this argument. First, the core elements of a psychologist's job can be specified in sufficient detail to enable an automated version to replace the human being. Not only can the automated version do the job, it will do it better, with less bias, fewer procedural errors in presentation, and with no burn out and fatigue. Therefore, there is a clear possibility that psychologists will be replaced by machines. These replacements are already in progress (cf. Innes & Morrison, 2017 for a review).

Second, some psychologists may still be required to continue to develop psychological theory and methodology. Psychologists with particular skills and insight may still be required, perhaps to provide the protocols of judgement required to upgrade the algorithms used to interpret the observational data. We are already seeing the algorithms *learning to learn*.

Third, the reduction in the psychological workforce will be dependent upon the analysis of the proportion of the psychologist's time is spent with these four components. We need to show how much time is spent on these activities. Already psychologists' roles are being changed to monitor the conduct of an electronic therapeutic intervention rather than act in a face-to-face role, with equivalent outcomes in the delivery of inter-CBT compared with face-to-face. With such changes come a range of issues which relate to the management of cases by exception and unfamiliarity with cases which lie "outside of the loop".

Fourth, there are implications for the education system. While not all psychology students wish to become professional psychologists, the large majority of them do. Therefore, the implications for the future training of psychologists are immense not only at postgraduate but at undergraduate levels. While there are other views within the discipline which do not predict the wholesale adoption of technology to deliver services, the 2019 Accreditation Standards (*Australian Psychology Accreditation Council*, 2018) are dependent upon the model outlined earlier and adopted in the training of psychologists. Alternative models have no presence in the scenario.

We note there are other less pessimistic views of the development of AI (e.g., Aoun, 2017). They do not, however, address the fact that the current model in psychology is based upon the development of a technological structure that is ready for automation. Levesque (2017) makes an argument for the importance of "commonsense" in the development of models, and we have already accepted the importance of common sense in our understanding of the development and implementation of AI. But this has to be at least partially opposed by the previous argument based upon the possibility of training intuition through the analysis of tacit knowledge. The entire analysis presented here is also based upon the adoption of assumptions about the direction and the causes of the accumulation of scientific knowledge, which are themselves based upon cultural forces (e.g., Collins & Evans, 2007), that can be challenged fundamentally. Recent developments in quantum cognition with implications for behavioural economics imply this even more emphatically (Orrell, 2018). Collins (2018) argues persuasively for a failure of AI to replace humans, but this fails to take account of the degree to which psychological practice has been simplified for delivery.

A final criticism of an analysis of the substitution of human judgement by AI is that AI cannot assume the creative mode of human thought; humans alone are capable of creating new ways of thinking, new forms of art and technology. Such an analysis does not account for the view that a Darwinian mode of thinking, based upon the blind variation of actions combined with selective retention of useful outcomes, as proposed by Campbell (1960), can account for the production of much of mankind's creative products, as supported empirically by Simonton (1999). Nor can it be in the analysis by Martindale (1990) in his work on *The Clockwork Muse* demonstrating how so much of human achievement in the arts, including painting and music, is predictable from a small number of operations and Burrow's (1987) mathematical analysis of the works of Jane Austin. Creativity can be achieved by AI and in a version of the Turing Test, the product created cannot be distinguished from a product produced by a human.

A reconstruction of psychological practice?

But a final rejoinder can be made. A behaviouristic and cognitive paradigm in psychology, which has resulted in the strong movement to automation, could be replaced by one which is more humanistic and oriented to the arts, as exemplified for many years by Koch (Finkelman & Kessel, 2000). Koch's approach has been debated interminably over the years (cf. Leary, 2001; Morawski, 2001) and never adopted but also never rejected. There is a place for debate and a reconfiguration of the standards developed for the curriculum in psychology, especially in Australia, that might mitigate the degree to which the processes of the robot can replace the processes of the human. One of the means whereby the march of the machines may be slowed is through the broadening and widening of knowledge and how that knowledge is applied to specific cases (e.g., Epstein, 2019). Accounts of the personal experience of therapists who have evolved different practices over years of treatment give vivid meaning to this possibility (cf. Marzillier, 2010) in stark contrast to the picture of professional psychology as practiced in many places (Newnes, 2011).

Consideration of this possibility also enables an association to be made with an earlier analysis in this chapter, namely that the essence of the development of artificial intelligence is the emergence of the universality of the processes, and not the specificity. The work of Tetlock (2005) on human expertise, based upon the thinking of Isiah Berlin (1953), emphasizes the superiority of the "fox" (who knows many things) over the "hedgehog" (who knows one big thing) in predicting developments in international relations. Epstein (2019) makes the same point more generally. Training in many things may give the impression of developing a superficial grasp of issues and problems and techniques. Broad training may, however, enable problem solving that is creative and innovative. Machines continue to develop at a rapid pace. It remains to be seen to what extent they may outperform humans in whatever domain we may examine.

Discussions within the domain of psychology continue around the concept of expertise and what the expert brings to the setting beyond many specific skills and techniques, akin to the proposal by Colvin (2015) of the inherent superiority of humans over machines. Tracey et al. (2014) discuss the "elusive good" that may comprise expertise while Vollmer, Spada, Caspar, and Burri (2013) dissect the value of university training and Schulte-Mecklenbeck, Spaanjaars, and Wittman (2017) actually dispute the diagnostic capacity of trained psychologists. The rise of AI within the context of psychology has brought to the surface for forensic examination the concept and understanding of expertise (Epstein, 2019; Eyal, 2019).

A coda

At the time of writing there is an emerging discussion that the excitement and trepidation about AI may be waning, in light of the difficulties which emerge in the research process (*The Economist*, June 2020). While not a forthcoming AI "winter" there is reference to an "AI autumn". Our analysis takes as it launch point, however, that human jobs, including the professions, have been changing for decades, due to technological developments (Graeber,

2019). Jobs have become more automated in their processes and can be replaced by machines. There may continue to be human traits and virtues that will lie beyond the capabilities of machines, but for a very large majority of the tasks currently performed by humans, machines will prevail.

References

Acemoglu, D., & Restrepo, P. (2019). Artificial intelligence, automation and work. In A. Agrawal, J. Gans, & A. Goldfarb (Eds.), *The economics of artificial intelligence: An agenda*. Chicago: University of Chicago Press.

Aoun, J. E. (2017). *Robot-proof: Higher education in the age of artificial intelligence*. Cambridge, MA: MIT Press.

Augoustinos, M., & Innes, J. M. (1990). Towards an integration of social representations and social schema theory. *British Journal of Social Psychology, 29*, 213–231.

Australian Psychology Accreditation Council. (2018). *Accreditation standards for psychology programs*. https://www.psychologycouncil.org.au/sites/default/files/public/Standards_20180912_Published_Final_v1.2.pdf

Autor, D. H., Levy, F., & Murnane, R. J. (2003). The skill content of recent technological change: An empirical exploration. *Quarterly Journal of Economics, 118*(4), 1279–1333.

Bailenson, J. (2018). *Experience on demand: What virtual reality is, how it works, and what it can do for you*. New York: W.W. Norton.

Barber, T. X., & Silver, M. J. (1968). Fact, fiction and the experimenter-bias effect. *Psychological Bulletin, 70*, 1–29.

Batson, C. D. (2011). *Altruism in humans*. New York: Oxford University Press.

Bem, D. J. (1965). An experimental analysis of self-persuasion. *Journal of Experimental Social Psychology, 1*, 199–218.

Bem, D. J. (1966). Inducing belief in false confessions. *Journal of Personality and Social Psychology, 3*, 707–710.

Berlin, I. (1953). *The hedgehog and the fox*. London: Weidenfeld and Nicholson.

Bless, H., & Burger, A. M. (2016). A closer look at social psychologists' silver bullet: Inevitable and evitable side effects of the experimental approach. *Perspectives on Psychological Science, 11*(2), 296–308.

Bloom, P. (2016). *Against empathy: The case for rational compassion*. New York: HarperCollins.

Bootle, R. (2019). *The AI economy*. London: Nicholas Brealey Press.

Boyd, R., & Holton, R. J. (2018). Technology, innovation, employment and power: Does robotics and artificial intelligence really mean social transformation? *Journal of Sociology, 54*(3), 331–345.

Brewer, W. F. (2012). The theory ladenness of the mental processes used in the scientific enterprise: Evidence from cognitive psychology and the history of science. In R. W. Proctor & E. J. Capaldi (Eds.), *Psychology of science: Implicit and explicit processes*. New York: Oxford University Press.

Bridle, J. (2018). *New dark age: Technology and the end of the future*. London: Verso.

Broad, E. (2018). *Made by humans: The AI condition*. Melbourne: Melbourne University Press.

Burrell, J. (2016, January–June). How the machine 'thinks': Understanding opacity in machine learning algorithms. *Big Data & Society*, 1–12.

Burrows, J. F. (1987). *Computation into criticism: A study of Jane Austen and an experiment in method*. Oxford: Clarendon Press.

Busemeyer, J. R., & Wang, Z. (2015). What is quantum cognition, and how is it applied to psychology? *Current Directions in Psychological Science, 24*(3), 163–169.

Campbell, D. T. (1960). Blind variation and selective retention in creative thought as in other knowledge processes. *Psychological Review, 67*, 380–400.

Campbell, D. T. (1963). Social attitudes and other acquired behavioral dispositions. In S. Koch (Ed.), *Psychology: A study of a science, investigations of man as socius* (Vol. 6, pp. 94–176). New York: McGraw-Hill.

Campbell, D. T. (1975). Degrees of freedom and the case study. *Comparative Political Studies, 8*, 178–191.

Campbell, D. T. (1994). The social psychology of scientific validity: An epistemological perspective and a personalized history. In W. R. Shadish & S. Fuller (Eds.), *The social psychology of science* (pp. 124–161). New York: Guilford.

Chomsky, N. (1971). The case against B.F. Skinner. *New York Review of Books, 17*(11), 18–24.

Christian, B. (2011). *The most human human*. New York: Doubleday.

Clegg, B. (2017). *Big data: How the information revolution is transforming our lives*. London: Icon.

Collins, H. (2010). *Tacit and explicit knowledge*. Chicago: University of Chicago Press.

Collins, H. (2018). *Artifictional intelligence: Against humanity's surrender to computers*. Cambridge: Polity Press.

Collins, H. (2019). *Forms of life: The method and meaning of sociology*. Cambridge, MA: MIT Press.

Collins, H., & Evans, R. (2007). *Rethinking expertise*. Chicago: University of Chicago Press.

Colvin, G. (2015). *Humans are underrated: What high achievers know that brilliant machines never will*. London: Nicholas Brealey.

Corti, K., & Gillespie, A. (2015). A truly human interface: Interacting face-to-face with someone whose words are determined by a computer program. *Frontiers in Psychology, 6*, 1–18. doi:10.3389/fpsyg.2015.00634

Cranney, J., et al. (2009). Graduate attributes of the 4-year Australian undergraduate psychology program. *Australian Psychologist, 44*, 253–262.

Crawford, J. T., & Jussim, L. (Eds.). (2018). *The politics of social psychology*. New York: Routledge.

Davies, P. (2018). *The demon in the machine*. London: Allen Lane.

deBruin, W. B., Parker, A. M., & Fischoff, B. (2020). Decision-making competence: More than intelligence? *Current Directions in Psychological Science, 29*, 186–192.

DeWall, F. (2016). *Are we smart enough to know how smart animals are?* New York: WW Norton and Co.

Dietvorst, B. J., Simmons, J. P., & Massey, C. (2015). Algorithm aversion: People erroneously avoid algorithms after seeing them err. *Journal of Experimental Psychology: General, 144*(1), 114–126. doi:10.1037/xge0000033

Duarte, J., Crawford, J., Stern, C., Haidt, J., Jussim, L., & Tetlock, P. (2015). Political diversity will improve social psychological research. *Behavioral and Brain Sciences, 38*, 1–58.

Edwards, L., & Veale, M. (2017). Slave to the algorithm: Why a right to an explanation is probably not the remedy you are looking for. *Duke Law & Technology Review*. Retrieved from https://heinonline.org/HOL/LandingPage?handle=hein.journals/dltr16&div=3&id=&page=

Elliott, A. (2019). *The culture of AI*. London: Routledge.

Epstein, D. (2019). *Range: Why generalists triumph in a specialized world*. New York: Riverhead Books.

Estes, W. (Ed.). (1954). *Modern learning theory*. New York: Appleton Century Croft.

Eyal, G. (2019). *The crisis of expertise*. London: Polity Press.

Farr, R. M., & Moscovici, S. (Eds.). (1984). *Social representations*. Cambridge: Cambridge University Press.

Ferster, C. B., & Skinner, B. F. (1957). *Schedules of reinforcement*. New York: Appleton-Century-Croft.

Finkelman, D., & Kessel, F. (2000). Sigmund Koch: Human agency and the psychological studies. In G. A. Kimble & M. Wertheimer (Eds.), *Portraits of pioneers in psychology* (Vol. 4, pp. 359–381). Washington, DC: American Psychological Society.

Flynn, J. R. (2009). *What is intelligence? Beyond the Flynn Effect* (Expanded ed.). Cambridge: Cambridge University Press.

Formosa, N. J., Morrison, B. W., Hill, G., & Stone, D. (2018), Testing the efficacy of a virtual reality-based simulation in enhancing users' knowledge, attitudes, and empathy relating to psychosis. *Australian Journal of Psychology, 70*, 57–65. doi:10.1111/ajpy.12167

Frey, C. B. (2019). *The technology trap*. Princeton: Princeton University Press.

Frey, C. B., & Osborne, M. A. (2013). *The future of employment: How susceptible are jobs to computerisation?* Oxford: Programme on the Impacts of Future Technology, University of Oxford.

Friedman, N. (1967). *The social nature of psychological research*. New York: Basic Books.

Galison, P. (1997). *Image & logic: A material culture of microphysics*. Chicago: University of Chicago Press.

Geertz, C. (1973). Thick description. In *The interpretation of culture: Selected essays*. New York: Basic Books.

Goff, P. (2019). *Galileo's error: Foundations for a new science of consciousness*. London: Rider Books.

Graeber, D. (2019). *Bullshit jobs*. London: Allen Lane.

Graesser, L., & King, W. L. (2020). *Foundations of deep reinforcement learning.* Boston: Addison-Wesley.

Greenwald, A. G. (2012). There is nothing so practical as a good method. *Perspectives on Psychological Science, 7*(2), 99–108.

Grinnell, F. (2009). *Everyday practice of science: Where intuition and passion meet objectivity and logic.* New York: Oxford University Press.

Guerin, B., & Innes, J. M. (1981). Awareness of cognitive processes: Replications and revisions. *Journal of General Psychology, 104,* 173–189.

Harnad, S. (1991). Other bodies, other minds: A machine incarnation of an old philosophical problem. *Minds and Machines, 1,* 43–54.

Herman, E. (1995). *The romance of American psychology: Political culture in the age of experts.* Berkeley and Los Angeles: University of California Press.

Hull, C. L. (1943). *Principles of behavior.* New York: Appleton Century Croft.

Inbar, Y., & Lammers, J. (2012). Political diversity in social and personality psychology. *Perspectives on Psychological science, 7*(5), 496–503.

Innes, J. M., & Fraser, C. (1971). Experimenter bias and other possible biases in psychological research. *European Journal of Social Psychology, 1,* 297–310.

Innes, J. M., & Morrison, B. W. (2017). Projecting the future impact of advanced technologies on the profession: Will a robot take my job? *Australian Psychological Society InPsych, 39*(2), 34–35.

Innes, J. M., &Morrison, B. W. (2020). Experimental studies of human robot interaction: Threats to valid interpretation from methodological constraints associated with experimental manipulations. *International Journal of Social Robotics.* doi: https://doi.org/10.1007/s12369-020-00671-8

Jacobucci, R., & Grimm, K. J. (2020). Machine learning and psychological research: The unexplored effect of measurement. *Perspectives on Psychological Science,* 1–8.

Jones, R. A., Linder, D. E., Kiesler, C. A., Zanna, M., & Brehm, J. (1968). Internal states or external stimuli: Observers' attitude judgments and the dissonance-self-persuasion controversy. *Journal of Experimental Social Psychology, 4,* 247–269.

Jureidini, J., & McHenry, L. B. (2020). *The illusion of evidence-based medicine: Exposing the crisis of credibility in clinical research.* South Australia: Wakefield Press.

Kaldy, Z., & Blaser, E. (2020). Putting effort into infant cognition. *Current Directions in Psychological Science, 29,* 180–185.

Kahneman, D. (2011). *Thinking fast and slow.* New York: Farrar, Straus and Giroux.

Kahneman, D., & Klein, G. (2009). Conditions for intuitive expertise: A failure to disagree. *American Psychologist, 64,* 515–526.

Kay, J., & King, M. (2020. *Radical uncertainty: Decision making for an unknowable future.* Hachette: Bridge Street Press.

Kazdin, A. E. (2008). Evidence-based treatment and practice. *American Psychologist, 63,* 146–159.

Kazdin, A. E., & Blasé, S. L. (2011). Rebooting psychotherapy research and practice to reduce the burden of mental illness. *Perspectives on Psychological Science, 6,* 21–37.

Klein, O., Doyen, S., Leys, C., daGama, P. A., Miller, S., Questienne, L., & Cleeremans, A. (2012). Low hopes, high expectations: Expectancy effects and the replicability of behavioural experiments. *Perspectives on Psychological Science, 7*(6), 572–584.

Koch, C. (2019). *The feeling of life itself.* Cambridge, MA: MIT Press.

Kovacs, K., & Conway, A. R. A. (2019). What is IQ? Life after "general intelligence". *Current Directions in Psychological Science, 28,* 189–194.

Kruglanski, A. W., & Gigerenzer, G. (2011). Intuitive and deliberate judgments are based on common principles. *Psychological Review, 118,* 97–109.

Leary, D. E. (2001). One big idea, one ultimate concern. *American Psychologist, 56,* 425–432.

Leichseuring, F., & Steinert, C. (2017). Is cognitive behavioral therapy the gold standard for psychotherapy? The need for plurality in treatment and research. *JAMA, 318*(14), 1323–1324.

Levesque, H. (2017). *Common sense, the Turing Test and quest for real AI.* Cambridge, MA: MIT Press.

Levin, D. T., Harriott, C., Paul, N. A., Zhang, T., & Adams, J. A. (2013). Cognitive dissonance as a measure of reactions to human-robot interaction. *Journal of Human-Robot Interaction, 2,* 1–17.

Li, J., Ju, W., & Reeves, B. (2017). Touching a mechanical body: Tactile contact with body parts of a humanoid robot is physiologically arousing. *Journal of Human-Robot Interaction, 6*, 118–130.

Lilienfeld, S. O., Lynn, S. J., Lohr, J. M., & Tavris, C. (Eds.). (2015). *Science and pseudoscience in clinical psychology* (2nd ed.). New York: Guilford.

Lilienfeld, S. O., Ritschel, A., Lynn, S. J., Cautin, R. L., & Latzman, R. D. (2014). Why ineffective psychotherapies appear to work: A taxonomy of causes of spurious therapeutic effectiveness. *Perspectives on Psychological Science, 9*, 355–387.

MacCorquodale, K., & Meehl, P. E. (1948). On the distinction between hypothetical constructs and intervening variables. *Psychological Review, 55*, 95–107.

MacCoun, R. J. (1998). Biases in the interpretation and use of research results. *Annual Review of Psychology, 49*, 259–287.

MacDorman, K. F., & Ishiguro, H. (2006). The uncanny advantage of using androids in cognitive and social science research. *Interaction Studies, 7*, 297–337.

Malabou, C. (2019). *Morphing intelligence*. New York: Columbia University Press.

Markova, I. (2014). Questioning interdisciplinarity: History, social psychology and the theory of social representations. In C. Tileaga & J. Byford (Eds.), *Psychology and history: Interdisciplinary explorations* (pp. 109–126). Cambridge: Cambridge University Press.

Martindale, C. (1990). *The clockwork muse: The predictability of artistic change*. New York: Basic Books.

Marzillier, J. (2010). *The gossamer thread: My life as a psychotherapist*. London: Karnac.

McAdams, D. P. (2015). *The art and science of personality development*. New York: Guilford.

Meehl, P. (1954). *Clinical versus statistical prediction: A theoretical analysis and review of the literature*. Minneapolis: University of Minnesota Press.

Miller, A. G. (1972). *The social psychology of psychological research*. New York: Free Press.

Miller, G. A. (2003). The cognitive revolution: A historical perspective. *Trends in Cognitive Science, 7*, 141–144.

Miller, T. (2019). Explanation in artificial intelligence: Insights from the social sciences. *Artificial Intelligence, 267*, 1–38.

Morawski, J. G. (2001). Gifts bestowed, gifts withheld: Assessing psychological theory with a Kochean attitude. *American psychologist, 56*, 433–440.

Morrison, B. W., Innes, J. M., & Morrison, N. M. V. (2017). *Current advances in robotic decision-making: Is there such a thing as an intuitive robot?* Australian Psychological Society Industrial and Organisational Psychology Conference, Sydney.

Muller, J. Z. (2018). *The tyranny of metrics*. Princeton: Princeton University Press.

Newell, B. R., & Shanks, D. R. (2014). Unconscious influences on decision making: A critical review. *Behavioral and Brain Sciences, 37*, 1–61.

Newnes, C. (2011). Toxic psychology. In M. Rapley, J. Moncrieff, & J. Dillon (Eds.), *De-medicalizing misery* (pp. 211–225). London: Palgrave Macmillan.

Nisbett, R. E., & Wilson, T. D. (1977). Telling more than we can know: Verbal reports on mental processes. *Psychological Review, 84*, 231–259.

O'Neil, C. (2016). *Weapons of math destruction*. London: Penguin.

Orrell, D. (2018). *Quantum economics: The new science of money*. London: Icon.

Orne, M. T. (1962). On the social psychology of the psychological experiment: With particular reference to demand characteristics and their implications. *American Psychologist, 17*, 776–783.

Orne, M. T. (1969). Demand characteristics and the concept of quasi-controls. In R. Rosenthal & R. L. Rosnow (Eds.), *Artifact in behavioural research* (pp. 143–179). New York: Academic Press.

Pastore, N. (1949). *The nature-nurture controversy*. New York: King's Crown Press.

Polanyi, M. (1958). *Personal knowledge*. London: Routledge.

Rahwan, I., et al. (2019). Machine behaviour. *Nature, 568*, 477–486. doi.org/10.1038/s41586-019-1138-y

Rasskin-Gutman, D. (2009). *Chess metaphors: Artificial intelligence and the human mind*. Cambridge, MA: MIT Press.

Reese, B. (2018). *The fourth age*. New York: Atria.

Rosenthal, R. (1976). *Experimenter effects in behavioural research* (English ed.). New York: Irvington.

Rosenzweig, R. (1933). The experimental situation as a psychological problem. *Psychological Review, 40*, 337–354.

Russell, S. (2019). *Human compatible: AI and the problem of control.* London: Allen Lane.

Sadler, M., & Regan, N. (2019). *Game changer: AlphaZero's ground breaking chess strategies and the promise of AI.* Alkmaar, The Netherlands: New In Chess.

Safina, C. (2020). *Becoming wild: How animal cultures raise families, create beauty and achieve peace.* New York: Henry Holt.

Scerri, E. (2016). *A tale of seven scientists and a new philosophy of science.* New York: Oxford University Press.

Schubert, A.-L., Nunez, M. D., Hagemann, D., & Vandekerckhove, J. (2018). Individual differences in processing speed predict cognitive abilities: A model-based cognitive neuroscience account. *Computational Brain & Behavior, 2*, 64–84.

Schulte-Mecklenbeck, M., Spaanjaars, N. L., & Wittman, C. L. M. (2017). The (in)visibility of psychodiagnosticians' expertise. *Journal of Behavioral Decision Making, 30*, 89–94.

Seaver, N. (2017, July–December). Algorithms as culture: Some tactics for the ethnography of algorithmic systems. *Big Data and Society*, 1–12.

Sejnowski, T. J. (2018). *The deep learning revolution.* Cambridge, MA: MIT Press.

Seligman, M. (2018). *The hope circuit: A psychologist's journey from helplessness to optimism.* Sydney: Penguin.

Shadish, W. R., Cook, T. D., & Campbell, D. T. (2002). *Experimental and quasi-experimental designs for generalised causal inference.* Boston: Houghton-Mifflin.

Shanteau, J., & Weiss, D. J. (2014). Individual versus domain expertise. *American Psychologist, 69*, 711–712.

Sharp, P. B., & Eldar, E. (2019). Computational models of anxiety: Nascent efforts and future directions. *Current Directions in Psychological Science, 28*(2), 170–176.

Shedler, J. (2010). The efficacy of psychodynamic psychotherapy. *American Psychologist, 65*, 98–109.

Shenhav, A., Musslick, S., Lieder, F., Kool, W., Griffiths, T. L., Cohen, J. D., & Botvinick, M. M. (2017). Toward a rational and mechanistic account of mental effort. *Annual Review of Neuroscience, 40*, 99–124.

Sherwood, J. J., & Nataupsky, M. (1968). Predicting the conclusions of negro-white intelligence research from biographical characteristics of the investigator. *Journal of Personality and Social Psychology, 8*, 53–58.

Simonton, D. (1999). Creativity as blind variation and selective retention: Is the creative process Darwinian? *Psychological Inquiry, 10*, 309–328.

Sinha, R., & Swearingen, K. (2002, April). *The role of transparency in recommender systems.* Paper presented at the CHI'02 extended abstracts on Human factors in Computing Systems, Minnesota.

Skinner, B. F. (1938). *The behaviour of organisms: An experimental analysis.* Oxford: Appleton- Century-Croft.

Skinner, B. F. (1953). *Science and human behaviour.* New York: Palgrave Macmillan.

Skinner, B. F. (1969, April, 20–25). The machine that is man. *Psychology Today*, 60–63.

Smith, R. E. (2019). *Rage inside the machine: The prejudice of algorithms and how to stop the internet making bigots of us all.* London: Bloomsbury Business.

Spearman, C. (1904). 'General intelligence' objectively determined and measured. *American Journal of Psychology, 15*(2), 201–293.

Susskind, D. (2020). *A world without work.* Milton Keynes: Allen Lane.

Susskind, R., & Susskind, D. (2015). *The future of the professions: How technology will transform the work of human experts.* Oxford: Oxford University Press.

Tetlock, P. E. (2005/2017). *Expert political judgment: How good is it? How can you know?* (New ed.). Princeton: Princeton University Press.

Thomas, J. G., & Sharp, P. B. (2019). Mechanistic science: A new approach to comprehensive research that relates psychological and biological phenomena. *Clinical Psychological Science, 7*, 196–215.

Tracey, T. J. G., Wampold, B. E., Lichtenberg, J. W., & Goodyear, R. K. (2014). Expertise in psychotherapy: An elusive good? *American Psychologist, 69*, 218–229.

Turing, A. (1950). Computing machines and intelligence. *Mind, 59*(236), 433–460.

Vollmer, S., Spada, H., Caspar, F., & Burri, S. (2013). Expertise in clinical psychology: The effects of university training and practical experience on expertise in clinical psychology. *Frontiers in Psychology, 4*, 1–12.

Von Neumann, J. (1958). *The computer and the brain.* New Haven: Yale University Press.

Walsh, T. (2018). *2062*. Melbourne: LaTrobe University Press.

Walsh, T., et al. (2019). *The effective and ethical development of artificial intelligence*. Report for the Australian Council of Learned Academies. Canberra, Australia: Australian Council of Learned Academies.

Wampold, B. E., & Imel, Z. E. (2015). *The great psychotherapy debate*. New York: Routledge.

Wann, T. W. (Ed.). (1964). *Behaviorism and phenomenology*. Chicago: University of Chicago Press.

Webb, E. J., Campbell, D. T., Schwartz, R. D., & Sechrest, L. (1966). *Unobtrusive measures: Nonreactive research in the social sciences*. Chicago: Rand McNally.

Westen, D., & Bradley, R. (2005). Empirically supported complexity: Re-thinking evidence based practice in psychotherapy. *Current Directions in Psychological Science, 14*, 266–271.

Wilson, T. D., Aronson, E., & Carlsmith, K. (2010). The art of laboratory experimentation. In S. T. Fiske, D. T. Gilbert, & G. Lindzey (Eds.), *Handbook of social psychology* (Vol. 1, pp. 51–81). Hoboken: Wiley.

Winograd, T. (1972). *Understanding natural language*. New York: Academic Press.

Woodley, M. A., te Nijenhuis, J., & Murphy, R. (2013). Were the Victorians cleverer than us? The decline in general intelligence estimated from a meta-analysis of the slowing of simple reaction time. *Intelligence, 41*, 843–850.

Woolfolk, R. L. (2015). *The value of psychotherapy: The talking cure in the age of clinical science*. New York: Guilford.

Yaniv, I., & Kleinberger, E. (2000). Advice taking in decision making: Egocentric discounting and reputation formation. *Organizational Behavior and Human Decision Processes, 83*(2), 260–281. doi:10.1006/obhd.2000.2909

Yeomans, M., Shah, A., Mullainathan, S., & Kleinberg, J. (2019). Making sense of recommendations. *Journal of Behavioral Decision Making*. doi:10.1002/bdm.2118

Young, J. E., Hawkins, R., Sharlin, E., & Igarajhi, T. (2009). Towards acceptable domestic robots: Applying insights from social psychology. *International Journal of Social Robotics, 1*, 95–108.

4

AI in the age of technoscience

On the rise of data-driven AI and its epistem-ontological foundations

Jutta Weber and Bianca Prietl

> Each new piece of miraculous apparatus has been heralded as the essence of a new (but usually short-lived) 'age' in the history of mankind. In its turn each machine metaphor has opened areas of both insight and radical blindness as it becomes a means of interpreting what happens in our world.
> Langdon Winner, *Autonomous Technology* (1977, 45)

> I am interested in the narratives of scientific fact – those potent fictions of science – within a complex field indicated by the signifier SF [science fiction; the authors].
> Donna Haraway, *Primate Vision* (1989, 5)

> Is there any point in understanding noisy data?
> Noam Chomsky, *Where Artificial Intelligence Went Wrong* (2012)

This chapter offers a critical discussion of the epistemological and ontological foundations[1] of AI. It begins with a short history of AI focused on the epistemological and ontological premises foundational to the three AI approaches that have dominated its historical development, namely, symbolic, connectionist, and data-driven AI. It then presents some early and more recent critiques of AI technologies that are informed by (critical/feminist) science and technology studies, including more recent developments in algorithm and critical data studies. After discussing some thoughts on how we are to understand the rise of data-driven AI, it concludes with some critical remarks about the current call for 'ethics in AI'. The overall aim of the chapter is to contribute toward a reflection on the all-too-often implicit assumptions entailed by AI per se and by its new instantiations, thus laying the analytical groundwork for shaping alternative AI technologies in the future.

From symbolic via connectionist to data-driven AI

Until recently, the history of AI has often been described as oscillating between two different approaches: *symbolic AI* as the dominant rational-cognitive approach on the one hand and *connectionist AI*, or 'sub-symbolic' approaches, on the other.

The former is based on formal logic and mathematics and draws on representation, causality, and deduction (Newell/Simon 1976). One of its central assumptions is the concept of the physical symbol system, according to which any intelligent system – human or machine – "must operate by manipulating data structures composed of symbols" (Russel/Norvig 2010, 18). Expert systems – artificial systems whose purpose is to reproduce knowledge – can be regarded as a classic example of this kind of AI: AI researchers sought to extract knowledge from experts by interviewing them and encoding the knowledge thus gained into logical rules to make it computable. It soon became clear, however, that static knowledge systems are rather difficult to build and are not especially robust (Norvig 2011). For this reason, as far back as the early 1980s, many regarded expert systems as a failure (Brooks 1986; Pfeifer/Scheier 2000).

The connectionist approach ranges from artificial neural network research to genetic algorithms and behavior-based robotics, and is rooted in, as well as inspired by, biology, psychology and the neurosciences. These approaches draw on correlation, induction, abduction and bottom-up strategies. They focus on behavior, learning, and self-organization while some work with concepts such as situatedness and embodiment. Warren McCulloch and Walter Pitts' artificial (learning) neural network (1943) is an early example of the biologically inspired approach. Another connectionist approach, Rosenblatt's famous 'Perceptron' (1962), which was a simple form of neural network, was vehemently criticized by Minsky/Papert (1969). Their critique heralded a lengthy period, from the late 1960s onward, in which the biocybernetic, connectionist approach lay dormant.

In the 1980s, however, the biocybernetic approach was revived in fields such as Artificial Life, biorobotics, and parallel distributed processing. In the course of this development, the focus of AI increasingly shifted from knowing to learning, from understanding reasoning as a high-level form of symbol manipulation toward solving problems with machine learning using so-called common-sense knowledge as a basis. It sought increasingly to deal with uncertainty and the 'theoryless' (Valiant 2014), a development paralleled by the introduction of new flexible databases (NoSQL), statistics-based methods of machine learning (e.g. genetic algorithms), and the usage of massive data that were now gathered from websites, search engines, online marketing, and similar sources.[2]

Data-driven AI is the dominant AI approach taken nowadays. It is based on machine learning (ML) from examples extracted via the analysis of massive amounts of (online) data, rather than building on logical rules.[3] More specifically, as one of the central pillars of data-driven AI, ML is "a method for finding patterns in data that are usefully predictive of future events but which do not necessarily provide an explanatory theory", as machine learner Leslie Valiant explains (2014, see 8). Its application is aimed primarily at aggregating "as much data as possible, in order to mine them for relevant patterns that allow the profiler to anticipate future behaviours" (Gutwirth/Hildebrandt 2010, 7). As the chances of finding 'relevant' patterns increase with the volume and size of the data collection, efforts are undertaken to (re)combine more data from diverse categories and multiple (online) sources in order to find new correlation patterns. Algorithm studies scholar Louise Amoore describes this logic of ML as the "imagination of possibilities" (Amoore 2013, 24). Interestingly, induction and abduction are used here instead of deduction to target the realm of the so-called theoryless (Valiant 2014) and not the traditional realm of the physical world:

> Machine learning is concerned with machines that improve with experience and reason inductively or abductively in order *to optimize, approximate, summarize, generalize from specific examples to general rules, classify, make predictions, find associations, propose explanations, and propose ways of grouping things.*
>
> *(Kovacs 2012, see 938f, emphasis added)*

Reason, that is, classical rational-cognitive analysis, is only used in the post-processing and post-analysis phase of machine learning but not in its methodological grounding (Erni/Fröhlich 2010; Valiant 2014). Today, most ML applications are not used to target phenomena in the physical world but social or cultural phenomena that occur in everyday life. The applications range from analyzing the preference behavior of consumers to identifying fraud strategies in credit card transactions to identifying 'terrorists'.

STS scholar Andrew Pickering has claimed that the biocybernetic approach is "an instantiation of a different paradigm from the one in which most of us grew up – the reductive, linear, Newtonian, paradigm that still characterizes most academic work in the natural and social sciences (and engineering and humanities, too)" (Pickering 2002, 413f). For him, "[c]ybernetics is all about this shift from epistemology to ontology, from representation to performativity, agency and emergence" (ibid., 414). Can this biocybernetic shift from logic to probability, from linearity to emergence, be regarded as a shift from classical Newtonian science to a new technorationality that seeks not so much to understand (fundamental principles) as to effectively engineer in the sense of developing the best solution possible for practical problems (Weber 2010, 2011)? Following Pickering's argument and keeping in mind the recent merging of biocybernetic AI approaches with probabilistic, data-driven approaches, the question arises: how do these epistemological and ontological changes in AI affect our understanding of the world and of ourselves? What are the foundations of these frameworks of thinking; what are their implicit norms and values and their societal impacts?

It seems important to understand these epistem-ontological shifts, their logics, effects, and consequences (Weber 2011), if we want to engage critically with AI.

Early critiques

Early symbol-processing AI was criticized for its belief that every aspect of human thinking could be reduced to logical formalism, i.e. that human thought (and everyday language) is computable (Weizenbaum 1976). The argument was that it ignores the fact that people learn through their embodied, language-mediated practices which are embedded in the everyday world and include implicit, context-bound knowledge that ensures they are able to find orientation in that world (Dreyfus 1972; Winograd/Flores 1987; Adam 1998). Although language has been increasingly technicized and technology today is mainly (computer) language-based, it is not the symbolic that AI is working with but formal languages involving numbers and processing rules, whose logic is different from that used to think, talk, and produce meaning. Turing machines and formal languages might be concise and coherent, but they are not meaningful (Weizenbaum 1976; Mersch 2006).

STS scholar Donna Haraway's work on technoscientific developments, which is at once optimistic and critical of their entanglement with the sociomaterial relations of power,[4] has inspired a diverse body of research on artificial intelligence and robots. This work enables us to better understand the changing "sociomaterial grounds of agency and lived experience of bodies and persons, of resemblance and difference, and of relations across the human/machine boundary" (Suchman 2008, 139). It demonstrates not only that AI is modeled on hierarchical, gendered assumptions (as, for example, when humanoid robots are given the highly stereotypical shape of women, infants, or pets) but also that gendered ontological, anthropological, and epistemological premises are enacted in the theoretical concepts that form the basis of AI development.

Feminist STS scholars Lucy Suchman, Barbara Becker, Alison Adam, and others have pointed out that symbolic AI works with a limited concept of intelligence, one equated solely with cognition. Thus, they shed light on the cultural assumptions enacted in the design of humanlike machines, particularly regarding the 'nature' of the human. They depict AI as a deeply conservative project that draws heavily on long-standing Western philosophical assumptions regarding the nature of human intelligence by focusing on the individual 'cognizer' as the point of origin of rational action, while under-privileging affectivity and bodily states as crucial to the specificity of the materially embodied and socially embedded subject. In this framework the 'cognizer' is modeled as the universal figure of 'man' rather than as an embedded and materially embodied subject (Suchman 1987; Becker 1992; Adam 1998). The problematic nature of this assumption already becomes apparent at the methodological level. For example, AI expert Alison Adam argues with regard to Herbert Simon's path-breaking book, *Human Problem Solving*, that the experiments conducted for his so-called general theory of intelligence, or 'information processing psychology', were:

> based on the behaviour of a few, technically educated, young, male, probably middle-class, probably white, college students working on a set of rather unnatural tasks [formal logic; chess playing; the authors] in a US university in the late 1960s and early 1970s.
>
> *(Adam 1998, 94)*

With regard to the early connectionist approach, Adam notes further that while there is a perceptible move away from strong rationalism – for example, knowledge is no longer modeled as propositionally structured (ibid., 45) – nevertheless, the system is still disembodied as the (implicitly male) operator supplies all the meaning for both input and output, including an understanding of skills and bodily knowledge, so that the system may be trained.[5] In her own research on social robotics, one of the authors (Weber 2005) also identifies a growing concern with questions of sociality, emotionality, and interaction within recent trends in robotics and the conceptualization of the human–machine relation. She argues that, while the 'weak' approach of so-called social robotics seeks to create machines capable of simulating emotions and sociality, it holds on to the traditional hierarchical master-slave relation between the expert/user and the machine. The 'strong' approach to social robotics, by contrast, seeks to create self-learning autonomous machines and builds on the highly gendered caregiver-infant relation between the user and the machine, thereby reifying traditional concepts of care and child-rearing. Modeling the human-robot relation in this way not only serves to exploit the user's time and dedication in helping the machine develop but also obscures the roboticists' own authorship of the human-robot relation. Sherry Turkle (1996) reaches a similar conclusion when describing a shift from rule-based to emergent models within the field of AI, according to which computers are imagined as developing children that learn from experience and interactions and thus build their intelligence from the bottom up. Whereas Turkle concedes that these connectionist computer systems no longer need to be programmed by means of centralized sets of rules but through 'learning-by-doing', Weber argues that every intelligent machine will still be based on rules, as rule-oriented behavior forms the material basis and makes up the fundamental functionality of these machines (2005, 214).

If we follow this argument, it means that the standardization of human behavior is a precondition for every computer model and software application, and this in turn gives rise to the question of which behavior is identified and enacted as the norm (i.e. as 'normal'), which human behavior is excluded from this conceptualization, and how both of these elements are intertwined with gendered, racist, classist, and ableist structures and symbolic systems. At the same time, new field of biologically inspired robotics pays great attention to the unpredictable and to chance. With iterative strategies of trial and error, biorobotics tries to support developments that might result in unpredictable but controllable machine behavior on the basis of emergent, or evolutionary, processes. Traditional ideas regarding the objectivity, neutrality, and reproducibility of experiments are increasingly called into question. The presumed self-organizing principles of the living are increasingly sought to be integrated into a new 'bottom-up' technique of control.

Before turning to the more recent critique of data-driven AI, it seems sensible to take a look at the structural setting within which AI is situated, as this has been problematized from its early days.

Sociopolitical context of AI

Although Donna Haraway takes an optimistic stance toward her analytical figure of the cyborg, "a cybernetic organism, a hybrid of machine and organism, a creature of social reality as well as a creature of fiction", she also remarks pointedly: "The main trouble with cyborgs, of course, is that they are the illegitimate offspring of militarism and patriarchal capitalism, not to mention state socialism" (2004 [1985], 10). The development of AI technologies has been heavily funded to date by military, defense, and intelligence organizations. A current example is the recently suspended cooperation between Google and the US Pentagon in Project Maven, a joint project to develop AI for interpreting video imagery that could be used to improve the targeting of drone strikes. While Google pulled out from Project Maven after an employee's protest letter against the participation of their employer in the development of warfare technology, tech giants are continuing to compete for multibillion-dollar defense contracts (Shane/Wakabayashi 2018). As this case shows, corporations active in the so-called new economy are gaining significance and influence when it comes to advancing AI technologies, as they control vast amounts of big (social) data as well as the technological infrastructure for generating, storing, and processing these data on which the development of AI depends today (boyd/Crawford 2012; Lyon 2004). Whereas critical data scientist Jim Thatcher (2014) argues with regard to the expanding data industry that big data are structured by capitalist interests, it is equally clear that, when it comes to the development of AI today, it is structured by both capitalist *and* military interests. Moreover, AI must be seen as the center of a military-industrial complex that US President Eisenhower warned against in his famous farewell address of 1961 (Eisenhower 1961). Media theorist James Der Derian (2009[2001]) even speaks of a rapidly growing military-industrial-media-entertainment network in the 21st century, which includes new digital media, the game and simulation industry, and other actors.

Taking further into account that its influential (corporate and military) actors are located for the most part in countries of the so-called global north, AI must be understood additionally as being situated within (post-)colonial structures (Hagerty/Rubinov 2019). This structural setting of AI is mirrored in the composition of the workforce responsible for developing AI as well as for whose perspectives and interests are taken into account in the development of AI technologies.

The workforce responsible for conceptualizing, designing, and developing AI is highly homogeneous: it constitutes a 'virtual class' consisting predominantly of relatively young, well-educated, socioeconomically privileged, white (Caucasian) or Asian men (Barbrook/Cameron 1996). At the same time, the largely invisible, less glamorous, low-skilled and low-paying work of so-called content moderation and simple data handling is done by a mostly anonymous (online) workforce comprised largely of people from the global south. Thus, the very foundations of AI are both gendered and globally divided, with many people around the world lacking the educational opportunities necessary to gain the skills required to participate in designing AI

(Hagerty/Rubinov 2019, 5). In addition to this, of course, there is all the unpaid work done by those of us with access to digital media technologies, which we hardly ever consider as work, given that it seems we are just 'using' these media technologies; in actuality, we are sharing data and creating content that can then be mined, repurposed, and traded. As "digital housewives" (Jarrett 2015) we provide unpaid (re)productive consumer labor for capitalist companies to exploit, but we also take part – albeit often unknowingly or even unwillingly – in creating big data sets that are at the heart of today's AI developments.

The data sets that are central for developing smart AI technologies today are, however, often unrepresentative of large parts of the world's population – namely, the elderly, the less affluent, the disabled, women, people of color, and those from the so-called global south – because there is a penchant for data that originates in and 'represents' North America and (Western) Europa as well as data on 'privileged' members of these societies. Thus, the data sets that are foundational to AI developments reinforce the exclusion of the interests and needs of vulnerable social groups across the globe, and, in doing so, reproduce historically established relations of dominance, marginalization, and subordination (Lyon 2004; Hagerty/Rubinov 2019). As a consequence, for example, while algorithms used in medical research are improving the identification of skin cancer, they are doing so only in relation to lighter skin-tone samples.

Current critique of (big) data-driven AI

With the rise of so-called big data, promoted as establishing a new regime of truth (for a critical assessment, see Beer 2016), data-driven AI has gained additional momentum in recent years. Advocates of big data analysis promise that more and better knowledge will be produced:

> Before big data, our analysis was usually limited to testing a small number of hypotheses that we defined well before we even collected the data. When we let the data speak, we can make connections that we had never thought existed.
>
> *(Mayer-Schönberger/Cukier 2013, 14)*

As this quote rather pointedly states, the concept of big data promotes the idea of a "data-driven rather than knowledge-driven science" (Kitchin 2014, 1). It thereby renews "the primacy of inductive reasoning in the form of a technology-based empiricism" (Mazzocchi 2014, 1250) and idealizes a data fundamentalist approach to knowledge production, as critical data scientist Kate Crawford (2013) has called it.

This *data fundamentalism* rests on at least two equally controversial premises: first, "the belief that life can be captured and modeled by data or even fully transformed into it" (Thatcher 2014, 1768) and, second, the assumption that objectivity is the result of a subject-free and therefore neutral production of knowledge. Both ideas have been heavily criticized within STS as constituting specifically modern ideals of science.[6] Proclaiming that "raw data is an oxymoron", Lisa Gitelman (2013) – and other scholars engaged in Critical Data Studies – have more recently revived the debate on how to understand data as a sociocultural, and highly political, construct. In contrast to the idea of data simply depicting and, thus, representing reality or nature, data is conceptualized as being the product of numerous practices of categorization and classification, the production of comparability, and the demarcation between what gets to be included and what does not, between what is considered as relevant and what is not – in other words, as a necessarily selective reduction of (social) reality. In their influential book, *Sorting Things Out*, STS scholars Geoffrey Bowker and Susan L. Star (1999) argued that data is never independent of the categories and stratifications that make up the sociocultural order of society and is therefore easily coupled with hierarchical differentiations and power relations. As a result, the focus on modeling, abstraction, and standardization that is central to any formal epistemology tends to ignore aspects of reality that do not fit the definition of the norm(al). Regarding the quantification of care work in hospitals, for example, they argued further that the quest for numbers led to the neglect of emotional work, which is usually done by women and 'other Others', as Haraway coined the term, such as the small talk conducted between a nurse and her (or, less often, his) patient, or a smile directed at them – work that is difficult to quantify and model using data. Others draw comparable lessons from historical experiences of quantification in human geography or social physics: the call for numerical representation is considered to favor mechanistic conceptions of the world that focus on singular codifiable components of reality, ignoring their interrelatedness, complexity, variability, and disparity (Barnes/Wilson 2014, 10). Numerical approaches to knowledge production have further been criticized as being less suited to capture relations of power, inequalities, or cultural and symbolic phenomena (Kitchin 2014, 8; Mazzocchi 2014). Additionally, it has been argued that data is 'performative': it constitutes the very 'reality' it supposedly merely represents. Building on these arguments, it has been proposed that data and society should be conceptualized as being *co-constitutive* (Houben/Prietl 2018).

The naïve promotion of a data fundamentalist approach to knowledge production within data-driven AI[7] also seems to ignore the long-standing insights of critical STS according to which there is no such thing as neutral and objective knowledge production but only "situated" truth claims that are highly contingent, depending on the sociomaterial context as well as on the subject producing the knowledge. Feminist work in STS has further argued that the modern Western ideal of science rests on the notion of a rational, non-situated, and bodyless subject of knowledge that has been constituted in contrast to the notion of emotionally bound and physically situated 'others', namely, women and people of color. Thus, the notion of objectivity has to be considered as a 'view from nowhere' that is ultimately androcentric as well as Eurocentric. Such a view has long served to legitimize the exclusion of women and people of color from academia and continues to marginalize forms of knowledge and modes of reasoning that are based on lived bodily experience and oral traditions (Haraway 1988).

Another characteristic of data-driven approaches to AI is the *correlationism underlying machine learning* approaches. Data-driven AI implements a shift from understanding or explaining a phenomenon – that is, asking *why* or *how* questions – to generating probabilistic predictions about a phenomenon that supposedly make it possible to describe or predict its future occurrence, as Chris Anderson (2008) famously proclaimed in his editorial letter for *WIRED* titled *The End of Theory*: "Who knows why people do what they do? The point is they do it, and we can track and measure it with unprecedented fidelity". According to this idea, reasoning increasingly moves from "data gathered about the past to simulations or probabilistic anticipations of the future that in turn demand action in the present" (Adams et al. 2009, 255), thereby establishing a "regime of anticipation" (ibid.) that is based on "post-explanatory pragmatics" (Andrejevic 2014, 1675). Put differently, turning to machine learning techniques goes hand in hand with giving up on explanatory theories and using pattern recognition to predict future behavior. A key technique within this context is regression analysis: here, algorithms search for patterns in large data sets by calculating how different variables correlate within this data set. By devising a model of this relationship, it becomes possible to predict how the variables identified will likely co-develop in the future. Thus, data-driven AI operates on the assumption that patterns found in data from the past enable us to predict (and govern) the future. The correlationism underlying this approach offers the possibility of finding patterns that do not originate in stereotypical classifications (such as women being more social than men). As Geoffrey Bowker (2014) argues, however, this advantage quickly turns into a disadvantage when the knowledge generated *fails to understand* the correlations identified and instead (mis)takes them as positivistic expressions of the truth. In other words, when AI affirms existing sociocultural structures, it turns into a sociomaterial apparatus of self-fulfilling prophecies, thereby unfolding conservative tendencies rather than fostering more objective decisions (Prietl 2019b).

As noted previously, *machine learning* gives up on explanatory theories and uses pattern recognition to predict future behavior. The post-Newtonian rationality, or 'technorationality', informing ML (Weber 2011; Suchman/Weber 2016) is based on a mapping of our world that is as complete as it can possibly be due to the collection and mining of any and every data source available. It is based on the exploitation of the unpredictable and unknown as well as on automated practices of tinkering. As such, it does not analyze the problem and deduce a solution but rather maps out a search area, defines border conditions, and uses processes of trial and error to solve problems that need not to be understood but solved or engineered. In contrast to this, the classical natural sciences worked – at least according to their own view of themselves, though this was often not true for their practices – with an experimental perspective on causal relations, a theoretical perspective on natural laws, and a mathematical perspective on general principles. They relied on empirical research conducted on the basis of measurement with instruments and well-established theories (cf. Cassirer 1957[1929]; Grammelsberger 2010). Starting from the diversity of phenomena, the purpose of the natural sciences has long been systematic observation and empirical-instrumental research with the aim of ordering the world in a rational way on the basis of theoretical concepts. Against this background, data-driven AI looks more like a 'theoryless' endeavor based on common sense as well as analogies and abduction, as it seeks to capture everyday knowledge that cannot be processed using mathematics or formal logic. Asking "what it is about common sense that logic fails to capture", Valiant argues that the problem is "a result of mathematical logic requiring a theoryful world in which to function well", whereas "[c]ommon sense corresponds to a capability of making good predictive decisions in the realm of the theoryless" (Valiant 2014, see 58). Mathematics and formal logic are devalued as the "idea that *common sense is somehow superior to reason*" (ibid., emphasis added) becomes fashionable.

Interestingly, this is turned into a theory of the general nature of the 'theoryless', when Valiant argues in his well-known book *Probably Approximately Correct* (sic!) that ML deals with the unsystematic, the non-linear, the affective, and the orderless. And, though this new pragmatic approach leaves traditional rational-cognitive foundations by the wayside, Valiant seeks to justify this by referring to evolution, claiming that 'humankind' has naturally used machine learning techniques throughout its entire history to cope with the 'theoryless' (Valiant 2014).

Last but not least, data-driven AI is deeply embedded within what scholar and publicist Evgeny Morozov (2013) has called *techno'solutionism'*. Research concerned with the digital avant-garde of Silicon Valley, one important birthplace of AI, notes that a "solutionist ethos" is prevalent among the relevant actors. The utopias being portrayed around digital data technologies depict the world as being full of 'bugs' that need to be 'fixed'. The preferred means to do so are technological ones, especially ICTs, digital technologies and, last but not least, AI. The core idea of the *techno'solutionism'* promoted here is that every problem, including social problems, can ultimately be reduced to a series of small and therefore manageable problems for which technological solutions can then be found. The optimistic belief in technological progress in combination with libertarian ideals and a deep distrust of established politics draws on the so-called Californian ideology that has become prominent throughout the second half of the 20th century (Barbrook/Cameron 1996). The Californian ideology sees 'politics' as an outdated form of democracy; instead of political debate and the building of public opinion, a virtual '*agora*', a digital public space of public discussion, is to be established where everyone is supposed to participate and speak his or her mind freely and equally, thereby paving the way for democratization, decentralization, and emancipation. To make this vision come true, two things are needed according to high-tech solutionism: humans need to live up to their full potential, which is supposed to be enabled by networking, the distribution and sharing of information and, therefore, equal access to knowledge and technology. Additionally, all institutions that hinder or restrict the free unfolding of human potential, such as bureaucracy, are to be removed and a strict meritocracy is to be established. While this may sound good in theory, the protagonists involved seem to fail to recognize not only existing inequalities in access to education and digital technologies but also the reproduction of power asymmetries and social inequalities in virtual spaces (e.g. Paulitz 2005; Zillien/Hargittai 2009). Likewise, the well-documented effect that the meritocratic ideal stabilizes existing social inequalities due to its disregard of the deeply embedded structural inequalities in society (Becker/Hadjar 2017) is not problematized any further, but a deeply anti-political stance is fostered. As Barbrook and Cameron (1996, 49–50) argue, this may be due to the fact that the protagonists of the New Economy themselves form a privileged "virtual class" that is rarely affected by racism, social inequality, or poverty. More importantly, however, this anti-political solutionism has profound consequences, as it privileges a focus on allegedly anti-political, purely factual aspects of reality and social life, thus ignoring the highly political and, therefore, inequality-relevant notions of the world we live in. Remembering the lack of sensitivity toward power asymmetries and social inequalities of data-driven AI, one of the authors (Prietl 2019a, 10–21) argued that the current approaches in AI development run the risk of mistaking the perspective of a privileged view for a universal perspective, rendering those in marginalized positions (once again) invisible.

Thus, exposing data-driven AI to a (feminist) critique of rationality shows that its epistemological foundations are anything but neutral. On the contrary, they embody a specific approach to the world that transports certain possibilities of knowing and is itself not neutral but rather favors specific worldviews, perceptual styles, and the reproduction of existing social inequalities, as Donna Haraway has argued for technoscientific artifacts in general. Current forms of data-driven AI do so by (1) privileging phenomena that are easily transformed into (numerical) data and (distinct) categories and that are, therefore, more readily amenable to processing algorithmically; by (2) promoting the generation of probabilistic knowledge about specific possible worlds (and not others), instead of engaging critically with our contemporary world and questions of why specific phenomena have (not) come about; and by (3) favoring the presumably non-political analyses of so-called facts over sociopolitically informed, situated, and normative debate (Prietl 2019a, 22).

Discussion

Given the contemporary hype around data-driven AI, which often conflates it with machine learning, it seems important to ask how these new technologies can also be seen as the expression of specific societal formations and pressing issues – an approach philosopher Gilles Deleuze propagated in his famous 'postscriptum of the control society' (Deleuze 1992). He interprets technologies not as an a priori but as the expression of the *zeitgeist*, of the ontological self-interpretation of a specific time and of a specific sociohistorical constellation of society, humans, and machines. According to this, we can ask why machine learning has become hegemonic in the last decade. Why are its forms of knowledge production – correlation, analogy, or abduction – so attractive? And how are power and knowledge entangled in the data-driven knowledge regime?

We find a renewed positivism built on the symbolic authority of data, which renders the results of such big data analyses extremely difficult to object to successfully (for the symbolic capital of numerical data, see Heintz 2010).[8] We are already familiar with this kind of authority in relation to statistics, which traditionally focused on the past while data-driven AI/ML focuses on prediction and anticipation – or even "premediation", as media theorist Richard Grusin argues: in the face of an "increasingly threatening future of geopolitical, environmental, and now economic dangers" (Grusin 2010, 134), people in Western societies are preoccupied with mediating every object, (inter)action, or event to "protect us from the kind of negative surprises that might await us in an un[pre; the authors]mediated world" (ibid., 127). Drawing on Foucault and Deleuze, Grusin argues that we are seeing a profound shift in the contemporary biopolitical regime toward a (neoliberal) governmentality with its strategies of control, management, and securitization. This move is accompanied by a "proliferation of networked media technologies so that the future cannot emerge into the present without having been premediated in the past" (ibid., 126). The cultural desire for anticipation and premediation thrives on and drives the development and use of networked media and – we would argue – especially that of data-driven AI. The monitoring of electronic interactions and the transactions of media networks that provide material for data analytics is supposed to register and prevent potential disruptions to the given sociopolitical order.

The mapping of a broad variety of possible futures via premediation, however, means that only specific options are offered, and some are more supported by the protocols and reward systems of AI (and other technological systems) than others. But processes of premediation could also be seen as technological discourses and practices which "turn open spaces of possibility into 'test environments preparing for techno- and sociological change'" (Kaerlein 2012). Premediation helps us to experience problematic political events, technological practices, or sociotechnical discourses as normal and regular. At the same time, the anticipation of possible worlds or events as well as practices of forethought fuels the production of ideas and innovations in (neoliberal) capitalism:

> [T]he aim is to produce a certain anticipatory readiness about the world, a perceptual style which can move easily between interchangeable opportunities, thus adding to the sum total of intellect that can be drawn on. This is a style which is congenial to capitalism.
>
> *(Thrift 2007, 38)*

Outlook

Throughout the last few years, reports of racist risk assessment tools employed in the US criminal justice system, of sexist recruiting tools, or of highly stereotypical digital assistants have highlighted the fact that AI programs are far from being neutral and objective.[9] In reaction to these numerous reports about discriminatory AI technologies and the ensuing public outcry, there has been a call for *ethics* in AI. So far this has mostly taken the form either of self-regulatory approaches, such as the implementation of ethical frameworks, guidelines, or boards that are supposed to ensure the development of responsible, non-discriminatory, and fair AI, or of endeavors to create moral machines and fair algorithms by building ethical considerations into AI technologies that enable them to act ethically themselves.[10] Design theorist Mona Sloane (2019) has criticized the hype around ethics as a panacea for remedying biases in AI, arguing that it functions as a smokescreen for carrying on with business as usual. Rather than initiating a genuine push toward social justice and equality, ethics are largely employed to gain a competitive advantage between companies, industries, or nations. And, last but not least, they are deployed because they are not enforceable by law and thus remain a gesture of goodwill.

The currently prevailing focus on ethics also appears problematic on an epistemological level due to conceptual shortcomings of how inequality/injustice is thought about in this context:[11] First, the focus on ethics assumes the existence of a rational and autonomous human being as the subject of (un)ethical behavior and, thus, takes a person's intent as key to identifying discrimination or wrongful doing. This idea of 'man' is highly andro- and Eurocentric. Focusing on the supposedly willful actions of individuals also means losing sight of the broader societal contexts within which actions take place. Put differently, a focus on free ethical choices for action largely ignores the social structures and symbolic orders in which people are situated and that pre-structure their choices, as well as the alternatives available to them in the first place. Second, the aforementioned understanding of (un)ethical behavior often translates into a rather narrow causal conception of discrimination, according to which efforts to construct non-discriminatory AI focus on identifying errors to be fixed, i.e. specific data sources, technical features, or human biases that are understood as the discrete roots of the unfair result in question.[12] This causal thinking, again, largely ignores the social structuring of technology as well as its own structuring role and, thus, closes down the space for criticizing and challenging inequality as a complex, sociocultural, historical, and emergent phenomenon that is deeply intertwined with AI technologies. Third, disregarding inequality as a complex, multi-dimensional phenomenon goes hand in hand with a single axis thinking centered on disadvantage with regard to a rather small set of legally protected social attributes such as race, gender, or age. As a consequence, such efforts fall short when it comes to accounting for the intersecting effects of discrimination and the more complex coupling of AI with social inequalities. In addition, the focus on the (un)fair distribution of (material) resources ignores the question of what counts as a resource in the first place, what is considered to be fair distribution, and how these terms can be operationalized in order to meet the need for formalization, which is foundational to AI technologies. Instead, the ways that AI itself not merely informs decisions but is bound up in the production of sociocultural meaning and practices are black-boxed.

Considering these points of critique, a turn to critical (feminist) STS perspectives seems fruitful. This would imply a shift in focus from questions of justice to questions of *inequality*. This means focusing on understanding how AI is entangled with social relations of power and inequality as well as symbolic hierarchies, and how AI takes part in reproducing these sociocultural structures by pre-structuring the production of hierarchically positioned subjects, social practices, and ways of living. It means, among other things, asking: *Who* takes part in developing AI and in designing AI technologies? *Which perspectives* and whose wishes and needs are represented in the design of AI? *Which norms and values* become materialized in AI, and *which ways of living* are favored and privileged compared to others that are marginalized or ignored altogether?

Besides understanding the complex interplay between AI and social relations of power and inequality, a (critical/feminist) STS perspective demands that we *take responsibility* for the development, design, and implementation of AI technologies. In her *Manifesto for Cyborgs*, Donna Haraway (2004 [1985], 33) summons the marginalized and subordinated to seize "the tools to mark the world that marked them as other". She depicts the vision of an "elsewhere", a better world that no longer rests on hierarchical dualistic thinking, a world made possible – among other things – by the rise of technosciences that defy the illusion of stable dualisms such as human vs. animal, nature vs. culture, or men vs. women. This utopia, however, is not to be mistaken with claiming neutral objectivity for feminist perspectives; on the contrary, Haraway (1988) explicitly rejects the possibility of any perspective being 'innocent', as she understands that *every* knowledge and truth claim is "situated" within social relations of power. Nevertheless, she argues for starting with the perspectives of those who are marginalized and subordinated, because they are less prone to misunderstand their perspective as a universal 'view from nowhere'. Haraway thus argues that we should reflect upon and make our own situatedness as a subject of knowledge a prerequisite for objectivity, because only this allows us all to be held accountable. With Haraway we can, thus, no longer hold on to the idea of neutral knowledge or artifacts, as these are always political in one way or another. Returning to AI, this means giving up the ultimately impossible search for non-biased technologies and instead focusing on how to *intervene responsibly* in their development and design; it means working toward taking into account a broad and diverse range of perspectives, needs, and demands in order to design AI technologies that are appropriate with respect to society's heterogeneity and complexity; and it means striving for an AI that dismantles and reduces existing relations of power and binary dualisms rather than stabilizing and reinforcing them. Last, but not least, it means talking less about the technologies we can produce and more about those that we *should* and *want* to produce.

Notes

1 Theory relies on meta-theoretical principles or orienting strategies. These principles or strategies contain epistemological premises as well as ontological options. The former give answers to questions such as how can knowledge be produced, what qualifies as knowledge/truth, how can truth claims be made, and what constitutes the subject of knowledge production. The latter lay down what set of things, entities, events, or systems are regarded as existing. Accordingly, ontology refers to these decisions and is not necessarily related to an essentialist argumentation. As AI centers around the question of knowledge production, considering the epistemological and ontological assumptions that go into its construction is paramount.
2 Peter Norvig, AI expert and research director at Google, claims that: "The fundamental tools of A.I. shifted from Logic to Probability in the late 1980s, and fundamental progress in the theory of uncertain reasoning underlies many of the recent practical advances" (Norvig 2011).
3 Although it is useful to differentiate analytically between these two approaches, it is important to keep in mind that many AI artifacts bring these frameworks together. For example, the Pitts/McCulloch approach of an artificial neural network, mentioned previously, can be seen as a hybrid of symbolic and connectionist AI because it is based on knowledge of basic physiology and brain structures but also works with propositional logic and Turing's theory of computation (Russell/Norvig 2010).
4 For an overview of selected articles see Haraway 2004.
5 For a critique of the "Sense-Act-Think paradigm" in these more recent approaches to AI, see also Hayles 2003.
6 Historians of science have described how the idea that 'nature should speak for itself' became dominant throughout the 19th century in modern Western societies. Whereas personal judgement was considered an important prerequisite for any scientist in the 18th century, the new notion of 'mechanical' or 'non-interventionist' objectivity (Daston/Galison 1992) disavowed the scientist as the subject of knowledge production. In contrast to the machines and technical apparatuses of observation and measurement that were proliferating at that time, the scientist was portrayed as a source of prejudice and misinterpretation and, thus, as a threat to the supposedly pure image of nature. With the replacement of the human body with technical artifacts, numerical data became increasingly important for the production and communication of scientific knowledge. Since numbers can be communicated independently (or so it seems) from the individuals, places, times, and contexts of their production, they swiftly came to be regarded as the ideal manifestation of neutral objectivity (Heintz 2010).
7 Interestingly, there appears to be a revival of promises of objectivity and neutrality in the context of big data analyses that have long been questioned even within AI and robotics research. Confronted with this discrepancy, one of the authors (Prietl 2019a: 22) has argued that the proliferating objectivity claims can be understood as discursive strategies for claiming epistemological authority in the course of establishing and institutionalizing big data methods, whereas the limits of big data analysis are hardly ever openly discussed, because they conflict with dominant popular ideals of 'objective' science.

8 Bettina Heintz (2010: 172) argues that an objection to numerical results requires either the availability of alternative numbers or a fundamental critique of the numbers in question, which in turn requires knowledge about their production.
9 For an overview, see the pioneering book *Weapons of Math Destruction* (2016) by mathematician Cathy O'Neil; see also Redden/Brand (2019) https://datajusticelab.org/data-harm-record/.
10 An analysis of statements about ethical AI development issued by key government, corporate, and civil actors in this field shows that they rely heavily on deterministic ideas according to which AI is inevitably coming and that it will disrupt the established social order and people's everyday lives. As a consequence, "'better building' is [presented as] the only ethical path forward" (for a critical discussion, see Greene/Hoffmann/Stark 2019: 2128), leaving no room to discuss alternative developments.
11 For a thorough critique from the perspective of moral and political philosophy, see Binns 2018; from the perspective of legal anti-discrimination efforts, see Hoffmann 2019.
12 As a consequence, current approaches to fair machine learning focus on 'pre-processing,' 'in-processing,' and 'post-processing' techniques, with the aim of eliminating biases in training data, in the data-mining or machine learning algorithm, as well as in the resulting algorithmic (decision-making) system (Binns 2018: 79; Hajian/Domingo-Ferrer 2013).

References

Adam, Alison (1998): *Artificial Knowing. Gender and the Thinking Machine*. London/New York: Routledge.

Adams, Vincanne/Murphy, Michelle/Clarke, Adele E. (2009): Anticipation: Technoscience, Life, Affect, Temporality. In: *Subjectivity* 28, 246–265.

Amoore, Louise (2013): *The Politics of Possibility. Risk and Security Beyond Probability*. Durham/London: Duke University Press.

Anderson, Chris (2008): The End of Theory: The Data Deluge Makes the Scientific Method Obsolete. *Wired Magazine* 16(7). Last access July 24, 2019 under www.wired.com/2008/06/pb-theory/.

Andrejevic, Mark (2014): The Big Data Divide. In: *International Journal of Communication* 8, 1673–1689.

Barbrook, Richard/Cameron, Andy (1996): The Californian Ideology. In: *Science as Culture* 26(6/1), 44–72.

Barnes, Trevor J./Wilson, Matthew W. (2014): Big Data, Social Physics, and Spatial Analysis: The Early Years. In: *Big Data & Society* 1(1), 1–14.

Becker, Barbara (1992): *Künstliche Intelligenz*. Frankfurt/New York: Campus.

Becker, Rolf/Hadjar, Andreas (2017): Meritokratie – Zur gesellschaftlichen Legitimation ungleicher Bildungs-, Erwerbs- und Einkommenschancen in modernen Gesellschaften. In: Rolf Becker (Ed.) *Lehrbuch der Bildungssoziologie*. Wiesbaden: VS Verlag, 37–62.

Beer, David (2016): How Should We Do the History of Big Data? In: *Big Data & Society* 3(1), 1–10.

Binns, Reuben (2018): What Can Political Philosophy Teach Us about Algorithmic Fairness? In: *IEEE Security & Privacy*, May/June, 73–80.

Bowker, Geoffrey C. (2014): The Theory/Data Thing. In: *International Journal of Communication* 8, 1795–1799.

Bowker, Geoffrey C./Star, Susan Leigh (1999): *Sorting Things Out. Classification and Its Consequences*. Cambridge, MA/London: MIT Press.

boyd, danah/Crawford, Kate (2012): Critical Questions for Big Data. Provocations for a Cultural, Technological, and Scholarly Phenomenon. In: *Information, Communication & Society* 15(5), 662–679.

Brooks, R. (1986): Achieving Intelligence Through Building Robots. A.I. Memo 899. Last access November 5, 2019 under https://people.csail.mit.edu/brooks/papers/AIM-899.pdf.

Cassirer, Ernst (1957[1929]): *The Philosophy of Symbolic Forms. Volume Three: The Phenomenology of Knowledge*. New Haven: Yale University Press.

Chomsky, Noam (2012): Where Artificial Intelligence Went Wrong. An Extended Conversation with the Legendary Linguist. An interview by Yarden Katz. *The Atlantic*, November 1, 2012. Last access November 4, 2019 under www.theatlantic.com/technology/archive/2012/11/noam-chomsky-on-where-artificial-intelligence-went-wrong/261637/?single_page=true.

Crawford, Kate (2013): The Hidden Bias in Big Data. In: *Harvard Business Review*, April 1, 2013. Last access November 4, 2019 under https://hbr.org/2013/04/the-hidden-biases-in-big-data.

Daston, Lorraine/Galison, Peter (1992): The Image of Objectivity. In: *Representations* 40(Autumn), 81–128.

Deleuze, Gilles (1992): Postscript on the Societies of Control. In: *October* 59, 3–7.

Der Derian (2009[2001]): *Virtuous War. Mapping the Military-Industrial-Media-Entertainment Network*. 2nd edition. New York: Routledge.

Dreyfus, Hubert L. (1972): *What Computers Can't Do. A Critique of Artificial Reason*. New York: Harper & Row.

Eisenhower, Dwight David (1961): Farewell Address. On the Military-Industrial Complex and the Government-Universities Collusion, January 17, 1961. Last access November 4, 2019 under www.panarchy.org/eisenhower/farewelladdress.html.

Erni, Daniel/Fröhlich, Jürg (2010): Postprocessing. Making Technical Artifacts More Intelligible. EASST Conference 2010 (EASST 2010): 'Practicing Science and Technology, Performing the Social'. The European Association for the Study of Science and Technology, September 2–4, University of Trento, Track 8: Probing Technoscience.

Gitelman, Lisa (Ed.) (2013): *Raw Data is an Oxymoron*. Cambridge, MA: MIT Press.

Grammelsberger, Gabriele (2010): *Computerexperimente. Zum Wandel der Wissenschaft im Zeitalter des Computers*. Bielefeld: transcript.

Greene, Daniel/Hoffmann, Anna Laura/Stark, Luke (2019): Better, Nicer, Clearer, Fairer: A Critical Assessment of the Movement for Ethical Artificial Intelligence and Machine Learning. In: *Proceedings of the 52nd Hawaii International Conference on System Sciences*, 2122–2131.

Grusin, Richard (2010): *Premediation: Affect and Mediality after 9/11*. London/New York: Palgrave Macmillan.

Gutwirth, Serge/Hildebrandt, Mireille (2010): Some Caveats on Profiling. In: Serge Gutwirth/Yves Poullet/Paul De Hert (Eds.) *Data Protection in a Profiled World*. Dordrecht/Heidelberg/London/New York: Springer.

Hagerty, Alexa/Rubinov, Igor (2019): Global AI Ethics: A Review of the Social Impacts and Ethical Implications of Artificial Intelligence. Last access November 4, 2019 under https://arxiv.org/abs/1907.07892.

Hajian, Sara/Domingo-Ferrer, Josep (2013): A Methodology for Direct and Indirect Discrimination Prevention in Data Mining. In: *IEEE Transactions on Knowledge and Data Engineering* 25(7), 1445–1459.

Haraway, Donna (1988): Situated Knowledge: The Science Question in Feminism and the Privilege of Partial Perspective. In: *Feminist Studies* 14(3), 575–599.

Haraway, Donna (1989): Introduction: The Persistence of Vision. In: id. (Ed.) *Primate Visions. Gender, Race, and Nature in the World of Modern Science*. New York: Routledge, 1–15.

Haraway, Donna (Ed.) (2004): *The Haraway Reader*. New York/London: Routledge.

Haraway, Donna (2004 [1985]): A Manifesto for Cyborgs: Science, Technology, and Socialist Feminism in the 1980s. In: id. (Ed.) *The Haraway Reader*. New York/London: Routledge, 7–45.

Hayles, N. Katherine (2003): Computing the Human. Turbulente Körper, soziale Maschinen. In: Jutta Weber/Corinna Bath (Eds.) *Feministische Studien zur Wissenschaftskultur*. Opladen: Leske & Budrich, 99–118.

Heintz, Bettina (2010): Numerische Differenz. Überlegungen zu einer Soziologie des (quantitativen) Vergleichs. In: *Zeitschrift für Soziologie* 39(3), 162–181.

Hoffmann, Anna Laura (2019): Where Fairness Fails: Data, Algorithms, and the Limits of Antidiscrimination Discourse. In: *Information, Communication & Society* 22(7), 900–915.

Houben, Daniel/Prietl, Bianca (Eds.) (2018): *Datengesellschaft. Einsichten in die Datafizierung des Sozialen*. Bielefeld: transcript.

Jarrett, Kylie (2015): *Feminism, Labour and Digital Media: The Digital Housewife*. New York/London: Routledge.

Kaerlein, Timo (2012): Premediated Regimes of Surveillance. Practices of Preemptive Crime Reduction in Minority Report and Law Enforcement. Unpublished manuscript.

Kitchin, Rob (2014): Big Data, New Epistemologies and Paradigm Shifts. In: *Big Data & Society*, 1(1), 1–12.

Kovacs, Tim (2012): Genetics-Based Machine Learning. In: Grzegorz Rozenberg/Thomas Bäck/Joost N. Kok (Eds.) *Handbook of Natural Computing*. Berlin/Heidelberg: Springer, 938–986.

Lyon, David (2004): Globalizing Surveillance: Comparative and Sociological Perspectives. In: *International Sociology* 19, 135–149.

Mayer-Schönberger, Viktor/Cukier, Kenneth (2013): *Big Data. Die Revolution, die unser Leben verändern wird*. München: Redline.

Mazzocchi, Fulvio (2014): Could Big Data Be the End of Theory in Science? In: *EMBO Reports* 16(10), 1250–1255.

McCulloch, W. S./Pitts, W. (1943): A Logical Calculus of the Ideas Immanent in Nervous Activity. In: *Bulletin of Mathematical Biophysics* 5(4), 115–137.

Mersch, Dieter (2006): *Einführung in die Medientheorie*. Hamburg: Junius.

Minsky, Marvin/Papert, Seymour (1969): *Perceptrons: An Introduction to Computational Geometry*. Cambridge, MA: MIT Press.

Morozov, Evgeny (2013): *To Save Everything, Click Here. Technology, Solutionism and the Urge to Fix Problems that Don't Exist*. New York: Public Affairs.

Newell, Allen/Simon, Herbert A. (1976): Computer Science as Empirical Inquiry: Symbols and Search. In: *Communications of the ACM* 19(3), 113–126.

Norvig, Peter (2011): The Machine Age. In: *New York Post*, February 13, 2011. Last access November 4, 2019 under https://nypost.com/2011/02/13/the-machine-age/.

O'Neill, Cathy (2016): *Weapons of Math Destruction*. New York: Broadway Books.

Paulitz, Tanja (2005): *Netzsubjektivität/en. Konstruktionen von Vernetzung als Technologien des sozialen Selbst*. Münster: Dampfboot.

Pfeifer, R./Scheier C. (2000): *Understanding Intelligence*. Cambridge, MA: MIT Press, 2nd edition.

Pickering, Andrew (2002): Cybernetics and the Mangle: Ashby, Beer and Pask. In: *Social Studies of Science* 32(3), 413–437.

Prietl, Bianca (2019a): Die Versprechen von *Big Data* im Spiegel feministischer Rationalitätskritik. In: Diana Lengersdorf/Jutta Weber (Eds.) *Gender, Schwerpunktheft Gender, Technik und Politik 4.0*, 3, 11–25.

Prietl, Bianca (2019b): Algorithmische Entscheidungssysteme *revisited*: Wie Maschinen gesellschaftliche Herrschaftsverhältnisse reproduzieren können. In: Anna-Lena Berscheid/Birgit Riegraf/Ilona Horwath (Eds.) *Feministische Studien, Sonderheft Cyborgs Revisited*, 37, 303–319.

Redden, Joanna/Brand Jessica (2019): Exploring Social Justice in an Age of Datafication. Last access November 4, 2019 under https://datajusticelab.org/data-harm-record/.

Rosenblatt, Frank (1962): *Principles of Neurodynamics: Perceptrons and the Theory of Brain Mechanisms*. Washington, DC: Spartan Books.

Russell, Stuart J./Norvig, Russell (2010): *Artificial Intelligence. A Modern Approach*. Upper Saddle River, NJ: Pearson.

Shane, Scott/Wakabayashi, Daisuke (2018): 'The Business of War': Google Employees Protest Work for the Pentagon. In: *The New York Times*, April 4, 2018. Last access November 4, 2019 under www.nytimes.com/2018/04/04/technology/google-letter-ceo-pentagon-project.html.

Sloane, Mona (2019): Inequality Is the Name of the Game: Thoughts on the Emerging Field of Technology, Ethics and Social Justice. In: *Proceedings of the 2nd Weizenbaum Conference*, 1–9.

Suchman, Lucy (1987): *Situated Plans and Actions. The Problem of Human Machine Communication*. Cambridge/New York: Cambridge University Press.

Suchman, Lucy (2008): Feminist STS and the Sciences of the Artificial. In: Edward J. Hackett/Olga Amsterdamska/Michael Lynch/Judy Wajcman (Eds.) *The Handbook of Science and Technology Studies*. Cambridge, MA/London: MIT Press, 139–165.

Suchman, Lucy/Weber, Jutta (2016): Human–Machine Autonomies. In: Nehal Bhuta Susanne Beck/Robin Geiss/Hin-Yan Liu/Claus Kress (Eds.) *Autonomous Weapon Systems. Law, Ethics, Policy*. Cambridge: Cambridge University Press, 75–102.

Thatcher, Jim (2014): Living on Fumes: Digital Footprints, Data Fumes, and the Limitations of Spatial Big Data. In: *International Journal of Communication* 8, 1765–1783.

Thrift, Nigel (2007): *Non-Representational Theory. Space Politics Affects.* London/New York: Routledge.

Turkle, Sherry (1996): *Life on the Screen: Identity in the Age of the Internet.* London: Weidenfeld & Nicholson.

Valiant, Leslie (2014): *Probably Approximately Correct. Nature's Algorithms for Learning and Prospering in a Complex World.* New York: Basic Books.

Weber, Jutta (2005): Helpless Machines and True Loving Care Givers: A Feminist Critique of Recent Trends in Human-Robot Interaction. In: *Journal of Information, Communication and Ethics in Society* 3(4), 209–218.

Weber, Jutta (2010): Making Worlds. Epistemological, Ontological and Political Dimensions of Technoscience. In: *Poiesis and Praxis. International Journal of Ethics of Science and Technology Assessment* 7, 17–36.

Weber, Jutta (2011): Blackboxing Organisms, Exploiting the Unpredictable. Control Paradigms in Human–Machine Translation. In: Martin Carrier/Alfred Nordmann (Eds.) *Science in the Context of Application. Boston Studies in the Philosophy of Science.* Cham: Springer, vol. 274, no. 6, 409–429.

Weizenbaum, J. (1976): *Computer Power and Human Reason: From Judgment to Calculation.* Oxford, England: W. H. Freeman & Co.

Winner, Langdon (1977): *Autonomous Technology. Technics-out-of-Control as a Theme in Political Thought.* Cambridge, MA/London: MIT Press.

Winograd, Terry/Flores, C. (1987): *Understanding Computers and Cognition: A New Foundation for Design.* Reading, MA: Addison-Wesley.

Zillien, Nicole/Hargittai, Eszter (2009): Digital Distinction: Status-Specific Types of Internet Usage. In: *Social Science Quarterly* 90(2), 275–291.

5

Work, employment and unemployment after AI[1]

Ross Boyd

There are few, if any, domains of contemporary life where concerns about the prospects of profound disruption by AI and advanced robotics have registered as strongly – be it in academic, policy or popular discourse – as that of work and employment. This should not surprise. It was in relation to the institution of work, itself a product of the (first) industrial revolution and fledgling capitalism, that most people in the early modern period would experience firsthand what Berman (1982; 18) referred to as the 'maelstrom' of modern life: the dislocating experiences brought about by the constellation of revolutions in economic life, scientific and political thought and practice, demography and the urban surround, and in cultural self-awareness. And for many it would be questions about the future of work that would continue to excite their greatest concern as the modern world continued to cycle through successive phases of disruption and renewal, including subsequent industrial revolutions.

Why so much worry about work? In his well-known essay *Work: The Key Sociological Category?* the German social and political theorist Claus Offe (1985; 129–150) set out three interrelated reasons why classical social science set 'work' as a cornerstone of social inquiry. The first was the emergence, in the 19th century, of the historically unprecedented social categories of 'work' and 'the worker'. The key mechanisms here included the separation of work as a discrete activity from the sphere of extended household production and the emergence of a clear division between private property and wage labour. Accordingly, the regulation of this newly 'free' labour shifted away from the normative ties of feudal obligation oriented to production for use, and towards the structural necessity of earning a wage in the newly conceived market for labour, driven by what Max Weber would refer to as 'the whip of hunger'. Second, the pre-modern, aristocratic hierarchy of 'noble' activities (those giving expression to a 'meaningful life') and 'vulgar' activities (those engaged out of necessity or which at best were purely utilitarian) was successfully challenged and even reversed. The combined effects of the protestant reformation and the bourgeois revolution, among other things, resulted in acquisition by means of market exchange (and even the compulsion to accumulate) acquiring a new ethical status. Finally, the emergence of work (or the capacity to work) as a marketable commodity, along with this new moral underwriting of acquisitiveness, give rise to a dominant means-ends rationality – be it in terms of the calculative rationality exemplified in Weber's analysis of double-entry bookkeeping or the technical rationality of the factory system (Marx) – as well as to distributive conflicts among the competing rationalities of 'capital' and 'labour'. Accordingly,

> (s)evered from the household and traditional forms of association, and deprived of political protection, wage labour was linked to the capitalist organization and division of labour, as well as to the processes of pauperization, alienation, rationalization and organized and disorganized forms of (economic, political and cultural) resistance inherent within these processes. All these developments consequently became the obvious pivot around which social-scientific research and theory formation rotated, and from which emanated all subsequent theoretical concern with social policy, family and moral systems, urbanization and religion.
>
> *(Offe, 1985; 132)*

At a time when a cluster of developments – the emergence of a post-industrial service society, the de-skilling of much production work, labour market dualisation and discontinuities in employment biographies – were having profound impacts on work and employment, Offe (ibid.) wondered whether 'work' as a social institution was losing its social organizing power and, hence, its significance as a social scientific concept and category.

Of course, scholarly worries about the future of the concept of work, and a possible fading of its descriptive and explanatory powers, are of an entirely different order to those of people worried about losing their jobs and for whom work is far from an abstract concept. For these people – reflecting upon what the new economic dispensation emerging with yet another wave of automation might have in store for them – 'work' remains a very salient consideration: as a livelihood necessity and provider of a (more or less) dignified existence; a means of discharging obligations to family and community; a source of social status and connection, self-fulfilment and self-expression; or a platform upon which to demonstrate skills, knowledge and talents.

My discussion commences with a brief history of concerns about automation, incorporating automation anxiety and other anticipations of a possible post-work society. I will then analyse contemporary debates centred specifically on the impacts and implications of AI and advanced robotics for work and employment, following this debate from an initial preoccupation primarily with the impacts of automation on aggregate levels of employment and unemployment through to more granular recent analyses of work and workplace change centred on human–machine interaction. Finally, I will identify a number of new issues emerging on the advancing frontier of 'AI and the future of work' debates.[2]

Background: a very brief history of concern about automation and work

Debates over the influence of AI-powered technologies on the 2016 US Presidential election were dominated by claims of Russian interference by way of industrial scale troll farms, the leaking of files and emails hacked from various Democratic Party servers, and what became known as the Facebook-Cambridge Analytica data scandal. Far less consideration has been given to the possible role played in the election by the negative effects of automation on employment and work, and the subsequent embrace of a radical populist right-wing platform promising to upset the political status quo on the part of workers angry and anxious about their prospects. In a recent study that sought to link the economics of automation to its social costs and political ramifications, Frey, Berger and Chen (2017) identify a positive correlation, of sorts, among groups whose work and employment has been hurt by automation and support for Donald

Trump, who had pledged to bring back jobs in manufacturing and mining that had long been automated away or were at considerable risk of following suit. This assertion of a link between the distributive implications of automation and the rise of right-wing populism has subsequently found support in other national contexts (Im et al., 2019; Kurer and Palier, 2019), which led to the argument that we are currently witnessing, as a response to contemporary AI-powered automation advances, "(riots) against the machines by democratic means" (Frey, Berger and Chen, 2017; 17).

The phrase 'riot against the machine' places contemporary debates over AI-powered automation, work and employment firmly within the context of a much longer and deeper set of historical processes. A few years after Jacques Vaucanson delighted (in 1738) the members of the Académie des Sciences, the royal court of France and the Parisian public alike with his displays of automata – 'The Flute Player', 'Pipe-and-Tabor Playing Shepherd', 'Tambourine Player' and 'Defecating Duck' (Riskin, 2003) – he was stoned and spat on by weavers in the streets of his hometown, Lyon, for having also developed the world's first automated loom (subsequently refined and widely deployed by Jacquard in 1804). Eli Whitney's development of the cotton gin in 1793 (following Joseph Eve's earlier roller gin) raised concerns about job losses due to its speed in preparing raw cotton for spinning, although in the southern US states this concern centred more on the impact these labour-saving machines might have on the price of slaves (Shiller, 2019; 8–9). The 'riot against the machine' motif is, however, most commonly associated with the 1779 Lancashire machine-breakers, the Luddite uprisings (1811–1816) and Captain Swing riots (1830–1832) in Britain. Here concerns about the impacts of mechanisation on employment in the rural textile industries, in concert with other grievances (low wages, poor working conditions, competition from migrant labour and, more generally, social changes associated with the advent of industrial capitalism), combined with the absence of any democratic opportunities to seek remedy by more peaceful means, led to often violent protests provoking equally, if not more, violent responses from authorities (Mantoux, 2013; Mokyr, 2009).

It is important when reviewing this history – just as it is when engaging contemporary debates – to avoid any simplistic zero-sum narrative in which automation entails a straightforward replacement of humans by machines. And care needs to be taken to untangle the short-term from long-term effects of mechanisation, as well as to attend to considerable variety among the forms that labour displacement can take. This said it cannot be my purpose to provide more than a cursory summation of some of the main historical tendencies here. It is certainly the case that the (first) industrial revolution caused considerable social and economic dislocation. This was especially so for certain categories of workers, most notably the artisanal weavers and knitters in small rural workshops who rapidly disappeared with the advent of new town-based textile factories. Even so the overall demand for labour grew, both in the factories as well as the agricultural workforce supplying the factories with raw materials. In a particularly perverse development, recently referred to as the Cotton Gin Paradox (a specific application of the 1885 Jevons Paradox), contrary to initial fears about price depreciation, the US slave population actually increased five-fold between the late 1790s and 1850, as vast tracts of land were cleared and cotton planted to meet the demands of the new mills (Curran, 2013). More, mechanisation did bring into existence new occupations (e.g. mechanics) and the factory system and broader market economy with which it was entangled increased demand for jobs such as supervisors, managers and accountants (Mokyr, Vickers and Ziebarth, 2015). Nevertheless, while there was strong growth in both output per worker and profits, wage growth was effectively non-existent between 1780 and 1815 (what is known as the Engels' pause), and it took until the mid-1850s for industrialisation to furnish a higher standard of living for the working classes than existed before the changes (although this also varied according to occupation and region, and needed to be reckoned against changes in hours worked and work intensity (Feinstein, 1998; Voth, 2000; Allen, 2009).

The ambivalence attending the early experiences of industrialisation registered clearly in the work of key political economic thinkers throughout the 19th century. In 1821, for example, David Ricardo was moved to add a new chapter, 'XXXI: On Machines', to the third edition of his major text *On the Principles of Political Economy and Taxation*. Here he walked back his earlier assertions that gains from applying technology to the processes of production would produce an increase in net income to the benefit of all, conceding instead that mechanisation, through changing the demand for labour, "may increase the net revenue of the economy. . . (and) . . . at the same time render the population redundant, and deteriorate the condition of the labourers" (Ricardo 1821; 469). Writing at the other end of the 19th century Alfred Marshall, in his *Principles of Economics*, argued that mechanisation, through increasing the scale and complexity of manufacturing, would act as a driver of employment and creator of new jobs – these often monotonous but providing (in the factory surround) social stimulation in addition to a wage. It was in 'The Fragment on Machines', taken from the seven notebooks written across 1857–8 now known as the *Grundrisse*, that Karl Marx revealed arguably the fullest appreciation of the ambivalent impacts of the mechanisation of production. Here the same technologies that under capitalism rendered the worker's labour a mere abstraction of more fulfilling activity, regulated entirely by the movement of machines, could be harnessed, Marx argued, to provide for abundance and liberate workers from the excruciations of drudgery in the transition to a post-scarcity, post-capitalist world.

For the better part of the 20th century, similar concerns could be found in scholarly, public and popular discourse, although often inflected in ways to reveal if not entirely new aspects at least a novel emphasis on themes less prominent in the debates of the preceding century. In *Ulysses* James Joyce would have the peripatetic Bloom neatly sum up what was at issue as he looked out a window on that day in Dublin in July 1904:

> A pointsman's back straightened itself upright suddenly against a tramway standard by Mr. Bloom's window. Couldn't they invent something automatic so that the wheel itself much handier? Well but that fellow would lose his job then? Well but then another fellow would get a job making the new invention?
>
> *(cf Askt, 2013; 2)*

Writing around the same time, Karel Capek introduced 'the robot' in his world-famous play 'R.U.R.'. Both the figure and the term – derived from the Czech *robota*, meaning 'forced labour' – is reminiscent of historical slave narratives and the dehumanisation attending the institution of slavery. For Capek's play explicitly foregrounds how processes designed to strip away 'humanness' were considered necessary conditions for the cheap, compliant source of labour underpinning a global robot economy that spared humans all labour save for that undertaken willingly for individual self-fulfilment – at least until the robots revolted and killed them all (Rhee, 2018; 17–24).

It would, however, be John Maynard Keynes, in his 1930 essay *Economic Possibilities for our Grandchildren*, who would most decisively introduce into automation debates the new twin emphasis on the potentials of technology to relieve the burdens on the labouring classes while enhancing the quantity and quality of their leisure – even while coining the term 'technological unemployment'. According to Keynes (1972) the joint effects of techno-scientific innovation, the mechanism of compound interest and capital growth that had steadily gained momentum from around the time of the Renaissance furnished the conditions whereupon, major disruption aside, his grandchildren's generation would be in a position to neutralise 'Adam's Curse': the fundamental human economic problem of survival 'by the sweat of one's brow'. Of course, the conditional 'major disruption aside' was well placed – the year following the essay's publication saw the onset of the Great Depression, closely followed by Word War Two and the massive dislocations this caused. Nevertheless, in the light of the mid-1950s through to the early 1970s, the historical processes Keynes had described seemed to have resumed and be running a course close to that which he had charted. Here the prospect of a post-scarcity world seemed realisable in an epoch marked by the significant levels of automation entailed in systems of Fordist mass production, the (necessarily) accompanying mass consumption, and a host of historically specific social-structural and cultural features across the societies of the West (mass education, the rise of white collar occupations and a bureaucratically employed middle class, the growing inter-articulation of organised labour, organised capital and a state increasingly oriented to planning interventions, the progressive expansion of the welfare state, the remediation of many of the urban dis-amenities of the 19th century, and a valorisation of science and technology: for a more detailed analysis of these features, see Lash and Urry, 1987).

In the 1930 essay Keynes argued that, having dispensed with Adam's Curse, two further problems would emerge as a consequence. First, there was the problem of technological unemployment where the application of labour displacing technology was occurring faster than society's capacity to redirect affected labour into new areas. He considered this, however, an unfortunate yet temporary side effect of success in resolving the economic problem. It was here that a second problem presented, however. Having won this long-dreamt-of freedom from toil how, Keynes asked, would people occupy this leisure in ways that would not result in lives dominated by idle distraction? He suggested that the remaining work available be distributed across the population at an estimated 15 hours per week (this perhaps also partially addressing the question of lost income that Keynes does not broach) which would prompt lives lived 'well' ('wisely', 'agreeably') instead. In the period identified here, in which for most of the West historically unprecedented low levels of unemployment obtained, the equation of automation with enhanced leisure time was put forward more vigorously than in the preceding century as an alternative to a future wherein progressive automation was equated with immiseration and despair, although concerns about technological unemployment certainly did not disappear.

By the time two of the pioneers of AI, Herbert Simon in 1965 (*The Shape of Automation*) and Marvin Minsky in 1967 (*Computation*), famously predicted that within one or two decades machines would match most human intellectual capabilities and be, therefore, able to do any work that humans could do, the 'leisure/post-work society' debate was already well established. Throughout the 1950s and 60s, and into the 70s a host of notable figures – from Marcuse, Theobald, Riesman and Fromm to Vonnegut, Dumazalier, Touraine, Bell and Gershuny – would take up positions ranging between leisure forming a prerequisite for genuine freedom through to work as essential to human fulfilment (for a comprehensive summary of these and other positions see Veal, 2009; 25–55). Yet while more roseate visions of a post-work society were put forward in the latter decades of the 20th century (e.g. Rifkin, 1995), the mood overall appeared to take a sombre turn following the mass deployment of first generation industrial robots in the 1980s – these automating many of the remaining labour intensive tasks in manufacturing – along with the introduction of computer software into white collar workplaces. For sure, this mood itself was not fed by new forms of automation alone – the transformation of the global trading system, the emergence of a fully fledged global division of labour and the subsequent offshoring of much Western manufacturing played a significant role as well. So too did the transformation of welfare state policies. Where these had once been conceived as instruments of social cohesion, mitigating the socially corrosive effects of free market liberalism, they would subsequently function more as instruments of social and cultural division (Taylor-Gooby, 2016). During these times the spectre of places like Youngstown, Ohio, provided forbidding glimpses of what the world might be like were machines to truly obviate the need for workers once and for all. On September 19, 1977, Youngstown's steel mills, which had once made the city one of the most prosperous in the country, started to close as US manufacturing shifted abroad. In only five years the entire industry, along with 50,000 jobs and well over a billion dollars in wages, had been removed from the regional economy, destroying the social and cultural cohesion of the city – leaving prison construction a rare growth industry (Thompson, 2015).

As of the late 20th century it was nonetheless the case that automation in its various forms had generated more jobs than it had destroyed. This is not to say that this had been cost free. Indeed, short-term dislocations in which entire occupations may be wiped out, skills depreciated and wages depressed are not rare in the history of machines replicating tasks once performed by human labour. We thus do well not to glibly downplay the considerable pain and distress to individuals and communities that surely does accompany automation. Yet it nonetheless remains the case that in all periods up to the present not all workers get displaced by any given innovation and long-term gains are had in the form of new jobs created, new occupations and skills and generally rising wages (Mokyr, Vickers and Ziebarth, 2015). The principle mechanisms here are well known. Not only do new technologies increase demand for types of labour associated with its own production, maintenance and integration into production systems and organisational structures (as Leopold Bloom grasped well) but, through the product innovation that technological innovation enables, entirely new economic sectors are brought into being. How does this pattern square with the advent of AI?

The contemporary debate – key themes, key thinkers

"Is this time different?" This constitutes the overarching question framing debates on the impacts of AI on work, employment and unemployment. On one level – one focussed on the technological capabilities of new AI-powered systems marrying machine learning algorithms and big data to advanced robotics, sensors and other actuators – it is getting increasingly difficult to avoid answering this question with an emphatic "Yes"! The development of advanced conversational user interfaces has, for example, enabled the automation – at least in a substantial part – of a whole range of tasks that previously required a significant component of human-human interaction – be this as virtual personal assistants, the use of conversational agents in public and private service delivery, human resources management and online sales. Likewise, the ability of machine learning algorithms to condense a wide array of uncertainties and risks into compact sets of weighted probabilities has seen them employed (often controversially) to make decisions about, inter alia, applications for credit, loans or insurance, and secure borders and city streets, as well as to shape individual behaviour in relation to consumption choices – that is, on tasks previously considered to require human judgement. More complex systems combining multiple smart-technologies (including AI and advanced robotics along with the internet of [industrial] things, smart materials, biotechnologies and nanotechnologies) that are either beginning to be rolled out or are in advanced trials – for instance I4.0 or the automatisation of mobilities systems – promise significant departures from previous forms of automation in manufacturing and transport through enabling machine self-monitoring and self-correction along with the development of machine-readable environments (Eubanks, 2018; O'Neil, 2016; Yeung, 2017; Weking et al., 2020; Elliott and Boyd, 2020; Everuss, 2021). Yet, as Edgerton (2007) reminded us some time ago, every new technology depends significantly upon the continuing functioning of existing systems, meaning that 'the new' blends both established and innovative technologies in a variety of combinations. The newly emerging systems do, therefore, need to be seen as layered over the top of existing technological systems, perhaps most notably those of electrification and telecommunications (Elliott, 2019) but can also be considered to be subject to established economic strategies, political priorities and cultural expectations even as they disrupt these.

Still this is not really what the question, "Is this time different?" asks after – at least in the initial asking. Put baldly, it asks whether the deployment of AI-powered technologies in workplaces will result in unprecedented job losses and the profound social transformations this might precipitate? Or will this deployment follow the pattern of short-term dislocations and long-term gains observed for the automations of the past? In order to follow the ways these debates have evolved I will divide the discussion here into two parts. The first focuses on the broader implications for employment, unemployment and hence work as a social institution and the political, social and cultural implications of this. The second looks more closely at the ways AI technologies are being integrated into workplaces and the implications this has for the organisation and experience of work from the perspective of a deepening human–machine interaction.

Employment, unemployment and social transformation

In 2013, at a workshop on 'Machines and Employment' hosted by the Oxford University Engineering Sciences Department and the Oxford Martin Programme on the Impacts of Future Technology, the economist and economic historian Carl Benedikt Frey and machine learning researcher Michael A. Osbourne presented a paper in which they discussed the results of a study they had conducted into the susceptibility of a range of US occupations to AI-powered automation. This entailed applying a model of actual and prospective machine capabilities (in areas such as machine learning, data mining, image and speech recognition and predictive analytics) to the occupational task and worker attribute requirements for the 702 occupational classifications in the US O★NET database (in actuality they used 70 occupations as a training data set to develop their own algorithm that then analysed the remaining 632 occupations). They reported that, according to their analysis, 47% of US occupations were potentially at risk from the advanced automation associated with AI (Frey and Osbourne, 2013). Replications of their method produced similarly startling figures for the UK (40%), Australia (40%) and Japan (49%). The authors were quick to hedge their findings about with numerous qualifiers: that this was purely an estimate of the exposure of existing jobs to these new technologies based upon a technology capabilities approach; and, that they made no claims about how far and how fast AI development and dissemination would go, nor how many jobs this would actually destroy. The headline figure of 47% stripped of these qualifications, nonetheless, certainly made and continues to make headlines, lending an ostensibly hard-edged empirical warrant to both scholarly and popular discourse and announcing the arrival of an age wherein an ever-expanding range of cognitive as well as physical capabilities being acquired by machines was making serious inroads into the world of work – be this for better (Brynjolfsson and McAfee, 2011, 2014; Srnicek and Williams, 2016) or worse (Ford, 2015; Spencer, 2016; Sachs and Kotlikoff, 2012).

In a relatively recent analysis Robert Holton and I (Boyd and Holton, 2018) critically evaluated the debate as it stood at the time we were writing. We concluded that an impressive expansion of machine capabilities was evident, and that this was enabling the automation of a far wider range of workplace tasks than ever before, including many non-routine cognitive tasks that had previously been the sole prerogative of humans. This may present real challenges with respect of employment, including in the service sector (which has been responsible for a considerable proportion of employment growth over recent decades) and even the professions, as suggested by Susskind and Susskind (2015; see also Innes and Morrison, 2020). So, we argued, it certainly appeared that a transformation of work and employment was underway. However caution against hyperbolic declarations about a catastrophic decline in employment was also definitely required. With respect of service employment, for example, changes were clearly evident; however, this did not represent a general threat, with some positions extremely vulnerable (e.g. accountants) and others (e.g. hairdressers) far less so (Haldane, 2015). More, AI-enabled technologies tend to be used to automate parts of an occupation's suite of tasks – not the whole suite. In a wide-ranging study of over 2,000 work activities spanning some 800 occupations Chui, Manyika and Miremadi (2016) found that within many jobs a significant portion of work activities – in some cases up to 45% – could be automated. This, of course, means that at least 55% of these work activities would still require human capabilities. For example, healthcare – including diagnostic decision-making and high-precision medical procedures – is being transformed by the application of algorithms, big data, sensors, 3D printing and the like. Yet as Meskó (2019) suggests, far from replacing medical practitioners, these technologies enhance the capacity of physicians to bring together cutting-edge medical science and clinical best practice where historically there had been a gap between these. Finally, many of the technologies entailed were still at an experimental or trial stage, with their specific workplace applications and likely impacts on work and employment difficult to specify (Boyd and Holton, 2018).

More generally, it is increasingly apparent that aggregate estimates of the impact of automation on job numbers do not provide the best insights into transformations of work and employment attendant upon the deployment of AI. Willcocks (2020) recently tracked changes in estimates of possible employment effects related to automation for the five years from 2013 to 2018. Arguably the most notable feature here is the considerable variation in the estimates themselves – from Frey and Osbourne's 47% of US jobs at risk in 2013, the 2016 Forrester Research (16% of US jobs lost by 2025, offset by 9% new jobs by 2027) and OECD reports (9% of US and European jobs at risk within a decade), through to reports in 2018 by the World Economic Forum (surveying 313 companies in 20 countries: 0.98 million jobs lost and 1.74 million created by 2022) and the McKinsey Global Institute (for 800 occupations, 2,000 work activities across 46 countries 15% or 400 million workers displaced by 2030, offset by the creation of between 390 million and 590 million jobs through improved healthcare, rising incomes, investment in infrastructure, energy transitions and greater marketisation of unpaid work). The usefulness of these estimates is clearly limited. As Willcocks suggests, these types of projections depend on what one measures (occupational requirements vs. specific tasks and activities), whether the potential job creation effects of automation (and other factors) are considered and offset against losses, and the timescales involved. In addition, the speed and extent to which these technologies are deployed and, hence, the type and severity of their impacts on employment will be heavily influenced by a range of factors including demographic trends, policy settings, investment priorities and socio-cultural expectations, among other things (discussion follows).

Problems of abstraction and a lack of nuance associated with a focus on employment aggregates as a measure of the impacts of advanced automation on work have been picked up by a number of prominent labour economists. David Autor (2019), for instance, has extensively documented the way measures of aggregate job losses (and jobs created) miss much about the ways digital technologies have, for quite some time, been changing the compositional pattern of employment in terms of the distribution of workers among high-, middle- and low-skilled jobs, with significant consequences for wage inequality. Whilst based on US data, Autor's observations are consistent with those for Europe and Australia (Borland and Coelli, 2017). Specifically, whereas the automation entailed in earlier periods of mass production provided opportunities for both blue and white collar workers and professionals, digital automation has tended to displace middle-skill workers – those performing cognitive and non-cognitive routine tasks that are readily codifiable – in occupations such as sales, office and administrative support, production, craft and repair. This hollowing out of 'the middle' has resulted in a polarised, 'hourglass' shaped pattern to the distribution of employment where high education/high wage and low education/low wage jobs are growing at the expense of middle-skill jobs. Somewhat surprisingly low-paid service and manual jobs have been least affected by digitalisation. This is because the task abilities in such positions – for instance situational adaptability, face-to-face communications, physical dexterity and many forms of visual recognition – are beyond current AI capabilities while only requiring moderate levels of education on the part of the people performing them. Here the major impact for workers does not entail levels of employment per se but rather a decline in wages (or more generally the labour share of national income) and conditions of employment, thus increasing economic inequality.

Likewise, Daron Acemoglu and Pascual Restrepo (2020) take issue with the standard economic approaches to technological progress (noted earlier) wherein technological progress, through increasing aggregate productivity, raises aggregate demand for labour (this more than compensating for falls in a few sectors). This account, they consider, is both descriptively suspect and unduly optimistic. For Acemoglu and Restrepo digital automation is not necessarily intended to increase labour productivity. It can do this by augmenting and, in so doing, complementing worker productivity. But it is often explicitly designed to substitute for labour. This can result in a suppression of labour demand, although reductions in costs can also prompt an expansion of output leading to an increase in demand for non-automated labour and hence the reinstatement of displaced workers. In any event the likely result is a decrease in the labour share of national income, even if aggregate employment remains around the same levels as before the introduction of these technologies. However, they continue, the potential for a double jeopardy for labour also exists in the form of 'so-so' technologies, those that are good enough to be adopted and displace workers but not good enough to yield sufficiently strong productivity gains to redress diminished labour demand (e.g. self-service kiosks or automated customer service). For Acemoglu and Restrepo what is noticeably absent in contemporary discussions over AI and the future of work is the question, "are we investing in the 'right' type of AI, the kind with the greatest potential for raising productivity and generating broad-based prosperity?" (p. 25). I will return to their discussion on the "right" type of AI in the following section.

For now, I want to briefly follow Acemoglu and Restrepo's observation that there are choices over the type of AI we decide to build, meaning that this is not preordained, to where it points out a further problem with aggregate estimates of the effects of AI on employment. As already indicated these estimates most often entail the form of matching current or prospective technological capabilities to (variously) occupational skill requirements, tasks or activities. There is a strong – if perhaps unwitting – element of technological determinism to this approach. In *Ironic Technics* Don Ihde (2008) discusses the 'designer fallacy', the problematic assumption that the future uses of any technology follow the original intentions of its designers. This is problematic, Ihde argues, given that a technology's future uses and effects are mediated by a variety of factors ranging from the historical and cultural contexts in which the technology's development and dissemination is embedded through to the specific material and operational properties of the technologies themselves (as evident in the forms of 'resistance' encountered in experimental and testing settings). For Ihde the, "complex sets of relations between multiple inputs into developing technologies. . . [lead to] . . . multiple, multistable possibilities for any single technology" (p. 23).

In our evaluation of the AI/future of work debate, Robert Holton and I resolved upon an approach that placed complexity and uncertainty squarely at the centre of analysis, thereby bringing social, cultural, political and economic processes into the frame (Boyd and Holton,

2018). In what is one of the most rigorous and comprehensive longitudinal studies of AI diffusion, Compagni, Mele and Ravasi's (2015) research on the deployment of surgical robots in Italy between 1999 and 2010 underscores the value of such an approach. In brief, these researchers found that the decisions – among surgeons, health policymakers and administrators from large or small, public or private hospitals and across regional settings – to be early adopters, subsequent adopters or non-adopters of these technologies depended on a variety of considerations in which assessments of technological capabilities figured but were by no means decisive. Other important factors included a desire to expand into new markets for surgery on the part of smaller hospitals, peer-group fears about falling behind with respect of 'exemplary practice', various pressures from regional politicians or hospital owners and cost-benefit anxieties around large investments.

AI and the organisation and experience of work

> Change the technology and you change the task, and you change the nature of the worker – in fact you change the entire population of people who can operate a system.
>
> (Mindell, 2015; 13–14)

As it has evolved, the focus of debate over AI and the future of work – among scholars at least – has shifted away from estimations of the overall number of jobs likely to be lost or gained and towards changes at the level of the organisation and in the nature and the experience of work, with a strong focus on human–machine interaction. There definitely remains a residuum of earlier concerns with what AI can or cannot do and hence what tasks might be realistically essayed to machines and what to humans in the emerging organisation of work – although this is appropriately scaled down from the macro level of analysis and with extrapolations of findings suitably muted. Pettersen (2019), for instance, provides a detailed account of the situated practices of knowing, learning, communicating and responding to varied interactional contexts entailed in what is commonly referred to as 'knowledge work'. She argues that the capacity to solve complex, often vaguely defined problems, or to develop creative interpretations, adjust to new challenges and move seamlessly between contexts in situations characterised by high degrees of uncertainty clearly demarcates one domain (among others) in which AI will not, for the foreseeable future, challenge human capabilities. Taking a somewhat different approach, Willcocks (2020) argues that increases in work intensification observed since the 2008 financial crisis are of a magnitude that cannot be solely attributed – as it often has been – to firms choosing to 'sweat their assets'. Looking closely at workplace studies involving advanced automation, he identifies three developments that are already driving work growth: an explosion of data from mobile devices and the internet of things; a massive increase in audit, regulation and bureaucracy across government agencies and business sectors accompanying this data explosion; and, a dramatic rise in cybersecurity problems requiring human in addition to technological solutions.

Nevertheless, the emphasis does seem to be moving more in the direction of exploring what is going on in terms of new forms of human–machine interaction. As the robotics engineer (and historian of engineering) David Mindell (2015) puts it:

> The most advanced (and difficult) technologies are not those that stand apart from people, but those most deeply embedded in, and responsive to, human and social networks.
>
> (p. 9)

As technologies progress, he continues, people move into ever more intimate relations with their machines. This, I would immediately add, does not always break in the direction of a progressive enhancement of the organisation or experience of work.

For Mindell, drawing on his experiences pioneering automated vehicle systems for oceanic and space exploration, as well as with driverless cars and automated piloting systems, these innovations profoundly alter the nature of work tasks and, hence, skill and knowledge requirements, education and even the demographic characteristics of those who enter particular occupational groups. Here what were once physical tasks, for instance keeping one's hands on controls and senses engaged directly with one's surround, evolve into cognitive tasks utilising visual displays. The experience of presence changes as well, as evident in the situation of US Air Force UAV pilots, at once physically at some distance from the battlefield, housed in remote ground-control stations, and simultaneously immersed more deeply in it (than conventional pilots flying high above the conflict) on account of advanced sensor systems. While the extreme environments of the ocean depths, outer space and the battlefield may appear quite removed from the work experiences of most people, Mindell insists many of the challenges – for example processes of switching in and out of automatic mode and the complex relations of trust this entails – have much in common with increasing automation in the daily round. The rethinking of notions of control and presence, and of (often highly gendered) cultural understandings of the nature of the work entailed, certainly has much in common with a number of the large iron ore operations in Western Australia where most of the mine operations, along with port facilities and around 1,000 km of rail lines connecting them, are run from a state-of-the-art remote operations facility 2,000 km south in Perth. Here the new 'miners' engaged in design, technology development and deployment, planning, as well as monitoring and even remotely maintaining (at times using virtual-reality technologies) mining operations, are drawn from multiple professional and disciplinary backgrounds (Gollschewski, 2015).

More generally, opportunities for creatively utilising AI platforms to do more than merely automate ever more tasks previously done by people (and therefore diminish labour share, increase inequality and depress labour demand) have emerged over recent years. Acemoglu and Restrepo (2020; 29–30; see also Autor, Mindell and Reynolds, 2019) consider a few examples:

- In education AI can collect and process data in real time with respect of the ways students respond on measures of performance and in terms of their cognitive and emotional reactions across topics as well as, importantly, in relation to different teaching styles. Recommendations for individualised teaching programmes are thus able to be developed, this both improving educational outcomes through enhanced responsiveness to student needs and increasing the demand for labour given the need for teachers with a diverse range of skills.
- AI applications for gathering and processing information can, as with the example of education, enhance the range and precision of diagnostic and treatment services healthcare providers can offer, similarly increasing productivity and labour demand.
- Advanced manufacturing companies (e.g. Tesla) are recognising that full automation is counterproductive given humans are still better at performing certain categories of tasks. However, industrial robotics and humans do not always mesh well, largely due to the degrees of precision robotic technologies require as well as for safety reasons. Accordingly, the use of interactive, augmented reality interfaces enabling workers to perceive, monitor and control the work process can enable elaborate worker-machine collaborations on high-precision design and production tasks.

In 2016 IBM, seeking to leverage the performative potential of its 'Watson' AI to gain a greater share of highly competitive digital marketplaces, whilst remaining well aware of popular concerns about AI, devised the category of 'New Collar' jobs. These IBM defined as,

> roles in some of the technology industry's faster growing fields – from cybersecurity and cloud computing to cognitive business and digital design – that do not always require a traditional degree . . . [but rather] . . . the right mix of in-demand skill-sets.
>
> *(cf Cox, 2020; 825)*

IBM would subsequently lobby US state and federal legislators to provide tax credits for firms and debt relief for workers participating in New Collar training programmes, this leading to the New Collar Job Act, 2017 (yet to be passed). As Cox (2020) notes, the overarching narrative is one of IBM engendering enhanced worker autonomy through AI augmentation, this prosthetically enabling them to perform an ever-expanding range of work tasks and, accordingly, to position themselves favourably in high-demand sections of the labour market. It cannot be my purpose here to discuss Cox's concerns about IBM's attempts to elongate its 'economy of learning', nor indeed to quibble over the rather simplistic (self-sufficient, self-determining) account of autonomy – human or machine – appealed to by IBM and other players (see Holton and Boyd, 2019). What is worth focusing on briefly is the idea of ongoing self-reinvention, and the notion of the entrepreneurial worker this implies, that Cox (2020; 833–834) identifies within the New Collar narrative. Here I would certainly not contest the possibility that the work experiences of IBM New Collar workers match, as reported, the affirmational rhetoric of a heightened experience of autonomy, or a widening horizon of opportunity. What I would want to do is open up the discussion to studies that point the way for other contexts in which the same rhetoric of enhanced autonomy and entrepreneurialism is applied to the situation of people whose work tasks and workplaces are extensively mediated by AI applications, but where worker's experiences and the affirmative rhetoric diverge considerably.

A significantly new set of developments centre on the emergence of cloud-based digital platforms (Google and Facebook being the best known) which, through providing the infrastructure upon which a variety of other commercial platforms can be established, are prompting a profound reconfiguration of market and working arrangements, as well as dramatically changing the ways value is created and captured (Kenny and Zysman, 2016). The various names given to these developments – from Sharing Economy and Creative Economy to Gig Economy, Precariat or 1099 Economy (referring to the US Internal Revenue Service form for independent contracting) – indicate that there is considerable disagreement about their beneficence. For the enthusiasts these technologies enable a whole new class of small producers – or proto-entrepreneurs – engaging both directly and flexibly with their clients, forming open communities of creation (Wikipedia, open source software) and realising the commercial value of underutilised personal assets (Uber, Lyft, Airbnb). For others the digital platforms that match workers to tasks merely increase the incidence of fragmented, part-time, poorly compensated and unprotected precarious employment (ibid.). Of course, such practices are not entirely new. Even if organised algorithmically the actual work arrangements have much in common with the putting-out system that predated the industrial revolution. Accordingly, Kenny and Zysman argue – in a manner similar to Acemoglu and Restrepo – that while technologies can frame choices, raise questions and present challenges, the ultimate impact of these new technological systems will be shaped by political and economic choices about the types of AI that will be developed, with an eye to questions about how markets, businesses and work arrangements ought to be organised and for whose benefit.

Discrepancies between the affirmative rhetoric of entrepreneurial selves or creative communities and the everyday experiences of people whose working lives are intricately bound by with the needs of AI-powered automated systems are cast in even starker relief once we consider the hidden human labour that is necessary to close the gaps between what AI technologies can do and the full range of actual task requirements entailed in given work environments. This is especially so for those environments that do not conform to the ideal conditions for automation (e.g. highly structured, closed and rules-based decision systems, clean data and so forth). In an analysis of the integration of AI into the mundane, yet dynamic, settings of retail grocery and farm management, Mateescu and Elish (2019) demonstrate how the labour entailed in 'human infrastructures' – "the integral human component of a socio-technical system without which that system cannot properly function" (p. 12) – is masked by the attribution of intelligence to the technologies themselves. In grocery, for example, human labour can be seen to augment, attend to the needs of and generally provide the appearance of intelligence and autonomy on the part of self-checkout systems – replacing batteries, unjamming or cleaning parts, updating outdated codes, modifying speaking patterns to be intelligible to smart speakers, chaperoning relations between machines and consumers and so forth. These worker's reconfigured skillsets, they continue, also include diagnosing shopper confusion, managing customer flows or spotting potential theft, all the while overseeing arrays of multiple self-service machines. Yet these new skills often go unacknowledged, are undervalued and, as such, tend to also be undercompensated (see also Ekbia and Nardi, 2017).

Taking in a more global purview Mary Gray and Siddharth Suri (2019) document how forms of hidden 'ghost' labour, not just algorithms, undergird so many of the operations of the digital economy. Mediated by on-demand platforms these workers, for instance, may screen 'flagged' content (pornography, violence and hate speech) on social media platforms, rate search engine matches with user requests to train AI, clean duplicate listings on recommendation sites, or provide translations and transcripts of TED talk videos. This work is, in other words, often anything but 'mindless', and includes much that would elsewhere be referred to as 'knowledge work'. On Gray and Suri's account these workers, moreover, manage to creatively craft social connections using the same digital platforms that have often been designed to isolate them from one another – for example, convening online forums in which they share their understandings of opaque systems and task instructions. And it is the case that some platforms will provide workers with collaboration tools, consistent schedules and even career ladders whilst advancing business goals. Which demonstrates, they argue, that the tendencies to conceal and devalue the labour upon which automated systems so often depend, and to treat the workers involved (by Gray and Suri's estimates there are at least several million globally, and this number is expanding year on year) as expendable and interchangeable, is (once again) a choice, framed or informed, but not determined by the technologies themselves.

Conclusion: the future prospect

What might we take forward from this discussion to equip us for ongoing debates over AI and the future of work and employment? I would suggest, in the first place, that paying too much attention – as tends to be the case with much popular discussion – to estimates of job losses accompanying the dissemination of AI technologies, even if offset by employment gains, is to plough a field of diminishing returns. Not only are such estimates hostage to a legion of contingencies, but they miss much that is important in the way of transformations in the domain of work that are, as indicated in the preceding section, better approached through attending to changes in human–machine interaction. This includes the way some very old work practices (e.g. putting out or piece work) are finding new opportunities in the affordances offered by new digital technologies.

To write of affordances is (in the second place) to recognise the new technological capabilities occasioned by AI – how they enable and mediate all manner of experience or activity, and can thus be rightly acknowledged as our partners in social, including workplace, interaction – without losing sight of the very human choices and decisions about, for instance, investment in the development of some technologies over others, and the manners of their integration into specific business models, organisational forms and work arrangements that the more excited rhetoric of 'autonomous systems' can obscure. This includes the choice to recognise, or not, the 'human infrastructure' that remains integral to the functioning of autonomous machine systems, and the oftentimes egregious consequences this can have for the workers involved.

In this chapter, and elsewhere, I have made a point of accentuating the radical uncertainty and complexity that attends the development and dissemination of all technologies, not the least being those that fall under the head of AI. Attempting to anticipate future directions for research in the field thus needs to be treated with a high level of caution. Yet the 'unforeseen' itself can – and indeed has – present as an emerging topic. In a recent essay Autor and Reynolds (2020) suggest that the COVID-19 pandemic might be challenging conventional understandings of automation, employment and inequality in the US. They identify four developments that might shape and condition an increasingly automated post-COVID economy: an expansion in the use of telepresence and remote working, highlighting the possibilities for the virtual workplace; urban de-densification, in part precipitated by telepresence (along with changing consumption practices), with a corresponding negative impact on janitorial, hospitality, security and other service jobs; a significant increase in small- to medium-size business failures leading to a greater concentration of employment in large firms; and, automation forcing, be it the accelerated roboticisation of meatpacking or warehouse cleaning or the use of aerial drones for delivery and surveillance purposes. While these developments, Autor and Reynolds argue, have significant negative implications for low-wage work, and hence economic inequality, they note that this is not a foregone conclusion, with the enormous government investments throughout the pandemic providing a model for the type and scale of public investment that might mitigate the costs of future automation.

Beyond this we might consider a potential renewal of interest in topics that have received scant attention in current automation debates. Smids, Nyholm and Berkers (2019), for example, observe that while the topic of 'meaningful work' has received some recent attention, this has not really incorporated any discussion on how work satisfaction, worker well-being and other related concerns have been impacted by the integration of robotics and AI into workplaces. Similarly, there is ample scope to revisit earlier debates on leisure time, and the realm of freedom, in the context of advanced automation, including proposals such as Ulrich Beck's "counter-model to the work society" (Veal, 2020).

Notes

1 This chapter is developed from research funded by the Australian Research Council Discovery Project Grant DP180101816 'Industry 4.0 ecosystems: a comparative analysis of work-life transformation'.
2 For the purposes of this chapter I will use, as a working definition, the approach to AI developed in Holton and Boyd (2019), following Bell (2018). This gathers the component features of AI under five main headings: big data; algorithms; machine learning; sensing; and logic/rationale. Rather than constituting a highly integrated and orderly arrangement of these dimensions, this model presents a rather more disorderly, internally discordant and uncertain bundle of processes. More, these processes are treated as being at once technological, social, political, economic and cultural.

References

Acemoglu, D. and Restrepo, P. (2020) The wrong kind of AI? Artificial intelligence and the future of labour demand, *Cambridge Journal of Regions, Economy and Society*, 13(1): 25–35.

Allen, R.C. (2009) Engels pause: Technical change, capital accumulation, and inequality in the British Industrial Revolution, *Explorations in Economic History*, 46(4): 418–435.

Askt, D. (2013) What can we learn from past anxiety over automation, *The Wilson Quarterly*, 37(3): 1–6.

Autor, D. (2019) Work of the past, work of the future, NBER Working Paper No. 25588, available at: http://groupelavigne.free.fr/nber25588.pdf.

Autor, D., Mindell, D. and Reynolds, E.B. (2019) *The Work of the Future: Shaping Technology and Institutions*, Cambridge, MA: MIT Taskforce on the Work of the Future.

Autor, D. and Reynolds, E.B. (2020) *The Nature of Work after the COVID Crisis: Too Few Low-Wage Jobs*, Cambridge, MA: MIT Task Force on the Work of the Future/Brookings Institute, available at: www.brookings.edu/wp-content/uploads/2020/08/AutorReynolds_LO_FINAL.pdf.

Bell, G. (2018) 'Decolonizing artificial intelligence' Fay Gale lecture University of Adelaide September 2018, available at: www.assa.edu.au/event/fay-gale-lecture-2/.

Berman, M. (1982) *All that Is Solid Melts into Air*. New York: Simon and Schuster

Borland, J. and Coelli, M. (2017) Are robots taking our jobs? *Australian Economic Review*, 50(4): 377–397.

Boyd, R. and Holton, R.J. (2018) Technology, innovation, employment and power: Does robotics and artificial intelligence really mean social transformation? *Journal of Sociology*, 54(3): 331–345.

Brynjolfsson, E. and McAfee, A. (2011) *Race Against the Machine: How the Digital Revolution is Accelerating Innovation, Driving Productivity, and Irreversibly Transforming Employment and the Economy*, Lexington, MA: Digital Frontier Press.

Brynjolfsson, E. and McAfee, A. (2014) *The Second Machine Age*, New York: Norton.

Chui, M., Manyika, J. and Miremadi, M. (2016) Where machines could replace humans – and where they can't (yet), *McKinsey Quarterly*, June, available at: www.mckinsey.com/~/media/McKinsey/Business%20Functions/McKinsey%20Digital/Our%20Insights/Where%20machines%20could%20replace%20humans%20and%20where%20they%20cant/Where-machines-could-replace-humans-and-where-they-cant-yet.pdf.

Compagni, A., Mele, V. and Ravasi, D. (2015) How earlier implementations influence later adoptions of innovations, *Academy of Management Journal*, 58(1): 242–278.

Cox, C.M. (2020) Augmenting autonomy: 'New collar' labor and the future of tech work, *Convergence: The International Journal of Research into New Media Technologies*, 26(4): 824–840.

Curran, E. (2013) The cotton gin paradox, available at: https://transitionvoice.com/2013/04/the-cotton-gin-paradox/.

Edgerton, D. (2007) *The Shock of the Old*, London: Profile.

Ekbia, H.R. and Nardi, B.A. (2017) *Heteromation, and Other Stories of Computing and Capitalism*, Cambridge, MA: MIT Press.

Elliott, A. (2019) *The Culture of AI*, London and New York: Routledge.

Elliott, A. and Boyd, R. (2020) The transformation of mobility: AI, robotics and automatization, in M. Büscher et al. (eds.), *Handbook of Research Methods and Applications for Mobilities*, Cheltenham and Camberly: Edward Elgar, pp. 241–250.

Eubanks, V. (2018) *Automating Inequality*, New York: St Martins Press.

Everuss, L. (2021) The new mobilities paradigm and social theory, in A. Elliott (ed.), *Handbook of Social and Cultural Theory*, London and New York: Routledge.

Feinstein, C.H. (1998) Pessimism perpetuated: Real wages and the standard of living in Britain during and after the industrial revolution, *Journal of Economic History*, 53(3): 625–658.

Frey, C., Berger, T. and Chen, C. (2017) Political machinery: Automation anxiety and the 2016 U.S. Presidential election, available at: www.oxfordmartin.ox.ac.uk/downloads/academic/Political%20Machinery-Automation%20Anxiety%20and%20the%202016%20U_S_%20Presidential%20Election_230712.pdf.

Frey, C.B. and Osbourne, M.A. (2013) The future of employment: How susceptible are jobs to computerisation, available at: www.oxfordmartin.ox.ac.uk/downloads/academic/The_Future_of_Employment.pdf.

Ford, M. (2015) *The Rise of the Robots*, New York: Basic Books.

Gollschewski, M. (2015) Case study: Automation and Australia's future workforce, in *Australia's Future Workforce?* Melbourne: CEDA.

Gray, M. and Suri, S. (2019) *Ghost Work: How to Stop Silicon Valley from Building a New Global Underclass*, Boston, MA: Houghton Mifflin Harcourt.

Haldane, A. (2015) 'Labour's share', speech to the trades union congress, London, URL (consulted 22 May 2016), available at: www.bankofengland.co.uk/publications/speeches/2015/864.aspx.

Holton, R. and Boyd, R. (2019) 'Where are the people? What are they doing? Why are they doing it?'(Mindell) Situating artificial intelligence within a socio-technical framework, *Journal of Sociology*.

Ihde, D. (2008) *Ironic Technics*, Copenhagen: Automatic Press/VIP.

Im, Z.J., Mayer, N., Palier, B. and Rovny, J. (2019) The "losers of automation": A reservoir of votes for the radical right? *Research & Politics*.

Innes, J.M. and Morrison, B. (2020) Can we predict the outcomes of deep learning algorithms that simulate and replace professional skills? Understanding the threats of artificial intelligence, in K. Andrews et al. (eds.), *Innovation in a Changing World*, Perth, WA: Navitas, pp. 163–176.

Kenny, M. and Zysman, J. (2016) The rise of the platform economy, *Issues in Science and Technology*, xxxii(3), available at: https://issues.org/the-rise-of-the-platform-economy/.

Keynes, J. M. (1972) *Collected Writings Volume 9: Essays in Persuasion*, London: Macmillan.

Kurer, T. and Palier, B. (2019) Shrinking and shouting: The political revolt of the declining middle in times of employment polarization, *Research & Politics*.

Lash, S. and Urry, J. (1987) *The End of Organized Capitalism*, Cambridge: Polity.

Mantoux, P. (2013) *The Industrial Revolution in the Eighteenth Century: An Outline of the Beginnings of the Modern Factory System in England*, New York/London: Routledge.

Mateescu, A. and Elish, M.C. (2019) *AI in Context: The Labor of Integrating New Technologies*, New York: Data & Society Research Institute, available at: https://datasociety.net/wp-content/uploads/2019/01/DataandSociety_AIinContext.pdf.

Meskó, B. (2019) The real era of the art of medicine begins with artificial intelligence, *Journal of Medical Internet Research*, 21(11): e16295.

Mindell, D. (2015) *Our Robots, Ourselves*, New York: Viking.

Mokyr, J. (2009) *The Enlightened Economy: An Economic History of Britain 1700–1850*, New Haven: Yale University Press.

Mokyr, J., Vickers, C. and Ziebarth, N.L. (2015) The history of technological anxiety and the future of economic growth: Is this time different? *Journal of Economic Perspectives*, 29(3): 31–50.

Offe, C. (1985) *Disorganized Capitalism*, Cambridge: Polity.

O'Neill, C. (2016) *Weapons of Maths Destruction*, New York: Crown Books.

Pettersen, L. (2019) Why artificial intelligence will not outsmart complex knowledge work, *Work, Employment and Society*, 33(6): 1058–1067.

Rhee, J. (2018) *The Roboytic Imaginary: The Human and the Price of Dehumanized Labor*, Minneapolis: University of Minnesota Press.

Ricardo, D (1821) *On the Principles of Political Economy and Taxation* (3rd edition), London: John Murray.

Rifkin, J. (1995) *The End of Work*, New York: Putnam.

Riskin, J. (2003) The defecating duck, or, the ambiguous origins of artificial life, *Critical Inquiry*, 29(4).

Sachs, J. and Kotlikoff, L. (2012) *Smart Machines and Long-term Misery*, Working paper w18629, Cambridge, MA: National Bureau of Economic Research.

Shiller, R. J. (2019) *Narratives about Technology-Induced Job Degradations Then and Now*, NBER Working Paper No. 25536, Cambridge, MA: National Bureau of Economic Research.

Smids, J., Nyholm, S. and Berkers, H. (2019), Robots in the workplace: A threat to – or opportunity for – meaningful work, *Philosophy and Technology*, 33: 503–522.

Spencer, D. (2016) Work in and beyond the second machine age, *Work, Employment, and Society*, 1–11.

Srnicek, N. and Williams, A. (2016) *Inventing the Future: Postcapitalism and a World without Work*, New York: Verso.
Susskind, R. and Susskind, D. (2015) *The Future of the Professions*, Oxford: Oxford University Press.
Taylor-Gooby, P. (2016) The divisive welfare state, *Social Policy and Administration*, 50(6): 712–733.
Thompson, D. (2015) A world without work, *The Atlantic*, July/August, available at: www.theatlantic.com/magazine/archive/2015/07/world-without-work/395294/.
Veal, A.J. (2020) Is there enough leisure time? Leisure studies, work-life balance, the realm of necessity and the realm of freedom, *World Leisure Journal*, 62(2): 89–113.
Veal, A.J. (2009) *The Elusive Leisure Society. School of Leisure*, Sport and Tourism Working Paper 9 (4th edition), Sydney: University of Technology, Sydney, available at: http:// datasearch.uts.edu.au/business/publications/lst/index.cfm and at www.leisuresource.net.
Voth, H.J. (2000) *Time and Work in England 1750–1830*, Oxford: Clarendon Press.
Weking, J., Stöcker, M., Kowalkiewicz, M., Böhm, M. and Krcmar, H. (2020) Leveraging industry 4.0 – A business model pattern framework, *International Journal of Production Economics*, 225.
Willcocks, L. (2020) Robo-apocalypse cancelled? Reframing the automation and future of work debate, *Journal of Information Technology*, 35(4): 286–302.
Yeung, K. (2017) 'Hypernudge': Big data as a mode of regulation by design, *Information, Communication & Society*, 20(1): 118–136.

6

Affects after AI

Sociological perspectives on artificial companionship

Michaela Pfadenhauer and Tobias Lehmann

Introduction

This chapter discusses sociological perspectives on the formation of social and emotional relationships with artefacts and related basic questions of sociality arising against the background of technological developments in the field of "social robotics", and prompted by the notion of "artificial companionship", in particular. In a first instance, the term "social robotics", hints at the development of robotic technologies that are envisioned to be employed in various situations of everyday life rather than in more isolated spheres such as industrial production or as in the case of field robotics (cf. Meister, 2014). Moreover, "social robotics" refers to the efforts undertaken by computer scientists, engineers, and psychologists, among others, to equip technologies with features that are intended to enable technological artefacts to behave in (seemingly) human-like ways, by adequately (or: sufficiently credibly) enacting as well as responding to social and emotional cues, for instance, via technologies enabling artificial sensory perception or the development of "emotional intelligence" (cf. Meister, 2014; von Scheve, 2014; Broadbent, 2017; McDuff & Czerwinski, 2018; Sarrica et al., 2019). In particular, the contribution centers around the notion of "artificial companionship" as it has been associated with technological artefacts that are envisioned to form long-term, emotional relationships with their human users (cf. van Oost & Reed, 2011; Böhle & Bopp, 2014; von Scheve, 2014; Pfadenhauer, 2014, 2015). The notion of "artificial companionship" in this sense is treated here as an ideal-typical starting point for sociological considerations regarding emergent forms of "human-robot-sociality" and their implications for the formation of emotional bonds between humans and robots that have been enabled by recent developments in social robotics.

From a sociological perspective, the development of social robots and their increasing availability prompt a range of questions concerning their potential to introduce new dynamics into the fabric of social relationships, as concerns have been raised whether social robots might actually have the potential to substitute for human-human interactions altogether, how the acceptance of social robots relates to broader dynamics in contemporary society, and how these dynamics play into people's dealings with the new technologies on the market (e.g., Turkle, 2010, 2011; Pfadenhauer, 2015; Fortunati, 2018). So, how to characterize people's envisaged and actual relationships with robots? How do people engage with these technologies, what motivates them to do so, what attributes do they ascribe to their robotic counterparts in interaction, and, in turn, how do these ascriptions reflect back on the patterns of interaction with these technologies? And it is not only the implications that social robotics yield in regard to the experiences of their *users* that become of interest but also the experiential backgrounds, intentions, and corresponding imagined or intended uses on the side of the *designers* who shape these technologies in the first place, the ways they translate their aspirations into the design of robotic artefacts, and the ways in which the design of social robots relates to users' perceptions of and dealings with these artefacts.

The contribution is structured as follows: first, the notions of social robotics and artificial companionship are introduced and discussed with a view on what distinguishes these technologies from other forms of robotics, their prevalent contexts of application, and the visions behind their development (1). Second, major tenets of sociological discourse on social robotics and artificial companionship are discussed, referring to their general status as "nonhumans" in social theory, exemplary sociological accounts of social robots and artificial companions "in action" more specifically, as well as regarding diagnoses of broader cultural patterns that accompany their development and use (2). Third, an account of artificial companions as "vehicles to cultural worlds of experience" (Pfadenhauer, 2014, 2015) is elaborated on in more detail, advocating a sociology of knowledge perspective for the analysis of people's dealings with social robots, the meanings attributed to social robots, and the latter's role in the everyday life and experience of their users (3).

1 Social robotics and artificial companionship

The development of social robots has been described as a new sub-field in the emerging field of "service robotics" which can be put in contrast with earlier applications of robotics in industrial and field settings (cf. Meister, 2014). In scientific discourse, discussion and development of "social robots" is a relatively recent phenomenon, with the concept having been taken up only in the last few decades, since the late 1990s. Since then, a number of definitions of what constitutes a social robot have been proposed and, since roughly the years 2014–2015, increased emphasis has been put on the problem as to what exactly defines the "sociality" of social robots (Sarrica et al., 2019). While definitions of social robots have somewhat varied, Sarrica et al. (ibid., p. 11) identify a number of commonly shared features that are usually evoked in scientific discourse:

> Overall, social robots are described as autonomous or semi-autonomous physical bodies that generally possess human- or animal-like qualities. In particular, these embodied agents perceive and respond to environmental cues, engage in social interactions, communicate, cooperate, learn, make decisions and perform actions. All these abilities become 'social' inasmuch as they are enacted by robots and evaluated by humans according to the community's goals and social norms.

The most pertinent area of application for social robots that has been promoted so far lies in the push to employ social robots in the care of elders. This has prominently been justified by a rhetoric of urgency regarding the ageing of society and corresponding needs to take care of the older parts of the population, not least in the face of problems of increasing social isolation, instances of loneliness, and lacking human personnel (Broadbent, 2017; Pedersen et al., 2018).

But also, for educational purposes (e.g., in language learning) and in the treatment of children with autism, social robots are conceived as potential supportive technologies (Broadbent, 2017). At the same time, applications of social robots in care arrangements that involve children and elders have prompted ethical concerns regarding robots' potential to "deceive" users by simulating social relationships that vulnerable people might come to rely on for emotional support; and related to this have been fears of "substitution" (i.e., the worry that the use of robots in care arrangements might deprive recipients of care of their human contacts; cf. van Oost & Reed, 2011). Furthermore, social robots have been developed as shopping mall guides, in the form of robotic toys and pets, robotic sex dolls, or as conversational agents as part of home entertainment systems (cf. Broadbent, 2017; Royakkers & van Est, 2015; McDuff & Czerwinski, 2018). As Fortunati (2018, p. 2674) argues, the development of social robotics thus represents a shift in the spatial dissemination of robots in society at large, which increasingly move out of industrial settings and into the domestic sphere of care and reproductive processes: The development of robotics is

> no longer confined to the industrial setting and workers but [has] expanded to the home and to social services, and as a consequence, to the elderly, children, women, and disabled people. In this vision, the targets of this new wave of robotics are the so-called 'weak social subjects,' and the labor that robots are required to address is immaterial and material care.

Hence, "the sectors that are likely to be penetrated by robots in the future are the reproduction sectors: domestic settings, healthcare, entertainment, education, communication and information, and the public sphere".

From a sociological point of view, strictly speaking, it can be argued that the notion of a social robot is in fact "a pleonastic definition since each technology is in itself social" (Fortunati 2018, p. 2679). To state the obvious, any technology is built by humans, with more or less clearly defined (social) purposes in mind, and with more or less clearly identifiable social implications and feedback mechanisms that come into effect with the introduction of new technologies. More specifically, concerning the capacity of artefacts to be perceived as agents to form social relationships with, a range of observations attest to a seemingly unlimited imagination on the side of humans to endow nonhuman, including inanimate, entities with qualities rendering them amenable for social interaction – often discussed under the header of "anthropomorphism" (cf. von Scheve, 2014; Broadbent, 2017). In the realm of technology more specifically, research on the "media equation" has shown "that people treat computers and other technologies as if they were human even though they know this is not the case", e.g., applying "stereotypical social categories, such as gender, ethnicity, and in-group and out-group status, when interacting with computers", or "overlearned social behaviors, such as politeness" (Broadbent, 2017, p. 640), and similar observations have been made regarding people's interactions with robots (ibid.).

In that broad sense, social robots are not as such more or less social than any other type of robot – or even than any other type of (nonhuman) entity. Insofar as the notion of social robotics refers to the development of an increasingly consolidated and coherent research field, then, a more precise criterion to delineate the field of social robotics would be to refer to the first-order constructions of researchers who aim to constitute an area of research in its own right, as against other fields of robotics (cf. Meister, 2014). In that sense, as Fortunati (2018, p. 2679) puts it, "it would be more correct to define social robots as robots that are *designed to be social*" (emphasis added). From a technological point of view, on the other hand, the design of social robots faces distinct challenges in comparison to other areas of application of robotic systems. As Meister (2014, p. 110) points out:

> Unlike Industrial Robots, which repeatedly do the same things in an accurately defined surrounding, and unlike Field Robots, which operate far away from humans, Service Robots are thought to operate in the habitat and in the presence of the most disturbing and unpredictable elements imaginable: ordinary human beings.

Or, to put it slightly differently, social behaviour and the actions to be carried out by social robots (e.g., care labor) appear to be less amenable to formalization than the tasks dealt with in other areas of robotics, and therefore entail specific challenges to social robots' design (cf. Fortunati, 2018).

Social robots are meant to fulfill a range of purposes, and they come in various shapes, sizes, and degrees of technological sophistication (cf. Meister, 2014; Royakkers & van Est, 2015; Broadbent, 2017; McDuff & Czerwinski, 2018). One of the most intriguing aims in this regard is to design artefacts that could serve as "artificial companions" to their human users (cf. van Oost & Reed, 2011; Böhle & Bopp, 2014; von Scheve, 2014; Pfadenhauer, 2014, 2015). In their discourse-analytical study, Böhle and Bopp (2014) demonstrate that since the beginning of 2000 the artificial companion metaphor has served as a guiding vision for a "new and emerging technology" in the interdisciplinary field of service robotics, artificial intelligence, and human-computer interaction. Of interest in the development of artificial companions "as either physical or digital entities is that they are sociable in some way, i.e. they have the potential to form social relationships with their human users or owners" (von Scheve, 2014, p. 68). Companionship implies that this type of bond is not merely situation-specific but rather cross-situational. Robotics researchers (and not only they) like to term it a "social relationship". For instance, among European projects on artificial companionship in the field of health care for the elderly, Böhle and Bopp (2014, p. 162) found a number of different connotations of the term *companion* – namely, "a guardian", "an assistant", and "a partner". In contrast to projects that take a monitoring or assistive approach to companionship, those that focus on partnership stress the emotional aspect. In other words, they aim to achieve the expression of emotionality on the part of the technological artefact and the evocation of feelings in the human counterpart.

Von Scheve specifies the notion of artificial companionship in more detail, summarizing the core elements usually highlighted in the literature on artificial companionship (2014, p. 68): first, "companions are supposed to be able to interact and communicate verbally or non-verbally with humans and 'understand' or even 'befriend' them, ideally in a 'humanlike' way"; second, "[a]rtificial companions should have some kind of 'personality' or be 'personally rich', have motivational concerns, be proactive, and – very generally – be believable and consistent in their behavior"; third, "sociability is usually seen as involving the capacity for emotionality and in particular to form emotional bonds with users", involving two basic capabilities: on the one hand, "artificial companions should exhibit emotional behavior and react emotionally to users' actions", and, on the other, they "should be capable of detecting and reacting to the emotions of their users in appropriate, i.e. socially acceptable ways" (ibid.). Commonly associated design features of artificial companions are then a "robotic" component "representing the autonomy of the device or agent"; a "social" component (in terms of an artificial companion's capability to interact with its users via various modalities, e.g., visual, auditory, or tactile channels); and a "humanoid" component "which means that a system is able to stimulate humanlike behavior and/or morphology" (ibid.).

The notion of artificial companionship, as a guiding vision and with a view on its technical realization, on the one hand, provides a paradigmatic case for sociological deliberations concerning new robotic technologies and their implications for novel forms of human-robot social relationships and in particular their emotional and affective dimensions. On the other hand, the artificial companion metaphor requires attention because such guiding visions serve not only as means of communication within the scientific community but also as vehicles for getting attention in the world beyond academia – and therefore they have an inherent normative power to shape one future among many possible futures of robotic technologies and humans' relationships with them (cf. Böhle & Bopp, 2014).

2 Sociology, "human-robot sociality", and emotions

So far, sociological engagements with social robotics have been rather rare. As Christian von Scheve notes, consideration of the affective and emotional qualities of interacting with nonhuman entities (such as robots) and their implications for the changing fabric of social relationships has so far largely been neglected in favor of the more basic question as to which status within social theory may be attributed to nonhuman entities in the first place: "In terms of sociological theory and social theory more generally, . . . interactions with nonhumans are primarily discussed in view of whether these are 'valid' social interactions at all" (2014, p. 80). Discussions of what may aptly be taken as constituting "social entities" as such has proven to be a vital battleground for social theorists of various backgrounds. At the same time, according to von Scheve, the "actual *social relationships* people form with artifacts" (ibid., p. 74; original emphasis) have received relatively little attention.

Especially within a Weberian paradigm according to which social action is defined to take place in a space of reciprocally oriented meaningful action, nonhuman entities have had no place to be considered as truly social actors (cf. von Scheve, 2014). There are, however, theoretical developments that have opened up new perspectives on this basic issue in social theory. Centering on the notion of "the social" in relation to material (or virtual) entities, these discussions are not necessarily concerned with robotic technologies as such, but they do inform basic understandings in regard to theorizing the nonhuman that by extension also apply to the field of interest at hand. In considering the status of nonhumans in social theory, roughly three prevalent approaches to the problem of "human-nonhuman sociality" can be distinguished (cf. Muhle, 2018 who himself proposes a systems theoretical approach to the problem; for a similar discussion of related approaches, see Pfadenhauer, 2014): First, along the lines of Actor-Network Theory, it has been argued that "the social" must not be restricted to the realm of human action in the first place but has to be conceptualized as an inherently hybrid collective of human and nonhuman actants. The agentic interrelations between these, that is, the networks they unfold, are given priority over anthropocentric conceptions of human action. Sociality is distributed among humans and nonhumans alike, stripping human action of its privileged place in social theory altogether. This approach stands in stark contrast to, second, a broadly conceived social constructivist perspective, according to which sociality is a matter of historically contingent attributions of sociality and agency to nonhuman entities by culturally situated human actors. The status of "proper" social actor within this perspective, however, typically remains reserved for humans. Third, sociality has been conceived of in terms of a gradualized spectrum of human and nonhuman agencies contributing to a given program of action, somewhat assuming a middle ground between the first and second positions.

Besides such basic considerations regarding the fundamentals of social theory and the non-human, in the meantime there have also been attempts to address the phenomenon of social robotics more directly, and, again, in varying ways. To begin with, the contributions of Meister (2014) and Alač et al. (2011) provide good examples for contrasting approaches that have been taken to the sociality of social robots, which could be labeled "internalist" on the one hand, and "externalist" on the other. Thus, Meister (2014) is concerned with devising an "architectural blueprint" for the "robot sociologicus". To do so, Meister draws on Hartmut Esser's theory of social action, with reference to the notion of generalized expectations and the routine character of most social activity. According to this view, whether or not a robot is capable to successfully act as a social actor depends on the alignment of its actions with the generalized expectations held by the social actors with whom the robot is confronted in a given situation. Importantly, the "idea of the robot sociologicus is not about artificial sociality in a substantial sense" but about the "transfer of an abstract principle to the architecture of a robot or the modeling of man-robot interaction" (Meister, 2014, p. 128). In other words, it does not touch upon the question of whether a robot is "really" social, but rather if it is capable to act in a *sufficiently competent* manner in situations of human-robot interaction. The key to competent action in this perspective lies in the internal architecture of the robot and its capability to process, memorize, and learn to adapt to generalized expectations of social actors on various levels, ranging from the enactment of the social role to the recognition of broader cultural norms and values.

Diametrically opposed to Meister's proposal is Alač et al.'s (2011) study of the collective enactment of a robots' sociality in the design process. Drawing on an ethnomethodological framework, among others, Alač et al. claim that to understand "the robot's social character means one has to look beyond the robot's computational architecture and its human-like appearance and behavior" and thus "that the social effects of the robot cannot be explained in terms of the designers as demiurgic beings" (ibid., p. 897). That is, the authors argue against a straightforward connection between roboticists' efforts to optimize the internal architecture of a robot on the one hand, and people's perception of its social character, on the other. Rather, the appearance of a robot's sociality is the outcome of a "multiparty interactional coordination" that "allows a technological object to take on social attributes typically reserved for humans" (ibid., p. 894). Drawing on their observations from a laboratory study of a design process in social robotics, the authors (ibid., p. 919) then argue that

> the robot is in fact social, but its social character does not exclusively reside inside the boundaries of its physical body or in its programming. . . . As the roboticists, toddlers, and their teachers engage in the design practice, the robot becomes a social creature in and through the interactional routines performed in the 'extended' laboratory.

Especially concerning the dimension of emotion and affect, an important stimulus for debates in sociology concerning the potential of artificial companions to change the fabric of social relations in contemporary society has been the work done by Sherry Turkle (cf. von Scheve, 2014; Pfadenhauer, 2015). Not least complicating the boundary between (virtual) social media technologies and (embodied) social robotics, Turkle has promoted the argument that people increasingly tend to substitute face-to-face relationships with other humans by such that are either mediated by technology or dispense of human relations altogether by instead forming emotional bonds with inanimate objects such as artificial companions (cf. Pfadenhauer, 2015). Turkle (2010) advances three cultural trends that accompany her observations. These are: first, a general "culture of simulation" (ibid., p. 9) prevailing in modern societies, which gradually relegates notions of 'authenticity' from a hitherto desirable attribute to the realm of taboo;

second, a cultural emphasis that is increasingly put on the appropriateness of observable outward behaviour, rather than on "human inner states" (ibid., p. 8); and, third, a generalized "fatigue" with human relations brought about by increasing emotional and social demands both in private life and in work that renders relationships with robots amenable alternatives to interactions with other humans which are often perceived as more stressful (cf. von Scheve, 2014). To this argument attest a number of Turkle's ethnographic observations of people's encounters with robotic technologies, and companion systems in particular:

> Importantly, her observations suggest that many people (primarily children and the elderly) act towards artificial companions in perfectly 'social' ways with little differences to interactions with humans. It also seems that for many, the distinctions between aliveness and inanimateness become blurred and they perceive some robots and artificial companions as (almost) 'living' things. . . . Moreover, Turkle . . . reports that many perceive interactions with artificial companions as less stressful, demanding, and exhausting than interactions in human relationships and in many cases would prefer interacting with robots to interactions with humans.
>
> *(von Scheve, 2014, p. 74)*

Christian von Scheve (2014) and van Oost and Reed (2011), starting from similar observations, provide further exemplary sociological framings of humans' interactions with social robots, both with an explicit emphasis on the dimensions of affect and emotion which lie at the core of visions of artificial companionship and their supposed potential to form long-term relationships with humans.

Drawing on Randall Collins' theory of interaction, ritual chains, and Jonathan Turner's sociological theory of emotion, von Scheve (2014) argues that

> emotional gratification and the fulfilling of certain transactional needs are crucial for actors to repeatedly engage in social interactions with others . . . and for the social relational implications that (positive) emotional energy implies, namely solidarity and feelings of belonging as a basis for the formation of relationships.
>
> *(ibid., pp. 76–77)*

In particular, participants in interaction rituals experience emotional gratification when they share a focus of attention as well as a common mood, both of which von Scheve suggests to be "amongst the phenomena users tend to attribute or ascribe to artificial companions" (ibid., p. 77). Further, we already hinted at humans' apparent propensity to anthropomorphize all sorts of animate and inanimate entities (cf. von Scheve, 2014; Broadbent, 2017). However, according to von Scheve, the ascription of a shared mood and focus of attention "is a process that probably does not apply to any inanimate object" but is facilitated by artificial companions' capacities to move and perform relatively autonomous action, and that seem to occur also in some interactions with animals and pets, especially dogs (ibid., p. 77).

Importantly, von Scheve's argument does not rely on whether ascribed emotional experiences (i.e. the perception of shared moods in artificial companions) do indeed have an authentic basis. Instead, von Scheve draws on a "shallow model of emotion" arguing that "[t]o account for the requirements of shared moods, the impression that artificial companions have emotions *at all* is crucial". Hence, "the mere impression that an artifact is emotionally responsive in the first place (e.g., via facial or verbal expressions) might suffice to generate outcomes of emotional energy" (ibid., p. 78). Similar to the argument provided by Meister (2014), this conception therefore circumvents "the hard problems of AI" by drawing attention to the outcomes of interactions with robots, rather than to the inherently human or nonhuman (cognitive or emotive) aspects of the interaction. In that sense, the design of artificial companions, at least in the foreseeable future, "rel[ies] more on implementing 'doing emotion' than on technically realizing the whole bottom-up architecture of human emotion" (von Scheve, 2014, pp. 79–80).

Van Oost and Reed (2011) take as a starting point for their sociological conceptualization of robot companions a criticism of prevalent "single point" frameworks employed in human-robot interaction (HRI) studies, that is, the latter's focus on bilateral interactions which suppose "an idealized relationship based upon communicative action between two essentially isolated individuals" suggesting "a singular relationship between an isolated robotic artifact and an emotional human being". In this view, "[t]he robot is seen to evoke in the human a vast array of emotions that result in intimate ties between person and human" (ibid., p. 11). However, as van Oost and Reed argue, this conception largely ignores the "wider social context with different actors and stakeholders involved" (ibid., p. 13), which all contribute to the shaping of human-robot interaction dynamics. Referring to research on robots in health care organizations and particularly their deployment in different medical units, they argue the shortcomings of this approach. Such research has shown considerable variability regarding the acceptance of robots in different departments of a hospital where different workflows, patient profiles, and interpersonal relations structure daily practices. Drawing inspiration from ecological and organizational analyses of technology, van Oost and Reed therefore propose to refine HRI studies by reference to Actor-Network Theory, arguing that "[a]dequate appropriation of new artificial companion technology will . . . depend . . . on how companion robots fit in and transform the wider actor-network that constitutes the care setting". Emotional bonds are then "not only a matter of bilateral relation between user and companion, but also a matter of *distributed emotional agency* over the whole complex care network, the robotic companion being only one actor" (ibid., p. 16; original emphasis).

To fully grasp the "contemporary appeal of artificial companions" (Pfadenhauer, 2015), it is necessary to go beyond situations of immediate interactions between humans and robots, and to also consider the broader social and cultural trends in which they take place. The previously discussed trends identified by Turkle (2010) are one way in which human-robot interactions have come to be contextualized. In one way, they are reminiscent of sociological diagnoses relating to ongoing processes of individualization in contemporary (Western) society and corresponding changes in the nature and structure of social relationships that challenge and overburden humans (cf. Pfadenhauer, 2015). In another way, they attest to processes that relate to the technological dimension of new robotic technologies more specifically, and the ways these have increasingly become a part of everyday life and experience. Fortunati, for instance, discusses various forms of "proto-robotization of the immaterial sphere in society", arguing that

> [t]he robotization of the domestic sphere can take place because a series of processes, developing through smartphones and the Internet and addressing individuals, have silently reshaped the general attitude toward automation. In the new millennium, individuals are trained to feel themselves as appendages of a society transformed through widespread automatization and/or robotic systems.
>
> *(2018, pp. 2682–2683; see also Pfadenhauer, 2015,*
> *for a discussion of related diagnoses)*

Fortunati (2018, pp. 2682–2685) calls on five interrelated areas of this "proto-robotization": 1) in terms of *communication* via the Internet, human communication has increasingly come to take place in a space that narrows communication down to the cues transmittable via electronic media, and bots have contributed to a standardization, simplification, and trivialization of respective social interactions; 2) concerning the consumption of *information*, automation processes become apparent in the introduction of algorithms to more efficiently deliver reporting to be consumed in everyday life; 3) *social behaviours* have become automated in so far as "[t]he multitudes' thoughts, tastes, emotions, confidences to friends, declarations of love, sexual preferences, strategies of dating, purchases and sales, ideological adhesions, and so on are nowadays subject to the mediation of online platforms, services and applications". For instance, one effect of this has been the simplification of respective interactions, as exemplified by the binary logic of the like/dislike button, which "has enabled billions of people to participate in several forms of self-expression and communication but at the cost of reducing their complexity and particularity"; 4) the *human body* increasingly becomes a site of robotization associated with new kinds of self-presentation, fashion, and beauty; and, finally, 5) also the *machines people are already familiar with* in their everyday life (such as cars, domestic appliances, ICTs) are getting increasingly robotized, as can be seen, for example, in current trends towards the development of automated driving technologies. Similar processes are pointed out by Pfadenhauer (2015), particularly with reference to pervasive processes of "medialization" and "mediatization" as a crucial background for humans' contemporary interactions with robots, as will be discussed in the next section.

3 Social robots as vehicles to cultural worlds of experience

This section lays out a conceptualization of artificial companions as "vehicles to cultural worlds of experience" (drawing on prior publications by Pfadenhauer, 2014, 2015). The argument starts with the phenomenon of "universal projection" (Luckmann, 1983), humans' ubiquitous capability to animate their material surroundings, which in the case of (social) robotics gains further traction against the background of largely mediatized life-worlds in contemporary societies. Social robots understood as such "vehicles to cultural worlds of experience", from the perspective of the sociology of knowledge, can be analyzed as both "objectivations" and "institutions" (cf. Berger & Luckmann, 1966), interacting with their users' experiential backgrounds, as well as more broadly shared stocks of knowledge circulating in society. While many concerns in the field of social robotics suggest a focus on the concrete interaction with a social robot (cf. van Oost & Reed, 2011), the sociology of knowledge approach to social robotics advanced here thus seeks to broaden the perspective by calling for a systematic consideration not only of the actual contexts of use of social robotic systems but also of the experiential backgrounds of their users and designers in a broader sense. Rather than asking for standardizable features of robotic systems, and the definite parameters of a situation that would allow for considering a particular human–machine interaction as "socially believable" or "valid", therefore, the adopted perspective holds that what a technology eventually turns out to be regarded as being and how it actually becomes embedded in (everyday) contexts of use is never determined by its technical design alone. Rather, its performative deployment always also relates to the interplay of first-hand experiences and interpretation offers made available by others. The sociology of knowledge approach discussed in the following thus constitutes a change of perspective. Attention is shifted away from the question of what robots (allegedly) do – namely, communicate and interact – and what they (allegedly) do to us – namely, transform us into beings who expect less from sociality (cf. Pfadenhauer, 2015). The focus is directed towards the question of what we do with robots when, or to the extent that, we incorporate them into our activities. Of particular interest here are a) the meanings which are objectified in technical artefacts, b) the importance which materiality gains via institutionalization, and c) the meanings that users associate with these technical artefacts by using them as vehicles to cultural worlds of experience.

Universal projection is the term Thomas Luckmann (1983) uses to denote human beings' innate capacity to project their own "living body" – a synthesis of consciousness and corporeality – onto everything they encounter in the world. What is characteristic about the evidence of this universal projection or "personifying apperception" (Wundt, 1896, cited in Luckmann, 1983, p. 51) is the fact that it is always "circumstantial" – that is, an interpretation on the part of the individual. As Luckmann (ibid., p. 53) argues, "I do not directly experience the 'inside' of the thing to which the sense 'living body' is transferred". This applies equally to the projection of the sense "living body" onto inanimate objects and conscious beings. However, the living body of another subject is registered not only as a part of one's environment but also as a "field of expression" of that subject's experiences (Schütz, 1972, p. 153). The intriguing consequence is that "the other can be, in principle, everything the actor is oriented to intentionally" (Knoblauch, 2013a, footnote 20).

According to Luckmann (1983, p. 55), this universal projection is called into question, when objects display physiognomic immobility (1), when they are immobile (2), and when they cannot communicate (3). The significance of Luckmann's deliberations for researching social robotics becomes obvious if we consider that by taking the exact opposite of each point on his list, one obtains the very dimensions that are being intensively researched in the field of social robotics, namely: flexible physiognomy (dynamic mimicry) (1), mobility (autonomous rather than externally controlled spatial movement) (2), and communication ability (verbal and gestural skills) (3). These same factors are also echoed by Sherry Turkle in her research on children's encounters with social robots. Thus, in *The Second Self*, Turkle (1984, p. 41) notes that the factors prompting children to locate robotized language computers "between the inanimate and the animate" are: autonomous motion, that is, the execution of spatial movements that are not initiated by the user; automatic language output that can be interpreted as the ability to converse; and the expression of apparent emotionality by means of technical features reminiscent of facial expressions, gestures, and vocalizations (see also von Scheve, 2014; Broadbent, 2017).

The concept of "mediatization", on the other hand, captures both quantitative (the omnipresence of media – "medialization") and qualitative dimensions (the ways in which media technology overcomes spatial and temporal borders – "mediation") of changes in communicative action (Knoblauch, 2013b). Central to these processes is what Knoblauch (ibid., p. 310) refers to as "the transgression of what used to be the primacy of the face-to-face situation". Besides the spatiotemporal experiential distance, which is overcome via media communication, an essential characteristic of the indirectness of mediatized communicative action is a certain degree of anonymization. That is to say, the interlocutor is perceived only as a type, and communication calls for greater typecasting. In other words, it proceeds in a more stylized manner or to a greater extent within "communicative forms" (i.e. the results of communicative action "which constitute the institutions of the communicative culture of a society", ibid., p. 297) than is the case in a face-to-face situation.

Just as some interaction partners in face-to-face situations are of interest only as incumbents of a particular role (e.g., salesperson or mail carrier), so too in mediatized communication does one encounter only a "segment" of the personality of the other person. This is related to both the mode of communication (e.g., on the telephone, one perceives the voice of the other person but not their facial or gestural expressions), and to the interaction partners themselves. Irrespective of how multifaceted my relationship to a person may be, mediatized communication allows me to address him in the role and for the purpose that is relevant to me at a particular point in time: as my intimate partner, to send a message of endearment; as my roommate, to remind him to put out the garbage can; as the local expert, to find out how to get from A to

B; as the man of manners, to seek advice on etiquette, etc. Seen in this way, even though many artificial companion technologies (at least at the present time) seem rather limited in the range of "communicative offers" they are capable of making, mediatized communication may be seen to facilitate the cultivation of exactly such restricted, but in a sense less diffuse, relationships, which are attuned to one's needs and mood at a particular point in time.

Against this double background of human's inert capacity for animating their surroundings, on the one hand, and the pandering conditions of mediatization that encourage them to do so in the case of social robots in particular, on the other, artificial companions are neither humans' counterparts in social relationships nor are they a meaningless medium for shaping social relations. Rather, we argue that the fascination of robots as a new technology stems from what Goffman calls the "astounding complex", which he defines as follows:

> An event occurs or is made to occur that leads observers to doubt their overall approach to events, for it seems that, to account for the occurrence, new kinds of natural forces will have to be allowed or new kinds of guiding capacities.
>
> *(1974, p. 28)*

This allows us to immerse ourselves in fantasy worlds – and robots are obviously one of many suitable vehicles for this purpose. Their suitability is enhanced by the fascination that all novelties exert.

With these vehicles, the framework conditions for such exceptional worlds of experience are prefabricated *by others* for consumption by the experiencing subject (cf. Hitzler, 2008). Both Scholtz's (2008) reports of his experiences with his AIBO (a robotic pet released by Sony in 1999 and discontinued in 2006), and the many comments by children about their Tamagotchis, Furbies, My Real Babies, etc. cited by Turkle (2011), show that this world of experience is also perceived by the experiencing subject as prefabricated, or made available, by others. Turkle (2011, p. 57) reports that eight-year-old Brenda claimed "in a knowing tone that 'people make robots and . . . people come from God or from eggs, but this doesn't matter when you are playing with the robot'". And Scholtz's (2008) account of his experiences with his AIBO shows that not only children but also many adults are willing to allow themselves to be transported via robots to these new cultural worlds of experience that are communicatively generated and sustained. This also means that these users redefine, or explain away, design- and construction-related imperfections so that they do not impair the special experience.

For instance, although AIBO's zoomorphic design lends itself to comparison with a household pet, this analogy is pointedly undermined by a number of design decisions. For example, no version of AIBO relieves itself; in contrast to Tamagotchi, an explicit reference to death was avoided (Scholtz, 2008, p. 218); and when the pet autonomously approaches the charging station and self-docks, no associations with feeding or sleeping are prompted. However, various elements, such as light-emitting diodes and acoustic signals, are aimed at creating the impression – at least temporarily – of an alive other. This is evidenced by Christopher Scholtz's entries in the research diary he kept while he was living with an AIBO. For example, the entry on 31 July 2003 reads:

> Aibo's movements make a stronger impression than those of simple electrical robots. . . . His real movements make sounds that can be located exactly in the room and transmit vibrations in a way that no loudspeaker system can. I am sitting on the bed beside Galato, . . . his tail is wagging the whole time. This produces slight vibrations, which are transmitted via the mattress and which I can feel. I have a strong feeling that there is a living thing

beside me; all cognitive concepts fail in this case; one reacts to something like this directly and without reflection.

(2008, p. 235; our translation)

Contrasting with such observations, on the other hand, are situations in which the AIBO's behaviour provoked irritations regarding the impression of its aliveness and the situationally felt reciprocity between AIBO and its owner. As Scholtz (2008, p. 247) noted in his field journal on 4 November 2003 (our translation):

I was standing in the bathroom and looking into my room through the half-open door. He was sitting there and I called out [his name]. . . . He turned his head completely to the right and looked at me. Whether it was a coincidence or not, it was a very strong effect, I could not but regard him as being alive. However, he then turned his head back to the forward position, looked up expectantly, and wagged his tail as if someone was standing in front of him. That showed that the fact that he located me was probably a coincidence after all.

Observations like the ones just referred to are the reason why we assign plausibility to Scholtz's thesis (2008, pp. 296 ff.) that the appeal of such entertainment robots has to do with "playing with ambiguity", in other words, with accepting the semblance of animate rather than inanimate material, of contingency rather than causality, etc. This willingness to engage with the artefact allows us to immerse ourselves briefly in a world of experience. Artificial companions (such as avatars, toys, etc.) are vehicles to such worlds. When worlds of experience are prefabricated and experienced as prefabricated, Hitzler (2008) classifies them as *cultural* worlds of experience that are communicatively generated and sustained. The thesis of the robot as a vehicle to such worlds of experience implies both the orientation towards a fascinating, impressive, irritating, absorbing object and the capacity of human consciousness to regard this object as something different and exceptional and to relocate to a thereby constituted world of experience. The way in which we interpret the object depends on its configuration or design but it is not pre-determined. The notions of "objectivation" and "objectification" allow to further elaborate on this point.

Generally speaking, objectivation means "the embodiment of subjective processes in the objects and events of the everyday life world" (Schütz & Luckmann, 1973, p. 264). These events can be verbal utterances or, as in the case of the finger-pointing example, physical acts, such as gestures or facial expressions. However, subjective processes are not embodied only in forms of expression and actions but also in objects, in the sense of the results of actions. Materialization is a fundamental stage in the process by which "the externalized products of human activity attain the character of objectivity" (Berger & Luckmann, 1966, p. 78). Objectification, then, is a) the process in which the individual apprehends the subjectively meaningful things that he externalizes – that is, the things that he does, says, shows, or produces – and makes them part of his consciousness, and b) the process that makes subjective knowledge social, that is intersubjectively accessible: "Because they [objectivations, MP] are products of action (*Erzeugnisse*), they are *ipso facto* evidence (*Zeugnisse*) of what went on in the mind of the actors who made them" (Schütz, 1972 [1932], p. 133). Whether a robot is perceived as a product or as evidence of what went on in the mind of the maker is a question of interpretation. The person to whom it is presented as a product can interpret it as an object per se, that is, as independent of its maker. If he focuses his attention on what went on in the mind of the maker then he can regard it as evidence (cf. ibid.).

An artificial companion, then, is a suitable vehicle to cultural worlds of experience because – or if – we treat it as a product endowed with a "universal meaning . . . that is independent of its maker and the circumstances of its origination" (Schütz, 1972 [1932], p. 135). This interpretation is encouraged mainly by its designation as a *social* robot, by the instructions for use, and by the interpretation schemata made available by the media. Besides this "objective meaning" (ibid.) of the product, we also endeavor to grasp its subjective meaning, in other words, *"the meaning-context within which the product stands or stood in the mind of the producer"* (Schütz, 1972 [1932], p. 133, original emphasis), and the conscious experiences which that person had (ibid., p. 135). However, an understanding of the objective-meaning context does not suffice as a basis for inferring subjective meaning because objective meaning "is abstracted from and independent of particular persons" (ibid., p. 135) and therefore refers back to a highly anonymous ideal type of producer. As Schütz (1972, p. 84 f.) points out, "My experiences of things and events in the life-world, of tools and artifacts in the broadest sense, contain references to the social world – to the world of my contemporaries and my forefathers".

Berger and Luckmann (1966) focus more on institutionalization than on this specific aspect of objectivation. An institution generally refers to "a 'permanent' solution to a 'permanent' problem of a given collectivity" (ibid., p. 87). These permanent solutions to fundamental problems are a product of interaction. They arise when a person solves a problem the same way for such a long time that it becomes a routine and these routinized actions are apprehended by another person as a certain type of action sequence by a certain type of actor: "Institutionalization occurs whenever there is a reciprocal typification of habitualized actions by types of actors. Put differently, any such typification is an institution" (ibid., p. 72). The process of habitualization is followed by a typification process in the course of which habitualized actions become independent, as it were. In other words, they detach themselves from the concrete life problems and concrete actors and become part of the common stock of knowledge. In this form they are passed on to the next generation. However, they are not only taught but also explained and justified as being expedient and appropriate. In other words, they are cognitively and normatively legitimated.

Following Rammert (2006), within the approach proposed here it is suggested that robots can be analytically located as institutions – that is, as patterns of problem-solving actions that serve as orientation and are transferred from generation to generation as knowledge. Technical artefacts, such as robots, are institutions in the sense that they always imply a certain way of dealing with them that is considered expedient and appropriate (cf. Rammert, 2006). Moreover, an institution not only regulates how an activity is typically carried out but also what actors (for example, technicians, nurses, consumers, patients with dementia) participate in the execution of these activities. And these actors participate as role players – in other words, with only part of their personality.

As an illustrating – albeit at this point speculative – example for the interplay between functional design features of social robots and people's appropriation of them as vehicles to cultural worlds of experience, Dautenhahn's (2007) analysis of the two main paradigms underlying "socially intelligent" robots is instructive. Under the "caretaker paradigm", humans take care of robots and learn social behaviour in the process. The "companion paradigm", by contrast, regards robots as caretakers who respond to humans' needs. However, under this paradigm, the artefact is conceived of as a companion only in the narrow sense of the word, namely as an assistant or a servant. According to Becker et al. (2013), most of the robotic devices currently established on the market – such as AIBO, Pleo, and, above all, PARO, the baby seal pet-therapy robot designed for use in nursing homes and hospitals – fit the caretaker paradigm. This is because artefacts suited to this purpose make high demands on the outward appearance – which is often zoomorphic – whereas the demands on sensors, active components, and mechanics are lower. By encouraging people to take care of a technical artefact, devices of this type are supposed to stimulate the kind of pro-social behaviour that people with autism have not developed and people with dementia gradually lose. Robots that fit the companion paradigm, on the other hand, must be able to support individual behaviours through personalization. This calls for high-tech machines that can operate safely in a relatively unstructured environment.

The norming character of this technology as an institution seems to be inversely proportional to its sophistication. In the caretaker paradigm humans are required to adapt to the robot, whereas the companion paradigm holds out the prospect of a technology that can adequately adapt to human idiosyncrasies and relevancies. To put it bluntly: Robots that fit the caretaker paradigm appear rather to activate the aspect of coercion exercised by institutions, whereas robots that fit the companion paradigm offer several options for usage. And as companion robots respond to humans' needs, they tend, first, to be more personified and, second, to be more sophisticated. However, it seems that robots which fit the companion paradigm would be superior as vehicles to worlds of experience. This argument, however, is of course yet to be confirmed by empirical investigation, and it might also be the case that different users respond in different ways to the features indicated by Dautenhahn's (2007) typology.

Concluding remarks

Many discussions concerning the introduction of social robots into everyday life oscillate between two opposing perceptions of robots' capabilities, and the benefits and potential dangers associated with them: "On the one hand, robots are often seen as competitors of humans, and their limitations are exaggerated in order to demonstrate that they are much less than humans" as a "reassuring strategy that aims to convince people that they are the undisputed protagonists of the society" – while, on the other hand, often by their designers, "robot's virtues are exaggerated" (Fortunati et al., 2018, p. 149). While the trope of the (social) robot nowadays has come "to circulate with the regularity of consumable goods", it has been noted that as robotic technologies increasingly pervade everyday culture, "the majority of the European population conceptualizes robots on the basis of cultural inputs such as science fiction literature, movies, and cartoons" which largely inform people's first interactions with respective technologies (ibid., 2018, pp. 143, 142). That many encounters with actually existing robots are, in fact, frequently perceived as rather "poor and disappointing" may therefore be attributed to a "tension between the imagery in the media and the pragmatic experience of actual interactions with robots today" (Sarrica et al., 2019, p. 4). Such tensions are obviously not least a result of the great (technological) difficulties to be overcome in the development of social robots in the sense envisaged by their engineers but presumably also due the heterogeneity of users and their varying expectations and experiential backgrounds.

While expectations directed towards the development of social robots vary widely, much (sociological) discourse has focused on whether or not robots may actually be perceived as valid social actors to begin with, or how to (sociologically) meaningfully describe interactions between humans and robots. Many approaches ask whether in actual interactions "anthropomorphizing" or "emotional relationships" are indeed realized, and thus, in a sense, ask about the conditions of successful social interaction between humans and machines. The sociology of knowledge perspective on social robotics takes up these points but also asks in what contexts of experience and in relation to which stocks of knowledge "successful" or "unsuccessful" interactions between humans and robots take place, what concrete meaning these interactions have from the perspective of designers and users, and how they become empirically manifest in the cultural worlds of experience constituted in specific interactions between humans and robots. An influential trope in discourse on social robotics has been Sherry Turkle's (e.g., 2011) argument concerning the potentially harmful effects of humans' interactions with artificial companions, as they may divert people from engaging with more meaningful interactions with other humans. On the other hand, although we do not want to exclude this possibility in detail, we are interested in the manifold and diverse ways in which social robots such as artificial companions may become appropriated as vehicles to cultural worlds of experience.

References

Alač, M., Movellan, J., & Tanaka, F. (2011). When a robot is social: Spatial arrangements and multimodal semiotic engagement in the practice of social robotics. *Social Studies of Science*, *41*(6), 893–926.

Becker, H., Scheermesser, M., Früh, M., Treusch, Y., Auerbach, H., Hüppi, R. A., & Meier, F. (2013). *Robotik in Betreuung und Gesundheitsversorgung*. ETH Zurich.

Berger, P. L., & Luckmann, T. (1966). *The social construction of reality*. Penguin Books.

Böhle, K., & Bopp, K. (2014). What a vision: The artificial companion. A piece of vision assessment including an expert survey. *Science, Technology & Innovation Studies*, *10*(1), 32.

Broadbent, E. (2017). Interactions with robots: The truths we reveal about ourselves. *Annual Review of Psychology*, *68*(1), 627–652.

Dautenhahn, K. (2007). Socially intelligent robots: Dimensions of human – robot interaction. *Philosophical Transactions of the Royal Society B: Biological Sciences*, *362*(1480), 679–704.

Fortunati, L. (2018). Robotization and the domestic sphere. *New Media & Society*, *20*(8), 2673–2690.

Fortunati, L., Sarrica, M., Ferrin, G., Brondi, S., & Honsell, F. (2018). Social robots as cultural objects: The sixth dimension of dynamicity? *The Information Society*, *34*(3), 141–152.

Goffman, E. (1974). *Frame Analysis*. Harvard University Press.

Hitzler, R. (2008). Von der Lebenswelt zu den Erlebniswelten Ein phänomenologischer Weg in soziologische Gegenwartsfragen. In *Phänomenologie und Soziologie* (pp. 131–140). VS Verlag für Sozialwissenschaften.

Knoblauch, H. (2013a). Alfred Schutz' theory of communicative action. *Human Studies*, *36*(3), 323–337.

Knoblauch, H. (2013b). Communicative constructivism and mediatization. *Communication Theory*, *23*(3), 297–315.

Luckmann, T. (1983). On the boundaries of the social world. In T. Luckmann (Ed.), *Life-world and social realities* (pp. 40–67). Heinemann.

McDuff, D., & Czerwinski, M. (2018). Designing emotionally sentient agents. *Communications of the ACM*, *61*(12), 74–83.

Meister, M. (2014). When is a robot really social? An outline of the robot sociologicus. *Science, Technology & Innovation Studies*, *10*(1), 107–134.

Muhle, F. (2018). Sozialität von und mit Robotern? Drei soziologische Antworten und eine kommunikationstheoretische Alternative. *Zeitschrift für Soziologie*, *47*(3), 147–163.

Pedersen, I., Reid, S., & Aspevig, K. (2018). Developing social robots for aging populations: A literature review of recent academic sources. *Sociology Compass*, *12*(6), e12585.

Pfadenhauer, M. (2014). On the sociality of social robots. A sociology-of-knowledge perspective. *Science, Technology & Innovation Studies*, *10*(1), 135–154.

Pfadenhauer, M. (2015). The contemporary appeal of artificial companions: Social robots as vehicles to cultural worlds of experience. *The Information Society*, *31*(3), 284–293.

Rammert, W. (2006). Die technische Konstruktion als Teil der gesellschaftlichen Konstruktion der Wirklichkeit. In D. Tänzler, H. Knoblauch, & H.-G. Soeffner (Eds.), *Zur Kritik der Wissensgesellschaft* (pp. 83–100). UVK Verlagsgesellschaft.

Royakkers, L., & van Est, R. (2015). A literature review on new robotics: Automation from love to war. *International Journal of Social Robotics*, *7*(5), 549–570.

Sarrica, M., Brondi, S., & Fortunati, L. (2019). How many facets does a "social robot" have? A review of scientific and popular definitions online. *Information Technology & People*, *33*(1), 1–21.

Scholtz, C. P. (2008). *Alltag mit künstlichen Wesen: Theologische Implikationen eines Lebens mit subjektsimulierenden Maschinen am Beispiel des Unterhaltungsroboters AIBO*. Vandenhoeck & Ruprecht.

Schütz, A. (1972). *The phenomenology of the social world*. Northwestern University Press.
Schütz, A., & Luckmann, T. (1973). *The structures of the life-world* (Vol. 1). Northwestern University Press.
Turkle, S. (1984). *The second self: Computers and the human spirit*. Simon & Schuster.
Turkle, S. (2010). In good company? On the threshold of robotic companions. In Y. Wilks (Ed.), *Close engagements with artificial companions: Key social, psychological, ethical and design issues* (pp. 3–10). John Benjamins.
Turkle, S. (2011). *Alone together: Why we expect more from technology and less from each other*. Basic Books.
van Oost, E., & Reed, D. (2011). Towards a sociological understanding of robots as companions. In M. H. Lamers & F. J. Verbeek (Eds.), *Human-robot personal relationships* (pp. 11–18). Springer Berlin Heidelberg.
von Scheve, C. (2014). Interaction rituals with artificial companions: From media equation to emotional relationships. *Science, Technology & Innovation Studies, 10*(1), 65–83.

7
Anthropology, AI and robotics

Joffrey Becker

The technical advances in artificial intelligence and robotics fuel many predictions and controversies. They appear as a good mean to represent how natural processes work. But they also convey representations about how humans think these processes, which redefines the relations between science, technology and nature by shifting the boundaries separating living bodies from their mechanical imitations. This challenge raised by research practices invites us to think not only about how natural processes become artifacts but also about the new place occupied by the techniques of artificial intelligence and robotics and their effects on social links. Of course this shift doesn't come from nowhere.

Since the late eighteenth century, the advent of industrial machinism has induced a deep transformation of the relationship our species always had with techniques. It involves a form of desensitization (Ingold, 1988), which establishes a separation between conception and realization. Using machines that imitate human action, the work itself can be thought independently of human action onto matter. The techniques slowly becomes technology. The practice becomes algorithm and the work activity can now be thought through the mere forces it needs, putting the ability of the human hand and skillful work aside. In this context, the ability to manipulate tools is transferred to the machines as the body itself becomes a mechanism, or even a tool, in the production chain.

With artificial intelligence and robotics, engineering is no longer just about designing artifacts which imitate and exceed the ability of human workers. Nowadays machines are more sensitive than ever before. They "see", "listen", "learn", "make decisions", and they tend to integrate more and more spaces once reserved to human beings. Homes, hospitals, elderly care centers, banks, schools, administrations, cities or even battlefields are now concerned by a process of a mass automatization. How can anthropology help this shift? What is at stake and how can we address the socio-technical systems relating humans to so-called intelligent devices? Artificial intelligence and robotics convey many representations about the evolution of life and techniques, the human body, communication, social relations and more broadly on organizations and society. They constitute therefore a privileged object for anthropological inquiry.

Joffrey Becker

1 A framework for anthropology

Robots and artificial intelligence–based artifacts raise the interest of an increasing number of actors. They convey conflicting ideas about the future. And, in a way, these visions are always associated with their image. A first vision promises a bright future. Machines, at once friends and slaves, construct for us a world freed from work; a world of leisure, where technology can potentially enable us to access immortality. Another, darker, promises the opposite. It's a world where humans have been overtaken by tools that perform better than them.

Research performed today by specialists is in some way always crossed by these hopes and fears, and always plays on the domestic universe or the themes of cooperation and assistance, relying on the dreamlike world of techno-scientific utopia while seeking to protect it from its risks. Everything must be done to ease their acceptance in our daily lives. Because the fear associated with the presence of intelligent devices is also that of their inventors; a fear that these machines could amplify technophobic feels, naively reminding us of the time of machine breakers[1] (Hobsbawm, 1952). In such a case, the most reluctant national economies could not challenge countries where public and private actors have already heavily invested in these technologies.

Doubts persist, sometimes relayed by roboticists and computer scientists themselves. Are robots our friends or our enemies? Should we be afraid of these machines? Robotics and artificial intelligence are perhaps even crossed by older anxieties, the fear of the figure of double, of objects that could come to life, the Promethean fear of exceeding the limits of the human experience. A dark magic seems at work when it comes to these machines, which can only be countered by the implementation of other techniques of enchantment in order to allow humans to project on these artifacts a kind of trust that machines are yet unable to experience. Artificial intelligence and robotics take shape between the dreams of entrepreneurs and the nightmare that we could one day live in a society of automatons. How can anthropology help understand this inherent complexity associated to research and development in computer sciences and mechanical engineering?

Jessica Riskin (2003) has shown how the paradoxical dynamics of the imitation of nature, already evoked in Aristotle's *Physics*, accompany a general transformation of nature and the rise of engineering during the progressive industrialization of Europe. This movement combines, she stresses, a mimetic and a pragmatic approach (Riskin, 2003:625). It relies on the mechanical simulation of natural functions, and initially consisted in the technical ability to replace the workforce of animals and humans with artificial ones. This characteristic transformation of machines, which progressively transformed human movements into artificial forces, then energy, is still based on the study of the most functional aspects of natural organizations. But now, computer automatization is moving that mechanistic analogy even further, considering artificial sensing and information processing. Relying on the notion of feedback, so-called intelligent devices are continuously informed by events perceived from their environment, transforming informational inputs into behavioral outputs. Bio-inspired objects thus aim to consider both biology and technology.

As Susan Leigh Star noted, if these artifacts constitute boundary objects which can be understood from multiple points of view while maintaining continuity in their identity, the research practices they lean on try to reach two main purposes (Star, 1988:38). They first constitute an attempt in intelligence which seeks to create a human or a broader biological simulacrum. They also constitute an attempt in intelligibility which seeks to produce objects that could be used and understood easily by humans. A key aspect of their existence is the referential role these objects play. As tools for simulation, they put into question our own ability to figure what human or animal identity consists in. And as interactive objects they are to be recognized as potential social partners.

Following these two main directions, this chapter will address the ways anthropologists consider the issues raised by artificial intelligence and robotics. It will try to show how the anthropological research conducted on these disciplines seeks to establish the very conditions of the emergence of the referential role played by so-called intelligent machines and how it affects social relations. In so doing, this chapter will try to connect the emerging issues of artificial intelligence and robotics with classical approaches in anthropological theory. To what extend do so-called intelligent systems constitute references which invite us to think about but also to act on natural or social processes? Can one imagine that an artificial body, by simulating an inner activity or any sign of a subjectivity, can produce an effect of identity? What is at stake and how can we qualify the technical devices relating humans to machines?

The following section will deal with the anthropology of science, starting from the history of automatons. It will then focus on Stefan Helmreich's work on artificial life (Helmreich, 1998). This part will show how anthropology is addressing the social and cultural issues of computer science, and more particularly the links between "life as it is" and "life as it could be". We will also see that making artifacts to understand and control life processes crosses a broader anthropological reflection on life (Pitrou, 2014; Coupaye & Pitrou, 2018). The next part will then turn to an ambiguity raised by artificial intelligence and robotics in their attempt to artificially reproduce life and its processes. Starting with John Searle's famous Chinese room issue, we will see that the questions associated with representation in robotics are closely related to the status it has in art. Because of the technical opacity of machines, so-called intelligent agents appear in a blur made of technology of enchantment and enchantment of technology (Gell, 1992).

We will then address the work made around the particular aesthetics of machines and the effects they produce on humans. Considering the work of Lucy Suchman on human–machine reconfigurations (Suchman, 2007), we will also discuss the experiments conducted by anthropologists on the uncanny associated with robots (Grimaud & Paré, 2011). This will lead us to consider what so-called intelligent machines convince us to believe. The fifth part will thus deal with the way artificial agents connect with anthropological works on symbolism, ontology and animism. Focusing mainly on the work of Denis Vidal this section will consider anthropomorphism and the perception mechanisms involved during an encounter with a robot (Vidal, 2007, 2016). To conclude this chapter, we will try to extend the limits of a human-centered approach, which appears to be dominant in anthropology.

2 Artificial lifeforms: the anthropology of science perspective

The anthropology of artificial intelligence and robotics can be understood first as an inquiry on the representations linked to the construction of models of what life is. It follows the path of the anthropology of science field and asks questions closely related to the constitution of knowledge associated with the construction of models and artifacts.

How are artifacts constructed to act as ontological references? What links do they create with the biological entities they imitate? The history of automatons shows very clearly how early science relied on such simulations of biological processes. These artifact-based approaches of living processes have slowly contributed to the emergence of the representation of animal as machine, for instance in Descartes' writings, and a century later in La Mettrie's. The automatons constructed by French engineer Jacques Vaucanson, such as "The Flute Player" or the "Defecating Duck", are good examples of how an object can be conceived as an attempt in artificial lifeform.

In Vaucanson's work, the movement of the automatons tries to show that life is the result of organic functions. More than a simple imitation of a flute player or an artificial duck able to eat, drink, digest and defecate, and clean off its wings and feathers, thus imitating in various ways a living duck, the Vaucanson's automatons rather give shape to the mechanical principles involved in flute play or digestion by dissolution. Thanks to wheels, axes, levers, cords, pulleys, valves or bellows, their movements draw analogies between vital functions and artificial mechanisms though they are not able to describe them in detail. Though the duck has once been described as a mere coffee grinder, these automatons, however, enable a curious looping effect. They give the impression of their autonomy and the life that is attached to it. This effect has been well studied by Jessica Riskin. Her study on Vaucanson's work, but also on the broader impact automatons had on early life science, showed how such objects were specifically conceived to illustrate new theories in biology during the eighteenth century (Riskin, 2003). Automatons are, in fact, part of a long historical tradition which experiments widely on representing life processes by designing artificially living machines. This way to design artifacts and models that represent life is still a core element in what constitutes research in artificial intelligence and robotics today.

Anthropologist Stephan Helmreich has been among the first social scientists to address the question of simulation in informatics. At the end of the 1980s, he started a vast inquiry on the work of pioneers in what is now called artificial life. By looking closely at the conceptions involved in artificial lifeforms at the SFI research institute on complex systems in Santa Fe, New Mexico, Helmreich drew a critical yet rich portrayal of the work done on artificial life.

Published in 1998 under the title *Silicon Second Nature*, the study conducted by Helmreich doesn't directly address the research done today in artificial intelligence and robotics throughout the world. However, this pioneering inquiry remains of importance for those who want to better understand how life processes can be imitated. The first reason is that such a study gives access, from the inside, to the field of artificial life by directly relying on researchers whose influence today continues to be determinant in bio-inspired complex systems research. The second reason is that this inquiry works on methods employed to describe living processes that are still operating in today's laboratories, mainly in the field of artificial intelligence. These methods mostly consist of the development, adaptation and evolution of populations of algorithms or automatons in simulated environments like Tierra, Polyworld or Echo. They are essentially used by researchers like Thomas Ray, Mark Bedau or Chris Langton to put into question notions like autopoiesis or emergence.

Since its beginning, computer simulation has served as a didactic base on which to make models about life processes. The community studied by Helmreich seeks to go beyond that. It put into question the limits of life itself by trying to reproduce its mechanisms into computers. How should these researchers construct non-living biological systems? What role does their own culture and representations play in that work? How, for instance, did Thomas Ray, the creator of Tierra, manage to think that the creatures evolving in a virtual environment could be considered *as if* they were living?

The construction of such environments appears to constitute a good substrate for practicing analogy. An artificial ecosystem like Tierra is thus perceived by its creator as an instance of species evolution and natural selection which takes the memory of computers for its medium. According to its designer, this software forms an appropriate experimentation tool which invites one to review and extend theories in biology and evolution. As a biologist, Ray conceived Tierra by following simple rules. His software generated populations of small codes that reproduce by copying themselves into the memory slots of the computer. These populations are then progressively erased from the memory thanks to another program that plays the role of natural selection. These elementary rules, Ray says, create more complex dynamics, highlighting the impression that the interacting agents in the simulation are autonomous and reinforcing the argument that they are good models to think living organisms.

In fact, identity between programs and living organisms is closely related to an analogy which finds its source in the manner in which life can be imagined. On the one hand, organisms and programs share a common structure which is born from the notion of genetic coding. On the other hand, those two are conceived from the idea that genes, like programs, are made of information. This reduction of organisms to genes, and genes to bits of information, makes analogy possible. But it also raises a boundary. Do these artificial lifeforms ultimately come from life or mimesis?

This question is of importance when it comes to better understanding our relationship with artificial lifeforms, whether they are software-based interfaces or robots. As Helmreich himself points out, following Dominique Lestel and Isabelle Stengers, the impression of life emerging from their activity (and the emotions that follow this impression) implies an aesthetic in which living organisms and their imitations tend to be confused. This very particular aesthetic brings nature to technical processes and simultaneously brings culture to life. The mutual intertwining between technical and natural processes, as Helmreich suggests, goes beyond mere epistemological questions to embrace broader anthropological concerns.

Informatics models of "life as it could be" are deeply influenced by culturally embedded representations, linked to the notions of gender, kinship, sexuality, race, economics, cosmology, myths and to the political and social contexts from which a situated understanding of these notions is possible. The story of life told by researchers may appear as a quite naive anthropological narrative. But it shows that the representations of life is transforming in the margins of nature. In that "second nature", Helmreich notes, life processes appear to depend exclusively on Judeo-Christian white male–centered values. They also imply reproduction techniques that are left mostly under the control of men. These simulation machines constitute then limit-biologies that are informed by cultural processes (Helmreich, 2011). Artificial lifeforms are in fact closely associated with a long history of object production techniques and cultural practices toward life management.

Indeed, all human societies develop theories about what life is. But they also deal with making it intelligible by constructing artifacts that share common properties with it. Perig Pitrou recently showed how understanding life through analogy with making objects is of importance among the Mixe of the Mexican state of Oaxaca (Pitrou, 2014). Craftwork helps humans to understand what life is. Technical activity, for instance pottery-making, is an actual entry point which can make the inherent complexity of natural processes more intelligible and then helps gain control on them. Among the Mixe, Pitrou observed, life can be understood through the activity of pottery-making while the living person is seen as an artifact to be built. This circularity between living beings and artifacts can be found not only in South America but also in many places all over the world. As a sum of the processes that humans try to understand, describe and control life, technique is becoming an object for anthropological inquiry.

Beyond any essentialist approach on life, Ludovic Coupaye and Perig Pitrou recently showed that a pragmatic approach, based on the concepts and methods of the anthropology of techniques and material culture (for instance the study of local techniques), can help to describe the analogies used to understand life processes and thus help refine ethnographic description (Coupaye & Pitrou, 2018). Inheriting from the French anthropological tradition of technique and materiality studies, Coupaye and Pitrou propose that, in order to understand the circumstances in which technique and life are closely entangled, it is necessary to scrupulously consider the set of procedures and devices employed by humans to coordinate the action of the various agents surrounding them. It is thus necessary to be attentive to the sequences which make that coordination effective, say the authors. If, as Coupaye and Pitrou noted, any operation on the living is also an interaction with the living, the same appears to be true with artificial intelligence and robotics. Beyond a mere set of operations that contribute to the construction of machines *as if* they were animated by processes which can be found in nature, so-called intelligent devices are also demonstrators. As we have seen, one of their main purposes is to simulate life processes in order to understand them. However, studying the cultural aspects which equip the scientists' views on life doesn't reveal their eventual effectiveness during an interaction. How can such objects be perceived? How do we deal with such simulations?

3 The "As if" issue: art and the limits to simulation

Simulations in robotics and artificial intelligence, and their concordance to reality, raise many issues which are central in computer science and robotic research. How similar are the human brain and the computer? How can an autonomous machine be programmed? What could its learning consist of? How could it "feel" the world around it and even understand us? As Alan Turing pointed out, these questions are associated with how the regulation of information in artificial systems can constitute an evidence of their intelligence. Though these questions seem mainly related to the relation between scientific culture and the epistemology of science, they are also raising unexpected concerns directly linked to the limits of representations, art and aesthetics, and even magic. Let's take a classic example from artificial intelligence history.

Researchers in artificial intelligence have, since the middle of the twentieth century, faced the question of the representation of intelligence. Their successes were obtained by manipulating symbols and producing effects of intelligence. But it was not possible to consider their programs as truly intelligent. This is the case of a very famous conversational agent called Eliza. Conceived by Joseph Weizenbaum between 1964 and 1966, this project aimed to solve fundamental technical problems. It consists of a dialogue program designed to read and answer messages written on a computer by a human user. The sentence entered by the user is analyzed by the system, which searches for each word in a kind of dictionary. It is then split into keywords and then transformed according to associated rules. If no keyword is found, the program applies a previous transformation. The resulting text is then displayed to the user. The rules adopted to make Eliza converse were conceived on the model of Carl Rogers' psychotherapy. The program works well to get humans to talk and it shows how much they believe the machine is able to reason by itself.

Eliza appears to be able to converse with a human. But it gives this feeling only because of specific programming rules, regardless of the meaning and relevance of the exchange. While it remains a useful tool for testing hypotheses on the human mind, it can't be compared to the brain and, therefore, does not constitute an explanation in itself. A thought experiment may allow us to grasp this problem; the "Chinese Room" described by John Searle (1980).

Let us suppose, Searle writes, that someone is locked into a room where there are documents written in Chinese. Suppose that this person knows absolutely nothing about the Chinese language so the written signs given to her are of no significance. Suppose again that someone provides another set of Chinese written documents to this person along with rules written in her mother tongue. These rules help to make associations between the first set of documents and the second. Suppose now that a third quantity of documents is given with similar instructions. The person should now be able to make associations between the different piles of documents and answer any questions. Outside the room where the person is locked, the answers will be considered to be coming from a Chinese-speaking person. And no one will know that they are the result of the application of rules concerning the manipulation of unknown symbols. Intelligence here is not at work, says Searle. And a machine that could apply a similar set of rules should not be considered as intelligent. Its understanding of such a situation would not be incomplete or partial. It would simply be null.

The criticism raised by Searle invites us to think about how early computer scientists considered intelligence through a computational approach which considers simulation to be a form of duplication, and which considers the activity of the mind independently from the activity of the body, consequently highlighting an underlying dualism in the scientific models of intelligence. The stance adopted by John Searle has provoked very strong reactions in the community of researchers, especially among the proponents of a strong artificial intelligence. But it found some echo with the ideas of Joseph Weizenbaum. He had himself repeatedly confronted the orthodoxy of his community about the shared desire to understand and replicate human intelligence in a mechanical way. For Weizenbaum, the intelligence of a machine would remain alien compared to that of a human, consisting in a syntactic way to deal with rules while human intelligence is able to make sense of the world.

Progressively, computer scientists admitted that computational architectures were far removed from their biological models. The brain activity would not be conceivable through a mere operation of calculation anymore. The interest in research shifted to a connectionist description of neural activity. Initiated at the beginning of the 1940s, in particular with the work of Warren McCulloch and Walter Pitts, the connectionist attempt in intelligence was first discussed when Josiah Macy Jr's foundation organized the series of conferences inaugurating cybernetics between 1942 and 1953, then by the advocates of the computational approach during what is considered as the founding event of artificial intelligence at Dartmouth College in 1956.

Programming using a connectionist approach turns an interest in symbol manipulation into an interest for the rules of management of individual operations created by networks of artificial neurons. Thanks to these, computer scientists managed to program computers "learn" to play backgammon or, recently, the game of Go. Neural networks are very much used today for different artificial learning tasks. However, if it seems reasonable to think that a machine could learn from the imitation of real neurons, applying such a technique is raising issues. In actual fact, computer scientists have to program how their systems make their own decisions. The risk in such a situation is introducing bias and artifacts in their algorithms or, even worse, creating something like a homunculus which certainly automatizes the decision process but, in fact, would transfer the programmer's agency into the computer. The difference between autonomy and automatism (or more accurately between science and fiction) is at stake here. This difference makes it difficult to know to what extent computer programs are intelligent in comparison to what extent they simply produce the effects of intelligence, as Weizenbaum and Searle discuss.

As is the case with many complex technical objects, robots and artificial intelligence–based programs remain black boxes. Forming a real node that brings the disciplines together, robotics and artificial intelligence remain barely accessible, even sometimes to the people familiar with their techniques. They are characterized by a sumptuous opacity (Latour, 2010:22). This opacity, however, shouldn't be understood as a mere attempt to mislead the public even if, at first glance, it appears to be the result of a skillful mix of technology of enchantment and enchantment of technology (Gell, 1992). These objects invite us to consider not only new methods for experimentation on natural processes but also new means for looking at the problems related to our own humanity. Though there are limits to their resemblance of the bodies they imitate, they can help to increase knowledge about ourselves: an anthropology which, paradoxically, built the understanding of what makes us human by sketching (and in so doing playing with) our own image (Becker, 2015). Artificial intelligences and robots have, therefore, strong connections with art practice and aesthetics.

So-called intelligent devices of all kinds are characterized by a gap between what they are and the natural processes they represent. This gap is closely associated with imitation and figuration (Marin, 1994:252–266). Thus, it is not surprising that art history has worked this theme since its beginning.[2] It is well known that imitating nature in art is crossed by ambiguity. On the one hand, imitating is about producing a double of what is meant to be represented. On the other, imitation is about transcending the original. Imitation in art is about magic and illusions, about creating a fragile effect, giving the feeling that someone is there as a working representation and simultaneously creating simulacrum (Marin, 1994:311). The relation between what exists in nature and the technical means by which it can be represented is, as Helmreich already remarked, of an aesthetic purpose (Becker, 2015).

In art, the problem raised by representation is far more than a matter of what is true or what is false. The important thing is that, as art historian Ernst Gombrich noted, the concordance between the model and its representation is obtained gradually, at the end of a long process depending exclusively on the artists' choices (Gombrich, 1960:62). A representation will always be imprecise, but it always contributes to the definition of what is represented. Symmetrically, the one who's looking at an art object will recognize more or less easily the familiarity the representation has with the original and will eventually imagine what the representation is missing to make it appear complete. Gombrich insists on these two aspects of imitation. On the one hand, we humans are able to describe reality using technical means. On the other, as spectators, we are also able to project on the representation elements of a ghost perception which then takes parts into the processes of classification and interpretation that define imitation (Gombrich, 1960:174). The role of anthropology is also to explore what happens when such a relation occurs.

As Jessica Riskin showed, the quality of being of the automatons of the Classical Age, or at least the relation they illustrate between their activity and observations in nature, consists of creating the conditions for a speculative way of thinking to emerge (Riskin, 2003). These relations were linked to the opposition between opacity and transparency, and they were directly related to the techniques used when constructing machines. Indeed, automatons of the eighteenth century were arousing curiosity and they were surrounded by mystery concerning their functioning. They were not only increasing the interest in nature among scientists. They were not only philosophical kinds of toys for scholars. They were part of a much larger excitement for techniques which were meant to revolutionize industry. Automatons grab attention. They were entertaining. And they contribute to the dramatization of animal and human vital functions (Riskin, 2003) in a very theatrical way, sometimes by using magic tricks (Metzner, 1998). Automatons, as we were about to see, were also objects that make believe.

4 Objects that "behave": interactions studies and experiments

Artificial intelligences and robots are not only interesting from the perspective of the anthropology of sciences and techniques. Because of their particular aesthetic they also raise interest in other domains of inquiry in anthropology. Their interactive purpose and their effects need to be understood from an interactional perspective. So-called intelligent machines show something about the relations we have with them but also through them. In terms of interactions, studies shows that humans are reluctant to stick to the plan initially conceived by the designers.

Lucy Suchman studied these relations in a book first published in 1987 under the title *Plans and Situated Actions*, then expanded her investigation in a second edition published in 2007.

The problem she addresses is in regards to the relationship between complex system designers and users. How can a machine explain how it works? The study that Suchman conducted focuses on communication between humans and machines. In particular, it focuses on the role of artificial intelligence and expert systems used to ease communication through planning and, more particularly, on the relationship between the planning activity and what humans do with the plan. It shows that so-called intelligent objects can't manage to make us act according to a previous plan. Planning is not a determinant for action. It is rather a resource used by human actors which helps them to think about what they are doing. Suchman shows that communicating with a machine, through its artificial intelligence, is far more complicated than one can imagine. A machine relies on rudimentary forms of communication that are very far from the subtle forms we use in our daily lives with peers. Such machines are defined by their qualifications. What are they able to do and what aren't they? How should we consider agents imitating human life? What do we share with them and what do we not?

Exploring human–machine interaction at the interface of their relation, Lucy Suchman aimed to show that anthropomorphic machines contribute to a new definition of the human body. Studying the work done at the MIT MediaLab's Personal Robotics Group, she focused her observations on the methods employed to figure human beings, more particularly by looking closely on the work done on the Kismet robot. Conceived of by Cynthia Breazeal, this robot is inspired by research on children's social development. The software architecture of the robot is made of many systems whose combination helps the machine to react to stimuli by expressing basic emotions. It is said that such a robot learns from experience and thus that it has the capability to have natural interactions with humans. In fact, Suchman notes, a huge difference exists between natural communication and that which we could have with this machine. To the non-expert eye, the robot remains a black box. If this machine contributes, like many, to playing with the frontiers of living and non-living, the uncanny feelings associated with its presence will also be a matter of interest for anthropology.

Named after Sigmund Freud and Ernst Jentsch works on the uncanny, Masahiro Mori's concept of Uncanny Valley is a central element in the communication issues addressed in robotics and artificial intelligence (Mori, 1970). Mori's idea is simple: The more the robots look like us, the more we are inclined to accept their presence. But when they resemble us too much, and when with a gesture they reveal their mechanical nature, they create a feeling of uncanniness in us. At this point, the curve correlating the appearance of an anthropomorphic robot and the acceptance or rejection feelings we have in their presence widens: the curve, in short, resembles a valley.

Anthropologist Emmanuel Grimaud and scenographer Zaven Paré explored this valley, experimenting on Professor Hiroshi Ishiguro's Geminoïd robot (a world-known surrogate of himself) in Japan with the help of computer scientist Ilona Straub. Realizing that the bizarre relations that had risen from the presence of Professor Ishiguro's machine are closely linked to a matter of representation and theater, E. Grimaud, Z. Paré and their German colleague engaged in a whole series of tests and experiments which aimed to understand what effects could appear from the animation of the robot. Their work moves from the questions initially raised by the anthropology of life (Helmreich, 1998) to questions related to the representations directly set through the activity of the machine (Grimaud & Paré, 2011). Which kind of theater does the robot play? Which presence does it stage?

Grimaud and Paré note that this presence is ghostly. It is that of the team of engineers whose tasks of conception and programming has been converted into machine activity. It is then that of the person who controls the robot. The peculiarity of Geminoïd is that it serves as a telepresence instrument. Ishiguro designed it with the idea of being able to attend conferences without leaving his laboratory. That's why the robot's appearance is that of Professor Ishiguro himself, constituting a kind of mechanical twin. Seated behind a console that records the movements of his face, the sound of his voice and allows him to perceive the environment surrounding the robot, Professor Ishiguro can use his machine to converse with distant people. However, this system despite its sophisticated complexity does not exactly transcribe the movements it must mimic in a remote environment. The presence of the robot is thus, and finally, related to the way the system itself manages (not without difficulty) to capture the activity of the person trying to control it and set the machine in motion.

This very particular presence can be seen not only through the programmed animation cycles of the machine but also through its errors, bugs, twitches and vibrations. Consequently, the complex network of presences visible through the robot's activity leads to an exercise of qualification which requires the person who controls it to learn to use the facial recognition system and the one who faces the robot to overcome the strangeness of its movements. The Geminoïd appears as strange semi-living creature. It is also something to play with. The playfulness of this robot is actually a central matter, which indicates strong connections between robotics and theater. The machine, like the puppet, has long been a source of inspiration for theatrical avant-gardes (Grimaud & Paré, 2011; Becker, 2015). But the robot made by Ishiguro introduces something new. Like the perceived action of the comedian, it relates to the body experience, making spectators infer about its character. But it does so on a pointillist mode, "coming to life" intermittently and eventually confusing people (sometimes by chance) for only a few seconds. Although it has been made to look realistic, it constantly oscillates between a frightening creature and the body of Professor Ishiguro.

Interacting with robots and artificial intelligence agents is about inferring human properties onto an object even if their resemblance to us seems poor (Heider & Simmel, 1944). They invite us to distinguish between life and non-life by deciphering their apparent behavior. In this way, robots and artificial intelligences join a much larger collection of objects which has retained the interest of anthropologists since the very beginning of the discipline.

5 A pathway to symbolism: compared ontology and the question of animism

Though they come from scientific knowledge on natural processes, whether they are motor, cognitive, emotional or social, it is not very surprising that so-called intelligent devices can be thought of in a symbolic way by people who interact with them or watch them react. Inference and beliefs are actually key steps in the interactions we can have with these objects even especially because it is difficult to compare them with the social interactions we have in our daily lives. As Searle noted, it is easy for everyone to suppose that a machine can be intentional. If a robot behave like we would do, one can suppose that it can experience inner states like ours and then must have in itself a mechanism which is able to produce such states (Searle, 1980:365). But what are these beliefs referring to? Are they a symptom of a human inclination for irrationality? Or are they rather part of a cognitive strategy? Do we become animist when interacting with such objects?

Machines are in some ways just like fetishes. They are captivating. But they also establish a relationship founded on the challenge, for someone who interacts with them, to overcome the subtleties that have been employed by their designers to make them appear alive. We contemplate their inner lives. Alfred Gell highlighted that, in order to understand such situations, the observer remains captive of his perception because of the indecipherable nature of what forms, in reality, such objects. The objects appear as a maze, leading the observer into a desperate attempt to give sense to what is perceived. This results in a cognitive blocking which originates from the observer's attempt to reconstruct, step by step, what has been done by the creator to conceive the object (Gell, 1998). Those objects are an entry point into symbolic processes. But the focalization they produce is not the only way they enter the vast body of issues associated with symbolism and, more particularly, how inferences can be compared with other object-based symbolic processes studied by anthropologists. As Dan Sperber noted, such processes also rely on evocation by leaning on memory (Sperber, 1975). Humans then have to both displace their attention by focusing on the object's action and search for familiarity (Becker, 2015) in order to open a frame for an analog-type of communication to occur (Bateson, 1966).

Denis Vidal described a very similar type of interaction when comparing robots and the representations of gods (Vidal, 2007). He remarked that the interactions which take place between humans and local deities of the northwest of India closely resemble the interactions we have with social robots. Looking at the erratic movements of a wooden structure carried by men, movements meant to bring answers to people's questioning, Vidal found that such a structure shared four main aspects with social robots. Robots are first provided with an anthropomorphic dimension. They also give rise to specific modes of interaction, which imply inferences about their behavior, the way they react, their sociability, their emotions, or their intentions. They then form the support of beliefs regarding their autonomy in relation to their designers. Finally, they are the subject of debate and speculation concerning the principles that animate them, regardless of the inferences of humans toward them. Extending the observation in robotics laboratories, Denis Vidal laid the foundation for a transversal and comparative approach that integrates robots into a much larger group of artificial creatures (Vidal, 2016). This comparative ontology actually works directly on the notion of anthropomorphism, marking a new stage in the history of this notion.

Anthropomorphic thought is indeed the subject of a long reflection that crosses the perspectives of anthropology as well as those of psychology and the arts. This notion covers a set of conceptions that vary in time and according to cultures. Why do we attribute the traits of our humanity to the things around us? Denis Vidal rightly notes that this idea is, sometimes still today, associated with a kind of vice or cognitive immaturity. In the nineteenth century, anthropomorphism appeared as a step in the evolution of societies. Anthropomorphism, often confused with animism, is considered to be an indicator of the movement of societies toward civilization. In the works of the French psychologist Jean Piaget, the notion designates a crucial step in the development of children. This link between the individual immaturity of the child and that which, for a long time, characterized the societies described as primitive persisted, Vidal emphasized, until the 1990s.

More recent works (Guthrie, 1995; Boyer, 1996) have, for instance, showed that anthropomorphic thought constitutes a completely rational strategy, and perhaps is the best suited when we have to manage novelty and uncertainty. It also forms a very effective way to stabilize representations of supernatural entities in human groups while making communication with them possible. For D. Vidal, the question of anthropomorphism must, however, be tackled without either a naturalist or a culturalist approach. This question really takes a new turn if we consider the multiple ways societies play with the categories used to order the world around them. The notion of anthropomorphism thus has to gain in heuristics if we think about it through a comparative ontology. By comparing different kinds of relations to what appear to us as autonomous objects, it is possible to not only consider the ways humans make the distinctions between human and non-human existences in a shared environment, but also the ways in which those distinctions are the object of transgressions everywhere. These transgressions show how the categories are in fact unstable and, because of their indeterminate nature, form a substratum where entities can develop and maintain themselves culturally.

Experimenting with human–machine interactions with the robot Berenson at the Quai Branly Museum, Vidal showed that the main issue when encountering an anthropomorphic robot is how to measure its autonomy and limits. This measure aims to verify that the machine is indeed one. However, once the mechanical nature of the robot is confirmed during interaction, this does not prevent humans from behaving with him as if it were a "person" (Vidal, 2016).

How could we understand this paradoxical attitude? As Vidal suggests, by establishing continuities between the human inner processes and those of machines and, simultaneously, by noting that a discontinuity exists between our appearance and theirs, the human-robot interactions reveal that a renewed form of animism is at work. Philippe Descola has shown that animism implies such a relationship of continuity and discontinuity (Descola, 2005). In animist societies, if the set of existing non-humans is endowed with an interiority identical to that of humans, it is mainly on the basis of a morphological difference that the relations of identity and otherness will be established. One can imagine that relations with robots could easily be compared to that occurring in animist worlds. But this is in fact absolutely not true.

In the world of animism, people not only project the attributes of a person onto non-human beings but also the specific sociability that is established between members of the same species, of different species, or between living beings and artifacts (Viveiros de Castro, 2014; Kohn, 2013; Santos-Granero, 2009). The "person" status which is inferred during an encounter with a robot seems to be as much marked by instability as by uncertainty. It seems to emerge from an identity that is as complex as it is cumulative, the ontology of a machine undergoing various transformations during the very time of the interaction (Becker, 2015; Becker, André & Dutech, 2019). Although machines seem to have a perceptual world of their own and their boundaries can be limited, the experiments conducted in the field of human-robot interactions show that attributing the quality of a subject to a machine does not necessarily imply that one is aware of the social relations that might prevail in a robot society, as this would be the case in the type of animist ontological inference describe by Descola (2005).

As we have already seen, regardless of its form or the principles that animate it, a machine always appears to us as a black box. These objects, because of the very partial knowledge we have of their internal mechanism, act upon us as true catalysts of beliefs. However, the perceptual mechanisms involved in encounters between humans and robots remain partially unknown, as the curators of the Persona exhibition at the Quai Branly Museum in Paris note in their introduction of the exhibition catalog (Grimaud et al., 2016). It is then important to ask "Who is there?" when such an encounter occurs. It is also important to address the parameters that favor the perception of a presence in a given situation and, above all, what makes this presence assimilable to known families of humans, animals, spirits, divinity, ghosts, and so on (Grimaud et al., 2016:13).

6 The limits of the human-centered approach: from agents to complex systems

This chapter has dealt with different approaches used in anthropology to better understand the issues raised by artificial intelligence and robotics. It presented how the discipline follows the two main prospects of artificial intelligence shown by Susan Leigh Star (1988). Studying how these objects are made and how cultural processes are embedded into scientific representations of life, anthropologists documented an attempt in reproducing natural phenomenons. Focusing then on the relations one can have with such devices, researchers in anthropology are confronted with the inherent difficulties met by computer scientists and roboticists in their attempt to produce intelligibility and natural interaction.

These two main dimensions of anthropological inquiry raise an issue, which is progressively gaining interest within in the field. When working on the tools of robotics and artificial intelligence, one of the main problems is that the human form is at the core of most of the studies on so-called intelligent or autonomous devices. This anthropocentric approach is, in fact, a perspective that focuses on the dynamics of attachment to anthropomorphic (or more broadly biomorphic) machines without, however, replacing these machines in the larger robotics and artificial intelligence landscape where they remain, despite their visibility, still largely in the minority. The literature produced in the human and social sciences deals for instance with the question of anthropomorphism in robotics by considering categories of heterogeneous phenomenons which find their source in the imitation of the human body.

Considering their conception or the effects they produce, the anthropomorphic systems form strange links with the human. For example, these simulations of living beings place the living subjects and objects that can be possessed on the same level (Richardson, 2016). They are screens on which our fantasies are projected. They form a place where natural processes and the human body reinvent themselves (Helmreich, 1998; Suchman, 2007). Because of their inability to grasp the complexity of social relations or to make sense of the world around them, they appear as anthropomorphic traps in which we would be quite willing to fall (Vidal, 2016).

These issues cross those raised by the perspective of robotics and artificial intelligence. For instance, the activity of such machines engages those who observe them in a game that consists of making assumptions of the social qualities of the robot while trying to grasp its potential interiority. Roboticists and computer scientists who work on the cognition of human–robot interaction and social robotics have understood this well. Through the study of mental models that humans have about autonomous agents, cognitive theories about interaction, and work on the expression of emotions and the recognition of human activities, they aim to facilitate the relationships that are built between humans and machines. Based on the observation that human–machine interactions follow the rules of social interactions between humans, empathy became a major issue in their studies, which led to agents whose form, behavior and processes invite their users to recognize the human in them (Becker, André & Dutech, 2019).

These devices are primarily considered for their resemblance to the human body, for the inferences they make raise in us or for the social frame that is gradually invented around them. These agents, like the autonomy that is associated with it, arouse mixed feelings of fascination, confusion, strangeness and uneasiness. The fascination engendered by machines hides the means and ideas which are at the origin of their actions. The purposes for which they are made remain unknown. Their presence, we have suggested, is actually more complex than it seems. If one can see the centrality that anthropology gives to the human figure in the study of the interaction between humans and machines, it is now time to include machines that don't necessarily resemble the human body in order to see how their activity has even deeper implications for societies.

It is important to better understand what the new revolution promised by the designers of robots and artificial intelligences could consist of. Although difficult to anticipate, its consequences on social life must be given special attention. Anthropologists have already pointed out how much the techniques employed by roboticists and computer scientists are subject to their own epistemic approaches, visions of life, evolution processes, social relations and, consequently, to the culture of research teams. These approaches imply that one should be attentive of the representations conveyed through the conception of so-called intelligent machines. For instance, inquiring on the materialities of information (Dourish, 2017) is a good way not only to consider and to confront the visions of the future conveyed by computer sciences and mechanical engineering but also to address the many questions that machines are already able to raise. In order to better understand what constitutes these systems' agency, and what place are they assigned us to (Akrich, 1987), anthropology has to focus on the complex socio-material networks it weaves.

Without doing this, anthropologists risk falling into a naive prospective, somewhat blinded by problems that have no place in the social world. Are robots our friends or our enemies? Should they have rights? Will artificial intelligences still need us? Must we program them to respect the moral rules written by science-fiction author Isaac Asimov? Do sex-bots have breakdowns? These sometimes fascinating, disturbing or amusing questions take us away from the concrete implications that robots and artificial intelligences already have on our social environments.

The field of inquiry explored by designers of robotic and computer systems goes far beyond a mere interest for life simulation and face-to-face interactions. From home automation to intelligent cities and to robotic dairy farms to remote settlements on the moon or Mars, much of the research conducted in this field shows how, based on data acquisition and mining, it is possible to optimize the performance of systems that are now conceived as hybrid. The tools of computer science and robotics seek their way to organize relationships. It is now no longer just a question of living alongside machines. It is also a matter of living inside them.

High technologies deserve interest not only for the curiosity they arouse but also for the connections they show. Computer science and robotics are at the intersection of many social worlds and although they are part of a modern imaginary, they have been understudied by anthropologists. Since at least the end of the First World War these objects are mediating stories. But now they are becoming part of our daily lives, these machines need to be fully studied, understood and criticized.

Notes

1 Far from conventional wisdom on luddism, Eric J. Hobsbawm showed that machine breaking in England's early factories not only affected machinery but also raw materials, finished products, and even the private property of employers. These revolts are not hostile to machines, and therefore to the technical progress they represent. They are part of a movement to defend wages.
2 At least since Giorgio Vasari published his book, *The Lives of the Most Excellent Painters, Sculptors, and Architects* between 1550 and 1558, and, more particularly, when he evokes the competition between Donato and his friend Brunelleschi.

References

Akrich Madeleine, 1987, "Comment décrire les objets techniques?" *Techniques et culture*, 9:49–64

Bateson Gregory, 1966, "Problems in Cetacean and Other Mammalian Communication", in K. S. Norris (ed), *Whales, Dolphins, and Porpoises*, Berkeley – Los Angeles, University of California Press:569–578

Becker Joffrey, 2015, *Humanoïdes, Expérimentations croisées entre arts et sciences*, Nanterre, Presses Universitaire de Paris Ouest

J. Becker, V. André, and A. Dutech, 2019, "Une expérience sur la qualification des comportements d'une lampe robotique", *Techniques & Culture* [Online], http://journals.openedition.org/tc/10771

Boyer Pascal, 1996, "What Makes Anthropomorphism Natural: Intuitive Ontology and Cultural Representations", *Journal of the Royal Anthropological Institute*, 2(1):83–97

Coupaye Ludovic, and Pitrou Perig, 2018, "Introduction. The Interweaving of Vital and Technical Processes in Oceania", *Oceania, Special Issue: Living Beings and Artifacts: Vital and Technical Processes in Oceania*, 88(1):2–12

Descola Philippe, 2005, *Par delà nature et culture*, Paris, Gallimard

Dourish Paul, 2017, *The Stuff of Bits, An Essay on the Materialities of Information*, Cambridge, MIT Press
Gell Alfred, 1992, "The Technology of Enchantement and the Enchantement of Technology", in Coote Jeremy and Shelton Anthony (eds), *Anthropology, Art and Aesthetics*, Oxford, Clarendon Press:40–63
Gell Alfred, 1998, *Art and Agency, An Anthropological Theory*, Oxford, Clarendon Press
Gombrich Ernst, 2002 (1960), *L'art et l'illusion, Psychologie de la représentation picturale*, Paris, Phaidon
Grimaud Emmanuel, and Paré Zaven, 2011, *Le jour où les robots mangeront des pommes, conversations avec un geminoïd*, Paris, Éditions Pétra
Grimaud Emmanuel et al., 2016, *Persona, étrangement humain*, Paris, Musée du quai Branly – Actes Sud
Guthrie Stewart E., 1995, *Faces in the Cloud, a New Theory of Religion*, Oxford and New-York, Oxford University Press
Heider Fritz, and Simmel Marianne, 1944, "An Experimental Study of Apparent Behavior", *The American Journal of Psychology*, 57(2):243–259
Helmreich Stefan, 1998, *Silicon Second Nature, Culturing Artificial Life in a Digital World*, Berkeley – Los Angeles, University of California Press
Helmreich Stefan, 2011, "What Was Life? Answers from Three Limit Biologies", *Critical Inquiry*, 37(4):671–696
Hobsbawm Eric J., 1952, "The Machine Breakers", *Past & Present*, 1:57–70
Ingold Tim, 1988, "Tools, Minds and Machines: An Excursion in the Philosophy of 'Technology'", *Techniques et Culture*, 12:151–176
Kohn Eduardo, 2013, *How Forests Think: Toward an Anthropology Beyond the Human*, Berkeley – Los Angeles, University of California Press
Latour Bruno, 2010, "Prendre le pli des techniques", *Réseaux*, 5(163):11–31
Marin Louis, 1994, *De la représentation*, Paris, Gallimard – Le Seuil
Metzner Paul, 1998, "Robert-Houdin and the Vogue of the Automaton-Builders", in *Crescendo of the Virtuoso. Spectacle, Skill, and Self-Promotion in Paris during the Age of Revolution*, Berkeley – Los Angeles, University of California Press:160–210
Mori Masahiro, 1970, "Bukimi no Tani (the Uncanny Valley)", *Energy*, 7(4):33–35
Pitrou Perig, 2014, "Life as a Process of Making in the Mixe Highlands (Oaxaca, Mexico): Towards a 'General Pragmatics' of Life", *Journal of the Royal Anthropological Institute*, 21(1):86–105
Richardson Kathleen, 2016, "Sex Robots Matters: Slavery, the Prostituted, and the Rights of Machines", *IEEE Technology and Society Magazine*, 35(2):46–53
Riskin Jessica, 2003, "The Defecating Duck, or The Ambiguous Origins of Artificial Life", *Critical Inquiry*, 29(4):599–633
Santos-Granero Fernando (ed), 2009, *The Occult Life of Things, Native Amazonian Theories of Materiality and Personhood*, Tucson, University of Arizona Press
Searle John R., 1980, "Minds, Brains, and Programs", *The Behavioral and Brain Sciences*, 3(3):417–424
Sperber Dan, 1975, *Rethinking Symbolism*, Cambridge, Cambridge University Press
Star Susan Leigh, 1988, "The Structure of Ill-Structured Solutions: Boundary Objects and Heterogeneous Distributed Problem Solving", in Les Gasser and Michael N. Huhns (eds), *Distributed Artificial Intelligence*, vol ii, London – San Mateo, Pitman, Morgan Kaufmann Publishers:37–55
Suchman Lucy, 2007, *Human–Machine Reconfiguration, Plan and Situated Action*, 2nd Edition, Cambridge, Cambridge University Press
Vidal Denis, 2007, "Anthropomorphism of Sub-Anthropomorphism? An Anthropological Approach to Gods and Robots", *Journal of the Royal Anthropological Institute*, 13(4):917–933
Vidal Denis, 2016, *Aux frontières de l'humain, Dieux: figures de cire, robots et autres artefacts*, Paris, Alma Éditeur
Viveiros De Castro Eduardo, 2014, "Perspectivisme et multinaturalisme en Amérique indigène", *Journal des anthropologues*, 138–139:161–181

8
Ethics of artificial intelligence[1]

Vincent C. Müller

Artificial intelligence (AI) is a digital technology that will be of major importance for the development of humanity in the near future. AI has raised fundamental questions about what we should do with such systems, what the systems themselves should do, what risks they involve and how we can control these.

After the background to the field (1), this article introduces the main debates (2), first on ethical issues that arise with AI systems as *objects*, i.e. tools made and used by humans; here, the main sections are privacy (2.1), manipulation (2.2), opacity (2.3), bias (2.4), autonomy & responsibility (2.6) and singularity (2.7). Then we look at AI systems as *subjects*, i.e. when ethics is for the AI systems themselves in machine ethics (2.8) and artificial moral agency (2.9). Finally we look at future developments and the concept of AI (3). For each section within these themes, we provide a general explanation of the *ethical issues* and we outline existing *positions* and *arguments*, then we analyse how this plays out with current *technologies* and finally what *policy* consequences may be drawn.

1 Historical and intellectual background

Some technologies, like nuclear power, cars or plastics, have caused ethical and political discussions and significant policy efforts to control the trajectory these technologies – usually only once some damage is done. In addition to such 'ethical concerns', new technologies challenge current norms and conceptual systems, which is of particular interest to philosophy. Finally, once we have understood a technology in its context, we need to shape our societal response, including regulation and law. All these features also exist in the case of the new technology of AI – plus the more fundamental fear that they may end the era of human control on planet Earth. The task of an article such as this is to analyse the issues, and to deflate the non-issues.

The ethics of AI and robotics has seen significant press coverage in recent years, which shows support for this kind of work, but also may end up undermining it: the press often talks as if the issues under discussion were just those that future technology will bring, and as though we already know what would be most ethical and how to achieve that. Press coverage thus focuses on risk, security (Brundage et al. 2018) and prediction of impact (e.g. on the job market). The result is a discussion of essentially technical problems that focus on how to achieve a desired outcome. Another result can be seen in the current discussion in policy and industry focuses on image and public relations – where the label "ethical" is really not much more than the new "green", perhaps used for "ethics washing". For a problem to qualify as a problem for AI ethics would require that we do *not* readily know what is the right thing to do. In this sense, job-loss, theft or killing with AI are not a problem in ethics, but whether these are permissible under certain circumstances *is* such a problem. This article focuses on the genuine problems of ethics where we do not readily know what the answers are.

A last caveat is in order for our presentation: The ethics of AI and robotics is a very young field within applied ethics, with significant dynamics but few well-established issues and no authoritative overviews – though there are beginnings (Bryson 2019; European Group on Ethics in Science and New Technologies 2018; Floridi et al. 2018; Gibert 2019) – or policy recommendations (AI HLEG 2019). So this chapter cannot just reproduce what the community has achieved thus far but must propose an ordering where little order exists.

The notion of 'artificial intelligence' is understood broadly here, as any kind of artificial computational system that shows intelligent behaviour, i.e. complex behaviour that is conducive to reaching goals. This means we incorporate a range of machines, including those in 'technical AI' that show only limited abilities in learning or reasoning but excel at the automation of particular tasks, as well as machines in work on 'general AI' that aims at creating a generally intelligent agent.

AI somehow gets under our skin further than other technologies – thus the field of 'philosophy of AI'. Perhaps this is because the goal of AI is to create machines that have a feature central to how we humans see ourselves, namely as feeling, thinking, intelligent beings. The main purposes of an artificial intelligent agent involve sensing, modelling, planning and action, but current AI applications also include perception, text analysis, natural language processing (NLP), logical reasoning, game-playing, decision support systems, data analytics, predictive analytics, as well as autonomous vehicles and other forms of robotics. AI may involve any number of computational techniques to achieve these aims; be that classical symbol-manipulating, inspired by natural cognition, or machine learning via neural networks.

Historically, it is remarkable that the term "AI" was used as above ca. 1950–1975, then it came into disrepute during the 'AI winter', ca. 1975–1995, and narrowed. As a result, areas such as 'machine learning', 'NLP' and 'data science' were often not labelled as 'AI'. Since, ca. 2010, the use has broadened again, and at times almost all of computer science and even high-tech is lumped under 'AI'. It is now a name to be proud of, a booming industry with massive capital investment, and on the edge of hype again.

While AI can be entirely software, robots are physical machines that are subject to physical impact, typically through 'sensors', and they exert physical force onto the world, typically through 'actuators', like a gripper or a turning wheel. Accordingly, autonomous cars or planes are robots, and only a minuscule portion of robots are 'humanoid' (human-shaped), like in the movies. Some robots use AI, and some do not: Typical industrial robots blindly follow completely defined scripts with minimal sensory input and no learning or reasoning.

Policy is only one of the concerns of this article. There is significant public discussion about AI ethics, and there are frequent pronouncements from politicians that the matter requires new policy – which is easier said than done. Actual technology policy is difficult to plan and to enforce. It can take many forms, from incentives and funding, infrastructure, taxation, or good-will statements, to regulation by various actors, and the law. Policy for AI will possibly come into conflict with other aims of technology policy or general policy. Governments, parliaments, associations and industry circles in industrialised countries have produced reports and white papers in recent years, and some have generated good-will slogans ('trusted/responsible/

humane/human-centred/good/beneficial AI'), but is that what is needed? For a survey, see Jobin, Ienca, and Vayena (2019) and our list on PT-AI Policy Documents and Institutions.

For people who work in ethics and policy, there is probably a tendency to overestimate the impact and the threats from a new technology, and to underestimate how far current regulation can reach (e.g. for product liability). On the other hand, there is a tendency for businesses, the military and some public administrations to 'just talk' and do some 'ethics washing' in order to preserve a good public image and continue as before. Actually implementing legally binding regulation would challenge existing business models and practices. Actual policy is not just an implementation of ethical theory but subject to societal power structures – and the agents who do have the power will push against anything that restricts them. There is thus a significant risk that regulation will remain toothless in the face of economic and political power.

Though very little actual policy has been produced, there are some notable beginnings: The latest EU policy document suggests 'trustworthy AI' should be lawful, ethical and technically robust, and then spells this out as seven requirements: human oversight, technical robustness, privacy and data governance, transparency, fairness, well-being and accountability (AI HLEG 2019). Much European research now runs under the slogan of 'responsible research and innovation' (RRI) and 'technology assessment' has been a standard field since the advent of nuclear power. Professional ethics is also a standard field in information technology, and this includes issues that are relevant here. We also expect that much policy will eventually cover specific uses or technologies of AI and robotics, rather than the field as a whole (Calo 2018). In this article, we discuss the policy for each type of issue separately, rather than for AI or robotics in general.

The issue of which impact AI will have on employment is not discussed in this article since there is a separate entry in this handbook on the topic.

2 Main debates

In this section we outline the ethical issues of human use of AI and robotics systems that can be more or less autonomous – which means we look at issues that arise with certain uses of the technologies, which would not arise with others. It must be kept in mind, however, that technologies will always cause some uses to be easier and thus more frequent, and hinder other uses. The design of technical artefacts thus has ethical relevance for their use, so beyond 'responsible use', we also need 'responsible design' in this field. The focus on use does not presuppose which ethical approaches are best suited for tackling these issues; they might well be virtue ethics rather than consequentialist or value-based. This section is also neutral with respect to the question whether AI systems truly have 'intelligence' or other mental properties: It would apply equally well if AI and robotics are seen merely as the current face of automation.

2.1 Privacy

Here is a general discussion about privacy and surveillance in information technology (e.g. Macnish 2017; Roessler 2017), which mainly concerns the access to private data and data that is personally identifiable. Privacy has several well-recognised aspects, e.g. 'the right to be let alone', information privacy, privacy as an aspect of personhood, control over information about oneself, and the right to secrecy (Bennett & Raab 2006). Privacy studies have historically focused on state surveillance by secret services but now include surveillance by other state agents, businesses and even individuals. The technology has changed significantly in the last decades while regulation has been slow to respond (though there is the General Data Protection

Regulation [GDPR 2016]) – the result is a certain anarchy that is exploited by the most powerful players, sometimes in plain sight, sometimes in hiding.

The digital sphere has widened greatly: All data collection and storage is now digital, our lives are increasingly digital, most digital data is connected to a single Internet, and there is more and more sensor technology in use that generates data about non-digital aspects of our lives. AI increases both the possibilities of intelligent data collection and the possibilities for data analysis. This applies to blanket surveillance of whole populations as well as to classic targeted surveillance. In addition, much of the data is traded between agents, usually for a fee. At the same time, controlling who collects which data, and who has access, is much harder in the digital world than it was in the analogue world of paper and telephone calls. Data collection, sale and use are shrouded in secrecy.

The data trail we leave behind is how our 'free' services are paid for – but we are not told about that data collection and the value of this new raw material, and we are manipulated into leaving ever more such data. The main data-collection for the 'big 5' companies (Amazon, Google/Alphabet, Microsoft, Apple, Facebook) appears to be based on deception, exploiting human weaknesses, furthering procrastination, generating addiction and manipulation (Harris 2016). The primary focus of social media, gaming and most of the Internet in this 'surveillance economy' is to gain, maintain and direct attention – and thus data supply.

Many new AI technologies amplify these issues. For example, face recognition in photos and videos allows identification and thus profiling and searching for individuals. There are additional techniques for identification, e.g. 'device fingerprinting', which are commonplace on the Internet (sometimes revealed in the 'privacy policy'). Together with the 'Internet of things', the so-called smart systems (phone, TV, oven, lamp, virtual assistant, home, etc.), the 'smart city' (Sennett 2018) and 'smart governance', robots are set to become part of the data-gathering machinery that offers more detailed data, of different types, in real time, with ever more information. These systems will often reveal facts about us that we ourselves wish to suppress or are not aware of: they know more about us than we know ourselves. In the last sentence of his bestselling book *Homo Deus*, Harari (2016) asks about the long-term consequences of AI: "What will happen to society, politics and daily life when non-conscious but highly intelligent algorithms know us better than we know ourselves?"

In effect, this surveillance and attention economy "is the business model of the Internet" (Schneier 2015), sometimes called 'surveillance capitalism' (Zuboff 2019). It has caused many attempts to escape from the grasp of these corporations, e.g. in exercises of 'minimalism', or through the open source movement, but it appears that present-day citizens have lost the degree of autonomy needed to escape while fully continuing with their life and work. We have lost ownership of our data, if 'ownership' is the right relation here.

Privacy-preserving techniques that can largely conceal the identity of persons or groups are now a standard staple in data science; they include (relative) anonymisation, access control (plus encryption) and other models where computation is carried out with fully or partially encrypted input data; in the case of 'differential privacy', calibrated noise to encrypt the output of queries is added (Abowd 2017). While requiring more effort and cost, such techniques can avoid many of the privacy issues. Some companies have also seen better privacy as a competitive advantage that can be leveraged and sold at a price.

One of the major practical difficulties is to actually enforce regulation, both on the level of the state and on the level of the individual who has a claim. They must identify the responsible legal entity, prove the action, perhaps prove intent, find a court that declares itself competent and eventually get the court to actually enforce its decision. Well-established legal protection of rights such as consumer rights, product liability and other civil liabilities or protections of intellectual property rights is often missing, or hard to enforce, in digital products. This means that companies with a 'digital' background are used to testing their products on the consumers, without fear of liability, while heavily defending their intellectual property rights.

In sum, we have an ever-growing data collection about users and populations – to such an extent that these systems and their owners know more about us than we know ourselves. We users are manipulated into providing data, unable to escape this data collection and without knowledge of data access and use. We are not even able to enforce our legal rights because we are unable to identify a legal entity and hold it accountable. We have lost control. The surveillance economy is a scandal that still has not received due public attention.

2.2 Manipulation

The ethical issues of AI in surveillance go beyond the mere *accumulation* of data and direction of attention: They include the *use* of information for problematic purposes. One of these is manipulation behaviour, online and offline – mostly aiming at the user's money. Of course, efforts to manipulate behaviour in a way that undermines autonomous rational choice are ancient, but they may gain a new quality when they use AI systems. Given users' intense interactions with data systems and the deep knowledge about individuals this provides, we are vulnerable to manipulation and deception – referred to as 'nudges'. With sufficient prior data, algorithms can be used to target individuals or small groups with just the kind of input that is likely to influence these particular individuals.

Many advertisers, marketers and online sellers will use any legal means at their disposal, including exploitation of behavioural biases, deception and the generation of addiction (Costa & Halpern 2019) – e.g. through 'dark patterns' on web pages or in games (Mathur et al. 2019). Such manipulation is the business model in much of the gambling and gaming industries but it is also spreading to other areas, e.g. to low-cost airlines. Gambling and the sale of addictive substances are highly regulated but online manipulation and addiction is not. Manipulation of online behaviour is becoming a core business model of the Internet.

Furthermore, social media are now the prime locations for political propaganda. This influence can be used to steer voting behaviour, as in the Facebook-Cambridge Analytica 'scandal' (Woolley & Howard 2017) and – if successful – it may harm the autonomy of individuals (Susser, Roessler, & Nissenbaum 2019).

Improved AI 'faking' technologies turns what was once reliable evidence into unreliable evidence – this has already happened with digital photos, sound recordings and video, and it will soon be quite easy to create (rather than alter) 'deep fake' text, photos and video material with any content desired. Soon, sophisticated real-time interaction with persons over texting, phone or video will be faked, too. So, we cannot trust digital interaction, but we are at the same time increasingly dependent on it.

The policy in this field of privacy and manipulation is struggling to catch up with technical and social developments. Civil liberties and the protection of individual rights are under intense pressure from business lobbying, secret services and other state agencies that depend on surveillance. Actual legal protection from surveillance and manipulation has diminished massively as compared to the pre-digital age (of letters, analogue telephones and oral conversations). While the EU GDPR has strengthened privacy protection somewhat, the US and China prefer growth with less regulation, likely in the hope that this provides a competitive advantage. It is clear that state and business actors have increased their ability to watch and to manipulate people with the help of AI technology and will continue to do so to further their particular interests – unless reined in by policy in the interest of general society (GDPR 2016).

2.3 Opacity

Opacity and bias are central issues in what is now sometimes called 'data ethics' or 'big data ethics' (Floridi & Taddeo 2016). Automated AI decision support systems and 'predictive analytics' operate on data and produce a decision as 'output'. This output may range from the relatively trivial to the highly significant: "this restaurant matches your preferences", "the patient in this X-ray has completed bone growth", "application to credit card declined", "donor organ will be given to another patient", "bail is denied", or "target identified and engaged". Data analysis is often used in 'predictive analytics' in business, healthcare and other fields, to foresee future developments – since prediction is easier with AI, it will also become a cheaper commodity.

It appears that AI systems for automated decision support are part of a power structure where it will often be impossible for the affected person to know how the system came to this output, i.e. the system is 'opaque' to that person. If the system involves machine learning, it will typically be opaque even to the expert, who will not know how a particular pattern was identified, or even what the pattern is. Bias in decision systems and datasets is exacerbated by this opacity. So, at least in the cases where there is a desire to remove bias, the analysis of opacity and bias go hand in hand, and the political response has to tackle both issues together.

Many AI systems rely on machine learning techniques in (simulated) neural networks that will extract patterns from a given dataset, with or without 'correct' solutions provided; i.e. supervised, semi-supervised or unsupervised. With these techniques, the 'learning' captures patterns in the data and these are labelled in a way that appears useful to the decision the system makes, while the programmer does not really know *which* patterns in the data the system has used. In fact the programs are evolving, so when new data comes in, or new feedback is given ("this was correct", "this was incorrect"), the patterns used by the learning system change. What this means is that the outcome is not transparent to the user or programmers: It is opaque.

There are several technical activities that aim at 'explainable AI' and, more recently, a DARPA programme (Gunning 2018) and the AI4EU project on 'human-centred AI' (AI4EU 2019, 100–187). This does not mean that we expect an AI to 'explain its reasoning' – doing so would require far more serious moral autonomy than we currently attribute to AI systems (see Section 3.2). In the EU, some of these issues have been taken into account with the GDPR, which foresees that consumers, when faced with a decision based on data processing, will have a legal "right to explanation" – how far this goes and to what extent it can be enforced is disputed (Wachter, Mittelstadt, & Russell 2018). Zerilli, Knott, Maclaurin, and Gavaghan (2019) argue that there may be a double standard here, where we demand a high level of explanation for machine-based decisions despite the abilities of humans to explain and provide reasons sometimes not reaching that standard themselves.

The politician Henry Kissinger pointed out that there is a fundamental problem for democratic decision-making if we rely on a system that is supposedly superior to humans but cannot explain its decisions. He says we may have "generated a potentially dominating technology in search of a guiding philosophy" (Kissinger 2018). The political angle of this discussion is presented by O'Neil in her influential book *Weapons of Math Destruction* (O'Neil 2016).

2.4 Bias

Bias typically surfaces when unfair judgements are made because the individual making the judgment is influenced by a characteristic that is *actually* irrelevant to the matter at hand, typically a discriminatory preconception about members of a group. So, one form of bias is a learned cognitive feature of a person, often not made explicit. The person concerned may not be aware of having that bias – they may even be honestly and explicitly opposed to a bias they are found to have (e.g. through priming, cf. Graham & Lowery 2004).

Apart from the social phenomenon of learned bias, the human cognitive system is generally prone to having various kinds of 'cognitive biases', e.g. the 'confirmation bias': Humans tend to interpret information as confirming what they already believe. This second form of bias is often said to impede performance in rational judgement (Kahnemann 2011) – though at least some cognitive biases generate an evolutionary advantage, e.g. economical use of resources for intuitive judgement. There is a question whether AI systems could or should have such cognitive bias.

A third form of bias is present in data when it exhibits systematic error, e.g. one of the various kinds of 'statistical bias'. Strictly, any given dataset will only be unbiased for a single kind of issue, so the mere creation of a dataset involves the danger that may it be used for a different kind of issue and then turn out to be biased for that kind. Machine learning on the basis of such data would then not only fail to recognise the bias, but codify and automate the 'historical bias'. Such historical bias was discovered in an automated recruitment screening system at Amazon (discontinued in early 2017) that discriminated against women – presumably because the company had a history of discriminating against women in the hiring process. The problem with such systems is their bias combined with humans placing excessive trust in the systems. The political dimensions of such automated systems in the US are investigated.

One use of prediction is in 'predictive policing', which many fear might lead to an erosion of public liberties because it can take away power from the people whose behaviour is predicted (Eubanks 2018; Ferguson 2017). It appears, however, that many of the worries about policing depend on futuristic scenarios where law enforcement foresees and punishes planned actions, rather than waiting until a crime has been committed (like in the 2002 film *Minority Report*). Actual 'predictive policing' or 'intelligence led policing' techniques mainly concern the question of where and when police forces will be needed most – which is something a police force has always done. Whether this is problematic depends on the appropriate level of trust in the technical quality of these systems, and on the evaluation of aims of the police work itself. Perhaps a recent paper title points in the right direction here: "AI ethics in predictive policing: From models of threat to an ethics of care" (Asaro 2019).

There are significant technical efforts to detect and remove bias from AI systems, but it is fair to say that these are in early stages (see UK Institute for Ethical AI & Machine Learning, Yeung & Lodge 2019). It appears that technological fixes have their limits in that they need a mathematical notion of fairness, which is hard to come by (Whittaker et al. 2018, 24ff).

2.5 Deception and robots

Human-robot interaction (HRI) is an academic field in its own right that now pays significant attention to ethical matters, the dynamics of perception from both sides, and both the different interests present in and the intricacy of the social context, including co-working. Useful surveys for the ethics of robotics can be found in: Calo, Froomkin, and Kerr 2016; Lin, Abney, and Jenkins 2017 and Royakkers and van Est 2016.

While AI can be used to manipulate humans into believing and doing things, it can also be used to drive robots that are problematic if their processes or appearance involve deception, threaten human dignity or violate the Kantian requirement of 'respect for humanity'. Humans very easily attribute mental properties to objects, and empathise with them, especially when the outer appearance of these objects is similar to that of living beings. This can be used to deceive humans (or animals) into attributing more intellectual or even emotional significance to robots

Ethics of artificial intelligence

or AI systems than they deserve. Some parts of humanoid robotics are problematic in this regard (e.g. Hiroshi Ishiguro's remote-controlled Geminoids), and there are cases that have been clearly deceptive for public-relations purposes (e.g. Hanson Robotics' "Sophia"). Of course, some fairly basic constraints of business ethics and law apply to robots, too: product safety and liability, or non-deception in advertisement.

There are cases, however, where human-human interaction has aspects that appear specifically human in ways that can perhaps not be replaced by robots: care, love and sex.

The use of robots in healthcare for humans is currently at the level of concept studies in real environments, but it may become a usable technology in a few years, and has raised a number of concerns for a dystopian future of de-humanised care (Sparrow 2016). Current systems include robots that support human carers/caregivers (e.g. in lifting patients or transporting material) and robots that enable patients to do certain things by themselves (e.g. eat with a robotic arm) as well as robots that are provided to patients for companionship and comfort (e.g. the 'Paro' robot seal). For an overview, see van Wynsberghe (2016). It is not very clear that there really is an issue here, since the discussion mostly focuses on the fear of robots de-humanising care, but the actual and foreseeable robots in care are for classic automation of technical tasks as assistive robots. They are thus 'care robots' only in a behavioural sense of performing tasks in care environments, not in the sense that a human 'cares' for the patients. Some robots that pretend to 'care' on a basic level are available (Paro seal) and others are in the making. A system that pretends to care would be deceptive and thus problematic – unless the deception is countered by sufficiently large utility gain. Perhaps feeling cared for by a machine can be progress in some cases?

Another area of discussion are sex robots: It has been argued by several tech optimists that humans will likely be interested in sex and companionship with robots and be comfortable with the idea (Levy 2007). Given the variation of human sexual preferences, including sex toys and sex dolls, this seems very likely: The question is whether such devices should be manufactured and promoted, and whether there should be limits to use (Danaher & McArthur 2017; Devlin 2018). Humans have long had deep emotional attachments to objects, so perhaps companionship or even love with a predictable android is attractive, especially to people who struggle with actual humans, and already prefer dogs, cats, a computer or a *tamagotchi*. In all this there is the issue of deception, since a robot cannot (at present) mean what it says or have feelings for a human. Having said that, paying for deception seems to be an elementary part of the traditional sex industry. Finally, there are concerns that have often accompanied matters of sex, namely consent, aesthetic concerns and the worry that humans may be 'corrupted' by certain experiences. This may seem old-fashioned, but it is likely that pornography or sex robots support the perception of other humans as mere objects of desire, or even as recipients of abuse – and thus ruin a deeper sexual experience.

2.6 Autonomy and responsibility

There are several notions of autonomy at play in the discussion of autonomous systems. A stronger notion is involved in philosophical debates where autonomy is the basis for responsibility and personhood. In this context, responsibility implies autonomy, but not inversely, so there can be systems that have degrees of technical autonomy without raising issues of responsibility. The weaker, more technical, notion of autonomy in robotics is relative and gradual: A system is said to be autonomous with respect to human control to a certain degree (Müller 2012).

One question is the degree to which autonomous robots raise issues to which our present conceptual schemes must adapt, or whether they just require technical adjustments. In most jurisdictions, there is a sophisticated system of civil and criminal liability to resolve such issues. Technical standards, e.g. for the safe use of machinery in medical environments, will likely need to be adjusted. There is already a field of 'verifiable AI' for such safety-critical systems, and for 'security applications'. Technical associations like the Institute of Electrical and Electronics Engineers and the British Standards Institution have produced 'standards', particularly on more technical problems such as data security and transparency. Among the many autonomous systems on land, on water, under water, in the air or in space, we discuss two samples: autonomous vehicles and autonomous weapons.

Autonomous vehicles hold the promise to reduce the very significant damage that human driving currently causes – with approximately 1 million humans being killed per year, many more injured, the environment polluted, soil sealed with tarmac, cities full of parked cars, and so on and so on. However, there seem to be questions on how autonomous vehicles should behave, and how responsibility and risk should be distributed in the complicated system the vehicles operates in. There is some discussion of 'trolley problems' in this context. In the classic 'trolley problems' (Woollard & Howard-Snyder 2016, section 2), various dilemmas are presented: The simplest version is that of a trolley train on a track that is heading towards five people and will kill them unless the train is diverted onto a side track. But on that track there is one person who will be killed if the train takes that route. 'Trolley problems' are not supposed to describe actual ethical problems or to be solved with a 'right' choice. Rather, they are thought-experiments where choice is artificially constrained to a small finite number of distinct one-off options and where the agent has perfect knowledge. These thought-experiments are used as a theoretical tool to investigate ethical intuitions and theories – especially the difference between actively doing vs. allowing something to happen, intended vs. tolerated consequences, and consequentialist vs. other normative approaches (Kamm & Rakowski 2016). This type of problem has reminded many of the problems encountered in actual driving, and in autonomous driving. It is doubtful, however, that an actual driver or autonomous car will ever have to solve trolley problems. While autonomous car trolley problems have received a lot of media attention, they do not seem to offer anything new to either ethical theory or the programming of autonomous vehicles.

Our second example is *military robots*. The notion of automated weapons is fairly old: "For example, instead of fielding simple guided missiles or remotely piloted vehicles, we might launch completely autonomous land, sea, and air vehicles capable of complex, far-ranging reconnaissance and attack missions." (DARPA 1983, 1). This proposal was ridiculed as 'fantasy' at the time (Dreyfus, Dreyfus, & Athanasiou 1986, ix), but it is now a reality, at least for more easily identifiable targets (missiles, planes, ships, tanks, etc.). The main arguments against (lethal) autonomous weapon systems (AWS or LAWS), are that they support extrajudicial killings, take responsibility away from humans and make wars or killings more likely (Lin, Bekey, & Abney 2008, 73–86). The crucial asymmetry where one side can kill with impunity, and thus has fewer reasons not to do so, already exists in conventional drone wars with remote-controlled weapons (e.g. US in Pakistan). Another question seems to be whether using autonomous weapons in war would make wars worse, or perhaps make wars less bad? If robots reduce war crimes and crimes in war, the answer may well be positive and has been used as an argument in favour of these weapons (Müller 2016). Arguably the main threat is not the use of such weapons in conventional warfare but in asymmetric conflicts or by non-state agents, including criminals. A lot has been made of keeping humans "in the loop" or "on the loop" in the military guidance on weapons (Santoni de Sio & van den Hoven 2018). There have been discussions about the difficulties of allocating responsibility for the killings of an autonomous weapon, and a 'responsibility gap' has been suggested (esp. Sparrow 2007), meaning that neither the human nor the machine may be responsible. On the other hand, we do not assume that for every event there is someone responsible for that event, and the real issue may well be the distribution of risk (Simpson & Müller 2016).

2.7 Singularity

In some quarters, the aim of current AI is thought to be an 'artificial general intelligence' (AGI) – this notion is usually distinguished from traditional notions of AI as a general purpose system, and from Searle's notion of 'strong AI': "computers given the right programs can be literally said to *understand* and have other cognitive states" (Searle 1980, 417).

The idea of the *singularity* is that if the trajectory of artificial intelligence towards AGI reaches up to systems that have a human level of intelligence, then these systems would themselves have the ability to develop AI systems that surpass the human level of intelligence, that is they are 'superintelligent'. Such superintelligent AI systems would quickly self-improve or develop even more intelligent systems (Chalmers 2010). This sharp turn of events after reaching superintelligent AI is the 'singularity' from where onwards the development of AI is out of human control and hard to predict (Kurzweil 2005, 487). Bostrom (2014) explains in some detail what would happen at that point, and what the risks for humanity are.

The fear that "the robots we created will take over the world" had captured human imagination even before there were computers. It was first formulated by Irvin Good:

> Let an ultraintelligent machine be defined as a machine that can far surpass all the intellectual activities of any man however clever. Since the design of machines is one of these intellectual activities, an ultraintelligent machine could design even better machines; there would then unquestionably be an 'intelligence explosion', and the intelligence of man would be left far behind. Thus the first ultraintelligent machine is the last invention that man need ever make, provided that the machine is docile enough to tell us how to keep it under control.
>
> *(1965, 33)*

The argument from acceleration to singularity is spelled out by Kurzweil (1999), who points out that computing power has been increasing exponentially, i.e. doubling about every two years since 1970 in accordance with 'Moore's Law' on the number of transistors, and will continue to do so for some time in the future. Kurzweil predicted that by 2010 supercomputers will reach human computation capacity, by 2030 'mind uploading' will be possible, and by 2045 the 'singularity' will occur. In addition to Moore's Law there is also the actual increase in the funds available to AI companies in recent years. There are possible paths to superintelligence other than computing power increase, e.g. the complete emulation of the human brain on a computer (Kurzweil 2012), biological paths, or networks and organisations (Bostrom 2014, 22–51). Despite obvious weaknesses in the identification of 'intelligence' with processing power, Kurzweil seems right that humans tend to underestimate the power of exponential growth.

The participants in this debate are united by being technophiles, in the sense that they expect technology to develop rapidly and bring broadly welcome changes – but beyond that, they divide into those that focus on benefits (e.g. Kurzweil) vs. those that focus on risks (e.g. Bostrom). Both camps sympathise with 'transhuman' views of survival for humankind in a different physical form, e.g. uploaded on a computer (Moravec 1990). They also consider the prospects of 'human enhancement', in various respects, including intelligence – often called "intelligence augmentation" (IA). It may be that future AI will be used for human enhancement, or will contribute further to the dissolution of the neatly defined human single person.

The argument from superintelligence to risk requires the assumption that superintelligence does not imply benevolence. This is contrary to Kantian traditions in ethics that have argued higher levels of rationality or intelligence would go along with a better understanding of what is moral and a better ability to act morally (Chalmers 2010, 36f). Arguments for risk from superintelligence say that rationality and morality are entirely independent dimensions – this is sometimes explicitly argued for as an "orthogonality thesis" (Bostrom 2014, 105–109).

Criticism of the singularity narrative has been raised from various angles. Kurzweil and Bostrom seem to assume that intelligence is a one-dimensional property and that the set of intelligent agents is well ordered in the mathematical sense – but neither discusses intelligence at any length in their books. Generally, it is fair to say that despite some efforts, the assumptions made in the powerful narrative of superintelligence and singularity have not been investigated in detail. Philosophically, one interesting question is whether or not singularity is on the trajectory of actual AI research (e.g. Brooks 2017; Müller forthcoming). This discussion raises the question whether the concern about 'singularity' is just a narrative about fictional AI based on human fears. But even if one *does* find negative reasons compelling and the singularity not likely to occur, there is still a significant possibility that one may turn out to be wrong. So, it appears that discussion of the very high-impact risk of singularity has justification *even if* one thinks the probability of such singularity ever occurring is very low.

Thinking about superintelligence in the long term raises the question whether superintelligence may lead to the extinction of the human species, which is called an "existential risk" (or XRisk): The superintelligent systems may well have preferences that conflict with the existence of humans on Earth, and may thus decide to end that existence – and given their superior intelligence, they will have the power to do so (or they may happen to end it because they do not really care). These issues are sometimes taken more narrowly to be about human extinction (Bostrom 2013), or more broadly as concerning any large risk for the species – of which AI is only one (Häggström 2016).

In a narrow sense, the 'control problem' is how we humans can remain in control of an AI system once it is superintelligent (Bostrom 2014, 127ff). In a wider sense it is the problem of how we can make sure an AI system will turn out to be positive, in the sense we humans perceive it (Russell 2019); this is sometimes called 'value alignment'. How easy or hard it is to control a superintelligence depends to a significant extent on the speed of 'take-off' to a superintelligent system. One aspect of this problem is that we might decide a certain feature is desirable but then find out that it has unforeseen consequences that are so negative that we would not desire that feature after all. This is the ancient problem of King Midas who wished that all he touched would turn into gold.

Discussions about superintelligence include speculation about omniscient beings, the radical changes on a 'latter day' and the promise of immortality through transcendence of our current bodily form – so they have clear religious undertones (Geraci 2010). These issues also pose a well-known problem of epistemology: Can we know the ways of the omniscient? Opponents would thus say we need an ethics for the 'small' problems that occur with actual AI and robotics, and less for the 'big ethics' of existential risk from AI.

2.8 Machine ethics

Machine ethics is ethics for machines, for 'ethical machines', for machines as *subjects*, rather than for the human use of machines as *objects*. It is often not very clear whether this is supposed to cover all of AI ethics or to be a part of it (Floridi & Saunders 2004; Moor 2006; Wallach & Asaro 2017). Sometimes it looks as though there is the dubious inference at play here that if machines act in ethically relevant ways, then we need machine ethics. Some of the discussion in machine ethics makes the very substantial assumption that machines can, in some sense, be ethical agents responsible for their actions, or 'autonomous moral agents'. It is not clear that there is a consistent notion of 'machine ethics' since weaker versions are in danger of reducing 'having an ethics' to notions that would not normally be considered sufficient (e.g. without 'reflection' or even without 'action'); stronger notions that move towards artificial moral agents may describe a – currently – empty set. So, in this chapter, we present ethical issues (discussed earlier) and the notion of moral agency in artificial systems (discussion follows), but we do not expand it to machine ethics.

2.9 Artificial moral agents

If one takes machine ethics to concern moral agents, in some substantial sense, then these agents can be called 'artificial moral agents', having rights and responsibilities. However, the discussion about artificial entities challenges a number of common notions in ethics and it can be very useful to understand these in abstraction from the human case (cf. Powers & Ganascia 2020). If the robots act, will they themselves be responsible, liable or accountable for their actions? Or should the distribution of risk perhaps take precedence over discussions of responsibility?

Several authors use 'artificial moral agent' in a less demanding sense, borrowing from the use of 'agent' in software engineering, in which case matters of responsibility and rights will not arise. James Moor (2006) distinguishes four types of machine agents: ethical impact agents (example: robot jockeys), implicit ethical agents (example: safe autopilot), explicit ethical agents (example: using formal methods to estimate utility), and full ethical agents ("can make explicit ethical judgments and generally is competent to reasonably justify them. An average adult human is a full ethical agent"). Several ways to achieve 'explicit' or 'full' ethical agents have been proposed, via programming it in (operational morality), via 'developing' the ethics itself (functional morality) and, finally, full-blown morality with full intelligence and sentience (Allen, Smit, & Wallach 2005; Moor 2006).

In some of these discussions the notion of 'moral patient' plays a role: Ethical *agents* have responsibilities while ethical *patients* have rights, because harm to them matters. It seems clear that some entities are patients without being agents, e.g. simple animals that can feel pain but cannot make justified choices. On the other hand it is normally understood that all agents will also be patients (e.g. in a Kantian framework). Usually, being a person is supposed to be what makes an entity a responsible agent, someone who can have duties and be the object of ethical concerns, and such personhood is typically a deep notion associated with free will (Strawson 2004) and with having phenomenal consciousness.

Traditional distribution of responsibility already occurs: A car maker is responsible for the technical safety of the car, a driver is responsible for driving, a mechanic is responsible for proper maintenance, the public authorities are responsible for the technical conditions of the roads, and so on. In general, "The effects of decisions or actions based on AI are often the result of countless interactions among many actors, including designers, developers, users, software, and hardware. . . . With distributed agency comes distributed responsibility." (Taddeo & Floridi 2018, 751). How this distribution might occur is not a problem that is specific to AI.

Some authors have indicated that it should be seriously considered whether current robots must be allocated rights (Danaher 2019; Gunkel 2018). This position seems to rely largely on criticism of the opponents and on the empirical observation that robots and other non-persons are sometimes treated as having rights. In this vein, a 'relational turn' has been proposed: If we relate to robots as though they had rights, then we might be well advised not to search whether they 'really' do have such rights (Coeckelbergh 2010). This raises the question how far such anti-realism or quasi-realism can go, and what it means then to say that 'robots have rights' in a human-centred approach.

There is a wholly separate issue regarding whether robots (or other AI systems) should be given the status of 'legal entities', or 'legal persons' – in the sense in which natural persons, but also states, businesses or organisations are 'entities', namely that they can have legal rights and duties. The European Parliament has considered allocating such status to robots for civil liability (Parliament 2016) but not criminal liability, which is reserved for natural persons. It would also be possible to assign only a certain subset of rights and duties to robots. In environmental ethics there is a long-standing discussion about the legal rights for natural objects such as trees (Stone 1972).

In the community of 'artificial consciousness' researchers believe there is a significant concern whether it would be ethical to create such consciousness, since creating it would presumably imply ethical obligations to a sentient being, e.g. not to harm it and not to end its existence by switching it off – some authors have called for a "moratorium on synthetic phenomenology" (Bentley, Brundage, Häggström, & Metzinger 2018, 28f).

3 Future developments

The singularity thus raises the problem of the concept of AI again. It is remarkable how imagination or 'vision' has played a central role since the very beginning of the discipline at the 'Dartmouth Summer Research Project' (1956). And the evaluation of this vision is subject to dramatic change: In a few decades, we went from the slogans "AI is impossible" (Dreyfus 1972) and "AI is just automation" (Lighthill 1973) to "AI will solve all problems" (Kurzweil 1999) and "AI may kill us all" (Bostrom 2014). This not only created media attention and PR efforts but it also raised the problem of how much of this 'philosophy and ethics of AI' is really about AI rather than about an imagined technology. As we said at the outset, AI and robotics have raised fundamental questions about what we should do with these systems, what the systems themselves should do, and what risks they have in the long term. They also challenge the human view of humanity as the intelligent and dominant species on Earth. We have seen issues that have been raised and we will have to watch technological and social developments closely to catch the new issues early on, and to develop a philosophical analysis, as well as to learn for traditional problems of philosophy.

Note

1 This chapter is based on Vincent C. Müller, Ethics of artificial intelligence and robotics, in Edward N. Zalta (ed.), *Stanford encyclopedia of philosophy* (Palo Alto: CSLI, Stanford University, forthcoming), http://plato.stanford.edu/

References

Abowd, J. M. (2017). How will statistical agencies operate when all data are private? *Journal of Privacy and Confidentiality*, 7 (3), 1–15.
AI4EU. (2019). Outcomes from the strategic orientation workshop (Deliverable 7.1). *ai4eu.eu* (28.06.2019).
AI HLEG. (2019). High-level expert group on artificial intelligence: Ethics guidelines for trustworthy AI. *European Commission* (09.04.2019). Retrieved from https://ec.europa.eu/digital-single-market/en/high-level-expert-group-artificial-intelligence

Allen, C., Smit, I., & Wallach, W. (2005). Artificial morality: Top-down, bottom-up, and hybrid approaches. *Ethics and Information Technology*, 7 (3), 149–155. doi: 10.1007/s10676-006-0004-4

Asaro, P. M. (2019). AI ethics in predictive policing: From models of threat to an ethics of care. *IEEE Technology and Society Magazine*, 38 (2), 40–53. doi: 10.1109/MTS.2019.2915154

Bennett, C. J., & Raab, C. (2006). *The governance of privacy: Policy instruments in global perspective* (2nd ed.). Cambridge, MA: MIT Press.

Bentley, P. J., Brundage, M., Häggström, O., & Metzinger, T. (2018). Should we fear artificial intelligence? In-depth analysis. *European Parliamentary Research Service, Scientific Foresight Unit (STOA), March 2018(PE 614.547)*, 1–40. Retrieved from www.europarl.europa.eu/RegData/etudes/IDAN/2018/614547/EPRS_IDA%282018%29614547_EN.pdf

Bostrom, N. (2013). Existential risk prevention as global priority. *Global Policy*, 4 (1), 15–31.

Bostrom, N. (2014). *Superintelligence: Paths, dangers, strategies*. Oxford: Oxford University Press.

Brooks, R. (2017). The seven deadly sins of predicting the future of AI (07.09.2017). Retrieved from https://rodneybrooks.com/the-seven-deadly-sins-of-predicting-the-future-of-ai/

Brundage, M., Avin, S., Clark, J., Toner, H., Eckersley, P., Garfinkel, B., . . . Filar, B. (2018). The malicious use of artificial intelligence: Forecasting, prevention, and mitigation. *FHI/CSER/CNAS/EFF/OpenAI Report*, 1–101. Retrieved from https://arxiv.org/abs/1802.07228

Bryson, J. J. (2019). The past decade and future of AI's impact on society. In Anonymous (Ed.), *Towards a new enlightenment: A transcendent decade*. Madrid: Turner – BVVA.

Calo, R. (2018). Artificial intelligence policy: A primer and roadmap. *University of Bologna Law Review*, 3 (2), 180–218. http://dx.doi.org/10.2139/ssrn.3015350

Calo, R., Froomkin, M. A., & Kerr, I. (Eds.). (2016). *Robot law*. Cheltenham: Edward Elgar.

Chalmers, D. J. (2010). The singularity: A philosophical analysis. *Journal of Consciousness Studies*, 17 (9–10), 7–65.

Coeckelbergh, M. (2010). Robot rights? Towards a social-relational justification of moral consideration. *Ethics and Information Technology*, 12 (3), 209–221. doi: 10.1007/s10676-010-9235-5

Costa, E., & Halpern, D. (2019). The behavioural science of online harm and manipulation, and what to do about it: An exploratory paper to spark ideas and debate. *The Behavioural Insights Team Report*, 1–82. Retrieved from www.bi.team/publications/the-behavioural-science-of-online-harm-and-manipulation-and-what-to-do-about-it/

Danaher, J. (2019). Welcoming robots into the moral circle: A defence of ethical behaviourism. *Science and Engineering Ethics*. doi: 10.1007/s11948-019-00119-x

Danaher, J., & McArthur, N. (Eds.). (2017). *Robot sex: Social and ethical implications*. Boston, MA: MIT Press.

DARPA. (1983). Strategic computing – New-generation computing technology: A strategic plan for its development an application to critical problems in defense (28.10.1983). Retrieved from www.scribd.com/document/192183614/Strategic-Computing-1983

Devlin, K. (2018). *Turned on: Science, sex and robots*. London: Bloomsbury.

Dreyfus, H. L. (1972). *What computers still can't do: A critique of artificial reason* (2nd ed.). Cambridge, MA: MIT Press.

Dreyfus, H. L., Dreyfus, S. E., & Athanasiou, T. (1986). *Mind over machine: The power of human intuition and expertise in the era of the computer*. New York: Free Press.

Eubanks, V. (2018). *Automating inequality: How high-tech tools profile, police, and punish the poor*. London: St. Martin's Press.

European Group on Ethics in Science and New Technologies. (2018). Statement on artificial intelligence, robotics and 'autonomous' systems. European Commission, Directorate-General for Research and Innovation, Unit RTD.01 (09.03.2018). Retrieved from http://ec.europa.eu/research/ege/pdf/ege_ai_statement_2018.pdf

Ferguson, A. G. (2017). *The rise of big data policing: Surveillance, race, and the future of law enforcement*. New York: NYU Press.

Floridi, L., Cowls, J., Beltrametti, M., Chatila, R., Chazerand, P., Dignum, V., . . . Vayena, E. (2018). AI4People – An ethical framework for a good AI society: Opportunities, risks, principles, and recommendations. *Minds and Machines*, 28 (4), 689–707.

Floridi, L., & Saunders, J. W. (2004). On the morality of artificial agents. *Minds and Machines, 14*, 349–379.

Floridi, L., & Taddeo, M. (2016). What is data ethics? *Philosophical Transactions of the Royal Society A, 374* (2083).

GDPR. (2016). General data protection regulation: Regulation (EU) 2016/679 of the European parliament and of the council of 27 April 2016 on the protection of natural persons with regard to the processing of personal data and on the free movement of such data, and repealing directive 95/46/EC. *Official Journal of the European Union, 119* (04.05.2016), 1–88. Retrieved from http://data.europa.eu/eli/reg/2016/679/oj

Geraci, R. M. (2010). *Apocalyptic AI: Vision of heaven in robotics, artificial intelligence and virtual reality*. Oxford: Oxford University Press.

Gibert, M. (2019). Éthique artificielle (version grand public). In M. Kristanek (Ed.), *Encyclopédie Philosophique*. Retrieved from http://encyclo-philo.fr/etique-artificielle-gp/

Good, I. J. (1965). Speculations concerning the first ultraintelligent machine. In F. L. Alt & M. Ruminoff (Eds.), *Advances in computers* (Vol. 6, pp. 31–88). New York and London: Academic Press.

Graham, S., & Lowery, B. S. (2004). Priming unconscious racial stereotypes about adolescent offenders. *Law and Human Behavior, 28* (5), 483–504. doi: 10.1023/B:LAHU.0000046430.65485.1f

Gunkel, D. J. (2018). The other question: Can and should robots have rights? *Ethics and Information Technology, 20* (2), 87–99. doi: 10.1007/s10676-017-9442-4

Gunning, D. (2018). *Explainable artificial intelligence (XAI)*. Defense Advanced Research Projects Agency. Retrieved from www.darpa.mil/program/explainable-artificial-intelligence

Häggström, O. (2016). *Here be dragons: Science, technology and the future of humanity*. Oxford: Oxford University Press.

Harari, Y. N. (2016). *Homo deus: A brief history of tomorrow*. New York: Harper.

Harris, T. (2016). How technology is hijacking your mind – From a magician and google design ethicist. *medium.com, Thrive Global* (18.05.2016).

Jobin, A., Ienca, M., & Vayena, E. (2019). The global landscape of AI ethics guidelines. *Nature Machine Intelligence, 1* (9), 389–399. doi: 10.1038/s42256-019-0088-2

Kahnemann, D. (2011). *Thinking fast and slow*. London: Macmillan.

Kamm, F. M., & Rakowski, E. (Eds.). (2016). *The trolley problem mysteries*. New York: Oxford University Press.

Kissinger, H. A. (2018). How the enlightenment ends: Philosophically, intellectually – in every way – human society is unprepared for the rise of artificial intelligence. *The Atlantic* (06.2018). Retrieved from www.theatlantic.com/magazine/archive/2018/06/henry-kissinger-ai-could-mean-the-end-of-human-history/559124/

Kurzweil, R. (1999). *The age of spiritual machines: When computers exceed human intelligence*. London: Penguin.

Kurzweil, R. (2005). *The singularity is near: When humans transcend biology*. London: Viking.

Kurzweil, R. (2012). *How to create a mind: The secret of human thought revealed*. New York: Viking.

Levy, D. (2007). *Love and sex with robots: The evolution of human-robot relationships*. New York: Harper & Co.

Lighthill, J. (1973). Artificial intelligence: A general survey. In *Artificial intelligence: A paper symposion*. London. Retrieved from www.chilton-computing.org.uk/inf/literature/reports/lighthill_report/p001.htm

Lin, P., Abney, K., & Jenkins, R. (Eds.). (2017). *Robot ethics 2.0: From autonomous cars to artificial intelligence*. New York: Oxford University Press.

Lin, P., Bekey, G., & Abney, K. (2008). Autonomous military robotics: Risk, ethics, and design. *US Department of Navy, Office of Naval Research* (20.12.2008), 1–112.

Macnish, K. (2017). *The ethics of surveillance: An introduction*. London: Routledge.

Mathur, A., Acar, G., Friedman, M., Lucherini, E., Mayer, J., Chetty, M., & Narayanan, A. (2019). Dark patterns at scale: Findings from a crawl of 11K shopping websites. *Proceedings of the ACM Human-Computer Interaction, 3* (81), 1–32.

Moor, J. H. (2006). The nature, importance, and difficulty of machine ethics. *IEEE Intelligent Systems, 21* (4), 18–21.

Moravec, H. (1990). *Mind children*. Cambridge, MA: Harvard University Press.

Müller, V. C. (2012). Autonomous cognitive systems in real-world environments: Less control, more flexibility and better interaction. *Cognitive Computation, 4* (3), 212–215. doi: 10.1007/s12559-012-9129-4

Müller, V. C. (2016). Autonomous killer robots are probably good news. In E. Di Nucci & F. Santoni de Sio (Eds.), *Drones and responsibility: Legal, philosophical and socio-technical perspectives on the use of remotely controlled weapons* (pp. 67–81). London: Ashgate.

Müller, V. C. (forthcoming). *Can machines think? Fundamental problems of artificial intelligence*. New York: Oxford University Press.

O'Neil, C. (2016). *Weapons of math destruction: How big data increases inequality and threatens democracy*. Largo, ML: Crown.

Parliament, E. (2016). Draft report with recommendations to the commission on civil law rules on robotics (2015/2103(INL)). *Committee on Legal Affairs* (31.05.2016).

Powers, T. M., & Ganascia, J.-G. (2020). The ethics of the ethics of AI. In M. D. Dubber, F. Pasquale, & S. Das (Eds.), *Oxford handbook of ethics of artificial intelligence*. New York: Oxford University Press.

Roessler, B. (2017). Privacy as a human right. *Proceedings of the Aristotelian Society, 2* (CXVII).

Royakkers, L., & van Est, R. (2016). *Just ordinary robots: Automation from love to war*. Boca Raton: CRC Press and Taylor & Francis.

Russell, S. (2019). *Human compatible: Artificial intelligence and the problem of control*. New York: Viking.

Santoni de Sio, F., & van den Hoven, J. (2018). Meaningful human control over autonomous systems: A philosophical account. *Frontiers in Robotics and AI, 5* (15). doi: 10.3389/frobt.2018.00015

Schneier, B. (2015). *Data and Goliath: The hidden battles to collect your data and control your world*. New York: W. W. Norton.

Searle, J. R. (1980). Minds, brains and programs. *Behavioral and Brain Sciences, 3*, 417–457.

Sennett, R. (2018). *Building and dwelling: Ethics for the city*. London: Allen Lane.

Simpson, T. W., & Müller, V. C. (2016). Just war and robots' killings. *The Philosophical Quarterly, 66* (263), 302–322. doi: 10.1093/pq/pqv075

Sparrow, R. (2007). Killer robots. *Journal of Applied Philosophy, 24* (1), 62–77.

Sparrow, R. (2016). Robots in aged care: A dystopian future. *AI & Society, 31* (4), 1–10.

Stone, C. D. (1972). Should trees have standing – Toward legal rights for natural objects. *Southern California Law Review, 2*, 450–501.

Strawson, G. (2004). Free will. In *Routledge encyclopedia of philosophy* (29.02.2004). Retrieved May 2005, from, www.rep.routledge.com/article/V014

Susser, D., Roessler, B., & Nissenbaum, H. (2019). Technology, autonomy, and manipulation. *Internet Policy Review, 8* (2). doi: 10.14763/2019.2.1410

Taddeo, M., & Floridi, L. (2018). How AI can be a force for good. *Science, 361* (6404), 751–752. doi: 10.1126/science.aat5991

van Wynsberghe, A. (2016). *Healthcare robots: Ethics, design and implementation*. London: Routledge.

Wachter, S., Mittelstadt, B. D., & Russell, C. (2018). Counterfactual explanations without opening the black box: Automated decisions and the GDPR. *Harvard Journal of Law & Technology, 31* (2).

Wallach, W., & Asaro, P. M. (Eds.). (2017). *Machine ethics and robot ethics*. London: Routledge.

Whittaker, M., Crawford, K., Dobbe, R., Fried, G., Kaziunas, E., Mathur, V., . . . Schultz, J. (2018). AI now report 2018. Retrieved from https://ainowinstitute.org/AI_Now_2018_Report.html

Woollard, F., & Howard-Snyder, F. (2016). Doing vs. allowing harm. *Stanford Encyclopedia of Philosophy*. Retrieved from https://plato.stanford.edu/archives/win2016/entries/doing-allowing

Woolley, S., & Howard, P. (Eds.). (2017). *Computational propaganda: Political parties, politicians, and political manipulation on social media*. Oxford: Oxford University Press.

Yeung, K., & Lodge, M. (Eds.). (2019). *Algorithmic regulation*. Oxford: Oxford University Press.

Zerilli, J., Knott, A., Maclaurin, J., & Gavaghan, C. (2019). Transparency in algorithmic and human decision-making: Is there a double standard? *Philosophy & Technology, 32* (4), 661–683. doi: 10.1007/s13347-018-0330-6

Zuboff, S. (2019). *The age of surveillance capitalism: The fight for a human future at the new frontier of power*. New York: Public Affairs.

9
Human–machine interaction and design methods

Naoko Abe

1 Introduction: overview of human–machine interaction – from computer to robot

This chapter addresses human–machine interaction and its associated conceptual frameworks and design methods. Human–machine interaction is a study of the interaction between humans and machines. By machine we mean "any kind of dynamic technical system or real-time application, including its automation and decision support equipment and software . . . [in relation to] many diverse application domains" (Johannsen, 2009). The more specific research fields of human-computer interaction and human-robot interaction can be encompassed under the umbrella of human–machine interaction. Human-computer interaction (HCI) is a field of study aiming at understanding and improving human interaction with computer-based technologies via computer interfaces (Kiesler and Hinds, 2004). The study of HCI covers a variety of research themes on usefulness, usability, acceptability, social impact of technology and potential harm of its use. Its targeted area of application covers mobile computing devices, Web and Internet services, games and network systems (Kiesler and Hinds, 2004). While human-computer interaction deals principally with a user's relation with computational and digital media, the specificity of human-robot interaction (HRI) is bound to a person's relation with embodied machines having varying degrees of 'intelligence'. This physicality of machines distinguishes human-robot interaction from human-computer interaction and directs research towards specific questions related to robot embodiment and interaction (Bartneck, 2020).

Since the development of personal computers and their commercialisation in the late 1970s, human-computer interaction has been exerted now for about 40 years. A widely accepted definition of HCI is given by the Association for Computing Machinery (ACM), which organizes the ACM Special Interest Group on Computer-Human Interaction (SIGCHI), as the following:

> a discipline concerned with the design, evaluation and implementation of interactive computing systems for human use and with the study of major phenomena surrounding them.
> *(SIGCHI Group: U.S., 1992)*

HRI as a research and scientific discipline is slightly younger than HCI, as it emerged in the mid-1990s and early years of 2000 (Goodrich and Schultz, 2007). The origin of the term "HRI" can be traced to the 1950 novel *I, Robot*, where science fiction writer Isaac Asimov stated his Three Laws of Robotics as follows:

> A robot may not injure a human being or, through inaction, allow a human being to come to harm.
> A robot must obey the orders given it by human beings except where such orders would conflict with the First Law.
> A robot must protect its own existence as long as such protection does not conflict with the First or Second Law.
>
> *(1950)*

Asimov raises questions in his stories which became central to HRI research such as "How much will people trust robots?", "What kind of relationship can a person have with a robot?", and "How do our ideas of what [it] is [to be] human change when we have machines doing humanlike things in our midst?" (Bartneck, 2020).

Human-computer interaction research dwells on the usability of computer technology and interactive interfaces, whereas human-robot interaction research aims to develop robots that communicate socially and interact with people in everyday life settings. Both HCI and HRI are intrinsically interdisciplinary research fields situated at the intersection of engineering, social sciences, and design. Cross-disciplinary approaches are therefore key for designing technologies and experiences that meet user needs and expectations through seamless interaction.

This chapter addresses the foundations of human-computer interaction and human-robot interaction. These are independent research fields; the first is practiced mainly in computer science and information technology, while the latter is associated principally with robotics and mechatronics. Nevertheless, both share common concerns, challenges, and visions. Moreover, the fact that artificial intelligence (AI), which was developed by computer scientists, has been adopted into many engineering areas including robotics is likely to lead to a gradual merging of the HCI and HRI research fields.

The prime aim of the chapter is to provide scholars and students in the social sciences with basic concepts and methodologies to be useful for an initial step in the field. It is designed to present fundamental concepts and theories, and principal methodologies which structure and direct the research agenda and process. Furthermore, the chapter discusses current limits and major difficulties in human-computer/robot interaction research. The chapter concludes with a discussion of future perspectives in the field. The importance of an interdisciplinary approach is again stressed as a key to overcoming current obstacles in the field.

Readers should note that the term "human–machine interaction" can be read as interchangeable with "human–computer/robot interaction" throughout the chapter.

2 Establishing interaction between human and machine: design theories

Establishing a successful interaction between humans and machines is an important goal in human–machine interaction. By a "successful" interaction, we mean that the communication and exchange between humans and intelligent artefacts unfolds safely, bidirectionally, and seamlessly. Such interaction is also expected to offer users positive and pleasant experiences, allowing them to engage in a long-term 'relationship' with objects, which would warrant a long-lasting use for suppliers in the marketplace. In this sense, an intelligent object should be more than a simple tool for a specific task, integrated in our daily life as a sort of social entity. Design of such interactive objects relies on the development and implementation of various interactional channels into the machine to transmit information and facilitate communication.

2.1 Affordances

The concept of affordances provides a key framework for examining the subject-object relationship that define the capabilities of both parties to be considered in the design of the interaction. The term "affordances" was conceptualised and defined by the American psychologist James Gibson in his book *The Senses Considered as Perceptual Systems* (1966), in addressing the inherent relationship between living organisms and their environments. According to Gibson,

> the affordances of the environment are what it offers the animal, what it provides or furnishes, either for good or ill.

This concept has been slightly amended and applied to design research by design engineer Donald Norman. By Norman's interpretation (1988), "affordances" refer to the relation between the properties of an object and the capability of the user that determine how the object could possibly be used. Affordances represent sensory features of an object such as shape, colour, material and so on, that intuitively imply its functionality and possible use to users, so defining the possibilities of a user's interaction with the object. Affordances offer clues that let users know how to use an object and undertake proper actions. Well-designed interfaces or artefacts thus facilitate the user's understanding of how to use them. The concept of affordances provides designers or researchers with a framework within which to configure the human–machine interaction, considering the user's expectations and perceptions as well as the contexts where the interaction is supposed to occur. It also allows them to identify what kind of properties should be adopted within digital devices or artefacts to secure adequate ways of user engagement with them.

2.2 Interactive design for computer interfaces

Well-known functions in interactive computer devices include haptic devices such as keyboards and touch screens, speech and auditory recognition systems, and gesture recognition. The keyboard is one of the earliest computer interfaces; even today, ergonomic aspects of its shape and materials can be significant components of an effective interface design. The touch screen is a more advanced form of haptic device and its application extends over smartphones, personal computers, game consoles, information panels and so on. Speech and auditory recognition is a process that takes a digital representation of speech, or detects the presence/absence of speech, and transcribes it into written text. Although speech recognition by itself does not understand or interpret what has been said, it merely converts a recorded representation of speech into a textual representation ready for further processing. Its application has been mainly developed for controlling digital devices through spoken language or for dictation applications. Gesture recognition is achieved through a sensing and computing system that monitors a person's movement, allowing a human to interact with a computer. Kinect, a device developed by Microsoft to sense and monitor human gestures applied to a game controller, is one of the most famous examples of application of this system.

2.3 Interactive embodied machine: a social robot

As an interactive physical machine, a social robot is a main subject of study in the field of human-robot interaction. Human-robot interaction aims to render machines interactive, even social, through robot embodiment equipped with multiple communication channels and intelligence to understand complex social environments. Social robots are designed:

> to engage people in an interpersonal manner, often as partners, in order to achieve positive outcomes in domains such as education, therapy, or health, or task-related goals in areas such as coordinated teamwork for manufacturing, search and rescue, domestic chores, and more.
>
> *(Breazeal et al., 2016)*

and

> to interact with people in human-centric terms and to operate in human environments alongside people. Many social robots are humanoid or animal-like in form, although this does not have to be the case.
>
> *(Bartneck, 2020)*

Developing such robot competencies requires a number of elements to be considered and developed, including the morphology of the robot, the role of non-verbal communication and the demonstration of emotion.

2.3.1 Form and appearance

One's appearance conveys many things to others before any deliberate communication occurs. By the same token, a robot's morphology enables people to frame their interaction with it before the interaction begins. The embodiment of a robot can be designed in many different forms including anthropomorphic, zoomorphic, machinic and infantile forms. Anthropomorphic forms are classified into two types of robot; so-called humanoid and android. The former has a human-like body shape, usually bipedal but also includes wheeled-locomotion robots such as Pepper. Android robots are characterised by a realistic human-like appearance, with realistic skin, hair, teeth and so on. For example, roboticist Hiroshi Ishiguro is a pioneer in the field of android robot research and has constructed a very realistic replica of himself called Geminoid HI.[1] Inspired by animals, Zoomorphic robots include a famous dog-shaped companion robot by Sony "AIBO" – a social robot "Leonardo" having the form of an imaginary animal developed by social roboticist Cynthia Breazeal at the Massachusetts Institute of Technology, a seal-like robot "Paro" developed by the National Institute of Advanced Industrial Science and Technology in Japan as a therapeutic device for patients in hospitals and elderly care facilities, and a type of legged-robot "Spot" providing quadrupedal dog-like locomotion from Boston Dynamics and so forth. Application of zoomorphic robots is wide-ranging from healthcare to industry. By machine-like robot we mean that a robot's shape is neither anthropomorphic nor zoomorphic. The home vacuum cleaner "Roomba" and home assistant intelligent devices such as Alexia, Google Home, and Jibo are included in this category.

Social robots can rely on infantile features that can be characterised as "cute". Indeed, cuteness has a biological function as it triggers adult responses for protecting or nursing. Konrad Lorenz, an Austrian ethologist and Nobel Laureate in physiology and medicine, states that juvenile features such as large eyes and a retreating chin evoke affective feelings in humans; a response to cuteness that has developed over the course of evolution. Infantile features can be adopted into a robot design as a strategy to draw human attention towards the robot. The project on "infanoid" robots lead by Hideki Kozima (Kozima et al., 2009) is a noteworthy example where a minimalist, interactive and cute-looking robot called "Keepon" was developed for assisting children and persons on the autism spectrum by capturing their attention and encouraging interaction.

Designers of social robots therefore need to take into consideration the effects of form and appearance on a person's appreciation, reaction and possible positive or negative interaction with a robot. The negative effect of robot appearance is the subject of the well-known Uncanny Valley theory advocated by Japanese roboticist Masahiro Mori (1970) five decades ago. The theory addresses the correlation between robot human-like appearance and people's psychological reaction towards the robot's appearance. Mori supposes that the more human-like a robot becomes, the more likable it is, until the likability decreases drastically and people experience negative feelings vis-à-vis a robot at the point where robot appearance becomes very realistic and indistinguishable from a human. Mori calls this abrupt descent the "Uncanny Valley". According to Mori, this phenomenon may be amplified by the motion of the robots. The theory is highly relevant in the design of robot morphology and in understanding the significance of anthropomorphic features. However, it is important to note that Mori's concept is no more than a presumption based on his experiences as a prosthetic roboticist five decades ago, when humanoid or android research robots did not yet exist. Although many researchers have attempted to justify Mori's assumption through the study of computer graphic avatars and robot faces, the Uncanny Valley theory remains unproven half a century after it was advocated.

2.3.2 Non-verbal communication

The role of non-verbal communication is extremely important for interaction between humans and robots, and several non-verbal signals are widely applied to the design of interactive robots. Non-verbal communication, as developed in cultural anthropology and psychology, refers to all modes of communication where the message and information are transmitted implicitly without using spoken words (Mehrabian, 1972). It includes the communicational functioning of bodily activity, gesture, facial expression, posture and spacing, touch and smell, and of those aspects of utterance that can be considered apart from the referential content of what is said (Kendon et al., 1981).

How a robot moves is one of the most important and challenging aspects in HRI. The area of research called "Kinesics", which designates the study of communication and interaction through the bodily movement of interactants, has been developed by anthropologist Ray Birdwhistell (1970). For instance gesture, which is a semantic action pattern, functions to provide additional information that is not captured in speech, non-pronounced feeling and thoughts. In HRI, human gestures are largely adopted into humanoid robots to render them more anthropomorphic and likable to humans in order to increase the willingness of people to interact with them (Salem et al., 2012). Robot motion plays an important communicative role for a person collaborating with a robot as it can provide cues that assist in inferring the robot's intention from its movement, allowing smooth task-based interaction (Dragan et al., 2015). Gaze and eye movement also provide subtle cues for managing social interaction. Their functions are to signal one's interest, attention or understanding. For instance, robot eye movement renders communication with a person more fluid (Imai et al., 2003) and facilitates turn-taking in conversation (Mutlu et al., 2012). Mimicry and imitation are also strategies to be applied in HRI. Mimicry is an unconscious replication of another's behaviour while imitation occurs consciously. These communication modes assist in learning new behaviours and social norms specific to a certain group, conveying group identity, and manipulating or persuading others (Chartrand and Bargh, 1999). An interesting research result on the effect of robot mimicry on people's behaviour shows that a robot that mimicked people's facial expressions and displayed socially contingent head poses received more monetary donations than a robot that did not display such behaviour (Wills et al., 2016).

The use of interpersonal space is also commonly applied to HRI. The term "proxemics" was coined by Edward T. Hall (1990), an American cultural anthropologist, to refer to the study of the human use of space in a relation to others and in different cultural and social contexts. Interacting people are expected to adhere to social norms in terms of their placement in situated space. Therefore, an appropriate use of space is crucial to a successful interaction because the misuse can generate negative psychological experiences and trigger anxiety, discomfort, and even a "fight or flight" response in people. The concept of proxemics offers roboticists a basis for designing a robot's behaviour in space and in response to people sharing the same space. The way that a robot approaches people, its placement with respect to them and its trajectory in social contexts need to be carefully considered and programmed in a dynamic interaction because these elements exert influences on people's behavioural responses and perceived experiences (Mizumaru et al., 2019). Likewise, Kendon develops the "F(facing)-formation" which is a study on the formation of bodily orientation in a group governed by social implicit norms (Kendon, 1990). The F-formation concept contributes to the configuration of robot path approaching a group of people and the variation of people's experiences with different robot approach paths (Ball et al., 2015).

Haptic interaction – that is, any form of interaction by touch – potentially offers a psychological support function, such as comfort, reassurance or consolation. It also indicates an affiliation or social group wherein touching each other is accepted among members. Moreover touch can play a role as a parameter to define power or dominance in a relationship (Henley, 1977). In HRI, haptic interaction is applied principally to therapeutic uses of robots. For instance, the seal-like robot Paro is designed to be touched and caressed by patients in a hospital as a therapeutic care tool.

2.3.3 Emotion

Emotion – considered to be a result of evolution – contributes significantly to providing appropriate solutions for human survival. Emotion conveys information both about the environment and one's potential future actions. As a result it facilitates individual choice of adaptive response to environmental changes and allows people to share important information with each other. Emotion is a major focus in HRI research, both as the capability of a robot to recognise human emotion and as its capability to express "emotions". The recognition and transmission of affect via facial expression is one of the most highly studied areas. Ekman and Friesen listed seven facial expressions of emotion that are recognisable universally across cultures: anger, contempt, disgust, enjoyment, fear, sadness and surprise (Ekman and Friesen, 1972). These facial expressions were encoded by Facial Action Coding Systems (FACS) which describes visually discernible facial movements (Ekman and Friesen, 1972). FACS allows robot facial expressions to be designed by implementing subtle mechanical muscle movements (Nieuwenhuisen et al., 2010). Recognition of human emotion by a robot is still, however, challenging because of the subtleties of human facial expressions and individual variations in facial features and expressions that make it difficult to achieve highly accurate emotion recognition (Bartneck, 2020).

3. Design methods in human–machine interaction

A variety of approaches and methods have been elaborated and employed in the design of active interaction between users and artefacts. The designer and researcher must choose a suitable approach to their goal, research questions, and problems to be solved, together with a relevant method for collecting and analysing data.

3.1 Human/user-centred approach

Human- or user-centred approaches to interaction design place a user at the heart of the design research. According to the International Organization for Standardization (ISO 9241–210:2019, 2019), human-centred design is defined as:

> an approach to interactive systems development that aims to make systems usable and useful by focusing on the users, their needs and requirements, and by applying human factors/ ergonomics, and usability knowledge and techniques.

While human-centred design elevates human properties such as needs, capacities, perceptions, psychological traits and limitations to higher priorities in the design of any type of object, user-centred design focuses on a problem-solving process that analyses how a target user may utilise the product, and on the environment where the product is used. Both design processes commonly build upon participatory methods where end-users or actors as proxies for real users are involved in the design process, adopting scenario-based and prototype-based approaches where a model of a product is tested and evaluated by participants in association with a predefined context.

3.1.1 Participatory design, user experience design, and design thinking

Participatory design refers to a method emphasising the involvement of the end-user of a product from the very beginning of the design process. User experience (UX) design aims to create useful, accessible and aesthetic artefacts or interfaces enhancing the user's interactivity with products and stimulating effective and intuitive usage to offer meaningful and positive experiences to users. Design thinking is characterised by a non-linear and iterative process emphasising design from the perspective of the user, and has been applied to diverse fields including design, engineering, education, business, health and so forth. The design thinking process as defined by the Stanford d.school (Stanford d.school, n.d.) involves five steps: empathise, define, ideate, prototype and test. The first stage: "empathise" aims to understand the users, or other concerned group, and the problems to be solved via "putting oneself in another's shoes" through observation, interview and contextual analysis. The "define" step involves identification of the principal problem, synthesising the information gathered in the first phase and formulating a problem statement as a concise description of the problem based on insights of the users and their needs. The "ideate" stage generates ideas, assumptions and innovative solutions to the problem identified in the problem statement. Brainstorming is a prominent technique during this stage. The "prototype" stage is an experimental phase where possible and improved solutions for the identified problems are constructed. The designers can produce sample models in various forms and materials utilising paper prototyping, videos, role-playing activities and so on. The last stage, "test", aims to conduct an evaluation of the prototype generated by real users or concerned parties and to obtain feedback on proposed solutions. This step allows for the generation of further

Human–machine interaction, design methods

problems and the redefinition of the problem and solution. This five-step process can iterate as needed to reach the best understanding of the problems and the best solutions to them.

3.1.2 Questionnaires

User experiences with designed artefacts and their perceptions of them can be measured using questionnaires. A user experience questionnaire (UEQ) allows users' experiences to be evaluated according to the following six factors: 1) attractiveness: overall impression of the product; 2) perspicuity: easy to learn, easy to understand; 3) dependability: predictable, secure; 4) efficiency: fast, organised; 5) novelty: creative, innovative and 6) stimulation: exciting, interesting (Laugwitz et al., 2008). The questionnaire contains 26 items scored on a seven-point Likert scale. The Godspeed Questionnaire Series (GQS) was developed by social roboticists to measure human perception of a robot in five dimensions that are important to the design of human-robot interaction, including anthropomorphism, animacy, likeability, perceived intelligence and perceived safety (Bartneck et al., 2009). The questionnaire contains a series of questions asking the user to rate her/his impression of the robot on a five-point Likert scale according to items such as fake/natural; machine-like/human-like; unconscious/conscious; artificial/lifelike and so on.

A human- or user-centric approach privileges people's perceptions and experiences throughout the process of designing interactive devices. Participatory design, user experiences and design thinking are largely applied by computer scientists and design researchers to develop and enhance the usability of interactive interfaces. Although a human-centred approach is increasingly being employed in human-robot interaction, especially in the areas of health and education, the method is still new and typically challenging because users often lack knowledge of achievable technological competencies of robots that can lead to unrealistic user ideas, while researchers have little knowledge of users' needs in the context of the usage. (Bartneck, 2020).

3.2 Experiment in a laboratory or survey in a natural context?

The difficulty in adopting a human- or user-centred approach to HRI lies in the fact that a robot is still a very complex artefact requiring highly specialised computational and mechatronic solutions in the hardware, software, sensors and actuators that allow the machine to generate appropriate controlled physical motion. Moreover, investigating human-robot interaction in a natural context remains challenging because so few robots have been commercialised and used in everyday life by laypeople. Consequently, experiments conducted in laboratories are a dominant method in HRI research, although methods for observing and analysing user practice in contexts of authentic robot use do exist. The experimental laboratory setting allows designers and researchers to conduct studies that ensure safe control of a robot's performance while acquiring a variety of measurements.

3.2.1 Experimental technique: Wizard of Oz

Wizard of Oz is a technique widely applied in HCI as well as HRI to investigate targeted interaction between humans and machines in a laboratory setting. In the Wizard of Oz technique – named after the American children's novel *The Wonderful Wizard of Oz* where a powerful wizard was in truth an ordinary old man who was operating machinery to be seen as magical – a robot is presented to experimental participants as having high-level decision-making abilities, whereas it is actually manually controlled by a hidden assistant. This method allows a participant to experience highly competent interactive performances from a robot during experiments, without the need for the robot to perform autonomously. For instance, one can use this method to investigate conversational communication with robots where the robot can respond fluently to a participant in a realistic and human-like way. The technique is particularly useful for early analysis of people's perceptions or reaction to future advanced competencies of machines that are under development, or to competencies that have not yet been fully applied to real interaction. Moreover, it can be also used for examining a user's acceptance of certain robot behaviours and to assist in defining the research direction in the design of effective interaction.

3.2.2 Ethnographic method

Ethnography is a qualitative method developed in anthropology and sociology and used since the beginning of the practice of human–machine interaction to survey user behaviours and practices with regard to artefacts in a natural context. The principles of the ethnographic method are based on a natural setting – the method is based on fieldwork: a holistic approach that considers the underlying values, goals and beliefs of people; a descriptive method by which the lifeways or practices of people are to be understood; and the consideration of each person's point of view (Giacomi et al., 1993). Though this method, a researcher attempts to understand the logic of human behaviours and the meaning of the activities and practices of people in relation to the environment that surrounds them. For instant, the ethnographic method has been employed by anthropologist Lucy Suchman in early human-computer interaction studies carried out at the pioneer computer sciences application research centre: Xerox PARC (Palo Alto Research Center). Suchman's aim is to examine to what extent peoples' courses of action depend on artefacts and social circumstances through observation of subject behaviours and analysis of conversations between studied subjects (Suchman, 2006).

In more recent research, Forlizzi uses the ethnographic method to investigate the usage of a Roomba robotic vacuum cleaner in comparison with a classical stick-type vacuum cleaner in six households over 12 months (Forlizzi, 2007). Through semi-structured interviews with family members, analysis of visual diaries completed by the families, and visits to households, the ethnographic investigation allows the author to reveal the implication of the robot on the behaviour of family members. For example, the presence of the robot changed the organisation of cleaning by elder people, and encouraged the participation of men and children in cleaning when compared with the stick-type of vacuum cleaner (Forlizzi, 2007).

The contribution of ethnography to HMI is that the method allows a designer or researcher to access real settings where a product will be used, and to learn about users and their practices in that setting. It provides "ecological validity" as a complement to quantitative studies, giving wider latitude for interpreting numerical data (Nardi, 1997). Gaining evidence about users and their environments through ethnography is crucial to prevent possible prejudices that the designer might otherwise impose on users because technological artefacts can exercise certain power in shaping peoples' practices and interaction with them (Giacomi et al., 1993).

4 Understanding human–machine interaction

Studying human–machine interaction makes it possible to understand the logic of human behaviour and interpretation of the facts and reality surrounding them during dynamic interaction with a machine. Understanding human–machine interaction is also comprehending humans. The following section introduces theories, principally developed in the social sciences of psychology, anthropology and sociology, that address the characteristics and properties of humans in response to a machine in the context of their interaction with it.

4.1 Human responses to machine by media equation theory

Humans tend to behave towards machines in the same way as they behave towards other humans. In early studies of human-computer interaction, Reeves and Nass (1996) investigated how people treat media such as computers and televisions. In one of their experimental studies on politeness, a group of participants accomplish a learning task assisted by a computer through text-based interaction. After task completion one half of the group is asked to evaluate the computer's performance by using the same computer, while the remainder of the group answers the same question using a computer that they have not interacted with. Reeves and Nass find that the participants who evaluated the computer's performance using the same computer scored its performance more positively than the group who evaluated the computer's performance using the new computer; that is, people tend to be more polite to the computer with which they have established a relationship rather than to the unknown computer. Reeves and Nass conclude that people tend to respond to media in the same way as they respond to humans and develop the concept of the "media equation". As a communication theory, the media equation reveals that people react to media as "they would either to another person by being polite, cooperative, attributing personality characteristics, such as aggressiveness, humour, expertise, and even gender." Furthermore, the authors discover that these attitudes in people occur in an automatic manner without conscious awareness. Nass and Moon state that these behaviours are a result of people relying on scripts drawn in their past, overlearned as ingrained habits and behaviours in their life rather than seeking the cues that reveal the asocial nature of a machine (Nass and Moon, 2000). While Nass and Moon reject an assumption of anthropomorphism, where people anthropomorphize computers and therefore apply social rules and behaviours to the computer (Nass and Moon, 2000), a few social cues such as interactivity, language and attribution of a personal role are sufficient to trigger mindless social responses of people to machines.

The media equation theory is widely known in human–machine interaction, although its reliability is questioned. Goldstein et al. (2002) addresses people's politeness to small computers or smart phones under similar experimental conditions to Nass and Reeves. Contrary to the latter's finding, Goldstein's study shows that the number of 'likes' decreased and number of 'dislikes' increased in the computer-present condition whereas the number of 'likes' increased and number of 'dislikes' decreased in the computer-absent condition. Regarding interaction with a robot, Bartneck et al. (2005) applied a famous Stanley Milgram experiment on human obedience behaviours where subjects are asked to administer electric shocks to other humans, to study how people treat a robot. The result of the study is that all participants chose to administer the highest voltage shock to the robot, compared with only 40% in Milgram's original study. The conclusion is drawn that people do not treat a robot as their congener and have less concern with abusing a robot than with abusing other humans (Bartneck et al., 2005), marking a limitation of the media equation.

4.2 Context of human–machine interaction

The study of context, where technological artefacts are used as key elements to understand the relations between artefacts, individuals and a social group, has been developed by anthropologists.

Situated action models developed by anthropologist Lucy Suchman (1987), focus on the emergent and contingent features in human activities; that is, on peoples' responses to surprising moments that occur in the course of interacting with a machine. Instead of centring on formal properties of artefacts, structured social relations, or the established social or cultural values of users and rational problem-solving or prior established plans, situated action models place people's improvised and creative problem-solving process in response to a unique situation at the heart of the analysis of human–machine interaction to account for real human activity.

As opposed to situated action, activity theory focuses on goal-oriented actions which can be performed in various ways to fulfil an aim. Activity theory defines artefacts broadly as a media of actions including instruments, language, signs and machines, by which people need to control their own behaviour (Kuutti, 1991). In activity theory, the notion of context is both external and internal. According to Nardi,

> What takes place in an activity system composed of object, actions, and operation, is the context. Context is not an outer container or shell inside of which people behave in certain ways. People consciously and deliberately generate contexts (activities) in part through their own objects; hence context is not just 'out there'.
>
> *(Nardi, 1995)*

The context is not only an external resource surrounding the user but is also internal; that is, people transform themselves through the development of their ability to use an artefact. This developmental process in which a person is changed is considered as a context as well as an activity (Nardi, 1995).

While situated action models dismiss reflective action – an individual's goals, plans or mental representation by stressing spontaneous actions – activity theory emphasises one's motivation and purposefulness as elements which could influence the interpretation or perception of a situation. Both theories agree to qualify a relation between an individual and an artefact as asymmetric. In activity theory, people and things are intrinsically inequivalent, while in a situated action framework, the relation between human and artefact is asymmetric because humans are able to adjust for contingency but objects are not. Moreover, both theories consider significantly the context where action is being undertaken as the prime resource for analysing the interaction. Situated action models invite the analyst to take into account the context where people are actually and spontaneously doing the flux of the action, while the activity theory considers internal context, that is, subjectivity and the intent of an individual underlying one's actions as well as external context (Nardi, 1995).

4.3 Sociological perspectives in human–machine interaction

Sociological perspectives and theories are also performed in human–machine interaction investigation and its design research. In Vertesi's (2015) ethnographic work at the National Aeronautics and Space Administration (NASA) over more than two years, she investigates the relation between scientists and engineers and the two robotic rovers which have been sent to Mars for the purpose of geological exploration. Through detailed observations of the workspace and analysis of discourses of NASA's scientists and engineers participating in the project, she uncovers a unique social order deployed in a team, its production and maintenance through the embodiment to visualisation. Scientists and engineers aspire to "see like the Rover"; that is, people "learn, imitate, and demonstrate what it is like to be a Rover on Mars", adopting and embodying the robot's sensibilities and mobilities on Mars when they interpret and examine the digital images sent from the robots (Vertesi, 2012). Vertesi's study demonstrates that the practice of "seeing like the Rover" of those who are involved in NASA's project is a collective organisational practice which generates and maintains social order in the laboratory.

Abe et al. (2019) aims to introduce sociological theory to the design of human-robot interaction, especially to collaborative robot research. While existing approaches to human-robot collaboration typically focus on how to build robots that can work safely and fluently with humans on joint tasks, Abe et al. point out that how people experience interaction with a robot and interpret its behaviour as collaborative or non-collaborative relies on an interactionism theory from microsociology. Microsociology is a branch of sociology specialising in social interaction and structure of small social units in everyday situations. In microsociology the interaction between individuals is a primary source of information from which to understand their behaviour, perception and decisions. The approach of Abe et al. is drawn from a recent study of Chartier et al. (2017) on the uncertainty of social rules; that is, the moment of breakdown of the social rule in the course of the interaction between individuals. Chartier's research interrogates how people may perceive a gesture as violent during interaction with others in a friendly context such as a pillow fight. The originality of Chartier's research is to analyse the process of the interpretation of a violent gesture through the interaction performed between players. The research demonstrates that there is no gesture that is intrinsically violent; instead, when one person makes a gesture which is not expected by his/her interactant, this situation creates an uncertainty between them that leads to a negative interpretation of the partner's gesture. By applying Chartier's approach, Abe's research emphasises the process of the interaction with a robot during a shared task, and the moment where an expected interaction fails. The contribution of this research to the field of collaborative robot studies in HRI is an approach that calls attention to interpretation of experiences as positive or negative and an understanding that a person constructs meaning of collaboration during interaction with a robot.

5 Discussion and limitations in human–machine interaction

Designing machines to interact with humans, or humanising machines, may cause unanticipated problems and unexpected effects not only on an individual but also on our human society. Indeed, developments in HMI are closely related to ethical, legal and social issues. The use of intelligent or autonomous machines in society calls into question power relationships such as "Who makes decisions, machine or user?". Moreover, the structure and organisation of social life as business models and education systems could be jeopardised by pervasive implementation of such technologies in human society. Therefore, human–machine interaction studies are required to take into consideration potential harm associated with successful development and deployment of intelligent or autonomous machines.

5.1 Emotional attachment to machines

It becomes a serious question when a machine enacts an affective role because a relationship fed by emotional attachment could comprise many issues. This is the case with the use of therapeutic robots in the care of elders or patients in hospital, and companion robots as a possible remedy for solitude. Those robots are supposed to, to a certain extent, fulfil the emotional needs of those people. For instance, the use of a seal-like, fluffy, cute-looking robot, Paro, as a tool for multi-sensory behavioural therapy for dementia patients in nursing homes is widely debated in terms of ethical concerns (Sabanovic et al., 2013). Paro is certainly an effective tool to stimulate those patients in a positive way; however, dementia patients may not be able to recognize that the robot is not a real animal. Accordingly, does that mean that the robot deceives people and manipulates them emotionally?

There is another anecdote which enlivened public and media debate regarding the emotional bond between a person and a machine. A Japanese man in his thirties claims to be married to a young female virtual character Hatsune Miku featured in a Gatebox. A Gatebox is a virtual home assistive robot though which users can control some electric devices at home from a distance, such as turning on a room light, and enjoy virtual conversations with the character inside the Gatebox. Interviewed by the Japanese media,[2] he said that since adolescence, he has speculated on "life without getting married to a real women" because in doing so he can avoid uncertain factors associated with a real marriage and family life. He adds in the interview that living with a virtual character releases him from the uncertainty in human-human relationships and makes him feel at ease and less stressed. This affair gave rise to controversy not only in terms of sexism such as a female character who serves a male master as a home keeper but also in terms of the possible substitution of humans by a virtual AI character. *Objectophilia* is a form of sexual attraction towards objects, seen in the Greek myth of Pygmalion where a sculptor falls in love with the women-shaped statue he has carved. AI permits the machine to become more and more personalised through extended interaction with the user. In turn the user can experience a sort of unique relationship with his/her object. The question that can be posed from this case is whether objectophilia could be considered and accepted in a society as a part of sexual diversity like other forms of sexuality.

Although social robots are expected to build affective relationships with users by having human-like forms and communication skills, emotional liaison with such robots becomes controversial with regard to ethical issues and the nature of human-human relationships. We can observe here a kind of paradox in human–machine design. Potential harm and negative impacts of AI, robots and intelligent devices in our lives and on society remain uncertain, with some social scientists warning that the use of technological devices and networks services are factors that could fundamentally transform our way of living in relation with others (Turkle, 2011). Further discussion is necessary.

5.2 Difficulty for successful long-term relation with a social robot

While research on human-robot interaction progresses and the expectation of its utility value in daily life grows, cases in real life are still limited and social robots are facing difficulties in commercialisation and market success. For instance, home assistive robots such as Anki, Jibo and Kuri that were commercialised in the $USD 500–900 price range came to an end of production and left the market. While the failure of those social robots in the market could be attributed to a lack of real need, or to an immaturity of technological development leading to unsatisfying user experiences, or to a gap between the over-promise of the product and its delivered capability, Hoffman (2019) argues that the prime reason for the failure is the 'longevity problem' of sustaining a long-term use-case for the products. Indeed, the robotics industry is dominated by engineers and computer scientists, and Hoffman argues for the importance of involving artists and designers in the industrial development of social robots from the early stages of product development because "design is a front-loaded activity that studies human behavior and works in artful ways to combine elements of history, aesthetics, ethics, psychology, and engineering to create products we want to use" (2019). This view pointing out the importance of interdisciplinary collaboration not only for developing meaningful research platforms but also to improve success in real markets is largely supported in the HRI community (Caudwell et al., 2019). Different disciplines can bring multiple perspectives, methodologies and understandings to human–machine interaction and the holistic design of interactive machines. An interdisciplinary approach is therefore required more than ever for the sake of successful long-term usage of social robots.

6 Conclusion: perspectives on our future with intelligent machines

What issues are to be addressed in future work on human–machine interaction? With the progress of AI and robotics, machines are gaining more and more artificial cognition, potentially leading to humanised characters with a pretence of personality. The boundary between the specificities of machines and those of humans will blur as progress continues. This speculation drives us to question what is the specific nature of humans, which machines do not have, in terms of intelligence, creativity or productivity and what is it to be human in the end. Nowadays it is inevitable and unimaginable to build our lives without any form of technologically intelligent artefacts because we cannot reverse the flow of powerful technological development. The challenge remains to answer such questions as "How can humans live in harmony with intelligent machines?" and "What kind of artificial intelligence should, or should not be, developed and embedded in machines?"

These questions need to be answered primarily from a human-centred perspective. Likewise, a society-centred approach will also be demanded. The development and deployment of technology are strongly linked to concerns which each society has. Moreover, individual behaviours towards the machine are grounded in cultural factors including religious beliefs, gender-based values and ideological choices. Successful adoption of technologies, including acceptance and trust in intelligent systems depends on how we can understand these social and cultural factors. While international initiatives addressing the standardisation of ethical guidelines for designing, manufacturing and using AI[3] are recognised as important, the value of a cross-cultural approach to understanding people's attitudes to, and expectations of, the technology needs further acknowledgement.

Human–machine interaction is a promising scientific research field addressing cutting-edge technology and involving experts and researchers from various disciplines. In reaching beyond a fundamental research subject, HMI researchers must engrave on their minds the following question: "Who is the technology for?". The example of Japanese start-up company Ory Laboratory and their project on an avatar robot "Orihime-D" is noteworthy.[4] The project offers to people suffering from amyotrophic lateral sclerosis (ALS) disease which paralyses their body, a job at a café through the operation of a robot remotely controlled by their eye movements. The robot is teleoperated from their homes by sufferers called "pilots" who take orders and serve clients at a café. The project aims to overcome personal mobility limitations and to encourage and support the social integration of physically disabled people by means of technology. We can learn from this initiative that technology has the potential for making the impossible possible by offering such an opportunity to disabled people. The development of intelligent systems should not only aim to automate various existing systems, but rather it should advance and enable novel possibilities for humanity, society and our relationships with others.

Finally, as addressed in the previous section, HMI requires increased collaboration with multiple disciplines and the involvement of the public, industry and policymakers. Citizen- and society-centred approaches will be crucial to long-term success. Cross-disciplinary collaboration will contribute to the advance of successful human–machine interaction as this depends on multiple and complex factors as discussed in this chapter. A holistic approach and analysis that combines different perspectives and methods are also key, not only to successful interaction but also to identify and reduce potential gaps between the designer's purpose and the user's needs and usage in a real context, because what engineers are aiming at with regard to technological advancement could be different from the end-user's expectation as well as the ways in which the machine is really used. An interdisciplinary approach is therefore essential to prevent unanticipated results. The interdisciplinary endeavour is not straightforward and a continuing dialog between disciplines is necessary to reach mutual understanding and work together for further advancement.

Notes

1 Geminoid HI https://robots.ieee.org/robots/geminoidhi1/, accessed 6 November 2020.
2 Interview: https://bizspa.jp/post-59884/, accessed 6 November 2020.
3 International initiatives include: "IEEE Global Initiative on Ethics of Autonomous and Intelligent Systems" in April of 2016; "Ethically aligned design, 1st edition, 2019, the IEEE global initiative"; an international conference on "AI: Intelligent Machines, Smart Policies" organised by OECD in 2017, "Principles of robotics" published by the Engineering and Physical Sciences Research Council in 2010 (https://epsrc.ukri.org/research/ourportfolio/themes/engineering/activities/principlesofrobotics/, accessed 6 November 2020.
4 Ory Laboratory: http://ces15.orylab.com, accessed 6 November 2020.

References

Abe N, Rye D and Loke L (2019) A Microsociological Approach to Understanding the Robot Collaborative Motion in Human-Robot Interaction. In: *Proceedings of the 31st Australian Conference on Human-Computer-Interaction*, Fremantle, WA Australia, 2 December 2019, pp. 407–411. ACM. DOI: 10.1145/3369457.3369503.

Asimov I (1950) *I, Robot*. New York: Gnome Press.

Ball A, Rye D, Silvera-Tawil D, et al. (2015) Group Vs. Individual Comfort When a Robot Approaches. In: Tapus A, André E, Martin J-C, et al. (eds) *Social Robotics*. Cham: Springer International Publishing, pp. 41–50. DOI: 10.1007/978-3-319-25554-5_5.

Bartneck C (2020) *Human-Robot Interaction: An Introduction*. Cambridge; New York, NY: Cambridge University Press.

Bartneck C, Kulić D, Croft E, et al. (2009) Measurement Instruments for the Anthropomorphism, Animacy, Likeability, Perceived Intelligence, and Perceived Safety of Robots. *International Journal of Social Robotics* 1(1): 71–81. DOI: 10.1007/s12369-008-0001-3.

Bartneck C, Rosalia C, Menges R, et al. (2005) Robot Abuse – A Limitation of the Media Equation. In: De Angeli A, Brahnam S and Wallis P (eds) *Abuse: The Darker Side of Human-Computer Interaction: An INTERACT 2005 Workshop*. Rome, September 12, 2005, pp. 54–57. Available at: http://www.agentabuse.org/Abuse_Workshop_WS5.pdf

Birdwhistell RL (1970) *Kinesics and Context: Essays on Body Motion Communication. Conduct and Communication*. Philadelphia: University of Pennsylvania Press.

Breazeal C, Dautenhahn K and Kanda T (2016) Social Robotics. In: Siciliano B and Khatib O (eds) *Springer Handbook of Robotics*. Cham: Springer International Publishing, pp. 1935–1972. DOI: 10.1007/978-3-319-32552-1_72.

Caudwell C, Lacey C and Sandoval EB (2019) The (Ir)relevance of Robot Cuteness: An Exploratory Study of Emotionally Durable Robot Design. In: *Proceedings of the 31st Australian Conference on Human-Computer-Interaction*, Fremantle, WA Australia, 2 December 2019, pp. 64–72. ACM. DOI: 10.1145/3369457.3369463.

Chartier G, Berthoz A, Brian É, et al. (2017) Violence and Uncertainty: Interactional Sketches for a Cognitive Analysis of Violent Actions. *Social Science Information* 56(2): 198–219. DOI: 10.1177/0539018417694772.

Chartrand TL and Bargh JA (1999) The Chameleon Effect: The Perception – Behavior Link and Social Interaction. *Journal of Personality and Social Psychology* 76(6): 893–910. DOI: 10.1037/0022–3514.76.6.893.

Dragan AD, Bauman S, Forlizzi J, et al. (2015) Effects of Robot Motion on Human-Robot Collaboration. In: *Proceedings of the Tenth Annual ACM/IEEE International Conference on Human-Robot Interaction – HRI'15*, Portland, Oregon, USA, 2015, pp. 51–58. ACM Press. DOI: 10.1145/2696454.2696473.

Ekman P and Friesen WV (1972) *Emotion in Human Face*. Cambridge: Ekman, Paul; Cambridge University Press.

Forlizzi J (2007) How Robotic Products Become Social Products: An Ethnographic Study of Cleaning in the Home. In: *Proceedings of the ACM/IEEE International Conference on Human-Robot Interaction*, p. 129. ACM Press. DOI: 10.1145/1228716.1228734.

Giacomi J, Mosher A, Swenton-Wall P, et al. (1993) Ethnographic Field Methods and Their Relation to Design. In: Schuler D and Namioka A (eds) *Participatory Design: Principles and Practices*. Hillsdale, NJ: L. Erlbaum Associates, pp. 123–155.

Gibson JJ (1966) *The Senses Considered as Perceptual Systems*. Boston, MA: Houghton Mifflin.

Goldstein M, Alsiö G and Werdenhoff J (2002) The Media Equation Does Not Always Apply: People are not Polite Towards Small Computers. *Personal and Ubiquitous Computing* 6(2): 87–96. DOI: 10.1007/s007790200008.

Goodrich MA and Schultz AC (2007) Human-Robot Interaction: A Survey. *Foundations and Trends® in Human-Computer Interaction* 1(3): 203–275. DOI: 10.1561/1100000005.

Hall ET (1990) *The Hidden Dimension*. New York: Anchor Books.

Henley N (1977) *Body Politics: Power, Sex, and Nonverbal Communication*. Englewood Cliffs, NJ: Prentice-Hall.

Hoffman G (2019) Anki, Jibo, and Kuri: What We Can Learn from Social Robots That Didn't Make It. In: *IEEE Spectrum*. Available at: www.talp.upc.edu/content/ieee-spectrum-anki-jibo-and-kuri-what-we-can-learn-social-robots-didnt-make-it.

Imai M, Ono T and Ishiguro H (2003) Physical Relation and Expression: Joint Attention for Human-Robot Interaction. *IEEE Transactions on Industrial Electronics* 50(4): 636–643. DOI: 10.1109/TIE.2003.814769.

ISO 9241–210:2019 (2019) Ergonomics of Human-System Interaction – Part 210: Human-Centred Design for Interactive Systems.

Johannsen G (2009) Human–Machine Interaction. In: Unbehauen H and UNESCO (eds) *Encyclopedia of Life Support Systems: EOLSS. 18 Volume 21: Control Systems, Robotics and Automation Elements of Automation*. Rev. 1.1. Oxford: eolss Publishers Co., Ltd.

Kendon A (1990) *Conducting Interaction: Patterns of Behavior in Focused Encounters*. Cambridge; New York: Cambridge University Press.

Kendon A, Sebeok TA and Umiker-Sebeok DJ (eds) (1981) *Nonverbal Communication, Interaction, and Gesture: Selections from Semiotica*. Approaches to semiotics 41. The Hague; New York: Mouton Publishers.

Kiesler S and Hinds P (2004) Introduction to This Special Issue on Human-Robot Interaction. *Human – Computer Interaction* 19(1–2). Taylor & Francis: 1–8. DOI: 10.1080/07370024.2004.9667337.

Kozima H, Michalowski MP and Nakagawa C (2009) Keepon: A Playful Robot for Research, Therapy, and Entertainment. *International Journal of Social Robotics* 1(1): 3–18. DOI: 10.1007/s12369-008-0009-8.

Kuutti K (1991) Activity Theory and its Applications to Information Systems Research and Development. In: Nissen H-E, Klein H-K, and Hirschheim RA (eds) *Information Systems Research: Contemporary Approaches & Emergent Traditions: Proceedings of the IFIP TC8/WG 8.2 Working Conference on the Information Systems Research Arena of the 90's Challenges, Perceptions, and Alternative Approaches: Copenhagen, Denmark, 14–16 December 1990*. Amsterdam; New York, NY: North-Holland, Distributors for the U.S. and Canada, Elsevier Science Pub. Co.

Laugwitz B, Held T and Schrepp M (2008) Construction and Evaluation of a User Experience Questionnaire. In: Holzinger A (ed) *HCI and Usability for Education and Work*. Berlin; Heidelberg: Springer Berlin Heidelberg, pp. 63–76.

Mehrabian A (1972) *Nonverbal Communication*. 3rd ed. 2009. Piscataway, NJ: Transaction Publishers.

Mizumaru K, Satake S, Kanda T, et al. (2019) Stop Doing it! Approaching Strategy for a Robot to Admonish Pedestrians. In: *2019 14th ACM/IEEE International Conference on Human-Robot Interaction (HRI)*, Daegu, Korea (South), March 2019, pp. 449–457. IEEE. DOI: 10.1109/HRI.2019.8673017.

Mori M (1970) The Uncanny Valley. *Energy* 6(4): 33–35.

Mutlu B, Kanda T, Forlizzi J, et al. (2012) Conversational Gaze Mechanisms for Humanlike Robots. *ACM Transactions on Interactive Intelligent Systems* 1(2): 1–33. DOI: 10.1145/2070719.2070725.

Nardi BA (1995) Studying Context: A Comparison of Activity Theory, Situated Action Models, and Distributed Cognition. In: Nardi B (ed) *Context and Consciousness: Activity Theory and Human-computer Interaction*. Cambridge, MA: The MIT Press.

Nardi BA (1997) The Use of Ethnographic Methods in Design and Evaluation. In: Helander M, Landauer TK, and Prabhu PV (eds) *Handbook of Human-Computer Interaction*. Amsterdam; New York: Elsevier, pp. 361–366.

Nass C and Moon Y (2000) Machines and Mindlessness: Social Responses to Computers. *Journal of Social Issues* 56(1): 81–103. DOI: 10.1111/0022-4537.00153.

Nieuwenhuisen M, Stückler J and Behnke S (2010) Intuitive Multimodal Interaction for Domestic Service Robots. In: *ISR/ROBOTIK 2010, Proceedings for the joint conference of ISR 2010 (41st Internationel Symposium on Robotics) und ROBOTIK 2010 (6th German Conference on Robotics), 7–9 June 2010, Munich, Germany – Parallel to AUTOMATICA*, 2010, pp. 1–8. Available at: http://ieeexplore.ieee.org/document/5756823/.

Norman DA (1988) *The Design of Everyday Things*. 1st Basic Paperback. New York: Basic Books.

Reeves B and Nass CI (1996) *The Media Equation: How People Treat Computers, Television, and New Media like Real People and Places*. Stanford, CA; New York: CSLI Publications; Cambridge University Press.

Sabanovic S, Bennett CC, Wan-Ling, C, et al. (2013) PARO Robot Affects Diverse Interaction Modalities in Group Sensory Therapy for Older Adults with Dementia. In: *2013 IEEE 13th International Conference on Rehabilitation Robotics (ICORR)*, Seattle, WA, June 2013, pp. 1–6. IEEE. DOI: 10.1109/ICORR.2013.6650427.

Salem M, Kopp S, Wachsmuth I, et al. (2012) Generation and Evaluation of Communicative Robot Gesture. *International Journal of Social Robotics* 4(2): 201–217. DOI: 10.1007/s12369-011-0124-9.

SIGCHI (Group: U.S.) (ed) (1992) *ACM SIGCHI Curricula for Human-Computer Interaction*. New York: Association for Computing Machinery.

Stanford d.school (n.d.) An Introduction to Design Thinking Process Guide. Available at: http://web.stanford.edu/~mshanks/MichaelShanks/files/509554.pdf (accessed 6 November 2020).

Suchman LA (1987) *Plans and Situated Actions: The Problem of Human–Machine Communication*. Cambridge [Cambridgeshire]; New York: Cambridge University Press.

Suchman LA (2006) *Human – Machine Reconfigurations: Plans and Situated Actions*. 2nd ed. Cambridge: Cambridge University Press. DOI: 10.1017/CBO9780511808418.

Turkle S (2011) *Alone Together: Why We Expect More from Technology and Less from Each Other*. Paperback first published. New York, NY: Basic Books.

Vertesi J (2012) Seeing like a Rover: Visualization, Embodiment, and Interaction on the Mars Exploration Rover Mission. *Social Studies of Science* 42(3): 393–414. DOI: 10.1177/0306312712444645.

Vertesi J (2015) *Seeing like a Rover: How Robots, Teams, and Images Craft Knowledge of Mars*. Chicago; London: The University of Chicago Press.

Wills P, Baxter P, Kennedy J, et al. (2016) Socially Contingent Humanoid Robot Head Behaviour Results in Increased Charity Donations. In: *2016 11th ACM/IEEE International Conference on Human-Robot Interaction (HRI)*, Christchurch, New Zealand, March 2016, pp. 533–534. IEEE. DOI: 10.1109/HRI.2016.7451842.

Part II
Fields of artificial intelligence in social science research

10

Management and organisation in the age of AI

Roman Batko

Introduction

Although the origins of artificial intelligence and robotics date back more than 60 years – the term "artificial intelligence" was first used at the Dartmouth Conference organised in 1956 by such figures as, among others, Marvin Minsky and John McCarthy – it is in the last decade that they have gained extraordinary popularity, becoming one of the most important determinants of the development of research disciplines, including management science.

As the authors of *AI for Management: An Overview* write:

> AI has many functions, including, but not limited to:
>
> - Learning, which includes approaches for learning patterns from data. Two main types of learning are unsupervised and supervised. In unsupervised learning, the computer learns directly from raw data, whereas with supervised learning, human input is provided to label or identify important aspects of the data to define the training. Deep learning is a specialized class of primarily supervised learning built on artificial neural networks;
> - Understanding, which includes techniques for knowledge representation required for domain-specific tasks, such as medicine, accounting, and law;
> - Reasoning, which comes in several varieties, such as deductive, inductive, temporal, probabilistic, and quantitative; and
> - Interacting, with people or other machines to collaboratively perform tasks, or for interacting with the environment
>
> *(Gil et al., 2020, p. 4)*

So, the task of AI is to use computers for reasoning, pattern recognition, learning and inference. It is these functions, assigned solely to the capabilities of the human brain, and not to machines, that arouse great interest, as well as – on the one hand, hope, and, on the other hand, a dystopian prediction of the end of civilisation and the catastrophe that may be brought by the artificial intelligence and robots.

The aim of this chapter is to show both the roots of the metaphorical inspiration that management and organisation science draw from the potential of AI and the practical overcoming of the constantly present paradoxes and aporetic tensions that are difficult to reconcile in the analogue reality. When analysing the current conditions of management and organisation in the age of AI, we also look to the foreseeable future to analyse the phenomena that are likely to come soon.

Digital transformation, extending in practice the classical understanding of space and time, allows for a different look at contradictions, and often simply eliminates them, because this tension does not show up in the world of zeros and ones. Thus, in the Age of AI, space and time, which for centuries have not been subject to any reflection other than philosophical, are redefined. Digital time is non-linear – you can stop it, slow it down or speed it up, and have the processes multiply and run automatically, 24/7, without breaks resulting from human rest, hesitations or error. The same applies to digital space, which exists as virtual and augmented, where material and visible resources are supplemented with invisible ones in addition to big data and algorithms, whereas cyberspace, by nature non-territorial, does not adapt as easily as a specific real space to management with its classic tools and techniques.

The former "modernity" of management was defined by symbols such as the Ford factory, the Weberian bureaucracy, the panopticon with watchtowers and constant control of inmates, or – as Bauman showed in *Modernity and the Holocaust* – by the concentration camp. Such modernity struggled with contingency, diversity and ambiguity, and therefore with every form of individual freedom and autonomy (Bauman, 2000). In today's postmodernity of management, we are dealing with "an individualized, privatized version of modernity, with the burden of pattern-weaving and the responsibility for failure falling primarily on the individual's shoulders" (Bauman, 2000, pp. 7–8), hence the incredible development of entrepreneurship and start-ups springing up like mushrooms.

For decades, management has been focused on market mechanisms, efficiency as well as technical and economic rationality. This has undoubtedly contributed to the growing expectation that the "analogue" management, still largely governed by Taylor's principles established over a century ago, will gain a new impetus. Not only will it be modern but it will also allow mankind to cope with the increasingly intense challenges of globalisation and the negative impact on the environment directly threatening the planet, and it will create paths of more sustainable development, alternative to the ones we have known so far. The next chapter of these awakened hopes is being written right before our very eyes. Due to the COVID-19 pandemic, management is no longer just a set of tools and knowledge for optimising work organisation and achieving business goals but has become co-responsible for creating and managing processes to save the world from both biological and economic collapse.

The postmodernity of management, especially in the Age of AI, is associated with the impression that social development leads us somewhere beyond modern institutions, towards institutions built on different assumptions. When prioritising these assumptions, Giddens points out first and foremost the epistemological uncertainty typical to postmodernity and the history deprived of purposefulness, which are followed by the inability to defend any vision of progress (1990). Giddens' original theory did not assume the appearance of "postmodernity" at all, replacing it by another phase of modernity – radically transforming the everyday experience – which he defined as "late modernity". When describing it, Giddens focuses primarily on concepts such as trust and risk. The importance of trust in the late modernity results from the emergence of complex expert systems and technologies that most people are no longer able to understand, while having to use them on a daily basis. This is the aforementioned consequence of the separation of time and space, which occurred in late modernity.

Hence the misunderstanding of the world created by the media, complex financial systems, the functioning of corporations and all global operations, ever faster forms of transport, space expeditions, nuclear energy – today we would also add: global computer network covering the world, telecommunications mobility, or the power of AI algorithms. Giddens defines trust as a 'protective cocoon' which stands guard over the self in its dealings with everyday reality (1991, p. 3) in the modern world based on the so-called risk culture. Risk is of particular importance in a society that breaks with the past and traditional ways of operating and is faced with a future that is both open and dubious (Giddens, 1991). Giddens points out that modernity has become a naturally unstable reality and that our life goes on in an "atmosphere of risk". Organisations have to operate in such a reality, and one of their most important tasks today is to manage risk in such a way as to reduce the likelihood of its negative effects in the public space. This applies in particular to transparency, ethical aspects and corporate social responsibility – also for the environment and the well-being of employees or, more broadly, stakeholders. This is somewhat in line with the diagnosis of Elliott (2018), who writes about systemic self-correction of the market:

> The claim is that the age of AI and its major new phase of technological innovation should be managed through developing and implementing market solutions, especially around systemic self-correction of the market which presents opportunities for policy responses whilst avoiding restrictive regulation that might endanger freedom of expression and media autonomy. This necessitates structural change focused on greater transparency and accountability of social media and associated digital organizations by way of instruments such as industry codes of conduct and measures to facilitate third-party fact-checking and verification projects.
>
> *(p. 197)*

Main axes of digital transformation

Jean Baudrillard (1994) prophetically remarked that simulacra supersede reality, signs refer to nothing but themselves, the copy can no longer be distinguished from the original. Doubling – the state in which simulacra created by the media or the Internet have the same and sometimes greater rights to exist than the reality around us – makes our ideas seem just as real as the reality itself. Reality becomes a hyper-reality in which images multiply in isolation from facts and their meanings. Going even further, we can say that the organisation exists only in transmission; it becomes an avatar of itself. Such activities – virtualising the space – are perfectly visible today, for example in the ever-growing importance of e-commerce and marketplaces, as well as the avatarisation of management by the invisible (seemingly because the effects of its operation are actually very real and visible) AI. The transformation of the space and attributes of classical organisation is one of the challenges faced by management science, that for almost all its history have been solving problems in "really" existing organisations of infrastructural nature. The key moment, in which it was recognised that there is no single reality cognisable with sensory perception, was when the model was admitted to be equal to reality. The whole discussion on the fact that "the map is not the territory" no longer matters as result of the use of computer modelling, prototyping without the need to create real equivalents of cars, bridges, airplanes and so on to be later produced. The binary reality, created from the code and not from the matter, has become equal in rights. Digital copies of machines – known as "digital twins" – are a prime example of this fact (Neugebauer, 2019). They exist in virtual space but are equipped with all the features that may be relevant to their operation in real conditions. This enables improvement and optimisation of the operation, and at the same time searches for weaknesses and possible failures.

The narratives of modernism used to be dominated by the myth of progress, change and objectivity. This myth has been deconstructed in recent years. It turns out that progress also has a terrifying reverse – destruction of the environment, social engineering hostile to the individual or deepening social inequalities. Change is treated as a linguistic fetish of the modernisation that justifies any action of the stronger, instead of being a way to achieve valuable social goals. Modernity was synthetically expressed by Zygmunt Bauman, who called it "obsessively legislating, defining, structuring, segregating, classifying, registering and universalising" (Bauman, 1995, p. 244). Bell, author of *The Coming of Post-Industrial Society*, on the other hand, believes that postmodern discourse begins with the advent of the post-industrial era. This era is characterised by such phenomena as the increase in the importance of theoretical knowledge, which is used for the development of technology, the increase in the importance of the knowledge class, the economy of information prevailing over the economy of goods and the primacy of services over products (Bell, 1999). As Alain Touraine writes, in a post-industrial society, the basic conflict between labour and capital ceases to be the most important, and it is the fight against the growing power of technocracy that becomes the most important (1971). Technocracy is a systemic sign of the post-industrial era, and many of its features are clearly present today, in the Age of AI, along with the usurpation of interference in almost every area of human activity through not only established law but also automated and algorithmised, self-learning control mechanisms causing an unprecedented erosion of trust. While the first industrial revolution mechanised production using hydro and steam energy, the second brought mass production using electricity, and the third was characterised by automation and computerisation, the digital transformation of not only organisations but of almost all areas of our lives, radically changes classically defined concepts in organisational and management science. It introduces completely new terms describing previously unknown phenomena (e.g. Cyber-Physical System, Industry 4.0, artificial intelligence, Deep learning, big data, blockchain, e-commerce) and also expands the semantic fields of some terms that in "analogue times" were used by organisational studies (Batko and Baliga-Nicholson, 2019).

Digital transformation is building a future in which the boundaries between the physical, digital and biological worlds are blurred, with AI being a great part of that. It also changes the most important areas of management, creating new business models, recognising the increasing importance of technological and disruptive innovation, which eliminates the existing ways of operating. Anthony Elliot (2018) called it the "technological tsunami" and there is a lot of evocative power in this metaphor. Tsunami is an unstoppable element, to survive its passage you have to be either prepared or able to act instinctively and save yourself in a difficult moment. When the water finally recedes, nothing will ever be the same. Other aspects of digital transformation in management include a new approach to human resources, which also takes into account non-human factors, which are more and more common in organisations, as well as the need to be part of strategic government programs in the field of using artificial intelligence (AI) to accelerate social and economic development by states (Bounfour, 2016).

Digital transformation closely related to the company's business strategy allows for a different look at the boundaries of the organisation, including supply chains and cooperation networks. Today, it is no longer unusual that the supplier and the recipient never get to know each other in person and all transactions take place in the digital environment. Likewise, in the case of business scalability the transition from a start-up to a global company operating on world markets may take a disproportionately short period of time, counted even in months, not years. The same applies to the pace of introducing products to the market and building a distribution or marketing network, especially that the source of value for the customer and the market here is mobility combined with real-time aggregation and processing of data supported by AI algorithms (Bharadwaj et al., 2013).

The use of intelligent and networked technologies not only ensures cost reduction but also generates additional revenues by creating a new market, and new products and services, as well as an innovative distribution network that, through the use of digital channels, exceeds the time and financial constraints associated with building a traditional distribution network, which until recently only large global concerns could actually afford. Thanks to the implemented AI solutions, transactions become faster and friendlier in their simplicity and transparency for the user, and at the same time repeated errors are eliminated. Intuitive systems of user recognition and payment authentication, recommendations of products complementary to the order placed in e-commerce, the possibility of using algorithmic incentives consisting in generating discounts, bundling and many others, leads to customer loyalty as a result of transactional ease, understood as convenience, while at the same time such that the customer is included in the community recommending the product.

Critical thinking about digital transformation, and thus about radical change, is somehow inscribed in human behaviour, prioritising stability and well-recognised environment, which makes the process of digital revolution quite problematic. It is slowed down, on the one hand, by the lack of knowledge combined with the ease of seeing in the latest achievements of science some magical elements and the primal fear of the incomprehensible and, on the other hand, by the lack of market readiness for radical change and lobbying of major players who have invested big money in their technological solutions and are not content with the fact that innovation is disruptive to their businesses. Even though it is meeting resistance, the "technological tsunami" will soon seize every area that is still protected.

Literature review

The small number of indexed research papers proves how recent is the topic of the relationship between management and AI. When searching by the topic "AI and management" in the Web of Science Core Collection in November 2020, we get only 148 records. At the same time, the freshness and attractiveness of this topic made books on AI and related social phenomena instantly become bestsellers. Such was the case with *Race Against the Machine* (2011) by Brynjolfsson and McAfee and its continuation *The Second Machine Age: Work, Progress, and Prosperity in a Time of Brilliant Technologies* (2014), where authors, analysing the dynamic contribution of digitisation in social life and the first examples of the use of AI in business, optimistically predict that soon machines will be able to do almost anything human beings are able to do now. Bostrom (2014) writes about superintelligence being the intellect that cognitively surpasses humans in literally every field, and analyses the consequences of the fact that machine processing will significantly surpass the processing of biological nature. Robotisation is the topic of the famous book by Ford: *Rise of the Robots: Technology and the Threat of a Jobless Future* (2015). Fleming (2019) also deals with a similar topic. We can see great interest in the subject of algorithmic management related to the issue of bias and control (Kellogg et al., 2019; Lambrecht and Tucker, 2019; Lange et al., 2019). In order to describe the coexistence of humans and AI, Tegmark (2017) introduces the term Life 3.0, while Elliott (2018) shows how "the culture of AI" changes almost all aspects of our social life, from politics to sexuality. Kai-Fu Lee (2018) writes about the growing importance of Asia, especially China, in the race for world supremacy thanks to the strategic use of AI. Davenport's *The AI Advantage* (2018) is a more practical guide, showing how companies can use AI to gain business benefits and competitive advantage.

Harari's books take best-selling positions, including *Homo Deus* (2018) devoted to the vision of the future. The futurologist Ray Kurzweil (2005) has created the concept of "singularity" to predict the rapidly approaching point where artificial intelligence will become more powerful than that of humans. The influence of technological innovations on the economy is investigated by Rifkin, the controversial author of the concept of "the zero marginal cost society", who heralded – although not being the first one to do so – the final decline of capitalism replaced by a cooperative community (2015). A separate trend in the discussion about the role of AI – or more broadly about the digital revolution – in changing the labour market and the future of job can be seen in works of such authors as Schwab (2017) and Susskind and Susskind (2015) among others. *The Future of Management in an AI World,* edited by Canals and Heukamp (2020), is discussing in the strict sense the topic included in the title itself. As the two authors write, "in this new AI-based world, companies need to rethink their purpose, strategy, organizational design, people development, and decision-making processes" (Canals and Heukamp, 2020, p. VI). Iansiti and Lakhani (2020) in their book *Competing in the Age of AI, Strategy and Leadership When Algorithms and Networks Run the World* claim that:

> AI is becoming the new operational foundation of business – the core of a company's operating model, defining how the company drives the execution of tasks. AI is not only displacing human activity; it is changing the very concept of the firm.
> *(Iansiti and Lakhani, 2020, p. 8)*

Attempting to order the main threads appearing in the research literature devoted to the relationship between AI and management, Vesa and Tienari (2020) cite several authors of reference for such topics as: artificial intelligence and intelligent agent programs construed as disruptive technologies, AI in the transformation of work, the future of society, debate about the destabilisation caused by machine learning and algorithmic decision-making. The authors focus on the way the functioning of AI technologies results in reinforced biases, creates "echo chambers", and violates privacy whilst lacking public scrutiny and transparency, as well as on the conceptualisations of artificial superintelligence seen as an example of existential disruption (Vesa and Tienari, 2020, p. 2).

Famous artificial intelligence ancestor

Management can also mean the process of reading an organisation as text and symbolic network of signs and metaphors (Gadamer, 1975). Hermeneutics can help us interpret the relationship between management and AI, but before we see the consequences of using such a metaphor, let us take a look at the famous AI ancestors, namely the Golem (Batko, 2013). The figure of Golem (which in Hebrew means *a formless creation, not yet formed*) is present in Kabbalistic Jewish thought, but his truly original sources can be found in the Bible, where the word "golem" appears in The Book of Psalms and is translated as embryo. In the Talmud, the *golem* is already "animated" and resembles a human being (Glinert, 2001). The desire to create a "second Adam" who would outweigh the human being and at the same time serve the community, emerged among Jews especially in times of danger, and inspired Jewish folklore. The legend of Golem, a figure made of clay, is best known in its version coming from a book by Gustav Meyrink published in 1915 and the film adaptation by Paul Wegener (1920). According to this legend, Golem was made by the 16th-century Rabbi Judah Loew ben Bezalel, known as The Maharal, who, thanks to his knowledge of Kabbalah, created a powerful defender of the persecuted Jewish diaspora in Prague. The creature was brought to life by putting in his mouth a piece of paper with the magic word *emet* (truth), while erasing the first letter – *aleph* and leaving the word *met* (death) meant depriving the monster of life. Golem, used by his master as a servant for all housework, grew more and more, and its inhuman size began to inspire fear. This prompted the rabbi to annihilate him. The most important and permanent elements of the story can be presented as follows: the community, unable to cope with its problems, creates an artificial entity with superhuman strength to serve and protect it; over time, the monster breaks free from the domination of its creator and grows in strength; an increasingly frightened community uses a trick to correct its mistake and annihilate the Golem. I do not know if it is a coincidence or rather the genius loci of Prague, but in 1920 – several hundred years after the legendary Golem was destroyed by its creator Rabbi Loew in the attic of the Old New Synagogue – one of the most important Czech writers of the 20th century, Karel Čapek, brings to life a robot – produced by R.U.R. or Rossum's Universal Robots (Čapek, 2005). A character from his stage play will introduce to the science fiction literature and, at the same time, to many modern languages the concept of a *robot*. Čapek uses the legend of Golem and creates its modern version. In 1920, the famous scientist Rossum has come to a small, isolated island to devote himself to research into marine biology, working on synthetic but living tissue. He discovers such a material and begins work on the imitation of nature, and creates a robot that, although made of synthetic materials, looks like a human being. Robots are manufactured to replace humans in the toughest jobs and, since machines do not tire out, the benefits of a purchase are obvious, so the demand grows and hundreds of thousands of machines are bought. Čapek's play, variously assessed from an artistic point of view, expressed concerns about the domination of technology over man. The rebellion of robots, the destruction of humanity and, finally, the healing force inherent in love are the most important messages of this piece. Norbert Wiener, one of the founders of cybernetics and computer science, interpreted the story about Golem in a similar way – in his book *God and Golem, Inc.* (1964), he called the machine a modern equivalent of Golem. Referring to the Prague legend, Wiener noticed that the story of Golem foreshadowed a problem, which nowadays becomes crucial, namely the relationship between humans and machines. Almost at the same time, Gershom Scholem, a philosopher and expert on Jewish mysticism, described the computer as a modern representation of the Golem. When giving a speech at the ceremony of connecting the first computer at the Weizmann Institute in Israel, in 1965, Scholem called it "Golem One" (Sherwin, 2007, s. 134). This is how, traveling through time, the immortal Golem first became a robot, and finally fused with the digital machine, creating its digital avatar. Virtual reality is a simulacrum of reality. As Baudrillard writes, simulation means substituting reality for the signs of reality, as well as operations in which, instead of a real process, it is the operational double, a sinless, programmable homeostatic sign-forming machine of this process that comes to the fore (Baudrillard, 1994). Today, the role of Golem, which inspires both admiration for his predicted omnipotence and fear of losing control over its actions, is played by the AI. Another emanation of thinking about humans overcoming their limitations is the idea of Übermensch by Nietzsche "Thus spoke Zarathustra" (1885/2009). The modern interpretation of this concept is brought by transhumanism that creates a being overcoming human limitations – a human–machine, called cyborg. Such an extension of human potential is to be a response to the increasing threats related to the environment, natural disasters and pandemics. Improving humans may be the only chance of saving them. There is another dimension to this discussion, namely a feminist interpretation of transhumanism. Donna Haraway (1991) has challenged the traditional attribution of technology and culture to men and nature to women.

 The dystopian trend characterised by fear of technology has its source also in the novel by the English writer and poetess of the Romantic period Mary Shelley, who published in 1818 a novel, *Frankenstein*, about the tragic fate of the scientist-philosopher Victor Frankenstein, who, while working on the mystery of immortality, discovers the possibility of restoring the life of the dead and even creating an ideal human. The tragic nature of the experiment remains to this day an inspiration for many pop-culture realisations, and the word Frankenstein itself personifies the horror of human hopes to become a god. Nowadays, such images of pop culture as *The Terminator* – an American science fiction film, directed in 1984 by James Cameron, about people fighting with cyborgs for survival, or the Wachowskis' film *The Matrix* (1999), the plot of which is based on the idea that humanity created artificial intelligence, but machines broke out of their control and turned against the creators, make up a certain interpretive framework for the development and social acceptance of AI.

Management in the age of AI – paradox, trust, control and algorithms

Paradox as a driving force in management

Paradox is, in a sense, natural to management (Clegg et al., 2002). On the one hand is the desire for supervision, control, strict planning and division of tasks to ensure efficiency, on the other hand is the expectation of independence, creativity, experimentation and the search for risky opportunities that best reflects the constant tension that accompanies managerial decisions. This is not the only paradox. The COVID-19 pandemic has brought a new dimension to another dilemma: whether to allow greater mobility of employees or stick to the stationary work. Remote work has become common (of course, where it was possible), setting new tasks, both in the field of innovations or inventions supporting remote work, and managerial tasks consisting of managing employees with whom contact is only virtual combined with assessing the effects of their work. The economic benefits of the virtualisation of work are confronted with the problems of a social and psychological nature that are caused by the isolation of employees and hindered group work resulting in the synergy effect being difficult to achieve. Standards developed in most companies work well in such situations, but they are neither improved nor developed, because creativity and innovation emerge much easier in group processes. The matter of autonomy and control remains a separate issue, discussion to follow. AI generates far-reaching changes in the organisation of work and people, concerning mainly:

- Work organisation – changes in this field concern the way companies work and organise themselves. While the more traditional companies try to adapt to technologies introducing teleworking or mobile working, the digital native companies present a more agile work organisation based on projects, collaborative spaces and crowdsourcing. This flexibility is reflected by the workplace (the employee can work anywhere), the working hours (at any time), the relationship between the employer and employee, and even in the approach (such a flexibility allows companies to find in the market the right person they need for a specific task). This has led to the emergence of digital platforms that incorporate mechanisms to confirm the identity of the service provider and the reliability of participants.
- Work-life relationship – due to changes in the work organisation, activities are kept separate from the physical space, building and schedule. Working hours are no longer relevant as what counts is the result achieved. And if, on the one hand, it seems to contribute to the work-life balance because tasks are performed with the convenience of a professional in mind, on the other hand, it means that people are always connected and available, which eliminates barriers between work and family life, which can be a problem if the working specialist is unable to set boundaries for themselves.

- Work, communication and collaboration model – the digital transformation also affects the way people work, communicate and collaborate. Teamwork is gaining in importance because knowledge, understood as a resource, can only be developed within a group. New ways of teamwork and collaboration, enhanced by technology (virtual teams), will emerge. Organisational structures will be replaced by project work and self-organising teams, as traditional hierarchies are too rigid and slow to respond to challenges.
- Productivity and talent management – the increase in the use of technology at work leads to an increase in the need for digital competences. Computer skills will be needed in all professions. In addition, routine tasks will be automated, increasing the demand for cognitive, problem-solving and creativity competences to successfully deal with tasks that are not automated. Moreover, markets will be more dynamic, requiring people to constantly adapt to new situations and be more flexible. This will lead to an investment in lifelong learning as the lifetime of the knowledge is permanently shorter. A certain level of resilience is also crucial.
- Organisational hierarchies – digital transformation is changing the balance of power in an organisation. Technologies empower employees to be more involved in decision-making by engaging them – in real time – in a variety of topics and decisions. Increased responsibility at work is favoured by increased access to information and greater transparency of information, facilitating finding contacts, people for specific topics/tasks and direct contact with several interlocutors (inside and outside the organisation), which seems to flatten the hierarchical levels (Mesquita et al., 2019).

Trust, digital control and privacy in the Age of AI

Almost 60 years ago – when the development of technology was viewed from a completely different perspective than it is today – Max Horkheimer already saw the dangers it would bring. Although technical knowledge widens the horizon of thinking and acting, the autonomy of the individual subject, his ability to resist the expanding apparatus of mass manipulation, the power of his fantasy, and independent judgement are clearly disappearing (Horkheimer, 2012). This mosaic of populist governments, fake news creating an alternative reality, "filter bubbles" limiting cognitive competences and building a false image of the world consists also of the mechanisms of automatic supervision of the activity of citizens on a national scale and employees on a company scale. Thus, the "disappearance of the autonomous subject" is achieved not only through manipulative mechanisms but also through omnipresent control run by AI algorithms programmed to detect deviations, anomalies and any non-compliance with the adopted standard. Exercising control is one of the fundamental functions of management. Organisational structures, processes and rules enable managers to control the chaos which could otherwise easily eclipse cooperation. Over the recent decades, however, the control mechanisms have escalated beyond any reasonable proportions, becoming the modern embodiment of the original panopticon (Taylor, 2015). There is a growing tendency to monitor all employee activity (including non-work-related behaviour) by means of oppressive calculating equipment which records every computer click, every second of a telephone conversation, and the exact time spent away from one's desk. According to Foucault, man is held captive by the control machine equipped with an apparatus for observation, recording and training. Today these very concepts, if slightly euphemised, constitute the cornerstone of scientific management. This, however, has no bearing on the fact that control is one of the fundamental functions of management. In the famous passage in Don *Quixote* where the main hero fights windmills (an economic artefact) thinking that they were mythological evil giants, the machines defeat him – the representative of a medieval spirit and holder of an old-fashioned and cavalier code of honour (Czarniawska, 2005). Modern windmills are cybercontrol artefacts. Control, and its synonymous expressions – such as check, superintend, supervise, counteract, monitor, regulate, verify, restrain, discipline, auditing, validate – are among the most commonly used by management science. The very fact that English language dictionaries give the word "manage" as one of the synonyms to "control" shows how close these concepts are on both semantic and pragmatic levels (Batko, 2016).

In Philip K. Dick's 1956 science fiction short story "The Minority Report" we encounter a criminal justice agency – "Precrime" – whose task is to identify and eliminate persons who will commit crimes in the future; in today's world, such actors, operating on the premise of precognition, appear to be a very realistic and not fictional concept at all. As early as the 1980s, long before the mass computerisation and hyper-invigilation which followed the trauma of 11 September 2001, Shoshana Zuboff, in her critically acclaimed book *In the Age of the Smart Machine: The Future of Work and Power* (1988), pointed out the connection between panoptic power and modern management strategies and the consequences ensuing from applying horizontal panopticism in an organisation. From a manager's perspective Zuboff recognises a new danger here – when behavioural complexity and versatility of attitudes and values are replaced with "black-and-white" or "zero-one" attitudes which become subject to the tyranny of gathered data interpreted by an algorithm, the focus shifts from human beings to numbers gauging every employee's efficiency.

Another aspect of the issue of trust and control in management is a phenomenon called by Bauman the adiaforisation (Bauman and Lyon, 2013), i.e. the separation of systemic procedures and actions from reflection on the effects they will cause. The responsibility then becomes, as Hannah Arendt calls it, "itinerant responsibility" or "nobody's responsibility", which can have a significant impact on decisions made. At the same time, the development of technology that collects and processes information, relieving people from making decisions, somehow "takes away" responsibility and guilt. Unmanned drones select all by themselves the targets to be killed, and the potential error leading to deaths of innocent people will shift the blame to the imperfection of technology and, under applicable law, will not be considered a crime. The operator can easily justify the lack of moral dilemmas with the enormous amount of information and the inability to control it flawlessly (Bauman and Lyon, 2013). The managerial revolution we are currently dealing with takes the responsibility for supervising subordinate employees from middle management and transfers it – through self-control mechanisms – to the employees themselves.

Algorithmic management

The European Commission (2019, p. 1) defines artificial intelligence as "systems that display intelligent behaviour by analysing their environment and taking actions – with some degree of autonomy – to achieve specific goals." As a scientific discipline, AI includes a range of techniques, including machine learning (e.g., Deep learning and reinforcement learning), machine reasoning, and robotics (European Commission, 2019). It is easy to notice that we can actually equate AI and management, which can also be defined as a system leading to the achievement of the intended goals. Therefore, let us look at algorithms, which are not only the most advanced management tools but primarily a universe aiming at autonomy through machine learning and auto-correction.

A big change will take place in the work environment of organisations using AI in their processes. According to Deloitte's Report, "Talent and Workforce Effects in the Age of AI"

(Hupfer, 2020) there are new roles in the organisation that can be called "AI translators". These are employees who look for the right language and ways to build understanding between technical employees and others:

- business leaders tasked with solving business problems by articulating the needs related to building AI-based systems, as well as interpreting the results from these decision support systems; most large corporations find it difficult to make the right decisions on time;
- change management experts, whose role is to implement changes and help integrate organisational processes and business models with artificial intelligence algorithms;
- user experience designers – the task of this group of employees is to make use of the user experience to make navigation in AI systems more user-friendly for the target audience;
- subject-matter experts, who will use their knowledge to develop AI systems and make them more and more professional with each stage.

(Hupfer, 2020)

In general, algorithms are supposed to help us navigate through an increasingly complex and fragmented environment. In this process, the search and content recommendation system are of key importance. However, the impact of the algorithms is much greater, as these are the algorithms that create social reality, shared knowledge and belief systems. This mainly applies to search engines whose algorithms function as constructors and codifiers of knowledge. They also play the role of the guardian and provider of the freedom/self-determination of users in the network and of control over that self-determination. The power of algorithms has important social consequences:

- seeking information from other people is replaced by questioning machines. Search engines are becoming part of the culture, an essential omnibus that knows the answers to all questions;
- people's ability to reflect is getting limited;
- distorting reality – the image resulting from web searches is incomplete and unsystematic;
- attention stratification – big business entities are more visible in search results;
- non-transparency – search engine and social media algorithms are kept secret, they are variable and it is not known what results they are promoting and will be promoting in the future;
- consolidating digital exclusion – petrifying differences in skills necessary for conscious search;
- promoting ideology which claims that new technology will solve social problems.

(Batko and Kreft, 2017)

Future of AI management

The International Federation of Robotics reports in the World Robotics 2020 Industrial Robots report that as much as 2.7 million industrial robots are already working in factories around the world, which means an increase by 12% year on year. Sales of new robots remain high, with 373,000 units sold worldwide in 2019. The global economic crisis related to the

COVID-19 pandemic will undoubtedly affect sales of industrial robots in 2020 (IFR, 2020); a significant decline is to be expected in the short term. In the medium term, this crisis will stimulate digitisation, creating growth opportunities for the robotics industry worldwide. The long-term outlook remains excellent. This is not the only form of the mass virtualisation of the business area. Przegalińska (2016) points to three basic levels of independence of virtual beings. The essence of mimetic virtualisation is copying real artefacts, devices and organisations. In this case, AI is not creative and its purpose is to imitate existing beings. The difference, of course, consists in reliability, constant availability and speed in data processing. A more advanced type is creative virtualisation, which refers to the creation of digital artefacts that have no counterpart outside of digital reality. In the future, objects created in this way may, but not necessarily, be recreated in the real reality. We would then be dealing with a reversal of the mimetic process – reality that imitates virtual creations. This is where we find the greatest field for invention, which is scrupulously utilised by start-ups looking for a niche that would give them a competitive advantage. The most advanced form is autonomous virtualisation, which consists in self-learning, self-organisation and reproduction of proven solutions. It is this type of virtualisation that takes the form of machine learning AI and it is the most desirable from the point of view of digital transformation.

The digitisation of the world takes place through the use of many elements that change the offline reality into the digital one, using the Internet of Things, more and more sensors, cameras and other intelligent devices. The data obtained from these sources is categorised and analysed by Deep learning. Thus, perceptual AI blurs the boundaries between the real and virtual world. Equipping AI with "sight and hearing" is already radically changing our lives through the ability to collect information remotely and make various management decisions on this basis. The fourth wave of AI, called autonomous, will combine the ability of machines to optimise through the use of complex data sets together with information from sensors equipped with artificial intelligence, which promises a completely new quality. The use of artificial intelligence will be based not only on an attempt to understand the surrounding world but also on its active shaping. Robotisation will therefore gain a completely new dimension; automatic production lines, which today require programming, monitoring and supervision by humans, will be able to optimise their activities on the basis of processed algorithmic data and to constantly improve planning, production and logistics processes (Kai-Fu- Lee, 2018).

The real problems that meta-level management has to face are:

- health, longevity;
- fairer redistribution of wealth;
- climate and environmental protection;
- renewable and alternative energy sources.

In each of these areas, we can see how the old paradigm is radically changed by the application of modern digital and AI technologies.

Artificial intelligence will also develop with the help of advanced heuristic strategies (the name comes from the Greek verb "to discover") which allow for selective searching of the problem area, which means using a small amount of data to solve very complex problems, especially where obtaining complete information is not possible. Predicting on the basis of fragmented data from many alternative scenarios together with recommendations as to which of them are the most likely and can bring the best solutions to problems is extremely useful in medicine and in finding answers to the challenges of deadly diseases, especially cancer, or the urgent need to develop a pandemic vaccine virus, as we have just witnessed. The UK's first Longevity AI Consortium (LAIC), established at King's College London, declares that:

> Modern deep learning techniques used to develop longevity and ageing predictors offer new possibilities for diverse data types. This will enable a holistic view to identify novel geroprotectors, biomarkers, drug discovery and biotechnology in the longevity, healthcare and pharmaceutical industry. . . . We will employ a variety of AI-based methods to explore patterns that have significant potential to impact longevity, healthy ageing, age-related diseases and targeted therapeutics from biomedicine to social and economic sciences.
>
> *(Kings College London, 2020)*

AI can also bring about a massive democratisation of specialised services and make them accessible to people who previously could not use them, for example in the field of medical diagnosis. In addition to areas such as banking, insurance or other sectors of the economy based on large data sets, the analysis of which can optimise decisions, and thus obviously improve the company's operations and maximize financial results, AI can be used also to improve and democratise public services. Smart city is a space where people and highly advanced technologies meet. The idea of a smart city generally boils down to ensuring that the quality of life is a good available to all residents. Another example is AI seeking fairer taxes. As Heaven (2020) writes, "In one early result, the AI found a policy that – in terms of maximizing both productivity and income equality – was 16% fairer than a state-of-the-art progressive tax framework studied by academic economists." The undeniable potential of AI is revealed in the analysis of data on issues such as energy management, water management, carbon footprint management, and waste management, as well as drawing conclusions and predicting actions to protect the climate and the environment. The development of autonomous means of transport supported by AI, as well as smart agriculture contributes to the effective use of the environment, and thus its protection. Closely related to this is another issue, namely renewable and alternative energy, such as wind, sun, geothermal energy, biomass or hydropower. Based on multi-factor data, artificial intelligence algorithms create models for the optimal use of weather conditions to achieve energy efficiency, as well as to analyse risks and, finally, optimise processes in the control of renewable energy systems.

The confrontation of the traditional approach to standardisation, personified by ISO – the International Organization for Standardisation – with the machine-developing AI logic promises to be interesting. It is relatively easy to standardise Weak AI (Narrow AI), formatted to solve very precisely defined problems, not exceeding the set framework. That is actually what is happening: the ISO/IEC/JTC 1/SC 42 subcommittee on artificial intelligence has published five standards dedicated to big data and one ISO/IEC TR 24028: 2020 standard "Information technology – Artificial intelligence – Overview of trustworthiness in artificial intelligence". It will be different if the expectations are fulfilled and a strong AI (artificial general intelligence) is created as an intelligent system with true awareness that is capable of thinking and reasoning in the same way as the human. Strong AI can not only assimilate information, as does weak AI, but also modify its own functioning, i.e., it is able to autonomously reprogram to perform any (not previously programmed) task. Strong AI will radically change the rules of the game, including all elements of human management. Not only techno-enthusiasts such as Kurzweil, the promoter of the singularity idea, or Demis Hassabis, the boss and co-founder of DeepMind, but also sceptical scientists surveyed by Nick Bostrom, author of *Superintelligence: Paths, Dangers, Strategies* (2017) predict the emergence of strong AI around 2030 on, and singularity in the 2040s. We are talking about a future that is by its nature unpredictable, but we also have strong grounds to believe that work on artificial intelligence, supported by artificial intelligence already involved in research today, together with the amazing computing power of quantum computers in the coming years will significantly change the world of management. The AI management is coming.

References

Batko, R. (2013). *Golem, Awatar, Midas, Złoty Cielec: organizacja publiczna w płynnej nowoczesności*. Wydawnictwo Akademickie Sedno.

Batko, R. (2016). Panopticon – Cybercontrol in Liquid Modernity: What Does Control Really Mean in Contemporary Management? In R. Batko & A. Szopa (Eds.), *Strategic Imperatives and Core Competencies in the Era of Robotics and Artificial Intelligence*. Business Science Reference (IGI).

Batko, R., & Baliga-Nicholson, K. (2019). Digital Innovation as the Key Factor in Changing Organizational Identity into a Digital Organizational Identity. *Problemy Zarządzania*, 17(4), 84.

Batko, R., & Kreft, J. (2017). The Sixth Estate – The Rule of Algorithms. *Problemy Zarządzania*, 15(nr 2 (68), cz. 2), 190–209.

Baudrillard, J. (1994). *Simulacra and Simulation*. Minneapolis, MN: University of Michigan Press.

Bauman, Z. (1995). O parweniuszu i pariasie, czyli o bohaterach i ofiarach nowoczesności. In E. Rewers (Ed.), *Pojednanie tożsamości z różnicą?* Biegańskiego: Wydawnictwo Humaniora.

Bauman, Z. (2000). *Liquid Modernity*. Cambridge: Polity Press.

Bauman, Z., & Lyon, D. (2013). *Liquid Surveillance: A Conversation*. Cambridge: Polity Press.

Bell, D. (1999). *The Coming of Post-industrial Society*. New York: Basic Books.

Bharadwaj, A., El Sawy, O. A., Pavlou, P. A., & Venkatraman, N. (2013). Digital Business Strategy: Toward a Next Generation of Insights. *MIS Quarterly*, 37(2), 471–482. JSTOR.

Bostrom, N. (2017). *Superintelligence: Paths, Dangers, Strategies*. Oxford: Oxford University Press.

Bounfour, A. (2016). *Digital Futures, Digital Transformation: From Lean Production to Acceluction*. Cham: Springer International Publishing.

Brynjolfsson, E., & McAfee, A. (2012). *Race Against the Machine: How the Digital Revolution is Accelerating Innovation, Driving Productivity, and Irreversibly Transforming Employment and the Economy*. Digital Frontier Press.

Brynjolfsson, E., & McAfee, A. (2014). *The Second Machine Age: Work, Progress, and Prosperity in a Time of Brilliant Technologies*. New York: W. W. Norton & Company.

Canals, J., & Heukamp, F. (Eds.). (2020). *The Future of Management in an AI World: Redefining Purpose and Strategy in the Fourth Industrial Revolution*. London: Palgrave Macmillan.

Čapek, K. (2005). *R.U.R. (Rossum's Universal Robots)*. eBooks@Adelaide The University of Adelaide Library.

Clegg, S. R., da Cunha, J. V., & e Cunha, M. P. (2002). Management Paradoxes: A Relational View. *Human Relations*, 55(5), 483–503.

Czarniawska, B. (2005). Don Quixote and Capitalism in Poland. On the Cultural Context of Organising. In B. Czarniawska-Joerges & P. de Monthoux (Eds.), *Good Novels, Better Management: Reading Organizational Realities in Fiction*. New York: Routledge.

Davenport, T. H. (2018). *The AI Advantage How to Put the Artificial Intelligence Revolution to Work*. Cambridge: MIT Press.

Elliott, A. (2018). *The Culture of AI: Everyday Life and the Digital Revolution*. New York: Routledge.

European Commission. (2019). *A definition of Artificial Intelligence: Main Capabilities and Scientific Disciplines* [Text]. Retrieved from https://ec.europa.eu/digital-single-market/en/news/definition-artificial-intelligence-main-capabilities-and-scientific-disciplines

Fleming, P. (2019). Robots and Organization Studies: Why Robots Might Not Want to Steal Your Job. *Organization Studies*, 40(1), 23–38.

Ford, M. (2015). *Rise of the Robots: Technology and the Threat of a Jobless Future*. New York: Basic Books.

Gadamer, H.-G. (1975). *Truth and Method*. New York: Seabury Press.

Giddens, A. (1990). *The Consequences of Modernity*. Palo Alto: Stanford University Press.

Giddens, A. (1991). *Modernity and Self-identity: Self and Society in the Late Modern Age*. Palo Alto: Stanford University Press.

Gil, D., Hobson, S., Mojsilović, A., Puri, R., & Smith, J. R. (2020). AI for Management: An Overview. In J. Canals & F. Heukamp (Eds.), *The Future of Management in an AI World: Redefining Purpose and Strategy in the Fourth Industrial Revolution*. London: Palgrave Macmillan.

Glinert, L. (2001). Golem! The Making of a Modern Myth. *Symposium*, *55*(2), 78–94.

Harari, Y. N., & Harari, Y. N. (2018). *Homo Deus: A Brief History of Tomorrow*. London: Harvill Secker.

Haraway, D. J. (1991). *Simians, Cyborgs, and Women: The Reinvention of Nature*. New York and London: Routledge.

Heaven, W. D. (2020). An AI Can Simulate an Economy Millions of Times to Create Fairer Tax Policy. *MIT Technology Review*. Retrieved from www.technologyreview.com/2020/05/05/1001142/ai-reinforcement-learning-simulate-economy-fairer-tax-policy-income-inequality-recession-pandemic/

Horkheimer, M. (2012). *Critique of Instrumental Reason*. New York: Verso.

Hupfer, S. (2020). *Talent and Workforce Effects in the Age of AI*. Deloitte.

Iansiti, M., & Lakhani, K. R. (2020). *Competing in the Age of AI: Strategy and Leadership When Algorithms and Networks Run the World*. Cambridge, MA: Harvard Business Review Press.

IFR. (2020). *IFR Presents World Robotics Report 2020*. IFR International Federation of Robotics. Retrieved December 8, 2020, from https://ifr.org/ifr-press-releases/news/record-2.7-million-robots-work-in-factories-around-the-globe

Kellogg, K. C., Valentine, M. A., & Christin, A. (2019). Algorithms at Work: The New Contested Terrain of Control. *Academy of Management Annals*, *14*(1), 366–410.

King's College London. (2020). *King's College London – Longevity AI Consortium*. Retrieved December 8, 2020, from www.kcl.ac.uk/health/research/divisions/cross/ark/ai-in-ageing-research

Kurzweil, R. (2005). *The Singularity Is Near*. London: Penguin Books.

Lambrecht, A., & Tucker, C. E. (2019). Algorithmic Bias? An Empirical Study into Apparent Gender-Based Discrimination in the Display of STEM Career Ads. *Management Science*, *65*, 2966–2981.

Lange, A.-C., Lenglet, M., & Seyfert, R. (2019). On Studying Algorithms Ethnographically: Making Sense of Objects of Ignorance. *Organization*, *26*(4), 598–617.

Lee, K.-F. (2018). *AI Superpowers: China, Silicon Valley, and the New World Order*. Boston: Houghton Mifflin Harcourt.

Mesquita, A., Oliveira, L., & Sequeira, A. (Eds.). (2019). *The Future of the Digital Workforce: Current and Future Challenges for Executive and Administrative Assistants*. Cham: Springer.

Neugebauer, R. (Ed.). (2019). *Digital Transformation*. Wiesbaden: Springer Vieweg.

Nietzsche, F. (2009). *Thus spoke Zarathustra*. Auburn, WA: Wilder Publications, Thrifty Books.

Przegalińska, A. (2016). *Istoty wirtualne: jak fenomenologia zmieniała sztuczną inteligencję*. Krakow: Towarzystwo Autorów i Wydawców Prac Naukowych Universitas.

Rifkin, J. (2015). *Zero Marginal Cost Society: The Rise of the Collaborative Commons and the End of Capitalism*. New York: St Martins Press.

Schwab, K. (2017). *The Fourth Industrial Revolution*. Davos: World Economic Forum.

Sherwin, B. L. (2007). Golems in the Biotech Century. *Zygon: Journal of Religion & Science*, *42*(1), 133–143.

Susskind, R., & Susskind, D. (2015). *The Future of the Professions: How Technology Will Transform the Work of Human Experts*. Oxford: Oxford University Press.

Taylor, S. S. (2015). Controls and Constraints. *Organizational Aesthetics*, *4*(1), 1–3.

Tegmark, M. (2017). *Life 3.0: Being Human in the Age of Artificial Intelligence*. London: Allen Lane and Penguin Random House.

Touraine, A. (1971). *The Post-industrial Society. Tomorrow's Social History: Classes, Conflicts and Culture in the Programmed Society*. London: Random House.

Vesa, M., & Tienari, J. (2020). Artificial Intelligence and Rationalized Unaccountability: Ideology of the Elites? *Organization*. https://doi.org/10.1177/1350508420963872

Wiener, N. (1964). *God and Golem, Inc: A Comment on Certain Points Where Cybernetics Impinges on Religion*. Cambridge: MIT Press.

Zuboff, S. (1988). *In the Age of the Smart Machine: The Future of Work and Power*. New York: Basic Books.

11

Ambivalent places of politics

The social construction of certainties in automated mobilities and artificial intelligence

Sven Kesselring and Carolin Schönewolf

The advent of artificial intelligence in mobility and transport is driven by "reflexive modernization" (Beck et al., 2003) and is as serious as the big bang often associated with it. The transformation of social worlds and the fundamentals of social interaction, namely communication and mobility, sneak into everyday lives and businesses – often unseen and unrecognized. This "metamorphosis" enters through the backstages of societal developments and technological inventions. So far, it does not disrupt and interfere brutally in people's routines and practices. The socio-technological change in mobility and transport which comes along with the new concepts of automated vehicles and automated mobilities:

> implies a much more radical transformation in which the old certainties of modern society are falling away and something quite new is emerging. To grasp this metamorphosis . . . it is necessary to explore the new beginnings, to focus on what is emerging from the old and seek to grasp future structures and norms in the turmoil of the present
>
> *(Beck, 2016, p. 3)*

In this sense, as much as we would like to agree with the dictum of artificial intelligence being the "technological tsunami" (Elliott, 2019) of our days, we would rather prefer an interpretation of a more subpolitical or societally subcutaneous restructuring and reframing of fundamental processes and perceptions of societies and their ideas, imaginaries and visualizations of future mobilities. This chapter elaborates on the fine-grained staging of automated mobilities and the fabrication of the images, the symbolic communications and our visual understandings of advanced technologies in mobility and transport, that is to say the relations of mobility, automation and artificial intelligence.

The emergence of every technology is not that abstract a process but rather full of very concrete and tangible factors making the technological development subject to experience. These factors can be quite material and physical such as the battery for an electric vehicle or the high-tech dashboard of an automated car. It can also be regulatory as the ratification of a law for autonomous mobility. But, it can also be political as territorial restrictions for automobiles with certain characteristics, i.e. a congestion charge in urban environments for non-electric automobiles. However, before and next to all these factors are shaping technologies, mainly unseen, and placed on the societal "backstage" as Goffman (1956) puts it. Understanding the Goffmanian concept of backstage calls for thorough investigation underneath the surface of immediate visibility and plausibility. It needs sociological analysis, so to say, behind the curtains of expert systems, industrial policies and public governance. This can be done in the form of a sort of policy analysis and argumentative discourse analysis as, for example, in a recent study conducted by (Servou, 2020). Based on comprehensive argumentative discourse analysis Servou (2020) shows how corporate, engineering, politics and planning actors and stakeholders fill the "void" of automated mobilities in the two specific cases of Munich and Stuttgart, Germany. This chapter follows a different approach and applies a methodology of deciphering strategies that make the invisible visible and which aim from transforming uncertainties and insecurities into pictures, images and "imaginaries" of possible mobility futures (Jasanoff, 2015). It is the place where one can find how and with which processes the technology development play is being staged – in front of the curtains. The play on stage here in this text is the one of "mobilities, automation and artificial intelligence" (Elliott, 2019; Freudendal-Pedersen et al., 2019). In the following we will show this play comes with an extraordinary opulent scenery which makes it a perfect example to analyze and decipher the construction of an automation technology on the backstage.

The backstage of automated mobilities is the place the "politics of ambivalence" (Beck et al., 1999). It is characterized by multiple uncertainties and insecurities on the side of the actors. Not only does automation call into question the more than 100-year-old path dependencies of automobility; it also challenges the main concepts of the automobile culture and its industries, namely the unity of the owner and driver of an automobile, the so called driver-owner (Diez, 2018, 3–4). Together with "vehicles-on-demand", automated mobilities are expected to "herald the end of the driver-owner age and give a new face to the automotive industry" (Diez, 2018, 2). This leads to a conflictual and antagonistic discursive structure between disruptive practices of "everything new" and the "business as usual" routines at work. What clashes here are socially sedimented traditions, embedded routines and the need for a reduction of complexities on the one hand and disruption, structural change and systemic innovation on the other. In the light of this very (first) modern "structural ambivalence" (Bauman, 1991; Beck, 1992) one can ask: Is "purification" (Bauman, 1991), the elimination and even extinction of deviant interpretations and alternative strategical orientations still the predominant modern paradigm for coping with uncertainties? One of the cases where this can be seen is in Knie's seminal study (1994). In it Knie analyzes purification strategies of the automotive industry by looking into the decades-long struggle of coalitions in favor of the Otto engine over the Wankel engine. In Latour's terms this can be interpreted as the victory of one actor-network over another which is what leads to the disappearance of one technological option from the market and its fading out from technology development processes and innovation.

How does this become compatible and how can this be controlled in a way that consistent strategic orientations become plausible, possible and legitimate in the end? How can disorder, uncertainty and insecurity be translated and transformed into coherent actions and policies? How does the chaos on the backstage end up in an almost perfectly staged play – i.e. about automation technologies? And, subsequently, how do actors from business, planning and political worlds create new and reliable certainties for a future of automated mobilities?

One of the strategies with which actors tackle the problem of uncertainties in the construction of new technologies is grounded in making technology futures available, robust and plausible through visualisations such as films, pictures, artworks and installations. Specifically in "a social world that is not just mediated but mediatized" (Couldry and Hepp, 2017, p. 15) these visualizations become increasingly a constitutive element in the social construction of realities. The construction of certainties in the discursive transformation of automated mobilities takes place not only through interdependencies of the spoken word, the political, the material, the social and so forth but more and more through the consumption and perception of visual materials provided by the Internet and on platforms such as YouTube, Vimeo, Instagram, Facebook, Snapchat and others.

A contradiction in terms, it seems, is: How can something be made visually available that lies in the uncertain future? And why is this relevant from a social science perspective on automation technologies ("they are only films")? "This leads us back to the year 1994" when Mitchell (1994) postulated the *pictorial turn* for the first time. This iconic turn was followed by several contributions on the impact of the visual (Zuev and Krase, 2017; Knoblauch et al., 2008; Tuma, 2013; Reichertz and Englert, 2011; Lüdeking, 2005; Reichle, 2007). In the center of all these arguments the visual is understood as socially constructed and at the same time it is constructing the social vice versa; it is a "specific and central part of a social construction of reality" (Lucht et al., 2013, p. 12). Furthermore, it is emphasized that the visual and the production of knowledge (e.g. about technologies) are inseparable (Lucht et al., 2013) (Kaiser et al., 2010). Thus, from a perspective of sociology of knowledge, it is not only about the relation of the visual and knowledge, but also about the relation of the visual and (un)known unknowns (about the concepts of knowledge see Böschen and Wehling 2012).

Films show how certain actors envision and imagine the future and what they consider as desirable. "The process of envisioning plays an important role within transition processes. . . . A transition vision is a future image with transformative characteristics" (Grin et al., 2010, p. 206). This is why the practice of envisioning and visualizing the future of automated mobilities is not just a peripheral or marginal element in the discourse. As we will demonstrate later on it is rather a key framing practice that actively produces mobility futures and prepares political, economic and civil society stakeholders together with the wider public for the materialization and the implementation of technologies in everyday life and business.

However, visualizations are by no means unambiguous. Quite obviously, as we all know from modern art, they are open for interpretation to a certain amount. Taking the multiplicity of perspectives into account and making this an integral element of the analysis is crucial, therefore. Different actors visualize multiple perspectives which have diverging relevances and meanings (Lucht et al., 2013). At the same time, visuals can have multiple effects on the observer. Visualizing technological futures can appear quite diverse as a communication tool, in advertising, in expectation management, as answers to expected fears, in communication with partners, with strategy tools and much more (Lösch, 2010). At the same time, they shape the view of what is shown and are thus highly relevant for understanding current configurations of technological futures. Manderscheid (2018) points out the relevance of understanding visualizations of technological futures of mobility in social contexts. She critically examines visualizations of anticipated technologies as realizations of current processes. They can be understood as temporal determinations of the film producers for a future in the uncertain present of multiple futures of technology.

The production of technological mobility futures: entering the backstage of visualization strategies

The films awaken the image of a predefined future. When we listen, for example, to policy makers and business leaders we hear them refer to clear-cut mobility futures, precisely defined

Ambivalent places of politics

and obvious in shape. By looking closer at the backstage in a methodologically controlled way we can understand how mobility futures are being constructed. The picture this reveals is the full-blown ambivalence of, for example, the films that visualize these futures in images, words, metaphors and symbols. Here we sum up two main points showing the fruitfulness of the visual sociology applied:

1. The price for the certainties presented to the audiences is a significant *reduction of complexity*. On the production and procedural side complexity gets transformed into the simplicity of a clean figurative language and ambivalence converts into unambiguity and clarity. Movie products must find a visual language and a system of signs, gestures and symbols that enables the producers to process and translate the openness and multiplicity of the future and connects it to the addressees' life worlds and their lived realities.
2. Movies and the whole toolbox of techniques of film making have the tendency to *make sense* to conceptualizations of automated futures (Kautt, 2017) even if the producers do not have an equally clear cut idea of what exactly this future might look like.

We will illustrate in the following examples of films produced by the automotive industry these two basic characteristics of the social construction of technology-based mobility futures through media and film. Table 11.1 shows the empirical basis of the analysis and lists 13 films of automated mobilities futures produced by Original Equipment Manufacturers and suppliers of the automotive industry.

Table 11.1 Overview of the film material

Date Upload	Film Title	Producer Car Manufacturer, Supplier, etc.	Availability Social media, Company Website etc.	Popularity Klicks (Status 06.11.2020)	Voice-over Yes/No
12.01.2014	Autonomous Driving on Highway	Continental Automotive Global (supplier)	YouTube	3.009 YouTube (YT)	No
10.06.2014	Volkswagen Urban Mobility 2030	Volkswagen (car manufacturer)	YouTube DailyMotion (DM)	Original video no longer available (new upload on YT 256; DM 179)	Yes
17.03.2015	The F015 Luxury in Motion Future City – Mercedes-Benz original	Mercedes-Benz (car manufacturer)	YouTube DailyMotion Company Website	276.110 (YT)	No
14.09.2015	Automated Driving – Cruising Chauffeur	Continental Automotive Global (supplier)	YouTube	2.922 (YT)	No
27.10.2015	Together We Ride	Nissan (car manufacturer)	YouTube DailyMotion Company Website	339.704 (YT)	No

(*Continued*)

175

Table 11.1 (Continued)

Date Upload	Film Title	Producer Car Manufacturer, Supplier, etc.	Availability Social media, Company Website etc.	Popularity Klicks (Status 06.11.2020)	Voice-over Yes/No
05.01.2016	Demo of the BMW iVision Future Interaction	BMW (car manufacturer)	YouTube	28.541 (YT)	No
04.01.2017	Future Mobility Lifestyle, 20XX	Panasonic (supplier)	YouTube Company Website	40.852 (YT)	No
13.03.2017	Toyota Concept-i / Concept Movie	Toyota (car manufacturer)	YouTube Vimeo Company Website	40.587 (YT)	No
14.07.2017	zFAS: Wie das Herzstück für das pilotierte Fahren funktioniert	Audi (car manufacturer)	YouTube Company Website (Audi Media Center)	66.868 (YT)	No
30.08.2017	The future of mobility/ smart vision EQ fortwo	smart (Car Manufacturer)	YouTube DailyMotion Vimeo Company Website	205.531 (YT)	No
21.02.2018	2018 CES	Future Mobility and the Niro EV	Kia	Kia (car manufacturer)	YouTube Company Website	8.282 (YT)	No
07.03.2018	Working to Shape the Future of Mobility	Renault (car manufacturer)	YouTube Twitter DriveMag	3.296 (YT)	No
20.03.2018	Siemens Road Solutions	Siemens (supplier)	YouTube Vimeo	5.634 (YT)	No

In order to enter the backstage of social construction and carve out sociological surplus and lessons learned from films about technology futures the analysis is guided from three epistemological questions developed in Schönewolf (2020). These three questions are being put to the empirical material in order to decipher the mostly hidden agenda and message driven by the backstage of ambivalence:

a   What has been left out from the film in order to make sense of the technology? Instead of merely describing what can be seen in the movies we rather put the process of reducing complexities and the producers' strategies of simplifying the envisioned future to center stage.
b   What is placed in the center of attention in the films? This is closely linked to the first question and aims for focusing on the producers' decisions of how to construct a main message and a specific social reality for the future of mobilities based on automation and artificial intelligence.
c   What social reality is created this way? As in other projects conducted by the authors the material has been investigated to understand the "social futures" (Urry, 2016) behind technological mobilities as presented in the films.

The following section mainly presents insights from a detailed analysis of films produced by the automotive industry about autonomous vehicles. It gives an example of what it means to deconstruct the backstage of producing technological mobilities futures. The detailed methodological conception and derivation of the methodology and the research design is documented in Schönewolf (2020).

The invisible: reduction of complexity by omitting social aspects

In order to increase the societal plausibility and acceptance of automated futures certain factors are left out by the producers of visualizations, namely the films. What is left out usually represents (social) complexity.

In the following, three examples are used to give an insight into the techniques and strategies of how automated futures are produced by making crucial social elements invisible.

The invisible 1: alternative mobility concepts

Here, the future of mobility is not only imagined as automated but often also as shared mobility. On the one hand, companies are aligning their strategies to the new sharing business models (Kesselring et al., 2020; Sumantran et al., 2017). On the other hand, cities are pinning great hopes on sharing systems as a solution to the challenges of today's urban traffic (Cohen and Shaheen, 2016; Hensher et al., 2020). While shared driving systems are highly valued in public discourse, in the communication of industry as well as municipalities, car-sharing concepts are almost completely absent in the visualizations that focus on automated driving. Although the films partially address the challenges of urban infrastructure and high traffic volumes, the visions of the automobile industry presented in the movies are based primarily on the individual, non-shared and private use of cars. This contrast between communicated expectations and strategic orientations of the automobile industry results in an underrepresentation of the interdependencies between different automobility concepts such as car-sharing and automated-driving technologies.

In addition to the absence of alternative automobility concepts such as car-sharing, the films are characterized by the absence of alternative means of transport independent of the automobile. In contrast to the expectations and agendas of urban leaders and city planners, public transport and active mobility (walking, cycling, the use of micromobilities, etc.) play a clearly subordinate role in the films. Aspects strongly emphasized in the films are the new urban order through the further and smart predominance of the car and external communication of vehicles as in car2x, car2car, car2infrastructure and so on. The almost comprehensive absence of other modes of transportation is striking and supports the framing of automobility as the predominant system in the urban environment. Thus, the technology of automated driving is visualized not only as independent from other mobility concepts beyond automatization but also imagined outside of actual urban infrastructure. Those practices of visualizing a technology "outside" and "independent" from social reality, which are in the realization only possible with the use of fiction, seem to be necessary methods in order to bring the technology into being.

The invisible 2: urban multidimensionality

The pictorial implementation of certain technical features like external communication of the vehicles by light and sound signals again support the predominance of the car in the urban context. This is accompanied by traffic conditions that are characterized by an omission of current elements in traffic. This utopia of uniformity comes along with the absence of infrastructural elements such as traffic jams, road works and accidents. Instead, what is staged here is the "zero-friction society" (Hajer, 1999) and seamless mobility. The autonomous vehicles in the films rarely face unclear and confusing moments in traffic or technically challenging situations. This is made possible by the limitation of the amount of other road users, especially those without a mechanical shell. In the depiction of (urban) social situations people are usually not present (e.g. KIA Motors, 2018) or they do not move, at all (e.g. Renault, 2018). However, traffic elements of the same kind, vehicles, are also radically limited in most films (e.g. Toyota, 2017), allowing the autonomously driving car to move freely through a clean and tidy urban space.

The underrepresentation of traffic complexities goes hand in hand with the presented designs of urban spaces. The films construct a version of an automated high-tech future and transport simultaneously visions of future cities and traffic.

The staging of the city and the way future traffic is shown differ greatly sometimes. The films address quite different elements of the city: people, architecture, traffic, streets, nature and so on. The implementation of these elements then results in different urban systems and how people can move and live within those cities.

By designing clean urban surfaces by omitting and underrepresenting contemporary urban elements, the future of the city is not only visualized in a less complex way, it is also literally partly redesigned. Some films create completely new concepts of urban infrastructure and transport. One film, for example, shows the resolution of streets and traffic signs (Mercedes-Benz, 2015). Instead of traffic signs and streets, the automobile projects traffic elements such as crosswalks onto the ground and allows pedestrians to walk in front of the car. It becomes an ordering element in the urban infrastructure. Thus, the dominant element in these newly designed urban futures is (or remains) the automobile. City, space and traffic are treated very differently in the films and thus imply various consequences for life in these cities and traffic systems. The films, which all deal with the future of automated driving, show that technology contributes to the production of public space. The city and traffic regulations are being redesigned. The new orders of traffic and dominant elements in public space sometimes have far-reaching consequences for civil society. This is not only relevant for the construction of new technologies, such as light communication of automated vehicles, but also for urban planning.

The invisible 3: diversity

Besides the co-production of the technology of autonomous driving, traffic and urban space, the films transport visualizations of social inequality through the selectivity of the imagined users. A recurring theme in the public discourse on new technologies and changes in mobility is "mobility for all" (Deutscher Städtetag 2018). Connected to this is the hope for a mobility supply that can work against current circumstances of social inequality – caused by access to mobility opportunities, vehicles and services. Automated driving, in conjunction with electric mobility and sharing models, is intended to give people with disabilities, the elderly and poor people access to mobility. The films give no answer to this hope, which is linked to automated mobility. Instead, they create pictures of non-diverse social reality. Fictitious protagonists are presented as the users of the new mobility technology. They can be typified as *Western, white and wealthy* (WWW). Mostly men appear as well-dressed sophisticated people who live in beautiful houses. From the way they talk and gesticulate, the viewer learns that they are successful professionals and quite often on the way to work in high-rises made from steel and glass.

Also, here automated mobilities are embedded in a zero-friction world and social environment. It is constructed as a technology that stands for liquid Western-oriented social groups with excellent access to financial capital, education and social capital. What we do not see are people of different colors, poor people, obese people, sad people, marginalized social groups and people in need of help. Automated driving is framed to be a premium exclusive product, not one of easy or even free access to a wider society. Instead, social inequality emerges as a normality and the picture and sign language used in the movies supports and manifests uneven distribution of mobility opportunities and accesses.

The recurring pattern of the *Western, white and wealthy* comes along with another characteristic: the future of automated mobilities designed in these films is not only WWW but also profoundly masculine (e.g. Panasonic, 2017; Mercedes-Benz, 2015; Audi AG., 2017). Non-male protagonists are not visible in almost any of the films. Instead the visualizations reproduce traditional gender roles by implicitly reconciling professional activity and success with masculinity.

Many of the films represent new forms of social prioritization. This takes place on a technical level on the one hand and on a social level on the other. On the technical level, such prioritization is realized, for example, via contested parking space (e.g., Volkswagen Group, 2014, see Table 11.1). On the social level, prioritization is implemented by the mobility users (e.g. smart, 2017). Only a few films address the topic of mobility of the elderly or people with disabilities. None of the films address the future pricing schemes of the visualized mobilities. There is no indication at all that the new mobilities will be accessible for financially weaker classes and as to whether this will have any positive impact on their mobility.

Almost without exception the films exclude any cultural diversity. The WWW users of the autonomously driving vehicles move around in spaces, infrastructures and architectures of clearly westernized design and aesthetics.

The producers' decisions to draw culturally and geographically homogeneous pictures is clearly remarkable, since many of them are not embedded in the cultural and geographical society shown – for example, the Japanese car manufacturer Toyota which had the second largest car sales in the world in 2019. In addition, this is considerable, since large parts of the world's drivers do not have the same characteristics as white Westerners and some of the most important markets are located in Asia, for instance.

While debates about "mobility for all" are held in connection with the technological advances of autonomous driving, social inequality continues and is manifested in the films. When acknowledging the power of images and visions for the "view of the world" (Coenen, 2010, p. 83), it is important to question how films about automated futures shape social reality. The films construct a social reality in which Western, white and wealthy men have excellent access to new technologies of mobility. Their lives become easier, more efficient and safer. Through the performativity of the films, social inequalities are not only manifested in film but also inscribed in technology.

What is left out in order to make sense of the technology? By making certain aspects about the future of autonomous driving invisible in the films, the complexity of the technology is reduced. That which is not placed at the centre of the films stands for diversity and ambiguity. The omission, simplification and unambiguity of this multiplicity can be described as a reduction of social complexity. The invisible empty trips, the non-existent or hardly existing car sharing, and the underrepresentation of alternative traffic concepts leads to an isolated presentation of the technology of automated vehicles. In addition, it is represented as isolated within the system of the city. While the future of public transport is a central argument in public debates, it is hardly or not at all visually included in the analyzed films. This isolation of the vehicle from space and elements that shape the city society is made clear by its lack of complexity. Only the absence of complex traffic situations and the challenges that characterize traffic make it possible for the autonomous vehicle to act independently, as depicted in the films.

The visible: making sense through emotionalizing automation

The gap created by the reduction of complexity is filled with emotional connotations of technology, automation and artificial intelligence. These connotations serve as a response to anticipated fears and anxieties from society about the new technologies and the rise of artificial intelligence in everyday life.

"More than a machine – a partner"

In fact, cars always have been "anthropomorphized" (Urry, 2004, p. 26) and have often been treated as people by giving them names, conceiving them as additional members of the family and so forth. In movies such as Disney's *The Love Bug* from 1968 with Herbie the pearl-white, fabric-sunroofed Volkswagen Beetle or *Chitty Chitty Bang Bang*, a musical also from 1968 with a vintage car as the main actor, emotional attachment is applied to the technical artefact of an automobile. This is also seen with Henry Ford's groundbreaking Model T from 1908 that was given nicknames such as "Tin Lizzie" and "Leaping Lena".

Films about automated vehicles and mobility aim to solve another emotional problem. People's fear of vehicles being driven by artificial intelligence or a machine they cannot control are addressed by bringing in a new dimension: the character of a vehicle, often described in traditional automotive magazines as the product of speed and acceleration, the driving experience, the roaring of the engine and so forth, is redefined by applying quite an old strategy. Vehicles are presented as caring machines – compassionate, tactical or even funny. These attributes initially do not line up with the primary characteristics of the machine – a cold, rational and efficient apparatus. As mentioned before, the connection between emotions and vehicles has been in existence for many years (e.g. Sheller, 2004) (Sachs, 1992). The new dimension comes in where the car becomes the companion and friend that enables the individual to realize personal projects and plans. Automated vehicles are seen as futuristic machines that follow a hidden set of rules and algorithms instead of the drivers orders. In this sense, such emotional vehicles are new and are subject to artists' and producers' creativity. The vehicles characterized in the films differ greatly in their characteristics. We divide these characteristics into to categories: *discrete robots* and *intervening humanoids* (see Figure 11.1).

The poles represent two extremes, defined firstly by their character traits (mechanical, cooperative, human) and secondly by their social or personal impact (assisting, life-changing). A vehicle that is machine-like in its appearance – that is, not emotional, empathetic or careful – appears as a discrete robot. The vehicle has no (human) name. It is comfortable and practical but not life-changing. The second extreme, the intervening humanoid, is staged as human-like – that is, compassionate, unpredictable, emotional. The vehicle bears a human name and

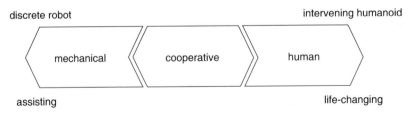

Figure 11.1 Character poles of the vehicles
Source: own illustration

establishes a relationship with its owner or user. It influences how the users arrange their everyday life, how they move, when they sleep, what music they listen to – the intervening humanoid is life-changing.

In the illustration, the partnership is attributed to various forms, which not only lie between human and machine but also address the animal world. An automobile manufacturer, for example, refers to a white horse (Toyota, 2017). After a short introduction the film *Toyota Concept-I I Concept Movie* starts with the slogan "More than a machine – a partner" (Toyota, 2017). The next scene shows a white horse and a child approaching together. The child becomes the human protagonist in the film, and the horse is the analogy of the vehicle and the metaphor for a constant companion throughout the protagonist's life. The final scene is dedicated to the white horse again, now free in the desert, strong and proud. With the desert and animalistic elements, producers not only connect to the natural but also the history of mobility. Before the development of automobiles and the invention of the bicycle and the railroad, the horse was the primary means of human transportation (Virilio, 1978; Featherstone, 2004). The horse in the film shows a naturalization of a mechanized interaction between human and machine. In other examples a relationship based on human attributes is established. What these relationships always have in common, however, is a friendly and cooperative relationship with the vehicle. Visualizations of this kind contribute to the emotionalization of the imagined technology. It serves as a direct response of the producers to anticipated fears from society about automation technology.

Safety

Panasonic summarizes its vision of the future of automobility as "safe, reassuring and comfortable" (Panasonic, 2017). Nissan has a similar view: "smarter, safer, easier" (Nissan, 2015). Safety is a topic in ten of the films and is addressed directly or suggested by the driving style of the vehicles and the communication between them.

The (added) value of safety is primarily created with technological solutions. The abilities of automated vehicles exceed that of humans. This is shown visually by sovereign bypassing and the early detection of obstacles. On a textual and linguistic level, safety is demonstrated by the decrease in accidents (Renault, 2018; Elliott *et al.*, 2019). However, the films do not explain to the consumers how the vision of safer traffic can be achieved. The future seems to be set, predefined and unambiguous. Only the pathway how to get there remains unclear and vague.

Safety is a shared narrative of the actors in the discourse of automated driving. The hope of increased safety not only serves as the emotional acceptance work directed to public discourse but also as legitimation work for the actors who are working on the technology (Schönewolf, 2020). With reference to American movement research, Keller notes that actors in social discourses select strategic interpretative frameworks to increase their mobility potential (Keller, 2011; Snow and Benford, 1999; Benford and Snow, 2000). Safety is an interpretative framework that provides information on how the expectations of autonomous driving are constructed linguistically and symbolically by the actors and how they currently construct the future of technology. To reconstruct the safety rationale, it is fruitful to question the meaning of security. This leads directly to its counterpart: risk. Like the narrative of safety, the narrative of risk is defined by cultural and social attributions of meaning (Douglas, 1992; Dollinger, 2016; Dollinger and Schmidt-Semisch, 2016; Eisch-Angus, 2016). Risk and safety are interrelated; risk is defined as a violation of safety and safety is legitimized by protection against risk (Dollinger, 2016; Dollinger and Schmidt-Semisch, 2016). In the case of autonomous driving, risk exists with the "human" (driver), whereas safety is connoted by the "mechanical" (automobile). Thus, the construction of safety not only loads a new technology with positive meanings and connotations but also generates uncertainties about current (technological) systems. The risk posed by the absence of these automation technologies thus becomes intolerable (Dollinger, 2016). The counterpart of risk not only creates its own positive legitimation or acceptance of the technology, it also provides it with an element of quality (Kaufmann, 2012, p. 258) that can give relevance to the technology. Attributions, meanings and appeals of this kind create expectations about what is considered safe and what is risky regarding (automated) automobilities. The connotation of autonomous driving as being safer than a human driving creates a re-accentuation (Bender, 2004, p. 147) away from comfort, luxury or innovation and towards a new necessity and standard of road traffic. Who can reject safety? The new accentuation exceeds the functional value of the technology and thus aims to create acceptance not only for the individual user of an automated vehicle but for all participants in traffic.

The value of safety is linked to the hope of better traffic for motorists and other road users. This makes it a supposedly unbeatable argument for the technology. But the narrative of the safety offered by automated vehicles does not hold up. The ambivalence when it comes to technology becomes apparent when the conditionality of safety is considered: Who is safe and who is not, actually? What creates the need of safety? What is the price of safety? These questions all remain unanswered in the films which leaves the viewers in a state of uncertainty and ambivalence.

But what is placed in the center of attention in the films? By making certain aspects visible about the future of autonomous driving, meaning has been attributed to the technology. To create this meaning, rational as well as emotional arguments have been used. The rational arguments take shape in the form of safety and efficiency. They appeal to the public's reasoning and aim to highlight the advantages of the technology over current forms of automobility which appear to be imperfect and unsafe in comparison to the new high-tech mobilities.

In addition, the cinematographic staging of naturalized connections between the human and the machine and the demonstration of joyful family life leads to an emotionalizing of technology. The rational, cool and mechanical visualizations are supplemented by strong emotional connotations. On the backstage of the affectual techniques is the assumption that feelings have positive effects on the success of the advertised technology or the final product (e.g. Kreutzer and Merkle, 2008; Plassmann, 2006; Trippe, 2013). In the automotive industry movie-based advertising conveys messages and appeals to emotions to elicit reactions from the consumer. The messages about the technology of autonomous driving sent out via the movies are positive throughout. They create images of privacy, joy and familiarity by referring to stories well known from advertising films in the industry. This becomes apparent through retrospective observations of car advertisements of the last several decades. The marketing and promotion of cars has always been influenced by current socio-political debates. Neumaier (2017) highlights this aspect in a historical review of car advertising in Western Germany and the USA in the 1970s. He examines the topic from the perspective of the energy crisis, resource consumption, environmental pollution and road safety. These issues were subject to heated public debates at the time. He ultimately arrives at the conclusion that there is an ambivalent attribution of rationality in the coded advertisements (Neumaier, 2017). The messages were constructed in such a way that functions and emotions were now closely linked (Neumaier, 2017, p. 47). Neumaier thus provides an example of the marketing strategies explained previously: the interaction of emotional messages and rational arguments.

Advertising films currently circulating in the automotive industry can be considered ambiguous. The films are not just rationally and objectively connoted explanatory films, nor are they purely emotionally appealing entertainment. They often show both: efficiency, productivity, safety as rational and joy, driving pleasure, family as emotional. There is no clear-cut line between reason and emotion.

Thus, making sense by visualizing certain aspects of the films leads to a recourse to old pictures, especially regarding emotional connotations. This emotional argument not only serves the marketing of a product or a brand, it also shapes the current technology of automated mobilities. An emotional machine with human or animalistic traits creates a framing of the technology as something beautiful, supportive and cooperative.

Compatibilization – do not be afraid!

What social reality is created here and is ushered into societies' perceptions of mobility and automation? The development of new technologies comes with a high degree of uncertainty and ambivalence for the social actors involved. In dealing with these uncertainties and the lack of knowledge, multiple strategies have been applied to disambiguate the technological futures of the automation technologies in the present. This co-production of knowledge by audiences and film makers about the technological future has a symmetrical effect: it shapes current practices and prepares us for the future.

The investigation of the backstage showed that the films reduce complexity by making it invisible. The resulting vacuum is filled with the visualization of meaningful narratives. In their composition, the reduction of complexity only results in a compatible image through simultaneously emotionalizing what is automated by machines.

It is particularly significant that although new concepts of technology are conveyed, social aspects have remained rigid. This is not a specific feature of technological futures in the automotive industry. Rather it is a typical characteristic of future visions (Kröger, 2014; Benford, 2010). The dichotomy between technological and social futures can be observed, particularly, in the science fiction genre. Technology historians and science fiction scientists, such as Fabian Kröger or Karlheinz Steinmüller, point out that technology and social issues are not conceived of together but separately (Kröger, 2014; Steinmüller, 2010). The result, they argue, is the unification of new technologies with old social patterns (Steinmüller, 2010, p. 29). The discussion of the visible and invisible elements of the films supports this argument. Next to the utopian images of automation technology, the visualization of the social context appears conserved. Not only gender relations but also traffic and automobility practices remain fundamentally in the present.

Grotesquely familiar stories and images of automobility, especially when taking old pictures and images into account, are by no means disruptive to the futures designed. The films, which are partly familiar and traditional, serve to emotionalize the expected futures. They call out to the public consumers of the films: "Do not be afraid!" The moving images provide an active and creative approach to the construction of technology. In the context of automobility, the iteration of old images in a new guise is an iteration of old systemic elements. In sum, the production and publication of fictional films about automated futures is the attempt of industrial and innovation politics, and specifically of the automotive industry, to socially construct certainties and deal with ambiguities and insecurities in relation to new technologies as well as the value of automation and AI in mobilities.

Visualization of future technologies are shaping social realities and are thus in need of being questioned by social science. In the investigation of automation technologies and artificial intelligence social science has the responsibility to not fall into the trap of compatibilization through fiction and investigate the backstage before the play is ultimately staged.

Conclusion

The aim of this chapter was to investigate and explain the sophisticated strategies behind the emergence of automated mobilities and the metamorphosis of technology-based social futures. Quite obviously, the automotive industry and the production of visualizations target the emotional and affectual constitution of trust in and the social acceptance of large-scale technological systems and the expert systems attached to them (see i.e. Giddens, 1997; Perrow, 2011). As in other fields of automation and artificial intelligence, the rise of the new and the disappearance of the old is socially constructed in a way that it stimulates familiar and often cozy connotations and associations. This is also the technique behind designing robots for medical care as innocent and infant-like machines and humanoid creatures. The biblical quote "Do not be afraid!" shows the dimension of the subcutaneous and subpolitical message that is transported here. It targets a subconscious level of understanding and experiencing technology and its presence in everyday life.

References

Audi, A.G. (2017): zFAS. Wie das Audi-Herzstück für das pilotierte Fahren funktioniert. Available at: www.youtube.com/watch?v=R26iby1LHoM (accessed 27 January 2020).

Bauman, Z. (1991): *Modernity and Ambivalence*. Cambridge: Polity Press.

Beck, U. (1992): *Risk Society: Towards a New Modernity, Theory, Culture & Society*. London: Sage.

Beck, U. (2016): *The Metamorphosis of the World: How Climate Change Is Transforming Our Concept of the World*, 1. Aufl. Cambridge: Polity.

Beck, U.; Bonß, W.; Lau, C. (2003): The Theory of Reflexive Modernization: Problematic, Hypotheses and Research Programme. *Theory, Culture & Society*, Vol. 20, No. 2, pp. 1–34.

Beck, U.; Hajer, M.A.; Kesselring, S. (Eds.) (1999): *Der unscharfe Ort der Politik*. Opladen: Leske + Budrich.

Bender, Gerd (2004): Heterogenität als Koordinationsproblem. Technikentwicklung in einem Verbundprojekt. In: Jörg Strübing, Ingo Schulz-Schaeffer, Martin Meister und Jochen Gläser (Hg.), *Kooperation im Niemandsland. Neue Perspektiven auf Zusammenarbeit in Wissenschaft und Technik*. Berlin: Springer, S. 137–161.

Benford, Gregory (2010): *The Wonderful Future that Never Was. Flying Cars, Mail Delivery by Parachute, and Other Predictions from the Past*. New York: Hearst Communications.

Benford, R.D.; Snow, D.A. (2000): Framing Processes and Social Movements: An Overview and Assessment. *Annual Review of Sociology*, Vol. 26, No. 1, pp. 611–639.

Böschen, Stefan; Wehling, Peter (2012): Neue Wissensarten. Risiko und Nichtwissen. In: Sabine Maasen, Mario Kaiser, Martin Reinhart und Barbara Sutter (Hg.): *Handbuch Wissenschaftssoziologie*. Wiesbaden: Springer Fachmedien Wiesbaden, S. 317–327.

Coenen, Christopher (2010): Deliberating Visions. The Case of Human Enhancement in the Discourse on Nanotechnology and Convergence. In: Mario Kaiser, Monika Kurath, Sabine Maasen und Christoph Rehmann-Sutter (Hg.), *Governing Future Technologies. Nanotechnology and the Rise of an Assessment Regime*. Cham: Springer, S. 73–87.

Cohen, A.P.; Shaheen, S.A. (2016): *Planning for Shared Mobility, PAS Report*, Vol. 583. Chicago, IL: American Planning Association.

Couldry, N.; Hepp, A. (2017): *The Mediated Construction of Reality*. Cambridge and Malden, MA: Polity.

Deutscher Städtetag (2018): Nachhaltige Mobilität für Alle. Online verfügbar unter http://staedtetag.de/presse/mitteilungen/085685/index.html (accessed 27 January 2020).

Diez, W. (2018): *Wohin steuert die deutsche Automobilindustrie?* 2., überarbeitete und aktualisierte Auflage. Berlin and Boston: De Gruyter Oldenbourg.

Dollinger, Bernd (2016): Sicherheit als politische Narration. Risiko-Kommunikation und die Herstellung von Un-/Sicherheit. In: Bernd Dollinger und Henning Schmidt-Semisch (Hg.): *Sicherer Alltag? Politiken und Mechanismen der Sicherheitskonstruktion im Alltag*. Wiesbaden: Springer Fachmedien Wiesbaden, S. 57–80. Online verfügbar unter https://doi.org/10.1007/978-3-658-07268-1_3.

Dollinger, Bernd; Schmidt-Semisch, Henning (Hg.) (2016): *Sicherer Alltag? Politiken und Mechanismen der Sicherheitskonstruktion im Alltag*. Wiesbaden: Springer Fachmedien Wiesbaden.

Douglas, M. (1992): *Risk and Blame: Essays in Cultural Theory*. London and New York: Routledge.

Eisch-Angus, Katharina (2016): "One Hell of a Big Story": Zur Narrativität der Sicherheitsgesellschaft. In: Bernd Dollinger und Henning Schmidt-Semisch (Hg.): *Sicherer Alltag? Politiken und Mechanismen der Sicherheitskonstruktion im Alltag*. Wiesbaden: Springer Fachmedien Wiesbaden.

Elliott, A. (2019): *The Culture of AI: Everyday Life and the Digital Revolution*. Milton: Routledge.

Elliott, A.; Kesselring, S.; Eugensson, A. (2019): In the End, It Is Up to the Individual. *Applied Mobilities*, Vol. 4, No. 2, pp. 1–7.

Featherstone, Mike (2004): Automobilities – An Introduction. *Theory, Culture & Society* Vol. 21 No. 4, pp. S. 1–24.

Freudendal-Pedersen, M.; Kesselring, S.; Servou, E. (2019): What Is Smart for the Future City? Mobilities and Automation. *Sustainability*, Vol. 11, No. 1, pp. 1–25.

Giddens, A. (1997): *The Consequences of Modernity*. Cambridge: Polity Press.

Goffman, Erving (1956). *The Presentation of Self in Everyday Life*. New York: Doubleday.

Grin, J.; Rotmans, J.; Schot, J.; Geels, F.W. (2010): *Transitions to Sustainable Development: New Directions in the Study of Long Term Transformative Change, Routledge Studies in Sustainability Transitions*, Vol. 1. New York, NY: Routledge.

Hajer, M.H. (1999): Zero-Friction Society. *Urban Design Quarterly*, No. 71, pp. 29–34.

Hensher, D.A.; Ho, C.Q.; Mulley, C.; Nelson, J.D.; Smith, G.; Wong, Y.Z. (2020): *Understanding Mobility as a Service (MaaS): Past, Present and Future*. Amsterdam, the Netherlands: Elsevier.

Jasanoff, Sheila (2015a): Future Imperfect. Science, Technology, and the Imaginations of Modernity. In: S. Jasanoff and S.-H. Kim (Eds.), *Dreamscapes of Modernity. Sociotechnical Imaginaries and the Fabrication of Power*. Chicago and London: The University of Chicago Press, S. 1–47.

Jasanoff, S. (2015b): Imagined and Invented Worlds. In: S. Jasanoff and S.-H. Kim (Eds.), *Dreamscapes of Modernity: Sociotechnical Imaginaries and the Fabrication of Power*, Chicago and London: The University of Chicago Press, 321–341.

Kaiser, Mario; Kurath, Monika; Maasen, Sabine; Rehmann-Sutter, Christoph (Hg.) (2010): *Governing Future Technologies. Nanotechnology and the Rise of an Assessment Regime*. Cham: Springer.

Kaufmann, Franz-Xaver (2012): *Sicherheit als soziologisches und sozialpolitisches Problem. Untersuchungen zu einer Wertidee hochdifferenzierter Gesellschaften*. Münster: LIT Verlag (Zivile Sicherheit. Schriften zum Fachdialog Sicherheitsforschung).

Kautt, York (2017): Grounded Theory as a Methodology and Method of Analyzing Visual Communication. *Forum Qualitative Sozialforschung/Forum: Qualitative Social Research,* Vol. 18, No. 3.

Keller, R. (2011): *Diskursforschung*. Wiesbaden: VS Verlag für Sozialwissenschaften.

Kesselring, S.; Freudendal-Pedersen, M.; Zuev, D. (Eds.) (2020): *Sharing Mobilities: New Perspectives for the Mobile Risk Society, Networked Urban Mobilities*. New York, NY: Routledge.

KIA Motors (2018): 2018 CES | Future Mobility and the Niro EV | Kia. Online verfügbar unter www.youtube.com/watch?v=ODDjhryjZk8, zuletzt geprüft am 27.01.2020.

Knie, A. (1994): *Wankel-Mut in der Autoindustrie. Anfang und Ende einer Antriebsalternative*. Berlin: Sigma.

Knoblauch, Hubert; Baer, Alejandro; Laurier, Eric; Petschke, Sabine; Schnettler, Bernt (2008): Visual Analysis. New Developments in the Interpretative Analysis of Video and Photography. *Forum Qualitative Sozialforschung/Forum: Qualitative Social Research,* Vol. 9, No. 3.

Kröger, Fabian (2014): Die Zukunft, die nie eintrat. Über die Nützlichkeit filmischer Zukunftsbilder des autonomen Fahrens für die Prospektive. In: *TATuP Zeitschrift für Technikfolgenabschätzung in Theorie und Praxis* 23 (1), S. 9–12.

Lösch, Andreas (2010): Visual Dynamics. The Defuturization of the Popular "Nano-Discourse" as an Effect of Increasing Economization. In: Mario Kaiser, Monika Kurath, Sabine Maasen und Christoph Rehmann-Sutter (Hg.), *Governing Future Technologies. Nanotechnology and the Rise of an Assessment Regime*. Cham: Springer, S. 89–108.

Lucht, Petra; Schmidt, Lisa-Marian; Tuma, René (Hg.) (2013): *Visuelles Wissen und Bilder des Sozialen*. Berlin: Springer.

Lüdeking, Karlheinz (2005): Was unterscheidet den pictorial turn vom linguistic turn? In: Klaus Sachs-Hombach (Hg.), *Bildwissenschaft zwischen Reflexion und Anwendung*. Köln: Von Halem, S. 407–426.

Manderscheid, Katharina (2018): From the auto-mobile to the driven subject? Discursive assertions of mobility futures. In: *Transfers* 8 (1), S. 24–43.

Mercedes-Benz (2015): The F 015 Luxury in Motion Future City – Mercedes-Benz Original. Available at: www.youtube.com/watch?v=SlfpZmCCZ_U (accessed 27 January 2020).

Mitchell, W.J.T. (1994): *Picture Theory: Essays on Verbal and Visual Representation*. Chicago: University of Chicago Press.

Neumaier, Christopher (2017): Vom Gefühl zum Kalkül? Autowerbung in Westdeutschland und den USA während der 1970er-Jahre. In: *Zeitgeschichte Digital*. Online verfügbar unter https://zeitgeschichte-digital.de/doks/frontdoor/deliver/index/docId/1077/file/ZF_3_2017_541_559_Neumaier.pdf, zuletzt geprüft am 27.01.2020.

Nissan (2015): Together We Ride. Available at: www.youtube.com/watch?v=9zZ2h2MRCe0 (accessed 27 January 2020).

Panasonic (2017): Future Mobility Lifestyle, 20XX. Available at: www.youtube.com/watch?v=KbqGA_78pIc (accessed 27 January 2020).

Perrow, C. (2011): *Normal Accidents: Living with High Risk Technologies*. Princeton: Princeton University Press.

Reichertz, Jo; Englert, Carina Jasmin (2011): *Einführung in die qualitative Videoanalyse*. Wiesbaden: VS Verl. für Sozialwissenschaften.

Reichle, Ingeborg (2007): Kunst-Bild-Wissenschaft. Überlegungen zu einer visuellen Epistemologie der Kunstgeschichte. In: Ingeborg Reichle, Steffen Siegel und Achim Spelten (Hg.), *Verwandte Bilder. Die Fragen der Bildwissenschaft*. Berlin: Kunstverlag Kadmos, S. 169–189.

Renault (2018): Working to Shape the Future of Mobility | Groupe Renault. Available at: www.youtube.com/watch?v=J02Ws94QuW8. Aufgerufen 06.12.2019 (accessed 27 January 2020).

Sachs, W. (1992): *For Love of the Automobile: Looking Back into the History of Our Desires*. Berkeley: University of California Press.

Schönewolf, C. (2020): *Vereindeutigung von Technikzukünften: Von der tradierenden Disruption autonomer Automobilität*. Cham: Springer.

Servou, E. (2020): Automated Driving in the Policymaking: The Productivity of the Void. Dissertation, Technische Universität München und Hochschule für Wirtschaft und Umwelt, München und Geislingen.

Sheller, Mimi (2004): Automotive Emotions. Feeling the Car. *Theory, Culture & Society*, Vol. 21, No. 4–5, pp. S. 221–242.

smart (2017): The Future of Mobility | Smart Vision EQ fortwo. Online verfügbar unter www.youtube.com/watch?v=4Afk82PW_Y4, zuletzt geprüft am 27.01.2020.

Snow, D.A.; Benford, R.D. (1999): Alternative Types of Cross-National Diffusion in the Social Movement Arena. In: D. della Porta, H. Kriesi, and D. Rucht (Eds.), *Social Movements in a Globalizing World*. London: Palgrave Macmillan.

Steinmüller, Karlheinz (2010): Science Fiction. Eine Quelle von Leitbildern für Innovationsprozesse und ein Impulsgeber für Foresight. In: *Foresight. Between Science and Fiction*, S. 19–31.

Sumantran, V.; Fine, C.; Gonsalvez, D. (2017): *Faster, Smarter, Greener: The Future of the Car and Urban Mobility*. Cambridge: MIT Press.

Toyota (2017): Toyota Concept-i/Concept Movie. Available at: www.youtube.com/watch?v=8IyPVK31j2o (accessed 27 January 2020).

Tuma, René (2013): Visuelles Wissen. Die Videoanalyse im Blick. In: Petra Lucht, Lisa-Marian Schmidt und René Tuma (Hg.), *Visuelles Wissen und Bilder des Sozialen*. Berlin: Springer, S. 49–69.
Urry, J. (2004): The 'System' of Automobility. *Theory, Culture & Society*, Vol. 21, No. 4–5, pp. 25–39.
Urry, J. (2016): *What Is the Future?*, 1. Aufl. Cambridge and Malden, MA: Polity.
Virilio, Paul (1978): *Fahren, fahren, fahren*. Berlin: Merve-Verl.
Zuev, Dennis; Krase, Jerry (2017): Visual Sociology. In: *Sociopedia*. Online verfügbar unter www.researchgate.net/publication/323595992_Visual_sociology, zuletzt geprüft am 27.01.2020.

12
Smart environments

Maja De Neergaard and Malene Freudendal-Pedersen

Introduction

The experience of being in a smart environment is everywhere and increasing daily. To many people, this is most manifested inside their homes as everyday technologies are increasingly becoming more connected and more sensitive to our individual uses. Internet sales are rising to the general middle class. This increased connectivity enables our electronic gadgets to respond to our immediate needs and comfort, be it in relation to heating, lighting, music, shopping, and so on. Today, when buying a washing machine, it is no longer enough to consider the number of spins, noise level, and energy efficiency. It is also necessary to consider its ability to download additional washing cycles, how to remote start the machine, and so forth. To some, this is exciting and interesting, and to others, it brings about a tedious complexity to everyday life and a demand for a response even if insufficiently knowledgeable of the task. The experience of smart environments is also manifested outside our homes. This is especially true if we live in a larger city, where the technologies and infrastructures of the urban environment are increasingly run, programmed, and managed using digital data, algorithms, and artificial intelligence (AI). In both the global north and global south, cities undergoing this digital transformation are commonly referred to as 'smart cities'. This chapter discusses the social science perspective on smart environments, and the phenomenon of smart cities serves as an example.

This chapter is divided into three parts. Beginning the chapter is an outline of some of the history and intellectual development behind the notion of smart environments. First, the smart environment is an idea that stems from computer and technology science and only lately has received mention in social sciences. However, the notion does not exist as a definite concept as such but rather recurs empirically as smart homes, smart health, or smart cities. Tracing the concept's intellectual development in social science is no straightforward task; therefore, instead, we briefly outline the history of the notion of 'environment'. Bringing forward this context is interesting because it clarifies the significant differences and understanding between technological and social science perspectives. Following this, the chapter argues why 'smart cities' are a useful example of smart environments from a social science perspective – even if 'smart homes', 'smart health', or 'smart workplaces' could also serve as examples.

In the second section, the chapter outlines and discusses the major claims and contributions in the field through a select number of empirical and theoretical perspectives aiming to represent an all-around (even if not complete) picture of the smart city literature. The section is divided into five headings focusing on the smart city as a corporate model for digital innovation, the tension between urban planning and smart city experiments, the everyday approach taken as an example of the current literature on smart urban mobility, the inequality and social diversity concerning the smart city, and finally, the need for embeddedness and contextualisation of smart city research. The final section outlines the future perspectives in the field and presents some of the criticisms and the suggested ways forward.

Some historical and intellectual underpinnings

Smart environments in computer and technology science

To grasp the intellectual development of the notion of a 'smart environment', a sketch of its conceptual and historical underpinnings is useful. Originally, the notion stemmed from the technical and computer sciences. As defined by Cook and Das (2004), a smart environment has the ability 'to acquire and apply knowledge about an environment and also to adopt to its inhabitants in order to improve their experience in that environment' (p. 3). Similarly, Kirste (2006) outlined an understanding where smart environments 'are physical spaces that are able to react to the activities of users, in a way that assists the users in achieving their objectives in the environment' (p. 322). What we understand from this is that the environment is a space, such as a home, workplace, or city, and that inhabitants or users are somehow assisted in their experience and in achieving their objectives with being in that space. As Kirste further explained, the purpose of the adjective 'smart' is to highlight 'the environment's capability to select its actions based on the user's objectives and not just on the current sensor data' (2006, p. 322). What we understand from this is that, in the given environment, some property can sense and respond to the inhabitant or user to offer assistance. Accordingly, as Kirste explained, 'the environment has to have a certain level of understanding of the *user's* view of the world' (2006, p. 322). In summary, we have an environment, such as a given space, that not just comprises its usual material properties but is equipped with digital properties that actively interact with the user. Traditionally, in technical and computer sciences, a smart environment is a construct that is programmed, designed, manipulated, and adapted to the specified needs and behaviours of a given user.

'Environment' and 'lifeworld' in social science

Outlining the intellectual history of smart environments from a social science perspective is somewhat different. First, the ontological understanding of smart environments in technical and computer sciences is different from that stemming from the social sciences (and humanities). A key turning point is how the different traditions understand 'the user's view of the world'. Second, while the concept does not have its intellectual history in the social sciences, the verb 'environment' does. The notion of 'environment' has a long theoretical history and is a fundamental concept for human (and non-human) beings in the world.

The idea of 'environment' has developed as a concept that concerns human (and non-human) experience and behaviour. In its two most notable original treatments, the environment first appears as the German term '*Umwelt*' in the work of philosopher Edmund Husserl and appears slightly later in the work of biologist Jakob von Uexküll. Although these cases are in two different disciplinary contexts, the term designates the fundamental surroundings of a human or animal. The notion has since travelled, and von Uexküll's *Umwelt* has entered present-day bio-semiotics and Husserl's *Umwelt* soon transformed into the phenomenological concept of *lifeworld* and has since been a founding concept for much theorisation of the human experience and its relation to its surroundings. When Husserl and von Uexküll developed their understanding of the environment, von Uexküll intended to enhance our understanding of the sensibilities and sense-making of non-human organisms, whereas Husserl was critical of the naturalism in the natural sciences and intended to develop a fundamentally different mode of understanding of the human experience. In recent decades, the notion of a lifeworld has been theorised, among others, by anthropologist Tim Ingold (2000), who aimed to bridge evolutionary and phenomenological directions (in anthropology) and made a central contribution to the present-day theorisation of the relationship between humans (and non-humans) and their environment. The second notable original treatment emerges with the philosopher of science and technology Don Ihde (1990), who conducted original work on human-computer interaction, also contributed greatly to the theorisation on lifeworld, articulating a substantial understating of relations between technology and the human experience. Whether evolutionary, phenomenological, or both, a long-held association between the environment and lifeworld and a deep appreciation of the environment/lifeworld exist as designating a fundamental premise of being – a fundamental mode of orchestration that existence necessarily and inescapably brings about. As is clear, the technical 'environment-as-construct' is highly different from the social 'environment-as-given' concept with immediate implications of whether and how the environment may be manipulated according to certain aims.

Major claims and contributions

The smart city, as proclaimed by Townsend (2013), represents 'the biggest building boom humanity will ever undertake' (p. 2). To meet demand, Townsend reported that India needs to build a new Chicago every year, and the government plans to build 100 smart cities. Similarly, in China, to follow up with the 12 million immigrants annually moving to cities from the countryside, the government plans to build 20 smart cities every year (Townsend, 2013). The advent of the smart city gained momentum immediately after the financial crisis in 2008 and is based on the belief that sustainable development can be reached through the technological innovation and digital transformation of the urban sphere.

In this chapter's discussion of the intellectual development of smart environments in social science, the phenomenon of smart cities is used as an example of a smart environment. Within the social sciences, the field of research on smart cities has grown exponentially during the past decade and has expanded among different disciplines (e.g. geography, sociology, and political science), different disciplinary traditions, and different academic intentions (e.g. professional, explorative, or critical). One element that has dominated the field is the (loudly voiced) inability to effectively define what a smart city is. It is a built form, a digital 'layer', a discourse, a brand, and increasingly, an urban environment in which people live. The discussion that follows touches upon all these different meanings, critiques, and associations. For now, we draw on just one of the attempts to summarise a smart city. According to Townsend, smart cities are 'places where information technology is combined with infrastructure, architecture, everyday objects, and even our bodies to address social, economic and environmental problems' (2013, p. 15).

Corporate smart city and its major critique

Within smart city literature, the promise of innovation is frequently connected to an 'engineering logic', where the aim is to optimise the social layout, the urban infrastructure and network, and (at least) parts of human interactions (Willis & Aurigi, 2018). A widespread understanding of smart environments is as 'coded spaces' (Kitchin, 2015) that facilitate self-learning in socio-technical environments based on information technology and AI. The idea is that the applied software facilitates the efficient use of space, infrastructure, and energy, creating user-friendly and sustainable environments (Rochet, 2018). These notions echo those of the smart environment in computer and technology science mentioned previously.

Another equally widespread understanding is the notion of smart cities as 'assemblages of technologies' that increase administrative efficiency, competitiveness, and social inclusion (Willis & Aurigi, 2018; Allwinkle & Cruickshank, 2011; Deakin, 2013). The effect of being smart also involves urban governance, inter-urban competition, and social responsibility.

A third understanding, associated with critical scholarship, presents the smart city as a case of 'corporate storytelling' (Söderström, Paasche, & Klauser, 2014). The idea of the smart city is a highly ideological concept that promises to make cities more environmentally sustainable and efficient, economically prosperous, and efficiently governed while hiding existing cultural, social, and economic problems (Hollands, 2008). This is an analysis of 'smart as [a] marketing strategy rather than actual products' (Wiig, 2016). The critique of corporate storytelling does not merely reflect the point made earlier regarding the need for context but is an important case of how the rhetoric is an actual driver. In its ability to transcend and blur the lines between brand, product, and existing socio-material reality, the discourse promotes the use of technology as a new and progressive idea.

Fourth, the current smart city strategies:

> outsource environmental and social resilience to the global technology sector. They increase the power of those already powerful elites who set the global technological agenda and marginalise opportunities for subversion, democratic engagement, and alternative strategies for environmental and social progress.
>
> *(Viitanen & Kingston, 2014, p. 815)*

These trends place entirely new pressures on cities and urban governance. The digitalisation of the city is not only about the technological solutions but about foreseeing their fallouts and understanding the business models they come with. In many ways, as Viitanen and Kingston argued, the smart city risks becoming a 'privatised' city.

As is clear, a major part of the literature has emphasised the importance of how, irrespective of the definition of 'smart', the key driver of the digitalisation of urban space comes from the industry. Kitchin (2014) called it 'the corporatisation of city governance and a technological lock-in'. As the industry's smart city initiatives involve a persistent focus on the scalability of initiatives, it also reduces the individual city to a mere testbed (Kitchin, 2014). As Townsend (2013) argued, '[t]oday big technology companies have usurped a leading role in shaping our visions for future cities' (p. 93) and 'by labelling their own visions of cities as "smart", technology giants today paint all others as inferior' (2013, p. 107).

As an example, Daimler's promotion of automated vehicles (under the argument of increased safety) does not focus on selling an object (the automated vehicle) but instead presents a future vision of a smart city. What is depicted is no longer focused on the car in a secluded environment but instead focuses on a bird's-eye view, displaying a dense urban environment with houses, cafés, cultural institutions, and an array of different types of mobility. The types of mobility include pedestrians, cycles, e-scooters, and mass transit, indicating a sustainable transport system, but it also clearly maintains an auto-logic hierarchy where car-only environments are dominant. The Daimler example underlines what Datta (2016) pointed out when saying that urbanisation has become a 'business model'. The smart city, it is argued, 'is not driven by visionary architects and planners but rather by the corporate sector seeking to create new global markets' (Datta, 2016, pp. 55–56). In contrast to the modernist utopias of the mid-century West, urban planning smart cities 'are not dreamt ideal cities but big business' (ibid.).

Urban planning and smart city experiments

With its inherent promises, it is no wonder that most cities are eager to employ the benefits of digital technologies. Consequently, this opens up the influence of technology corporations on urban planning, urban development, and urban governance that continues to grow and influence the everyday lives of citizens. These approaches to what the smart city is or can be in the future are strongly criticised for enforcing a 'techno centric planning paradigm' (Hajer, 1999; Miciukiewicz & Vigar, 2012; Canzler & Knie, 2016). Similarly, Miciukiewicz and Vigar (2012) pointed out that these technology-led solutions are considered 'carriers of political capital' and 'magic bullets' for meeting the carbon reduction goals by many policymakers, leading to a depoliticisation of urban transportation policymaking. The critique centres on the need to reassess the concept of smart cities in a wider socio-political perspective and infuse its discourse with an understanding of all aspects of cities and not only which technologies we can put into them. Hollands (2008) framed this lack of a wider perspective as the new clothing of urban entrepreneurialism, which hides the negative side effects that this implementation of new technologies can have on cities. Urban planning and policy become apolitical, and technological solutions that are not context-dependent can be sold to any political regime (Söderström et al., 2014).

Moreover, Graham and Thrift (2007) argue that infrastructure is often misrepresented as something fixed and stable. The popular assumptions are rooted in 'deep infrastructural ideologies of the West – which tend to normalise a ubiquitously networked urbanism' (p. 13). Such 'cultures of normalised and taken-for-granted infrastructure [assume] perfect order, completeness and homogeneity' (p. 10). Instead, infrastructure is leaky, partial, and heterogeneous. Interruptions to service are commonplace. Governmental institutions play an important role in promoting a shift towards sustainable cities or human cities through encouraging technological innovation, investing in sustainable infrastructure, and facilitating debates on changing the automobility system as a whole. This opens up a field for experiments and tactical urbanism, which enables politicians, planners, and citizens to develop new ways of being mobile and getting together.

The 'smart' in everyday life – an example of smart urban mobility

Mobilities in multiple forms, such as technological, geographic, digital, social, and cultural, shape cities and the urban environment. In many ways, this is driven by rapidly growing technological developments that are becoming an integrated part of the urban space and are changing the pulses and pace of the urban environment. The mobilities paradigm questions the 'rational' paradigm in planning that still understands the future of mobilities and cities, or the smart city, as centred on increasing the efficiency of technology with a focus on connectivity, integration, and social cohesion. The critique of the rational planning paradigm has a long history that began decades before the advent of the mobilities paradigm. One of the critique's most known protagonists, Jane Jacobs, argued how the modernist rationality resulted in 'cleaning out' the city of all its charm and history, networks, and social relations. Instead, she argued, the role of planning should be to support and balance the already-existing dynamics in the city and to establish equilibrium where it was not present. Ideals like those of Jane Jacob's have become increasingly relevant as our urban environments become smarter because sometimes the questions regarding 'why and for what' seem to be missing, and 'because we can' becomes the reason for implementing smart environments. This is very often argued with the claim that smart environments will make cities and their mobilities more sustainable.

This is an opportunity worth exploring. However, many of the smart mobilities solutions are dominated by car producers with solutions centred on the combination of connected, autonomous, shared, and electric mobility based on digital platforms (e.g. Volkswagen 'Together 2025'; BMW ACES; Daimler CASE). In the big picture, when we include lifecycle analysis and externalities, this iteration of the system of automobility is not a sustainable solution. The car has dominated the urban environment for the last 100 years, and it seems that smart environments are working along these lines as well.

As Canzler and Knie (2016) pointed out, reassessing the relation between automobiles and the urban environment is necessary:

> The automobile with its combustion engine was only the first generation appliance. Its broad success, however, has forced us to consider alternatives and re-interpret the product with the help of digital technologies. From a sociological perspective, the fixation with safeguarding the current product paradigm will, sooner or later, have to give way to a new generation of transportation.
>
> (p. 65)

Indeed, when taking as a starting point the socio-cultural and everyday life perspective, smart environments can also be about 'old' solutions, such as facilitating bike lanes and pedestrian and urban dwelling spaces, making them top priority on the roads. Strongly promoted by the Danish architect Jan Gehl, this type of thinking has been labelled the 'human city' as an expression of a city where the human scale sets the parameters of urban planning. What makes a human city is that the speed is low enough for people to interact with their surroundings so that people can see, smell, and experience at close proximity. To Gehl, this means walking or cycling or at least travelling at a maximum speed of 20 km/h. It is also about the scale of the urban environment, such as open facades at ground level (stores, small gardens in front of apartments, coffee shops, and so forth), roads that are not too wide, and squares (broad roads with car divides, narrow ones connect). This of course means less space for cars and necessitates solutions moving away from individual ownership towards mobility-as-a-service. It replaces individual ownership and provides an alternative between public transport and the individual car. Such solutions can be an important part of a (smart) urban environment that is not only about rational efficiency and seamless movement but also about everyday life and the human scale.

Inequality and the smart city

A notable absence in both smart city discourse and in 'actually existing' smart urban environments is the attention to the diversity of urban citizens. As Engelbert, van Zoonen, and Hirzalla (2019) argued, citizens represent different interests and needs, but these are rarely stated in the smart city discourse. For decades, feminist urban scholars have been scrutinising patriarchal urban development and have raised questions regarding how to develop an inclusive city, but according to Sangiuliano (2015), smart cities are generally not attentive to gender inequalities.

In continuation of this vein, scholars have started to ask whether the digital transformation of urban space leads to a more inclusive city or whether it builds upon or even reinforces exclusionary power relations (Gilbert, 2010; Datta & Odendaal, 2019; Elwood & Leszczynski, 2018). The contributions to the field are still limited, but the questions they raise are central from a social science perspective. There is a substantial need for increased awareness in social sciences of the types of exclusionary mechanisms of gender, class, ethnicity, age, and so on that the digitalisation of the urban environment involves. What are the social norms? What is the moral economy? How are urban and digital inequalities being produced or reproduced?

Embeddedness and contextualisation

One of the reasons for the large interest in and power of the smart city discourse is based on its inherent promise as a means to act on urgent problems in cities. However, the smart city discourse has developed as a 'one-size-fits-all narrative' that hides the conflicts, antagonisms, and inconsistencies in urban environments (Kitchin, 2015). In tracing the development and import of 'smart' in urban planning, it is clear that a lack of research exists that clarifies what the rise of 'smartness' in urban environments will become.

Smart city activities are also about social, cultural, political, economic, architectural, and ecological challenges. Appreciating the continued importance of critical work, Kitchin (2015) called for how the field would benefit from developing 'detailed genealogies of the concept and initiatives', more in-depth empirical case studies of specific smart city initiatives, more 'comparative research that contrasts smart city developments in different locales', and better 'collaborative engagement with various stakeholders' (p. 132). A need remains for sustained societal contextual differentiation regionally, politically, and socially.

In a similar vein, Shelton, Zook, and Wiig (2015) called for engagement with the 'actually existing' smart city visions and implementations in particular places, arguing how much research so far has been based on the more extraordinary cases. Hajer et al. (2015) argued for a policy approach to sustainability that lies beyond what they call 'cockpitism', where the aim is to be closer to what the urban realm is when it is not only viewed from above but also experienced and understood in all its materialities and embodiment of human encounters. In the past years, the ongoing scholarship bears on exactly these concerns and on the growing recognition of how the digitalisation of urban space is a highly context-specific process that demands detailed empirical study to detangle the complex and situated processes.

Numerous aspects make cities different from each other. In response to this, one example is the edited volume by Karvonen, Cugurullo, and Caprotti (2019) that represents several studies in a host of different places that aim to unpack and contextualise smart city initiatives, showing individual differences. In discussing the differences and particularities when developing smart solutions in the global north vis-à-vis the global south, Aurigi and Odendaal (2020) argued how place-based approaches are necessary to enhance the social sustainability of the city. If only the technical aspects of smart cities are in the foreground, 'the qualities of place and the human agency that crucially contribute to city-making' become invisible (ibid., pp. 1–2).

Future perspectives

The field of the smart environment as manifested in the smart city and smart mobilities literature is very much a field in development, both empirically and theoretically. In this final section, some major areas that need future development are outlined.

Difference and particularity

As outlined previously, the field is characterised by a decade of social science (and particularly urban studies) scholarship that has critically examined the discourse, initiatives, and ideological underpinnings of corporate smart city solutions and promises. In the past years, the field has begun to develop a broader scope of empirically detailed studies with greater social, political, and geographical differentiation. More systematic knowledge of the differences involved is needed when developing smart solutions. For instance, what does implementing smart solutions in existing urban structures through retrofitting vis-à-vis on green field locations from the bottom up mean? Existing urban structures have numerous restrictions, for instance, in relation to the automated car. Many older European cities have inner-city districts where sharp segregation between different modes of transport is not possible, and they have several streetscapes with shared spaces.

First, it is worth discussing whether automation on these streets makes any sense. In an entirely newly developed urban agglomeration, there is an opportunity to design streetscapes that make the implementation of the automated car possible. This requires a serious discussion of what kind of city this would create and whether this is a city with human qualities. Neither method for these two urban settings would demand many different solutions, and perhaps some that can be transferred. In addition, it is essential to consider the relationship between everyday practices with these technologies and be aware that new urban developments also provide the best opportunities to change everyday practices.

Second, what are the characteristics of digital solutions in large cities and small municipalities? How and to what extent are the involved inhabitants 'digitally dressed' to meet new digital infrastructures? For instance, what are the levels of welfare, education, and digital literacy, to mention a few aspects? All this knowledge is essential to avoid ending up in a situation in which we insert digital technologies into a city, and they are not used optimally. This is not optimal from a sustainability outset. Some of the more recent research has also suggested that urban smartness should be understood as a process. Here, the focus is on how the creation of the new urban digitalised fabric is happening through small-scale initiatives, where the forms of participation and governance, in more or less complex forms, play a key role.

A third key aspect of the needed emphasis on difference and particularity is how different practices and traditions of urban governance affect smart solutions. In what ways does it matter if a city has a strong or a weak tradition of comprehensive planning and regulation? What is the influence, if any, of user involvement and participatory cultures? Finally, there is a continued need to theorise the intersection of smart environments and everyday life. At the beginning of the chapter, the notion of 'lifeworld' was introduced, as it characterised a major branch of social science approaches to everyday life. The lifeworld tradition is one place to start, but the major future perspective is that the social sciences take part in forming the analysis of smart environments through their theoretical legacies of anti-naturalism, anti-subjectivism, and the human/non-human intertwinement. One example is the recent involvement of Stengers' (2005) notion of 'the idiot' that emphasises the dangers of slipping into a reductionist view of a 'proper' subject (Tironi & Valderrama, 2018).

Cross-disciplinary and cross-sector approaches

While attention is being focused on the future perspective of differentiation, a substantial need exists for more cross-disciplinary approaches within research and development of smart cities (and more broadly, smart environments). It seems the field is still, to a large degree, working on the old premise that technical and natural sciences provide the 'real' knowledge and that social sciences and humanities are secondary. The exponential growth of digital technologies, the speed with which they develop, and the enormous financial interests and governance implications it raises are easier handled with a positivist ontology that provides measurable answers, assessments, and models. This leaves the social sciences and humanities to provide the 'afterthought' and critique of what is already implemented.

However, to understand how and why things matter to people, social sciences and humanities must be part of developing the digital environments from the onset. New digital technologies hold considerable promise concerning sustainability and climate change issues, but technology is never better than the way it is used. The development of new technology must go hand in hand with a firm and context-specific understanding of the associated everyday practices. Presently, this is probably the most decisive criticism and future perspective of the field, but one that cannot be solved from within the field alone.

Within debates of sustainability, this dilemma is well known. One of the major experiences is how sustainability strategies must be strongly rooted in both urban governance and the networks of stakeholders in civil society, cities, and businesses. No 'technical fix' exists for societal problems, and the corporate smart city discourse could also benefit from this premise. According to Urry (2016), when designing 'desirable futures', the focus should stem from the outset in specific social settings containing a thorough analysis of the social and historical conditions. In line with this, Freudendal-Pedersen and Kesselring (2016) argued for thinking with transdisciplinary and cross-sectoral methodologies when focusing on all the aspects of cities and not only on which technologies that can be put into them.

Conclusion

The critical scholarship on smart cities has made a substantial contribution to the social sciences' understanding of how digital technologies are significantly transforming cities. This is not a new phenomenon, and the potentially negative effects that new information and communications technology and networked infrastructure have on cities have long been recognised (see, e.g. Graham & Marvin book on Splintering Urbanism from 2001). Nevertheless, the recent literature addresses how the proclaimed effects from digital technology are circumscribed within an entire ideology of how data, algorithms, and AI can solve even social, environmental, and economic problems and provide for better, cost-efficient urban governance. The global recognition of climate challenges (with the upsurge in austerity politics in many urban governments) has resulted in a historical momentum for the rapid influence of digital technology. The literature on smart cities is also an example of the remaining divide between technology/natural science and social science approaches to digital technology, AI, and smart environments.

In the case of smart cities, this is reinforced in the industry-led developments promoting the vision of smart cities as a solution to social and climate problems. The major critique is that this corporate smart city is a 'one-size-fits-all model' that reduces social problems and diminishes geographical differences and that computing models and algorithms that use such data to cure urban inefficiencies cannot stand alone. Smart environments, whether as smart cities, smart homes, or smart workplaces, force us to continuously ask and understand how the digital revolution is transforming society. This chapter outlines some of the convergences and divergences between contemporary social theory/science and the digital solutions using the smart city discourse as an example and argues for the substantial need for contextualisation and place-dependent analysis to mature our understanding and the future design of the everyday networked society.

It seems relevant to ask the question whether any alternative to the smart citizens who wish to be guided through the urban environment efficiently and safely exists. In *Liquid Life*, Bauman (2005) stated that we lack the driving force to create new utopias because of the fragmentation of late-modern lives and these processes are making individuals and artefacts into objects of consumption. 'Liquid life means constant self-scrutiny, self-critique and self-censure. Liquid life feeds on the self's dissatisfaction with itself' (Bauman, 2005, pp. 10–11). A life that creates dissatisfaction leaves no room for common utopias. We could argue that smart environments fit well into the state of modern lives. It symbolises an inherent state of paralysis, with no possibility of creating social learning because modern society has shaped us into individuals with a primary focus on unlimited freedom and the possibility to purchase whatever we desire. This quite pessimistic view might be true for some, and here, being smart and guided by the urban environment makes sense. However, we also see different values and dreams for shaping the future, which rest within the fragile irrationalities that make everyday life work. The real problem is if these values and dreams disappear and if we forget how to play and live beyond the existing frames. The human city is not about smartness, it is about meetings, interactions, and a slow pace.

References

Allwinkle, S., & Cruickshank, P. (2011). Creating smart-er cities: An overview. *Journal of Urban Technology*, *18*(2), 1–16.

Aurigi, A., & Odendaal, N. (2020). *Shaping smart for better cities: Rethinking and shaping relationships between urban space and digital technologies*. Cambridge, MA: Academic Press.

Canzler, W., & Knie, A. (2016). Mobility in the age of digital modernity: Why the private car is losing its significance, intermodal transport is winning and why digitalisation is the key. *Applied Mobilities*, *1*(1), 56–67.

Cook, D., & Das, S. K. (2004). *Smart environments: Technology, protocols, and applications* (Vol. 43). Hoboken, NJ: John Wiley & Sons.

Datta, A. (2016). The smart entrepreneurial city: Dholera and other 100 utopias in India. In S. Marvin, A. Luque-Ayala, & C. McFarlane(Eds.), *Smart urbanism: Utopian vision or false dawn* (pp. 51–70). London: Routledge. https://doi-org.zorac.aub.aau.dk/10.4324/9781315730554

Datta, A., & Odendaal, N. (2019). Smart cities and the banality of power. *Society and Space*, *37*(3), 387–392.

Deakin, M. (2013). *Smart cities: Governing, modelling and analysing the transition*. London: Routledge. https://doi.org/10.4324/9780203076224.

Elwood, S., & Leszczynski, A. (2018). Feminist digital geographies. *Gender, Place & Culture*, *25*(5), 629–644.

Engelbert, J., van Zoonen, L., & Hirzalla, F. (2019). Excluding citizens from the European smart city: The discourse practices of pursuing and granting smartness. *Technological Forecasting and Social Change*, *142*, 347–353.

Freudendal-Pedersen, M., & Kesselring, S. (2016). Mobilities, futures & the city: Repositioning discourses – changing perspectives – rethinking policies. *Mobilities*, *11*(4), 575–586.

Gilbert, M. (2010). Theorizing digital and urban inequalities: Critical geographies of 'race', gender and technological capital. *Information, Communication & Society*, *13*(7), 1000–1018.

Graham, S., & Thrift, N. (2007). Out of order: Understanding repair and Maintenance. *Theory, Culture & Society*, *24*(3), 1–25.

Hajer, M. (1999). *Zero-friction society*. Retrieved from May 29, 2014, from www.rudi.net/books/11454

Hajer, M., Nilsson, M., Raworth, K., Bakker, P., Berkhout, F., de Boer, Y., . . . Rockström, J. (2015). Beyond cockpit-ism: Four insights to enhance the transformative potential of the sustainable development goals. *Sustainability*, *7*(2), 1651–1660.

Hollands, R. G. (2008). Will the real smart city please stand up? *City*, *12*(3), 303–320. https://doi.org/10.1080/13604810802479126.

Ihde, D. (1990). *Technology and the lifeworld. From garden to earth*. Bloomington: Indiana University Press.

Ingold, T. (2000). *The perception of the environment: Essays on livelihood, dwelling and skill*. London: Routledge.

Karvonen, A., Cugurullo, F., & Caprotti, F. (Eds.). (2019). *Inside smart cities. Place, politics and urban innovation*. Abingdon, OX and New York, NY: Routledge.

Kirste, T. (2006). Smart environments. In E. Aarts & J. Encarnação (Eds.), *True visions. The emergence of ambient intelligence* (pp. 321–337). Berlin and Heidelberg: Springer. https://doi.org/10.1007/978-3-540-28974-6.

Kitchin, R. (2014). The real-time city? Big data and smart urbanism. *GeoJournal, 79*(1), 1–14.

Kitchin, R. (2015). Making sense of smart cities: Addressing present shortcomings. *Cambridge Journal of Regions, Economy and Society, 8*(1), 131–136. https://doi.org/10.1093/cjres/rsu027.

Miciukiewicz, K., & Vigar, G. (2012). Mobility and social cohesion in the splintered city: Challenging technocentric transport research and policy-making practices. *Urban Studies*. https://doi.org/10.1177/0042098012444886.

Rochet, C. (2018). *Smart cities: Reality or fiction*. London and Hoboken: Wiley.

Sangiuliano, M. (2015). *Gender and social innovation in cities. SEiSMiC gender action plan & toolkit*. Drammen, Norway: European Centre for Women and Technology.

Shelton, T., Zook, M., & Wiig, A. (2015). The "actually existing smart city". *Cambridge Journal of Regions, Economy and Society, 8*(1), 13–25.

Söderström, O., Paasche, T., & Klauser, F. (2014). Smart cities as corporate storytelling. *City, 18*(3), 307–320.

Stengers, I. (2005). The cosmopolitical proposal. In B. Latour & P. Webel (Eds.), *Making things public* (pp. 994–1003). Cambridge, MA: MIT Press.

Tironi, M., & Valderrama, M. (2018). Unpacking a citizen self-tracking device: Smartness and idiocy in the accumulation of cycling mobility data. *Environment and Planning D: Society and Space, 36*(2), 294–312.

Townsend, A. (2013). *Smart cities. Big data, civic hackers, and the quest for a new utopia*. New York, NY: W.W. Norton & Company.

Urry, J. (2016). *What is the future?* Cambridge: Polity Press.

Viitanen, J., & Kingston, R. (2014). Smart cities and green growth: Outsourcing democratic and environmental resilience to the global technology sector. *Environment and Planning A, 46*(4), 803–819.

Wiig, A. (2016). The empty rhetoric of the smart city: From digital inclusion to economic promotion in Philadelphia. *Urban Geography, 37*(4), 535–553.

Willis, K. S., & Aurigi, A. (2018). *Digital and smart cities*. Abingdon, OX and New York: Routledge.

13

Models of law and regulation for AI

Nicolas Petit and Jerome De Cooman

Introduction

This chapter discusses models of law and regulation of artificial intelligence (hereafter, "AI").[1] The goal is to provide the reader with a map of the law and regulation initiatives towards AI. Most law and regulation initiatives display, on their face, heterogeneity. Yet they often have common foundations. This chapter surveys the four main models of law and regulation of AI that emerge (I), describes their strengths and weaknesses (II), discusses whether technological evolution should be addressed under existing or new laws (III), and puts forward a fifth model of law and regulation based on externalities with a moral twist (IV).

I Survey of law and regulation models for AI

In the literature, legal scholars and practitioners come to the question of law and regulation of AI through four mental models. That is the black letter law model (A), the emergent model (B), the ethical model (C) and the risk regulation model (D). We describe each of these models, and discuss specific applications to AI.

A Black letter law model

In a black letter law model, the focus is on how existing laws apply to an AI system.[2] By black letter law, we mean of entire body of positive law, that is judicial and statutory law. In his seminal book *Theorie der juristischen Argumentation*,[3] Robert Alexy explained that legal discourse tries to resolve the question of what is mandatory, allowed or prohibited by answering practical questions not in a general way but instead taking into account the restrictions driven by legal frameworks composed of binding norms.[4]

The black letter law model starts from the identification of the relevant law, to which it confronts the matter of fact involving an AI system.[5] In practice, the matter of fact will often be an AI use case leading to a dispute.

In a black letter approach, the analysis is either conducted within a field of the law or across several fields of the law. In the first case, the disciplines most commonly looked at in

Table 13.1 Description of law and regulation model

	Black letter law	Emergent	Ethical	Risk regulation
Timing	Reactive	Proactive	Proactive	Proactive
Discussion	Descriptive	Normative	Normative	Normative
Approach	Statutory and doctrinal interpretation => what the law is	Normative => what the law should be	Teleological when deontological ethics Ontological when consequentialism	Cost-benefit analysis, with possible precautionary principle
Example	Legal personhood and intellectual property		Citizens' scoring and facial recognition	
Issues	Irrelevance	Redundance	Ethics lobbying Ethical relativism Ethics shopping	Knee-jerk regulation

the law and AI scholarship are product safety (including cyber security) and liability, consumer protection, intellectual property, labour law, privacy, civil liability, criminal liability, legal personhood, insurance and tax law. A particularly visible example of a disciplinary approach is the rights-based approach. Under a rights-based approach, a subset of legal and regulatory obligations pertaining to human rights, the rule of law and democracy are deemed so important that they become the main focus of inquiry in discussions over the law and regulation of AI systems.[6]

One disciplinary issue discussed under the black letter law model is whether AI-created inventions[7] or works of art can benefit from intellectual property (IP) rights, and who is their owner.[8] Consider an AI-created song. Under copyright law, courts insist that the work exhibits a "modicum of creativity", reflects the "author's intellectual creation" or constitutes the exercise of "non-mechanical, non-trivial skill and judgment".[9] A debate exists today on whether the originality requirement prevents the allocation of copyrights to intelligent machines.[10] Similarly, in the area of patent law, an innovation is protected on the condition that it involves an "inventive" step. As a rule, inventiveness means non-obviousness to a person skilled in the art. In layman's terms, a non-obvious discovery is one that is unexpected. But where should we set the benchmarks for "non-obviousness" and "skill in the art", when one contemplates the introduction of AIs capable of "recursive self-improvement"?[11] What is not obvious to a man skilled in the art may be trivially evident for a super intelligent machine.

But the black letter law model also raises transversal issues that cut across various fields of the law. For example, can AIs be granted legal rights to litigate, contract or own property, including IP?[12] The parallels in discussions about the legal personhood of humans, corporations, international organizations and innate objects like trees are unmistakable.[13]

The black letter law approach is dominated by teleological questions. To solve fictional cases, courts and legislatures often consider the goals of the law.[14] For example, legal personhood was granted to corporations in order to promote economic exchange. A question that will therefore arise will be: should AIs be granted legal personhood to promote economic exchange, as was done for corporations? Similarly, a certain degree of legal personhood has been recognized to trees on grounds of sustainable development. In turn, it may be asked whether AI legal personhood is likely to contribute to the conservation of global resources.

B Emergent model

The emergent model asks whether AIs raise new issues that require the creation of "a new branch of law".[15] The assumption is that AI systems produce emergent phenomena.[16] Concretely, the emergent model asks whether AI systems' unique economic,[17] ethical[18] and scientific concerns require *sui generis* legal prohibitions or exonerations of AI.[19] An emergent model is often at work behind books, articles and commentaries on "the law of driverless cars",[20] "the law of drones",[21] or "the law of robots".[22]

Often, the intellectual inquiry under the emergent model focuses on classes of AI applications. The *Stanford Artificial Intelligence and Life in 2030 Report* (the "Stanford Report") provides a good illustration.[23] The Stanford Report purports to highlight how AI applications bring "specific changes affecting the everyday lives of the millions of people who inhabit them".[24] It focuses on eight domains where AI is deemed to have the greatest impact: "transportation, service robots, healthcare, education, low-resource communities, public safety and security, employment and workplace, home/service robots, and entertainment".[25] From this, the Stanford Report enumerates nine broad categories of legal law and policy that AIs tend to raise: privacy, innovation policy, civil liability, criminal liability, agency, certification, labor, taxation and politics.

The Stanford Report displays commonalities as well as discrepancies with the black letter law model.[26] Some topics that were absent, irrelevant or subjacent in the black letter law model are prominent in the emergent model. This is the case of the legal arrangements governing certification (e.g., professional licensing requirements), taxation (e.g., how automated compliance reduces infringements to the law) and politics (e.g., voting and deliberation processes). And in the emergent model, the legal issues are framed as general topics that cut through several legal fields. Innovation policy is, for example, the umbrella framework under which liability issues, freedom of speech and patent law are discussed.

The emergent model is more focused on questions of *ex ante* legal design.[27] By this, we mean how to code an AI system to address a prospective legal issue.[28] This is distinct from the black letter law model, which focuses on legal arrangements for *ex post* frictional cases. One reason for this difference may be that technology-untrained lawyers are less comfortable discussing how to turn legal rules into computer code.

In addition, discussions under the emergent model are often more normative. Experts discuss "*Should* the law . . ." questions, while in the black letter approach they descriptively ask "*Does* the law . . ." questions. The emergent model thus gives a more explicit exposition to technological optimism or pessimism, which is often implicit in black letter law discussions.

The issue of whether AIs and robotic applications deserve legal rights brings understanding to what the emergent approach is concretely. Under this approach, one looks at technological outcomes, and applies a kind of Turing test to establish whether legal personhood can be granted. This approach was the one followed by Professor Lawrence Solum in a much-cited article when he considered the following thought experiment: "Could an artificial intelligence serve as a trustee?".[29] It is also the one followed when one asks whether an AI created song is approximates human art.[30]

Compared to the black letter law model, the emergent model is ontological. Since existing laws are often out of the picture, their goals are not considered. The intellectual inquiry focuses on understanding what the technology is. In the AI context, this is often done by reference to human intelligence.[31] The discussion focuses on a reflection on ourselves, and what makes us human.[32] And this is not neutral. Consider the idea of granting legal personhood to AIs. The emergent model may be biased in favor of anthropomorphic AI systems (robots like Asimo) or symbolic ones (softbots like Siri, Alexa or Cortana). Studies have shown that individuals treat computers like they behave with other human beings.[33] Evolutionary biology shows that people tend to treat as human what is like human. As Levy explained:

> if our children see it as acceptable behaviour from their parents to scream and shout at a robot or to hit it, then . . . our children might well come to accept that such behaviour is acceptable in the treatment of human beings.[34]

C *Ethical model*

A third popular model focuses on ethics as the fundamental component of any law and regulation of AI systems. Ethics are the part of practical philosophy that deals with moral dilemmas. AI systems implicate mostly a field of ethics known as normative ethics.[35] The purpose of normative ethics is to create moral norms distinguishing the good and the bad. Applied ethics are also relevant to AI systems. Applied ethics analyze specific moral problems (e.g. abortion, euthanasia and now specific AI applications of like citizen scoring or facial recognition).

Normative ethics has three sub branches: virtue ethics, consequentialist ethics and deontological ethics. All three infuse debates over the law and regulation of AI systems.[36] Virtue ethics consider that happiness requires the practice of moral qualities in daily life. Aristotle singled out wisdom, justice, intelligence and moderation. Moreover, virtue ethics imply a "golden mean". Courage, for example, is the middle ground between cowardice and recklessness.[37] In an AI context, the requirement of transparency is an example of virtue ethics. And the middle ground reached by the requirement of explicability is a good illustration because it requires some accountability, but not to the point of mandating exhaustive disclosure.

Deontological ethics consider that compliance with ethical duties determine whether an action is right or wrong, regardless of its consequences.[38] For example, assistance to homeless people (the intention) is rightful even if it implies a reduction of wealth for the benefactor (the consequence). Kant identified some "categorical imperatives".[39] A classical example given are the obligation to tell the truth or to treat humans with dignity.[40] The EU Guidelines on AI embrace a Kantian spirit when they state "AI is not an end in itself, but rather a promising means to increase human flourishing".[41] AI is a tool that should serve humanity, not the opposite. Deontological ethics sometimes lead to paradoxes. Always tell the truth is a categorical imperative. But what if a murderer rings at the door and asks an AI home assistant, "Where is your owner"?[42] The idea of ethical duty regardless of consequences is dangerous. The road to hell is paved with good intentions.

Consequentialism focuses on impacts. Rightfulness depends on a cost-benefit analysis.[43] Consequentialism is egoist when the costs and benefits are examined from the perspective of the agent that acts. It is altruist when the examination takes place from the perspective of society excluding the agent.[44] And it is utilitarist when the impact on society as a whole is considered.[45] A degree of consequentialism transpires from the European Guidelines on AI. One of their stated objectives is "to maximise the benefits of AI systems while at the same time preventing and minimizing their risks".[46]

The ethical model of law and regulation is technology neutral. Ethical recommendations adopted towards computational technologies like AI emulate solutions previously adopted in relation to biological technologies. Across the world, AI ethics tend to converge on the principles of beneficence, non-maleficence, autonomy, justice and explicability.[47] These principles come directly from bioethics, with the exception of explicability.[48] A debate exists today on whether it is right to draw inspiration from bioethics for AI systems. For example, while the interests of a patient and a doctor might be aligned, the same is not true for the developer of AI systems and its user.[49] Moreover, the regulatory environment of biotechnologies and AI differ widely, leading to distinct ethical requirements. For example, the regulatory framework in place in the health sector prevents hospitals from putting budgetary constraints before the interest of the patient.[50] By contrast, no such incentive constraint exists for AI.[51] Self-reliance on developers' willingness to respect ethical principles is key. Yet, research suggests that ethical statements have little or no impact on their daily practice.[52]

D Risk regulation model and the precautionary principle

A fourth model of law and regulation of AI systems is risk regulation. By risk regulation, we mean attempts to reduce the probability of occurrence *or* the levels of harms arising from events inherent in technology. In a White Paper on AI, the European Commission (EC) takes a clear risk regulation approach when it calls for "a regulatory framework [that] should concentrate on how to minimize the various risk of potential harm".[53]

A risk regulation model of AI has several features. First, risk regulation proposes *ex ante* solutions. The goal is preventive, not corrective. Product design plays an important role, compared to insurance or liability. Red buttons, humans in the loop or sandboxing requirements in self-driving systems are possible examples.

Second, risk regulation mobilizes statistical evidence to evaluate risks.[54] For example, the German Data Ethics Commission proposed a pyramidal framework distinguishing five levels of risks, from the negligible (no special regulatory measure) to the existential one (complete or partial ban).[55] In that respect, risk regulation comes close to consequentialism and cost-benefit analysis: the higher the risk, the stronger the regulatory response.

That said, risk regulation's dependence on measurement encounters two limits. One, when calculation is impossible due to scientific uncertainty, precaution must prevail.[56] Absence of evidence does not mean evidence of absence. An event with uncertain probability but unsustainable consequences is unacceptable.[57] This is where the precautionary principle gets in the game.[58] In AI contexts, a precautionary logic inspires calls for red lines, bans or moratoria on applications like lethal autonomous weapons, citizen scoring or facial recognition. Science is not irrelevant in the precautionary approach. Science helps establish the causal link between the event and its consequences. Besides, a precautionary approach is more than extreme consequentialism. The precautionary principle is a moral duty to ensure that everything possible is done to avoid catastrophic risk.

Two, cultural, political and psychological factors also influence risk regulation.[59] The Frankenstein complex, that is the Western fear that the creature (e.g., an AI system) might one day outcompete and turn against its creator (humanity)[60] – a fear that Nick Bostrom calls the treacherous turn[61] – is strongly rooted in Western culture, to the point that it appears in the European Report on civil law rules on robotics.[62]

II Four fallacies of law and regulation for AI

The four models of law and regulation of AI exhibit dramatic shortcomings.

A The paradox of irrelevant law

The paradox of irrelevant law concerns the black letter law model. Lawyers conjecture frictional rule-implementation cases with imperfect comprehension of the underlying technology. Because lawyers need case studies to apply their deductive discipline, they tend to rely on science-fiction to generate facts. Many scholarly works on AI and the law, for example, start with a discussion of Asimov's Three Laws of Robotics. But because science-fiction is what it is,[63] lawyers miss out on relevant technological evolutions by focusing on fictional ones. The best example of this is driverless car. The dominant hypothesis in most science-fiction work prior to 2000 envisioned the period 2015–2025 with men and women driving flying hover cars, not a driverless one.[64] Had legal experts changed the law, we would today have a detailed, useless law of flying cars.

The black letter law model also leads to irrelevance due to blind spots. Reasoning from existing rules focuses our attention in the wrong directions. Our laws are abstract commands designed on the basis of specific representations of the state of the world and its trajectories.[65] Too much reliance on the black letter approach undermines the necessary development of novel legal fields in a context of emergences.[66] The following example illustrates the point. Assume that an AI ends up dominating the world.[67] Should society introduce a "law of humans" which affords minority rights to humans and protects our species from intelligent machines in case this ominous prediction ever comes true? However, some of us cannot see this necessity today because all our laws embody the non-secular postulate that human conscience is special and makes us superior to machines, animals and other entities. As a result of this cultural a priori, our laws are essentially more about how humans treat non-humans (and in particular machines), and not about how non-humans (and in particular machines) treat humans.

B *The problem of redundant law*

A fundamental aspect of emergent models of law and regulation of AI is to treat the technology as novel. As a result, emergent models of law and regulation often assume the existence of gaps in the law, or that AI systems operate in a lawless world.

Judge Easterbrook famously called this intellectual attitude the "law of the horse".[68] The expression derides the tendency to adopt new and *ad hoc* law when technologies emerge – in the 19th century, the horse. Today, AI. The problem of the law of the horse is easy enough to see. Assume an AI-assisted robot gardener causes damage when mowing the lawn. Do we need to legislate specific rules on robot gardeners to address liability issues? The answer is a sure no. *Nove sed non nova* – not a new thing but in a new way.

In so far as AI is concerned, the law of the horse problem is essentially one of redundancy. AI is imitative.[69] Marvin Minsky wrote that AI is the "science of making machines do things that would require intelligence if done by men".[70]

If, on the one hand, law A governs human behavior while law B governs AI behaviour and, on the other hand, AI tends to imitate human conduct, then law A tends to copy law B. This is the problem of redundant law.

Most scholars that work under the emergent model tend to overlook the problem of redundant law because they overestimate the capability of AI systems.[71] Human beings indeed have the tendency "to attribute programs far more intelligence than they actually possess (by any reasonably objective measure) as soon as the program communicates in English [or other natural language] phrases".[72] This bias feeds normative claims whereby new and *ad hoc* rules should be adopted for AI.

C *Ethics and the failure of good intentions*

The ethical model is uncontroversial in its ambitions. Yet, it is rife with problems in its implications. The first set of problems is ethics lobbying (or ethics washing). Ethics lobbying arises when private or public organizations use ethical debates to prevent, delay or even replace legislation.[73] The idea is to rule out binding laws in favour of softer ethical rules better suited to technological innovations.[74] This concern has been voiced in the EU, whose Guidelines on AI have been criticized on the ground that they neither embody, nor call for, enforceable legal requirements.[75]

The second set of problems concerns ethical relativism. Put simply, there is no single ethics.[76] What one considers as good or bad is, by definition, personal. There is no objective way to rank Aristotle's virtues versus Kantian categorical imperatives.

The trolley problem illustrates ethical relativism (though some dispute its relevance).[77] Consider a self-driving car, and place it in a situation in which there will be casualties. For example, the self-driving car must choose between two options: (1) continuing its course, and killing a mother and her baby who crossed on red or (2) changing course, and killing an old woman on the sidewalk. How should the self-driving car, and the programmers in charge of optimizing algorithms, decide? Under the consequentialist approach, should it favour the younger or the older? Or should we randomize the decision of the self-driving car because it is what is closest to a human reaction?[78]

To answer these questions, the Massachusetts Institute of Technology (MIT) conducted a large-scale ethical study called the Moral Machine Experiment. The study sought to assess individuals' preferences in response to various death toll scenarios – for example, when an autonomous vehicle should hit a wall to avoid a pedestrian who crossed the road illegally.[79] The findings of the MIT study confirm the absence of universal ethics.[80] Three clusters of ethical values emerged, in the West,[81] the East[82] and the South.[83] Individualistic cultures prefer sparing the many, while collectivist cultures tend to spare older members of the population.[84] And pedestrians who cross illegally have higher survival chances in countries which are "poorer and suffer from weaker institutions, presumably because of their experience of lower rule compliance and weaker punishment of rule deviation."[85]

The third set of problems is ethics shopping. In a globalized world, companies can choose to locate their AI research operations in countries with weak ethical standards. In turn, companies can export weakly ethical AI systems to other jurisdictions, a practice known as ethics dumping.[86] As an importer of AI systems, the European Union was invited to rely on certification mechanisms to ensure that imported products have not been developed in countries with low ethical standards.[87]

D Knee-jerk regulation

Knee-jerk regulation arises from an unwarranted application of the precautionary principle in response to realized risks and popular outcry.[88] The 2011 Fukushima nuclear disaster is a case in point. It combines a known "dread risk" (radioactivity), an intervening event (the disaster itself) and a reaction of stigmatization (essentially, by the public opinion).[89] In several Western countries, nuclear technology has been blamed and not Japan's exposition to seismic hazard.[90] As a result, some countries relatively unexposed to seismic and weather events have introduced nuclear exit policies, and turned to fossil fuel energies as an alternative.[91]

The potential for knee-jerk regulation of AI systems is easy to foresee. Consider the case of a deficient AI airliner autopilot and assume that society displays a lower tolerance threshold for accidents caused by machines. In this context, it can be anticipated that society will respond to any crash with a prohibition of fully or partly AI-operated planes and roll back to require a significant degree of human operation. This, in spite of existing evidence that human-operated flights may be significantly less secure than AI-assisted ones and that the source of the problem lies in the complex interaction between automated machines and humans.[92] Instead of prohibiting AI-assisted planes, regulation should seek to improve machine-human cooperation in ways that enhance safety.

The costs associated with knee-jerk regulation also increase incentives on lawmakers to regulate anticipatively rare events with extreme impact. The problem, however, is that some rare events which have an extreme impact can only be explained and predicted after their first occurrence – Nassim Taleb speaks about "black swan" events.[93] Focusing on black swans to avoid them or, at least, be prepared, is a waste of time and resources.[94] Rather, "learning to learn" is more important.[95] After the Asian tsunami in 2004, the world was awakened to the dangers of undersea earthquakes. But it appears that not everyone drew the correct implication of undersea earthquakes and tsunamis for nuclear power plants until 2011. Perhaps is this due to the fact that, as Taleb notes, we focus too much on specificities rather than generalities.[96]

III Law V policy for AI

The normative question of whether technological evolution can be addressed by the justice system under existing laws, or whether it requires developing public policy, and in turn new laws, has long been discussed in scholarly literature. In the early 20th century, Justice Holmes argued that the judicial process under the common law was apt to solve "social questions", and in particular, socio-scientific disputes, because what is really before the judge "is a conflict between two social desires, each of which seeks to extend its dominion over the case, and which cannot both have their way".[97] In contrast, and more recently, Spagnoletti has opposed that the legal system "is inadequately prepared to cope with socio scientific disputes",[98] in particular because adjudication exhibits interests through conflicts, and are thus ill suited to serve the public interest.[99] This issue can be conceptualized as whether one should have a dispute resolving or a policy implementing approach to the law and regulation of AI.[100]

A Against policy implementing approaches for AI?

There are three arguments against policy implementing approaches of AI law and regulation. The first is that regulation stifles AI innovation. For example, data minimization requirements embodied in privacy regulation undermine the performance of AI systems.[101] It is common knowledge that AI systems rely on large datasets.[102]

Such concerns have led Ryan Calo to support a specific immunity regime for AI and robotics manufacturers, close to the immunities enjoyed by firearms producers and website operators.[103] This means that AI systems should be safe, as designers remain liable under classic product safety laws but are immune from lawsuits for improper uses of their products. Such a selective immunity constitutes a trade-off between safety and incentives.

The second argument against policy is that interest groups capture regulation.[104] In the context of AI, one area with strong rent seeking potential by private interest groups is car insurance. In many countries, the law imposes insurance duties on the driver and/or user. With self-driving cars, the case for driver and/or user compulsory insurance is less compelling. There is less driver control, fewer accidents and lower damages at society level.[105] Of course, trees and snow still fall, causing casualties on the road. However, as autonomy progresses, allocating liability on the driver and/or user seems less justified, and a transfer to driverless car manufacturers is a more plausible option. Moreover, the insolvency concern that underpins the compulsory nature of insurance seems less problematic with car manufacturers.[106] The problem, of course, is that insurance companies have much to lose if compulsory driver and/or user insurance is abandoned. Their relative bargaining power against a handful of manufacturing companies is much lower than in relation to myriad individual drivers and/or users.[107] Last, car manufacturers exposed to hold-up conduct by insurance companies, may have incentives to vertically integrate into insurance services, rendering the insurance industry irrelevant in the long term. This situation incentivizes insurance companies to lobby in favour of an extension of compulsory driver and/or user insurance for self-driving cars.[108]

But public interest groups too can capture regulation. Public choice theory hints that government officials might favor technology that maximizes their own returns. Moses and Chan explain that instead of using the most useful AI technology, governments discharging law enforcement functions might focus on the most lucrative ones like technology that optimizes fining – or those that contribute with its enforcement activities.[109]

The last argument against public policy is that regulation cannot keep pace with technological progress. When adopted, it may already be obsolete.[110] Gemignani however notes that both law and public policy share this problem:

> the law generally reacts to issues only after they have become the center of a real controversy. Courts generally, and some courts exclusively, address a question of law only after an actual dispute involving that question has been brought before them. Legislation is also more often reactive than proactive. Yet in a society that seems to lurch from crisis to crisis, it is unclear whether such a strategy can avert eventual disaster. The danger of this reactive approach to technological advance becomes clear when dealing with robots and computers.[111]

Yet, public policy raises specific regulatory "pacing" questions because lawmakers must decide when to intervene. This is not the case for courts. Gregory Mandell calls this issue a "quandary": whilst a lawmaker would like to discourage research in harmful technologies and incentivize research in beneficial ones, the risks and opportunities created by emerging technologies cannot be "suitably understood until the technology further develops".[112] The regulatory process must therefore keep a degree of "connection", and wait for technology to develop so as to endow the social planner with enough knowledge.[113] However, as the lawmakers acquire the necessary knowledge, the technology is entrenched and it may be too late to act. This is known as the Collingridge paradox.[114]

This risk is discussed by Nick Bostrom as the "treacherous turn". This notion refers to the pivot point which is reached when a recursive self-improving AI becomes sufficiently strong enough to strike humans without warning or provocation.[115] In a matter of minutes, a malignant AI may consider that humans are threats to the achievement of its final values and turn against them avoiding the controls systems set by engineers. Bostrom uses the example of an AI designed to optimize production in a paperclip factory. Following a treacherous turn, the AI would proceed by first "converting the Earth and then increasingly large chunks of the observable universe into paperclips".[116] Elon Musk gave a similar speech when he tried to convince listeners that even a seemingly harmless AI system could have disastrous consequences.[117]

B Against existing dispute resolution for AI?

The drawbacks of developing public policy for AI should not lead to the conclusion that reliance on courts is sufficient. Public policy is a necessity because the alternative – case-by-case dispute resolution – is worse.[118] Prospects of litigation chill research and innovation incentives, too.[119] For example, Ryan Calo has warned of the risk of crippling legal liability regimes in the field of open robotics.[120] The same applies to AI. Uncertain liability rules act as disincentives to investment, and channel the flow of capital towards narrow functionality where producers can better manage risk, leaving general AI robotics underdeveloped. And the uncertain application of existing legal institutions at early phases of technological development does not allow the formulation of safe appropriability propositions required to attract venture capital.[121]

Besides, others insist on the potential of regulation to enable innovation. The Porter hypothesis states that strict environmental, health and safety standards prompt firms to improve their productivity, and finds that "properly designed [regulatory] standards can trigger innovation that may partially or more than fully offset the costs of complying with them".[122] In Porter's view, "tough standards trigger innovation and upgrading", and prompt firms to re-engineer. In addition, strict regulatory standards can promote market competition, by inducing firms to race for first movers' advantages.[123] In the AI field, Smuha mentions adoption of a fast-track migration policy for workers with an AI-related background.[124]

IV A fifth model? Externalities with a moral twist

Section I surveyed existing models of law and regulation for AI. This section describes a novel model. We propose to index the law and regulatory response upon the nature of the externality – positive or negative – created by an AI system, and to distinguish between discrete, systemic and existential externalities. The model brings together all existing models of law and regulation for AI in a consistent framework. Relating to Section III, deviations from existing law towards the creation of AI-specific law and regulation by public policy should be indexed on the type of externality generated by the technology. We introduce some key concepts first (A). We then discuss concrete applications (B).

A Key concepts

Let us start from the proposition that law and regulation of AI purport to address externalities. By externalities, we mean activities that inflict harm or provide benefits to third parties – for example, any party other than the AI system.

The proposition is rooted in mainstream public interest theory. The choice of this framework is not the result of convenience or coincidence but instead follows the underlying, and often implicit, paradigm of the four models of law and regulation AI discussed previously (with the exception, perhaps, of ethics).[125]

Two types of externalities can be distinguished. A negative externality occurs when an AI system imposes costs on third parties. A positive externality appears when an AI system provides benefits on third parties. Positive and negative externalities exist when the AI system (or its governor) fail to internalize or appropriate all or any of those benefits or adverse effects. Economic theory suggests that rational agents overinvest in the supply of activities that produce negative externalities. For example, AI developers may invest in AI systems that reduce the demand for labour and wages, without this being compensated by enough productivity gains that compensate technological unemployment or the delay in the introduction of other productivity enhancing technologies.[126] Conversely, the private sector may underinvest activities in basic and long-term AI research and development which yield positive externalities.[127] For example, manufacturers may not invest in ethical standards and "friendly AI" initiatives, because the benefits of this are largely appropriated by third parties. In both configurations, economic theory explains that a public interest-driven government can attempt to correct externalities through

Models of law and regulation for AI

the imposition of taxes, the allocation of subsidies or the promulgation of explicit legislative and administrative controls.[128]

Classifying an externality as good or bad involves a good deal of subjective judgment. The replacement of workers by AI systems and machines is a case in point. On the one hand, the externality can be seen as positive, since machines can work more efficiently and faster than people what may lead to a general reduction in prices.[129] On the other hand, it will increase the unemployment rate, and this constitutes a negative externality.

Building on the notion of externalities, we introduce hereafter a novel distinction between three types of externalities. The first type consists in *discrete externalities* (negative of positive). These externalities present the following non-cumulative properties. They are personal, random, rare or endurable. Personal externalities affect third parties at the individual agent level. Random externalities affect all and any third party with equal chance. Rare externalities exhibit low frequency of occurrence. Endurable externalities do not drastically impair the "quality of life" of those who are subject to it or do not radically improve it.[130]

A typical example of a negative discrete externality is a AI gardener whose visual recognition module dysfunctions and confuses the neighbor's cat with a parasite, ending up spraying the cat with toxic pesticide. A typical example of a discrete positive externality occurs if the AI gardener eradicates parasites at night.

The second type covers *systemic externalities*. They cover third party harm or benefits with the following non-cumulative properties: local, predictable, frequent or unsustainable. By local, we look at harm or benefit that affect a non-trivial segment of the population. By predictable, we envision harm or benefit that is foreseeable for a benevolent authority. By frequent, we consider a repeated occurrence of harm or benefit. By unsustainable, we refer to a non-transitory reduction or increase in well-being of the population class under consideration (given scarce resources). A durable rise in inequalities (poor get poorer, rich get richer) is a case in point.

An often discussed negative systemic externality consists of the substitution of man by intelligent machines on the factory floor (and the ensuing disappearance of many existing manufacturing jobs, adding pressure on workers' wages in the long term, etc.). Conversely, a less discussed though equally important positive systemic externality consists in the new complementary jobs that will be created by the introduction of intelligent machines and cognitive computing in industrial sectors (and the corollary reduction in manufacturing costs across the economy as well as transfers of productivity gains to consumers through lower prices).

The third group of externalities comprises existential threats and opportunities created by AIs and robotic applications. To denote their existential nature, we call them as "existernalities". Existernalities exhibit several cumulative properties: they are global, improbable, unpredictable and terminal. Global existernalities hit indiscriminately across geographies, demographics and societies. Improbable externalities are those that are usually dismissed by rational wisdom as fictional. Unpredictable externalities are those whose timescale and likelihood of occurrence are improperly assessed. Terminal existernalities have the potential to extinguish humanity as we know it.[131]

We talk of existential properties to denote both biological and philosophical concerns. Existernalities cover "acts which can cause large-scale destruction of lives and property".[132] But they also refer to "acts which can destroy the philosophical and ethical foundations upon which society is built".[133] Gemignani advocates pro-active regulation of existernalities.

Negative existernalities include the risk of human extinction,[134] maligned superintelligences,[135] lethal autonomous weapons, and other dystopian, Terminator-spirited scenarios of machine takeover. Positive existernalities include pure human enhancement,[136] cosmic endowment,[137] virtual immortality, and so on. Often, the boundary between a positive and negative existernality is a subjective issue. For instance, time-travel is seen by some as a threat for humanity, and by others as an improvement. Away from science-fiction, Kranzberg talks of dis-benefits and mentions:

> advances in medical technology and water and sewage treatment have freed millions of people from disease and plague and have lowered infant mortality, these have also brought the possibility of overcrowding the earth and producing, from other causes, human suffering on a vast scale.[138]

Gemignani provides an example of a law that seeks to address existernality: "Should there be a law that no machine which carries out a peculiarly human function, such as determining guilt or innocence, be permitted to take a human form?"[139] Gemignani appears concerned about the existential costs of delegating justice to anthropomorphic machines.

In Table 13.2, we list some examples of discrete and systemic externalities, as well as existernalities.

Admittedly, this classification is not perfect. A wide spectrum exists between systemic and discrete externalities. Take a malfunctioning self-driving vehicle that drives over a bystander by error and causes serious injuries. Ostensibly, the case does not fall into the "discrete" category because although the case is personal, random and rare, the impact on the family of the victim as well as the demonstration of a defect in the safety of technology prompt wider social concerns.

Table 13.2: Typology and examples of externalities

Discrete externality		
Negative	An industrial robot restarts abruptly and kills a worker on the factory floor.	
Positive	Drone spots thief on way to delivery destination, alerts law enforcement which stops the burglar.	
Systemic externality		Public interest
Negative	General reduction in privacy across society due to generalized operation of information-hungry AI systems	
Positive	Improved disaster responses and humanitarian systems thanks to AI monitoring of population w/o consent	
Existernality		
Negative	Permanent state of war following introduction of lethal autonomous weapons (LAWs)	
Positive	Acceleration towards technology frontiers: time-travelling; emulated minds; cosmic exploration	Existential

On the other hand, this illustration cannot be categorized under the "systemic" category since that accident is not frequent, nor local, neither unsustainable despite the fact it caused a decrease in the standard-of-living of the injured civilian.

B Normative implications

The normative implications from the previously discussed conceptual framework follow a logical progression from existing law to the development of public policy.

The resolution of discrete externalities should be left to existing laws. Society defers to the decentralized courts system which will process discrete externalities on a case-by-case basis. Disputes are solved *ex post* through the application of the general rules of property, contract and liability and other specific laws. This is acceptable because discrete externalities cannot affect society by any significant order of magnitude. Moreover, this regulatory approach is efficient because it allows a degree of decisional experimentation, benchmarking and cross-fertilization.

When more severe threshold effects are encountered with systemic externalities, society should contemplate public policy development. The question is whether *ad hoc* law or regulation ought to be adopted to correct the systemic externality. Here are some examples of such questions in relation to negative externalities: must a specific tax be introduced in automation-intensive industries subject to creative destruction?; must black-box[140] requirements be imposed on manufacturers of AI systems confronted with moral dilemmas like the trolley problem?; must specific privacy regulation be adopted on the second-hand AI systems market to protect data subjects, including previous governors? Likewise, examples abound for positive systemic externalities: given the public goods nature of infrastructure and collective action problems amongst competing producers, must subsidies be allocated for the construction of controlled environments for AI systems (for example, specific road infrastructure for driverless cars)?; should developers and manufacturers of generative AI technologies enjoy statutory immunity for damages caused by their inventions?[141]; should intellectual property regimes be relaxed to enable open, transparent and peer-scrutinized research processes in AI systems with the goal of friendly AI?

Regulatory responses to systemic externalities must be subject to *ex ante* and *ex post* impact assessment. By *ex ante* impact assessment, we refer to the prospective cost-benefit evaluation of future regulatory options. By *ex post* impact assessment, we consider retrospective cost-benefit measurement of experimented regulatory options. In both cases, society experiments with various regulatory options in dedicated zones of the real-life environment, and proceeds to evaluate the results of such tests. In Japan, for instance, the creation of so-called Tokku zones system has entitled robot manufacturers to conduct practical tests on public roads and environments.[142] This mixed *ex ante* and *ex post* approach limits risks of Collingridge type quandaries and reduces risks of disabling regulation.

Existernalities create concerns of such levels that they can be *ex ante* subject to law and regulation, without prior AI and robotic experimentation, implementation or realization. Given their global nature, the regulation of existernalities should tentatively be decided by international organizations. However, international organizations are often paralyzed by gridlock on existential issues (like peacekeeping or climate change) due to their wide membership. In the AI field, endless discussions have taken place at the United Nations over a proposed ban on the use of lethal autonomous weapons (LAWs). Regional institutions (like the EU) might be better forums for the initial regulation of existernalities. And yet, this is not a given. For example, the EU HLEG on AI failed to adopt red lines of research on AI consciousness, LAWs or citizen scoring systems.

In addition, the fact that externalities are "black swans" implies a degree of fatality in terms of our failure to anticipate them.[143] Conversely, knee-jerk regulatory responses cannot be excluded in democratic systems. Overall, a degree of expert and technocratic input in decision-making is therefore appropriate. In this context, the involvement of standard-setting organizations (like the IEEE, SAE, the ISO and many others) may play a useful contributive role to the definition of early positions on externalities. Last, objections to the costs of prohibitive *ex ante* intervention are not material, because the costs of type II errors (false negatives) in relation to externalities are higher than the costs of type I errors (false positives). A type II error occurs when we fail to remedy a serious existential risk in probability and/or intensity terms. A type I error occurs when we wrongly remedy a moot existential risk in probability and/or intensity terms. Immediately one understands that the cost of a type II error is existential, whilst this is not necessarily the case for a type I error. The cost of the latter is thus more acceptable than the cost of any type II error which will always be existential. But there is more. A type II error in relation to externalities is not reversible because humanity has disappeared. This excuses any and every type I error in relation to externalities.

Conclusion

This chapter has attempted to describe models of law and regulation for AI. Its main ambition is primarily descriptive: help readers make sense of developing legal frameworks in this ever-evolving, and quite anarchic, area of the law.

In addition, this paper has developed a normative case for a new model of law and regulation for AI. The model proposes to index the intensity of regulatory response upon the nature of the externality created by an AI application. When AI-generated externalities are discrete, societies should defer to *ex post* litigation before courts. When AI-generated externalities are systemic, societies' planners should envision *ex ante* regulation but carefully test and experiment. This meshes the benefits of anticipation and empiricism and avoids the Collingridge dilemma as well as disabling regulation problems. Last, when AI-generated externalities are existential, societies should consider *ex ante* intervention, and bring into it a degree of expert deliberation.

Our proposed model is not only about distinguishing levels of regulatory response based on a probabilistic reasoning and classification of externalities regarding their frequency, severity, and globality. It also overcomes the pitfall of the "tyranny of numbers" and the "aura of precision" by making ethical concerns central.[144]

Notes

1 AI, as a field, concerns itself with the construction of systems which are capable of rational behaviour in a given situation. See Stuart J. Russel and Peter Norvig, *Artificial Intelligence: A Modern Approach* (3rd ed., Pearson, 2010), 1–2 and 4–5. We acknowledge the fact that one must distinguish between artificial intelligence as a scientific discipline (AI) and artificial intelligence systems (AIS). While the former "includes several approaches and techniques, such as machine learning (of which deep learning and reinforcement learning are specific examples), machine reasoning (which includes planning, scheduling, knowledge representation and reasoning, search, and optimization), and robotics (which includes control, perception, sensors and actuators, as well as the integration of all other techniques into cyber-physical systems)", the latter "are software (and possibly also hardware) systems designed by humans that, given a complex goal, act in the physical or digital dimension by perceiving their environment through data acquisition, interpreting the collected structured or unstructured data, reasoning on the knowledge, or processing the information, derived from this data and deciding the best action(s) to take to achieve the given goal". See The European Commission's High-Level Expert Group on Artificial Intelligence, "A Definition of AI: Main Capabilities and Disciplines", definition

developed for the purpose of the AI HLEG's deliverables, April 8, 2019, available at <https://ec.europa.eu/newsroom/dae/document.cfm?doc_id=56341> accessed April 6, 2020, p. 8. This definition brings together artificial intelligence and (cognitive) robotics. Cognitive robotics refers to the "endowing of robots with more cognitive capabilities". See Stan Franklin, "History, Motivations and Core Themes", in Keith Frankish and William M. Ramsey (ed.), *The Cambridge Handbook of Artificial Intelligence* (Cambridge University Press, 2014), 25. Furthermore, we discuss both AIs and robots under the same intellectual aegis, even though we acknowledge the differences between those two technological fields. We do this not only because we conjecture a degree of convergence between both technologies, but primarily because intelligent machines in soft or hard envelopes have the ability to "act upon the world". See Ryan Calo, "Robotics and the Lessons of Cyberlaw" (2015) 103(3) *California Law Review*, 513–564.

2 This can be understood with a little green men metaphor. An alien from a distant planet sets foot on Earth. Most of Earth's clothing factories produce ready-to-wear suits for humans in calibrated sizes. Are human suits refitted; must they be stretched or adjusted? Or shall humans leave the alien naked?

3 Initially published in 1978 under the name *Theorie der juristischen Argumentation: Die Theorie des rationale Diskurses al Theorie der Juristischen Begründung* and translated in English by Ruth Adler and Neil MacCormick in 1989. See Robert Alexy, *A Theory of Legal Argumentation: The Theory of Rational Discourses as Theory of Legal Justification* (Clarendon Press, 1989).

4 Matthias Klatt, "Robert Alexy's Philosophy of Law as a System", in Matthias Klatt (ed.), *Institutionalized Reason: The Jurisprudence of Robert Alexy* (Oxford University Press, 2012), 5.

5 Robert Alexy, *Theorie der juristischen Agumentation: Die Theorie des rationale Diskurses als Theorie der juristischen Bedründung* (2nd ed, Suhrkamp, 1991), 307–309. Alexy's theory however claims that some cases cannot be handled only on the basis of those norms due to the fact the lawmakers are sometimes unclear. Matthias Klatt, "Robert Alexy's Philosophy of Law as a System", in Matthias Klatt (ed.), *Institutionalized Reason: The Jurisprudence of Robert Alexy* (Oxford University Press, 2012) 6.

6 Paul Nemitz, "Constitutional Democracy and Technology in the Age of Artificial Intelligence" (2018) 376(2133) *Philosophical Transaction of the Royal Society A: Mathematical, Physical and Engineering Sciences*; Filoppo A. Raso et al, "Artificial Intelligence & Human Rights: Opportunities & Risks" (September 25, 2018) Berkman Klein Center for Internet & Society at Harvard University; Karl M. Manheim and Lyric Kaplan, "Artificial Intelligence: Risks to Privacy and Democracy" (2019) 21 *Yale Journal of Law and Technology*, 106; Jessica Fjeld et al., "Principled Artificial Intelligence: Mapping Consensus in Ethical and Rights-based Approaches to Principles for AI" (January 15, 2020) Berkman Klein Center for Internet & Society at Harvard University; Mireille Hildebrandt, "The Artificial Intelligence of European Union Law" (2020) 21(1) *German Law Journal*, 74–79.

7 By AI-created invention, we mean an invention fully brought to existence by the AI, without human assistance.

8 Christophe Leroux and al., "Suggestion for a Green Paper on Legal Issues in Robotics" (*euRobotics*, December 31, 2012) <www.unipv-lawtech.eu/files/euRobotics-legal-issues-in-robotics-DRAFT_6j6ryjyp.pdf>: "Above mentioned legal IP systems are based on the fact that computers are inert tools, so that current intellectual property regimes usually only apply to humans or legal persons creations and not to creations coming from computers or inert tools. However, artificial technologies have advanced rapidly to the point that intelligent agents do not assist humans in the creation of works, but generate them autonomously. Thus, intelligent agents are capable of creativity". See also Ryan Abbott, "Hal the Inventor: Big Data and Its Use by Artificial Intelligence", in Cassidy R. Sugimoto et al (ed.), *Big Data Is Not a Monolith* (MIT Press, 2016); David Levy, *Robots Unlimited: Life in a Virtual Age* (A K Peters, Ltd. 2006), 396–397 (hereafter Levy, *Robots Unlimited*) and Michael Gemignani, "Laying Down the Law to Robots" (1984) 21(5) *San Diego Law Review*, 1054.

9 Elizabeth F. Judge and Daniel J. Gervais, "Of Silos and Constellations: Comparing Notions of Originality in Copyright Law" (2009) 27(2) *Cardozo Arts & Entertainment Law Journal*, 375–408.

10 A proxy is that a selfie taken by a monkey has been deemed unsusceptible of copyright protection because of lack of authorship. See, on this case, Joshua Jowitt, "Monkey See, Monkey Sue: Gewirth's Principle of Generic Consistency and Rights for Non-Human Agents" (2016) 19 *Trinity College Law Review*, 71–96.

11 For use of this term, see Nick Bostrom, *Superintelligence, Paths, Dangers, Strategies* (Oxford University Press, 2014) (Hereafter Bostrom, *Superintelligence*).

12 Samir Chopra and Laurence F. White, *A Legal Theory for Autonomous Artificial Agents* (University of Michigan Press, 2011), 155 (hereafter Chopra and White, *Legal theory for autonomous artificial agents*)

(conferring legal personhood necessitates a "decision to grant an entity a bundle of rights and concomitant obligations").

13 Christopher D. Stone, *Should Trees Have Standing? Law, Morality, and the Environment*, (3rd ed., Oxford University Press, 2010).

14 See Chopra and White, *Legal theory for autonomous artificial agents*, 186 ("the decision to accord or refuse legal personality (both dependent and, in function of increasing competence, independent) would ultimately be a result-oriented one for courts and legislatures alike, and cannot rest solely on conceptual claims").

15 Levy, *Robots Unlimited*, 397. To use again our little green men metaphor (see *supra* n 2), the emergent approach is comparable to a tailor-made suit factory. The exercise consists in designing cloth that suits the alien.

16 Ronald C. Arkin, *Behavior-based robotics* (MIT Press, 1998); Ryan Calo, "Robots in American Law" (February 24, 2016), University of Washington School of Law Research Paper No. 2016–04.

17 Ryan Calo, "Open robotics" (2011) 70(3) *Maryland Law Review*, 101–142 (hereafter Calo, "Open robotics").

18 Ethical arguments nurture demand for an all-out ban on research in relation to lethal automated weapons ("LAWs"). "Autonomous Weapons: An Open Letter from AI & Robotics Researchers" (July 28, 2015) <http://futureoflife.org/open-letter-autonomous-weapons/>: "Starting a military AI arms race is a bad idea, and should be prevented by a ban on offensive autonomous weapons beyond meaningful human control". See also The European Commission's High Level Expert Group on Artificial Intelligence, "Ethics Guidelines for Trustworthy AI" (April 8, 2019) <https://ec.europa.eu/newsroom/dae/document.cfm?doc_id=58477> (hereafter: "AI HLEG Guidelines"). For more on the ethical approach, see *Infra* No I.C.

19 In the computer science profession, there are concerns that "overly rigid regulations might stifle innovation", See *The Economist*, "You, Robot?" (*The Economist*, September 1, 2012). On this particular point, see *Infra* No III.A.

20 See Alex Glassbrook, *The Law of Driverless Cars: An Introduction* (Law Brief Publishing, 2017).

21 Michelle Bolos, "A Highway in the Sky: A Look at Land Use Issues That Will Arise with the Integration of Drone Technology" (2015) 2 *University of Illinois Journal of Law, Technology & Policy*, 411–436; Tziporah Kasachkoff and John Kleinig, "Drones, Distance, and Death", in George J. Andreopoulos, Rosemary L. Barberet and Mahesh K. Nalla (ed.), *The Rule of Law in an Era of Change* (Springer, 2018), 15–45.

22 Ryan Calo, A., Michael Froomkin, and Ian Kerr, *Robot Law* (Edward Elgar Publishing, 2016).

23 Artificial Intelligence and Life in 2030, One Hundred Year Study on Artificial Intelligence, Report of the 2015 Study Panel, September 2016.

24 Ibid.

25 Ibid.

26 For instance, the Stanford Report stresses that AI is very relevant in relation to "regulation" without though discarding its relevance for other sources of law like common law, federal law, local statutes or ordinances.

27 As explained previously, this refers to the *ex ante* coding of legal rules in AIs and robots at the design stage.

28 Olivier Boissier et al. "A Roadmap Towards Ethical Autonomous Agents" (*EthicAa*, 2015) <https://ethicaa.greyc.fr/media/files/ethicaa.delivrable.3.pdf>.

29 Lawrence B. Solum, "Legal Personhood for Artificial Intelligences" (1992) 70(4) *North Carolina Law Review*, 1231–1288.

30 Nina I. Brown, "Artificial Authors: A Case for Copyright In Computer-Generated Works" (2019) 20(1) *Columbia Science and Technology Law Review*.

31 Here, we fall in a complex philosophical discussion as to whether our criteria of choice is Wittgenstein "family resemblance" or Aristoteles theory of definition (known as predicable doctrine), which focuses on genus and specific essence. See Michael R. Ayers "Locke versus Aristotle on Natural Kinds" (1981) 78(5) *The Journal of Philosophy*, 247–272.

32 This issue has been thoroughly discussed by early philosophers since Aristoteles up until enlightenment. Those debates consist in a reflection of whether humans and animals are different by a matter of degree (as suggested by Darwin's theory of evolution, or are distinct in kind). Many properties have been underlined to denote the specificity of the human king: thought, language, instinct, self-consciousness, emotions, perfectibility, religion, vertical position, etc. For a good review (and rebuttal),

see Philalethes. "The Distinction between Man and Animals" (1864) 2(6) *The Anthropological Review*, 153–163.
33 See for an example reference to computer-human interaction: Clifford Nass and Scott Brave, *Wired for Speech: How Voice Activates and Advances the Human-Computer Relationship* (MIT Press, 2005), 3–4. See also Byron Reeves and Clifford I. Nass, *The Media Equation: How People Treat Computers, Television, and New Media Like Real People and Places* (Cambridge University Press, 1996); Mark Coeckelbergh, "Humans, Animals, and Robots: A Phenomenological Approach to Human-Robot Relations" (2011) 3(2) *International Journal of Social Robotics*, 197–204.
34 David Levy, "The Ethical Treatment of Artificially Conscious Robots" (2009) 1(3) *International Journal of Social Robotics*, 209–216.
35 There are three different branches of ethics: metaethics, applied ethics and normative ethics. See James Fieser, "Ethics", Internet Encyclopedia of Philosophy, <www.iep.utm.edu/ethics/>.
36 Jerome De Cooman, "Ethique et Intelligence Artificielle: l'exemple européen" (2020) 1 *Revue de la Faculté de Droit de l'Université de Liège*, 79–123.
37 Aristotle, *Nicomachean Ethics*, translated by W.D. Ross (Kitchener, 1999).
38 Markus Frischhut, *The Ethical Spirit of EU Law* (Springer 2019), 21(hereafter, Frischhut, *Ethical Spirit of EU Law*).
39 Independently of our desires: "I ought never to act except in such a way that I could also will that my maxim should become a universal law". Immanuel Kant, *Groundwork of the Metaphysics of Morals* (1785); in Karl Ameriks and Desmond M. Clarke (eds.), *Cambridge Texts in the History of Philosophy*, translated by Mary Gregor (Cambridge University Press, 1997), 15 (hereafter Kant, *Groundwork of the Metaphysics*). Kant was searching for rules we can universalise.
40 Ibid., 38–41
41 AI HLEG Guidelines, 4.
42 Helga Varden, "Kant and Lying to the Murderer at the Door . . . One More Time: Kant's Legal Philosophy and Lies to Murderers and Nazis" (2010) 41(4) *Journal of Social Philosophy*.
43 Frischhut, *Ethical Spirit of EU Law*, 23.
44 James Fieser "Consequentialist Theories", Internet Encyclopedia of Philosophy, <www.iep.utm.edu/ethics/#SH2c>.
45 Jeremy Bentham, *Introduction to the Principles of Morals and Legislation* (1789), reproduced in 2000 by Kitchener.
46 AI HLEG Guidelines, 4.
47 Luciano Floridi and Josh Cowls, "A Unified Framework of Five Principles for AI in Society" (2019) 1(1) *Harvard Data Science Review*, 5; Brent Mittelstadt, "Principles Alone Cannot Guarantee Ethical AI" (2019) 1 *Nature Machine Intelligence*, 501.
48 Ibid.
49 Mittelstadt, "Principles Alone Cannot Guarantee Ethical AI", 501.
50 Ibid., 502.
51 Except maybe for particular activities, like privacy or data protection, which are protected in Europe through the General Data Protection Regulation.
52 Andrew McNamara, Justin Smith and Emerson Murphy-Hill, "Does ACM's Code of Ethics Change Ethical Decision Making in Software Development?" (October 2018) Proceedings of the 2018 26th ACM Joint Meeting on European Software Engineering Conference and Symposium on the Foundations of Software Engineering, 729–733; Mittelstadt, "Principles Alone Cannot Guarantee Ethical AI", 504; Thilo Hagendorff, "The Ethics of AI Ethics – An Evaluation of Guidelines" (February 28, 2019) arXiv (Cornell University) <https://arxiv.org/abs/1903.03425>.
53 European Commission, "White Paper on Artificial Intelligence: A European Approach to Excellence and Trust" (February 19, 2020), COM(2020) 65 final, p. 10.
54 David Wright and John Copas, "Prediction Scores for Risk Assessment", in Robert Baldwin (ed.), *Law and Uncertainty: Risks and Legal Processes* (Kluwer International Law, 1997), 21–38.
55 Daten Ethik Kommission, "Opinion of the Data Ethics Commission (Executive Summary)" (October 2019) <www.bmjv.de/SharedDocs/Downloads/DE/Themen/Fokusthemen/Gutachten_DEK_EN.pdf?__blob=publicationFile&v=2> p. 19 fig. 2.
56 Roger Brownsword, *Rights, Regulation, and the Technological Revolution* (Oxford University Press, 2008), 118–119.
57 Joseph Norman and al., "Climate Models and Precautionary Measures" (forthcoming), Issues in Science and Technology and Laurence Boisson de Chazournes, "New Technologies, the Precautionary

Principle, and Public Participation", in Thérèse Murphy (ed.), *New Technologies and Human Rights* (Oxford University Press, 2009), 168–169.
58 Bridget M. Hutter, "The Attractions of Risk-Based Regulation: Accounting for the Emergence of Risk Ideas in Regulation" (March 2005), ESRC Centre for Analysis of Risk and Regulation, Discussed Paper No 33.
59 Lukasz Gruszczynski, *Regulating Health and Environmental Risks under WTO Law: A Critical Analysis of the SPS Agreement* (Oxford University Press, 2010), 20.
60 Sam N. Lehman-Wilzig, "Frankenstein Unbound: Towards a Legal Definition of Artificial Intelligence" (1981) 13(6) *Futures*, 442–457.
61 Bostrom, *Superintelligence*, 144–145.
62 "Whereas from Mary Shelley's Frankenstein's Monster to the classical myth of Pygmalion, through the story of Prague's Golem to the robot of Karel Čapek, who coined the word, people have fantasised about the possibility of building intelligent machines, more often than not androids with human features". Report from of January 27, 2017 with recommendations to the Commission on Civil Law rules on robotics, (2015/2103(INL)) <www.europarl.europa.eu/doceo/document/A-8-2017-0005_EN.html>.
63 We acknowledge the fact that sometimes, science-fiction stories are anticipative. For instance, Jules Vernes wrote a story on a travel to the moon. It was science-fiction at the time, it is no more nowadays.
64 With the notable exception of Isaac Asimov in Sally; Isaac Asimov, "Sally" (1953), Fantastic.
65 Take again the metaphor of the Alien (see *supra* n 2). His physiological condition may be different from ours. He may not need a suit at all. Instead, his physiological needs could be entirely different: for instance, he may be over sensitive to noise, and need soundproof helmets to cover its ears.
66 Jack M. Balkin, "The Path of Robotics Law" (2015) 6(1) *California Law Review Circuit*, 45–60. ("The new technology disrupts the existing scene of regulation, leading various actors to scramble over how the technology will and should be used. As people scramble and contend with each other over the technology, they innovate – not only technologically, but also socially, economically, and legally – leading to new problems for law. Instead of saying that law is responding to essential features of new technology, it might be better to say that social struggles over the use of new technology are being inserted into existing features of law, disrupting expectations about how to categorize situations").
67 Bostrom refers to this as the singleton scenario. See Bostrom, *Superintelligence*.
68 Frank H. Easterbrook, "Cyberspace and the Law of the Horse" (1996) *The University of Chicago Legal Forum*, 207–216.
69 McCarthy spoke about AI as the science of "programming computers to solve problems which require a high degree of intelligence in humans". John McCarthy, "Programs with Common Sense" (Stanford, 1959) <http://jmc.stanford.edu/articles/mcc59/mcc59.pdf>. He also made clear that "reaching human-level AI requires programs that deal with the common-sense informatic situation". John McCarthy, "Concepts of Logical AI" (Stanford, April 17, 2000) <http://www-formal.stanford.edu/jmc/concepts-ai.pdf>.
70 Marvin Minsky, *Semantic Information Processing* (MIT Press, 1968).
71 Ted Striphas, "Algorithmic Culture" (2015) 18(4–5) *European Journal of Culture Studies*, 395–412; Ian Bogost, "The Cathedral of Computation" (*The Atlantic*, January 15, 2015) <www.theatlantic.com/technology/archive/2015/01/the-cathedral-of-computation/384300/>.
72 Massoud Yasdani, *Artificial intelligence: Principles and applications* (Chapman and Hall, 1986), 326. See also Thomas J. Barth and Eddy Arnold, "Artificial Intelligence and Administrative Discretion" (1999) 29(4) *American Review of Public Administration*, 348: "it is one thing to independently think through and analyze a question posed by one's superior; however, it is quite another to raise additional unasked questions or take the initiative and provide unsolicited advice where warranted. Even the most sophisticated AI system ultimately may be flawed because it lacks curiosity – that is, the urge to investigate issues or ask questions on its own".
73 Thomas Metzinger, "Dialogue Seminar on Artificial Intelligence: Ethical Concerns" (March 19, 2019) <www.europarl.europa.eu/streaming/?event=20190319-1500-SPECIAL-SEMINAR1&start=2019-03-19T15:44:53Z&end=2019-03-19T15:56:00Z&language=en>; Nathalie Smuha, "The EU Approach to Ethics Guidelines for Trustworthy Artificial Intelligence" (2019) 4 *Computer Law Review International*, 101; Ben Wagner, "Ethics as an Escape from Regulation: From Ethics-Washing to Ethics-Shopping?" in Mireille Hildebrandt and Serge Gutwirth (ed.), *Being Profiling. Cogitas Ergo Sum*

(Amsterdam University Press, 2018); Paul Nemitz, "Constitutional Democracy and Technology in the Age of Artificial Intelligence" (2018) *The Royal Society Publishing*, https://royalsocietypublishing.org/doi/full/10.1098/rsta.2018.0089; Luciano Floridi, "Translating Principles into Practices of Digital Ethics: Five Risks of Being Unethical" (2019) 32 *Philosophy & Technology*, 188; Hagendorff, "The Ethics of AI Ethics"; Mittelstadt, "Principles Alone Cannot Guarantee Ethical AI", 501; Ryan Calo, "Artificial Intelligence Policy: A Primer and a Roadmap" (2017) 51 *UC Davis Law Review*, 399–436.

74 Ben Wagner, "Ethics as an Escape from Regulation", 84 ("Ethical frameworks that provide a way to go beyond existing legal frameworks can also provide an opportunity to ignore them").

75 Between the publication of the Draft (December 18, 2018) and the Report (April 8, 2019) on the European Ethics Guidelines, the document was open to a public consultation, in order to gather as many feedbacks as possible. All comments made during this open consultation are available at https://ec.europa.eu/futurium/en/system/files/ged/consultation_feedback_on_draft_ai_ethics_guidelines_4.pdf.

76 For an illustration, see Floris de Witte, "Sex, Drugs & EU Law: The Recognition of Moral and Ethical Diversity in EU Law" (2013) 50(6) *Common Market Law Review*, 1545–1578.

77 "Suppose you are the driver of a trolley. The trolley rounds a bend, and there come into view ahead five track workmen, who have been repairing the track. The track goes through a bit of a valley at that point, and the sides are steep, so you must stop the trolley if you are to avoid running the five men down. You step on the brakes, but alas they don't work. Now you suddenly see a spur of track leading off to the right. You can turn the trolley onto it, and thus save the five men on the straight track ahead. Unfortunately, . . . there is one track workman on that spur of track. He can no more get off the track in time than the five can, so you will kill him if you turn the trolley onto him. Is it morally permissible for you to turn the trolley?"; Judith Jarvis Thomson, "The Trolley Problem" (1985) 94(6) *The Yale Law Journal*, 1395–1415. Johansson and Nilsson argue that the trolley problem could in fact be solved by introducing self-driving cars. ("A key enabler to disarm the trolley problem is the ability of the self-driving vehicle to estimate its own operational capability for handling surprising situations, and adjust its own tactical behavior accordingly.") Rolf Johansson and Jonas Nilsson, "Disarming the Trolley Problem – Why Self-driving Cars Do Not Need to Choose Whom to Kill" (September 2016) Workshop CARS 2016 – Critical Automotive Applications: Robustness & Safety, Göteborg, Sweden.

78 The outcome of such accident is more driven by instinct and human reflex than by a personal ethical debate. In fact, "human drivers who survive a crash may not have realized that they were in a dilemma situation". See Edmon Awad, Sohan Dsouza, Richard Kim, Jonathan Schulz, Joseph Enrich, Azim Shariff, Jean-François Bonnefon and Lyad Rahwan, "The Moral Machine Experiment" (2018) 563 *Nature*, 59.

79 This experiment is available on <http://moralmachine.mit.edu/>.

80 "This platform gathered 40 million decisions in ten languages from millions of people in 233 countries and territories"; Awad et al., "The Moral Machine Experiment", 59.

81 The Western cluster contains "North America as well as many European countries of Protestant, Catholic, and Orthodox Christian cultural groups. The internal structure within this cluster also exhibits notable face validity, with a sub-cluster containing Scandinavian countries, and a sub-cluster containing Commonwealth countries"; "The Moral Machine Experiment" 61.

82 The Eastern cluster contains "many far eastern countries such as Japan and Taiwan that belong to the Confucianist cultural group, and Islamic countries such as Indonesia, Pakistan and Saudi Arabia"; Awad et al., "The Moral Machine Experiment", 61.

83 The Southern cluster contains "consists of the Latin American countries of Central and South America, in addition to some countries that are characterized in part by French influence (for example, metropolitan France, French overseas territories, and territories that were at some point under French leadership). Latin American countries are cleanly separated in their own sub-cluster within the Southern cluster"; Awad et al., "The Moral Machine Experiment", 61.

84 Awad et al., "The Moral Machine Experiment", 62.

85 Ibid.

86 See Floridi, "Translating Principles into Practices of Digital Ethics", 189; Charlotte Walker-Osborn and Callum Hayes, "Ethics and AI a Moral Conundrum" (*The British Computer Society*, June 11, 2018) <www.bcs.org/content-hub/ethics-and-ai-a-moral-conundrum/>; Metzinger, "Dialogue Seminar on Artificial Intelligence".

87 This idea is especially proposed by the European Commission's independent experts on AI. See AI HLEG Guidelines, 23 and Floridi, "Translating Principles into Practices of Digital Ethics", 190.

88 Also known as the "risk regulation reflex". Interestingly, knee-jerk responses work also in the other direction. President Obama mocked the Republicans calls for deregulation as a knee-jerk obsession: "Feel a cold coming on? Take two tax cuts, roll back some regulations and call us in the morning". See "Remarks by the President at the Democratic National Convention" (September 7, 2012) <www.whitehouse.gov/the-press-office/2012/09/07/remarks-president-democratic-national-convention>.
89 Emily Hammond, "Nuclear Power, Risk, and Retroactivity" (2015) 48(4) *Vanderbilt Journal of Transnational Law*, 1059–1082.
90 William J. Kinsella, "Being 'Post-Fukushima': Divergent Understandings of Sociotechnical Risk" (2015) Fukushima Global Communication Programme Working Paper Series.
91 Speaking of the impact of the Three Mile Island accident in the US, Kranzberg noted: "Yet the historical fact is that no one has been killed by commercial nuclear power accidents in this country. Contrast this with the 50,000 Americans killed each year by automobiles. But although antinuclear protestors picket nuclear power plants under construction, we never see any demonstrators bearing signs saying 'Ban the Buick'!"; Kranzberg, "Kranzberg's Laws", 552.
92 David A. Mindell, *Our Robots, Ourselves: Robotics and the Myths of Autonomy* (Viking Adult, 2015).
93 "What we call here a Black Swan (and capitalize it) is an event with the following three attributes. First, it is an outlier, as it lies outside the realm of regular expectations, because nothing in the past can convincingly point to its possibility. Second, it carries an extreme impact. Third, in spite of its outlier status, human nature makes us concoct explanations for its occurrence after the fact, making it explainable and predictable"; Nassim N. Taleb, *The Black Swan. The Impact of the Highly Improbable* (Random House, 2007), xvii–xviii (hereafter Taleb, *Black Swan*).
94 Ibid., xx–xxi.
95 Ibid., xxi.
96 Ibid.
97 Oliver Wendell Holmes, "Law in Science and Science in Law" (1899) 12(7) *Harvard Law Review*, reprinted in Oliver Wendell Holmes, *The Collected Legal Papers* (Harcourt, 1921), 210–43. See also, Elliott E. Donald, "Holmes and Evolution: Legal Process as Artificial Intelligence" (1984) 13(1) *The Journal of Legal Studies*, 113–146 ("The image of the common law that Holmes presents in 'Law in Science and Science in Law' is not of judges legislating rules. The architecture of the common law is not the product of conscious design choices by individual judges. It is rather the product of the logic of selection by a system, of an 'invisible hand' like that of the market, or of natural selection in biology").
98 Robert J. Spagnoletti, "Using Artificial Intelligence to Aid in the Resolution of Socioscientific Disputes: A Theory for the Next Generation" (1987) 2(1) *Journal of Law and Technology*, 101. Spagnoletti defines the legal system generally as a "method by which individual parties can present their interests and society can decide its own public policy".
99 Ibid. Spagnoletti adds two other reasons. First, "[t]he present legal system, consisting primarily of nonscientific personnel, is unskilled in the relevant areas of expertise needed to understand the technology". Second, socio scientific disputes involve "quality-of-life decisions" and those are "difficult because they typically involve personal value judgments".
100 Rafael La Porta, Florencio Lopez-de-Silanes and Andrei Shleifer, "The Economic Consequences of Legal Origins" 46(2) *Journal of Economic Literature*, 285–332.
101 Ira S. Rubinstein, "Big Data: The End of Privacy or a New Beginning?" (2013) 3(2) *International Data Privacy Law*, 74–87; Omer Tene and Jules Polonetsky, "Privacy in the Age of Big Data: A Time for Big Decisions" (February 2012), 64 *Stanford Law Review Online*, 63–69.
102 Randy Bean, "How Big Data Is Empowering AI and Machine Learning at Scale" (*MIT Sloan Management Review*, May 8, 2017) <https://sloanreview.mit.edu/article/how-big-data-is-empowering-ai-and-machine-learning-at-scale/>. It is interesting to note that these concepts – AI and Big Data – are more than intertwined. Because big date gets bigger every day, AI is use to capture and structure big data. See Daniel E. O'Leary, "Artificial Intelligence and Big Data" (2013) 28(2) *IEEE Intelligent Systems*, 96–99. Some authorities consider the possibility to regulate large sets of data. For instance, Article 5(c) of the General Data Protection Regulation stipulates that "personal data shall be adequate, relevant and limited to what is necessary in relation to the purposes for which they are processed ('data minimisation')". Regulation (EU) 2016/679 of the European Parliament and of the Council of April 27, 2016 on the protection of natural persons with regard to the processing of personal data and on the free movement of such data, and repealing Directive 95/46/EC (General Data Protection Regulation), Official Journal of the European Union, L 119/1. See also Robert D. Atkinson, "IP Protection in the Data Economy: Getting the Balance Right on 13 Critical Issues" (January 2019),

Information Technology & Innovation Foundation (ITIF) <http://www2.itif.org/2019-ip-protection-data-economy.pdf> "regulators began preventing companies from acquiring large amounts of data, this would delay or prevent many important technological advancements. For example, Tesla's self-driving technology, IBM Watson's ability to diagnose medical illness, and the Weather Company's weather predictions would all be impossible without massive amounts of data".

103 Calo, "Open Robotics" ("Congress should shield manufacturers and distributors of open robotic platforms from suit for what consumers do with their personal robots, just as it immunizes gun manufacturers from suit for what some people do with guns and websites operators for what users upload and post").

104 Anne O. Krueger, "The Political Economy of the Rent-Seeking Society" (1974) 64(3) *The American Economic Review*, 291–303.

105 More so if the law incrementally reduces individuals' freedom to drive. See Dan McCrum, "Insurers Will Destroy Themselves to Nudge US into Robot Utopia" (*Financial Times*, March 4, 2014) <https://ftalphaville.ft.com/2014/03/04/1787962/insurers-will-destroy-themselves-to-nudge-us-into-robot-utopia/>.

106 Michael G. Faure, "Economic Criteria for Compulsory Insurance" (2006) 31(1) *The Geneva Papers on Risk and Insurance Issues and Practice*, 149–168.

107 See "EU Considers New Insurance Laws for Driverless Cars" (*Euractiv*, 2016) <www.euractiv.com/section/digital/news/eu-considers-new-insurance-laws-for-driverless-cars/>.

108 By the same token, car manufacturers may lobby government so as to be insulated from all liability, and deflect it towards software developers.

109 Lyria Bennett Moses and Janet Chan, "Using Big Data for Legal and Law Enforcement Decisions: Testing the New Tools" (2014) 37(2) *University of New South Wales Law Journal*, 659: "Chan's research found that the most successful use of information technology for proactive policing was in support of traditional law enforcement: the use of mobile data systems in police cars to check for outstanding traffic offence warrants. The enthusiastic adoption of this technology is easily explained by its effectiveness, as evidenced by 'an exponential increase in the collection of fines as well as the imprisonment of fine defaulters'".

110 Consider a proposed Federal Aviation Administration (FAA) regulation that insists that unmanned aircraft system (UAS) must be limited "to daylight-only operations, confined areas of operation, and visual-line-of-sight operations". Now compare this with surveys reporting that pilots spend just seven minutes manually operating their planes in a typical flight. See John Markoff, "Planes Without Pilots" (*The New York Times*, April 6, 2015) <www.nytimes.com/2015/04/07/science/planes-without-pilots.html?_r=2>. No wonder why companies like Amazon, Intel and Google have railed against emerging drones delivery regulation, which they consider outdated. See Ben Popper, "What's Really Standing in the Way of Drone Delivery?" (*The Verge*, January 16, 2016) <www.theverge.com/2016/1/16/10777144/delivery-drones-regulations-safety-faa-autonomous-flight>.

111 Gemignani, "Laying Down the Law to Robots", 1046.

112 Gregory N. Mandel, "Regulating Emerging Technologies" (2009) 1(1) *Law, Innovation and Technology*, 75–92.

113 Roger Brownsword and Morag Goodwin, *Law and the Technologies of the Twenty-First Century. Texts and Materials* (Cambridge University Press, 2012).

114 David Collingridge, *The Social Control of Technology* (Francis Pinter Ltd., 1980). Biotechnologies in the large sense are an example. Whilst they promise many wonders in public health, nutrition and environmental protection, the creation of new eco-systems could precipitate the demise of animal or human species, create new diseases, etc.

115 Bostrom, *Superintelligence*, 144–145.

116 Ibid., 150.

117 At Vanity Fair's Conference, Elon Musk said: "Let's say you create a self-improving A.I. to pick strawberries, and it gets better and better at picking strawberries and picks more and more and it is self-improving, so all it really wants to do is pick strawberries. So then it would have all the world be strawberry fields. Strawberry fields forever"; Maureen Dowd, "Elon Musk's Billion-Dollar Crusade to Stop the AI Apocalypse" (*Vanity Fair*, March 26, 2017) <www.vanityfair.com/news/2017/03/elon-musk-billion-dollar-crusade-to-stop-ai-space-x>.

118 Epstein for instance poses the necessity of regulation: "At bottom, the proper inquiry never poses the stark choice of regulation versus no regulation". See Richard A. Epstein, "Can Technological Innovation Survive Government Regulation" (2013) 36(1) *Harvard Journal of Law & Public Policy*, 88.

119 Product liability litigation in relation to deficient medical devices is an often-heard worry.

120 Calo, "Open Robotics".
121 See Calo, "Open Robotics": "legal uncertainty could discourage the flow of capital into robotics or otherwise narrow robot functionality".
122 Michael E. Porter and Claas Van der Linde "Toward a New Conception of the Environment-Competitiveness Relationship" (1995) 9(4) *The Journal of Economic Perspectives*, 97–118.
123 Nicholas A. Ashford and Ralph P. Hall. "The Importance of Regulation-Induced Innovation for Sustainable Development" (2011) 3(1) *Sustainability*, 270–292. Pelkmans and Renda document empirical examples of enabling regulation. One of them is the regulation of end-of-life vehicles. Under the EU regulation, ambitious recycling targets were adopted far in excess of industry anticipations, including the reuse and recycling of 85% of cars by 2015. As a result, automotive manufacturers engaged in a virtuous cycle of innovation at design and planning stage. See Pelkmans and Renda, "Does EU regulation hinder or stimulate innovation?". The optimistic tone of the literature on enabling regulation shall however not obscure that firms may follow innovation strategies designed to evade the law. The 2015 Volkswagen NOx (nitrogen oxides) emission scandal highlights that when overly ambitious regulatory targets are adopted, firms have incentives to invest into technologies which game the enforcement system, including malicious software.
124 Nathalie A. Smuha, "From a 'Race to AI' to a 'Race to AI Regulation': Regulatory Competition for Artificial Intelligence" (*SSRN* December 31, 2019) <https://papers.ssrn.com/sol3/papers.cfm?abstract_id=3501410>.
125 See Daniel Weld and Oren Etzioni, "The First Law of Robotics (a Call to Arms)" (1994) 2 *AAAI*, 94, Proceedings of the Twelfth National Conference on Artificial Intelligence, 1042–1047.
126 Daron Acemoglu and Pascual Restrepo, "Robots and Jobs: Evidence from US Labor Markets" (2020) 128(6) *Journal of Political Economy*.
127 Executive office of the President National Science and Technology Council Committee on Technology, "Preparing for the Future of Artificial Intelligence" (October 12, 2016) <https://obamawhitehouse.archives.gov/sites/default/files/whitehouse_files/microsites/ostp/NSTC/preparing_for_the_future_of_ai.pdf>.
128 Richard A. Posner, "Theories of Economic Regulation" (1974) 5(2) *The Bell Journal of Economics and Management Science*, 335–358.
129 A price drop is not guaranteed though, since the cost of purchasing and controlling robots should be added to the equation.
130 What Bostrom calls a non-pure human enhancement. Nick Bostrom, "Existential Risk Prevention as Global Priority" (2013) 4(1) *Global Policy*, 15–31 (hereafter Bostrom, "Existential Risk Prevention").
131 The concept of "terminality" can be further delineated by distinguishing imminent terminal existernalities that lack the unpredictability property and distant existernalities which fulfill all four properties.
132 Gemignani, "Laying Down the Law to Robots", 1046.
133 Ibid.
134 See Ray Kurzweil, *The Singularity is Near: When Humans Transcend Biology* (Penguin Book, 2006). This also covers dehumanization through the blurring of distinctions between machines and humans.
135 See Bostrom, "Existential Risk Prevention".
136 Pure human enhancement goes beyond the restoration of destroyed human functions. Human enhancement is often opposed to therapy, which "aims to fix something that has gone wrong". But this distinction is not airtight. See Nick Bostrom and Rebecca Roache "Ethical Issues in Human Enhancement", in Jesper Ryberg, Thomas Petersen and Clark Wolf (ed.), *New Waves in Applied Ethics* (Pelgrave Macmillan, 2008), 120–152.
137 See Bostrom, "Existential Risk Prevention".
138 Kranzberg, "Kranzberg's Laws", 547.
139 Gemignani, "Laying Down the Law to Robots", 1050.
140 A black-box algorithm is an algorithm for which it is impossible to know how it reach a particular output from given inputs. According the High-Level Expert Groups on Artificial Intelligence, black-box requirements should be the implementation of explicability, traceability and auditability. See AI HLEG Guidelines.
141 For a precedent, see Senate Bill: S. 1458 (103rd) General Aviation Revitalization Act of 1994, known as GARA.

142 Yueh-Hsuan Weng, Yusuke Sugahara, Kenji Hashimoto and Atsuo Takanishi, "Intersection of 'Tokku' Special Zone, Robots, and the Law: A Case Study on Legal Impacts to Humanoid Robots" (2015) 7(5) *International Journal of Social Robotics*, 841–857.
143 Events that come as surprises to most, if not all. See Taleb, *Black Swan*.
144 Bob Heymand and Mike Titterton, "Introduction", in Bob Heyman, Andy Alaszewski, Monica Shaw and Mike Titterton (ed.), *Risk, Safety and Clinical Practice: Health Care Through the Lens of Risk* (Oxford University Press, 2008), 3 and 11.

14

Artificial intelligence and cyber-security

Matteo E. Bonfanti, Myriam Dunn Cavelty, and Andreas Wenger

Introduction

"Artificial Intelligence is Becoming a Key Weapon in the Cyber-security War" reads the title of a recent blog entry by a leading cyber-security company (Sentonas 2017). In this chapter, we ask: Is that so? If yes, in what ways? Moreover, what kind of social science literature is there to help us understand the implications of the connection between artificial intelligence (AI) and cyber-security?

In answering these questions, the chapter faces several challenges. First, neither cyber-security nor AI in cyber-security are well-developed fields of research in the social sciences. While this is changing in the case of cyber-security politics (Dunn Cavelty and Wenger 2020), we are far from observing any sustained academic research on AI in cyber-security in the non-technical disciplines. On the one hand, we can see this dearth as an opportunity: there are so many socially relevant but unanswered questions at the intersection between digital security and AI that it is a goldmine for researchers seeking to distinguish themselves. On the other hand, making scholarly contributions in an area where there is no stable academic base yet is difficult, especially for junior academics: it is easy to get lost in the vast possibilities of broad, exciting research questions and challenging to identify the body of literature one wants to contribute to. Not least, choosing outsider topics can have implications for an academic career: publishing articles about cyber-security and AI in high-ranked journals is difficult because it is hard to fulfil the disciplinary requirements for innovative theory, combined with matching data and rigorous methods.

The second major challenge for academia is that cyber-security and AI research are not only strongly interdisciplinary but also transdisciplinary. Because knowledge creation, innovation, but also relevant policy practices are determined not by scientific but by non-scientific stakeholder communities in the policy and the private sector, the majority of publications are not academic per se but have an applied policy focus. Working on such an applied topic can be a challenge for early career academics trying to find tenured positions because policy-related, applied work is not valued in many academic settings. That said, for academics seeking to transition to the private or the public sector, knowledge about cyber-security matters is an asset: too few experts exist who can speak with depth and authority about digital transformation, security, and social consequences.

Navigating these opportunities and challenges, this chapter discusses the convergence between AI and cyber-security in four main parts. We first situate cyber-security in the social sciences, showing how the field of research has only recently matured. In a second section, we show how the confluence between cyber-security and AI happened, highlighting how uncertain the actual effects on security are. Three possible application areas can be identified at this point in time, however, and they are discussed in section three. Considering some of the lessons and observations from the cyber-security field, we outline three interesting research clusters for AI and cyber-security research in the last section.

Cyber-security in the social sciences

The insecurity of cyberspace comes to society's attention through the regular reporting of data breaches and other cyber-related incidents in the media. However, not only is the frequency of such incidents increasing, but they also are getting more sophisticated and consequently more impactful in terms of financial or political damage. As a result, the majority of states treat cyber-security as a serious matter of national security. In the social sciences, cyber-security has therefore developed into a field of research in the discipline of international relations, security and strategic studies. In the first section, we describe how the treatment of cyber-security as "high politics" stems from a particular non-technical security conception that has emerged over the years. In a second section, we briefly discuss the latest trends in cyber-security politics research.

Cyber-security: from technical issue to high politics

What is cyber-security? This seemingly simple question does not have simple answers, not least because underlying technologies, threat perceptions, and countermeasures related to cyberspace keep evolving, changing both the concept and the related policy issues. The term cyberspace refers to a virtual, large-scale, dynamic domain of data exchange, sustained through a series of physical objects like computers, cables, or mobile phones and the corresponding software protocols. The technological details of this "space" and the opportunities and challenges this creates for human users are not fixed, with emerging AI technologies being a case in point. This means that we need to be sensitive to changes in the larger environment of cyber-security at all times.

On a basic level, the security of digital technologies is grounded in dedicated risk management practices developed by computer specialists to make computers and computer networks more secure. Seen from a technical viewpoint, cyber-security is primarily about the protection of confidentiality, integrity, and availability of data and information (the so-called CIA-Triad), also known as information security or information assurance practices. Yet, cyber-security is more than information security: rather than just seeking to protect information assets it also extends to humans and their interests (Von Solms and Van Niekerk 2013). Moreover, decisive for the elevation of the issue from a technical to a security political issue was the realization in the 1990s that a set of high-value assets, so called critical infrastructures, whose disruption or destruction could have severe consequences, were getting increasingly dependent on digital technologies for a variety of functions (Dunn Cavelty 2008). The related threat discourse that emerged consists of two interlinked factors: an outward-looking focus that sees an increasing willingness of malicious actors to exploit the weaknesses inherent in our societies without hesitation or restraint. This is coupled with an inward-looking focus on system-inherent vulnerabilities in (computer) systems. Beyond the technical, cyber-security is therefore also a type of security that refers to offensive and defensive activities of state and non-state actors in cyberspace.

Given the interconnection between computer networks, critical infrastructures, and national security, many nations are paying more attention to the strategic-military aspects of cyber-security. In the process, cyber-security is both securitized, meaning the establishment of an issue as belonging to the national security domain, often under the purview of the intelligence community, and militarized, best defined as "the growing pressures on governments and their armed forces to develop the capacity to fight and win wars in this domain" (Deibert 2011: 2). In a power political context, cyber-security serves the protection of national interests in cyberspace and the pursuit of wider security political goals through the exploitation of opportunities. Conceptualized like this, cyberspace is both a vulnerability-multiplier and a force-multiplier – a target (risk *to* cyberspace) and a weapon (risk *through* cyberspace) (Deibert and Rohozinski 2010).

Researching cyber-security politics

There used to be two strategic key concerns for early observers of conflict in and through cyberspace: the relatively low entry costs for disruptive cyber-"weapons" and the high vulnerability of critical infrastructures. In accordance, threat perceptions and policy debates in the 1990s and part of the early 2000s were dominated by the spectre of catastrophic high-impact, low-probability attack scenarios. Over time, however, experts began to shift their attention to the reality of persistent cyber-operations across the conflict spectrum. This was a consequence of emerging empirical evidence that state and non-state actors prefer to influence the larger information sphere before and during political disputes or conflicts, sometimes coupled with mildly disruptive attacks (Baezner 2018), whereas strategic cyberwar – defined as stand-alone, surprise attacks against critical infrastructures – failed to make an appearance.

The increase in the number of actual cyber-operations to study allowed international relations scholars to use "old" strategic studies concepts and test their applicability to the new domain (Kello 2017). Concepts such as cyber-coercion (Borghard and Lonergan 2017), cyber-deterrence (Lindsay 2015), or the offense-defence balance (Slayton 2016/17) get scrutinized or datasets of cyber-operations built (Maness and Valeriano 2019; Kostyuk and Zhukov 2019). What emerged as a consensus from such scholarly projects is that operating in cyberspace is more technically and organizationally demanding than the key strategic concerns of the 1990s suggested. Furthermore, after observing strategic restraint at the high end of conflict and permanent subversion at the low end of conflict, the role of actors *inside* the state came into focus. Differentiating between military and other actors, it was mainly the intelligence agencies and their particular practices that came into focus (Lindsay 2017). An observed change in the economic environment, mainly in cyber-security market dynamics, also led to attention on actors *beyond* the state, namely cyber-security companies. For example, researchers focus on how intelligence practices of private companies influence state policy and practice at the national and international levels (Egloff 2020a, 2020b; Maschmeyer 2020) or what roles private actors play in the emergence of international behavioural norms (Eggenschwiler 2021).

Overall, cyber-security research has reached beyond its already interdisciplinary boundaries into even more disciplines as it extends to new empirical questions. Researchers have begun to integrate concepts and explanatory mechanisms from international relations and security studies, international political economy, and intelligence studies. Science and Technology Studies (STS) offer a productive lens for understanding the mutual interplay between the technical and the socio-political sphere. Practice theory with its focus on technological possibilities and socio-technical processes allows integration of these different approaches at the empirical level. More data about cyber-operations by many different actors around the world and better tools to monitor and analyze this data are becoming available. While there is still ample room for theory development and theory testing, it is to be expected that the field continues to focus on rich empirical work (Dunn Cavelty and Wenger 2020).

Artificial intelligence meets cyber-security

It took more than a decade for cyber-security politics to mature as a field of study, with dedicated PhD programs and funding opportunities emerging. When looking at AI research in the social sciences, it is at least ten years behind that development. At the moment, AI research is dominated by technical, problem-solving projects that seek to create (marketable) solutions. More reflexive research focusing on the socio-political aspects of AI is very rare. However, certain dynamics and assumptions apparent in existing publications can help to make an informed judgement about where AI research at the intersection to cyber-security might be headed. In this section, we focus our attention first on policy developments, stressing mainly the involvement of governments in AI development and the impact of this on cyber-security conceptualizations and practices. We stress that the future of AI in cyber-security is highly uncertain due to the dynamical interaction between technological development and socio-political factors.

Policy developments as a driver

Over the last couple of years, AI has become hugely attractive for different stakeholders worldwide. The growing interest in AI is reflected by an increasing number of dedicated initiatives that are aimed at boosting the acquisition/provision of AI capabilities on the side of governments, in particular the sustaining/accelerating research and development of these technologies and fostering their application for cyber-security purposes (among others). Promising applications include cyber-threat detection, analysis, and, possibly, prevention and response. Western governments in general, and the US Defense Advanced Research Projects Agency (DARPA) in particular, have been funding fundamental research and development in AI and computer networks since the 1960s. However, driven by profit and visions of transformative AI, today, the private sector invests the largest amount of resources (human, technological, organizational, and financial) into the development and commercialization of AI. Subsequently, multinational technology firms, other private organizations, and academia are often at the forefront of AI innovation, whereas militaries and government agencies work towards leveraging these advances.

Governments have sought to sustain AI advancements through multiple policy mechanisms at least since 2016. They have invested in AI infrastructures, encouraged academic education and professional training, funded scientific research, and incentivized public-private partnerships and collaborations, as well as promoted standards through procurement or other policies. In consultation with the private sector and the broad civil society, they have in some cases sponsored the adoption of guiding principles or basic norms (e.g. fundamental rights, data privacy) to sustain "responsible" or "trustworthy" innovation in this technological field (European Commission 2019). In many countries – for example, China, the United Kingdom, Canada, India, Japan, France – governments orient their actions towards the acquisition of AI capabilities according to wide-scope national AI strategies, most of which address cyber-security as one promising field of application (Cussins Newman 2019: 34 ff; OECD.AI 2020). Further policy instruments or other technical documentation tackling sectorial applications of AI complement these strategies.

In general, governmental policies and their implementing actions pursue the threefold objective of: (i) encouraging the uptake of AI, (ii) maximizing its benefits, and (iii) minimizing the associated risks. As far as cyber-security is concerned, policies aspire to make AI capabilities available to relevant national cyber-security stakeholders (mainly public and private organizations) and ensure they can resort to these capabilities to gain an advantage over their competitors – an advantage which can make the difference in terms of power relations, that is, in terms of the capacity of such stakeholders to safeguard their assets and promote their interests in or through cyberspace.

Impact of AI development on cyber-security

The attention on AI suggests that governments largely believe in the transformative capacity of these technologies and are aware of the importance of mastering it in the coming years. It shows there are expectations for the role AI can play in shaping cyber-security and security in general. However, many aspects of this relationship are still unclear. For example: in what ways will AI enhance the protection of individuals, organizations, nations, and their cyber-dependent assets from hostile threat actors? How will it introduce novel vulnerabilities and enable additional typologies of actions? How will it induce cyber-security stakeholders to adapt to changing risk scenarios and opportunities? In addition, how will it require them to adopt additional measures on the technological, policy, regulatory, or other levels (Bonfanti 2021; Buchanan 2020)?

Providing a definitive answer to these questions is not easy. AI innovation is developing quickly under the pressure of multiple actors such as public/private researchers, developers, and providers; policy and regulatory authorities at the domestic or supranational level; security/military agencies; and the broader civil society. Anticipating the mid- to long-term outcomes of such development is hard. From a technical point of view alone, there have been previously unimagined improvements in the AI core infrastructures and components – that is, computing power, algorithms design, standard software frameworks for faster replication of experiments, and the availability of large datasets. Such improvements can be expected to continue, given the growing public and commercial investments in the field (Fischer and Wenger 2019). In addition, AI is not the only technology that promises to change cyber-security: there are further technologies displaying a similar transformative capacity such as quantum computing or homomorphic encryption. AI will interact with these technologies in a way that is impossible to predict. Therefore, we cannot establish the whole spectrum of possible interactions of AI with these technologies and foresee the overall impact on cyber-security.

Beyond the technical, advances in AI have a strong socio-technical component, which is more than the sum of technological capabilities and scientific/technical knowledge (Cussins Newman 2019: 6). Progress made in AI research and applications, and their implications for cyber-security, are inevitably shaped by the models of governance that will emerge from the formal/informal, fragmented/coordinated, and often unbalanced interactions among public authorities, private organizations, and the civil society. Progress will also be influenced and driven by these actors' assessments of the risks and opportunities stemming from the deployment of AI for cyber or other security purposes. Risks and opportunities are not to be understood in narrow technological terms only, for example, as strictly pertaining to the functioning of AI tools, their safety, and their efficiency. Rather, they will affect a range of different issues and communities. At a higher level of abstraction, they involve nations' economic integrity and well-being, social cohesion, diplomatic relations, or political stability. The governance of such risks and opportunities will therefore reflect individual and collective assessments, visions, values, interests, and challenges.

Possible mid- to long-term application areas

Given that the trajectory of AI innovation remains uncertain and is determined by the interaction between multiple players and forces, it is hard if not impossible to predict how it will affect cyber-security. In this section, we focus on some early and promising applications of AI to cyber-security, however, which allow us to make an informed, although general, guess about what to expect in the near-term future. Based on a review of selected scientific and technical literature, we present three possible application areas: we describe how AI may likely affect the cyber-threat landscape, discuss the existing challenges and opportunities stemming from the adoption of AI-based solutions to achieve cyber-defensive/offensive objectives, and present the role AI can play to sustain or counter cyber-information and influence operations. Mainly, AI is an enabling technology that can be deployed across many different domains, for civil and military purposes, as well as to do good or harm. Whether these applications are positive or negative will to a large degree depend on cyber-security stakeholders, in particular state-actors, and their ability and willingness to govern the risks and opportunities deriving from the AI-induced transformation of cyber-security.

AI and the cyber-threat landscape

The deployment of AI components for cyber-related purposes can affect the cyber-threat landscape in several ways. Absent the adoption of any substantial preventive measure, AI can expand existing cyber-threats (quantity), alter the typical character of these threats (quality), and introduce new and unknown threats (quantity and quality).

AI could expand the set of actors who are capable of carrying out malicious cyber-activities, the rate at which these actors can carry out the activities, and the set of plausible targets. This claim follows the efficiency, scalability, and adaptability of AI as well as the "democratization" of research and development in this field. In particular, the diffusion of AI components among traditional cyber-threat actors – states, criminals, hacktivists, and terrorist groups – could increase the number of entities for whom carrying out attacks may become affordable. Given that AI applications are also scalable, actors who possess the resources to carry out attacks may gain the ability to do so at a higher rate. New targets to hit may become worthwhile for them.

From a qualitative point of view, AI-powered cyberattacks could also feature in more effective, finely targeted, and sophisticated actions and attacks. Increased effectiveness derives from the attributes of efficiency, scalability, and adaptability of these solutions. Potential targets are more easily identified and scrutinized.

Furthermore, AI could enable a new variety of malicious activities that exploit the vulnerabilities these technologies introduced in the cyber-systems that integrate them. These vulnerabilities might be the cause of incidents or pave the way to both known and unknown malicious forms of exploitation (Patel et al. 2019). Exploits might consist of "data poisoning" attacks – injections into the training data that causes a learning algorithm to make mistakes – or "adversarial examples", digital inputs and real-life artefacts designed to be misclassified by machine-learning solutions. The latter are most effective if the parameters of the AI model are known (so-called white box attacks). However, they can also work without such knowledge, in "black box attacks" (Gu et al. 2019). Experts are aware that there is a wide range of potential malicious exploitations that has still to be fully explored. Some of these exploitations could be cyber-related. In this regard, cyber-security itself becomes relevant to AI research and development. To preserve the proper functioning, reliability, and integrity as well as to avoid nefarious effects, AI-integrated cyber-systems require safeguards from cyber-incidents or attacks. The adoption of cyber-security practices as well as the promotion of broad cyber-hygiene programs with specific requirements for AI research, development, and application is referred to as "Cyber-security for AI" (Spring et al. 2019: 11).

Defensive and offensive use: computer network operations

Many features of AI that make it appropriate for cyber-defence applications also make it suitable for cyber-offence. Therefore, in the next three to five years, one should expect organizations to adopt and implement AI-based cyber-defence capabilities to safeguard their assets, such as networks, information, and people, from adversaries who might leverage both AI and non-AI tools for offensive purposes. Similarly, there will be actors employing AI-powered cyber-offence capabilities to compromise targets who might engage in AI- or non-AI-integrated cyber-defence. In particular, AI-based cyber-capabilities may support activities aimed at protecting from or executing computer-network operations, be they attacks or exploitation. They will also likely support defence from or execution of so-called cyber-information and influence operations (Cordey 2019).

Both defence and offence can benefit from the deployment of AI to produce cyber-intelligence, that is, actionable knowledge to support decision making on cyberspace-related issues (Bonfanti 2018). Indeed, AI is able to integrate several functions of the cyber-intelligence process, in particular the collection, processing, and analysis of information (Galyardt et al. 2019). It can boost information gathering and widen its scope to multiple sources and several endpoints. It may also enhance the selection of information and corroborate it with additional data provided by other sources. AI can also support analysis by finding hidden patterns and correlations in processed data. By integrating AI capabilities into these functions, the cyber-intelligence process will likely advance in terms of automation and speed.

The ability of AI components to produce cyber-intelligence will translate into specific defensive applications at the tactical/technical and operational level of cyber-security. Operationally, AI could be used to retrieve and process data gathered from network security analysis programs and correlate them against other available information. Tactically, AI will increasingly support cyber-threat detection, analysis, and, possibly, prevention. In particular, it will upgrade Intrusion Detection Systems (IDS) aimed at discovering illicit activities within a computer or a network (Buczak and Guven 2016; Apruzzese et al. 2018). The same goes for spam and phishing detection systems as well as malware detection and analysis tools. As per the latter, AI will probably improve the discovery of modern and emerging malware, which can automatically generate novel variants to elude traditional rule-based identification approaches. It will help in attributing these variants to the correct malware family thanks to its capacity to recognize some hidden patterns, which are invisible to traditional or human-based analysis.

AI components will also integrate multifactor authentication or verification systems. These will help detect a pattern of behaviour for a particular user to identify changes in those patterns. Another promising target for tactical defensive application of AI is automated vulnerability testing, also known as fuzzing. Although promising, the described applications for anomaly and threat detection/analysis are tainted with both false negatives (Zetter 2019) and positives (Xin et al. 2018). As per the former, pilot testing or early deployment show they are still, and keep on being, a main problem. Even a false positive rate of 0.1% could account for hundreds of false alarms, which are unbearable for many organizations (Apruzzese et al. 2018).

AI applications will also be used for cyber-offensive purposes, that is, to compromise a target organization or user, its networks, and the data processed. They will enable more numerous and sophisticated cyberattacks. As in the case of defence, AI applications may generate cyber-intelligence to prepare and implement attacks. They may improve the selection and prioritization of targets for cyberattacks involving social engineering. These are attacks employing psychological manipulation of target users to get them to reveal specific information or perform a specific action for illegitimate reasons. Thanks to AI, potential victims' online information can be harvested and processed to automatically generate custom malicious websites, emails, and links based on profiling (Brundage et al. 2018).

AI components will also enhance adversarial vulnerability discovery and exploitation. They will prompt sophistication in malware designing and functioning, as well as support their obfuscation. AI-powered malware can evade detection and respond creatively to changes in the target's behaviour. They will function as an autonomous and adaptive implant that learns from its host in order to remain undetected, search for and classify interesting content for exfiltration, search for and infect new targets, and discover new pathways or methods for moving through a network and finding the key data that are the ultimate target of an attack. Already in 2018, IBM researchers developed a malware of this type, dubbed DeepLocker. This AI-powered malware conceals its intent until it reaches a specific victim. It carries out its malicious action as soon as the AI component identifies the target through indicators like facial recognition, geolocation, and voice recognition. What is unique about DeepLocker is that it uses AI (deep neural network) to unlock the attack (Stoecklin 2018).[1] Finally, AI will also be deployed to spoof authentication or verification systems, such as those integrating biometric identifiers (Patel et al. 2019).

Cyber-information and influence

AI will likely enhance the planning and running of cyber-information and influence operations. By supporting automation, it will boost digital information gathering as well as surveillance of targets' online behaviour (Bonfanti 2019). It will increase the set of tools available to inform and influence adversaries through and within cyberspace, especially by leveraging social media platforms (Patel et al. 2019: 22ff). With regard to the latter, AI can improve bots and social bots management as well as allow the production of messages targeted at those most susceptible to them (similar to behavioural advertisement; Brundage et al. 2018).

Following an ongoing trend, AI-based solutions, especially those integrating deep generative adversarial neural networks (GAN), will help to create manipulated digital content. Such content, known as synthetic media or deepfakes, consists of hyper-realistic video, audio, imagery, or text that are not easily recognizable as fake through manual or other conventional forensic techniques (Collins 2019). Once generated, synthetic media may be abused (Bonfanti 2020). Harmful employment is already abundant and documented in the media. For the most part, it consists of the deployment of AI-doctored videos for targeted online cyber-bullying, stalking, and defamation (Chesney and Citron 2018). Probably on the rise in the near-term is the weaponization of synthetic media for cyber-enabled blackmailing, scamming, corporate sabotage via market or other types of manipulative operations, and for political propaganda (Ajder et al. 2019). In these cases, synthetic media will play as add-ons to "individual/organisation-oriented" or "communities-oriented" information operations (Bonfanti 2020).

Although AI will integrate and enable these activities, it will also contribute to countering them. From a defensive point of view, AI can support the detection of and response to cyber-influence and information operations. It can help monitor the online environment, such as social media platforms; identify the early signs of malicious operations, such as increasing bots or social bots activities; in addition to discovering altered digital content, including synthetic media (Knight 2019; Collins 2019).

AI in cyber-security research in the social sciences: future avenues

The current literature on AI in the social sciences focuses on either AI politics or on AI governance. The discussion on AI politics looks at how and with what consequences states are treating AI as a strategic resource because they anticipate a significant impact of AI on the global distribution of economic, military, and political power (Fischer and Wenger 2019). Given this "high politics" connotation, the majority of research focuses on the impact of AI on military capabilities and on strategic stability (Haas and Fischer 2017). Just like the literature focusing on AI politics, the body of literature on AI governance is sparse. Due to the high potential stakes at play, there is a prime focus on the regulation of AI-enabled autonomy in weapons systems. Overall, the take of these contributions on technology is deterministic: they tend to portray security governance as reactive to future technological development that is following a fixed trajectory (e.g. Kralingen 2016).

There is a large tradition of seeing technology as naturalized driver of change in the international relations (IR) literature. It is taken to have unidirectional effects on matters of politics, whereas the social and political factors, which influence the shape, design, and use of security technologies, go largely ignored (Fritsch 2011). This notion has also negatively affected early cyber-security literature: very often, technological determinism combined with technological pessimism leads to largely overblown threat perceptions and a strong focus on worst-case, low-probability events to the detriment of more frequent but less spectacular occurrences. Fortuitously, this simplified perspective on technology and politics is changing: growing numbers of scholars explore the interaction between scientific practices, technological systems, and security politics in more recursive and dialectical ways (McCarthy 2018). This type of literature questions why one kind of technology is developed and not another, by whom, and why – and how it comes to be utilized in specific forms. In doing so, the literature has begun to produce increasingly sophisticated ideas of how technological innovation, framing, and appropriation interact with social and political processes in the security domain.

Fundamental for this type of conceptualization is the idea of "co-production" (Miller and Wyborn 2020). The concept of co-production rejects the strict technology/policy dichotomy of traditional deterministic views of technology. Elements and processes in international politics are inextricably linked with and jointly produced by technology and science. Technologies are not simply artefacts that appear from out of nowhere to exert influence but reflect social and political dynamics and decisions. Hence, co-production directs researchers' attention towards questions of how science, technology, and world politics are co-constitutive (Jasanoff 2004).

Though it is highly likely that the fast-changing dynamics of AI development in cyber-security and other security-relevant fields will sustain the domination of technical and problem-solving publications way into the future, it would be beneficial if the social sciences began to pay more sustained attention to a variety of topics as well. Drawing from observations previously made in the field of cyber-security politics research (Dunn Cavelty and Wenger 2020), we outline three broad avenues for future research in what follows. The first focuses on questions of power and strategy and has a clear link to IR and strategic studies research. The second focuses on the relationship between the development and design of technologies and the political possibilities and restraints that emerge from this, with a particular focus on the role of private, industry actors. The third is about the establishment of norms and good behaviour for security governance.

AI and changes on the strategic level

In this first cluster, the current literature on AI politics and AI governance can be taken as a starting point. Building on cyber-security research and the insights that emerged in the last few years, the key question is going to be whether and how emerging AI stabilizes or destabilizes power relationships in general and the effects of cyber-operations on national security and international stability more concretely. One important lesson – which also applies to musings about how other emergent technologies such as quantum computing revolutionize security (Lindsay 2020) – is that dual-use technologies always lead to multiple, contingent, and non-linear effects: they empower some actors and applications, while disempowering others. Who wins and who loses is not predetermined but needs to be established carefully via observations of the field. Unless we want to study threat politics, as in "who paints what kind of picture of the threat and with what political consequence", solid case studies of the usage of new technologies in conflictual settings are going to be paramount in order to establish what are and what are not the imagined effects of the interlinkage between cyber-security and AI on international security.

Most importantly, technological development trajectories should not be taken for granted but need to be observed. Overall, it is highly likely that cyber-security will grow further in importance as countries all around the world strive to shape digital transformation processes. The complexity of socio-technical systems will increase due to the ubiquitous digitalization and automation of technical processes. As these technical systems become more tightly coupled and integrate more aspects of society and economy, cyber-security concerns will inevitably expand to more policy fields at both the national and international level.

As an enabling technology with diverse applications in all areas of life, AI and cyber-security will be further interwoven. However, which issues emerge as particularly noteworthy is unclear at this point in time. The fact that there is considerable uncertainty regarding the tempo and scope of these technological developments creates new demands for research that maps, assesses, models, and forecasts technological possibilities. As social scientists, we need to understand the increasingly salient political and social aspects that will affect the patterns of cooperation and conflict in politics and society at the national and international level.

The co-constitution between technologies and politics

The second cluster focuses on the processes by which new technologies in the AI-field are designed, including attention on those who conceptualize, develop, and assemble, and train the technology. The development of technology is inherently political, as all stages of the design process and all the people involved are carriers of certain norms, assumptions, and ideas, all of which flow into the technology. This way, we can attempt to understand how the practices and implicit norms that enter a new technological design help to pre-structure political decisions later. Conversely, this insight also means that bottom-up governance processes focused on the design of technologies can complement top-down inter-governmental processes and are equally important in regulating new technologies (McCarthy 2018), which opens up interesting avenues, for example, for rethinking arms control.

The study of AI politics and governance can start integrating views on how preexisting entities, processes, practices, and actors are affected and transformed by science and technology and how they in turn adapt to, and thereby shape, science and technology. For example, an interesting research project would be to study and compare how AI is co-produced by an interplay between market dynamics, technological uncertainty, political perceptions, and arms race dynamics in different localities. Although the potential of AI, which is primarily driven by market dynamics, is still uncertain, policy makers in various countries are already treating AI as having significant value for the production of security and are basing their present actions on predictions about the future. Such decisions about the future are taken based on assumptions and beliefs.

Norms and governance

The new technologies will be primarily developed by global technology firms and the private sector. As a consequence, state actors will become more dependent on technology firms and independent technology experts, further transforming the relationship between public and private actors. In the field of national security, public actors will uphold their efforts to control the risk of escalation trough international cooperation. States cannot secure cyberspace on their own without taking into account market and social forces; yet no stable cyber-security governance framework will emerge without greater convergence on responsible behaviour among great powers.

As long as great powers disagree about what represents responsible use of cyber-operations in state interactions, and for that matter what forms of espionage and interference in the political process of other states through cyberspace are acceptable, little top-down progress will materialize. Bottom-up progress, on the other hand, presupposes that the actors become more visible for each other in order to successfully work together in a multistakeholder framework. Social science research can shed light on invisible actors and analyze the interaction between market dynamics and political dynamics in stabilizing cyberspace; it can evaluate if the socio-technical institutions that secure cyberspace reflect the tools and practices of public and private actors.

The key governance challenge at the domestic political level is how to overcome fragmentation of authority and accountability. Tighter coupling of technical systems and their growing interconnectedness with socio-political institutions creates growing demand for governance in networks, which in turn means that governments increasingly share responsibility with actors from business and society. The integration of policy into a coherent overall framework involves difficult trade-offs between security and privacy and creates horizontal and vertical coordination and cooperation problems across government and at the intersections between state, economy, and society. Research can evaluate how states can fine-tune their multidimensional roles. How states decide to regulate their technology base is, moreover, directly linked to how they anticipate this will influence their relative economic, political, and military power at the international level. Academics in this context can study how different (democratic and authoritarian) political systems balance regulation and market forces and what this means for state access to the private technology sector, export control systems of dual-use technologies, and screening mechanisms of foreign investment into the strategically relevant technology base.

Governments can play a significant role in addressing these risks and opportunities by managing and steering the AI-induced transformation of cyber-security. To influence the transformation, governments can also establish dynamic testing, validation, and certification standards of AI tools for cyber-related applications. At the international level, they can work towards common norms around AI research and development and consider smart constraints on the proliferation of knowledge and capabilities in this technological domain. Furthermore, they can foster a positive and inclusive governance of AI by operationalizing high-level principles, such as those adopted by the EU and the Organisation for Economic Co-operation and Development (OECD) for trustworthy AI.

Conclusion and outlook

Is artificial intelligence a new key weapon in the cyber-security war? The answer is: its role and effects are going to be ambivalent and warrant close attention in the coming years. It seems clear that AI will affect cyber-security in the following way: it will enrich the cyber-threat landscape – both in quantitative and qualitative terms. It will likely increase the number of cyber-threat actors, offer them additional exploitable vulnerabilities and targets, as well as boost their malevolent actions. Conversely, AI will contribute to defence from those threats by enabling the discovery of unknown vulnerabilities, the detection of malicious cyber-activities, and the implementation of countermeasures.

In sum, AI will support both cyber-defence and offence and it is difficult to establish whether defensive or offensive applications will benefit more. Clearly, it will depend on the capacity of public or private cyber-security stakeholders to master and leverage AI. It will also depend on their overall ability to identify, understand, and address the risks, threats, and opportunities stemming from the deployment of these technologies. It is our hope that future AI and cyber-security research will converge with the research that seeks to understand how technologies and world politics are co-constructed. Thereby, security technology can be endogenized into political processes and no longer taken to stand outside politics.

As AI takes on an ever more prominent place on the international policy agenda, and as IR and security scholars increasingly find themselves in the role of policy advisors, their engagement with the co-constitution of technology, science and politics will lead to a more nuanced policy discourse on the foreign policy and security implications of AI. Most crucially, such a conceptualization highlights that technologies and their use are always subject to economic, social, and political decisions and processes. This also means that no aspect of their development or use is inevitable. Rather, and even more so with a technology that is still dynamically evolving as we speak, scholars need to attune themselves to study the messy interaction between micro-politics and macro-politics without predetermining the effects.

Research at the intersection of cyber-security and AI needs to speak to a variety of other bodies of research in order to remain relevant to policy choices and cognizant of technological possibilities. The selection of interesting and pressing issues should happen without too many disciplinary constraints and institutional barriers, if possible. Universities can help the public actors at the national and international level to catch up in their technology competence, while educating the next generation of experts for society and industry. Academia can contribute to the study of cyber-security and AI and through its independent and peer-reviewed knowledge broaden the knowledge base for some of the difficult policy choices that lie ahead. Science can collaborate with the private and public actors in the development of evidentiary standards and norms that will underpin the future resilience of socio-technical systems, and in the negotiation and establishment of new norms and institutions that should govern the use and misuse of these systems.

Note

1 The malicious payload will only be unlocked if the intended target is reached. The AI model is trained to behave normally unless it is presented with a specific input: the trigger conditions identifying specific victims.

References

AI HLEG (High-Level Expert Group on Artificial Intelligence) (2019). A Definition of AI: Main Capabilities and Scientific Disciplines. A Document Prepared by the High-Level Expert Group on Artificial Intelligence. Available at https://ec.europa.eu/digital-single-market/en/news/ethics-guidelines-trustworthy-ai (last accessed on October 22, 2020).

Ajder, H., Cavalli, F., Patrini, G., and Cullen, L. (2019). The State of Deepfakes: Landscape, Threats, and Impact. Deeptracelabs. Available at https://regmedia.co.uk/2019/10/08/deepfake_report.pdf (last accessed on October 22, 2020).

Apruzzese, G., Ferretti, L., Marchetti, M., Colajanni, M., and Guido, A. (2018). On the Effectiveness of Machine and Deep Learning for Cyber Security. In Minárik, T., Jakschis, R., and Lindström, L. (Eds.), *10th International Conference on Cyber Conflict CyCon: Maximising Effects*, 371–390. Tallinn: NATO CCD COE Publications.

Baezner, M. (2018). *Hotspot Analysis: Synthesis 2017: Cyber-Conflicts in Perspective*. Zurich: Center for Security Studies (CSS), ETH Zurich.

Bonfanti, M. E. (2018). Cyber Intelligence: In Pursuit of a Better Understanding for an Emerging Practice. *Cyber, Intelligence, and Security*, 2(1): 105–121.

Bonfanti, M. E. (2019). An Intelligence-Based Approach to Countering Social Media Influence Operations. *Romanian Intelligence Studies Review*, 19–20: 47–67.

Bonfanti, M. E. (2020). The Weaponisation of Synthetic Media: What Threat Does This Pose to National Security? In CiberELCANO, No. 57, July. Available at https://css.ethz.ch/en/Themes/AI/all-publications/details.html?id=/t/h/e/w/the_weaponisation_of_synthetic_media_wha (last accessed on October 22, 2020).

Bonfanti, M. E. (2021). Artificial Intelligence and the Offence-Defence Balance in Cyber-Security. In: Dunn Cavelty, M., and Wenger, A. (Eds.), *Cyber-Security Politics: Socio-Technological Transformations and Political Fragmentation*. London: Routledge.

Borghard, E. D., and Lonergan, S. W. (2017). The Logic of Coercion in Cyberspace. *Security Studies*, 26: 452–481.

Brundage, M., Avin, S., Clark, J., et al. (2018). The Malicious Use of Artificial Intelligence: Forecasting, Prevention, and Mitigation. Available at https://maliciousaireport.com/ (last accessed on October 22, 2020).

Buchanan, B. (2020). A National Security Research Agenda for Cyber-security and Artificial Intelligence. Center for Security and Emerging Technology, CSET Issue Brief, May 2020. Available at https://cset.georgetown.edu/research/a-national-security-research-agenda-for-cyber-security-and-artificial-intelligence/ (last accessed on October 22, 2020).

Buczak, A. L., and Guven, E. (2016). A Survey of Data Mining and Machine Learning Methods for Cyber Security Intrusion Detection. *IEEE Communications Surveys Tutorials*, 18 (2): 1153–1176.

Chesney, R., and Citron, D. K. (2018). Deep Fakes: A Looming Challenge for Privacy, Democracy, and National Security. *SSRN Electronic Journal*. Available at papers.ssrn.com/ sol3/papers.cfm?abstract_id=3213954 (last accessed on October 22, 2020).

Collins, A. (2019). *Forged Authenticity: Governing Deepfake Risks*. Lausanne: EPFL International Risk Governance Center.

Cordey, S. (2019). Cyber-Influence Operations: An Overview and Comparative Analysis. CSS Risk and Resilience Reports. ETH Zurich. Available at https://css.ethz.ch/en/services/digital-library/publications/publication.html/c4ec0cea-62d0-4d1d-aed2-5f6103d89f93 (last accessed on October 22, 2020).

Cussins Newman, J. (2019). Toward AI Security. Global Aspirations for a More Resilient Future. Center for Long-Term Cyber-security (CLTC) White Paper Series. Available at https://cltc.berkeley.edu/wp-content/uploads/2019/02/CLTC_Cussins_Toward_AI_Security.pdf. (last accessed on October 22, 2020).

Deibert, R. (2011). Ronald Deibert: Tracking the Emerging Arms Race in Cyberspace. An Interview. *Bulletin of the Atomic Scientists*, 67 (2): 1–8. https://doi.org/10.1177/0096340210393703.

Deibert, R., and Rohozinski, R. (2010). Risking Security: The Policies and Paradoxes of Cyberspace Security. *International Political Sociology*, 4: 15–32.

Dunn Cavelty, M. (2008). *Cyber-Security and Threat Politics: US Efforts to Secure the Information Age*. London: Routledge.

Dunn Cavelty, M., and Wenger, A. (2020). Cyber Security Meets Security Politics: Complex Technology, Fragmented Politics, Networked Science. *Contemporary Security Policy*, 41 (1): 5–32.

Eggenschwiler, J. (2021). Big Tech's Push for Norms to Tackle Uncertainty in Cyberspace. In: Dunn Cavelty, M., and Wenger, A. (Eds.), *Cyber-Security Politics: Socio-Technological Transformations and Political Fragmentation*. London: Routledge.

Egloff, F. (2020a). Contested Public Attributions of Cyber Incidents and the Role of Academia. *Contemporary Security Policy*, 41 (1): 55–81.

Egloff, F. (2020b). Public Attribution of Cyber Intrusions. *Journal of Cybersecurity*, 6 (1). https://doi.org/10.1093/cybsec/tyaa012.

European Commission (2019). Communication "Building Trust in Human-Centric Artificial Intelligence". Available at https://ec.europa.eu/digital-single-market/en/artificial-intelligence.

Fischer, S., and Wenger, A. (2019). A Politically Neutral Hub for Basic AI Research. *ETH CSS Policy Perspective*, 7 (2): 1–4.

Fritsch, S. (2011). Technology and Global Affairs. *International Studies Perspectives*, 12: 27–45.

Galyardt, A., Gupta, R., DeCapria, D., Kanal, E., and Ettinger, J. (2019). Artificial Intelligence and Cyber-Intelligence: An Implementation Guide. Available at https://resources.sei.cmu.edu/asset_files/EducationalMaterial/2019_011_001_548767.pdf.

Gu, T., Dolan-Gavitt, B., and Garg, S. (2019). BadNets: Identifying Vulnerabilities in the Machine Learning Model Supply Chain. Available at https://arxiv.org/pdf/1708.06733.pdf.

Haas, M. C. and Fischer, S. C. (2017). The Evolution of Targeted Killing Practices: Autonomous Weapons, Future Conflict, and the International Order. *Contemporary Security Policy*, 38(2): 281–306.

Jasanoff, S. (2004). *States of Knowledge: The Co-Production of Science and the Social Order*. London and New York: Routledge.

Kello, L. (2017). *The Virtual Weapon and International Order*. New Haven, CT: Yale University Press.

Knight, W. (2019). Even the AI Behind Deepfakes Can't Save Us From Being Duped. *Wired*. Available at www.wired.com/story/ai-deepfakes-cant-save-us-duped/.

Kostyuk, N., and Zhukov, Y. M. (2019). Invisible Digital Front: Can Low-Level Cyber Operations Shape Battlefield Events? *Journal of Conflict Resolution*, 63: 317–347.

Kralingen, M. V. (2016). Use of Weapons: Should We Ban the Development of Autonomous Weapons Systems? *The International Journal of Intelligence, Security, and Public Affairs*, 18(2): 32–156.

Lindsay, J. R. (2015). Tipping the Scales: The Attribution Problem and the Feasibility of Deterrence against Cyberattack. *Journal of Cybersecurity*, 1(1): 53–67.

Lindsay, J. R. (2017). Restrained by Design: The Political Economy of Cybersecurity. *Digital Policy, Regulation and Governance*, 19: 493–514.

Lindsay, J. R. (2020). Demystifying the Quantum Threat: Infrastructure, Institutions, and Intelligence Advantage. *Strategic Studies*, 29(2): 335–361.

Maness, R. and Valeriano, B. (2019). See The Dataset Under. Available at https://drryanmaness.wixsite.com/cyberconflict/cyber-conflict-dataset

Maschmeyer, L. (2020). *Slow Burn: Cyber Conflict and Subversion in Ukraine*. Working Paper, 3 September 2020.

McCarthy, D. (ed.) (2018). *Technology and World Politics: And Introduction*. London: Routledge.

Miller, C., and Wyborn, C. (2020). Co-Production in Global Sustainability: Histories and Theories. *Environmental Science & Policy*, 113, 88–95. https://doi.org/10.1016/j.envsci.2018.01.016

OECD.AI Policy Observatory (2020). National AI Policies and Strategies. Available at https://oecd.ai/policy-areas

Patel, A., Hatzakis, T., Macnish, K., Ryan, M., and Kirichenko, A. (2019). Security Issues, Dangers and Implications of Smart Information Systems. Sherpa Project D1.3. Available at https://dmu.figshare.com/articles/D1_3_Cyberthreats_and_countermeasures/7951292

Sentonas (2017). Available at www.crowdstrike.com/blog/how-artificial-intelligence-is-becoming-a-key-weapon-in-the-cyber-security-war

Slayton, R. (2016/17). What Is the Cyber Offense-Defense Balance? Conceptions, Causes, and Assessment. *International Security*, 41(3), 72–109.

Spring, J. M., Fallon, J., Galyardt, A., Horneman, A., Metcalf, L., and Stoner, E. (2019). Machine Learning in Cyber-Security: A Guide. SEI Carnegie Mellon Technical Report CMU/SEI-2019-TR-005. Available at https://resources.sei.cmu.edu/asset_files/TechnicalReport/2019_005_001_633597.pdf.

Stoecklin, M. P. (2018). DeepLocker: How AI Can Power a Stealthy New Breed of Malware. Available at https://securityintelligence.com/deeplocker-how-ai-can-power-a-stealthy-new-breed-of-malware/.

Von Solms, R., and Van Niekerk, J. (2013). From Information Security to Cyber Security. *Computers & Security*, 38, 97–102.
Xin, Y., Kong, L., Liu, Z., Chen, Y., et al. (2018). Machine Learning and Deep Learning Methods for Cybersecurity. *IEEE Access*, 6, 35365–35381.
Zetter, K. (2019). Researchers Easily Trick Cylance's AI-Based Antivirus Into Thinking Malware Is 'Goodware'. Motherboard. Available at www.vice.com/en_us/article/9kxp83/researchers-easily-trick-cylances-ai-based-antivirus-into-thinking-malware-is-goodware.

15
Lethal autonomous weapons systems

Frank Sauer

As a field of research as well as an issue of diplomatic concern, autonomous weapons and questions surrounding their potential international regulation have undergone a remarkable development. What began in the early 2000s (Altmann, 2004, p. 71) as an academic niche concern, ended up high on the UN's arms control agenda not even ten years later. That is a steep trajectory, especially when compared to other arms control and disarmament issues and considering that autonomy in weapons system was only in its nascency when the UN addressed it in 2013. Any regulatory actions at the time would for the most part have been preventive. The UN context is also where the issue of weapon autonomy received the by now (unfortunately) common moniker "Lethal Autonomous Weapons Systems" – "LAWS", for short.

After having made its way to from academia into international arms control and disarmament fora, the issue gathered considerable interest in the media and in the general public as well – there was barely a newspaper article or TV broadcast on the topic that was not accompanied by the eye-catching metal grin of the Terminator.

LAWS attract interest from various scholarly disciplines. Today, there is a large body of literature analyzing weapon autonomy and its implications not only from engineering and computer science angles but from the perspective of international humanitarian law (IHL), international human rights law (IHRL), moral philosophy, arms control, and international norm development, to name just the most prominent fields of research.

Weapon autonomy is widely considered a military development of paramount importance. It has been aptly described as "the third revolution in warfare, after gunpowder and nuclear arms" (FLI, 2015) and arguably represents, in a sense of literally raising questions of life and death, the most consequential application of artificial intelligence (AI) in a military context. It seems safe to say that in the same way militaries were keen to adopt the steam engine, electricity, or electronics in the past, they hope to benefit in an equal manner from the transformative promise that AI holds today (DSB, 2016, pp. 6–11; Horowitz et al., 2018, pp. 3–5; Kania, 2020).

AI is a broad concept, with no uniform definition, and the goalposts of what is considered artificially intelligent are constantly shifting – yesterday's monumental AI breakthrough (such as computers playing chess) is just ordinary software today. A good rule of thumb – and the working definition adopted for this chapter – is to think of AI as allowing the automation of tasks that previously required human intelligence to complete.

The chapter will first outline the characteristics of weapon autonomy and identify the main advantages and opportunities connected to it from a military point of view. Then, the main challenges and criticisms will be presented, highlighting key contributors to that particular, interdisciplinary debate which by now has spanned the last 15 years. Afterwards, the emergence and the intricacies of the current focal point of the debate, namely the notion that LAWS require the retention of some form of human control over the use of force, will be discussed in more depth. Contributions from international relations (IR) scholars focusing on the development of the social norms and practices surrounding LAWS are presented in the subsequent, next-to-last section. Finally, the conclusion discusses potential future developments to be anticipated in terms of regulation and new international law.

Weapon autonomy: what is it, and what are the military incentives for increasing it?

The term "Lethal Autonomous Weapons Systems" is awkward. After all, neither "lethality" nor "autonomy" are decisive factors with regard to what is at stake. The military application of non-lethal force raises legal and ethical concerns as well (take the preventive prohibition against non-lethal, blinding laser weapons [Rosert and Sauer, 2020, pp. 6–9] as just one example), and the term autonomy is, philosophically speaking, inappropriately anthropomorphizing machines which have limited agency and are incapable of reasoning and reflecting as well as unable to take on responsibility. However, at this point the term LAWS is widely used as shorthand, as are notions such as "machines making decisions", and so this chapter will make use of them as well.

What is this – steadily increasing – "autonomy" in weapons systems? (Boulanin, 2016; Boulanin and Verbruggen, 2017; Roff, 2016). To conceptualize weapon autonomy, a functional understanding has found broad acceptance in scholarly literature. It is also gaining traction in the diplomatic debate at the UN's Convention on Certain Conventional Weapons (CCW) in Geneva, the main venue for the international discussion about a possible international regulation as well as a regular meeting place for scholars working on the issue. The functional understanding has emerged and found acceptance not least because two powerful voices in the LAWS discourse, the United States and the International Committee of the Red Cross (ICRC), have adopted it (DoD, 2017 [2012]; ICRC, 2016; Scharre, 2018).

From a functionalist point of view, the issue is best understood as one of autonomy *in* a weapons system, that is, of the machine rather than a human performing a certain function (or certain functions) during the system's operation (Boulanin and Verbruggen, 2017). One of the upshots of focusing solely on who – human – or what – machine – is performing specific functions is that separate definitions for "autonomy" and "automation" are not required. After all, there exists no clear delineation even in technical and engineering disciplines. In fact, the two terms can be – and often are – used interchangeably. A good example is the case of self-driving cars: The international Society of Automotive Engineers, for instance, stipulates six levels of driving automation while at the same time describing Level 5 as full vehicle autonomy.

A functionalist can also remain agnostic regarding the underlying technology that enables a system's autonomous functionality. Obviously, it is the various techniques and solutions spun into the military from the constantly ongoing civilian innovations in the field of AI that enable an increase in weapon automation (Horowitz, 2018, p. 39), that is, the weapon performing a variety of comparably complicated tasks with minimal or no human assistance or supervision. Computer vision would be the most prominent example for such a spin-in of commercial technology into the realm of military applications. But what matters from a functionalist point of view is solely that the task is performed by the machine, not how exactly it is enabled to do so – in other words, there is no need to get into the technological weeds to conceptualize what weapon autonomy is about.

Where and how exactly is autonomy in weapons systems taking effect? Every military operation concluding with an attack on a target can be systematized along discrete steps of a "kill chain" or "targeting cycle" (iPRAW, 2019). This includes a list of functions, namely finding, fixing, tracking, selecting, and engaging the target (as well as assessing the effects afterwards). A weapon which operates autonomously completes this entire targeting cycle – including the final stages of selecting and engaging the target with force – without human intervention (or supervision). A particular focus in the debate about LAWS lies on those last two functions, which the ICRC calls "critical functions" (ICRC, 2016, p. 7). That is because most of the political, legal, and ethical risks currently being scrutinized with regard to weapon autonomy derive from handing the control over the use of force from a human to a machine. Those will be discussed in the next section.

Weapon autonomy, including the critical functions, is not new, but recent innovations in AI allow its development and application on a much larger scale. In effect, it is only recently that autonomous targeting has started to leave its former military niche applications (the most prominent case being terminal defense systems used to quickly fire at incoming munitions) and become adopted across the board.

What is the major incentive for increasing autonomy? There is a whole range of driving factors behind it. Ronald Arkin at a very early stage introduced the notion that weapon autonomy would render warfare more humane overall. Machines know no fear, stress, or fatigue and are devoid of negative human emotions; they don't overreact, and they lack a self-preservation instinct. So even in the case of a surprise attack they could delay returning fire, the argument goes. They supposedly not only allow for greater restraint but eventually better discrimination between civilians and combatants as well, thus resulting in the potential to apply military force in stricter accordance with the rules of IHL (Arkin, 2009, 2010, 2012; Reeves, 2020).

Observers who expect autonomy to allow for an overall increase in IHL compliance despite current technical shortcomings – such as Kenneth Anderson and Andrew Waxman – generally argue in a two-step fashion. Such weapons, at first, would be used only in circumstances where no civilians or civilian infrastructure are present, thus removing the necessity of the machine having to discriminate between lawful and unlawful targets. Technology would later on, in a second step, have matured enough to fix the compliance issue and thus render the system able to perform IHL compliance on at least a human level on its own (Anderson et al., 2014, pp. 405–406; Anderson and Waxman, 2013, pp. 11–13; Schmitt and Thurnher, 2013, pp. 246–248).

A key feature of weapon autonomy is that it renders constant communication and control links optional. This yields several effects, all of which are best analyzed in the body of work put forward by Paul Scharre: One, if a system does not necessarily have to communicate with human operators, it can complete its mission even in situations where communication is degraded or denied and do so in a "radio silent" manner, rendering it harder for an adversary to detect. Autonomy thus adds to the overall military effort to manage the signatures of weapons systems and make them stealthier. Two, making human input optional is increasing force multiplication. In other words, one human can operate more than one, maybe even dozens, system at the same time. Autonomy-derived force multiplication could thus result in either a reduction of personnel costs or an increased effectiveness with the same body of personnel. Three, autonomy also allows for a large number of systems to move and operate in a coordinated manner. What is known as "swarming" describes a flock of systems implementing the three simple rules of separation, alignment, and cohesion during operation. This means that they avoid crowding and at the same time steer towards the average heading and position of their neighbors. The emergent behavior of such configurations of multiple weapons systems opens up a range of new possibilities because swarms are able to perform anti-access/area-denial missions or overwhelm an enemy's defenses. They are also, especially when consisting of numerous small systems, hard to defend against cost-effectively. Lastly, the most important incentive – and arguably the key driver for increasing weapon autonomy – is the increase in operational speed. The weapon functioning autonomously means that it completes the targeting cycle, that is, it fights, "at machine speed". This will always give it the upper hand over (remotely) human-operated weapons (Altmann and Sauer, 2017; Ekelhof and Persi Paoli, 2020a; Horowitz, 2019; Lachow, 2017; Scharre, 2014; Scharre, 2020, pp. 61–63, 105–110; Verbruggen, 2019).

Main criticisms: technological, ethical, legal, and strategic concerns

One of the earliest critics of autonomy in weapons systems was Noel Sharkey. As a roboticist, Sharkey was appalled by the prospect of the technology he helped develop being used for fighting wars. More importantly, he was deeply skeptical of the intended-use cases he found in publicly available military plans and road maps; he suspected political and military decision-makers were not sufficiently aware of the limits of the technology they intended to deploy, arguing: "Policymakers seem to have an understanding of AI that lies in the realms of science fiction and myth" (Sharkey, 2007). The inability of current-state AI systems to discriminate between combatants and innocent civilians and thus the inability to comply with IHL was – and remains – one of the key reasons for Sharkey (2008) to argue for a prohibition of weapon autonomy and a legally binding obligation to retain human control over weapons systems.

A second LAWS critic of the first hour was moral philosopher Rob Sparrow. He framed his skepticism about the real-world capacities of autonomous weapons in a set of more refined arguments, combining ethical and legal considerations. Drawing on just war theory in a path-breaking piece in 2007, Sparrow argued that a key requirement of fighting a just war is that a human being can be held responsible for the deaths occurring. However, with weapons operating autonomously over extended periods of time, it is unclear where the responsibility for killing eventually comes to rest. Since punishing the machine would be meaningless and punishing the commanding officer for actions of a machine she had no control over would be unfair, it followed for Sparrow that fielding autonomous systems would be inacceptable (Sparrow, 2007, 2009, 2015, 2016).

An early comprehensive overview over the state of the art of relevant military technology, legal, and ethical implications and potential future scenarios was put forward by Armin Krishnan (2009). In his book, four years before LAWS would even start entering the UN's arms control discussions, he already acknowledged the immense challenge of achieving regulation on the issue due to the revolutionary impact ascribed to robotics and automation by the military. He observed that:

> [i]t would be both ethically questionable and militarily unwise for Western states to simply renounce the use of armed military robots completely. At the same time, it would be very complacent and irresponsible to leave such a potentially very powerful military technology like military robotics largely unregulated", warning that "it will be challenging to bypass the various roads to hell.
>
> *(Krishnan, 2009, pp. 158, 167)*

Sparrow's, 2007 argument came to be known more widely – and was in fact popularized in the LAWS debate and beyond – as "the accountability gap". It was put forward more prominently and elaborated on extensively by Bonnie Docherty in her reports for Human Rights Watch (HRW) and the international Campaign to Stop Killer Robots. To derive a need for new international law from moral concerns and legal considerations not yet addressed explicitly in the existing body of international law, the Campaign leveraged the "Martens Clause" contained in various international legal documents. It states that "[i]n cases not covered [by] international agreements, civilians and combatants remain under the protection and authority of the principles of international law derived from established custom, from the principles of humanity and from the dictates of public conscience" (HRW, 2012, 2015). The potential harm to civilians resulting from the inability of LAWS to comply with the principle of discrimination contained in IHL in combination with the accountability gap formed the point of departure for the Campaign's work in diplomatic fora as well as in alerting and informing the general public.

Peter Asaro's work further illuminated the moral groundings of the legal case against LAWS by pointing out that "[u]nderlying the whole of body of law, and particular expressions of law, we find morality . . . and many legal norms coincide with moral norms" (Asaro, 2016, p. 371). A key contribution made by the philosopher Asaro is fully fleshing out a notion that was introduced to the UN by Special Rapporteur Christof Heyns (2013, p. 17), when LAWS were briefly discussed in the UN's Human Right Council, and in some more depth discussed early on by Mark Gubrud (2014). It is the notion that delegating life-and-death decisions on the battlefield to a machine infringes on the human dignity of the person being killed. This line of thought was later picked up not only by other scholars (Rosert and Sauer, 2019; Sparrow, 2016) but also the International Committee of the Red Cross (ICRC, 2016) which lent weight to it in the diplomatic arena of the UN. Asaro argued (2016, p. 385) that "[i]n the absence of an intentional and meaningful decision to use violence, the resulting deaths are meaningless and arbitrary". From this he derived the general duty "not to delegate to a machine or automated process the authority or capability to initiate the use of lethal force independently of human determinations of its moral and legal legitimacy in each and every case" (Asaro, 2012, p. 688). Finding a "technological fix" for LAWS' lack of IHL compliance is rendered immaterial by this much more fundamental objection by Asaro, Gubrud, Heyns, and others because it stipulates that delegating the decision to kill another human being to a machine is an evil in itself.

Paul Scharre was among the first to acknowledge and analyze the operational risks conjured up by fighting at machine speed. Drawing on the theory of "normal accidents" (Perrow, 1984), Scharre identified the risk of unintended escalation arising from unforeseen (inter-)actions of automated complex systems, making him one of the first scholars to explicitly spell out the risk of a "flash war" triggered algorithmically and at a pace that renders human intervention impossible. He thus identified the important potential of – and requirement for – humans remaining in the targeting cycle as a fail-safe mechanism and argued for man-unmanned teaming or "centaur warfighting" as a solution (Scharre, 2016; see also Scharre, 2019).

Physicist Jürgen Altmann and political scientist Frank Sauer later developed these notions further by mapping the risks identified by Scharre onto the strategic notions of arms race and crisis instability (Altmann and Sauer, 2017). This strand of the literature also analyzes the deeper implications of relying on AI and machine learning to operate weapons systems in the field, pointing out the specific limits and idiosyncrasies of the underlying technology, for instance regarding computer vision (Sauer, 2020). It is not only that; as the technology currently and for the foreseeable future stands, computer vision is unable to understand situational and social context, rendering its application error-prone with regard to appropriate action in unclear or ambiguous scenarios. What is more, every military will of course additionally try deception tactics and tamper with the autonomous systems of its adversary. Research on "adversarial examples" within the field of AI (Evtimov et al., 2017) suggests that computer vision will thus render LAWS uniquely susceptible to deception and spoofing (see, as only one example, the by now famous example of the turtle mistaken for a rifle, Athalye et al., 2017).

With their confluence model of deontologist (LAWS' current incompliance with IHL and their fundamental violation of the human right to dignity) as well as consequentialist arguments (LAWS' detrimental effects on international peace and stability), Daniele Amoroso and Guglielmo Tamburrini presented one of the strongest comprehensive scholarly combinations of ethical and legal considerations in critique of LAWS. Their work underlines the need to retain human control over weapons systems and suggests, by drawing on earlier work by Sharkey, thinking about this along the lines of levels of interaction between humans and machines – not unlike the levels of driving automation used in the automotive industry. The legal scholar Amoroso and the philosopher Tamburrini were also among the first to popularize the insight that operationalizing human control for weapons systems would have to depend on operational context and that there is no "one-size-fits-all" solution (Amoroso and Tamburrini, 2017, 2019). The current state of the debate about human control and how to implement it in practice is picked up in the next section.

A particularly original point of view was recently presented by computer scientists and human–machine interaction expert Missy Cummings (2020b) who expressed doubts about the actual transformative potential of AI in the military, harking back again to the technological skepticism accompanying some strands of the debate since the earliest days of Sharkey's warning about the limited applicability of AI in 2007. Cummings draws direct parallels to the commercial world, where current progress in AI and especially machine learning, while delivering qualified successes, has at the same time been completely overhyped – all whilst remaining "brittle" and limited in its application (Cummings, 2020a; on brittleness see also Marcus, 2018), even in its most advanced implementations such as computer vision. She highlights as a key example the automotive industry's overpromising on self-driving cars. "The inability of AI to handle uncertainty raises serious questions about how successful it will be in military settings", she points out (Cummings, 2020b). What is more, the hype spilling over from the civilian into the military world, she suggests, could lead countries to merely pretend to have AI capabilities – a "fake it till you make it" phenomenon sometimes also called fauxtomation in the commercial world, when start-up companies pretend to have developed some new "AI" product while actually selling customers either ordinary software or cheap human labor disguised as results derived from AI. Within the current geopolitical framework of the renewed great power rivalry between the US, China, and Russia, in combination with an uncurbed arms race, an overly hasty striven for AI-enabled armed forces and the accompanying pretension might end up perpetuating mutual misperceptions and unnecessarily inflating threat assessments. Quite ironically then, according to Cummings, the detrimental results for international peace and stability might be similar to what authors such as Scharre, Altmann, and Sauer expected, even though the revolutionary potential of military AI is largely overhyped and in reality much more limited than what most policymakers, military planners, and observers acknowledge.

Human control: the focal point of the LAWS debate

That dealing with the legal, ethical, and operational risks raises by LAWS would require an effort to retain human control and prevent full autonomy across the board was an insight early on in the discussion. In fact, the demand that "[h]umans should . . . retain control over the choice to use deadly force" was already contained in Bonny Docherty's very first report for

Human Rights Watch with which the Campaign to Stop Killer Robots was kicked off (HRW, 2012, p. 37). Nevertheless, the Campaign, modeling its key message after past humanitarian disarmament successes such as the bans achieved on anti-personnel landmines and cluster munitions, for the longest time kept framing the issue primarily as one of "banning killer robots".

Categorizing a type of weapon, counting, capping, and reducing its numbers or banning them altogether are tried-and-tested approaches in both nuclear and conventional arms control as well as humanitarian disarmament. However, this quantitative paradigm is not applicable in the case of LAWS.

The functional view on weapon autonomy suggests that the problem begins with conceiving of LAWS as a category. In other words, aside from the fact that maturing technology will make it possible to endow almost every weapons system with some capability of operating without human input, autonomy in military terms is a platform- and technology-agnostic function in a system of systems. Consequently, the degree of autonomy in any given component in this system of systems may vary from time to time; in other words, it may vary between different tasks performed by the same human–machine system. Activating autonomous mode, to put it bluntly, could be nothing but a checkbox ticked in the interface of a weapon's operation system at any point in time, rendering LAWS virtually indiscernible from remotely operated weapons by merely inspecting them from the outside. In sum, discerning "LAWS" (bad) from "not-LAWS" (good) in a categorical sense is simply not possible. The actual substance of the LAWS discussion is thus not one about a specific type of weapon; it is one about the coming human–machine relationship in 21st-century warfare (Rosert and Sauer, 2020, p. 14). Physicist Mark Gubrud (2014, p. 37) was one of the first scholars to point this insight out in unmistakably clear terms:

> Instead of arguing about how to define what weapons should be banned, it may be better to agree on basic principles. One is that any use of violent force, lethal or non-lethal, must be by human decision and must at all times be under human control.

In reports published by the British non-governmental organization (NGO) Article 36 (Moyes, 2016; Roff and Moyes, 2016), a leading member of the international Campaign to Stop Killer Robots, Richard Moyes and Heather Roff later developed this basic principle further by coining the term "meaningful human control". Roff and Moyes popularized the insight amongst scholars and diplomats that merely calling for "appropriate human judgment", the way the US's official doctrine on weapon autonomy does (DoD, 2017 [2012]), might not be sufficient and runs the risk of eventually diluting human involvement to a legally and ethically inacceptable degree. After all, in some cases not-human judgment might be considered "appropriate". "[A] human simply pressing a 'fire' button in response to indications from a computer, without cognitive clarity or awareness, is not sufficient to be considered 'human control' in a substantive sense", they argued (Roff and Moyes, 2016, p. 1), calling for a form of human control that is more substantial or "meaningful". Key requirements introduced by Moyes and Roff, among them that the technology used be predictable and reliable, that accurate information be provided to the user to give her situational awareness, and that there is an option for timely human intervention as well as that the human–machine relationship should generally speaking be conceived of as dependent on the context of use, remain key pillars of the debate LAWS and human control.

It is worth noting, however, that the introduction of the concept of meaningful human control was also met with criticism. For instance, Rebecca Crootof warned against sacrificing "potential gains in human safety" derived from weapon autonomy "to an overly-strict interpretation of what constitutes meaningful human control" (Crootof, 2016, p. 62). Clearly, the concept would never be politically accepted as a prompt to fall back behind the levels of automation in military systems already in existence. Various types of weapons, from the aforementioned terminal defense systems to cruise missiles to smart artillery shells, have been deployed for decades without human control or direct input regarding final target selection and engagement. Critics such as Crootof were of course right in pointing out that implementing (meaningful) human control should not be taken to mean (a return to) constant and direct human manipulation at all times.

This prompted forward-looking proponents of human control to work toward a more refined conceptualization of what meaningful human control could be and what it would look like depending on various circumstances on the modern battlefield. The International Panel on the Regulation of Autonomous Weapons (iPRAW), an independent expert group supported by the German government to advise the international community at the UN (and of which, full disclaimer, the author is a member), picked up where Moyes and Roff left off and suggested perceiving of human control as operationalizable both "in design" and "in use", that is, during the construction and setup as well as the operation of a weapons system (iPRAW, 2019).

This approach of differentiating between control in design and in use suggested by iPRAW is just one among several attempts to develop a coherent framework that acknowledges the shift of focus towards human control that Roff and Moyes had initiated. In the diplomatic language of the discussion at the CCW, the shorthand for the theoretical and practical goal of operationalizing human control became known as working on "the human element" or "human–machine touchpoints". This was accompanied by the notion that control would have to play a role over the entire "lifecycle" of a weapons systems – including political direction, research and development, testing, certification, deployment, use and post-use assessment (CCW, 2018, p. 13).

Merel Ekelhof and Giacomo Persi Paoli's (2020b) "iceberg model", published in a report for United Nations Institute for Disarmament Research (UNIDIR), aimed to capture exactly this holistic approach in more depth by outlining that autonomy and human control do not become relevant later, as during the system's operation, but earlier, in phases of the multi-tiered targeting process that contains various political, legal, and operational elements (see also Ekelhof, 2019).

Similarly, Ilse Verdiesen, Filippo Santoni de Sio, and Virginia Dignum proposed a comprehensive framework encompassing three concentric circles of engineering, sociotechnical, and governance perspectives on control. For any system to remain under control, their "technical layer describes the technical conditions required", their "socio-technical layer describes the operators' psychological and motivational conditions", and their "governance layer describes the political and institutional conditions and the oversight mechanisms required" (Verdiesen et al., 2021, pp. 15–16).

Lastly, a sophisticated and at the same time very elegant approach to human control was recently introduced by the ICRC and the Stockholm International Peace Research Institute (SIPRI). In their report, Vincent Boulanin, Neil Davison, Netta Goussac, and Moa Peldán Carlsson structure human control according to the who, what, when, and how:

> (1) Who is/are the human/s in control? The operator directly using the AWS, the commander in charge of the attack, the people in the broader command and control structure, or a combination of these? (2) What is under human control? The AWS as a whole, the critical functions of selecting and applying force to targets, or the consequences of the specific attack? (3) When should human control be exercised? Up to the point of activation of the AWS only, or during its operation as well? (4) How should human control be exercised? What form should the control take?
>
> *(Vincent Boulanin et al., 2020, p. 23)*

Important contributions to the field of international norm research

Scholars of IR took an almost immediate interest in the calls for a ban on weapon autonomy from different epistemic communities, the subsequent forming of the Campaign to Stop Killer Robots, and the emergence of the "proto-norm" of human control over the use of force.

Charli Carpenter (2011) analyzed "why" and "how" some issues become adopted by transnational advocacy movements whereas others remain overlooked. She highlighted especially the vetting power of key nodes – such as HRW and the ICRC – in international human disarmament advocacy networks. By conducting interviews with some of the scholars raising alarm about LAWS as well as members of the NGO community adopting "killer robots" as a new humanitarian disarmament issue, and by observing the diplomatic discussions at the UN herself for her book *Lost Causes*, Carpenter reconstructed how LAWS made their way out of the ivory tower and on to the top of the human security agenda (Carpenter, 2014, pp. 88–122).

By conducting a systematic comparative analysis of the process on LAWS and the two previous, successful weapons regulation campaigns against blinding laser weapons and anti-personnel landmines, Elvira Rosert and Frank Sauer concluded in her work that the messaging focus on civilian harm and the inability of LAWS to comply with the IHL principle of discrimination as well as the call for a "ban on killer robots" are suboptimal strategies for the Campaign to Stop Killer Robots. They suggested prioritizing fundamental ethical objections over IHL concerns and a focus on human dignity; and they argued that, instead of assuming that "killer robots" are a definable, bannable category of weapons, the Campaign would benefit from doubling down on and further strengthening its call for meaningful human control (HRW, 2020; Rosert and Sauer, 2019, 2020).

Criticizing constructivist approaches in IR for privileging deliberation over practice with regard to analyzing the emergence of norms, Ingvild Bode and Hendrik Huelss offer an analytical perspective focused on procedures and practices in which normativity surrounding LAWS emerges from their development, testing, and deployment. "Regardless of whether a ban will or will not be imposed, the practice of [L]AWS will already shape understandings of what is appropriate and thereby take the place of a more profound societal-political debate on what is normatively acceptable", they conclude (Bode and Huelss, 2018, p. 21).

Lastly, Denise Garcia's contributions from a perspective of global governance and international law shed light not only on the conditions for the emergence of what she calls "humanitarian security regimes". What is more, Garcia's work explicitly ties the discussion on regulating LAWS and the accumulation of collective risks (not unlike the ones emerging from nuclear weapons) to wider notions of "preventive security governance" and a clear normative interest in global peace and stability as well as a fostering of the "common good" for all of humanity (Garcia, 2015, 2016, 2018).

Conclusion: prospects for (international) regulation

The introductory section of this chapter described the swift climb that LAWS performed on the international arms control agenda. The discussion about a possible regulation of LAWS, and thus the creation of new international law to ensure the retention of human control over the use of force, has been underway since 2013 within the framework of the CCW. Seven years is not a long time in UN terms. At least, that's what the comparison to other arms control and humanitarian disarmament processes suggests. Efforts to ban cluster munitions, for instance, were beginning, somewhat depending on where one chooses to locate the earliest discussions, decades before the convention eventually entered into force in 2010.

Since 2013, thousands of scientists and representatives of civilian technology companies, the drivers of innovation in the field of AI, have sided with the NGOs assembled in the Campaign to Stop Killer Robots in warning about a potentially very dangerous paradigm shift in warfare. One of the most prominent warning voices was the late Stephen Hawking; others are Demis Hassabis and Mustafa Suleyman – the founders of Google's AI development company DeepMind – and Elon Musk. Physicist Max Tegmark and his Future of Life Institute facilitated open letters calling on the international community at the UN to act preventively (FLI, 2015, 2017).

However, it is not only the 2020 SARS-CoV-2 pandemic that has decelerated the deliberative process around LAWS at the CCW in Geneva. Regulating autonomy in weapons systems is especially difficult due to the enormous military significance ascribed to it, not solely but especially by the great powers. This sets LAWS apart from successful regulatory processes of the recent past, such as the aforementioned cluster munitions, anti-personnel landmines, or blinding laser weapons, with the latter one being achieved within the CCW framework. Modern military surveillance and weapons systems render landmines and cluster munitions dispensable, and blinding lasers always represented somewhat of an exotic capability that great powers could forego without great perceived military costs. Weapon autonomy is, Missy Cummings' skepticism about AI's true transformative potential notwithstanding, perceived differently by policymakers and military planners. As it currently stands, it appears as a development that simply is without alternative to most – just as Armin Krishnan foresaw in his 2009 book.

In addition, geopolitics in general are currently not conducive to achieving new arms control and disarmament breakthroughs. Existing multilateral and bilateral agreements and treaties are eroding, with some already lost – this list includes the terminated Intermediate Range Nuclear Forces Treaty (INF), the faltering Joint Comprehensive Plan of Action (JCPOA) with Iran, the contested Open Skies Treaty and, potentially soon, NewSTART – the only remaining bilateral nuclear arms control treaty between Russia and the United States. Getting a new binding international legal instrument out of the United Nations' CCW would be challenging in a normal, less frosty geopolitical landscape. The current global arms control winter makes it seem almost impossible.

One widely shared anticipation for the future deriving from the current state of affairs is that the LAWS process might end up leaving the UN framework at the end of 2021 – just as cluster munitions and landmine processes have done. The UN's CCW would – once again – have just served as an incubator. Historically, these stand-alone humanitarian disarmament efforts benefited from a critical mass of willing states as well as a "champion state" (Garcia, 2015) spearheading the movement. But with some 30 CCW States Parties currently calling for new international law, the momentum is not quite big enough yet; and while the "ABC-Group" consisting of Austria, Brazil, and Chile is consistently very vocal at the UN, a true champion state has not emerged yet either. Other regulatory actions are conceivable, of course: softer options range from a politically binding code of conduct to non-binding declarations to the simple sharing of best practices. And various kinds of laws, policies, and doctrines are possible domestically (Hynek and Solovyeva, 2021). But, with the way things stood at the end of 2020, the chances for achieving a broadly shared international, legally binding regulation are slim.

References

Altmann, J. (2004) 'Military Uses of Nanotechnology: Perspectives and Concerns', *Security Dialogue*, vol. 35, no. 1, pp. 61–79.

Altmann, J. and Sauer, F. (2017) 'Autonomous Weapon Systems and Strategic Stability', *Survival*, vol. 59, no. 5, pp. 117–142.

Amoroso, D. and Tamburrini, G. (2017) 'The Ethical and Legal Case Against Autonomy in Weapons Systems', *Global Jurist*, vol. 18, no. 1. https://doi.org/10.1515/gj-2017-0012.

Amoroso, D. and Tamburrini, G. (2019) *What Makes Human Control Over Weapon Systems "Meaningful"?* [Online]. Available at https://www.icrac.net/wp-content/uploads/2019/08/Amoroso-Tamburrini_Human-Control_ICRAC-WP4.pdf (Accessed 12 February 2019).

Anderson, K., Reisner, D. and Waxman, M. (2014) 'Adapting the Law of Armed Conflict to Autonomous Weapon Systems', *International Law Studies*, vol. 90, no. 386, pp. 386–411.

Anderson, K. and Waxman, M. (2013) *Law and Ethics for Autonomous Weapon Systems: Why a Ban Won't Work and How the Laws of War Can*, The Hoover Institution, Stanford University: Jean Perkins Task Force on National Security and Law Essay Series.

Arkin, R. C. (2009) 'Ethical Robots in Warfare', *IEEE Technology and Society Magazine*, vol. 28, no. 1, pp. 30–33.

Arkin, R. C. (2010) 'The Case for Ethical Autonomy in Unmanned Systems', *Journal of Military Ethics*, vol. 9, no. 4, pp. 332–341.

Arkin, R. C. (2012) 'Governing Lethal Behavior in Robots [T&S Interview]', *Technology and Society Magazine, IEEE*, vol. 30, no. 4, pp. 7–11.

Asaro, P. (2012) 'On Banning Autonomous Weapon Systems: Human Rights, Automation, and the Dehumanization of Lethal Decision-Making', *International Review of the Red Cross*, vol. 94, no. 886, pp. 687–709.

Asaro, P. (2016) 'Jus Nascendi, Robotic Weapons, and the Martens Clause', in Ryan Calo, A. Michael Froomkin and Ian Kerr (eds.), *Robot Law*, Cheltenham: Edward Elgar Publishing, pp. 367–386.

Athalye, A., Engstrom, L., Ilyas, A. and Kwok, K. (2017) *Synthesizing Robust Adverserial Examples* [Online]. Available at https://arxiv.org/pdf/1707.07397.pdf (Accessed 5 February 2018).

Bode, I. and Huelss, H. (2018) 'Autonomous Weapons Systems and Changing Norms in International Relations', *Review of International Studies*, online first, pp. 1–21.

Boulanin, V. (2016) *Mapping the Development of Autonomy in Weapon Systems: A Primer on Autonomy*, Stockholm International Peace Research Institute, SIPRI [Online]. Available at https://www.sipri.org/sites/default/files/Mapping-development-autonomy-in-weapon-systems.pdf (Accessed 17 January 2017).

Boulanin, V., Davison, N., Goussac, N. and Peldán Carlsson, M. (2020) *Limits on Autonomy in Weapon Systems: Identifying Practical Elements of Human Control*, Stockholm International Peace Research Institute [Online]. Available at https://www.sipri.org/sites/default/files/2020-06/2006_limits_of_autonomy.pdf (Accessed 2 June 2020).

Boulanin, V. and Verbruggen, M. (2017) *Mapping the Development of Autonomy in Weapon Systems*, Stockholm International Peace Research Institute, SIPRI [Online]. Available at https://www.sipri.org/sites/default/files/2017-11/siprireport_mapping_the_development_of_autonomy_in_weapon_systems_1117_0.pdf (Accessed 14 November 2017).

Carpenter, R. C. (2011) 'Vetting the Advocacy Agenda: Network Centrality and the Paradox of Weapons Norms', *International Organization*, vol. 65, no. 1, pp. 69–102.

Carpenter, R. C. (2014) *"Lost" Causes: Agenda Vetting in Global Issue Networks and the Shaping of Human Security*, Ithaca, Cornell University Press.

CCW (2018) *Report of the 2018 Session of the Group of Governmental Experts on Emerging Technologies in the Area of Lethal Autonomous Weapons Systems. United Nations Group of Governmental Experts of the High Contracting Parties to the Convention on Prohibitions or Restrictions on the Use of Certain Conventional Weapons Which May Be Deemed to Be Excessively Injurious or to Have Indiscriminate Effects* [Online]. Available at http://undocs.org/en/ccw/gge.1/2018/3 (Accessed 28 October 2020).

Crootof, R. (2016) 'A Meaningful Floor for "Meaningful Human Control"', *Temple International & Comparative Law Journal*, vol. 30, no. 1, pp. 53–62.

Cummings, M. (2020a) 'Rethinking the Maturity of Artificial Intelligence in Safety-Critical Setting', *Association for the Advancement of Artificial Intelligence (AAAI) Magazine* [Online]. Available at https://hal.pratt.duke.edu/sites/hal.pratt.duke.edu/files/u39/2020-min.pdf (Accessed 27 October 2020).

Cummings, M. (2020b) *The AI that Wasn't There: Global Order and the (Mis)Perception of Powerful AI: Texas National Security Review Policy Roundtable: Artificial Intelligence and International Security* [Online]. Available at https://tnsr.org/roundtable/policy-roundtable-artificial-intelligence-and-international-security/ (Accessed 15 June 2020).

DoD (2017 [2012]) *Directive 3000.09: Autonomy in Weapon Systems*, Washington, DC: Department of Defense.

DSB (2016) *Defense Science Board Summer Study on Autonomy*, Washington, DC: Defense Science Board.

Ekelhof, M. (2019) 'Moving Beyond Semantics on Autonomous Weapons: Meaningful Human Control in Operation', *Global Policy*, vol. 48, no. 1, p. 3.

Ekelhof, M. and Persi Paoli, G. (2020a) *Swarm Robotics: Technical and Operational Overview of the Next Generation of Autonomous Systems*, UNIDIR [Online]. Available at https://unidir.org/publication/swarm-robotics-technical-and-operational-overview-next-generation-autonomous-systems (Accessed 14 April 2020).

Ekelhof, M. and Persi Paoli, G. (2020b) *The Human Element in Decisions about the Use of Force*, The United Nations Institute for Disarmament Research [Online]. Available at https://unidir.org/sites/default/files/2020-03/UNIDIR_Iceberg_SinglePages_web.pdf (Accessed 28 October 2020).

Evtimov, I., Eykholt, K., Fernandes, E., Kohno, T., Li, B., Prakash, A., Rahmati, A. and Song, D. (2017) 'Robust Physical-World Attacks on Deep Learning Models', *arxiv.org*, https://arxiv.org/pdf/1707.08945.pdf, arXiv:1707.08945v4.

FLI (2015) *Autonomous Weapons: An Open Letter from AI & Robotics Researchers*, Future of Life Institute [Online]. Available at https://futureoflife.org/open-letter-autonomous-weapons/ (Accessed 31 August 2015).

FLI (2017) *An Open Letter to the United Nations Convention on Certain Conventional Weapons*, Future of Life Institute [Online]. Available at https://futureoflife.org/autonomous-weapons-open-letter-2017/ (Accessed 25 September 2017).

Garcia, D. (2015) 'Humanitarian Security Regimes', *International Affairs*, vol. 91, no. 1, pp. 55–75.

Garcia, D. (2016) 'Future Arms, Technologies, and International Law: Preventive Security Governance', *European Journal of International Security*, vol. 1, no. 1, pp. 94–111.

Garcia, D. (2018) 'Lethal Artificial Intelligence and Change: The Future of International Peace and Security', *International Studies Review*, vol. 20, no. 2, pp. 334–341.

Gubrud, M. (2014) 'Stopping Killer Robots', *Bulletin of the Atomic Scientists*, vol. 70, no. 1, pp. 32–42.

Heyns, C. (2013) *Report of the Special Rapporteur on Extrajudicial, Summary or Arbitrary Executions*, New York: United Nations General Assembly.

Horowitz, M. C. (2018) 'Artificial Intelligence, International Competition, and the Balance of Power', *Texas National Security Review*, vol. 1, no. 3, pp. 37–57 [Online]. DOI: 10.15781/T2639KP49.

Horowitz, M. C. (2019) 'When Speed Kills: Lethal Autonomous Weapon Systems, Deterrence and Stability', *Journal of Strategic Studies*, vol. 42, no. 6, pp. 764–788.

Horowitz, M. C., Allen, G. C., Kania, E. B. and Scharre, P. (2018) *Strategic Competition in an Era of Artificial Intelligence*, CNAS [Online]. Available at https://s3.amazonaws.com/files.cnas.org/documents/CNAS-Strategic-Competition-in-an-Era-of-AI-July-2018_v2.pdf?mtime=20180716122000 (Accessed 25 July 2018).

HRW (2012) *Losing Humanity: The Case against Killer Robots*, Human Rights Watch [Online]. Available at https://www.hrw.org/sites/default/files/reports/arms1112_ForUpload.pdf (Accessed 8 October 2018).

HRW (2015) *Mind the Gap: The Lack of Accountability for Killer Robots*, Human Rights Watch [Online]. Available at https://www.hrw.org/sites/default/files/reports/arms0415_ForUpload_0.pdf (Accessed 31 August 2015).

HRW (2020) *The Need for and Elements of a New Treaty on Fully Autonomous Weapons*, Human Rights Watch [Online]. Available at https://www.hrw.org/sites/default/files/media_2020/06/202006arms_rio_autonomous_weapons_systems_2.pdf (Accessed 29 October 2020).

Hynek, N. and Solovyeva, A. (2021) 'Operations of Power in Autonomous Weapon Systems: Ethical Conditions and Socio-Political Prospects', *AI & Society*, vol. 36, pp. 79–99.

ICRC (2016) *Autonomous Weapon Systems: Implications of Increasing Autonomy in the Critical Functions of Weapons*, Morges: International Committee of the Red Cross.

iPRAW (2019) *Focus on Human Control. iPRAW Report No. 5*, International Panel on the Regulation of Autonomous Weapons [Online]. Available at https://www.ipraw.org/wp-content/uploads/2019/08/2019-08-09_iPRAW_HumanControl.pdf (Accessed 12 February 2019).

Kania, E. B. (2020) *"AI weapons" in China's Military Innovation*, Washington, DC, Brookings: "Global China: Assessing China's Growing Role in the World" [Online]. Available at https://www.brookings.edu/wp-content/uploads/2020/04/FP_20200427_ai_weapons_kania_v2.pdf (Accessed 4 May 2020).

Krishnan, A. (2009) *Killer Robots: Legality and Ethicality of Autonomous Weapons*, Farnham: Ashgate eBook.

Lachow, I. (2017) 'The Upside and Downside of Swarming Drones', *Bulletin of the Atomic Scientist*, vol. 73, no. 2, pp. 96–101.

Marcus, G. (2018) *Deep Learning: A Critical Appraisal* [Online]. Available at https://arxiv.org/ftp/arxiv/papers/1801/1801.00631.pdf (Accessed 5 February 2018).

Moyes, R. (2016) *Key Elements of Meaningful Human Control* [Online]. Available at http://www.article36.org/wp-content/uploads/2016/04/MHC-2016-FINAL.pdf (Accessed 26 September 2017).

Perrow, C. (1984) *Normal Accidents: Living with High-Risk Technologies*, New York, NY, Basic Books.

Reeves, R. (2020) *The Ethical Upside to Artificial Intelligence*, War on the Rocks [Online]. Available at https://warontherocks.com/2020/01/the-ethical-upside-to-artificial-intelligence/ (Accessed 15 June 2020).

Roff, H. M. (2016) *Weapon Autonomy is Rocketing* [Online]. Available at http://foreignpolicy.com/2016/09/28/weapons-autonomy-is-rocketing/ (Accessed 10 May 2016).

Roff, H. M. and Moyes, R. (2016) *Meaningful Human Control, Artificial Intelligence and Autonomous Weapons*, Article 36 [Online]. Available at http://www.article36.org/wp-content/uploads/2016/04/MHC-AI-and-AWS-FINAL.pdf (Accessed 28 October 2020).

Rosert, E. and Sauer, F. (2019) 'Prohibiting Autonomous Weapons: Put Human Dignity First', *Global Policy*, vol. 94, no. 1, p. 42.

Rosert, E. and Sauer, F. (2020) 'How (not) to Stop the Killer Robots: A Comparative Analysis of Humanitarian Disarmament Campaign Strategies', *Contemporary Security Policy*, pp. 1–26.

Sauer, F. (2020) 'Stepping Back from the Brink: Why Regulating Autonomy in Weapons System is Difficult, Yet Imperative and Feasible', *International Review of the Red Cross – Special Issue on "Digital Technologies and War"*.

Scharre, P. (2018) *Army of None: Autonomous Weapons and the Future of War*, New York: W W Norton & Co.

Scharre, P. (2019) *Autonomous Weapons and Stability: Thesis Submitted in Fulfillment of the Requirements for the Degree of Doctor of Philosophy in the Department of War Studies Faculty of Social Science & Public Policy*, London, King's College London [Online]. Available at https://kclpure.kcl.ac.uk/portal/files/129451536/2020_Scharre_Paul_1575997_ethesis.pdf (Accessed 2 June 2020).

Scharre, P. (2020) *Autonomous Weapons and Stability: Thesis Submitted in Fulfillment of the Requirements for the Degree of Doctor of Philosophy*, King's College London [Online]. Available at https://kclpure.kcl.ac.uk/portal/files/129451536/2020_Scharre_Paul_1575997_ethesis.pdf (Accessed 13 June 2020).

Scharre, P. D. (2014) *Robotics on the Battlefield Part II: The Coming Swarm*, Center for a New American Security CNAS [Online]. Available at https://s3.amazonaws.com/files.cnas.org/documents/CNAS_TheComingSwarm_Scharre.pdf?mtime=20160906082059 (Accessed 30 January 2020).

Scharre, P. D. (2016) *Autonomous Weapons and Operational Risk*, Center for New American Security, CNAS Working Papers [Online]. Available at https://s3.amazonaws.com/files.cnas.org/documents/CNAS_Autonomous-weapons-operational-risk.pdf (Accessed 3 January 2016).

Schmitt, M. N. and Thurnher, J. S. (2013) '"Out of the Loop": Autonomous Weapon Systems and the Law of Armed Conflict', *Harvard National Security Journal*, no. 4, pp. 231–281.

Sharkey, N. (2007) 'Robot Wars Are a Reality', *The Guardian* [Online]. Available at https://www.theguardian.com/commentisfree/2007/aug/18/comment.military (Accessed 27 October 2020).

Sharkey, N. (2008) 'Grounds for Discrimination: Autonomous Robot Weapons', *RUSI Defence Systems*, vol. 11, no. 2, pp. 86–89.

Sparrow, R. (2007) 'Killer Robots', *Journal of Applied Philosophy*, vol. 24, no. 1, pp. 62–77.

Sparrow, R. (2009) 'Predators or Plowshares? Arms Control of Robotic Weapons', *Technology and Society Magazine, IEEE*, vol. 28, no. 1, pp. 25–29.

Sparrow, R. (2015) 'Twenty Seconds to Comply: Autonomous Weapons Systems and the Recognition of Surrender', *International Law Studies*, vol. 91, pp. 699–728.

Sparrow, R. (2016) 'Robots and Respect: Assessing the case against Autonomous Weapon Systems', *Ethics & International Affairs*, vol. 30, no. 1, pp. 93–116.

Verbruggen, M. (2019) 'The Question of Swarms Control: Challenges to Ensuring Human Control over Military Swarms', *EU Non-Proliferation and Disarmament Consortium. Non-Proliferation and Disarmament Papers*, no. 65.

Verdiesen, I., Santoni de Sio, F. and Dignum, V. (2021) 'Accountability and Control Over Autonomous Weapon Systems: A Framework for Comprehensive Human Oversight', *Minds and Machines*, vol. 31, pp. 137–163.

16
AI and worldviews in the age of computational power

Massimo Durante

> In Dasein's everydayness the agency through which most things come about is one of which we must say that 'it was no one'.
>
> (Martin Heidegger, *Being and Time*, 165)

The rise of computational power

We live in societies that are increasingly dependent on data processing. Data constitutes resources (inputs) with which we build specific representations of both reality and of ourselves, and these representations inform our decisions and actions (outputs). Data plays an extremely important role in many domains: from economics to politics; from ethics to law; from science to education, etc. We process data for an infinite number of purposes, from the marketing and sales of goods and services, to predicting and influencing network user preferences, promoting political agendas and seeking to sway voter opinions and decisions. We process data to determine a borrower's default risk and to set the terms of a legal sentence; to short-list job applicants for an interview that might change their lives. We process data to provide us with recommendations for books and restaurants, flights and hotels. We rely on data processing in countless circumstances, in order to meet even the minutest needs and demands of our *everyday* life (Durante, 2019; Elliott, 2019; Weinberger, 2019).

What is most striking is that we do almost none of this personally. We mainly entrust such tasks to machines, which use computational models to calculate decisions on our behalf. The availability of ever-increasing computational power (understood here as the power to process inputs and turn them into outputs) characterizes our data-driven societies. Computational power exerts a dramatic effect on our reality, for not only does it profoundly alter our world, but it changes us as well. Computational systems are not just instruments limited to processing data and producing outcomes: this instrumental representation of technology is fundamentally outmoded and inadequate. For reliance on this power also leads to the generation of new forms of knowledge and a different representation of reality: one that is now populated by autonomous artificial agents, smart devices, machines, Deep learning systems and robots. In other words, by an entire range of computational models that are capable of autonomous behavior and decisions. Because it affects our everyday life, computational power modifies and redesigns our forms of life. We are thus called upon to rethink the very concept of technology itself, which can no longer be understood solely in instrumental terms but must be mainly understood in terms of its environmental dimension:

> ICTs are not becoming more intelligent while making us more stupid. Instead, the world is becoming an infosphere increasingly well adapted to the ICTs' limited capacities. Recall how we set up a border wire so that the robot could safely and successfully mow the lawn. In a comparable way, we are adapting the environment to our smart technologies to make sure the latter can interact with it successfully. We are, in other words, wiring or rather enveloping the world.
>
> *(Floridi, 2014, 143)*

This radical transformation affects any agent. All agents need to understand and represent their own reality in order to make decisions and act, lest these decisions and actions be made and performed blindly. This is the case for any system capable of deciding, acting and interacting with the environment: human beings, animals, robots, or whatever other computational system that processes inputs and turns them into outputs. Of course, each computational system has its own way of doing things, depending on its unique knowledge base, prediction and representation of reality, and computing capacity. It is not uncommon for these forms of knowledge, prediction and representation to diverge. At times, they are even contradictory or hard to convey in a common language, based on a general epistemology. Despite these sometimes vast differences, however, such systems are likely to interact; this gives rise to intricate relationships that can have serious and relevant consequences. The result is an unpredictable proliferation of viewpoints – that is, ways of representing, predicting, and understanding reality – that produce diverse visions of the world, which are sometimes hard to make sense of and reconcile. The use of computational power also produces the "power to cleave of the digital" (Floridi, 2017, 123) by which:

> The digital 'cuts and pastes' reality, in the sense that it couples, decouples, or recouples features of the world – and therefore our corresponding assumptions about them – which we never thought could be anything but indivisible and unchangeable. It splits apart and fuses the 'atoms' of our experience and culture, so to speak. It changes the bed of the river, to use a Wittgensteinian metaphor.

Hence, human beings are no longer the only ones to have the capacity to represent, understand, and predict the world and act in it. More or less knowingly and deliberately, we are building a world, in which a multitude of different agents decide, operate, act and interact based on different epistemic models. Some agents operate syntactically, by means of enormous computational power, whereas others operate semantically, by making sense of the world. Some agents take decisions through powerful predictions, based on statistical correlation. Others connect cause and effect, based on the principle of causation. Still others also try to combine different approaches and capacities in new and unexpected ways, even if these ways remained grounded in different types of representation:

> The only real continuity between our old types of models and our new ones is that both are representations of the world. But one is a representation that we have created based on our understanding, a process that works by reducing the complexity of what it encounters. The other is generated by a machine we have created, and into which we have streamed oceans of data about everything we have thought might possibly be worth noticing. The

source, content, structure, and scale of these two types of representations are vastly, disconcertingly different.

(Weinberger, 2019, 62)

In a world of ceaseless interactions between human beings and computational systems, it becomes extremely difficult to distinguish one from the other. This raises a series of critical questions that lie at the juncture between technology, power and epistemology. In this scenario, we need to realize who is going to have to adapt to the representation of whom. If we increasingly delegate decisions and tasks to machines that operate based on specific computational models, do we need to adapt ourselves and our world to the functioning of such machines? What does such a move entail cognitively and socially? How far does it go ethically or legally? To what extent does it make us economically dependent on such machines?

The everyday revolution

The digital revolution prompted by the rise of computational power is not, in our opinion, something that is meant to take us to the Moon, replace human beings with androids or robots, create sci-fi scenarios such as in *The Matrix*, or program a *Person of Interest*–like machine. The digital revolution driven by computational power is an everyday revolution. It is thus all the more profound, unnoticed and widespread, and it deeply affects the fabric of our usual and daily habits and practices, that is, our everyday lives. Like all radical revolutions, the digital revolution takes root in our everyday life, so it is precisely at this level that its main effects deserve to be examined (Elliott, 2019, 8–9), namely, in relation to the forms of life that it is reshaping:

One way of describing the direction in which our own culture is moving is that many of us are starting to *adapt* what we might call a *digital form of life* – one which takes life in the infosphere for granted, precisely because the digital is so seamlessly integrated into our lives.

(Lynch, 2016, 10; emphasis added)

Often overlooked in the past, this perspective has gained traction, thanks also to its grounding in relevant philosophic stances. As has been recently remarked, both Heidegger and Wittgenstein, whose philosophies seem worlds apart, focused their attention and shed light on the everyday dimension of human life, in the pursuit of an authentic philosophy (Egen, 2019). Both philosophers were interested in how our beliefs, concepts and projects are deeply entrenched in our everyday practices, conditions and experiences. Let us see briefly how this sort of involvement plays a crucial role in our own lives. Without dwelling on the fact that *Dasein* involves "*a way of life* shared by the members of some community" (Haugeland, 2005, 423), it is worth recalling the question of, in Heidegger's words, "who it is that Dasein is in its everydayness" (*Being and Time*, Introduction to IV: 149). Everydayness, therefore, plays a crucial role in Heidegger's concept of Dasein, which we cannot fully expound on in the present context. However, let us give a brief account of this notion by making reference to an enlightening passage by Michael Wheeler (2011):

Dasein confronts every concrete situation in which it finds itself (into which it has been thrown) as a range of possibilities for acting (onto which it may project itself). Insofar as some of these possibilities are actualized, others will not be, meaning that there is a sense in which not Being (a set of unactualized possibilities of Being) is a structural component of Dasein's Being. Out of this dynamic interplay, Dasein emerges as a delicate balance of determination (thrownness) and freedom (projection). The projective possibilities available to Dasein are delineated by totalities of involvements, structures that . . . embody the culturally conditioned ways in which Dasein may inhabit the world.

Everydayness describes a situation that involves both the *having been thrown into the world* and the *possibilities for acting* available to Dasein (onto which it may project itself). In other terms, everydayness is the context within which the dynamic interplay between determination (thrownness) and freedom (projection) takes place: that is, the context in which Dasein's projective possibilities are delineated by the totalities of involvements, which *embody* the culturally conditioned ways in which Dasein may inhabit the world and thus make sense of it. In this sense, the dynamic interplay between determination and freedom that characterizes everydayness is, to put it differently, Dasein's form of life. If the structures of our involvements are modified, this also modifies how Dasein projects itself onto its possibilities. Let us reformulate this idea from a different standpoint.

Against this backdrop, what delineates human from artificial intelligence is not so much intelligence but rather our bodily experience of our form of life, since our mindset is perpetually involved in the contextual, dynamic interplay that grounds our everyday projects, beliefs, intentions, ideas, cognitive states, and that shapes our form of life. For this reason, AI computational models will not so much substitute or take over human intelligence, as they will change, in the long run, our human intelligence, to the extent to which they alter the contextual, dynamic and everyday interplay between determination and freedom, and hence, our bodily experience of our forms of life. Let us see how our forms of life may gradually be modified.

A form of life is, in fact, a contingent combination of syntactic and semantic rules. The complex interplay between syntactic and semantic rules is not always visible. On the contrary, it normally goes unnoticed: it is the hidden part of the iceberg. Our deep-seated habits and practices, our projects and possibilities, and our resistance toward as well as our attraction for what is new, are the most visible part. While at first sight computational power may seem to affect, change and reshape only our most superficial practices and possibilities, it actually touches upon this inner interplay most profoundly. It recasts how our (and not just our) possibilities are grounded in the totalities of our involvements. It changes syntactical rules and hence also changes how semantic rules interact with and are distinct from syntactical rules (how the process of semanticization is related to the process of calculation). If in addition to this shift in the interplay between syntactical and semantic rules the interplay between determination and freedom also changes, our forms of life cannot but be deeply affected.

On the one hand, if this change is too sweeping and sudden, and disrupts how we predict, represent and understand our world and ourselves, we will inevitably struggle to adapt to it. On the other hand, computational power may cleave us of our dependence on contextual factors. Because AI systems are not necessarily contingent upon contextual (social, cultural, historical, etc.) factors, AI systems could or should be built and be able to work without being inevitably affected by our "preconditions of understanding", or what Hans-Georg Gadamer referred to as human "prejudices" (Gadamer, 1989). The so-called AI for Good can also be understood as an attempt to free AI systems from human preconditions of understanding, cognitive biases and deep-seated prejudices. In so doing, AI systems may dramatically change how reality is represented, understood and processed.

The change driven by computational power is therefore basically epistemological. In this sense, changes in our habits and traditional ways of conceiving ourselves and the world – the tip of the iceberg we can see readily see on the surface – are the result of a deeper change, which concerns the interplay of determination and freedom, syntactic and semantic rules, knowledge and understanding, and which is reshaping our forms of life. It is with this larger, invisible part of the iceberg that we run into a complex and crucial problem of governance.

The governance of AI

The expression of "governance of AI" is an inaccurate moniker. We cannot – and maybe should not – try to govern the epistemological development of AI. We can – and probably should – regulate the effects of decisions and actions carried out by AI computational systems, which are increasingly impacting our lives. For instance, we need to deal with what may turn out to be unjust or unfair about these decisions. We cannot be satisfied with regulating these effects by simply optimizing the results produced by these systems. Governance is not just about optimization. We can and should regulate how AI computational systems operate and the contexts in which they do so: we must bring to light and discuss the implicit value choices that are embodied in the functioning of these systems and in the optimization of their results (Pagallo & Durante, 2016). It is exactly in this regard that Wittgenstein's idea of a form of life becomes crucial, since it allows us to appreciate how hard it is to criticize what works successfully and is embodied in our forms of life:

> A form of life, as I mean it here, is the myriad practices of a culture that create their philosophies, but also, in Stanley Cavell's words, their 'routes of interest and feeling, sense of humor, and of significance, and of fulfillment of what is outrageous, of what is similar to what else.' As I read him, Wittgenstein thought that once a set of practices is ingrained enough to become your form of life, it is difficult to substantively criticize them or even to recognize them as what they are. That's because our form of life is 'what has to be accepted, the given.' We can no longer get outside of it.
> *(Lynch, 2016, 10; who cites Cavell, 1969, 52; Wittgenstein, 1963, 226)*

The everydayness of computational power should not be left to mask how our forms of life are structured, preventing us from substantively criticizing them or even recognizing them for what they are. For this reason, we need to understand the interplay of determination and freedom, syntactic and semantic rules, and knowledge and understanding that reshapes our forms of life as a result of AI computational power. In other words, we should not consider decisions and operations undertaken by AI computational systems as different from ours, regarding them as inexplicable because they are driven by a different logic. We should seek to understand how our epistemology accounts for such decisions and operations. We should also be aware of the fact that it would be misguided to do otherwise, for in a liberal perspective we cannot hinder the innovative and disruptive development of AI. We cannot really bridle (let alone thwart) the proliferation of new viewpoints and the production of knowledge and understanding brought about by computational models. Of course, a different problem, which cannot be addressed here, is whether the production of knowledge and understanding created by computational power should remain in the hands of a few, giving rise to *information silos*, which produce both information and power asymmetries across society (Green, 2019; Webb, 2019; Foer, 2017; Durante, 2015).

Let us return to the issue of epistemology, since it is a crucial point to ponder in this context. As already mentioned, the impact of AI prompted by the rise of computational power is primarily an epistemological one, and one that concerns the forms of knowledge themselves, not merely the data and information they comprise. There is often some confusion about this from a theoretical standpoint: although these notions relate to each other, they are conceptually distinct. Let us briefly draw their conceptual perimeter in plain terms.

An item of data is basically a *lack of uniformity* in the world, a difference that signals a difference. While data can be processed at a syntactical level (and at a proto-semantic level), it cannot be processed per se at a semantic level. A black dot on a white screen or a red light seen in the middle of night provides us with data, but it is meaningless in and of itself. It merely signals a lack of uniformity that can be grasped and processed as such. Naturally we can attach a meaning to this lack of uniformity: a black dot on a white page, for instance, might be understood as a punctuation mark. As human beings and semantic engines, we can attach a meaning to and make sense of data, whereas machines, despite being extremely efficient and powerful syntactic engines, cannot. This means that a data-driven society is not necessarily a meaningful one. If we take more than a merely utilitarian view of society, meaning is more important than happiness.

Information is different from data. Information requires a process of signification, according to which x counts as y. Information – at least as understood in semantic terms – is thus data plus meaning (see Floridi, 2010, 22–25). Information requires a semantic dimension that is much more difficult to process; it requires a highly complex capacity, which is at present almost exclusively the domain of human beings. Meaning is what separates human beings from machines, and it constitutes human singularity. However, information is not enough. Information enables us to know a certain p, but it does not tell us why we know that p. An information-driven society does not necessarily provide us with all answers to all of our questions. As Wittgenstein taught us, any genuine investigation begins with questions, and the ability to formulate the right question is undoubtedly the most difficult part of any philosophical or scientific pursuit. We thus need to upgrade information to knowledge.

So, what is knowledge? We have already said that knowledge is not the equivalent of a mere set of data or information. While it is true that the sharing of data or information increases the number of people who possess that data or information, it does not necessarily increase knowledge itself. We see, then, that while knowledge requires data and information, it is never reducible to them. To put it plainly: knowledge is justified and actionable information (Lynch, 2016, 14):

> The old intelligent services adage is that knowledge is actionable information. Actionable information is information you can work with – that, in short, you can trust. Guesses are not actionable – even if they are lucky, precisely because they are *guesses*. What is actionable is what is justified, what has some ground. So: whatever else it is, knowledge is having a correct belief (getting it right, having a true opinion) that is grounded *or justified*, and which can therefore guide our action. Call this *the minimal definition of knowledge*.
>
> (Lynch, 2016, 14)

It is important to take note of these two aspects: knowledge is *justified* and *actionable* information. It can guide our actions *because* it offers us some ground to build on. It is crucial not to lose sight of the fact that action and justification are linked. In this sense, knowledge is not a mere account of reality, but a process that is literally fundamental for the construction of our world. Moreover, being able to justify a belief requires us to treat knowledge as a "network theory of account" (Floridi, 2011), according to which a new piece of information cannot properly be considered knowledge, although it can be once it is part of an appropriate network of relations with another information source:

> Each piece of semantic information is an answer to a question, which, as a whole, poses further questions about itself that require the right sort of information flow in order to be answered correctly, through an appropriate network of relations with some informational source.... It follows that, for relevant semantic information to be upgraded to knowledge, it is necessary to embed it in a network of equally relevant questions and correspondingly correct answers.
>
> *(Floridi, 2011, 278–279)*

As already remarked, having grounded or justified information throughout a network of equally relevant questions and correspondingly correct answers can guide our actions: justified and actionable information is information one can work with and build on. In this sense, knowledge is also teleological: that is, it serves specific purposes. It allows us to decide and act in the world on the basis of justified information and beliefs that allow us to interact with other agents on rational grounds. Changes in how we know and understand things in the world have a profound impact on our forms of life: this not only leads to a recombination of syntactical and semantic rules but, as a result, alters how we make decisions, act in the world and interact with other agents. Let us take a closer look at what this means. The epistemological impact of AI computational systems is important from three main standpoints.

1 Agency

Firstly, it affects how action takes place in the world. There is a deeply ingrained sense, which demands further reflection, that action is no longer the exclusive prerogative of human beings. This is the most salient trait of our times: agency is no longer just a human affair. AI computational systems are transforming the world at a dizzying pace: they act alongside us and often on our behalf. We find ourselves increasingly delegating actions to AI systems in a more or less deliberate and conscious way. Sometimes we are fully conscious of delegating our choices, but at other times, we do not even realize that when performing operations, exchanging messages or producing data online, this fact alone produces metadata and nourishes the functioning of computational systems, which process our data and execute operations, regardless of our will and awareness. Artificial *intelligence* is increasingly and relentlessly turning itself into artificial *agency*, where the ability to modify the world becomes more relevant and significant than the ability to mimic or replicate the modes of human reasoning. This is not just to say that engineering or weak AI prevails over cognitive or strong AI. It is also to say that computational power is such precisely because AI computational systems have their *own* modes of reasoning (world representation, knowledge, decision-making, understanding, learning by experience, etc.), which are no longer totally reliant on human ones. At a certain point, AI computational systems may be able to learn more from other AI computational systems than from human beings. This should not be shocking or scary to us. It is a just a matter of fact that we need to take into account, which reminds us that epistemology is an increasingly crucial part of any political, moral, legal or social issue. The computational race is directed toward deciding, acting and self-learning, and not toward intelligence as such.

2) Interaction

Secondly, it affects how interaction takes place in the world. Human beings are not only called upon to coordinate their actions with that of other agents, including artificial ones, but also with those agents' computational power. Indeed, artificial agency can set a standard for human action. This happens for several reasons: a) because we entrust tasks to machines that perform them more quickly and efficiently than we do, at the expense of gradually being deprived of the tasks and skills associated with them; b) because algorithmic counterfactuals (Pearl & Mackenzie, 2018; Wachter et al., 2018; Durante, 2019) allow us to measure and evaluate how we could or should have acted in certain situations; and c) because computational systems require us to adapt our behavior and the environment to the functioning of these systems. Computational systems interact and operate best in structured environments, which are different from typical human environments, which are mostly unstructured as most human activities are. Having to structure AI systems' activities and environments can be also very beneficial and challenging to human beings. In some cases, the process of programming a computational system makes us aware of certain problems. Human bias is just one example. Our decisions may often be driven by more or less ingrained cognitive biases that we are, as human beings, are quite good at obfuscating. When programming a computational system, programmers may be called upon to de-bias the knowledge basis or the training dataset on which an AI computational system is built.

3) Explanation

Thirdly, it affects how action is accounted for in the world. This may very well be the most decisive and problematic aspect. We have always tried to understand and explain reality, in order to make decisions and behave in the world. We have always tried to explain how things happen and hence how to predict and determine future events based on scientific causality. Similarly, we have also tried to explain and predict human actions, in order to assess and discourage behaviors deviating from social, moral or legal norms, by resorting to criteria of social, moral or legal imputation. Usually, we first try to explain, and then to act. Explanation has always been put at the service of the ability to design and build our own world. In a sense, humans believe that they are free to the extent that they can explain how things happen. Explanation has relieved human beings from the burden of supernatural or magical forces. It has made us free in that we can envisage the outcome of our actions.

A familiar example is that of the law. For purposes of the law, we need to foresee (at least to some extent) the legal consequences of our behaviors before we act. For instance, I should know beforehand what will normally happen in legal terms if I do not stop at a red light. In order to foresee the legally relevant consequences, we need to be able to figure out and explain the behavior that produces these consequences, and how it does so (this is true whether from an observer's or an agent's viewpoint). One also needs to explain how some consequences have been produced, when one is charged with a specific accusation. In this sense, we need explanations both to predict (*ex ante*) and to contest (*ex post*) the legally relevant consequences of a particular behavior. Of course, legal explanations are mainly intrinsic to the specific epistemological field of law (even if law is necessarily entangled with other epistemological fields: neuroscience, medicine, informatics, etc.). Against this backdrop, we need to know (through ex ante predictions or ex post explanations), in order to decide or to act.

As already remarked, knowledge is information that we can work with and build upon. By saying this, we do not mean that we understand knowledge only as a passive representation of the world according to the traditional stance of the observer's epistemology. On the contrary, we believe that the maker's knowledge is highly relevant (Durante, 2017), especially in technological and multi-agent systems (Floridi, 2018). According to this approach:

> Alice [the maker] is part of the system. As the ontic or factual source of *s*, Alice holds the information *p* as part of the system that brings about *s*. It follows that the maker's knowledge is knowledge of a system from within, not from without, consistent with the Aristotelian view that 'science est scire per causas'. This too is in stark contrast with the passive view we inherit from some modern epistemology, and the Cartesian tradition, which is based on a receptive perception of the world, rather than design, intervention, interaction, and control. The problem emerged in the nineteenth century German philosophy of technology, which correctly criticized Kant precisely because of his inability to see that, through technology, agents create, design, and manipulate objects in themselves, not just their phenomenal perceptions.
>
> *(Floridi, 2018, 481)*

In this sense, when the maker is an AI computational system (a type of agent that differs from us) that decides, acts and is, hence, capable of bring about *s*, the problem is whether we can turn this knowledge from within into knowledge for that which is not part of the system, that is, into knowledge we can account for, work with and build on. Let us return to the field of law. Nowadays, we can build AI computational systems that make screening decisions whose logic may seem to defy us. As recently remarked in more general terms:

> This reveals a weakness in our traditional basic strategy for managing what will happen, for the elements of a machine learning model may not have the sort of one-to-one relationship that we envision when we search for the right 'lever' to pull. When everything affects everything else, and when some of those relationships are complex and non-linear – that is, tiny changes can dramatically change the course of events – butterflies can be as important as levers. Overall, these changes mean that while models have been the stable frameworks that enable explanation, *now we often explain something by trying to figure out the model our machines have created.*
>
> *(Weinberger, 2019, 62)*

Against this backdrop, it is noteworthy that legal scholars investigate whether or not the right to explanation is currently recognized under the existing law (notably, in the General Data Protection Regulation) for decisions made by automated systems that no longer require human intervention (Wachter et al., 2017; Goodman & Flaxman, 2017; Pagallo, 2018). A right is a subjective position of claim that is always correlated to a subjective position of duty. So, in an information society, who has the *duty* to provide us with explanations for decisions made by automated systems that no longer involve human intervention? It is not our intention to enter into the legalities of this debate but rather to understand what it says about our society.

A right to explanation

It is important to note that the General Data Protection Regulation (GDPR) not only has a legal function but is also driven by social impetus. The regulation aims to renew and strengthen a possible social covenant based on trust between network users, institutional actors and private companies. This is best exemplified in recitals n. 6 and 7, which we cite here in their entirety:

(6) Rapid technological developments and globalization have brought new challenges for the protection of personal data. The scale of the collection and sharing of personal data has increased significantly. Technology allows both private companies and public authorities to make use of personal data on an unprecedented scale in order to pursue their activities. Natural persons increasingly make personal information available publicly and globally. Technology has transformed both the economy and social life, and should further facilitate the free of personal data within the Union and their transfer to third countries and international organizations, while ensuring a high level of the protection of personal data.

(7) Those developments require a strong and more coherent data protection framework in the Union, backed by strong enforcement, given the importance of creating the trust that will allow the digital economy to develop across the internal market. Natural persons should have control of their own personal data. Legal and practical certainty for natural persons, economic operators and public authorities should be enhanced.

Against this backdrop, the GDPR seems to establish (through a number of provisions: art. 14, 15, and 22; see also recital 71) a general principle in the digital governance of current information societies: individuals should not be subject to decisions made without human intervention, in the sense that they should at least be able to change or contest the decision. In this perspective, human beings should always be provided with an explanation when they bear the consequences of an automated decision. Let us briefly examine the main interpretations concerning whether or not the right to explanation exists in the GDPR.

On the one hand, there are those who do not recognize that such a right is guaranteed. Thorough analysis of the GDPR by some scholars led to the conclusion that it is impossible to gather indisputable evidence defending such a right from the fragmentary norms of the regulation (Wachter et al., 2017). On the other hand, there are those who assert the existence of such a right, making their claim on different bases. One must pay close attention, therefore, to the arguments underlying these sorts of interpretation. Bryce Goodman and Seth Flaxman (2017) have argued, for example, that the right to explanation can substantially be inferred from the requirement for providing the data subject with a meaningful explanation of the logic involved in making the decision (art. 14 and 15, GDPR). Explanation is understood here as being the logic behind the decision, and it is a fundamental component of the more general obligation to inform the data subject of automated decision-making process relying on the processing of personal data. Ugo Pagallo (2018) has, instead, argued that the existence of the right to explanation can be inferred, from a procedural standpoint, from the general right to defense – that is, from the inalienable need to provide the data subject with the right to fully challenge the automated decision (art. 22, GDPR). In other words, how can people actually defend themselves from the effects of decisions that significantly affect them without knowing (i.e., receiving an explanation about) how an AI system arrived at that decision?

This heated debate is further fueled by the various (legal, cognitive and technological) challenges involved in providing such explanations. Suffice it here to say that the requirement for explanation has already been captured under terms such as "transparency", "understandability", "explainability" and "explicability" (Floridi et al., 2018; for a critical view see Robbins, 2019) and the possibility of providing automated explanation has now been proposed (Doshi-Velez & Kortz, 2017). As already remarked, whatever interpretation and scope are made of the right to explanation, the GDPR is meant to set a general principle in the digital governance of AI computational systems: individuals should not be subject to automated decisions made without human intervention, unless they are able to change or challenge the decision.

We can interpret this principle in two ways. It can either be seen as a basic tenet of human civilization that aims to limit the process of automating decisions and to provide individuals with a meaningful form of control and a viable instrument of protection. This would be aimed once again at strengthening a climate of trust among network users, or more broadly, among members of the information society. Or else it can be interpreted, following Hegel, as the owl of Minerva, which only spreads its wings with the falling of the dusk (*post-factum*), and the eventually achieved awareness of the risks of automation collides with a reality that has already been determined and is past the point of no return. The law in this case would represent, as a social institution, the last bulwark against an unyielding trajectory: that of the growing delegation of decisions and actions to automated machines, which we can only partially understand and govern.

In our opinion, this principle should be correctly understood in its essential epistemological function: as a relevant filter through which to look, carefully and critically, at the world we are building. In other words, the GDPR reveals the existence of a central issue, an open question, which it helps us to envisage and understand; however, it would be unreasonable and unrealistic to believe that the law will be able to provide us with the only or main solution. The social function of law is not only deeply concerned with regulating human behavior but, first and foremost, with increasing human understanding by providing human beings with an institutional forum for discussion, interpretation and deliberation. If the law at present is so taken with the issue of explanation and human intervention in automated decisions, it is because this issue raises two essential and underlying questions that need to be reexamined and discussed: freedom and violence.

If the right to explanation is now being examined in epistemological terms, it is because behind the formation of knowledge, the freedom of individuals is at stake. It is not just a question of providing a legal remedy for those who intend to challenge automated decisions based exclusively on the automated processing of personal data. The stakes are much higher: they involve rethinking the very idea of freedom in a technological context where predicting, deciding and acting are no longer the exclusive prerogative of human beings. The issue of explanation calls into question, beyond the strictly legal framework, the meaning of freedom, whatever it means. We could just say about freedom what Saint Augustine said about time: "What then is time? If no one asks me, I know; if I want to explain it to someone who does ask me, I do not know". Therefore, whatever else it is, freedom may be understood in the present context in transcendental terms. In this sense, we are free, so to speak, not so much because we are able to freely determine the course of actions (with respect to which we could have decided and acted differently); we are free as human beings because and to the extent to which we are able to explain what happens to us (we have reasons for devising, choosing or justifying alternate possibilities). It is this reflective capacity to take a distance from the world, through explanation, that allows us not to be passively subjected to what happens to us in the world and to plan and justify certain courses of action in it. This is also very concrete, since explanations are not so much mere theoretical accounts of reality but rather conceptual tools that serve practical purposes, such as changing the world for some reason. To the extent that we are subject to the effects of acts or decisions, whose logic and functioning we are unable to meaningfully explain, we feel that we are losing touch with our own freedom, with its language and grounds.

Not only do we feel that our freedom is threatened but that, in a sense, we ourselves are threatened. We feel that there is something more or less perceptibly violent in a world where we bear the consequences of decisions or acts in which we have no voice. What kind of violence is this, that presents itself as totally anonymous and immaterial? Can it even be defined as violence? Although dissimilar, moral, social and psychological violence have a common conceptual ground that allows us to define the essence of violence. In every occurrence of the world violence, we tend to implicitly make a common reference not to *what* we experience but to *how* we experience something. As the moral philosopher Emmanuel Levinas (1990, 6) has pointed out:

> Violence is to be found in any action in which one acts as if the rest of the universe were there only to receive the action: violence is consequently also any action which we endure without at every point collaborating in it.

Violence is found in any action in which one acts with no regard for another member or instance of the universe. The conceptual core or the essence of violence is its radical *regardlessness*. Hence, violence is what turns an agent into a mere patient or what prevents a patient from becoming an agent. A patient is, thereby, deprived of the basic capacity of becoming an agent and thus of becoming a specific source of information. From an informational standpoint, violence is the deprivation of the critical capacity to be that specific source of meaningful information. The deprivation of this capacity is part of the individual rights of an informational agent, when it concerns its right not to be subjected to the consequences of automated decisions made without human intervention. This problem – the fact that human beings are part of an alienating context whose logic and functioning they cannot always understand, control and account for – once again strongly raises the issue of human dignity in the age of rising computational power.

Computational power and human dignity

As pointed out, computational power is characterized by the building of AI systems that make decisions and operate on the basis of their own particular logic and representation of reality, gradually adapting the world to their mode of functioning. The increasing proliferation of models, agents and points of view that the growth of computational power brings with it is certainly an element of enrichment and development; however, it also constructs a matrix of relationships in which human beings can no longer entirely determine the aims and values at stake. Humans are not only called upon to compare their representation of the world with that of computational models but are also a subject of those models' representation. If a bank uses a computer algorithm to create a profile of the *good borrower*, individuals will be torn between their objections to the automated construction of this profile and their interest in being subsumed within it (in a return to the traditional "voluntary servitude" [La Boétie, 1975], albeit under modern guise). In this sense, the impact of computational power has both an *extrovert*, or about the world, and an *introvert*, or about ourselves, aspect (to refer to Floridi's distinction as regards to the overall impact of science: Floridi, 2010, 8–9).

Computational power is neither conceived from a material standpoint (according to which power consists of a substantial set of means or resources) nor from a relational one (according to which power consists in the ability to determine the will of others, even in the face of an opposition, or to establish collective rules and to impose their respect, by virtue of general consent), nor even in metaphysical terms (as a result of privileged properties or positions). Computational power is to be conceived of as the ability to create the conditions of its enactment – that is, the conditions allowing this power to be fully exercised – by adapting the world to its logic and functioning. As in Foucault's *Microphysics of Power* (1991), computational power is not in principle localizable here or there nor does it operate according to precisely made plans (through the rigid distinction between those who wield it and those who are subjected to it), but, unlike that form of power, it may be, at least in part, appropriated by all those who can exploit it (such as *Big Tech*), which has been made collectively possible by the ongoing dissemination of data.

However, computational power cannot be merely interpreted as something that someone appropriates at a certain point in history. Computational power has taken a long period of time to develop, and required a lengthy gestation period. Floridi astutely observed that the modern period was witness to a constant and progressive transformation, according to which "thinking was reasoning, reasoning was reckoning, and reckoning could already be done by a Pascalina" (2014, 93). Over time, the idea has come to light that, in order to decide and act rationally, one must be able to calculate and process data and information, that is to say, to wield computational power. For many years, this ability was considered to be the exclusive prerogative of human beings, at least until the invention of computers. Machines have now outstripped us in this regard.

Although computational power has been a long time in coming, it cannot simply be said that it belongs to a given historical moment; on the contrary, this power can now be conceived of as a vector of history. Computational power is the engine of current history, which designates the perspective in which to interpret the main features of the impact of digitalization and the information revolution as "aspects of a single macroscopic trend", to quote Floridi: "This is the rocket that has made humanity travel from history to hyperhistory" (2014, 8). In this sense, computational power is a vector of history that deploys the conditions of its exercise, not only adapting the world to its logic and functioning but also reshaping our forms of life.

A parallel with economic power may perhaps serve to clarify the point. Imagine the case of an individual who has immense financial resources in the following two scenarios. In the first, it is absolutely forbidden to buy or sell anything: even if there are endless possibilities for doing so, the individual cannot exercise their power (not even to circumvent the existing prohibition). In the second scenario, no such prohibition exists: in principle, everything can be sold and purchased (with some limited exceptions). In this case, not only can the individual exercise their power, but they can also use it to overcome existing limits (by trying to buy people's favor or attention, bribing them or attempting to buy things that are not for sale). Here, power is exercised not only in its own right but also to build (or strengthen) the conditions favoring its exercise. Contemporary art, literature and cinema best express the essence of economic power in modernity, when representing our world as a place where everything can be sold and bought, included human values. Kant had already glimpsed the problem, in conceiving that human dignity has an intrinsic worth but not a market price, and is not an object of exchange (1998, 42):

> In the kingdom of ends everything either has a price or a dignity. What has a price can be replaced by something else as its *equivalent*; what on the other hand is raised above all prices and therefore admits of no equivalent has a dignity. What is related to general human inclinations and needs has a market price; that which, even without presupposing a need, conforms with a certain taste, that is, with a delight in a mere purposeless play of our mental powers, has a fancy price; but that which constitutes the condition under which alone something can be an end in itself has not merely a relative worth, that is, a price, but an inner worth, that is, dignity.

What cannot be replaced by something else, since it admits no equivalent, possesses a form of dignity. In our information society driven by computational power, everything risks being subjected to the logic and functioning of this power, which constitutes the condition under which hardly anything can be an end in itself. Against this backdrop, it is not difficult to foresee that as the visible effects of computational power become increasingly apparent, arguments about human dignity will abound.

Conclusions

AI worldviews have been examined in the light of the rising phenomenon of computational power. This is a new form of power. If data is the new oil, computational power is its engine and it has created a watershed in our information society. Computational power does not supplant previous forms of power such as economic, political, legal, social or informational. Instead, it lends those forms of power new tools and means of expression. The use of computational power reshapes the environment, and AI computational systems become strategic tools for us in adapting to the new technologically shaped environment and in extracting from that environment the energy and resources on which the individual and collective well-being of information societies ultimately depends. While this may lead to widespread improvements in living conditions, it may also aggravate existing power and information asymmetries, such that the rich become richer and the poor even poorer, and result in substantially undemocratic (or at least controversial) outcomes. The use of computational power produces new forms of knowledge, and knowledge, as we know, is in turn a form of power. The inherent circularity by which computational power contributes to producing the conditions of its own implementation still needs to be investigated. The everydayness of AI computational systems has a strong impact on our society. The impact brought about by these systems is first and foremost epistemological. It not only affects our habits and traditional ways of conceiving of ourselves and of the world, but also and above all affects the interplay of determination and freedom, syntactic and semantic rules, and knowledge and understanding, which is reshaping our forms of life. In so doing, computational power can redesign the very fabric of our reality and threaten human freedom, control and dignity.

We are just at the beginning of the plexus of questions and issues that the use of computational power is likely to raise.

References

Cavell S., *Must We Mean What We Say?* Scribner and Sons, New York, 1969.
De La Boétie E., *The Politics of Obedience: The Discourse on Voluntary Servitude*, Free Life Editions, New York, 1975.
Doshi-Velez F., Kortz M., Accountability of AI under the law: The role of explanation, in *Berkman Klein Center Working Group on Explanation and the Law, Berkman Klein Center for Internet and Society Working Paper*, 2017, accessible at: https://dash.harvard.edu/handle/1/34372584.
Durante M., The democratic governance of information societies. A critique to the theory of stakeholders, in *Philosophy & Technology*, 28(1), 11–32, 2015.
Durante M., *Ethics, Law and the Politics of Information. A Guide to the Philosophy of Luciano Floridi*, Springer, Dordrecht, 2017.
Durante M., *Potere computazionale. L'impatto delle ICT su diritto, società, conoscenza*, Meltemi, Milano, 2019.
Egen D., *The Pursuit of an Authentic Philosophy: Wittgenstein, Heidegger, and the Everyday*, Oxford University Press, Oxford, 2019.
Elliott A., *The Culture of AI. Everyday Life and the Digital Revolution*, Routledge, Abingdon-New York, 2019.
Floridi L., *Information. A Very Short Introduction*, Oxford University Press, Oxford, 2010.
Floridi L., *The Philosophy of Information*, Oxford University Press, Oxford, 2011.

Floridi L., *The Fourth Revolution. How the Infosphere is Reshaping Human Reality*, Oxford University Press, Oxford, 2014.

Floridi L., Digital's cleaving power and its consequences, in *Philosophy & Technology*, 30(2), 123–129, 2017.

Floridi L., What a maker's knowledge could be, in *Synthese*, 195, 465–481, 2018.

Floridi L., et al., AI4 people – An ethical framework for a good AI society: Opportunities, risks, principles, and recommendations, in *Minds and Machines*, 28(4), 689–707, 2018.

Foer F., *World Without Mind. The Existential Threat of Big Tech*, Penguin Books, London, 2017.

Foucault M., *Discipline and Punish: The Birth of the Prison*, Penguin, London, 1991.

Gadamer H.G., *Truth and Method*, 2nd rev. edn., trans. by J. Cumming and G. Barden, Crossroad, New York, 1989.

Goodman B., Flaxman S., European union regulations on algorithmic decision-making and to right to explanation, in *AI Magazine*, 38(3), 50–57, 2017.

Green L., *Silicon States. The Power and the Politics of Big Tech and What It Means for Our Future*, Counterpoint, Berkeley, 2019.

Haugeland J., Reading Brandom reading Heidegger, in *European Journal of Philosophy*, 13(3), 421–428, 2005.

Kant I., *Groundwork for the Metaphysics of Morals*, ed. and trans. by M. Gregor, Cambridge University Press, Cambridge, 1998.

Levinas E., *Difficult Freedom. Essays on Judaism*, The Athlone Press, London, 1990.

Lynch M., *The Internet of Us. Knowing More and Understanding Less in the Age of Big Data*, Liveright Publisher, London-New York, 2016.

Pagallo U. Algo-Rhythms and the Beat of the Legal Drum, *Philosophy and Technology*, 31, 507–524, 2018.

Pagallo U., Durante M. The Pros and Cons of Legal Automation and Its Governance, *European Journal of Risk Regulation*, 7, 323–335, 2016.

Pearl J., Mackenzie D., *The Book of Why: The New Science of Causes and Effects*, Basic Books, New York, 2018.

Robbins S., A misdirected principle with a catch: Explicability for AI, in *Minds and Machines*, 29, 495–514, 2019.

Wachter S., Mittelstadt B.D., Floridi L., Why a right to explanation of automated decisions-making does not exist in the general data protection regulation, in *International Data Privacy Law*, 7(2), 76–99, 2017.

Wachter S., Mittelstadt B.D., Russel C., Counterfactual explanations without opening the black box: Automated decisions and the GDPR, in *Harvard Journal of Law & Technology*, 31(2), 841–887, 2018.

Webb A., *The Big Nine: How the Tech Titans and Their Thinking Machines Could Warp Humanity*, PublicAffairs, New York, 2019.

Weinberger D., *Everyday Chaos. Technology, Complexity, and How We're Thriving in a New World of Possibility*, Harvard Business School, Harvard, 2019.

Wheeler M., Martin Heidegger, in *Stanford Encyclopedia of Philosophy*, Edward N. Zalta (ed.), first published 12 October 2011 (Last modified, Winter Edition 2018), accessible at: https://plato.stanford.edu/archives/win2018/entries/heidegger/.

Wittgenstein L., *Philosophical Investigations*, trans. by G.E.M. Anscombe, Basil Blackwell, Oxford, 1963.

17
Technogenarians
Ageing and robotic care[1]

Eric L. Hsu

Ageing, as a substantial body of sociological work has established (Peine and Neven, 2019), cannot be understood without some reference to technology. Technological developments, like the advent of various walking aids and mobile phones, have transformed how ageing is experienced and socially structured (Joyce and Loe, 2010). But equally, it is important to note how ageing has factored into how technologies are designed and utilized (Schulz et al., 2015), which the term, 'gerontechnology' (Graafmans, 2017), has been used to capture.

The primary aim of this chapter is to explore how one of the frontiers in gerontechnology is the advent of robotic technologies for aged care. This chapter employs a sociological approach. It is principally interested in the social dimensions of aged care robots.[2] It investigates how these gerontechnologies are socially motivated and constructed (Frennert and Östlund, 2014; Šabanović, 2010). Elder care robots, from this perspective, bear the imprints of specific values and cultures. Their use can engender new or exacerbate existing social problems, just as they can be used to address various kinds of social inequality.

This chapter begins by outlining how and why robots for older people are being developed in the contemporary era across different contexts. It then covers the ethical issues that have been raised about the use of these robotic technologies. Afterward, the chapter provides an overview of how the social and cultural sciences have critically investigated many of the assumptions that have been made about the future of aged care robots. Many works have called into question the idea that aged care robotics are going to be uniformly accepted and/or predominantly beneficial. The chapter concludes with a discussion of how the social and cultural study of aged care robots can be further expanded and deepened. This involves being more attuned to its mobile dimensions. The chapter also encourages further study on the ways in which aged care robotics has bearing on a myriad of other topics like environmental sustainability. Interventions of this kind are meant to underscore and expand the promise of social and cultural perspectives on the associations between robotics and ageing.

Robots as means to address the challenges of an ageing population

Why has the technological development of robots become such a key issue in the provision of care for older people in and across different parts of the world? In order to answer this question, we first need to consider how ageing more broadly has been framed and discussed. Numerous works have observed that the phenomenon of population ageing has become of one of the grand challenges facing numerous countries and regions in the 21st century (Lutz et al., 2008; Schoeni and Ofstedal, 2010). For example in the United States, predictions have been made that the number of Americans who are 65 years or older will double by 2050 (Pew, 2015). In Japan, this trend has been even more severely forecast, with Japan being designated by many as a 'super-ageing society' (Muramatsu and Akiyama, 2011). Demographic ageing has been identified as such a significant issue in many parts of the world because it is commonly associated with a number of social problems. Demographic ageing, for example, is thought to challenge the viability of existing health and care systems and it is also expected to lead to significant labor shortages (Harper, 2014).

As numerous studies have shown (Neven and Peine, 2017; Peine et al., 2015), technological innovations are frequently framed in many contexts as a remedy for the social problems associated with an ageing population. Robotic technologies have especially played a key role in the advancement of this movement and discourse (Frennert and Östlund, 2014; Pedersen et al., 2018). Robots are not only predicted to help make up the labor shortages resulting from demographic ageing, they are also thought to improve the lives of elderly people in very substantial and discrete ways.

Some scholarly work has sought to capture the vast array of robotic technologies that are in the process of being developed, which are meant to have applications and implications for the lives of older people (Broekens et al., 2009; Pedersen et al., 2018; Robinson et al., 2014; Shishehgar et al., 2018). Broekens et al. (2009) have drawn a useful distinction between robots that are service oriented and those that can act as companions. The latter is said to enhance the physical and psychological well-being of older people by providing them with a sense of companionship, while the former is more geared toward helping older people live more independent lives that are safe, sufficiently mobile, and connected with others.[3]

Robinson et al. (2014) have attempted to make further and more nuanced distinctions. For them, it is important to recognize that not all robots are 'social' ones. While some types of robots, such as companion robots and some service robots, are communicative and are able to be treated as social entities, other kinds of robots, like rehabilitations robots, lack these 'social' qualities.

Shishehgar et al. (2018) have undertaken a systematic review of how robots can impact the lives of older people and they have additionally identified nine key robot categories. In addition to there being 'companion' robots, Shishehgar et al. (2018) draw attention to the development of 'telepresent' robots, which help to facilitate communication for older persons. They also note the existence of 'manipulator service' and 'rehabilitation' robots, which either support the basic tasks of independent living through handling or carrying objects or provide older people with physical support and assistance. Robots, in Shishehgar et al.'s account, can also be used to monitor the health of older persons, which is related to but distinct from 'reminder' robots that aim to improve treatment and medication adherence and 'fall detection' robots that mitigate or inform others of fall occurrences. The last two types of robots for older persons identified by Shishehgar et al., are 'domestic' robots and robots that are geared to provide 'entertainment'. Domestic robots are designed to help older people with the chores they need to do and, like 'manipulator service' robots, they are intended to help people age in place. Robots that have the capacity to entertain older people are needed because older people experience adverse learning and/or cognitive effects when entertainment in their lives is lacking.

Overviews and studies of the robots that are being developed for aged care in the engineering and computing sciences have tended to paint a rather favorable picture (Sparrow and Sparrow,

2006). For example care robots, like other gerontechnologies, have been developed based on the belief that they will help older people live at home independently as long as possible.[4]

Advances in robotic technologies, like the ongoing advent of transit vehicles that involve an automated component, are also said to address the high levels of transport disadvantage that older people have been shown to experience (Holley-Moore and Creighton, 2015). Robots, from this perspective, are said to increase the autonomy that older people have, and older people, with the help of robots, are thought to be more socially connected to others.

Another benefit of developing aged care robots, or 'carebots', is their ability to help carers of older people, whether in professional care settings or within the familial home. Ishiguro (2017: 258–259) has established, for example, that there is a discourse in Japanese government policy documents concerning older persons that believes care robots can 'reduce the physical/mental burden of care work and can lessen care worker turnover'.

Relatedly, developing robots for aged care is further depicted as having benefits for economies. Not only does the innovation and production of robots involve the creation of high-tech jobs, the use of robots is also thought to reduce the amount of money national governments need to spend on care for the populations they look after. Taken together, this amounts to what Neven and Peine (2017) have termed, 'the triple win' discourse of ageing.

In the section that follows, we explore how ethical discussions of robotics have troubled and complicated accounts of aged care robots that are overwhelmingly positive in their outlook. Many scholarly works and commentaries have focused attention on the harmful and ethically questionable aspects of deploying and developing robotic technologies for aged care. But it should be noted that ethical analyses of gerontechnological robots have not simply been one-sided. Ethical defenses of robots have concomitantly been advanced, which have tried to expose some of the limitations of universal ethical pronouncements (Coeckelbergh, 2016; Vandemeulebroucke et al., 2018).

The ethical dilemmas of aged care robots

It is not hyperbole to say that a great deal of work has recently been produced in the social sciences, which investigates the ethical dimensions of developing and deploying robots in the context of aged care. This unfolding discussion has been highly varied in its scope and it is beyond the remit of this chapter to cover all the relevant terrain.[5] But some key points, especially relevant to the sociology of gerontechnology and robotics, merit consideration.

Vallor (2011: 254) has identified numerous key points of ethical concern that have been raised about 'carebots'. One revolves around the possibility that older people might be 'objectified' as problems through the use of robotic technologies. Objectification refers to the treatment of people 'as if they were a lump of dead matter: to be pushed, lifted, pumped or drained, without proper reference to the fact that they are sentient beings' (cited in A. Sharkey and Sharkey, 2012a). Carebots stand to do this by potentially reducing the amount of control and autonomy that older people have over their own lives.

Sharkey and Sharkey (2012b) and others (Decker, 2008) have discussed this possibility at some length. Their works highlight the possibility that carebots might unfairly restrict the actions and lives of older persons. Sharkey and Sharkey acknowledge that there might be instances when older persons might be rightfully prevented from engaging in certain activities, such as when an older person who has been diagnosed with suicidal tendencies takes out a knife from a kitchen drawer. But Sharkey and Sharkey are concerned that robots may not be up to the task of determining when it is appropriate to restrain someone's liberty in a justifiable manner. This partly has to do with the fact that 'robots are able to follow well-specified rules, but they are not good at understanding the surrounding social context and predicting likely intentions', especially in comparison to humans (Sharkey and Sharkey, 2012b: 272). Accordingly, this is why the autonomous aspects of care robots are ethically troublesome. We should avoid putting too much faith into the capacity of robots to manage the lives of older people, as this may be a way to erode the liberty and autonomy of older persons without due process.

In her account of how carebots have been ethically debated, Vallor (2011: 254) also has identified privacy as a key theme. Robots of all kinds that provide care to older people are likely to involve a monitoring component, whether that be to provide a certain level of companionship or to alert others when a fall has occurred. But Sharkey and Sharkey (2012b) contend that this feature of carebots also has the potential to unfairly intrude on the right to privacy that older people are entitled to.[6] Sharkey and Sharkey point out that older people may not always realize that their words and activities are being recorded. They may say or do things around robots that they would not like others to know about. And thus who has access to the data collected by robots and how long the data is stored for are issues that need to be ethically scrutinized.

According to Vallor (2011: 254), the ethical dimensions of roboticized aged care is further complicated by the possibility that carebots may reduce the amount of human contact experienced by older people. Sparrow and Sparrow (2006) have notably raised this as an ethical issue worthy of consideration. While robots stand to reduce the amount of work that human carers have to personally undertake to look after those they are responsible for (Decker, 2008), Sparrow and Sparrow and others have suggested that carebots can one day be used to replace human carers altogether or at least in some significant capacities. The two authors cite research that affirms the importance of human interactions in the lives of the elderly. When older people are socially isolated from others, there are clear indications that this generally reduces their quality of life.

According to Sparrow and Sparrow, we need to bear in mind that the isolating aspects of robots can come in a number of forms, some of which are more subtle than others. While it may be clear how harm can come from a robot taking the place of a loved one, it may be more difficult to recognize why it is problematic to deploy cleaning robots in institutional care settings. The concern is not simply that cleaning robots will not be able to adequately carry out their tasks. It is that their use might further deprive older people of human interactions, as 'it is often the cleaning staff who provide much of the "human contact" for [older] patients and residents' (Sparrow and Sparrow, 2006: 151).

But carebots should not be characterized as having only socially isolating effects. Sharkey and Sharkey (2012a, 2012b) argue that a more balanced and multifaceted view is needed. For them, to properly understand how carebots stand to affect how socially connected older people are to others, we also need to bear in mind the possibility that robots may also be used to facilitate new – or heighten existing – social interactions. This is evident in the way that some carebots, like robot pets, may give older people something to talk about with others. Robots that have a telepresence component can also help older people establish virtual interactions with their friends and family. And some robots that are mobility focused, such as those that improve the function and utility of wheelchairs, can help older people, at least from a technical point of view, access and move about spaces that help people feel more connected to others in their communities.[7]

This Janus-faced quality of the ethics of aged care robots is also present in one of the last themes identified by Vallor (2011). Vallor observes that the issue of deception has also featured prominently in ethical debates about aged care robotics. How, to what effect, or even whether it is fair to say that carebots deceive older people have garnered a plethora of ethical interpretations. One of the key positions within this discussion has been articulated by Sparrow and

Sparrow (2006). They note how the care provided by some kinds of robots might be based, in some fundamental way, on an illusion. According to them, robots, unlike humans, are most likely unable to display sincere concern or friendship to those around them. They can only give off the impression that the care they provide is genuine. Sparrow and Sparrow believe this is problematic for two reasons. The first is that it is a '(minor) moral failure' to be deceived about the world around us (Sparrow and Sparrow, 2006: 155). Additionally, Sparrow and Sparrow believe that being deceived is not conducive to having one's needs met. Only when there is a truthful understanding of the world, can we actually have our 'interests advanced, or our well-being served' (Sparrow and Sparrow, 2006: 155).

While numerous works have found utility and insight in Sparrow and Sparrow's warning that carebots can be harmfully deceptive, some divergent perspectives have emerged (Coeckelbergh, 2016; Wachsmuth, 2018). Coeckelbergh (2016), for instance, has found Sparrow and Sparrow's characterization of robotic care as being wrongly 'deceptive' as a gross over-simplification of how care is actually responsibly provided to older persons. For Coeckelbergh, deception is not something we should wholly try to avoid when it comes to elder care. While respecting the autonomy of older persons is what all care givers should aim for, there are circumstances where some 'deception may play a legitimate role' (Coeckelbergh, 2016: 460). This applies when an older person no longer has the capacity to act in an autonomous way, such as when someone develops a severe case of dementia. In these circumstances, deception may be justifiably used to prevent harm to them or others. Consequently, this means that a revaluation of the 'deceptive' aspects of carebots is needed. Rather than make a universal pronouncement that robots are ethically problematic because they possess a deceptive element, we should instead look to understand how the ethical issues of robot deception are contextual.[8]

This, in turn, speaks to Vandemeuelebroucke et al.'s (2018) observation that there are two distinct approaches in the ethical debate surrounding aged care robots. They characterize the first as being a kind of 'ethical assessment'. When scholars use this approach through the lens of deontology or principalism, they typically seek to evaluate whether or not the use of a specific technology upholds, furthers, or contradicts, certain values and principles. A strength of this is that it leads us to decide how technologies should be incorporated or utilized in our lives, such as in the realm of aged care.

However, there is a divergent yet complementary ethical approach to aged care robots, which has also been advanced, that is worthy of our consideration. Vandemeuelebroucke et al. label this approach as a type of 'ethical reflection'. This approach diverges from ethical assessment in that it does not regard technology as a 'collection of neutral instruments' (Vandemeulebroucke et al., 2018: 24). When scholars use this approach, they believe the technologies themselves influence the very values and principles that are used to judge them. In other words, the use of robots does not simply align with or diverge from what it means to provide good elderly care. Robots invite us, in some sense, to rethink and reflect on what good elderly care constitutes. A benefit of using this approach is that it avoids instituting a 'top-down' view of ethics. It does this by providing 'tools to go beyond a simple yes-or-no answer about care robot use and the consequences for aged practices and society' (Vandemeulebroucke et al., 2018: 24).

In Vandemeulebroucke et al.'s (2018) account, to properly grasp the nuances, complexities, and stakes of aged care robots, ethical assessment should be combined with ethical reflection. Critical evaluations of robotic technologies from a distance are needed but so are up-close empirical investigations of how robots are being developed and deployed to transform the lives of older people.

In the section that follows, we cover how research of this kind has emerged in the social and cultural sciences, in fields such as Science and Technology Studies (STS) (Frennert and

Östlund, 2014), history, and sociology. We explore how this growing body of work has been situated in a number of contexts around different types of technology and we also consider how various studies have produced new insights about how robotic technologies are developed and implemented in the context of aged care. It is not enough to simply say whether or not robots are ethically justifiable or problematic writ large. This determination must be made with some reference to specific contexts and the cultural systems in which robot technologies are embedded, which we now turn to consider.

The discontinuities and hidden social impacts of developing aged care robots

Just as the ethical discussion of the use of robots in aged care has been varied, so too has the social and cultural study of aged care robots been relatively diverse in terms of what it has investigated. One prominent strand of research has sought to investigate what older people actually think about the robotic care technologies that are being developed for them (Niemelä and Melkas, 2019; Smarr et al., 2014). This research has called into question the view that aged care robotics will be wholly socially beneficial. To varying extents, it has also cast doubt on the idea that robotic technologies will be uniformly accepted and adopted.

Studies in this vein have found that some types of robotics are perceived as being more dangerous and/or less useful than others. Niemelä and Melkas's (2019) study of a citizen panel of older people in Finland, for example, found that there was potential acceptance of robots in care settings but only in a secondary capacity. Study participants 'felt that robots could not replace humans in terms of presence, interaction and touch' (Niemelä and Melkas, 2019: 186). Smarr et al.'s (2012) small scale study of older people from one community in the United States also found that support for robots was limited to certain tasks. Study participants indicated that they were open to robots helping with instrumental tasks, such as giving medication reminders and helping with housework. But there was less interest in robots being involved in activities of daily living such as shaving, getting dressed, and walking.

Research focusing on user acceptance of aged care robots has additionally sought to solicit the views of care givers, family members, and medical professionals who populate the lives of older people. Forlizzi et al. (2011) have established that it is not enough to just understand what older people think about robots if we want to understand how and to what extent robots might become a part of their experience. We also need to understand the 'ecology', which elderly people are a part of.

Ishiguro's (2017) qualitative study of what care workers in Japan think about the use of some robotic care technologies has shown benefits of using this approach. Many of the care workers in her study indicated that they felt uncomfortable using a robotic transfer lift because this technology was not seen to provide a 'warm' enough level of care. Ishiguro found that perceptions of this kind may help to explain why robotic technologies so far have only been used on a very limited basis in Japanese care work.

Further complicating this picture is the fact that socio-demographic and contextual factors have also been found to affect the acceptance of aged care robots. Flandorfer (2012) has indicated that older people and the people around them should not be thought of as an homogeneous mass. Social variables like gender and class also play a role in determining how robots are viewed in the provision of elder care, and so too does societal context, as different societies seem to express some of their own distinct cultural attitudes toward robots (Nomura et al., 2008).[9]

Beyond just understanding how various people view robotics in aged care, some social and cultural researchers recently investigated how robotic technologies are actually being developed and implemented (Hsu et al., 2020; Neven, 2010). This research aimed to investigate whom is involved in the technology development process and how technology may be configured in certain ways that may be socially problematic.

Neven (2010) has notably conducted an ethnographic study of a company based in the Netherlands developing robotic technology with applications for the elderly. Neven (2010: 344) found that the developers of the robot were influenced by stereotypes of older people as being lonely and in need of 'physical, cognitive and mental health maintenance and support'. Older people who were asked to test the technology underdevelopment indicated they felt the robot was intended for someone who conformed to the stereotypical image of older people as being socially isolated and mentally and physically frail, which the test users themselves tended not to associate themselves with. Neven observed that this feedback did not ultimately make a strong impact upon the technology developers, as the developers mainly held on to the stereotyped images of older people that they initially had, which justified their design trajectory.

Hsu et al. (2020) have found this tendency to marginalize older people in the technology development process also present in their qualitative study of how roboticists in Japan are creating technologies for the elderly. Like Neven (2010), Hsu et al. (2020) sought to study the images that technology developers held of their users, using Akrich's (1995) seminal theory of 'user representations'. Hsu et al. found that Japanese robot developers tended to have a stereotyped view of older people. Roboticists commonly 'emphasized the physical and mental frailty, degradation, and/or deficit of older people when discussing the technologies they were working on' (Hsu et al., 2020: 3). Rarely, if ever, was ageing portrayed in a positive light.[10]

This was found to be significant for a number of reasons. User representations have been shown to have some influence on how technologies come to be used, which in turn has an effect on their social impacts. But user representations of aged care robots not only affect how the future might be constructed. They also have implications for the here and now. When technology developers hold and perpetuate images of older people that are stereotyped and problematic, this draws from but also informs how the elderly are socially positioned and valued. Weber (2005) has shown this to be the case when it comes to gender. When roboticists model human-robot interactions on social dynamics that may be stereotyped or negative – such as when robots are designed to look and behave like women to make them seem 'harmless' and 'friendly' – Weber asserts this has the potential to broaden or reinforce unequal social relations.

Hsu et al.'s (2020: 4) study partly attributed the stereotyped images of older people that Japanese roboticists held to the lack of input that older people had in the technology development process. Older people, in some cases, were not consulted at all by the participants of Hsu et al.'s study, or they were only given very narrow parameters from which to evaluate the technology that was presented to them. Some roboticists reported that they were able to 'test' their technologies on older people only by asking them simplistic questions, such as which robotic technologies they preferred.

Hsu et al. (2020) found there were manifold reasons why older people were not able to be more significantly involved in the technology design process. Some roboticists described not having enough resources or time to extensively engage with end users. Others reported not having sufficient expertise or social license to work with the people for whom they were developing the technologies.

Numerous works have not only sought to promote more participatory design approaches to aged care robots, they also have proposed ways this can and ought to come about (Leong and Johnston, 2016; Šabanović et al., 2015; Toms et al., 2019). Putting older people and their carers at the center of the design process is worthwhile because it can likely lead to 'more successful technical and social outcomes' (Šabanović et al., 2015: 106). Participatory design involves recognizing older people as 'innosumers' (Peine et al., 2014) and 'technogenarians' (Joyce and Loe, 2010). The elderly are not simply 'passive' consumers who must conform to the technologies that are presented to them. Rather they should be regarded as key actors and stakeholders in the technology development process.

Leong and Johnston (2016) note that at the core of participatory design is the practice of 'mutual learning'. Technologies should ideally be developed dialogically, and design paternalism should be avoided as much as possible. This means it may not be enough for robot developers to simply seek feedback from older people. As Peine et al. (2014) have noted, some efforts made by technology developers to solicit input from older people may still actually reinforce rather than challenge paternalistic design approaches. This occurs when there remains a strict division of labor between technology developers and older technology users. When technology developers retain ultimate authority about how to interpret and simplify the complex knowledge they have of the users they design technologies for, then this perpetuates – rather than opposes – some of the paternalistic tendencies that exist in gerontechnology (Peine, 2019).

Additionally, technology developers need to gain deeper insight into older people, beyond just understanding what robotic technologies they will accept. Salvini et al. (2010) have found that just because a technology is easy to use does not mean older people will actually incorporate it into their lives. Usability and acceptability need to be distinguished from one another, and more attention needs to be paid on the former than the latter.[11]

Frontiers in the social study of aged care robots: heterogeneity, sustainability, and mobility

While social scientific research on aged care robots has spanned a number of topics and contexts, many social aspects of robotic care technologies remain undertheorized and underinvestigated. As covered in earlier sections, a growing body of work in the social sciences has sought to understand how robots for aged care are being developed. With a couple of exceptions (Frennert, 2016; Neven, 2010), this research has tended to be more focused and less multifaceted in terms of the relevant social groups it has sought to undertake research on. Studies that have concentrated on technology developers (Hsu et al., 2020; Hyysalo, 2006), older persons (Smarr et al., 2014), or care workers (Ishiguro, 2017; Saborowski and Kollak, 2015; Wright, 2019) have indeed produced many valuable insights. But little is known about how these groups interact and interface with one another. Additionally, as Neven (2015: 345) notes, more research also needs to be conducted on the role the media plays in constructing robot futures for older people.

There is also a need for research to be more ongoing, longitudinal, and comparative. Šabanović (2014) has argued that the culture of robotics is mutative and is made up of diverse components. She has found that it is useful to frame the cultural elements of robotics in contexts like Japan as a type of 'repeated cultural assembly'. What it means to embrace an aged care robot is likely to transform and involve a diverse array of actors, meanings, skills, and infrastructures.

Kovacic's (2018) historical study of how Japan has attempted to forge a dominant national culture around robots highlights the dynamic nature of how robotic cultures can emerge and evolve. Kovacic notes that while it is tempting to presume some cultural contexts, like Japan, have an enduring predisposition to embrace some uses of robots, this overlooks the complexity and history of how robotic cultures form. While it is the case that some cultural discourses and practices become more prominent than others, we should not overlook the existence of other divergent cultural views and narratives.

This in turn speaks to what is powerful about social and cultural research on the theme of robotics in the context of aged care. It has the potential to illuminate social aspects of aged care robots that are underappreciated or oversimplified. Future research will continue to expand what the development of aged care robots is likely to have bearing on. Wright's (2019) study of care workers in Japan, for example, has established that robots not only stand to transform how care work for the elderly is constituted. It has implications for migration as well, which has commonly been glossed over in public discussions of ageing and robots.

The environmental impacts and implications of aged care robots likewise await more sustained and in-depth scholarly interest. To date, debates about the use of aged care robots have largely overlooked the topic of environmental sustainability. Little research has been directly undertaken on the energy consumption involved with aged care robots, particularly at the scale proposed by some companies or policymakers. Social and cultural research will be key to advancing knowledge on this very pressing issue. As Nicholls and Strengers's (2019) cultural study of robotic vacuum cleaners has shown, energy consumption related to robots – especially in home settings – is not only a technical matter. Rather, robotic technologies involve visions and representations of their usage that are related to changing cultural notions of what constitutes cleanliness, comfort, and convenience, which are associated with differing levels of energy consumption.

There is additionally great potential for social research on aged care robotics to further expand what we know about how power and social inequalities are being expressed in new ways through the use of robots and artificial intelligence (AI). Robots of all kinds – including ones involved in the provision of aged care – are being developed with varying levels of artificial intelligence built into them (Elliott, 2019). Some robots are being designed to operate in a more automated way, while others require significantly more human input to function. Social research stands to deepen understanding of what it actually means for aged care robots to become more artificially intelligent.

Rubeis's (2020) account of the risks of AI-driven elder care serves as a productive starting point. Rubeis has identified AI-based gerontechnology, which encapsulate robots, as potentially being depersonalizing, discriminatory, de-humanizing, and/or disciplinary. It should be noted that this may have something to do with the agency of the AI itself, as the mechanisms of AI cannot be reduced to or subsumed as human actions. Algorithms, which form a key part of AI technologies, should themselves be regarded as a kind of social actor (Just and Latzer, 2017). But this does not mean AI systems are wholly divorced from the social. Suchman (2007) has noted that robotic technologies driven by AI commonly take on an 'enchanted' quality. AI-driven robots sometimes appear to operate magically, as if they were fully autonomous. But yet, Wajcman (2017: 124–125) notes that this image of AI systems and robots commonly occludes the multitude of people who are tasked with creating, propping up, and steering the operation of AI technologies. There is a need in other words to not only learn more about how advanced AI robots exceed human control. We also need, in some respects, to flip the study of aged care robots on its head. Rather than just ask how AI-driven robots will provide care to older people, we should also explore what 'care' and upkeep needs to be provided to robots and AI systems (Saborowski and Kollak, 2015).

Finally, this chapter finds that there is an impetus for social and cultural studies of aged care robots to be more attuned to its glocal[12] and mobile dimensions. Thus far, the social and cultural study of aged care robots has either tended to be universalizing[13] or be based within a specific social context, most often within the conceptual boundaries of a nation-state such as the US or Japan. While it is relatively easy to understand why the former tendency is problematic, since universalizing robot cultures downplays cultural difference, the critique that nation-state-based studies also have shortcomings has not been as well-developed in the social and cultural study of robots.

One reason why we need to go beyond nation-based approaches to studying robotic cultures has to do with issues identified with methodological nationalism (Chernilo, 2006). Methodological nationalism, in its crudest expressions, presupposes that nation-states constitute discrete societal units that are the containers and drivers of social action. A key criticism of methodological nationalism in social research is that it presents an overly static and endogenous understanding of social change and behavior. It is less attuned to the ways in which societies as entities are exogenously constituted through and against cultural interchange and flows.

Urry (2000) has notably proposed that we focus on the phenomenon of mobility as a corrective. This has led to the establishment of what Sheller and Urry (2006) have termed, 'the new mobilities paradigm', an area of study that has underscored and elaborated the social significance and complexity of movement in all of its heterogeneous forms. To date, the theme of mobilities has not figured substantively into the study of aged care robots. But there are multiple reasons why adopting a mobilities focus might be fruitful in producing new insights and expanding research agendas.

Concentrating on the mobile aspects of aged care robots has the potential to reveal more of the under-appreciated impacts of using robots to provide care for older people. As discussed earlier, by modifying, enhancing, supplanting, and/or re-imaging technologies like the wheelchair or the motor vehicle, some types of robots are being developed that may transform how older people move about in the social world. A mobilities research lens is useful to apply here because it can tease out what is meaningful about those particular transformations, as movement facilitated by robots is not just a functional matter. It is also laden with cultural meaning and significance.

A mobilities focus can also attune researchers to the ways in which the development, uptake, and use of robotic gerontechnologies occurs between and within different contexts. Through her study of the ways in which anthropomorphic care robots from Japan have been introduced into the context of Denmark, Leeson (2017) has demonstrated how robot cultures can be interconnected with one another. Leeson found that technologies are not simply transplanted from one context into another in a straightforward manner. Transfers of technologies often lead to unforeseen usages and they can be multidirectional, which is to say that the originating context of an introduced technology does not simply remain static. This suggests that we should think of robotic cultures as constituting heterogenous elements that travel and traverse various contexts and spaces. A mobilities lens sensitizes us to the fact that these movements can be tracked and studied at different scales (Cresswell, 2010: 552). The culture of aged care robots not only involves macro components like governmental or corporate agreements to import technology, which may reflect geopolitical power imbalances and struggles, it also involves the transport of knowledge, skills, people, and objects.

Conclusion

This chapter has explored how there are growing associations between robots and ageing. Robots are thought to play an increasingly prominent role in the provision of elder care in many parts of the contemporary modern world. This chapter has explored what is potentially ethically problematic about the use of aged care robots. The ethical debate surrounding carebots for older people was shown to be multi-sided and not simply critical. Just as it is problematic to embrace robots in aged care in a wholesale fashion, dismissing them *in toto* or from a universalist position was also found to be worthy of pointed criticism (Vandemeulebroucke et al., 2018).

Eric L. Hsu

The social and cultural sciences have much to contribute to how we ethically assess and reflect upon the development of aged care robot technologies. Research that has been undertaken on how various social groups view and interact with robotic technologies has cast doubt on the idea that aged care robots will be wholly socially beneficial and uniformly accepted. There is a need to take into account socio-demographic factors (Flandorfer, 2012) and the interaction between various groups that make up the ecology of older people (Forlizzi et al., 2011). Further, there is a need to be critical and reflexive about the topics, people, and concepts under investigation. For example, learning about the 'acceptability' of robots may not give us an adequate understanding of how robots might factor into the lives of older people and those who surround them (Peine and Neven, 2011; Salvini et al., 2010).

This chapter established that there are a multitude of frontiers that await further exploration in the social and cultural study of robotic gerontechnologies. While valuable insights have been produced about the ways in which robotic technologies are being developed in various contexts and how technology design approaches might be more participatory, less is currently known about the links between aged care robots and topics like environmental sustainability. The mobile aspects of robots in aged care also await more sustained investigation. This refers to the underexplored view that robot cultures are constituted by heterogenous elements that involve movement within and between different contexts. Taken as a whole, these investigations are meant to further highlight the relevance of social and cultural perspectives of aged care robots. The social and cultural sciences stand to help people understand that the future of robots in aged care is not a fixed one.

Notes

1 This work was supported by the Toyota Foundation (TYTID D16-R-0242) and the Australian Research Council (DP180101816).
2 This chapter works with a definition of a robot provided by Pedersen et al. (2018). They use 'ideal terms' to define a robot as 'a machine that resembles a living creature with the ability to move independently and perform complex actions and/or interactions' (Pedersen et al., 2018: 2).
3 It should be noted that while service robots and companion robots are two categories of robots that have applications for older people, they do not exist in pure and exclusive forms (Broekens et al., 2009). For example, some robots are known to have both service and companion features.
4 See the work of Neven (2015) for an extended discussion of how technology developers have come to operate under the assumption that living independently at home should be one of the ultimate end goals of gerontechnologies.
5 For a more extended and in-depth account of how the ethics of aged care robots has been debated, see the work of Vandemeulebroucke et al. (2018) and Vallor (2011).
6 Sharkey and Sharkey (2012b: 270) cite Article 12 of the Universal Declaration of Human Rights: 'No one shall be subjected to arbitrary interference with his privacy, family, home, or correspondence, nor to attacks upon his honor and reputation. Everyone has the right to the protection of the law against interference or attacks'.
7 Bissell et al. (2020) trouble the idea that automated forms of mobility are likely to only decrease the amounts of transport disadvantage that some social groups have traditionally experienced. Robotic and automated technologies and transport systems are likely to also bring about new or reinforce existing forms of social inequality.
8 Coeckelbergh (2016), in fact, actually goes a step further than this. He questions whether 'deception' is even the right word to use given its pejorative connation.
9 Hsu et al. (2020) have found that developers of aged care robots should also be understood as a diverse collection of persons, who employ a myriad of design approaches.
10 See Durick et al. (2013) for an extended discussion of how crisis accounts of ageing are prevalent in gerontechnology design and why these accounts are problematic.

11 Peine and Neven (2011) argue that we should even go a step further. Peine and Neven explore the concept of the 'domestication' as a way to go beyond the discourse of 'usability' and 'acceptability'. For Peine and Neven (2011: 136), 'a focus on domesticability relaxes the assumption often found in usability approaches – at least in the way they are normally operationalized – that a technology is usable when users appropriate it in more or less exactly the way intended by designers. Domesticable technology, in contrast, is open to uses not foreseen by its designers'.

12 'Glocalization' is a term in globalization studies that describes the dynamic interface between global and local forces. See Hsu (2010) for a brief overview of this concept.

13 Some data from research exploring 'acceptance' or the 'ethics' of aged care robots have contained universalizing tendencies. Some studies have either underplayed or omitted discussion of the cultural environment. Additionally as Vandemeulebroucke et al. (2018) have noted, there have been some works that have taken a 'top-down' approach to analyzing the ethics of deploying robots for aged care.

References

Akrich M (1995) User representations: Practices, methods and sociology. In: Rip A, Misa T and Schot J (eds) *Managing Technology in Society: The Approach of Constructive Technology Assessment*. New York: Pinter, pp. 167–184.

Bissell D, Birtchnell T, Elliott A, et al. (2020) Autonomous automobilities: The social impacts of driverless vehicles. *Current Sociology* 68(1): 116–134. DOI: 10.1177/0011392118816743.

Broekens J, Heerink M and Rosendal H (2009) Assistive social robots in elderly care: A review. *Gerontechnology* 8(2). DOI: 10.4017/gt.2009.08.02.002.00.

Chernilo D (2006) Social theory's methodological nationalism myth and reality. *European Journal of Social Theory* 9(1): 5–22. DOI: 10.1177/1368431006060460.

Coeckelbergh M (2016) Care robots and the future of ICT-mediated elderly care: A response to doom scenarios. *AI & Society* 31(4). Springer London: 455–462. DOI: 10.1007/s00146-015-0626-3.

Cresswell T (2010) Mobilities I: Catching up. *Progress in Human Geography* 35(4): 550–558. DOI: 10.1177/0309132510383348.

Decker M (2008) Caregiving robots and ethical reflection: The perspective of interdisciplinary technology assessment. *AI & Society* 22(3): 315–330. DOI: 10.1007/s00146-007-0151-0.

Durick J, Robertson T, Brereton M, et al. (2013) Dispelling ageing myths in technology design. *Proceedings of the 25th Australian Computer-Human Interaction Conference: Augmentation, Application, Innovation, Collaboration, OzCHI 2013*, pp. 467–476. DOI: 10.1145/2541016.2541040.

Elliott A (2019) *The Culture of AI: Everyday Life and the Digital Revolution*. London: Routledge.

Flandorfer P (2012) Population ageing and socially assistive robots for elderly persons: The importance of sociodemographic factors for user acceptance. *International Journal of Population Research* 2012: 1–13. DOI: 10.1155/2012/829835.

Forlizzi J, Disalvo C, Gemperle F, et al. (2011) Assistive robotics and an ecology of elders living independently in their homes assistive robotics and an ecology their homes. *Human-Computer Interaction* 19: 24–59.

Frennert S (2016) *Older People Meet Robots: Three Case Studies on the Domestication of Robots in Everyday Life*. PhD Thesis, Doctoral Thesis (Compilation), Lund University.

Frennert S and Östlund B (2014) Review: Seven matters of concern of social robots and older people. *International Journal of Social Robotics* 6(2): 299–310. DOI: 10.1007/s12369-013-0225-8.

Graafmans J (2017) The history and incubation of gerontechnology. In: Kwon S (ed.) *Gerontechnology: Research, Practice, and Principles in the Field of Technology and Aging*. New York: Springer, pp. 3–11.

Harper S (2014) Economic and social implications of aging societies. *Science* 346(6209): 587–591.

Holley-Moore G and Creighton H (2015) *The Future of Transport in an Ageing Society*. London: International Longevity Centre.

Hsu EL (2010) Social theory and globalization. In: Elliott A (ed.) *The Routledge Companion to Social Theory*. London: Routledge, pp. 203–218.

Hsu EL, Elliott A, Ishii Y, et al. (2020) The development of aged care robots in Japan as a varied process. *Technology in Society* 63. Elsevier Ltd. DOI: 10.1016/j.techsoc.2020.101366.

Hyysalo S (2006) Representations of use and practice-bound imaginaries in automating the safety of the elderly. *Social Studies of Science* 36(4): 599–626. DOI: 10.1177/0306312706058426.

Ishiguro N (2017) Care robots in Japanese elderly care: Cultural values in focus. *The Routledge Handbook of Social Care Work Around the World*: 256–269. DOI: 10.4324/9781315612805.

Joyce K and Loe M (2010) A sociological approach to ageing. *Technology and Health*. 32(2): 171–180. DOI: 10.1111/j.1467-9566.2009.01219.x.

Just N and Latzer M (2017) Governance by algorithms: Reality construction by algorithmic selection on the Internet. *Media, Culture and Society* 39(2): 238–258. DOI: 10.1177/0163443716643157.

Kovacic M (2018) The making of national robot history in Japan: Monozukuri, enculturation and cultural lineage of robots. *Critical Asian Studies* 50(4). Taylor & Francis: 572–590. DOI: 10.1080/14672715.2018.1512003.

Leeson C (2017) *Anthropomorphic Robots on the Move: A Transformative Trajectory from Japan to Danish Healthcare*. University of Copenhagen. Available at: www.egv.dk/images/Projekter/Projekter_2013/Christina_Leeson_PhD_thesis_2017.pdf.

Leong TW and Johnston B (2016) Co-design and robots: A case study of a robot dog for aging people. *Lecture Notes in Computer Science (including subseries Lecture Notes in Artificial Intelligence and Lecture Notes in Bioinformatics)* 9979. LNAI: 702–711. DOI: 10.1007/978-3-319-47437-3_69.

Lutz W, Sanderson W and Scherbov S (2008) The coming acceleration of global population ageing. *Nature* 451(7179): 716–719. DOI: 10.1038/nature06516.

Muramatsu N and Akiyama H (2011) Japan: Super-aging society preparing for the future. *Gerontologist* 51(4): 425–432. DOI: 10.1093/geront/gnr067.

Neven L (2010) 'But obviously not for me': Robots, laboratories and the defiant identity of elder test users. *Sociology of Health & Illness* 32(2): 335–347. DOI: 10.1111/j.1467-9566.2009.01218.x.

Neven L (2015) By any means? Questioning the link between gerontechnological innovation and older people's wish to live at home. *Technological Forecasting & Social Change* 93. Elsevier B.V.: 32–43. DOI: 10.1016/j.techfore.2014.04.016.

Neven L and Peine A (2017) From triple win to triple sin: How a problematic future discourse is shaping the way people age with technology. *Societies* 7(3): 26. DOI: 10.3390/soc7030026.

Nicholls L and Strengers Y (2019) Robotic vacuum cleaners save energy? Raising cleanliness conventions and energy demand in Australian households with smart home technologies. *Energy Research and Social Science* 50(October 2018). Elsevier: 73–81. DOI: 10.1016/j.erss.2018.11.019.

Niemelä M and Melkas H (2019) Robots as social and physical assistants in elderly care: 177–197. DOI: 10.1007/978-981-13-7725-9_10.

Nomura T, Suzuki T, Kanda T, et al. (2008) What people assume about humanoid and animal-type robots: Cross-cultural analysis between Japan, Korea, and the... *International Journal of Humanoid Robotics* 5(1): 25–46. DOI: 10.1142/S0219843608001297.

Pedersen I, Reid S and Aspevig K (2018) Developing social robots for aging populations: A literature review of recent academic sources. *Sociology Compass* 12(6): 1–10. DOI: 10.1111/soc4.12585.

Peine A (2019) *Ageing and Digital Technology*. Springer Singapore. DOI: 10.1007/978-981-13-3693-5.

Peine A and Neven L (2011) Social-structural lag revisited. *Gerontechnology* 10(3): 129–139. DOI: 10.4017/gt.2011.10.3.002.00.

Peine A and Neven L (2019) From intervention to co-constitution: New directions in theorizing about aging and technology. *The Gerontologist* 59(1): 15–21. DOI: 10.1093/geront/gny050.

Peine A, Faulkner A, Jæger B, et al. (2015) Science, technology and the 'grand challenge' of ageing-understanding the socio-material constitution of later life. *Technological Forecasting and Social Change* 93. Elsevier Inc.: 1–9. DOI: 10.1016/j.techfore.2014.11.010.

Peine A, Rollwagen I and Neven L (2014) The rise of the 'innosumer'-rethinking older technology users. *Technological Forecasting and Social Change* 82(1). Elsevier Inc.: 199–214. DOI: 10.1016/j.techfore.2013.06.013.

Pew (2015) *Family Support in Graying Societies*. Washington, DC: Pew Research Centre.

Robinson H, MacDonald B and Broadbent E (2014) The role of healthcare robots for older people at home: A review. *International Journal of Social Robotics* 6(4): 575–591. DOI: 10.1007/s12369-014-0242-2.

Rubeis G (2020) The disruptive power of artificial intelligence. Ethical aspects of gerontechnology in elderly care. *Archives of Gerontology and Geriatrics* 91(April). Elsevier: 104186. DOI: 10.1016/j.archger.2020.104186.

Šabanović S (2010) Robots in society, society in robots: Mutual shaping of society and technology as a framework for social robot design. *International Journal of Social Robotics* 2: 439–450. DOI: 10.1007/s12369-010-0066-7.

Šabanović S (2014) Inventing Japan's 'robotics culture': The repeated assembly of science, technology, and culture in social robotics. *Social Studies of Science* 44(3): 342–367. DOI: 10.1177/0306312713509704.

Šabanović S, Chang W-L, Bennett CC, et al. (2015) A robot of my own: Participatory design of socially assistive robots for independently living older adults diagnosed with depression. In: Zhou J and Salvendy G (eds) *Human Aspects of IT for the Aged Population. Design for Aging*. Cham: Springer International Publishing, pp. 104–114.

Saborowski M and Kollak I (2015) 'How do you care for technology?' – Care professionals' experiences with assistive technology in care of the elderly. *Technological Forecasting and Social Change* 93. Elsevier Inc.: 133–140. DOI: 10.1016/j.techfore.2014.05.006.

Salvini P, Laschi C and Dario P (2010) Design for acceptability: Improving robots' coexistence in human society. *International Journal of Social Robotics* 2(4): 451–460. DOI: 10.1007/s12369-010-0079-2.

Schoeni RF and Ofstedal MB (2010) Key themes in research on the demography of aging. *Demography* 47: 5–15. DOI: 10.1353/dem.2010.0001.

Schulz R, Wahl HW, Matthews JT, et al. (2015) Advancing the aging and technology agenda in gerontology. *Gerontologist* 55(5): 724–734. DOI: 10.1093/geront/gnu071.

Sharkey A and Sharkey N (2012) Granny and the robots: Ethical issues in robot care for the elderly. *Ethics and Information Technology* 14(1): 27–40. DOI: 10.1007/s10676-010-9234-6.

Sharkey N and Sharkey A (2012a) The eldercare factory. *Gerontology* 58(3): 282–288. DOI: 10.1159/000329483.

Sharkey N and Sharkey A (2012b) The rights and wrongs of robot care. *Robot Ethics: The Ethical and Social Implications of Robotics*: 267–282.

Sheller M and Urry J (2006) The new mobilities paradigm. *Enviroment and Planning A* 38(2): 207–226. DOI: 10.1068/a37268.

Shishehgar M, Kerr D and Blake J (2018) A systematic review of research into how robotic technology can help older people. *Smart Health* 7–8. Elsevier: 1–18. DOI: 10.1016/j.smhl.2018.03.002.

Smarr CA, Mitzner TL, Beer JM, et al. (2014) Domestic robots for older adults: Attitudes, preferences, and potential. *International Journal of Social Robotics* 6(2): 229–247. DOI: 10.1007/s12369-013-0220-0.

Smarr CA, Prakash A, Beer JM, et al. (2012) Older adults' preferences for and acceptance of robot assistance for everyday living tasks. *Proceedings of the Human Factors and Ergonomics Society 56th Annual Meeting*, pp. 153–157. DOI: 10.1177/1071181312561009.

Sparrow R and Sparrow L (2006) In the hands of machines? The future of aged care. *Minds and Machines* 16(2): 141–161. DOI: 10.1007/s11023-006-9030-6.

Suchman L (2007) *Human–Machine Reconfigurations: Plans and Situated Actions*. Cambridge: Cambridge University Press.

Toms G, Verity F and Orrell A (2019) Social care technologies for older people: Evidence for instigating a broader and more inclusive dialogue. *Technology in Society* 58. Elsevier Ltd. DOI: 10.1016/j.techsoc.2019.01.004.

Urry J (2000) *Sociology beyond Societies: Mobilities for the Twenty-First Century*. London: Routledge.

Vallor S (2011) Carebots and caregivers: Sustaining the ethical ideal of care in the twenty-first century. *Philosophy and Technology* 24(3): 251–268. DOI: 10.1007/s13347-011-0015-x.

Vandemeulebroucke T, Dierckx de Casterlé B and Gastmans C (2018) The use of care robots in aged care: A systematic review of argument-based ethics literature. *Archives of Gerontology and Geriatrics* 74(August 2017). Elsevier: 15–25. DOI: 10.1016/j.archger.2017.08.014.

Wachsmuth I (2018) Robots like me: Challenges and ethical issues in aged care. *Frontiers in Psychology* 9(April): 2017–2019. DOI: 10.3389/fpsyg.2018.00432.

Wajcman J (2017) Automation: Is it really different this time? *British Journal of Sociology* 68(1): 119–127. DOI: 10.1111/1468-4446.12239.

Weber J (2005) Helpless machines and true loving care givers: A feminist critique of recent trends in human–robot interaction. *Journal of Information, Communication and Ethics in Society* 3(4): 209–218. DOI: 10.1108/14779960580000274.

Wright J (2019) Robots vs migrants? Reconfiguring the future of Japanese institutional eldercare. *Critical Asian Studies* 51(3). Taylor & Francis: 331–354. DOI: 10.1080/14672715.2019.1612765.

18
Big data and data analytics

Jo Bates

The emergence of social research about big data analytics

In 2012, it was claimed by IBM that 90% of all data in existence had been generated in the previous two years. This was, according to many, the era of "datafication" (van Dijck, 2014); a term used to refer to the processes by which masses of "big data" are generated about aspects of life that were not previously quantifiable. Vast reams of data were being produced by new technologies such as social media platforms (boyd and Crawford, 2012) and smart city infrastructures (Kitchin, 2013). The analytical possibilities of this process of datafication were significant, as became evident for much of the public in 2013 when Edward Snowden blew the whistle on the data-driven surveillance practices of the USA's National Security Agency and other countries' security services, illuminating how they had intercepted metadata relating to billions of phone calls and online interactions (van Dijck, 2014). By 2014, the term "big data" had been added to consultancy firm Gartner's annual hype cycle as the industry turned its attention to what this new resource might offer.

It wasn't only the tech sector and consultancy firms that were paying attention to these processes of datafication and the emergence of big data analytics. Even prior to the hype surrounding 'big data' that emerged around 2013, social scientists and humanities scholars had begun to question the implications of increasing amounts of 'transactional data' for their disciplines. Savage and Burrows (2007), for example, had pointed to a "coming crisis in empirical sociology". No longer was the social survey – the bread and butter method of quantitative sociologists – necessarily the best way to understand populations. Organisations were increasingly conducting their own in-house sociological research using the transactional data generated as consumers interacted with their systems. They observed how these data, which academic sociologists rarely had access to, offered much more fine-grained insights into, for example, people's social networks, than the resource intensive methods of academia.

Other observers noted both the significant potentials and challenges that "big social data" raised for the humanities (Manovich, 2011) and social sciences (Ruppert, 2013). Manovich (2011) observed that despite the interesting opportunities that such data opened up for the humanities, beyond researchers working in companies such as Facebook and Google, most had limited access to use of the data, and the skills required to answer interesting humanities questions using such data were not typically something that humanities scholars have. He observed the emergence of "new kinds of divisions" between "those who create data . . . those who have the means to collect it, and those who have expertise to analyze it" (p. 10). Ruppert (2013) made similar observations from the perspective of social science, calling for new modes of interdisciplinary collaboration that are able to develop innovations in methods that allow researchers to "innovatively, critically and reflexively engag[e] with new forms of data" (p. 270), and foster a "critique from within" that is able to grapple with issues of privacy, rights and ethics.

Beyond questions about the methodological implications of big data on academic social science and humanities, the gaze of scholars began to turn more generally in the direction of the emergent phenomena of big data analytics. Early contributions came from those whose work had positioned them close to the newly emerging technologies. danah boyd and Kate Crawford (2012), social scientists based at Microsoft Research, published an essay posing six "critical questions for big data", with a particular focus on social media data. They critiqued the claim of some within the tech sector that, with the advent of big data, numbers had begun to 'speak for themselves'. Instead, they recognised that the much heralded objectivity and accuracy of big data was misleading. Too often, they observed, patterns could be seen in big data where none actually existed, for example correlations between stock indexes and butter production in Bangladesh. Big data did not always mean better data, and understanding the sample was, in the age of big data, more important than ever. For example, it was vital to recognise that Twitter data did not represent all people – only what Twitter users chose to say on Twitter. Understanding big data in context, they argued, was crucial for interpretation, and just because researchers have access to data does not make it ethical to analyse it. Finally, they made similar observations to Manovich about the emerging divides related to which researchers had access to such data and the skills to analyse it, and which did not.

Urban geographer Rob Kitchin, was also beginning to pose similar questions with a focus on the emergence of Smart Cities. He questioned the claim that big urban data, often generated in 'Smart City' contexts, are neutral and lacking in ideology, noting that such data do not exist independently of, for example, ideas, people and social contexts. He also raised concerns about the surveillance dynamics of emergent Smart City infrastructures. He observed that as urban data systems became more centralised through Smart City developments, they also become more panoptic in design:

> rais[ing] the spectre of a Big Brother society based on a combination of surveillance (gazing at the world) and dataveillance (trawling through and inter-connecting datasets), and a world in which all aspects of a citizen's life are captured and potentially never forgotten.
> *(Kitchin, 2013, p. 11)*

These early interventions from social scientists also raised the question of what big data actually are. Much of the tech sector had adopted the 3Vs definition: big data were data that were so large in volume, variety and velocity that they could not be processed and analysed using standard data technologies. However, as Kitchin and McArdle (2016) observed definitions sometimes also involved other attributes such as exhaustivity, resolution, indexicality, relationality, extensionality and scalability (p. 2). Through examination of a number of supposedly 'big' datasets, Kitchin and McArdle (2016) observed that only a few datasets had all these traits and some were not even significant in volume or variety as the original 3Vs definition implied they ought to be. They concluded that 'big data' as a category of data needed to be further unpacked. Van Dijck (2014) also drew attention to the necessity to understand the ways in which metadata (data about data) make up big datasets, particularly in the wake of the Snowden revelations which identified how national security services apply big data analytics techniques to communications metadata.

Kitchin and McArdle (2016) were not alone in questioning what 'big data' are. Boyd and Crawford (2012) had already defined 'big data' not only as a technological and analytical phenomenon but also a mythological one. The mythology of big data that they embedded in their definition related to the widespread beliefs surrounding 'big data', specifically that big data "offer a higher form of intelligence and knowledge that can generate insights that were previously impossible, with the aura of truth, objectivity, and accuracy" (p. 663). Van Dijck referred to this mythology as "the ideology of dataism" (p. 198). As Beer (2016) argued social scientists and humanities scholars, "need[ed] to take the concept of 'big data' seriously . . . [and] explore the type of work that is being done by that concept" (p. 1), as well as the work being done by applications of so-called big data.

Emerging from these early provocations by social scientists and humanities scholars, a new sub-field of critical data studies, made up of researchers from disciplines including geography, media and communications and information studies, began to take shape. Work aiming to define the focus of the 'critical data studies' field was published in *Human Geography* (Kitchin and Lauriault, 2014 and Dalton and Thatcher, 2014) and *Communications* (Iliadis and Russo, 2016). A field specific journal was launched in 2014 – *Big Data and Society*, edited by sociologist Evelyn Ruppert; and field specific conferences were also launched – for example, 'Data Power' in 2015 (http://datapowerconference.org/) and 'Data Justice' in 2018 (https://datajusticelab.org/data-justice-conference/). While research interest in big data and related fields has expanded across the different disciplines of the social sciences and humanities in recent years, and many disciplinary conferences now have 'data' related tracks, the loosely formed sub-field of critical data studies provides a space in which transdisciplinary insights about 'big data' and related analytics are fostered. The following sections go on to discuss the major claims and developments in this field, as well as its principle contributions, criticisms and possible future developments.

Major claims and developments in the field: philosophical and political

As previously overviewed, researchers in the field have advanced a number of arguments in relation to big data and related analytics. Key arguments have been (1) philosophical in orientation, examining the epistemological and ontological claims and implications of big data, and (2) political in orientation, examining issues related to power and governance in the context of big data. While some contributions are more clearly philosophical or political, many researchers in the field draw on both philosophical and political arguments, to varying degrees, in order to advance their claims. This section begins first by considering philosophical critiques of, and insights about, big data, both epistemological and ontological. It then moves on to examine political claims about big data systems, including issues of dataveillance, discrimination, transparency and exploitation. The section finishes by exploring the implications for collective agency in the context of advances in big data analytics.

Philosophical critiques of big data

One of the early critiques that social scientists and humanities scholars advanced in relation to big data was an epistemological critique of the claim that big data had the capacity to generate new, superior forms of knowledge. Epistemology is the branch of philosophy that deals with the nature of knowledge, for example how it is created and what constitutes valid knowledge. The hype surrounding big data had included a number of claims about the far-reaching potential of big data to overturn earlier ways of creating knowledge. These arguments echoed some of the points made by sociologists Savage and Burrows (2007) in their paper on the coming crisis in sociology; however, they went further and with less nuance. Leading the way was an audacious claim made in 2008 by Chris Anderson – the editor of the tech magazine *Wired* – that big data analytics made the scientific method obsolete, that we should forget every theory generated by the natural and social sciences, and simply let the numbers "speak for themselves". His ideas caught on in some of the industry hype surrounding 'big data' in the following years, and, unsurprisingly, social scientists and humanities scholars took the bait and came down hard on Anderson's claims.

The epistemological critique of 'big data' centred on a number of key points:

1. **Data are never "raw", neutral or self-evident representations of the world.** Big data, in particular data generated as a by-product of some other activity (e.g. social media practices) or using sensors (e.g. location or environmental sensors), were often presented by big data advocates as an essentially accurate and truthful representation of phenomena, void of any social or political bias or interference. Early interventions from social scientists and humanities scholars often centred on this claim. Lisa Gitelman's (2013) edited collection, *"Raw Data" Is an Oxymoron*, was a key contribution to this debate. As was work by Kitchin (2013, 2014), boyd and Crawford (2012) and van Dijck (2014). All of these critiques advanced, in their own ways, the argument that data are never "raw", socially neutral representations of the world, rather they are manufactured in complex social contexts shaped by ideologies, beliefs, finance etc.

2. **The outputs of big data analytics are not neutral representations of the world.** Similar to the argument that data were not "raw", critics also recognised that the analysis of data and interpretation of patterns and relationships in data is also undertaken by people and shaped by their socio-cultural biases, assumptions, contexts (Kitchin, 2014; D'Ignazio and Klein, 2020)

3. **N ≠ all, data are always partial.** A frequent claim advanced in the hype of big data was that such data are comprehensive and offer full resolution; that there was no longer any need to sample because data represented the full population (n = all). Critics such as Kitchin (2014) and boyd and Crawford (2012) instead recognised that despite the increasing volume of datasets, big data were still always in some way partial representations of the world, and that it was vital to understand the ways in which any given dataset was incomplete in relation to whatever the analyst was trying to understand. In simple terms, a Twitter dataset only represents (likely a sub-set of) Twitter users and what they share on Twitter, and is not representative of the thoughts of the full population as some big data advocates assumed.

4. **Big data as a technology for knowledge production is theoretically driven.** While advocates had proclaimed that 'big data' meant the end of theory, critics re-joined with the observation that big data systems are not themselves free of theory and philosophy, rather they were created for a purpose and guided by an agenda, and the analytical techniques and algorithms they use are based upon scientific reasoning and established theories (Kitchin, 2014).

More recently, the epistemological debates around big data have drawn on feminist and decolonial lenses to illuminate some of the ways that historically constituted social injustices become embedded in the 'universalist' knowledge claims emerging from many big data systems. D'Ignazio and Klein's (2020) "data feminism" lens, for example, draws attention to who is engaged in the practice of data analytics, and what this may mean for the knowledge claims that are produced by the field. They observe that it is common for people from "dominant groups" to be the ones who do and benefit from big data analytics, and whose priorities tend to get turned into products.

Milan and Treré (2019), take this line of critique further to observe that the critique of big data analytics that has developed in the social sciences also has its own biased epistemology. They argue that research in the field has so far tended to "take as frame of reference the liberal democracies of the West, with their sociocultural substrate and long tradition of representative institutions, rule of law, and citizen involvement in public affairs". Those outside this frame of references, they argue – "the different, the underprivileged, the silenced, the subaltern, and the 'have nots'" who are not necessarily connected to particular geographical locations – have remained in a "blind spot" (p. 320), and their knowledges and experiences need to be centred.

As well as advancing an epistemological critique of big data and the hype and critique surrounding it, social scientists and humanities scholars have also explored the ontological dimensions of big data systems. Ontology refers to the philosophical study of the nature of being – for example, existence and reality – and how different entities relate to one another. Big data systems raise a number of ontological questions; for example, Ruppert (2013) asks what the implications of big data might be on the nature of who people are, as individuals and societies. Others have addressed the question of what entities make up a big data system, and what this might mean in relation to the social shaping and implications of big data. Kitchin, for example, advance the idea of a 'data assemblage'; a complex of socio-material entities including cultural (e.g. ideologies, beliefs, norms), social (e.g. regulations, communities) and material (e.g. technologies, infrastructures, investments) factors that all inter-relate to shape how data are produced, processed and used (Kitchin and Lauriault, 2014; Kitchin, 2014). This interest in the materiality of big data systems, both in terms of their constitution and implications, has been explored by a number of researchers in the field. For example, Bates et al. (2016) examine the socio-material constitution of data objects and flows in their work on 'Data Journeys', and Lupton (2018) draws on various theories of materialism to illuminate "the material and embodied dimensions of human – data assemblages as they grow and are enacted, articulated and incorporated into everyday lives".

As Couldry and Powell (2014) assert, the "mutual intertwining of human and material agency is hardly a new insight" (p. 3), but the observation takes on increased significance for research in a context in which big data practices are largely opaque to non-experts. Through drawing on a variety of materialist traditions, such scholars have avoided an idealist critique of big data systems which would understand big data to be driven only by things such as beliefs, ideas and discourses, to illuminate the complex assemblage of interrelated social and material factors that produce 'big data' and the work it does in the world. As articulated by Coté et al. (2016):

> This is not to suggest that Big Data – more specifically processes of datafication – are best or at all understood as socially constructed. Indeed, discursive analysis or unreconstructed social theory cannot fully grasp how data re-articulates the social, cultural, political and economic in a deeply recursive manner. Thus, any political reckoning must equally account for the materiality of data, alongside the logic guiding its processes and the practices that deploy its tools.
>
> *(p. 5)*

Political critique of big data

Beyond the philosophical questions around what data are, how they come to be, what work they do, and what kinds of knowledge claims it is possible to make with them, a further – and often related – focus of research about big data analytics has been the politics of data. While there is an underlying politics behind much of the work cited in the previous section, two papers published in 2016 and 2017 explicitly lay out the case for a focus on "data politics" within the field (Coté et al., 2016; Ruppert et al., 2017).

While stopping short of articulating a singular framework for illuminating data politics, Coté et al. (2016) instead argue that to "forensically unpack the value-laden information and knowledge" produced through data analytics, what is required is a "political critique [that] entails questions of data access, technological understanding and capacities, and the ability to critically examine the algorithms of data analytics" (p. 9). Not only was it vital to understand how data and their analysis are constituted in complex socio-material contexts, it was also crucial to pay attention to concentrations of economic power and ownership within the data economy, and how algorithms "enact new procedures of power and knowledge" (p. 8). While Coté et al's. (2016) conceptualisation of data politics remains focused on the political constitution of the outputs of big data analytics, Ruppert et al. (2017) place more emphasis on the ways in which data has been constituted as a political object with particular "powers, influence and rationalities". They argue that data has become political because it "reconfigures relationships between states and citizens" (p. 1). It has become "a force that is generative of . . . new forms of power relations and politics at different and inter-connected scales" (p. 2). In the big data era, virtual and actual worlds interact to produce subjects whose political rights become "objects of struggle" in the field of data politics.

While these approaches to defining 'data politics' have their differences, they are similar in their emphasis on issues of power, struggle and relations between different social groups. Within the wider literature on big data analytics, these issues are explored by authors who, on the one hand, frame big data in terms of its capacity for oppression through surveillance, discrimination, exploitation and a lack of transparency, and those that refocus this framing with an emphasis on agency and empowerment of citizens in the context of big data systems. The following section will outline these debates in more detail.

- **Surveillance, dataveillance and the data gaze.** Researchers of surveillance practices began to pay attention to data-driven systems earlier than many within the social sciences and humanities. For example, Louise Amoore's (2006) research on the expansion of "biometric borders" in the early 2000s which examined the ways in which personal data was increasingly being used to "classify and govern the movement of people across borders" (p. 341).

    Others have also worked to unpack the differences between traditional forms of surveillance and contemporary practices of "dataveillance". Kitchin (2013), for example, notes how while surveillance involves "gazing at the world", the term dataveillance emphasises the practice of "trawling through and interconnecting datasets" (p. 11), and in a piece published post-Snowden revelations, communications scholar Jose van Dijck (2014) noted that while "surveillance presumes monitoring for specific purposes" the dataveillance enabled by big data analytics "entails the continuous tracking of (meta)data for unstated preset purposes" (p. 205).

    In the Smart City context, Kitchin (2013) pointed to the ways in which big data systems were leading to a centralisation of urban surveillance systems in city control rooms, while in other contexts researchers observed that surveillance systems were becoming more distributed and less panoptic (Galic et al., 2015). These and other studies observed the different ways in which data-driven surveillance systems were shifting the relationship between state and citizens, and the ways that already marginalised citizens could become caught up in these systems, for example because the data and algorithms falsely concluded they were a national security risk. These novel forms of surveillance were not only perceived to impact the power relation between state and citizens but also consumers and commercial organisations such as platform companies (e.g. Google, Facebook).

- **Discrimination and biased systems.** As big data analytics systems were adopted in more and more areas of society it fast became apparent that the discriminatory and unjust impacts that had been observed in border control and state surveillance systems were also a feature of other types of big data systems. One area of significant research activity is related to bias in search engines. Using a variety of methodological approaches, researchers have observed how the results of search engines such as Google and Bing have significant racial and gendered biases (Noble, 2018; Otterbacher et al., 2017). What was quickly becoming apparent was that these systems and the data they were ingesting and learning from reflected, and in many cases exaggerated, the significant social injustices related to racism and sexism that are present within the societies that produced the data and systems. While some computer scientists have begun work to try and fix these biased systems (e.g. those engaged in work on 'FATE' [fairness, accountability, transparency and ethics]), many social scientists and humanities scholars are concerned that the kinds of technical fixes being proposed are unlikely to be sufficient to address such a complex socio-technical problem.

- **Exploitation and colonisation.** Scholars drawing on a Marxist understanding of social relations have long pointed to the exploitative dynamic that sits behind people's online activity, recognising internet users' online activity as a form of 'digital labour' that generates value for capitalist platform owners. More recently, some social theorists have expanded this critique to the wider big data context. Thatcher et al. (2016), for example, argue that the capturing of 'big data' about people is a form of accumulation by dispossession; an "asymmetric power relationship in which individuals are dispossessed of the data they generate in their day-to-day lives" (p. 990). A similar argument is put forward by Couldry and Mejias (2019), who also argue that the ways in which data is captured and processed by companies is a form of "appropriation". Both sets of authors argue that these processes of appropriation should be understood as a contemporary form of colonialisation that they term "data colonialism" (Thatcher et al., 2016; Couldry and Mejias, 2019). This understanding of big data as 'colonising' has also been proposed by theorists who adopt a different – non-Marxist – perspective. Ruppert et al. (2017), for example, argues that "data colonizes minds . . . [and] lifeworlds" (p. 5), and Milan and Treré (2019) adopt a decolonial lens to critique the ways in which research about big data analytics is biased towards a frame of reference centred on the liberal democracies of the West.

- **Black-boxed systems.** These issues of dataveillance, discrimination and exploitation are, Frank Pasquale (2015) argues, further compounded by a further colonisation: a colonisation by "the logic of secrecy" (p. 2). While big data systems have made citizens far more transparent to the watchful eyes of states and companies, these same institutions have in many cases become more secretive, particularly in relation to the functioning of the 'black-boxed' big data systems that increasingly inform their decision making. With a focus specifically on big data systems used in Wall Street (finance) and Silicon Valley (internet), Pasquale explores the different tactics firms use to keep secrets about their black-boxed systems and argues the case for transparency.

While there has been significant focus from social scientists and humanities scholars on the oppressive nature of big data systems, a further body of work has examined the possibilities of agency within this context. As Kennedy et al. (2015) assert in the introduction to a special issue on the topic of 'data agency', "thinking about agency is fundamental to thinking about the distribution of data power" (p. 2). Early contributions exploring such questions include Couldry and Powell's (2014) essay in which they argue for more attention to be paid to "agency and reflexivity" than theories which only emphasise oppressive forms of algorithmic power. They identify two ways in which this might be done. First, examination of the ways that community organisations can use data analytics to further their own agendas, for example NGOs such as Mapping for Change. Second, researching people's attempts to create an information economy that is "more open to civic intervention". They conclude by arguing that it might be important for those in the field to highlight not only the risks of big data systems but also the potential opportunities – "ambiguous as they may be" (p. 4). This line of argument is also presented by Taylor et al. (2014) in a paper that reports on ideas emerging from a workshop about how big data might become a "resource for positive social change in low- and middle- income countries (LMICs)" (p. 418). They argue that there are four potential opportunities big data offers in this context: "advocacy; analysis and prediction; facilitating information exchange; and promoting accountability and transparency" (p. 418), yet across these opportunities they recognise that there are challenges relating to issues of privacy and open data. They argue that it is crucial for civil society groups from LMICs to become engaged in the debates around big data practices.

Related to these debates around "data agency" others have explored how societies should respond to emergent data practices in ways that fit with normative values such as ethics and justice. Some of this work is happening in emergent interdisciplinary fields such as FATE, which brings together researchers working primarily in the fields of computer science, ethics and law to develop technical and legal interventions that mitigate against the risks big data analytics poses with regard to privacy and discrimination. However, as some social scientists and humanities scholars have observed, in this field concerns with big data can be framed quite narrowly as a specialist issue focused primarily on technical and legal solutions. Some social scientists have instead argued that responses to emergent data practices should be framed more broadly through centring the discussion on notions of "data justice" that "relate to long-standing social, political, economic and cultural issues" (p. 873), rather than being specifically technical problems requiring techno-legal solutions (Dencik et al., 2019)

A further line of debate within this area is whether ethics offers a satisfactory framework to address problems identified with big data analytics (Rességuier and Rodrigues, 2020). Many have observed how the discourse around data ethics has in recent years been co-opted by big tech companies and others in the tech sector to 'ethics wash' their products without any deep consideration of their social implications. Social scientists and humanities scholars have therefore questioned whether 'ethics' alone is sufficient to address the problems with big data analytics that researchers and social justice campaigns have observed. Dencik et al. (2019), for example, observe that there is a need to "position data in a way that engages more explicitly with questions of power, politics, inclusion and interests, as well as more established notions of ethics, autonomy, trust, accountability, governance and citizenship" (p. 874).

Principal contributions of the field: conceptual, methodological, empirical and community building

The major claims and research developments highlighted in the previous section can be understood as mapping onto a number of key contributions made by the field. Core contributions to knowledge are categorised here as (1) conceptual, (2) methodological and (3) empirical contributions. A fourth contribution is identified as the creation of research communities interested in critical examination of issues related to big data and analytics from social science and humanities perspectives.

Conceptual contributions

As Kitchin (2014) argued in his book *The Data Revolution*, "there is a need to develop conceptual and philosophical ways to make sense of data" (p. 25). In 2014, when the book was published, there was a relatively limited conceptual apparatus through which to make sense of the emergence of big data and related analytics, but it was not long before scholars stepped into the space with a variety of conceptual tools that could be used to help illuminate what was unfolding.

Early concepts tended to describe what observers saw. Terms such as "datafication" for example aimed to describe the unprecedented ways in which more and more aspects of life were being quantified through capture of data via devices and sensors. Similarly, the term "dataveillance" aimed to capture the shift that big data enabled in the context of surveillance allowing watchers to trawl through and interconnect databases (Kitchin, 2013, p. 11).

Researchers also began conceptualising the context that was shaping – and being shaped by – these emergent big data practices. Another contribution from Kitchin and Lauriault (2014) within this area was the concept of the "data assemblage". This concept aims to capture the ways in which big data systems are complexly intertwined with a variety of technical, political, social and economic apparatuses that "frame[] their nature, operation and work" (Kitchin and Lauriault, 2014, p. 7; see also Kitchin, 2014).

A further body of conceptual work has aimed at developing normative concepts that aim to promote a direction of travel for how societies respond to big data and analytics, as well as offering a space for critique of existing practices. The concept of "data agency" (Kennedy et al., 2015) introduced earlier, for example, emphasises the importance of paying attention to the important ways that data might be used by ordinary people in order to further their own agendas. Similarly, the notion of "data justice" (Dencik et al., 2019) moves beyond responses that are overly determined by technical and legal responses in order to offer a deeper political critique of what social justice might look like in a datafied society.

While it has been critiqued for its primarily Western orientation (e.g. Milan and Treré, 2019), the previous discussion reflects the beginnings of a conceptual framework developed by key scholars in the field of critical data studies that provides an initial tool box for researchers in the field to think with, and to adapt and further develop, as they undertake their own investigations into the implications of big data analytics on societies.

Methodological contributions

A further area of contribution has been in relation to advancing methods for conducting empirical research aimed at exploring the interrelation between the relationship between data and society. Lupton (2019, 2020) and colleagues have gathered together a variety of innovative methods that have been developed by researchers in different fields in order to examine the how people make sense of data in the contemporary era, as well as developing innovative methods of their own such as Data Letters and Data Kondo. They list a large number of methods from the field of human-computer interaction, including 3D printing of data, data selfies, data comics, among others, as well as highlighting a number of methods developed within the social sciences to explore these issues. One interesting feature of social science methodological innovations in this field has been a focus on mobility, and here we explore some of these methods in more detail.

One interesting methodological contribution that places an emphasis on mobility is that of data walks. Powell's (2018) "data walks" or "datawalkshop" method, draws on a tradition of methods that involve walking, including psychogeography. The approach is a participatory methodology, bringing together aspects of both research and public engagement, to engage people in discussion about the data processes that they observe in the urban environment, and exploring them from a particular perspective or matter of concern – for example, surveillance or discrimination. Jarke (2019) builds on this idea of the data walk in her co-design research with older adults in Germany. Through embedding data walks in her research process and evaluating the approach in the context of exploring open government data from the perspective of older citizens, she observes how data walks can be used in complementary ways to help answer questions at different stages of the design process of data-driven systems.

A different methodological approach that draws upon the idea of mobility is Bates et als.' (2016) data journeys methodology. With a focus on the mobility of data, the authors develop a methodological approach to capture the socio-material dynamics that shape the movement of data as they move between different sites from when they are initially created to when they are used in different contexts. Through following the data and using mobile ethnographic methods to capture cultures and contexts of the people that work with data in different places, they are able to shed light on some of the driving forces behind the circulation of data through interconnected big data systems.

Interesting methodological contributions are also starting to emerge through collaborations between social scientists or humanities scholars and computer scientists, some of whom have been inspired by critical debates about big data and analytics in recent years. Some of this work is visible at computer science conferences such as CHI (ACM Conference on Human Factors in Computing Systems) and ACM FAccT (ACM Conference on Fairness, Accountability, and Transparency). While a number of social scientists and humanities scholars have called for such collaboration, and have been actively involved in such work over recent years, there is still more scope for deepening methodological innovation through interdisciplinary engagement between the social and technical disciplines to examine the challenges of datafied societies and shape future developments.

Empirical contributions

While the work cited in this chapter has been primarily of a conceptual or commentary nature, many cited authors based their arguments on their in-depth empirical work that has often been written up in other papers. For example, amongst others, work by Kitchin on data dashboards in Dublin's Smart City; Amoore on data analytics in border control; Bates on the circulation of meteorological and climate data; Kennedy on public perceptions of organisations' data practices and governance. These empirical contributions have produced detailed and critical accounts of, for example, the ways in which complex social, cultural, political and economic factors interplay to provide a framework for how big data systems are envisioned and developed, and what the implications of this may be for societies. Much of this work evidences significant concerns and raises many questions about the unjust implications of emergent data practices for already marginalised social groups (e.g. Amoore, 2006), or illuminates how patterns of big data sharing and trading might be empowering already powerful agents such as financial companies in relation to societal challenges such as climate change (e.g. Bates et al., 2016).

Emergence of new research and activist communities

A final contribution of the field that can be identified relates to community building. Over the last few years there has been a flourishing of new spaces for people from different backgrounds to share and engage in dialogue about research and ideas related to big data analytics and society. Some of these have emerged from within academia – for example, the research journal *Big Data and Society* that was launched in 2013, and international conferences such as Data Power and Data Justice (in the social sciences and humanities), and ACM Conference on Fairness, Accountability and Transparency (in the computer sciences). Other groups have emerged from activist communities in which academics may or may not be involved. Examples, include Data for Black Lives and the Algorithmic Justice League in the USA, and Indigenous Data Sovereignty Networks in countries including the USA, Canada, Australia and New Zealand.

Key critiques of research in the field: politics, bias and empirical grounding

Critiques of research in this field tends to revolve around disagreements related to the differing political commitments and positionalities of researchers. For example, critiques are advanced that some research is not critical or normative enough, or that it emphasises technical or legal solutions that do not recognise or make explicit the ways in which issues identified reflect longstanding social, political, economic and cultural inequalities (Dencik et al., 2019). These critiques have been most obvious along disciplinary lines. For example, critical social scientists have argued that the techno-legal orientation of research communities such as FATE are limited to the extent that they do not fully grapple with the complex social realities of big data, but instead emphasise the development of technical methods to identify, measure and correct problems within big data systems.

Another critique has been that much work in the field has been strongly Western in orientation, with many of the key contributors being based in North American and European universities and drawing upon Western perspectives and theories in their work (Milan and Treré, 2019; Halkort, 2019). Some conferences have tried to address some of these concerns in an effort to decolonise the field, for example in selection of keynote speakers, conference themes and financial support for attendees from the 'global south', however there is still much work to be done to broaden and enrich the field beyond predominantly Western perspectives.

A final critique relates to the lack of empirical grounding in some research. For example, some theoretical or speculative work may make assumptions or exaggerated claims about the power of big data analytics that do not ring true for data scientists and practitioners that have more understanding of the technical and organisational limitations on some of the speculations that have been advanced by some scholars and journalists. These tensions between researchers with different disciplinary backgrounds and underlying philosophical commitments in the way they approach research can often work as a barrier to advancing interdisciplinary research that aims to better understand big data analytics as a socio-technical phenomenon.

Conclusion: the importance of critical data studies and anticipated future developments

Big data and related analytics technologies are likely to become more deeply embedded into different organisational and social contexts in the years to come. While some legal frameworks such as the EU's GDPR aim to curb some of the most significant risks to citizen's privacy and freedom, these laws have their limitations and often are a few steps behind the most recent technological developments. Academic fields such as critical data studies and FATE, and related activist communities, are therefore crucial to help society keep abreast of big data developments, offer critique of practices that risk unjust social consequences, and develop recommendations for how to resolve issues identified.

With some of the conceptual and normative groundwork now laid for the field of critical data studies, at least in the Western context, we might expect more in-depth empirical work to be added to that already produced by scholars in the field in the coming years, and some of this work will add its own conceptual and theoretical insights. Given the Western bias of the existing conceptual toolbox means it is "only partially able to grasp the obscure development, the cultural richness, and the vibrant creativity emerging at the margins of the 'empire'" (Milan and Treré, 2019, p. 321), we might also expect to see a flourishing of concepts, theories and empirical work that advances efforts to decolonise the field. Further, it is anticipated that we will see more interdisciplinary collaboration between those in the social and technical disciplines. Such collaboration would allow for both more forensic unpacking of the work of big data systems and those that develop them, as well as critical design research to advance the development of big data systems that are designed around values of social justice, rather than profit and social control.

References

Amoore, L. (2006) 'Biometric borders: Governing mobilities in the war on terror', *Political Geography*, 25, pp. 336–351.
Bates, J., Lin, Y. W. and Goodale, P. (2016) 'Data journeys: Capturing the socio-material constitution of data objects and flows', *Big Data and Society*, 3(2), pp. 1–12. doi: 10.1177/2053951716654502.
Beer, D. (2016) 'How should we do the history of big data?' *Big Data & Society*, 3(1), pp. 181–196. doi: 10.1177/2053951716646135.
boyd, d. and Crawford, K. (2012) 'Critical questions for big data: Provocations for a cultural, technological, and scholarly phenomenon', *Information Communication and Society*, 15(5), pp. 662–679. doi: 10.1080/1369118X.2012.678878.
Coté, M., Gerbaudo, P. and Pybus, J. (2016) 'Introduction. Politics of big data', *Digital Culture & Society*, 2(2), pp. 5–16. doi: 10.14361/dcs-2016-0202.
Couldry, N. and Mejias, U. A. (2019) 'Data colonialism: Rethinking big data's relation to the contemporary subject', *Television and New Media*. doi: 10.1177/1527476418796632.
Couldry, N. and Powell, A. (2014) 'Big data from the bottom up', *Big Data & Society*, 1(2). doi: 10.1177/2053951714539277.
Dalton, J. and Thatcher, J. (2014). 'What does a critical data studies look like, and why do we care? Seven points for a critical approach to big data', *Society and Space*. Available at: http://societyandspace.com/material/commentaries/craig-dalton-and-jim-thatcher-what-does-a-critical-data-studies-look-like-and-why-do-we-care-seven-points-for-a-critical-approach-to-big-data/ (Accessed: 23 December 2014).
Dencik, L., et al. (2019) 'Exploring data justice: Conceptions, applications and directions', *Information, Communication & Society*, Routledge, 22(7), pp. 873–881. doi: 10.1080/1369118X.2019.1606268.
D'Ignazio, C. and Klein, L. (2020) *Data Feminism*. MIT Press: Cambridge, MA.

Galic, S., et al. (2015) 'Bentham, Deleuze and beyond: An overview of surveillance theories from the panopticon to participation', *Philosophy and Technology*, 30, 9–37.

Gitelman, L. (2013) *'Raw Data' is an Oxymoron*. MIT Press: Cambridge, MA. Available at: https://mitpress.mit.edu/books/raw-data-oxymoron (Accessed: 17 August 2020).

Halkort, M. (2019) 'Decolonizing data relations: On the moral economy of data sharing in Palestinian refugee camps', *Canadian Journal of Communication*, 44(3).

Iliadis, A. and Russo, F. (2016) 'Critical data studies: An introduction', *Big Data & Society*, (December), pp. 1–7. doi: 10.1177/2053951716674238.

Jarke, J. (2019) 'Open government for all? Co-creating digital public services for older adults through data walks', *Online Information Review*. doi: 10.1108/oir-02-2018-0059.

Kennedy, H., Poell, T. and van Dijck, J. (2015) 'Data and agency', *Big Data and Society*, 2(2), pp. 1–7. doi: 10.1177/2053951715621569.

Kitchin, R. (2013) 'The real-time city? Big data and smart urbanism', *GeoJournal*, 79(1), pp. 1–14. doi: 10.1007/s10708-013-9516-8.

Kitchin, R. (2014). *The Data Revolution: Big Data, Open Data, Data Infrastructures and Their Consequences*. Sage: London.

Kitchin, R. and Lauriault, T. P. (2014) 'Towards critical data studies: Charting and unpacking data assemblages and their work (preprint)', *Geoweb and Big Data*, pp. 3–20. Available at: http://papers.ssrn.com/sol3/papers.cfm?abstract_id=2474112.

Kitchin, R. and McArdle, G. (2016) 'What makes big data, big data? Exploring the ontological characteristics of 26 datasets', *Big Data & Society*, 3(1).

Lupton, D. (2018) 'How do data come to matter? Living and becoming with personal data', *Big Data & Society*, 5(2). doi: 10.1177/2053951718786314.

Lupton, D. (2019) 'Data letters and data kondo'. Available at: https://livingwithpersonal.data.blog/2019/11/20/data-letters-and-data-kondo/.

Lupton, D. (2020) 'Innovative and creative methods for researching people's use and understandings of their data – A resource list'. Available at: https://livingwithpersonal.data.blog/2020/03/08/innovative-and-creative-methods-for-researching-peoples-use-and-understandings-of-their-data-a-resource-list/.

Manovich, L. (2011) 'Trending: The promises and the challenges of big social data', *Debates in the Digital Humanities*, pp. 460–475. doi: 10.5749/minnesota/9780816677948.003.0047.

Milan, S. and Treré, E. (2019) 'Big data from the south(s): Beyond data universalism', *Television and New Media*, SAGE Publications Inc., 20(4), pp. 319–335. doi: 10.1177/1527476419837739.

Noble, S. U. (2018) *Algorithms of Oppression: How Search Engines Reinforce Racism*. New York: New York University Press.

Otterbacher, J., Bates, J. and Clough, P. (2017) 'Competent men and warm women: Gender stereotypes and backlash in image search results', *Conference on Human Factors in Computing Systems – Proceedings* (May), pp. 6620–6631. doi: 10.1145/3025453.3025727.

Pasquale, F. (2015) *The Black Box Society: The Secret Algorithms That Control Money and Information*. Harvard University Press: Cambridge, MA.

Powell, A. (2018) 'Alison Powell on data walking', *TMG Journal for Media History*, 21(2), pp. 146–150. http://doi.org/10.18146/2213-7653.2018.371.

Rességuier, A. and Rodrigues, R. (2020) 'AI ethics should not remain toothless! A call to bring back the teeth of ethics', *Big Data & Society*, SAGE Publications Ltd, 7(2). doi: 10.1177/2053951720942541.

Ruppert, E. (2013) 'Rethinking empirical social sciences', *Dialogues in Human Geography*, 3(3), pp. 268–273. doi: 10.1177/2043820613514321.

Ruppert, E., Isin, E. and Bigo, D. (2017) 'Data politics', *Big Data & Society*, 4(2). doi: 10.1177/2053951717717749.

Savage, M. and Burrows, R. (2007) 'The coming crisis of empirical sociology', 41(5), pp. 885–899. doi: 10.1177/0038038507080443.

Taylor, L., et al. (2014) 'Big data and positive change in the developing world', *Policy & Internet*, 6(4), pp. 418–444. doi: 10.1002/1944-2866.POI378.

Thatcher, J., O'Sullivan, D. and Mahmoudi, D. (2016) 'Data colonialism through accumulation by dispossession: New metaphors for daily data', *Environment and Planning D: Society and Space*, 34(6), pp. 990–1006. doi: 10.1177/0263775816633195.

van Dijck, J. (2014) 'Datafication, dataism and dataveillance: Big data between scientific paradigm and ideology', *Surveillance and Society*, 12(2), pp. 197–208. doi: 10.24908/ss.v12i2.4776.

19
AI, culture industries and entertainment

Sam Han

Introduction

The role of artificial intelligence (AI) in contemporary cultural and entertainment industries speaks to its increasing ubiquity in specific fields but also everyday life more broadly. It reflects a singular fact: the intertwined nature of everyday life with technologies, in particular digital technologies, many, if not all, of which deploy some aspect of artificial intelligence. While the myth of AI still animates a great deal of public discourse – mostly having to do with the potential of a "machine takeover" of humanity and talks of "the singularity," there is, as other chapters in this volume surely suggest, a growing acknowledgement of AI's current proliferation in a variety of mundane features of everyday life (Kurzweil 2005). This too reflects a shift in the way in which discussions of AI, at least discursively, have been sublimated into other, adjacent, conversations, namely those debating big data, surveillance and algorithms, to name just a few.

One would not be entirely off base to think that these developments signal an evolution of the public understanding of artificial intelligence. After all, the specificity of discussions toward technologies, media and devices that deploy AI expresses a more grounded view of artificial intelligence as opposed to the baseless fears generated by films like *I, Robot*, and signals a greater sophistication in broad discussions about not only the technical aspects of AI but also its social implications. For instance, contemporary discussions around privacy and data protection amid growing methods of surveillance by states and corporations have not centered on technical aspects of data mining only. They have, in fact, focused on matters of freedom of expression and the right to privacy (Lomas 2020). While this is most certainly welcome news, this is not the case with all aspects of artificial intelligence.

AI's ability to demonstrate creativity, and this development's subsequent impact on creative and cultural industries, is still somewhat misunderstood, at least in the realm of public discourse. There are some reasons as to why this is so. For one, human creativity remains an enigma. The science of creativity (mostly based in the fields of psychology and neuroscience) is bedeviled by definitional questions around what counts as creativity, and also how one can recognize the creative from the banal (Konnikova 2014; Hsu 2020). In addition, creativity bears the responsibility of special status, viewed as the characteristic differentiator of humans as a species from others, adding more weight to these discussions.

Like "reason," or "intelligence," creativity is viewed as the basis of culture and cultural production, which are hallmarks of human specialness. Hence, to think about creativity is to think about what it means to be human – not only in some grand sense – but also specifically how the figure of the human being is situated within the context of technological modernity as not only an artist, capable of making singular cultural objects but as an industrialist, capable of producing culture *en masse*. Therefore, when artificial intelligence comes up as it pertains to the creative and cultural industries, "creativity," it is not only whether machines can be "creative," and thus able to produce art and culture, but also the rapidity and broad scope of its circulation, distribution and reception that animates discussion and debate. As this chapter will try to show, a major consequence of research into the impact of AI developments in the creative and cultural industries is how it affects our "measure" of humanity. Discussing AI's relationship to the cultural and creative industries unleashes the latent anxiety around human autonomy that is part and parcel of the uncertain human-technology relations of the contemporary period. If the creativity of AI can mirror that of a human being, on what grounds can we be sure of human specialness since machines can already work faster and more accurately?

It should be said from the get-go that "whether machines could be creative" and also "what sort of efficiency machines could offer" were issues that preceded the earliest forays into research that we would ultimately identify as "artificial intelligence." In fact, one could begin with the very beginnings of industrialization.

Although largely taught, and therefore understood, as part of the history of the Industrial Revolution, which spans the 18th and 19th centuries, the reckoning of humankind with the potential of mechanical production could be said to begin in earnest with the development of factory system, that is, with the rise of capitalism. One could see the surprise of the factory setting, with its loud noises, unending steam and moving parts (a far cry from the agrarian lifeworld of just a generation prior) in the photographs of Lewis Hine and Charlie Chaplin's *Modern Times* (1936). In one of Hine's most famous images, simply called "Steamfitter" (1920), one can see, in spite of the muscular man in the foreground with a wrench larger than his forearm, the pipes behind him domineer over him. Their presence, made more dramatic with them in the shadows, can be described as looming. For Hine, who was both a sociologist and social reformer, the intention was to show the dignity of the worker in spite of the alienating environment of the factory. In his other famous photographs, many of which depicted the horrors of child labor, one can see the smallness of the subject, whether a single child or a several children amid the machinery. Chaplin's film opens with an homage to this famous photo in a way. The main character gets caught up in the cogs of a comically large machine.

These artistic expressions thematize what Marx would detail in *The Economic and Philosophical Manuscripts*. It was not work as such that resulted in alienation but rather the toil of doing so in the conditions of the factory, doing the same task over and over again. What Marx points out, albeit elsewhere, is that the purpose of this repetitive revolution in work was to produce at an alarming rate. It was efficiency. The technological innovations of the industrial period revolutionized work, converting it into a generic form of effort- and time-expenditure called "labor." Whereas "work" was tied to specific crafts and vocations, "labor" was merely doing tasks. Hence, the model of compensation was bound to "labor-time" not skill, effort or how well the job was done.

What hovers over this entire transformation of human expenditure under the capitalist mode of production is the rate at which it was able to not only produce commodities but also reproduce them with precision. Alienated labor, therefore, was the necessary sacrifice for standardization and efficiency that came with industrialized capitalism.

AI, culture industries and entertainment

Even in this brief, Marxist retelling of formation of the mode of production, there is, I believe, a way of reading this rather well-trodden history through the lens of artificial intelligence. The very conditions of possibility for capitalism were set in motion by forging a particular kind of relationship between human capacity and machinery. The factory could do what humans on their own could not. While today the language that abounds is "machine learning," the magical qualities of industrialization, which utilized cruder technologies, raw materials and thermodynamics, had to do with its sheer power – maximum output – as well as the capacity for exactitude.

This chapter offers an all-too-brief exploration of artificial intelligence's impact on the creative, cultural and entertainment industries. Beginning with the historical development of the industrialization of culture, it offers an interpretive genealogy, which begins with the work of the Frankfurt School, specifically highlighting how technology and mechanical reproduction, figures into their conceptualization of the culture industry, suggesting it foreshadows some of the concerns that emerge later on with regard to artificial intelligence's impact on culture. It then proceeds to cover some of the key ideas in artificial intelligence research which focuses on creativity. Centering on the work of Margaret Boden, it discusses in greater detail what we mean by "creativity." It then moves on to some recent developments in the creative and cultural industries that utilize artificial intelligence, with a sustained analysis of key examples from Japan, a country that has been at the forefront of artificial intelligence development, especially as it pertains to culture and entertainment. After analyzing some of the criticisms of the increasing presence of artificial intelligence in the creative and cultural industries, the chapter concludes with some thoughts about future of AI and the creative industries.

1 The industrialization of culture: a possible pre-history of artificial intelligence

As mentioned earlier, the onset of industrialization and a capitalist mode of production had already disrupted a previous arrangement between human beings and nature, especially as it pertained to how human beings work. With greater sophistication in methods of mechanical reproduction, culture too had become subject to the standardization of the factory system. The scholars who have had the greatest impact in studying this development are the Frankfurt School. After all, Theodor Adorno and Max Horkheimer, the figures most readily associated with the Frankfurt School, are responsible for the term "the culture industry."

But even before they released the work that would contain the theory of the culture industry, there is the work of Walter Benjamin, who, while not exactly a formal member of the Institute for Social Research, was a major influence on the members. In particular, his famous essay on "mechanical reproduction" is of particular relevance here as it serves as an overview of the impact of reproduction on culture and art, in particular photography and cinema. For Benjamin, the fact that artwork can be reproduced mechanically, that is with speed and exactitude, represented "something new." What occurred in 1900, when technical reproduction was able to facilitate the transmission of artwork in a mechanical manner, was, according to him, a challenge to the "whole sphere of authenticity." If authenticity could be understood as "the essence of all that is transmissible from its beginning," from its "substantive duration to its testimony to the history which it has experienced," then what technical (or mechanical) reproducibility was able to do was cut off the work of art from historical time and space (Benjamin 2013, p. 221). Benjamin describes this as the decay of "aura," that is, a work's "presence in time and space, its unique existence at the place where it happens to be." "The technique of reproduction," he writes, "detaches the reproduced object from the domain of tradition" (Benjamin 2013, pp. 220–221).

He offers two features of mechanical reproduction – process and technical. In order to explain this further, Benjamin uses the example of photography, which, along with cinema, takes on a status of privilege throughout his analysis. "Process reproduction" is best explained by the development process of photographs, during which the photographer can "bring out those aspects of the original that are unattainable to the naked eye yet accessible to the lens, which is adjustable and chooses its angle at will" (Benjamin 2013, p. 220). There is also the possibility of "enlargement" through cropping. Process reproduction can produce images that, as Benjamin puts it nicely, "escape natural vision." The latter – technical reproduction – refers to copies. As Benjamin points out, a photograph can "place the original into situations which would be out of reach for the original itself" (Benjamin 2013, p. 220). He gives the example of a cathedral, which can now be located in "the studio of a lover of art" (Benjamin 2013, p. 221).

Benjamin's reading of the effect of reproduction focused on human sense perception. His lamenting of the degradation of aura is not baseless nostalgia but rather a sharply articulated understanding of the impact of media-technological change. In terms of photography, Benjamin suggests that mechanical reproduction has allowed the "masses" to "bring 'things' closer." This has the consequence, however, of audiences accepting reproductions rather than the original, giving the reproduction great epistemological weight. "Every day the urge grows stronger to get hold of an object at very close range by way of its likeness, its reproduction," he writes. In addition, there is the added issue of what Benjamin identifies as the growing "sense of the universal equality of things" (Benjamin 2013, p. 223). For him, this would result in a generalized degradation not only of aura but a lessening of artistic appreciation as audiences would merely see originals and their copies on the same plane. The "uniqueness" and "permanence" of the original could potentially be superseded by "transitoriness" of mechanical reproduction. This could, potentially, blur the distinction between "author" and "public," making it "merely functional" (Benjamin 2013, p. 232).

But the fear of the eradication of this line is not the only concern for Benjamin. As he notes in his analysis of cinema in particular, the way in which film transforms the nature of the viewer's engagement with the work of art is alarming. For him, mechanical reproduction results in "distraction" rather than "concentration." The latter is called forth when the viewer is "absorbed" by a work of art. The movies, with its techniques of close-ups, slow motion and all kinds of rapid movements such as gliding, floating and supernatural motions, could be seen to enhance this absorption. But Benjamin argues the contrary, calling this experience the "shock effect" (Benjamin 2013, p. 238). The engagement the shock effect of cinema produces is hardly one of criticality but rather like being enveloped into a building. Architecture, Benjamin writes, "[represents] the prototype of a work of art the reception of which is consummated by a collectivity in a state of distraction" (Benjamin 2013, p. 239). When we enter a building, we hardly think twice about it, simply naturalizing the structure's existence. We do not look at it with any sort of critical distance, making anyone who enters the building "an examiner, but an absent-minded one" (Benjamin 2013, p. 241).

This line of argument, regarding the effect of mechanical reproduction on human sense of perception, is mirrored by those influenced by Benjamin, especially Theodor Adorno. The arguments he made – both with Max Horkheimer and solo – can be seen to echo Benjamin's. While Benjamin deploys the term "mechanical reproduction," Adorno (and Horkheimer) use "industrialization" or "mass culture" (Horkheimer and Adorno 2007).

Although the obvious place to refer to when discussing "mass culture" is the collaborative work on "the culture industry," we can see even see elements of a similar thinking in other work published around the same time. In an article called "A Social Critique of Radio Music," Adorno describes the effect of "constant repetition" of classical music as turning a "living force" in to a "museum piece" (Adorno 1996, p. 230). For Adorno, the problem is partly to do with the context of music. The broadcasting of music on the radio decontextualizes the original place and space of music. He asks:

> Does a symphony played on the air remain a symphony? Are the changes it undergoes by wireless transmission merely slight and negligible modifications or do those changes affect the very essence of the music? Are not the stations in such a case bringing the masses in contact with something totally different from what it is supposed to be, thus also exercising an influence quite different from the one intended?
>
> *(Adorno 1996, p. 230)*

For Adorno, this is a product of a "commodity society," which speaks to the particular state of capitalism that favors "monopolized mass production of standardized goods" (Adorno 1996, p. 231). As music is subject to "standardization and mass production" it becomes altered. It "[ceases] to be a human force and is consumed like other consumers' goods" (Adorno 1996, p. 231).

When music is commodified, the audience does not truly listen to the music. They are actually experiencing "commodity listening," which Adorno describes as "a listening whose ideal it is to dispense as far as possible with any effort on the part of the recipient – even if such an effort on the part of the recipient is the necessary condition of grasping the sense of the music." He goes so far as to call it "ready-mix" music, with the listener "[suspending] all intellectual activity when dealing with music and is content with consuming and evaluating its gustatory qualities" (Adorno 1996, p. 231). In other words, music on the radio affects taste. When he asks, "Does the mass distribution of music really mean a rise of musical culture? Are the masses actually brought into contact with the kind of music which, from broader social considerations, may be regarded as desirable?" he is being facetious (Adorno 1996, p. 232). Not too long after, he describes radio as responsible for a "retrogression in listening."

What then is "retrogressive listening"? Adorno describes it thusly:

> Retrogressive listening to a symphony is listening which, instead of grasping that whole, dwells upon those melodies, just as if the symphony were structurally the same as a ballad. There exists today a tendency to listen to Beethoven's Fifth as if it were a set of quotations from Beethoven's Fifth. We have developed a larger framework of concepts such as atomistic listening and quotation listening, which lead us to the hypothesis that something like a musical children's language is taking shape.
>
> *(Adorno 1996, p. 233)*

In an earlier era, the listener was "eager to follow the most daring musical exploits" (Adorno 1996, p. 233). Today, the listener, under conditions of musical mechanical reproduction, "feels happy only if it is fed Beethoven's Seventh Symphony again and again" (Adorno 1996, p. 233). Radio then, as another "technique of musical reproduction," limits the taste of the listener (Adorno 1996, p. 232). Standardized music is forced upon him or her through the radio.

> This tendency in today's mass-produced music can be expressed in precise technical terms. Musical analysis can furnish us with plenty of materials which manifest, so far as rhythmical

> patterns, sound combinations, melodic and harmonic structures are concerned, that even apparently divergent schools of popular music, such as Sweet and Swing, are essentially the same. It can further be shown that their differences have no bearing on the musical essence itself. It can be shown that each band has assumed certain mannerisms with no musical function and no other purpose than to make it easier for the listener to recognize the particular band – such as, say, the musically nonsensical staccati with which Guy Lombardo likes to end certain legato phrases.
>
> *(Adorno 1996, p. 235)*

Adorno dubs this "the musico-technological control of sociological interpretation."

For Adorno, the industrialization of culture, and music in particular, manipulates the masses, in effect, limiting the exposure of the audience to different kinds of music, namely music that challenges rather than pleases. Mechanical reproduction, which in this case, is the recording and broadcasting of "good music," such as that of Beethoven, to a broad audience basically standardizes it, thus making it a commodity.

We can understand the perspectives of Benjamin and Adorno of the 1930s and 1940s as mirroring the concerns of not only intellectuals but others in the early decades of the 20th century. While the mythic power of technology did hold a great deal of promise in the public imagination of industrialized societies, nevertheless there was the underlying concern of its potential threat to "humanity" (Marx 2000), defined here, among Benjamin and Adorno, as something close to the degradation or limitation of aesthetic engagement resulting from commodification. Technological reproduction, therefore, is understood as servicing the production of commodities.

2 Creativity as the test of the human: the work of Margaret Boden

The relationship between the unprecedented reproductive capacity of industrial technology, for the theorists associated with the Frankfurt School as briefly discussed earlier, was determined by the dominance of the commodity form. The emphasis on what industrialization had wrought onto human forms of creative expression was clearly couched within Marxist conceptions of alienation. For researchers in artificial intelligence, such as Margaret Boden, who were investigating its relationship to creativity, the point of emphasis slightly differed. While the arguments from the industrialization of culture implied that that something human was being degraded, artificial intelligence research, on the other hand, pursued the question of whether technology would artificially *enhance* human capacity.

We can explore this tension in the work of Boden, which investigates the possibility of computers being creative. From the earliest days of computing, artificial intelligence has been a specter haunting the enterprise. As she notes, artificial intelligence is the "study of how to build and/or program computers to do the sorts of things which human minds can do" (Boden 2003, p. 14). If one looks at the earliest models of computing, including those from Charles Babbage and Ada Lovelace ("the analytical engine") in the 19th century all the way to Alan Turing's "Turing machine" in the 20th, one can see, in their very names, a sense of what these mathematicians and engineers perceived to be the capacity of these virtual machines. Babbage and Lovelace's "analytical engine," for instance, was theorized to analyze data in accordance to a programmer. In effect, the analytical engine could only order – not create – data (Boden 2003, p. 16). The Turing machine, likewise, was conceived as being programmed but with a greater degree of flexibility. According to Turing, a "computing machine" (his words) could read and adjust within a given set of rules depending on the circumstances (Boden 2003, p. 20). Turing's specific formal model had to do with the ability of a machine to read and alter symbols on a tape (the earliest form of memory). But currently, in the popular imagination, the "Turing test" has more purchase than any sort of detailed, technical description of how the Turing machine works. The Turing test is a way of determining whether a computer is able to act in a human manner. While for Turing and artificial intelligence research more broadly the test measured human "thinking," Turing himself actually had a broader sense of human capacity. Turing's example of the exchange involved in a typical Turing test reads more like a Turing scenario. It is, in actuality, a thought experiment whereby there is a computing machine, an interrogator and a human. A computer "passes" the Turing test if the human interrogator cannot tell whether the messages are coming from a human or not. In one of the most widely cited excerpts from Turing's description, there is a moment when the interrogator asks the computer or interlocutor to write a sonnet and subsequently asks follow-up questions.

> **Interrogator** In the first line of your sonnet which reads 'Shall I compare thee to a summer's day', would not 'a spring day' do as well or better?
> **Computer** It wouldn't scan.
> **Interrogator** How about 'a winter's day'? That would scan all right.
> **Computer** Yes, but nobody wants to be compared to a winter's day.
> **Interrogator** Would you say Mr. Pickwick reminded you of Christmas?
> **Computer** In a way.
> **Interrogator** Yet Christmas is a winter's day, and I do not think Mr. Pickwick would mind the comparison.
> **Computer** I don't think you're serious. By a winter's day one means a typical winter's day, rather than a special one like Christmas. (Copeland 2000)

Poetry back in the early 20th century, and today, occupies an interesting proxy for human creativity. One can see this in the development of poetry competitions that are effectively Turing tests. In 2015, inspired by Turing, the Neckom Institute for Computational Science at Dartmouth College in the United States organized several competitions that tested programmers' abilities to create works that would confuse the judge's ability to differentiate "human essence" from "computer code." In addition to one for sonnets, there are others for short stories and a mix (as in a DJ mix).

A poem, a short story or a mix "passes" the Turing test when the judges are unable to tell whether it was made by a human or a computer. Computer scientist Dan Rockmore, the director of the Neckom Institute, is clear about what these competitions are meant to measure. As he notes, he is neither "hoping a machine can generate an *average* short story" nor is he:

> looking for experimental short fiction. And similarly for a sonnet, I wouldn't be looking for a random collection of things that had the right meter and the right rhyme scheme, which . . . from some postmodern point of view might appear to be a great sonnet.
> *(Palca 2015)*

He's not looking for a sonnet that could have been written by Shakespeare or short story by Alice Walker or a mix by DJ A-Trak.

While he states that he is not looking for excellence, there is a clear rationale behind choosing poetry, fiction and music. These examples of human culture have what he calls a "that," which he strongly connects with "emotion." Poetry can "leave you with a lump in your throat." He goes on to explain why poetry has a privileged position in AI research on creativity.

> Poetry is a good place to move the end zone: it's rooted in the inspirational and the comical – *the deeply human* – and yet, in many of its forms, it edges toward the computational and algorithmic. Poetry even seems to have been implicit in the bold 1955 manifesto that first announced the field of artificial intelligence, declaring that "an attempt will be made to find how to make machines use language, form abstractions and concepts." The pioneers of A.I. never mentioned poetry outright, but, if you squint, you might see its spirit in their ambitions to investigate the 'rules' connecting human thought with word 'manipulation' and in their efforts to explore the relationship between creativity and randomness – not to mention in their grander goal of creating machines that would 'improve themselves.'
>
> *(Rockmore 2020)*

More specifically, a sonnet hits a "sweet spot." As Rockmore states, "they're a rich art form (good for poets) with clear rules (good for machines)." Even kids can learn to write sonnets since there is a specific meter and a template in terms of stanzas. Learning to write usually entails reading a lot of them. Thus, begins the process of mimicry.

The issue, however, is how much a machine needs to read in order to learn the template fully. Brains of children do not need much material to begin this process, as Rockmore points out. With computers, even the most sophisticated types of machine learning, such as neural networks, "need lots and lots of data in order to train, or become more accurate at a given task." Neural network architecture, while certainly the most cutting-edge form of machine learning as it is based on human brains, is successful when there is a given dataset that it works from. The example of language translation or image recognition, two functions done remarkably well by Google, relies on the fact that: "the Internet is full of words and photos for these neurons to train on *in silico*." Barring that, learning itself does not occur. As Rockmore concludes, "deep-learning machines need more inputs than the average school kid."

The Turing test, while widely accepted as the standard for "assessing artificial intelligence," has some drawbacks, especially when it comes to creativity and art. If the standard is whether the work passes for something produced by a human being, it falls short as this does not account for the amount of creative and cultural work today that already involves machine learning. One can think of digital photography, which has machine learning woven into many steps in the creation of an image, from in-camera auto-focusing (many of which have features like "eye detection" and "face detection") all the way to photo-editing software (many of which feature "skin smoothing"). These are all reliant upon computers learning and recognizing what is an eye or a face. If one takes a picture on a digital camera and adds slight edits on Adobe Lightroom or even on Instagram before posting it, how much of the picture's eventual "likes" (or hearts) can be said to be achieved by the human user? If we had to break it down into percentages, attributing "credit" for why a like is produced, it would be nearly impossible. Given this difficulty, what has animated researchers historically is what AI technologies may tell us about being human. As Boden writes:

> AI-concepts enable us to do psychology in a new way, by allowing us to construct (and test) hypotheses about the structures and processes that harmony may be involved in thought.
>
> *(Boden 2003, p. 6)*

Of course, if what AI is after is "creativity," specifically *human* creativity, one needs to figure out what that is, within the context of the human mind.

Boden's definition of creativity begins with its distinction from newness. Newness is merely novel whereas creativity is unpredictable. Newness, she argues, is merely a component of creativity. Ideas or "artefacts" must not only be new but also surprising and valuable (Boden 2003, p. 1). In spite of its many criteria, creativity, Boden argues, is not a "special activity" but rather an aspect of general human intelligence. It is not some magical activity resulting from divine inspiration that strikes out of the blue. Creativity is rooted in everyday abilities such as "conceptual thinking, perception, memory and reflective self-criticism" as well as "analogical thinking, searching a structured problem-space" (Boden 1998, p. 347).

Boden's typology of creativity contains three types: (1) combinational, (2) exploratory and (3) transformational (Boden 1998, p. 347). Combinational involves making "unfamiliar combinations of familiar ideas." Examples of this include poetic imagery, collage and analogies. As Boden notes, making novel combinations requires a rich store of knowledge (Boden 2003, p. 3). "Exploratory" involves the generation of novel ideas within a given structured conceptual space, which is normally "picked up from one's own culture or peer group." For Boden, this is the kind of creativity that artists and scientists engage in as it operates within existing "styles of thought." Lastly, there is transformational creativity, which impacts any given conceptual space so as to generate new structures. Boden at times calls this "re-routing" or "thinking the unthinkable" (Boden 2003, p. 6).

According to Boden, computer models of creativity are focused on the second type, that is, exploratory (Boden 1998, p. 349). For instance, in electronic music (which will be discussed in greater detail in the following section), where artificial intelligence was first deployed in earnest within the sphere of culture, there is still the inputting of musical conventions, including a "list of signatures: melodic, harmonic, metric, and ornamental motifs characteristic of individual composers" (Boden 1998, p. 351). These are "values" that must be "plugged in." In the case of EMI (experiments in musical intelligence), these are made up of conventions from Western music. As Boden points out

> [H]uman values – and therefore the novelties which we are prepared to approve as 'creative' – change from culture to culture, and from time to time. In some cases, they do so in unpredictable and irrational ways: think of the fashion-industry, for example, or of rogue memes like the back-to-front baseball-cap. Nor are value-shifts confined to trivial cases such as these: even Bach, Mozart, and Donne were ignored and/or criticized in certain periods.
>
> *(Boden 1998, p. 354)*

Beyond music, there are other examples that Boden points to. There is AARON, developed by Harold Cohen in the 1970s, which creates spontaneous drawings of abstract forms (Boden 2003, p. 151). Some of these could be understood to resemble rocks or sticks or even birds or beetles. This is done through a mixture of general and specific knowledge that has been inputted into the program (Boden 2003, p. 159). According to Boden, AARON meets the criteria of creativity (Boden 2003, p. 164).

Boden then asks (rhetorically) what a program must be like in order to appear creative (Boden 2003, p. 163). She responds by suggesting that it must "inhabit, and explore, a conceptual space rich enough to yield indefinitely many surprises," which meets the criteria for exploratory creativity. But she notes that "ideally, it should extend this space – or perhaps even break out of it, and construct another one." It should also produce results that are "individually unpredictable" although they should possess a consistent style. Moreover, the product should be generated by the program acting alone, "relying on its own computational resources rather than constant input from a human operator," and also needs to "be able to reconsider its past choices in deciding what to do next." Lastly, the results must be "aesthetically pleasing" (Boden 2003, p. 164). Although AARON seemingly checks all these boxes, it resembles a human artist "who has found a style, and is sticking to it" (Boden 2003, p. 164). An example Boden gives is how AARON has specific constraints on what a body looks like (Boden 2003, p. 160). The body-model is based on, for instance, two arms and two legs. This is clearly a limitation. There can be no other types of bodies.

The limits of AARON demonstrate what Boden describes as "bottlenecks" that still stand in the way of a full-fledged piece of creative expression made by artificial intelligence. The first is domain-expertise, which is necessary for mapping the conceptual space to be explored or transformed. The second, which is especially difficult, is the valuation of the result (Boden 1998, p. 355). For Boden, there is no AI system that has access to the "rich and subtly structured stock of concepts that any normal adult human being has built up over a lifetime."

3 AI in the contemporary culture industry and entertainment

While the aspects of Boden's work covered previously do not directly address more recent developments, when thinking about recent cultural and creative industries' attempts at incorporating artificial intelligence, the bottlenecks she identifies are nevertheless still relevant. Creating original pieces of art (or "content" as it is now called) is still a tall task for artificial intelligence (Steimle 2014). In the main, artificial intelligence can be seen in many of the content distribution methods of the cultural and creative industries. For instance, on streaming platforms such as YouTube and Netflix which together take up 24% of global internet traffic (Gold 2020) and video more broadly accounting for 60.6% (Sandvine 2019), there is the commonplace feature of "user experience personalization," where artificial intelligence is used to offer personalized content based on user activity. This is has become quite refined on Netflix but also YouTube, whose autoplay functioned has been accused of producing a "Rabbit Hole Effect," which suggests videos based on an algorithm (Feldman 2019). And it is precisely the algorithm, as both a technique and signifier, that has arguably become the aspect of AI technology that has garnered not only the most attention but also the greatest inroads into our everyday life.

Lev Manovich discusses this as "cultural AI." "Today," he writes, "industrial 'cultural AI' is built into devices and services used by billions of people." It is "everywhere." But, "instead of being an instrument of a single artistic imagination," the potential for which Boden's work emphasizes, "AI has become a mechanism for influencing the imaginations of billions" (Manovich 2019, p. 2). Hence, Manovich argues that cultural AI works in the realm of "aesthetics," that is, it helps "[guide] us towards choices preferred by the majority." AI works in the realm of what the sociologist Pierre Bourdieu would deem "taste." There are specific ways in which cultural AI operates. Manovich provides a taxonomy (Manovich 2019, p. 5).

1. Selecting content from larger collections: search, discovery, curation, recommendations and filtering
2. Targeting content (e.g. one-on-one marketing, behavioral targeting and market segmentation)
3. Assistance in creation/editing of new content (if we think of AI as intelligent in the biological senses we can all this "participation" in content creation)

4   Fully autonomous creation (e.g., AI composing music tracks in a particular style, writing business and sports news articles, creating visualizations from given datasets, designing websites, generating email responses)

What brings together nearly all of the items on this list is the recasting of human and non-human relations in both the consumption and production of culture. The first two items have to do with bringing specific bits of cultural content to specific audiences for them to consume. The latter two refer to how content creation is "aided" by AI. Simply put, both consumption and production are changing under conditions of "cultural AI."

To illustrate consumption, we can look at the case of Warner Bros., the giant American entertainment company, which was looking to market a beloved sitcom that originally aired in the 1990s that had been successful in syndication as well as in home DVD and video sales. The task set before Intel, the technology company known for making processors and employed by Warner Bros., was to enact "curation efficiency." Warner Bros. wanted to see "which scenes will best resonate with . . . target audiences" and also "what clips cue which emotions" all in the hopes of "[maximizing] the impact of . . . ongoing marketing efforts." To do so, Intel deployed artificial intelligence on "video metadata" to "improve content discovery and monetization." A key detail in curation efficiency, however, is the need for Intel's data scientists to develop a "training data set via crowdsourcing." Put simply, this means that any algorithm or program that can tag content with specific kinds of metadata requires information input – from human beings – in order to "train" it (Mohamed 2020). In this case, it was clearly about which emotions were "cued." There must be some form of "Deep learning."

While just one example of a single, albeit rather large, producer of cultural content, Warner Bros., speaks to the "consumption side" of cultural AI. There is, as mentioned, the production side as well (points 3–4 in Manovich's taxonomy). In order to illustrate those, we could look toward Asia, where, for instance, the governments of South Korea and Japan have invested heavily in AI (Cho and Lee 2020; OSA_DC 2020). The most obvious example is the virtual Japanese "idol" Hatsune Miku.

The term "idol" in Japan is used to refer to a type of personality that is very often a singer but also performs across genres and platforms. Idols are distinguishable in Japanese media culture due to the specific mechanisms of the system of scouting and development of young talent. One of the key aspects of idol culture in Japan is the nature of fandom. Specifically, one of the key points of Japanese fandom is the connection, largely based on fantasy and personality, forged between the audiences and the artists.

Hence, Hatsune Miku, Japan's first globally popular, virtual pop star was conceived – initially as a marketing ploy – as a mascot for Crypton Future Media, which makes music software. Initially, Crypton's CEO wanted to market software that he had made using a technology called Vocaloid 2. The Vocaloid programs were virtual voice programs. The first version had not done well, in part due to the generated voices not sounding very lifelike. Hiroyuki Itoh, the CEO, decided he was going to create an idol for the program, in hopes of boosting its marketing. Itoh hired a graphic novelist to create a character that was "cute but also slightly edgy, something that would attract young people" (Verini 2012). What resulted was Hatsune Miku, a 16-year-old girl weighing 92 pounds, described as having "long, thin legs, coquettish bug-eyes, pigtailed blue locks . . . and a computer module on her forearm."

When Vocaloid 2 was released, Crypton facilitated, on its website, the sharing of users' own creations using the software, and shortly thereafter, the deluge of crowdsourcing began, with users generating not only songs that featured the "voice" of Hatsune Miku but also "fan fiction," including background stories and various illustrations. This sort of participatory fan culture has given rise to what one critic has called Hatsune Miku's "wiki-celebrity," highlighting the importance of fan production in the Hatsune Miku phenomenon. There are 22,000 original songs written for her by her fans. Free software, called MikuMikuDance, was developed and released which allowed users to create 3D animations of Miku, helping to broaden Miku's visual identity. When Miku performs at concerts, Sega, the videogame developer, uses aspects of this crowdsourced work to produce 90-minute films.

Hence, Judith Bessant describes Miku as a "post-human pop star" (Bessant 2018, p. 33), owing in large part to the fact that the Miku phenomenon consists of not only corporate-driven content (as is the case with most Japanese "idols") but rather, in the main, "consumer-generated" that involve "amateur and professional composers, animators, artists, and fans in which a huge number of people mutually collaborate to create content." This means lyrics, music, illustrations and even video. Bessant makes the comparison to Wikipedia and YouTube but Bessant also speaks to extant fan cultures of Japan, including *dojin*, which are self-publishing circles, and also *otaku*, the subculture of super fans.

Kobayashi and Taguchi suggest that the Miku phenomenon shows evidence of a new type of user, one that is somewhat removed from the idea of "relatively passive users," who populate the comment sections of YouTube and social media. The users that make up Miku's universe are co-creators and co-producers. Kobayashi and Taguchi view it through the lens of systems theory:

> In Hatsune Miku's case, this feedback loop is narrated as a story in which, through the quantity and quality of content acting as a spur, all of the following increase: the number of products and services that construct the ecosystem, the number of creative users that produce things, and the number of interactive users that watch and comment on the content.
>
> *(Kobayashi and Taguchi 2019, p. 11)*

Jelena Guga describes Miku as a "product of digital information reproduction and participatory culture" (Guga 2014, p. 37). Miku is not only a celebrity but also a platform, "offering an ecosystem for a 'collective' to express itself artistically, by forming its specific aesthetics and canons of that expression" (Guga 2014, p. 41). Miku is therefore an example of what Pierre Levy one called "collective intelligence" in an early analysis of the internet (Levy 1999). While the idea of collective intelligence presumes *human* minds working together to contribute to something larger, we could modify that in the present context to include artificial sources of intelligence as well in view of the fact that Miku's existence is an interplay between machine-generated content (Miku's voice) and human creativity.

Hence, for many scholars of artificial intelligence, the use of AI in the cultural and creative industries still remains embedded in aspects of humanity. What technology – in this case artificial intelligence but one could say, more generally, digital culture – does is make the connection between humans more obviously mediated. In a sense, Manovich's taxonomy is not all that different from Boden's broader point regarding the limits of "pure AI" or the fourth item on Manovich's list. However, what is perhaps unique about Manovich's position is the emphasis on the recasting of human and non-human relations in the production and consumption of culture. What AI has done is not so much to automate humanity but to deepen its relationship with itself. And in this way, it can be seen as giving rise to different kind of aesthetic doxa, one which is less determined by elites, but one that which is closer to desire.

4 An uncanny valley?: critiques of AI-produced music and journalism

The cultural and creative industries' deployment of AI to automate and standardize aesthetic and artistic choices – or "curation efficiency" as Intel calls it – has been pointed to by contemporary cultural critics. Similar to the critiques by Benjamin and Adorno covered previously, they point out that the creeping in of AI into culture has resulted in cultural objects that are not quite human but rather something "uncanny," which Yair Rubinstein describes as "too close for comfort" (Rubinstein 2020, p. 85).

The term "uncanny valley" is credited to Masahiro Mori, a Japanese robotics and automation pioneer, and refers to the "unease often reported in response to almost-human images, whereby small discrepancies between reality and expectation are highlighted to the point of proving unease" (Avdeeff 2019, p. 4). In recent years, critical discussions of the "uncanny valley" have revolved around a song called "Daddy's Car," made in Flow Machines, Sony's software that uses AI to suggest melodies and chords among other musical elements. In 2016, Flow Machines sought to create songs that mimicked the style of specific artists' back catalogs. Unsurprisingly, as Sony is the owner of their catalog, the Beatles were selected. The resulting song, "Daddy's Car," was not intended to simply copy the Beatles. After all, where would one begin, when the Scousers themselves were influenced by American blues and R&B? Instead, the song was supposed to be mimic their "signature style." Style, as Boden argues, is something of an adherence to a structure. This, as Melissa Avdeef notes, is especially so in terms of popular music where "individual or authorial style" is developed "within . . . constraints" (Avdeeff 2019, p. 7). Put differently, style is something like "skills acquisition" rather than some kind of creative singularity. Flow Machines is able to collect "meta-information" on the songwriting style and run that through algorithmic machines (Rubinstein 2020, p. 81). It uses this information to generate melodic bits and pieces as well as chord progressions. These are then available for selection and sequencing. In this case, Sony revealed that the song was arranged by Flow Machines' artistic director, Benoit Carre. As Avdeef notes, "Daddy's Car" is an example of "augmented creativity" (Avdeeff 2019, p. 4), with artificial intelligence aiding a human creator.

While unremarkable artistically, the song has been a touchstone for debates around AI and creative production. Some have noted that the song is not really an autonomous creation since it was Carre who did a lot of the sequencing, making what are the key aesthetic decisions, much in the vein of sampling in much of contemporary music. Others suggest that its rather derivative sound speaks to the broader trend of declining standards in culture, especially with the onset of artificial intelligence in the production and consumption of culture.

This line of criticism has also extended to recent developments in what is called "automated journalism." Bloomberg News, for instance, uses a system aptly named "Cyborg" which is "able to assist reporters in churning out thousands of articles on company earnings reports each quarter." According to a report in the *New York Times*, "a third of the content published . . . uses some form of automated technology" (Peiser 2019). The *Associated Press*, *The Guardian Australia* and *Forbes* also use some kind of AI technology. While financial news seems to present the most instances of automated journalism, minor league baseball and high school football are also areas of coverage where news outlets have deployed some kind of AI.

In this case, the rationale behind using AI is to save the "creative tasks" of journalism to human writers. As the director of news partnerships at the *Associated Press* notes:

> The work of journalism is creative, it's about curiosity, it's about storytelling, it's about digging and holding governments accountable, it's critical thinking, it's judgment – and that is where we want our journalists spending their energy.

The use of AI for data collection and organization gives rise to a view of AI as a "productivity tool." Even with the data that is collected by AI, there is no "shiny robot banging out copy." In order to craft an "automated" news story, there is the work of editors and writers crafting several versions of a story. The supposed "threat" of AI to newsrooms is akin to the introduction of the telephone, according to the head of research and development at the *Wall Street Journal*:

> It gives you more access, and you get more information quicker. It's a new field, but technology changes. Today it's A.I., tomorrow it's blockchain, and in 10 years it will be something else. What does not change is the journalistic standard.

These comments assume that AI, as a technology, will not undermine the core journalistic standard of objectivity and factuality. But in fact there have been calls by professional fact-checkers (usually monitoring statements by politicians) who have developed automated fact-checking to "bring back the humans." For instance, the developers of Squash, a video app "that displays relevant fact-checks during a speech or debate when a candidate or elected official repeats a claim that has been checked." However, the developers of Squash have found that artificial intelligence needed human help in making the "final decisions about which fact-checks to display on the screen." This was also the case with ClaimBuster, which sifted through transcripts of speeches and statements by politicians but also selected and summarized which statements to fact-check to send out in an email to editors and reporters at major newspapers in the United States. To improve its take-up among journalists, ClaimBuster hired a university student to sift through the statements before sending it out in order to give "[the bot] some personality." The developers describe it as "[combining] automation and personalization" (Adair and Stencel 2020).

Thus, what we see from even the proponents of AI in music and journalism (two major components of the content industry today) is that the idea of AI as bearing the potential for what Boden would call "historical creativity," that is, producing something no one else has seen before, is no longer something held on to even in by its current mythologizers. Nevertheless, there seems to be another tendency, which is to see artificial intelligence as merely technological.

Jaron Lanier, one of the fiercest and most prominent critics of artificial intelligence, has tried to call out this trend by deeming artificial intelligence "an ideology, not a technology" (Lanier and Weyl 2020). In an article written with Glen Weyl, he points out that artificial intelligence is, in fact, not really a singular technology but rather a constellation of various techniques. What is given the name "artificial intelligence" today is based on merely a "subjective measure of tasks that we classify as intelligent." After all, in the decades before big data, there was artificial intelligence research happening on university campuses. But today, "artificial intelligence" is functionally synonymous with data scraping and data surveillance. Hence, Lanier concludes that artificial intelligence, when used as an umbrella term, is "marketing." Today, if any sort of software or technique is dubbed "AI," it benefits from "an air of magic." As a floating signifier, it obfuscates what it really is, which, according to Lanier, is an ideology that "[directs] thinking about the nature and use of computation."

What most concerns Lanier is the fact that AI, again, as ideology often "distracts from the responsibility of humans." In other words, AI ideology does not properly contextualize the place of humans in its work. For example, in everyday life, by the sheer fact of connecting on our mobile devices and computers, we are generating immense amounts of data. When private companies turn this data into commodities, this data is not considered "work" but rather, as Lanier stridently describes, "an off-the-books barter for certain free internet services." This "shadow work" amounts to a mirage, where we simply "ignore the man behind the curtain." Artificial intelligence is framed as autonomous when it is built off the back of human labor.

> 'AI' is best understood as a political and social ideology rather than as a basket of algorithms. The core of the ideology is that a suite of technologies, designed by a small technical elite, can and should become autonomous from and eventually replace, rather than complement, not just individual humans but much of humanity. Given that any such replacement is a mirage, this ideology has strong resonances with other historical ideologies, such as technocracy and central-planning-based forms of socialism, which viewed as desirable or inevitable the replacement of most human judgement/agency with systems created by a small technical elite.
>
> (Lanier and Weyl 2020)

This means that in order for AI to fully acknowledge its human basis, it must treat users as workers not customers. The "only alternative," he writes, is when workers are paid and become "citizens in full." For Lanier, this line of thinking stems not only from an empirical objection to how AI actually functions but also from a normative position regarding the "potential for AI." He actually does not care whether one rejects AI ideology based on the "humanist objection" – humans have a special place in the world – or the "pluralist objection" – everything depends on social context. What he wishes to point out is that an understanding of AI as *independence* from rather than an *interdependence* with humans is flawed.

It is notable that Lanier harkens back to an earlier era of industrial relations where organized labor had significant influence in society. "Workers who earn money also spend money where they choose; they gain deeper power and voice in society," he states. "They can gain the power to choose to work less, for instance. This is how worker conditions have improved historically." In reimagining the role of technology in human affairs, Lanier's argument poses somewhat of a departure from his earlier pronouncements of social media presenting a "digital Maoism" (Johnson 2006). In spite of the unexpected heel turn toward any sort of socialist rhetoric, it nevertheless raises the possibility of rethinking the other half of the stated subject of this chapter, which is AI and the creative and cultural industries.

What we can learn from Lanier and the critics of AI in the cultural and creative industries is that human "work" has expanded in the era of increased artificial intelligence but has become less visible and de-emphasized. Put differently, digital existence, which had become more cultural in the sense of the participatory culture of social media collapsing consumption and production of culture, has become an extension of the cultural and creative industries without recognition as workers. As is clear with the criticisms of End User License Agreements on YouTube and more recently TikTok, there is a great deal of revenue generated without content creators' recognition as employees in the traditional sense. The most famous and highly compensated among these are, depending on the platform, "partners" whereby the platform offers more lucrative revenue-sharing contracts. Even they, who are arguably the stars of these platforms, are not employees – meaning they do not have the usual protections and benefits associated with employment. But even among the rank and file users, AI is used to generate value. One does not need to upload anything on video-sharing platforms; he or she can simply watch videos, and their viewing habits are tracked by the platforms, populating its database and helping them refine their algorithm. In an era where production and consumption have merged into each other, technology users have become unsuspecting (and uncompensated) workers in the culture industry rather than simply duped consumers.

5 Rethinking the human: the future of AI in culture and entertainment

Thus far, this chapter has provided an investigation of artificial intelligence's impact on the creative, cultural and entertainment industries. Starting off with the work of the Frankfurt School, specifically Benjamin and Adorno, it argued that their work anticipated some of the concerns that emerged later with AI. It then moved on to the work of Margaret Boden in order to delve into what exactly "creativity" means when it is used in the context of AI and the cultural and creative industries. It then looked at some examples of the use of artificial intelligence in music and journalism and traced some critical perspectives.

The question of artificial intelligence in the realm of cultural and creative industries remains open to new and unexpected developments in the future. As mentioned several times over the course of this chapter, AI is already everywhere. Its novelty therefore is perhaps more ideological than technical, to recapitulate the terms used by Lanier. Thus, the future of AI is not only a matter of technological innovation but also the increasing level of cultural awareness of its impact on the culture and creative industries. Some key areas to keep track of in this regard are cultural variability, legality and affect.

The question of cultural variability (or lack thereof) goes back to the earlier criticisms of the industrialization of culture of the Frankfurt School, with fears of standardization and the development of what they call "mass culture" being the most obvious. The "pointy-edge" of high culture, that is, the critical, and even subversive, character of works of art would be blunted, resulting in easily digestible pieces of art. What's worse, according to Adorno and Horkheimer, this standardized, mass culture would reinforce the status quo not only making it tolerable for the masses, but even enjoyable. This would entail nothing short of the replacement of culture with entertainment.

While writers such as Lanier and Nicholas Carr bemoan the shallowing of our brains and the falling of cultural standards with the onset of "curation efficiency" facilitated by AI's "integration in cultural production and reception," Manovich has actually put forth the possibility that AI may not necessarily spell the "decrease in aesthetic variability." In fact, he asks whether it could increase it. This means, of course, thinking differently about variation, in particular how it is defined and measured. For Manovich, in assuming that everyone is producing similar cultural content in order to "play to the algorithm" (Cotter 2018), one has already given over AI – its techniques and affordances – to the industrialization (and, crucially, the classification) of culture spurred, in part, by large media platforms. For instance, when music streaming services, such as Spotify or Apple Music, create playlists, musical styles and artists that may not adhere to the genre as traditionally understood are categorized according to the platforms' own criteria. The practice of the culture industry in classifying artifacts, people and behavior is what Manovich calls "supervised machine learning." They usually reinforce the "taken-for-granted classifications and ways of seeing the world." "Unsupervised machine learning," to the contrary, could allow us to discover new categories and develop connections not considered before (Manovich 2019, p. 18). This entails the retention of large-scale cultural data sampling but also a new approach to capturing not only characteristics of the cultural object(s) but also its reception, use and circulation. In other words, Manovich is calling for the separation of culture from industry and the recovery of AI from the large media platforms by smaller, independent content creators.

In addition to cultural variability, the matter of legality and copyright remains crucial when considering the future of AI and the cultural and creative industries. As was the case when digital technologies opened up the possibility for greater sharing, sampling and remixing, copyright emerged as one of the key issues (Vaidhyanathan 2003; Lessig 2009). Similarly, when content is created by artificial intelligence, the question authorship rears its head. If artificial intelligence, such as in the case of "Daddy's Car," generates some aspects of a piece of music or art, but it also has the mark of human hands, to whom does the copyright (not to mention, royalties and other forms of credit) belong? If it is indeed shared, how is it divvied up?

This has become a live issue in South Korea, where there has been heavy investment into AI research by the state as well as its globally recognized technology firms. As it stands, the Copyright Act in South Korea only protects works which are "creative productions expressing *human thoughts and emotions*" (Cho and Lee 2020). Because of this, a cultural creation by AI is not protected under copyright law. There have been discussions among firms that work made by AI should be considered that of the company much in the way a freelancer's work is considered not hers. Despite the fact that industry watchers do not anticipate it changing anytime soon, it is notable that South Korean law enshrines human thoughts *and* emotions. In the context of South Korean law and culture, we can say that emotions are seen as the bedrock of humanity and human cultural expression. It is due to the *lack* of emotions that work done by AI is not protected by copyright.

How long until "affective computing" permeates the artificial intelligence landscape as it pertains to the cultural and creative industries is an open question. While Boden suggests that the methods for reading emotions in human beings is "still relatively crude," the prospect of affective computing reinforces the importance of emotion in the production of culture" (Boden 2016, p. 75). It seems, in time, that the definition of the human will be contested yet again by technological development. In 1964, Marshall McLuhan described media as "the extensions of man[sic]" in the 21st century and beyond, it may be appropriate to amend McLuhan's declaration to include media as the *reflection* of humanity – albeit with the caveat that what it means to be human has always been co-constituted by dominant technologies of the time.

References

Adair, B. and Stencel, M., 2020. A Lesson in Automated Journalism: Bring Back the Humans. *Nieman Lab*. Available from: https://www.niemanlab.org/2020/07/a-lesson-in-automated-journalism-bring-back-the-humans/

Adorno, T.W., 1996. A Social Critique of Radio Music. *The Kenyon Review*, 18 (3/4), 229–235.

Avdeeff, M., 2019. Artificial Intelligence & Popular Music: SKYGGE, Flow Machines, and the Audio Uncanny Valley. *Arts*, 8 (4), 130.

Benjamin, W., 2013. *Illuminations: Essays and Reflections*. New York: Schocken Books.

Bessant, J., 2018. *The Great Transformation: History for a Techno-Human Future*. London and New York, NY: Routledge.

Boden, M., 1998. Creativity and Artificial Intelligence. *Artificial Intelligence*, 103 (1–2), 347–356.

Boden, M., 2003. *The Creative Mind: Myths and Mechanisms*. London and New York: Routledge.

Boden, M., 2016. *AI: Its Nature and Future*. Oxford and New York: Oxford University Press.

Cho, W.H. and Lee, H.I., 2020. AI, Machine Learning & Big Data Laws and Regulations | Korea | GLI. In: *GLI – Global Legal InsightsInternational Legal Business Solutions*. London: Global Legal Insights.

Copeland, B.J., 2000. AlanTuring.net The Turing Test [online]. *AlanTuring.net*. Available from: www.alanturing.net/turing_archive/pages/Reference%20Articles/TheTuringTest.html [Accessed 1 November 2020].

Cotter, K., 2018. Playing the Visibility Game: How Digital Influencers and Algorithms Negotiate Influence on Instagram. *New Media & Society*, 21 (4), 895–913.

Feldman, B., 2019. YouTube Exec Denies the Existence of 'Rabbit Hole Effect'. *Intelligencer*.

Gold, H., 2020. Netflix and YouTube Are Slowing Down in Europe to Keep the Internet from Breaking. *CNN*.

Guga, J., 2014. Virtual Idol Hatsune Miku. In: *International Conference on Arts and Technology*. Cham: Springer, 36–44.

Horkheimer, M. and Adorno, T.W., 2007. *Dialectic of Enlightenment: Philosophical Fragments*. 1st ed. Stanford: Stanford University Press.

Hsu, H., 2020. How Can We Pay for Creativity in the Digital Age? *The New Yorker*, 14 September.

Johnson, S., 2006. Digital Maoism (Published 2006). *The New York Times*, 10 December.

Kobayashi, H. and Taguchi, T., 2019. Virtual Idol Hatsune Miku: Case Study of New Production/Consumption Phenomena generated by Network Effects in Japan's Online Environment. *Markets, Globalization & Development Review*, 3 (4).

Konnikova, M., 2014. Where Do Eureka Moments Come From? *The New Yorker*.

Kurzweil, R., 2005. *The Singularity Is Near: When Humans Transcend Biology*. New York: Penguin Publishing Group.

Lanier, J. and Weyl, G., 2020. AI is An Ideology, Not a Technology | WIRED. *Wired*.

Lessig, L., 2009. *Remix: Making Art and Commerce Thrive in the Hybrid Economy*. London: Bloomsbury.

Levy, P., 1999. *Collective Intelligence: Mankind's Emerging World in Cyberspace*. Cambridge, MA: Basic Books.

Lomas, N., 2020. Europe's Top Court Confirms no Mass Surveillance without Limits. *TechCrunch*.

Manovich, L., 2019. *AI Aesthetics*. Moscow: Strelka Press.

Marx, L., 2000. *The Machine in the Garden: Technology and the Pastoral Ideal in America*. Oxford: Oxford University Press.

Mohamed, F., 2020. Warner Bros. Taps Intel AI to Connect Content and Audience [online]. *Intel*. Available from: www.intel.com/content/www/us/en/artificial-intelligence/posts/warner-bros-taps-intel-ai-to-connect-content-and-audience.html [Accessed 1 November 2020].

OSA_DC, 2020. Artificial Intelligence in Japan (R&D, Market and Industry Analysis). *Medium*.

Palca, J., 2015. Shall I Compare Thee to an Algorithm? Turing Test Gets a Creative Twist. *NPR.org*.

Peiser, J., 2019. The Rise of the Robot Reporter. *The New York Times*, 5 February.

Rockmore, D., 2020. What Happens When Machines Learn to Write Poetry. *The New Yorker*.

Rubinstein, Y., 2020. Uneasy Listening Towards a Hauntology of AI-Generated Music. *Resonance*, 1 (1), 77–93.

Sandvine, 2019. Netflix Falls to Second Place in Global Internet Traffic Share as Other Streaming Services Grow [online]. Available from: www.sandvine.com/inthenews/netflix-falls-to-second-place-in-global-internet-traffic-share [Accessed 1 November 2020].

Steimle, J., 2014. What Is Content Marketing? *Forbes*.

Vaidhyanathan, S., 2003. *Copyrights and Copywrongs: The Rise of Intellectual Property and How it Threatens Creativity*. New York: NYU Press.

Verini, J., 2012. How Virtual Pop Star Hatsune Miku Blew Up in Japan. *Wired*, 20 (11).

20
AI, robotics, medicine and health sciences

Norina Gasteiger and Elizabeth Broadbent

Introduction

> [T]he computer as an intellectual tool can reshape the present system of health care, fundamentally alter the role of the physician, and profoundly change the nature of medical manpower recruitment and medical education – in short, the possibility that the health-care system by the year 2000 will be basically different from what it is today.
>
> Schwartz (1970: 1257)

The emergence of artificial intelligence (AI) has provided many opportunities for improvements in healthcare. Early expectations were for AI to change the role of physicians, recruitment and education, as exemplified in the quote opening the chapter. Now, AI has surpassed these predictions and has widespread use, from helping clinicians to make more accurate diagnoses to consulting patients remotely. Additionally, the development of AI has accelerated the growth of physical tools, such as wearables and robotics. Surgeries can now be performed with the assistance of robots, and social companion robots are used in aged care.

This chapter begins by briefly exploring the historical and intellectual development of AI and robotics, with a focus on health purposes. Major claims and developments, principal contributions to healthcare and major criticisms of using AI and robots in healthcare will be covered. This chapter ends by highlighting current perspectives and exciting developments for the future of AI and robotics in health and medicine.

Introducing AI and robotics

In this section, some common AI terms are explained, as applied to healthcare. AI, in brief, refers to machines simulating human intelligence. This depends on the analysis of big data which 'trains' machines, such as computer systems. The application of AI in healthcare is motivated by clinical need and real-life issues that are solvable through data use. AI algorithms may solve a problem or simplify the problem by assisting medical practice (e.g. giving recommendations for treatment). Ultimately, the purpose of applying AI to the health sector is to improve the delivery and quality of care, patient engagement and health outcomes.

Both medical and demographic data are used in AI systems. General demographic data include age, occupation, sex and income. Medical data refers to any information on the health and wellbeing of an individual including medical notes, clinical laboratory tests, electronic recordings from medical devices, physical examinations and clinical imagery. This data may be structured or unstructured, with use of either depending on the abilities and goals of the AI technique. Structured data are organised and standardised, such as laboratory results, smoking status and demographics. This helps to infer the possibility of a disease outcome or cluster patients' traits. Conversely, unstructured data are disorganised, lacking a predefined model of categorisation, and are often text-heavy. In health, the most obvious example is a doctor's clinical notes.

AI may also be virtual or physical (Hamlet & Tremblay, 2017). Virtual AI refers to the application of the buzzwords commonly associated with AI (natural language processing, machine learning, Deep learning and neural networks) to software or computer systems. Conversely, physical AI refers to the application of AI in concrete tools and technologies, including intelligent prosthetics and, importantly, robotics.

The word *robot* stems from the Czech word *robota*, meaning labourer (Hockstein et al., 2007). By definition, robots are machines that mimic and automate human behaviour. Robots may be autonomous, semi-autonomous or passive. They can be controlled directly or via teleoperation or telepresence. Teleoperation or 'telerobotics' refers to controlling robots remotely (i.e. in the same room). In contrast, telepresence is useful when one cannot be in the same location. Here, transnational control is possible.

Robots, like AI, can perform various health-related tasks. This help can be assistive in nature and is often not intended to replace human-delivered care. In hospital settings, mobile robots are used to prevent the spread of infections by cleaning surfaces. They are also used to perform essential but mundane tasks, such as sorting pills in pharmacies, delivering meals to inpatients and handling and organising test tubes in laboratories. Robots can help to provide direct care. Surgical robots, for example, assist surgeons in performing procedures more precisely and efficiently.

Robots may also provide companionship. For example, robots can promote patient-centred care, by acting as social companions in inpatient settings, homes or in residential care for older adults. Additionally, they can physically aid patients by lifting objects.

Historical and intellectual development

Robots and AI were not originally developed for the health sector. Nonetheless, they can play a crucial role in delivering patient-centred, efficient and safe care. It is important to understand the key milestones that fostered their development.

Early AI and robotics: 1940s and 1950s

Ideas regarding AI have been traced back to Grecian myths. However, two key events occurred much later, in the 1940s and 1950s, which are recognisable as definite roots of AI. First, Pitts and McCulloch conceptualised a mathematical model on what we now name the 'neural network' in 1943. Their most important findings understood how neurons fire and that they can learn and adapt their action over time (McCulloch & Pitts, 1943). The second key event is Alan Turing predicting machine learning in 1950, without naming it so (Mintz & Brodie, 2019).

Turing attempted to answer the question, 'Can a machine think?' which was both revolutionary and beyond his time, considering that computers were still being created. Turing also developed the 'Turing Test', a method of inquiring whether AI could exhibit behaviour indistinguishable to a human (Mintz & Brodie, 2019).

In 1956, John McCarthy first linked the term AI with the science and engineering of developing intelligent machinery (Amisha et al., 2019; Mintz & Brodie, 2019). Later in the 1950s, work on natural language processing began. This involves extracting information from unstructured data such as text or speech and processing it into structured data, which machines can interpret and use in machine learning (Fei Jiang et al., 2017).

Developments in robotics also commenced in the 1950s, although the concept can be traced back to early literary works by the Czech Capek brothers in 1917 and 1921 (Hockstein et al., 2007). Their ideas became a reality in 1958 when the first industrial robot was assembled for the automotive industry. General Motors introduced the *Unimate* robot for automating unpleasant tasks such as welding. This robot consisted of a single hydraulic manipulator arm.

The 1960s and 1970s

Machine learning and, consequently, neural networks and Deep learning were developed in the 1960s. Machine learning is an umbrella term that refers to statistical techniques for fitting models to structured data and the machine 'learning' from this data (Davenport & Kalakota, 2019). Machine learning can be supervised or unsupervised, depending on whether the outcome variable is known. Supervised learning refers to a known outcome variable and unsupervised to an unknown variable.

Neural networks and Deep learning are complex techniques of machine learning (Davenport & Kalakota, 2019). Artificial neural networks vaguely simulate how neurons in the brain would process signals. The purpose of this is to identify patterns across data by recognising key features. Deep learning draws on neural network models but incorporates many levels of features and variables (Davenport & Kalakota, 2019). Deep learning techniques are used to predict highly accurate outcomes. Progress in Deep learning also helped to improve other techniques, such as natural language processing.

Advances in natural language processing were led by Weizenbaum (1966), a computer scientist at the Massachusetts Institute of Technology (MIT). As an experiment, Weizenbaum (1966) developed ELIZA, a text-based natural language processing computer program that acted as a psychotherapist. ELIZA was, in essence, the first known chatbot and conversational AI to attempt the Turing Test.

Demand for robots in various sectors increased dramatically in the 1960s and 1970s. After the *Unimate* robot had its successful assembly line debut in 1961, other industries realised the potential for automating dangerous and mundane tasks. Space and deep-sea exploration, search-and-rescue missions, and military use further pushed for the development of robotics (Hockstein et al., 2007). However, the value of robots in the health sector had not yet been realised.

There is little knowledge of AI in health and medicine prior to 1970. Researchers at Stanford University were the first known to use an AI technique for health purposes, in their development of MYCIN (Davenport & Kalakota, 2019). MYCIN was a simple inference engine, using backward chaining and around 600 rules to identify bacteria that caused severe infections and to recommend antibiotics, based on patient traits such as body weight. This was the first clinical decision support system that could aid in diagnosis and treatment. However, MYCIN was never used in practice, partly due to ethical and legal concerns regarding the use of computers in health contexts. These concerns were reflected in other literature during the time.

For example, Schwartz (1970) raised concerns regarding the use of computers to 'appraise' clinicians. Similarly, Schwartz talks about the intrusion of computers resulting in the changing nature of the health workforce whereby the demand for highly skilled clinicians lessens as computers take on more of their work. Interestingly, these concerns are still commonplace today and will be addressed later in this chapter.

The 1980s and 1990s

The 1980s and 1990s were characterised by a surge of interest in AI, especially the application of neural networks, fuzzy set theory and Bayesian networks. Although fuzzy set theory was first developed in 1965, its use became more popular during this time period. Fuzzy set theory refers to the degree of membership an object has within a set. This technique is particularly useful when the available data are vague or imprecise. In contrast, Bayesian networks are an inferential modelling technique that allows users to make predictions and compute the probability of an outcome.

Rule-based expert systems similar to MYCIN were also developed (Davenport & Kalakota, 2019). One clinical decision support system was implemented into practice and continues to be used today. This system is DXplain, launched by the University of Massachusetts in 1986 (London, 1998). DXplain uses a modified form of Bayesian logic to generate possible diagnoses based on user-input on patient signs, laboratory results and symptoms. Potential diagnoses are then ranked to assist clinicians in making a final diagnosis. The original system contained information on approximately 500 diseases. The system became more comprehensive over time and featured 2,000 diseases in 1987, when it was available nationwide over dial-up Internet services, until 1995. At this point, it was also available as a stand-alone service that could be downloaded on PCs. The widespread use of the Internet pushed for DXplain to be available as a web-based service, which replaced all other forms of media in 1996. The DXplain system is still used today, primarily in the United States of America, for clinician education in medical schools.

The 1980s and 1990s resulted in a substantial advancement in the area of surgical robotics. In 1985 a prototype for a surgical arm capable of conducting a brain biopsy with 0.05mm precision was developed (Hockstein et al., 2007). This built the foundation for work on Neuromate, a robotic tool that received FDA approval in 1999. The Robodoc system was also used across Europe for hip replacements, beginning in 1992, but did not receive FDA approval. Robodoc is a computer-guided milling machine, used to drill the femoral bone during surgery (Hockstein et al., 2007).

Telerobotic systems, such as daVinci, were first used clinically in Belgium in 1997 (Ballantyne, 2002). The original daVinci system consisted of a visual console that provides a three-dimensional view of the site, hand-based control grips which allow the surgeon to move the instruments remotely and a three-armed robotic-controlled instrument drive system to perform the surgery. One of the three arms provides a binocular video of the operation. In 1999 the Zeus system was developed (Hockstein et al., 2007). This system was intended to perform telepresent surgeries, similar to daVinci.

The introduction of surgical robots resulted in a need for patient simulators to practise the new methods. Previous simulation methods involved using cadavers. Virtual reality (VR) simulations were introduced in 1990 as a less resource-intensive, repeatable, safer and more ethical alternative (Badash et al., 2016). Simulations could also be uploaded to robotic tools, such as the Robotic Surgical Simulator which helped teach surgeons to use the daVinci system and practice operations (Badash et al., 2016).

The last twenty years: 2000 to 2020

Innovative use of AI and robotics in healthcare continued to grow in the 2000s. In 2001 a surgeon sitting in New York, United States, used the Zeus system to perform a laparoscopic cholecystectomy on a patient in Strasbourg, France (Hockstein et al., 2007). This was a world-first for telepresent surgeries. While Zeus is no longer available, the daVinci system has since received FDA approval and is now used worldwide (Hockstein et al., 2007).

Development and implementation of patient-facing AI systems and robots have also increased. PatientsLikeMe, a web-based, AI-enabled community and research platform launched in 2004 (Okun & Wicks, 2018). Aimed at empowering individuals, those with health conditions can share their lived experiences and learn from others. The site has more than 650,000 members who have contributed 43 million data points. Machine learning and natural language processing techniques analyse patient-generated data to understand health conditions and make predictions.

Since 2005, companion robots like the fluffy baby harp seal, Paro, have been used in the homes of older adults with dementia (Shibata & Tanie, 2001). Younger populations also use robots, such as the two-foot-tall MEDi humanoid. MEDi helps to distract, ease pain and reduce stress for children receiving uncomfortable procedures, including vaccinations (Beran et al., 2013). MEDi ultimately acts as a friend to young children.

The AI Companion tool introduced in 2007 by Cogito uses natural language processing. This software can accurately detect symptoms of depression and post-traumatic stress disorder by analysing phone calls, text messages and the duration of calls. PatientsLikeMe and Companion are two of many examples of applying AI to create novel methods of diagnosis and care for patients. By 2016, most investments regarding AI were for healthcare applications in comparison with other sector (Amisha et al., 2019).

In 2020, a pandemic further accelerated the growth of AI and robotics. The severe acute respiratory syndrome coronavirus 2 (SARS-CoV-2) causing COVID-19 demanded the sudden need for the use of telehealth (remote) consultations, as many governments globally imposed a lockdown. Robots such as UVD robots (Blue Ocean Robotics) and AIMBOT (UBTech) played an important role in containing the pandemic. Robot-controlled non-contact ultraviolet (UV) surface disinfection sanitised hospital rooms from traces of the virus in China and Italy, taking only 10 minutes per room (Blue Ocean Robotics). In a hospital in Shenzhen, China, the mobile AIMBOT robot measured temperatures using infrared thermal sensors, with 99% accuracy from a 3.5 metre distance. It could also detect whether someone was wearing their face-mask properly and disinfect itself after contact with people.

Major claims and developments

Significant developments in the area of AI and robotics for health and medicine can be attributed to many key contributors. In AI, major developments include wearables, affective computing, relational agents and the Internet of Healthy Things. Similarly, the field of healthcare robotics has been advanced by autonomous, behaviour-based and companion robots.

Wearables

Wearable computing refers to computer-powered wearable items, such as clothing, earphones, shoes, socks, watches, wristbands and glasses (Jin, 2019). These technologies are considered 'smart' as they possess advanced functions, not unlike the abilities of smartphones. Importantly, wearables enable AI by generating large datasets on users that can be interpreted through machine learning techniques (Jin, 2019).

Known as the godfather of wearables, Alex 'Sandy' Pentland spearheaded the field of wearable medical technology, or as Pentland (2004) initially conceived it, 'healthwear'. By marrying the domains of psychology, computer sciences and engineering, wearables can provide an insight into people's behaviours and physiology. Pentland ultimately inspired and worked on popular wearables such as the Google Glass, fitness trackers and watches that can measure heart rate, blood pressure and record temperature.

The primary purpose of wearables was to monitor patients or the self (Pentland, 2004). By using data generated by wearables, models can be built on a patient's normal behaviour. Incoming data can then be used to monitor a patient and to identify irregular or concerning behaviour. Algorithms can also be used to diagnose, predict and inform clinician treatment plans. For example, wearables can monitor an elderly patient who is at risk of experiencing a fall (Jin, 2019). Smart watches and wristbands use accelerometers to collect data on a change in velocity, such as in the event of a fall. This data can be shared with carers, to alert them and hasten emergency care.

The widespread adoption and presence of wearables and IoHT (explained later in this section) have resulted in an almost obsessive self-tracking cultural phenomenon. This is explained by the concept of the 'quantified self' – the ability to quantify aspects of daily life, make meaning of this data and ultimately make changes for the better.

Affective computing and relational agents

By coining the concept of 'affective computing', Picard (1997) postulates that computers are capable of recognising a user's emotional state, responding to these emotions and expressing their own. Work in this field focuses on giving computer systems emotional intelligence, including empathy and self-awareness. Understanding a user's affective state can be achieved by using physiological measures, such as facial expression recognition, heart rate, and sensing skin conductance to identify arousal. Computers can be programmed to react to these cues and communicate emotions back to the user in a manner that appears empathetic.

These ideas were applied in the first affective wearable – the Q Sensor, developed by Affectiva, an organisation co-founded by Picard and el Kaliouby in 2009. The Q Sensor was a small device worn on a wristband. Used primarily to understand stress and predict outbursts by autistic children, it detected emotion through the skin, using skin conductance techniques. Small electrical changes in the skin were recorded and monitored by doctors, caregivers and patients themselves. This was based on the sympathetic nervous system's 'fight or flight' response, which increases physiological arousal resulting in increased heart rate and sweating. Increased moisture results in the skin being more electrically conductive, which sensors measure the strength of by sending an electrical pulse from one point of the skin to another.

Developments in wearable computers and affective computing have shifted our thinking from seeing computer systems as tools to seeing them as socially intelligent agents. This has ultimately paved the way for the relational computer agent. Relational agents leverage affective computing by building and maintaining long-term relationships with users. Bickmore (2003) describes relational agents as conversational, animated humanoid characters that use nonverbal (e.g. gaze and gesture) and verbal (e.g. speech and tone) modalities to simulate human interaction. Relational agents maintain relationships over multiple face-to-face interactions by remembering history and managing future interactions.

In health, relational agents may build trusting and caring relationships to facilitate behaviour change. For example, Bickmore et al. (2013) tested the effectiveness of a relational agent that played the role of an exercise coach that motivated and encouraged users to exercise more. Findings of the randomised controlled trial (RCT) with 263 older adults indicated that the agent was effective at increasing walking in the short-term.

The Internet of Healthy Things

The Internet of Healthy Things (IoHT) refers to connecting everyday objects to the Internet and for these objects to be able to transmit and use data, without human-to-computer interaction, for health purposes. Generating volumes of data is crucial for powering AI algorithms. Data from multiple sources can provide holistic understandings of a patient's health and may be used to produce models that can make more accurate predictions and recommendations for diagnosis or treatment.

Joseph Kvedar conceived the concept of connecting technologies to various aspects of the health system (i.e. tools, facilities and people) as 'connected health' (Kvedar et al., 2014). This revolutionised the delivery of telehealth (the delivery of healthcare at a distance), using technology. IoHT or connected health enables telehealth by seamlessly and efficiently sharing and using data, thus promoting the provision of continuous, patient-centred and virtual healthcare (Kvedar et al., 2014).

The potential for connecting technologies on IoHT infrastructure is vast and includes ubiquitous sensors, ingestibles, personal trackers, wearables, mobile devices, tablets, apps and social networks. This is exemplified in the Abilify MyCite ingestible (Otsuka Pharmaceutical Company), a novel method of tracking medication adherence for adults with schizophrenia or bipolar disorder. Abilify MyCite consists of an atypical antipsychotic aripiprazole tablet embedded with a small sensor (1mm x 1mm) and a patch sensor worn by the patient. Once ingested, the stomach's acid fluids activate a signal to the patch, which is forwarded to a patient's smartphone. The data is then sent to a cloud-based server which carers or clinicians can access through a web-based portal. Abilify MyCite was approved by the FDA in 2017.

Autonomous behaviour-based robotics

Autonomous robots perform tasks with a high degree of self-sufficiency. As a form of artificial intelligence, autonomy is achieved by making calculations based on data collected in specific situations, defining probabilities, making informed decisions and then acting or reacting. It is important to note that autonomous robots only perform actions that they have been programmed to do.

Rodney Brooks popularised actionist or behaviour-based autonomous robotics in the 1980s at MIT. By making sensorimotor links within environments, autonomous behaviour-based robots are able to correct their actions when they make mistakes (Brooks, 1990). This means that they rely on adaptability. Brooks founded the company iRobot in 1991, which produced Roomba in 2002 – a famous autonomous specialised vacuuming robot that promises to free up time by automating mundane household tasks. To vacuum, Roomba uses sensors and AI to learn and adapt to its environment (Mois & Beer, 2020).

Autonomous service robots like Roomba can alleviate the burden of tasks that may be too physically demanding for some individuals (Mois & Beer, 2020). Implemented in the homes of the elderly or disabled, behaviour-based service robotics can easily adapt to their environments and ultimately support independent living.

Companion robots

Social companion robots provide therapeutic benefits to users. Mimicking the success and acceptance of animal therapy, many companion robots look and behave like real animals.

However, they are easier to care for, especially by young children or older adults with dementia. Takanori Shibata, Chief Senior Research Scientist at the National Institute of Advanced Industrial Science and Technology in Japan, is a key contributor to this field. Arguably, Shibata's most notable work is the invention and commercialisation of Paro (Shibata & Tanie, 2001).

Paro is a robotic baby harp seal. Charged by a pacifier, the robot has five hours of battery time and weighs 2.55kg. Ubiquitous tactile sensors are placed under its antibacterial fur-like surface to measure contact. To simulate animal behaviour, Paro has sight (light sensors), balance and auditory sensors to recognise speech and the direction of the sound. Physically, the robot can move its neck, flippers, tail and eyelids (see Figure 20.1).

Figure 20.1 Paro the companion robot

Robots like Paro can replicate the psychological, physiological and social benefits of animal therapy. A cluster-RCT conducted with 415 older adults with dementia in Australia found that Paro improved mood states and agitation when compared to standard care (Moyle et al., 2017). Participants were also more verbally and visually engaged. Other research used a repeated measures design to explore the physiological effects of interacting with Paro in 17 older adults in rest-home and hospital-level care (Robinson et al., 2013). Blood pressure decreased significantly during the interaction, and diastolic blood pressure increased once Paro was removed, showing similar effects to animal therapy.

Principal contributions

Robotic systems and AI techniques have revolutionised healthcare delivery, how administrative activities are performed, and the extent to which patients are empowered and their preferences prioritised. These technologies have resulted in more accurate detection of disease, precise diagnoses and safer medical treatment. Simultaneously, clinicians can provide better quality and appropriate long-term care by using AI to predict treatment outcomes and prognosis. Administrative activities related to care can now be streamlined and partially automated, helping to ensure that no patient is forgotten and that care is continuous.

Through these technologies, care can be provided beyond geographical boundaries, and patient decision making can be made through telehealth and virtual consultations. Importantly, this level of care can be maintained until the end of life, as individuals can age at home, in familiar environments and within their communities.

Detection, diagnostics, treatment and prognostics

Common medical errors relate to the wrong administration, reaction to and dosing of medications (especially anaesthesia), and missed, inaccurate or delayed diagnosis and treatment. These errors are often caused by human factors (e.g. miscommunication) and are exacerbated by systemic issues regarding short-staffing of clinicians, long shifts leading to burnout and increasing demand. AI and robots support the delivery of high quality, personalised and safe medical care, from detecting conditions, supporting accurate diagnoses, identifying the most suitable treatment plans and calculating long-term prognosis and risk of recurrence. By automating and supporting aspects of medical care, AI and robots may alleviate some of the burden of clinicians; however, these technologies are not readily available yet.

Detection and diagnostics

Neural networks, Bayesian networks and decision trees can assist diagnosis. According to Loh (2018), AI directly competes with pathologists and radiologists, who similarly rely on detecting patterns across large datasets to make a diagnosis. However, in many cases, AI has outperformed humans. In one study, Google researchers found that AI was more accurate (89%) in detecting malignant tumours from images of breast cancer, compared to pathologists (73%) (Liu et al., 2017).

As AI is not flawless, conclusions should be reviewed by clinicians and used only to support human diagnosis. For example, Taylor et al. (2018) trained a neural network to detect moderate and large pneumothoraces (lung collapse due to air in the chest) from frontal chest x-rays. The AI correctly identified 90% of negative x-rays and was 80–84% accurate in detecting positive x-rays. This was useful for helping radiologists organise cases by priority of care

(Taylor et al., 2018). Efficient detection and diagnosis are crucial, as severe pneumothoraces require timely care.

The advancement of robotic technology has also led to the possibility of robot-assisted diagnoses, such as in endoscopies. Endoscopies are a non-surgical procedure used to detect bleeding, cancers, anaemia and inflammation in a patient's internal organs (oesophagus, small intestine, stomach and colon). Clinicians traditionally insert and manipulate the endoscope – a long tube that hosts a camera while the recorded imagery is presented on a television screen. Handheld manipulation requires extensive training and experience. During lengthy procedures it may produce a hand tremor and, consequently, impair the quality of the footage. Robots can steadily manipulate rigid and flexible endoscopes, allowing for clinicians to focus on detecting abnormalities using clearer imagery (Li & Chiu, 2018). These may be controlled by foot pedals, a joystick or voice command, thus decreasing possible miscommunication between the endoscope holder and leading clinician (Li & Chiu, 2018). Robot-assisted endoscopies are commonplace in some hospitals and an endoscopic arm is now also embedded in the daVinci system.

Treatment and prognostics

As discussed elsewhere in this chapter, robots can help to treat patients, such as by assisting surgeries (daVinci), and both robots and AI chatbots can provide therapy (for example, Paro and Woebot). AI, however, has the potential to help answer difficult questions pertaining to the delivery of high quality and personalised medical care. These may include: Is this medication safe, and at what dose? Which treatment will work best for this patient? Will this treatment work in the long-term? What is the prognosis and likelihood of a recurring event? By answering these questions, common medical errors can be avoided and health outcomes optimised.

Large datasets can help to identify when medications may not be safe to prescribe/administer, if they are safe, the most suitable dose and route of administration. Data may include current medical knowledge on dosage, side effects, reactions with other medications and good practice guidelines. This data, combined with patient information such as allergies, current medications and general medical history can guide clinicians on safe medication administration. AI is used to comb through the data, identify patterns and make recommendations. This could involve drug dosage algorithms or adverse warning effects when medications may harm a patient (Amisha et al., 2019).

Precision medicine is a popular application of machine learning techniques, whereby predictions are made off data to determine a successful, safe and personalised treatment plan for each patient. In precision medicine, treatments are chosen for each patient by accounting for their genetic, lifestyle and environmental factors, and a combination of data thereof. A crucial field of related study is pharmacogenomics – the study of how a patient's genes may affect their response to medications. Precision medicine requires collaboration between a team of specialists across medical fields and is therefore both resource- and time-intensive. AI can be more efficient as it does not rely on manual analysis. In a study, human experts took 160 hours to make a treatment plan for a patient with brain cancer (Wrzeszczynski et al., 2017). IBM's AI, Watson, took only 10 minutes to analyse a genome of the patient and make a comparable personalised plan (Wrzeszczynski et al., 2017). However, poor clinician adoption has slowed the application of AI techniques into clinical practice for precision medicine (Loh, 2018).

AI can also predict long-term prognosis and risk of recurring events. Prognosis refers to the likely course of a diagnosed condition, such as progression or recovery. For example, machine learning techniques can predict the progression of dementia (Mathotaarachchi et al., 2017). These assess amyloid PET scans or a combination of PET scans and cerebrospinal fluid and blood-based biomarkers. By analysing longitudinal data from electronic medical records, machine learning models can also predict events such as falls or hospital readmissions. Golas et al. (2018) developed a Deep learning algorithm by using data from 11,510 patients to predict 30-day hospital readmissions for patients with heart failure. The model was found to be superior to traditional techniques and was used to identify patients with risk for hospitalisation. This could have significant cost-saving benefits for clinical teams by ensuring that interventions are targeted at the most high-risk patients.

Management and administration

By automating duties, AI and robots can relieve staff from mundane and time-intensive tasks. Schwartz (1970) refers to administrative tasks as 'housekeeping activities' that are necessary to ensure practices and hospitals run smoothly. As previously mentioned, robots can assist hospital and lab staff by sorting pills and organising test tubes.

Administrative activities that employ AI tend to be online or digital. These include online check-ins, scheduling of appointments and hospital admissions, and digitising and organising medical records from previously paper-based physical records (Amisha et al., 2019). AI may also be used to determine immunisation dates for children and alert staff when reminder calls for follow-up appointments need to be made (Amisha at el., 2019). Human resource departments are also now using AI algorithms to promptly identify and recruit the most appropriate and experienced medical personnel. This is an often time-consuming task due to a general shortage of nurses and doctors.

Administrative tasks can be streamlined through automation, which frees up time for more complex issues to be resolved by humans. Human-dependent duties may include communicating with insurance companies, answering a patient's questions, interviewing a candidate for a job, liaising with clinical staff and ordering resources for the best price.

Telehealth

Telehealth is a broad term and may include virtual consultations, e-therapy, remote monitoring or patient management. Telehealth is a crucial mode of healthcare delivery for patients who live in rural or remote locations, cannot travel, are too ill or vulnerable to attend in-person care or during epidemics and pandemics of infectious diseases. Aside from making healthcare more accessible, telehealth also reduces indirect costs related to seeking care (e.g. travel), resulting in more affordable care.

AI and robotic technologies enable telehealth. This is exemplified in differing methods of providing remote consultations. Virtual consultations can be offered by clinicians instead of in-person appointments, by using video teleconference software and at-home monitoring systems (e.g. blood pressure devices or wearables). These systems may contain sensors to collect and transmit data in real-time to a website. AI conversational agents or 'chatbots', such as those in the GP at Hand (Babylon Health, 2019) app symptom checker, may also consult patients without the need of human supervision.

Chatbots are particularly helpful when patients are self-triaging, such as making the decision whether or not to see a doctor or seek emergency care. By using natural language processing, the chatbot in GP at Hand can respond appropriately. Deep learning enables messages to be interpreted and speeds up the process of searching the knowledge graph. The knowledge graph consists of a database with millions of data points representing current medical knowledge (i.e. symptoms and terminology), an individual's health records (medical history and previous interactions with the app), wearables synced to the app and conditions associated with geography and specific populations.

The chatbot may then refer patients to a video-based consultation through the app or make recommendations for self-care (see Figure 20.2). Patients can also replay their virtual appointment, book face-to-face appointments, have prescriptions sent to their local pharmacy and receive referrals through the app (Babylon Health, 2019). The triage chatbot in this app has been piloted and endorsed by the UK's NHS.

AI chatbots may provide mental healthcare remotely. Teletherapy (also known as e-therapy, e-counselling and cyber-counselling) refers to the online and distant delivery of mental healthcare. Teletherapy is convenient, affordable and more accessible to many individuals, especially those who may feel anxious when seeking mental healthcare in person. However, a major limitation of basic teletherapy is the inability to detect suicidal ideation or self-harming behaviours. Advanced teletherapy that uses AI algorithms can recognise these symptoms by using natural language processing and machine learning techniques to identify patterns across an individual's data (Loh, 2018).

Although basic e-therapy tools can be useful for mild mental health issues, they are often limited to providing generalised information and support to individuals. AI-powered teletherapy may be more personalised and engaging. The Woebot chatbot, for example, continually analyses data gathered during interactions to identify negative emotions and then provides tips on how to understand and reframe these sentiments. Woebot is available through Facebook

Figure 20.2 Image showing the triage and video consultation functions on Babylon's GP at Hand app

Source: Babylon

messenger and as an app. The AI-powered chatbot delivers evidence-based cognitive-behavioral therapy (CBT) to improve overall mood, anxiety and depression. In an RCT conducted by Fitzpatrick et al. (2017) with 70 college students (aged 18–28), Woebot significantly improved symptoms of depression over two weeks, compared to those using an information-only mental health eBook. Woebot was also successful at reducing anxiety (Fitzpatrick et al., 2017). Importantly, the chatbot refers users to seek 'higher-level care' if their mood does not improve over six weeks and upon identifying suicidal or self-harming tendencies presents information for crisis helplines. A similar chatbot, Tess, was inspired by ELIZA and developed by X2AI. Like Woebot, Tess can respond 24/7 and suggests helplines for crises and general stress-relief strategies. In an RCT with 74 participants, Tess significantly reduced symptoms of depression and anxiety compared to those receiving only information (Fulmer et al., 2018).

Remote patient monitoring (RPM) is another sub-field of telehealth that is enabled by AI and robotics. RPM involves the collection and transmission of health-related data for assessment and interpretation by clinicians. RPM may be used to support independent living, promote behaviours (e.g. medication adherence) or for particular conditions that require frequent monitoring. RPM technologies may detect changes that are indistinguishable by humans, and are therefore not reported by patients.

RPM may be a stand-alone or an additional function. Within the IoHT, home devices can be connected to the Internet via smart sensors, solely for RPM purposes. Non-invasive sensors within 'smart homes' may detect environmental changes (i.e. temperature, humidity, smoke), physiological signs (blood oxygen level, blood pressure, heart rate, body temperature) and movement. AI algorithms can be used to analyse incoming data against a model of normal behaviour. When abnormal activity occurs, RPM technologies can alert family, carers, health staff or emergency services to respond.

Homecare robots may also provide RPM. For example, iRobi, a telehealth robot designed to support people with chronic obstructive pulmonary disease (COPD) measures heart rate, breathlessness and quality of life weekly (Broadbent et al., 2018). Aside from RPM, iRobi educates users on COPD and reminds patients when to take their medications, use their inhalers, and do rehabilitation exercises. It also displays videos on how to perform these exercises and records adherence (see Figure 20.3). The robots were linked with smart inhalers that recorded inhaler use on a secure website.

In a pilot RCT with 60 COPD patients, Broadbent et al. (2018) reported that those using iRobi were significantly more adherent to their inhalers and rehabilitation exercises than those receiving standard care. By using smart inhalers and iRobi, data collected remotely can be used by clinicians to accurately and continuously monitor adherence, which is crucial to COPD care and delaying further lung damage.

Older people's health

Robotics and AI have majorly altered our approach to caring for the elderly. These technologies support ageing-in-place and independent living within aged-care communities. This significantly improves the quality of life for older adults due to enhanced social inclusion and connection (Barrett et al., 2012). Ageing-in-place also benefits families and carers, as it ensures continuity and familiarity of the environment, and promotes independence for both parties (Barrett et al., 2012). Additionally, ageing-in-place alleviates the burden on aged-care facilities and the economy.

A preference for ageing-in-place poses the opportunity for home-based social robots to assist older adults. Robinson et al. (2014) distinguish between two types of social robots: companion

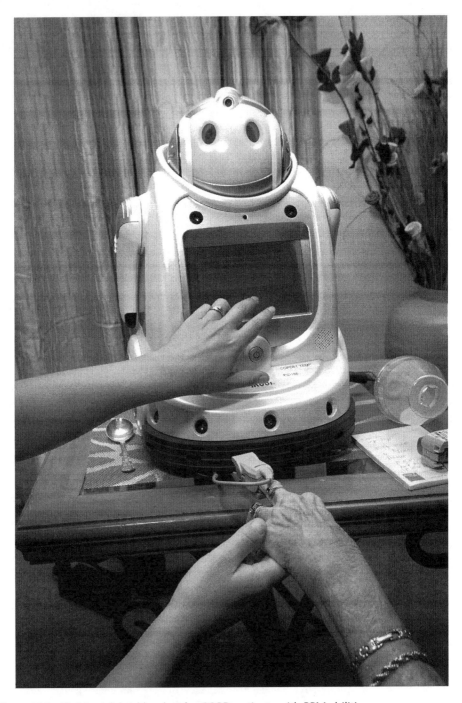

Figure 20.3 iRobi, a telehealth robot for COPD patients with RPM abilities

AI, robotics, medicine and health sciences

robots (e.g. Paro) and service robots, used to provide specific help. Used in the home, service robots may perform fetch-and-carry tasks and can help with physically demanding household chores, as demonstrated by vacuum cleaning robots, such as Roomba. Daily care robots can also provide reminders to older adults, who may struggle to remember to take medications, perform tasks or attend appointments, due to mild dementia or mild cognitive impairment.

Social robots may help to prevent the decline of cognitive functioning by delivering cognitive stimulation activities, such as games (Law et al., 2019). CompanionAble for example, is a service robot that provides reminders to older adults, enables users to video call their family or care assistants, and delivers cognitive training activities (Schroeter et al., 2013). Five older adults tested CompanionAble in their own homes and concluded it was both enjoyable to use and useful (Schroeter et al., 2013). Likewise, Bomy (see Figure 20.4) is a 60cm-tall, penguin-like mobile service robot that provides scheduled reminders to older adults, recognises their faces, brings them medications and delivers six cognitive stimulation games (Arin, 2019).

For older adults who experience memory loss and tend to wander, remote location monitoring enables functional independence while reducing stress on caregivers (Robinson et al., 2014). AI-enabled smartphone applications and smartwatches can locate an individual. For example, the iWander app is designed to track people with dementia by using GPS and communication (Sposaro et al., 2010). As individuals use the system, data is collected to build a model that reflects normal behaviour. Data is then analysed through Bayesian techniques to estimate the probability of wandering behaviour. Depending on the probability, the app will issue verbal prompts that direct the individual home. iWander will also notify the nominated caregiver with the location of the individual. A call can be performed between the wandering

Figure 20.4 Bomy, a social home-based service robot that provides reminders and delivers games

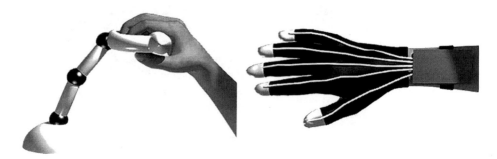

Figure 20.5 End-effector (left) and generic full-hand exoskeleton (right)

individual, caregiver and local emergency services. With ongoing use, the Bayesian network becomes increasingly accurate by learning and identifying behavioural patterns (Sposaro et al., 2010). The success of the iWander app, however, is dependent on individuals being able to use a mobile phone and remember to take it with them.

Robotics and AI may also be used to facilitate emergency and rehabilitative care for conditions associated with ageing. As previously discussed, AI-enabled wearables may help to predict or detect when an individual experiences a fall and communicate this to their carer (Jin, 2019). Robotic systems can also be used to engage older adults in stroke rehabilitation. Stroke rehabilitation tends to focus on strengthening muscles required for motor-skill movement and range-of-motion. Robotic-assisted rehabilitation supports individuals in repeatedly performing motions of the upper or lower limb, to regain function and strength.

End-effector and exoskeleton robotics are used in stroke therapy. Reviews conducted by McConnell et al. (2017) and Aggogeri et al. (2019) compare both types of robotics for the rehabilitation of hand movement in stroke survivors (see Figure 20.5). Specific movements include grasping, opening the hand and moving the wrist. End-effector robotic devices provide force to the distal location of the limb. This means they do not match the actual joint, so some movement will be restricted and abnormal. However, end-effector robots are easier to set up as the hands are adjustable to different sizes and are more usable for new patients. In comparison, exoskeletons are mounted on the patient, resulting in more natural movement, and better posture as the axes match the joints of the user.

Regardless, both types of therapy robots apply an intensive and accurate force, again and again. Advanced therapy robots can also collect data (e.g. on spasticity) and provide tactile feedback to improve movements. They can also help to alleviate the burden on therapists as they do not require constant supervision, thus enabling therapists to see multiple patients simultaneously or allow for remote, home-based care. Both types of robotics are used commercially, in conjunction with conventional therapy.

Main criticisms

Although AI and robotics pose significant benefits to the delivery of healthcare, their shortfalls are heavily criticised. Critiques regard their absence of human-like characteristics, limitations in data quality and potential for algorithm bias. Many people have reported ethical concerns such as privacy, confidentiality and accountability. Fear of replacement and loss of employment remain significant concerns. An amalgamation of these criticisms has resulted in hesitant adoption and slow uptake of many technologies.

Absence of human qualities

In the book *Alone Together* Sherry Turkle (2011) postulates that humanity is nearing a robotic moment, determined by the fact that people already filter companionship through technology. Accordingly, the subsequent stage of downplaying our emotional attachment to other humans will be through our acceptance of technologies as companions. Thereafter, robots will be employed as carers for children and in healthcare.

Turkle (2011), amongst others, openly criticises the acceptance of technology and observes that humans are quick to assign human-like qualities, even when the technology is limited. This is known as the 'ELIZA effect', named after the first chatbot ELIZA (introduced earlier in this chapter). Turkle writes about a study in which students conversed with the chatbot to assess its ability to be human-like. Rather than honestly describing its limited capacity and lack of human traits, they exaggerated its strengths. The results reflected that ELIZA was able to imitate human conversation, not because the chatbot actually could, but due to participants' desire for the computer to be lifelike.

In reality, AI tools and robots lack certain human attributes. The human qualities we perceive these technologies to possess are those we desire and hence falsely assign (Turkle, 2011). Robots cannot inherently empathise with patients. Similarly, AI systems lack traits such as creativity, comprehensive communication skills and critical thinking (Amisha et al., 2019). These traits are tacit knowledge, and cannot yet be easily taught, quantified and programmed into machines. The semblance of human caring can be programmed through eye gaze behaviors that suggest attention, and smiling that suggests friendliness, but these attributes are inferred by the user.

Data quality and bias

It is often said that an AI algorithm is only ever as good as the data it has access to. However, data quality and consequently bias in AI is a complex issue, deeply rooted in historical injustice and social inequities (Loh, 2018). Data availability results in bias, as some minority groups are under- or misrepresented in datasets. Algorithms are also often used for populations and within contexts they were not designed for. Consider, for example, an AI algorithm that detects melanoma (skin cancer) in photographs but is only programmed with images of white, male patients. When used for other populations, such as African American females, the algorithm can lead to results that are inaccurate, inconsistent and systematically prejudiced by containing gender and racial biases.

Within healthcare, bias in AI may result in inequitable (unjust) treatment, care and ultimately differential health outcomes between populations. In our example, the algorithm could contribute to late detection, misdiagnosis and worse health outcomes such as increased severity/spread of cancer and perhaps preventable mortality due to late, or no, diagnosis.

These issues have resulted in the emergence of the AI ethicist. An AI ethicist works with researchers and data scientists to detect algorithm biases or immoral behaviour and determine the long-term consequences of these biases. They then guide their teams on how to mitigate these.

Data quality and storage have also been critiqued within wearables, as sensors do not always collect reliable and accurate data. Generally, this is because they have been developed in lab or experimental settings and when worn casually (and sometimes incorrectly) pick up 'noise' – undesired environmental data (Jin, 2019). Small devices are often limited in regard to their battery life and data storage capacity. This can jeopardise the quality and quantity of data collected.

Privacy, confidentiality, accountability and deception

Technological advances give rise to ethical considerations for use and implementation. If unaccounted for, these concerns can prevent uptake and slow the adoption of AI and robotic systems. Privacy and confidentiality are crucial to protect sensitive health-related data from being shared, commercialised or misused. Medical providers have a legal obligation under national legislation to protect health data. Examples include the UK's Data Protection Act 2018, the USA's Health Insurance Portability and Accountability Act (HIPAA) 1996 and the New Zealand Health Information Privacy Code 1994. However, not many countries have updated their privacy acts to specifically cover new technologies of the digital age, such as facial recognition or natural language processing techniques, that could be used for malicious intent.

Concerns around privacy and confidentiality have been present for a long time. In 1970 Schwartz raised concerns regarding the use of computers to appraise clinicians covertly. In 2004, Pentland argued that cell phone signals could be used to track people. Nowadays, phones and wearables commonly collect GPS location data, which may be used to monitor and track individuals. Pentland (2004) suggested that ownership and control of data should be maintained by the user. For example, in the case of wearables, individuals should be able to decide whether they want to wear them, as opposed to sensors being placed in the surrounding environment. These issues remain relevant and complicated, as new technologies emerge and disappear quickly, bringing with them new challenges for maintaining patient privacy and confidentiality.

Accountability for technological problems must also be considered, as it is often unclear who would be accountable if technology fails. In health, failure could result in preventable injury, permanent disability or even death, especially during a robot-assisted surgery, or if sensors do not reliably measure a fall.

As technology becomes increasingly advanced, deception should be considered. Deception is not always black and white, and issues regarding this may be more problematic in some areas than others. Consider, for example, that an older adult with moderate dementia believes that their fluffy companion robot is an animal. This is seemingly harmless, given that companion robots are successful due to their ability to mimic the psychological and physiological benefits of animal therapy (Moyle et al., 2017; Robinson et al., 2013). Conversely, individuals with a history of attempted suicide may also not realise that the AI chatbot they are disclosing their mental health concerns to is in fact, not a human. Advanced chatbots may pick up suicidal ideation or self-harming tendencies, but limited chatbots may not. It is clear that transparency is crucial, especially in situations that may give rise to harm.

Loss of jobs

Job threat concerns and replacement are popular topics in the media, alongside headlines like, "Will robots take over the world?" These media reports may inadvertently reduce acceptance of robots by the general population. However, most AI and robots in healthcare are designed to work with humans, not to replace them.

Some argue that the widespread use of robots and AI will result in less demand for skilled clinicians (Schwartz, 1970). However, others argue for beneficial application within healthcare. For example, by alleviating workload, technologies can help to avert potential clinician burnout. Likewise, AI and robots may take on mundane and time-lengthy administration tasks. This enables medical staff to focus on the human side of care, such as taking more time with their patients and communicating with their team members. It also has to be recognised that new jobs are created with novel technologies.

Uptake and adoption

An amalgamation of the previously mentioned criticisms can result in poor uptake and slow adoption. However, there are many other reasons as to why technologies are not accepted nor used. Firstly, many AI algorithms and robots are developed and evaluated in experimental and research settings. Their performance within these theoretical settings may not always translate to real-world use (Loh, 2018). Their transferability to medical care settings may also be limited because regulations, policies, workflow and organisation preferences are not accounted for. Similarly, end users may not accept technologies that they do not perceive as useful, enjoyable, nor easy to use (Robinson et al., 2014). Development of intuitive technologies that transfer to real-life settings requires user-centred design and evaluation research that explores usability in the context, and with the target population it is developed for.

Secondly, health technologies may result in a temporary reduction in productivity and increase of cost for organisations, as systems need to be set up (i.e. transferring data and testing functions) and staff trained. Depending on digital literacy skills, staff may require long-term technical assistance. If technologies require a steep learning curve and significant changes to 'business-as-usual,' staff may push back. Additional staff may need to be hired to support implementation. If cheaper and simpler alternatives exist, these may be preferred. Traditional patient care provider payment structures are likely to be disrupted by new technologies and alternative ways to pay providers need to be developed.

Thirdly, many robot companies experience failure of uptake due to a multitude of interrelated problems. These include a lack of 'hype' or need for the product, limited funding, competition and a lengthy development time. Many cycles of development, trial and amendment are required to develop a minimum viable product. This is both costly and resource-intensive.

Current perspectives and future development

The future of AI in medicine holds much promise. Market trends forecast an increasing interest and investment in AI-enabled tools for health and medicine, including robotics. Current trends show that the global health-related AI market was valued at USD 2.5 billion in 2018 (Grand View Research, 2019). This is expected to grow at a compound annual growth rate of 41.5%, reaching USD 31.3 billion by 2025. Some countries in the Asia Pacific (Australia, Japan, South Korea, India, China and Singapore) are predicted to experience the most significant growth, accelerated by a rising number of start-up companies, government-led AI initiatives, adoption and improvements in their health technology infrastructure (Grand View Research, 2019). Ultimately, investment in research, development and implementation of AI is crucial to widespread acceptance, adoption and ultimately ubiquitous use by health organisations, clinicians and patients.

Future developments of health-related AI and robotics focus on containing pandemics, enabling telehealth through big data and wearables, virtual assistants, brain-computer interfaces and minuscule medical robots used within and outside of the body.

Containing pandemics

An important future application of AI is the prevention and containment of infectious disease outbreaks, such as the COVID-19 pandemic. Countries currently depend on medical facilities to identify, monitor and report patterns across new cases with similar symptoms. In 2004, Pentland predicted that infectious diseases like severe acute respiratory syndrome (SARS) or attacks using biological weapons might be detected earlier if individuals were monitored using AI-enabled wearables. Continuous monitoring may detect patterns across individuals before they present to hospital, by identifying similar symptoms and behaviours (i.e. lethargy, fever and not going to work). Early detection could enable a quicker response and easier containment.

Contact tracing for infected individuals could also be more accurate, by using mobile technologies. Contact tracing is crucial to containing infectious diseases, as those exposed to an infected individual often do not know that they may have been infected. Current contact tracing methods consist of government and public health professionals identifying and tracking anyone an infected case may have had contact with. Potential cases are then called to provide health and self-isolation information. Manual contact tracing is both time- and resource-intensive, especially when individuals cannot be contacted by phone.

During the COVID-19 pandemic, Singapore implemented a Bluetooth-enabled contact tracing app called TraceTogether. The app acts as a 'digital handshake' when users come into close proximity. Data on contact is also stored to alert users of potential infection in the future. However, adoption of TraceTogether was stunted in many countries, due to privacy concerns and doubt that enough of the population would be willing to use the app. A gradual increase in technology acceptance may lead to better uptake of similar community-driven contact tracing apps during future pandemics, as would addressing privacy concerns.

Developments in infectious disease robotics are still in relatively early stages, although the 2020 COVID-19 pandemic did accelerate their application into clinical environments. As seen by the AIMBOT and UVD robot, their main advantages include that robots cannot be infected and that they can disinfect themselves. More development and implementation of infectious disease robots in hospitals and public spaces is possible for future epidemics and pandemics.

Big data and wearables

Growth is also expected in the application of big data and the development of wearable technology. Big data now, and more so in the future may consist of an amalgamation of data gathered by wearables and mobile devices, with datasets growing, as individuals wear more GPS and sensor-embedded technology. Computational abilities to analyse big data and identify trends will become more advanced to reveal patterns and associations relating to human behaviour and health outcomes (i.e. risk prediction). This will also shift the traditional delivery of face-to-face healthcare to remote delivery, as telehealth and RPM are enabled, and as individuals are empowered to self-monitor.

Future developments in wearable technology concentrate on seamless integration of wearables into fashionable clothing and accessories that people want to wear continuously, as fashion trends influence sales and consumer demand. Technology and trends change rapidly, so engineers may develop timeless, permanent and less visible solutions such as clothing, body patches or implants embedded underneath the skin. Likewise, future development will promote long-term use by harvesting natural energy to maintain battery life. For example, future wearables may leverage solar exposure, body heat and kinetic energy through movement.

Artificial general intelligence, artificial superintelligence and emerging virtual assistants

Advances in AI focus on learning and sophisticated capabilities that are equal to, or outperform a human. Current AI is perceived as narrow (weak) (Pohl, 2015). Consider virtual assistants, such as Siri and Google Assistant, for example. These are capable of very specific household

AI, robotics, medicine and health sciences

tasks like turning on music and answering questions like, 'Where is the nearest pharmacy?' Their sole purpose is to assist users and make smartphones easier to use. Hence, they do not need to learn or perform a variety of tasks.

However, a lucrative market in virtual healthcare assistants is emerging to respond to a shortage of clinicians, especially nurses (Grand View Research, 2019). Virtual assistants may save up to 20% of the time attributed to unnecessary visits. Importantly, they also provide more accessible healthcare by conducting consultations, RPM and providing personalised care, based on previous interactions and medical history. Nevertheless, human qualities like reasoning and empathy are required for virtual healthcare assistants to deliver care that is synonymous to their human counterparts.

Virtual assistants currently scratch the surface on artificial general (strong) intelligence (AGI), whereby an AI's performance is equal to a human. AGI algorithms can reason, plan and solve problems and learn from experience, similar to humans (Pohl, 2015). An example of a company performing ongoing development in this field is Soul Machines, who develop autonomous human-like virtual assistants. The virtual humans are complete with unique personalities and dynamic computer-generated interfaces that can react and respond to human users, including interpreting and reciprocating emotions (Soul Machines, 2020).

These virtual humans are built using biologically motivated models, and can be applied in healthcare. For example, virtual humans have the potential to visually demonstrate biological and disease processes through advanced graphical models of anatomy and physiology, and to use these to engage and motivate people in healthy behaviours (Sagar & Broadbent, 2016). The Baby X project combines models of motor and neural systems to create a virtual infant that can naturally be interacted with. Baby X has a digital brain that allows her to sense, learn, adapt and communicate in a human-like manner (Figure 20.6).

Beyond AGI, engineers will eventually strive to develop artificial superintelligence (ASI) that outperforms humans (Pohl, 2015). It is contested whether machines will need to gain

Figure 20.6 Virtual human, Baby X, learning animals
Source: Soul Machines Ltd

consciousness to be considered as having ASI. If so, computers would be able to outperform humans intellectually, from philosophical reasoning to the application of mathematics and science. Importantly, self-aware ASI would be able to set goals and may work independently from humans. Some perceive self-aware ASI to be a threat to humankind. The application of ASI in health and medicine could, however, be revolutionary, as cures for complicated and burdensome illnesses could potentially be invented quickly, and ethical dilemmas could be well-reasoned.

Human brain-computer interfaces

Brain-computer interface (BCI) systems are a promising field that is advancing medical robotics and our understanding of human-robot interaction. BCI is a novel technology that uses physiological signs in the brain to activate and control external devices or computers (McConnell et al., 2017). These may use passive signals (e.g. staring at a light) or active signals (e.g. thinking about closing and opening a hand). Further, BCI may be invasive or non-invasive. Invasive BCI technology is implanted into the brain during neurosurgery. This allows for precise detection of individual neurons. Conversely, non-invasive technology often uses electroencephalography (EEG) or functional magnetic resonance imaging (fMRI) to detect brain signals.

Until recently, invasive implants dominated BCI applications, due to their ability to detect stronger signals and ultimately enable more precise control. In 2019 a team of researchers from Carnegie Mellon University developed a breakthrough for non-invasive BCI (Edelman et al., 2019). Their mind-controlled robotic arm was able to accurately and continuously track and follow a computer cursor, by using EEG. This innovation could have significant benefits for paralysed individuals or those with poor mobility. Similarly, as it avoids surgical and medical requirements related to implants, it can be widely implemented and made available on a commercial scale. For research benefits, it can also be tested on larger numbers of participants, compared to small cases in invasive BCI. This means that the technology is developed to be responsive to the needs of users. The BCI technology by Edelman et al. (2019) has already been tested in 68 subjects.

Aside from neuro-prosthetics and assistive robotics, future BCI developments include mind-controlled wheelchairs, verbal communication and motor neurorehabilitation (i.e. for stroke survivors). Benefits of BCI technology are promising but mostly originate from animal studies, pre-clinical testing and small experiments or case studies (McConnell et al., 2017). Future large-scale development and evaluation is required.

Minuscule medical robotics

Developments in medical robotics and biotechnology innovation include stream-lining platforms, telementoring (remote guidance by experts) and importantly, smaller instrumentation (Badash et al., 2016; Topol, 2019). Specifically, microrobotics and nanobots may provide healthcare from within the body while swarm robots collectively perform healthcare-related tasks.

Medical microrobots

Microrobots, by definition, are less than one millimeter in diameter. Magnetic fields steer microrobots through the natural pathways in the body, including blood vessels and the gastrointestinal tract. Potential applications include supporting treatment and diagnosis, such as by delivering medications to specific areas in the body.

In 2016 a research group in Germany introduced a remote-controlled Spermbot that fits itself to a slow sperm and guides it to the egg – a first in microrobotic fertility treatment (Medina-Sánchez et al., 2016). Another promising example by researchers from the Max Planck Institute for Intelligent Systems includes the mobile Millibot (Hu et al., 2018). Millibot is a soft inchworm-like robot with advanced locomotive capabilities. Controlled by external magnetic fields, Millibot can walk, roll, crawl, float and swim through different terrains (Hu et al., 2018). Importantly, Millibot can pick up an object such as medication, transport it through the digestive tract, urinary tract or heart surface and release it when needed (Hu et al., 2018). It may also unclog arteries. While microrobotics are still being evaluated, we may see the first clinical application in the foreseeable future.

Nanobots

Nanobots (nanites, nanorobots, nanoids, nanoagents) are smaller than microrobots, at the size of a nanometer (10^{-9} meters). Nanobots may help on a cellular level, by being programmed to diagnose, monitor and treat a range of diseases. Nanobots can be applied topically, or enter the body orally or through injections. In dentistry, nanobots may be introduced via a mouthwash or toothpaste (Rifat et al., 2019). Once in the mouth, they could identify and destroy pathogenic bacteria. Similarly, when applied topically, nanobots may be programmed to cure skin diseases by removing dead skin, replenishing and balancing oil and ultimately supporting the healing process.

Research has also shown that nanobots with embedded biosensors may enable more precise cancer treatment, as they are highly site-specific and unlike conventional therapies may be programmed to only destroy cancerous cells (Sivasankar & Durairaj, 2012). In other potential health-related applications, nanobots may help to fight the HIV virus and tetanus bacterium, assist surgeries from within the body and repair the structure of DNA for genetic disorders (Bhuyan & Bardoloi, 2016; Rifat et al., 2019; Sivasankar & Durairaj, 2012). Evidently, nanobots are perceived to have widespread potential for health applications. However, future use of nanobots, like microrobots, is reliant on successful human trials, as previous research has shown potential in animal trials. Manufacturing of nanobots is also extremely complicated due to their size (Rifat et al., 2019). Regardless, innovations in significantly smaller robotics may redefine what is perceived as 'minimally invasive' (Topol, 2019).

Swarm robotics

Natural swarm insects have inspired the development of swarm robots. Swarm robots consist of many small, autonomous but straightforward robots (i.e. micro- or nanorobots), each equipped with sensors, a transmitter and a receiver to communicate with one another. By interacting with each other and the environment, swarm robots perform behaviours collectively. A taxonomy of possible behaviours is presented by Schranz et al. (2020), who determine that swarm robots are capable of organising themselves spatially, navigating environments, making decisions and performing other miscellaneous behaviours (e.g. self-healing and self-reproduction).

Of relevance to health and medicine, nano-swarm robots may be able to collectively resolve blood clots or deliver targeted medications in the body (Rifat et al., 2019). Another use, outside of the body is to transport medical resources that would be too heavy, large or important for individual robots to carry. Examples may include urgent transportation of medications or human organs for transplant surgeries between hospitals or to difficult-to-reach locations and conflict zones. Swarm robots could transport these resources by collectively exploring environments and navigating them. Of note is the reliability of the technology. Swarm robots can detect faults in individual robots (i.e. hardware issues) and use machine learning algorithms to self-heal software issues (Schranz et al., 2020). They may also self-reproduce/replicate new robots, eliminating the need for engineers and ensuring that the swarm is large enough to perform tasks. However, while the potential for swarm robotics has been realised, future development and real-world industrial application of advanced swarm algorithms is required (Schranz et al., 2020).

Conclusion

The use of AI and robots in health and medicine has so far contributed to providing more accessible, efficient, high quality and patient-centred care. Living in a digital ecosystem undoubtedly tests our society, both in terms of ethical considerations, culture and social norms. However, whether through partial assistance or automation, AI and robotics assist clinicians to monitor, diagnose, and treat patients. Such technologies can empower patients to monitor their own health, provide additional options for accessing care and support, and may enable older people to live independently for longer. Through increasing investment, acceptance, cross-industry innovation and respectful collaboration between computer scientists, engineers, clinicians and patients, novel applications can be developed to further protect individual and population health outcomes.

References

Aggogeri, F., Mikolajczyk, T. & O'Kane, J. 2019. Robotics for rehabilitation of hand movement in stroke survivors. *Advances in Mechanical Engineering*, 11(4): 1–14.

Amisha, Malik, P., Pathan, M. & Rathaur, V.K. 2019. Overview of artificial intelligence in medicine. *Journal of Family Medicine and Practice*, 8(7): 2328–2331.

Arin, K. 2019. Using robotics in dementia prevention, care. *The Korea Herald*. 20 October. Available at www.koreaherald.com/view.php?ud=20191018000579

Babylon Health. 2019. GP at hand. Available at www.gpathand.nhs.uk/

Badash, I., Burtt, K., Solorzano, C.A. & Carey, J.N. 2016. Innovations in surgery simulation: A review of past, current and future techniques. *Annals of Translational Medicine*, 4(23): 453.

Ballantyne, G.H. 2002. Robotic surgery, telerobotic surgery, telepresence, and telementoring. Review of early clinical results. *Surgical Endoscopy*, 16(10): 1389–1402.

Barrett, P., Hale, B. & Gauld, R. 2012. Social inclusion through ageing-in-place with care? *Ageing & Society*, 32(3): 361–378.

Beran, T.N., Ramirez-Serrano, A., Vanderkooi, O.G. & Kuhn, S. 2013. Reducing children's pain and distress towards flu vaccinations: A novel and effective application of humanoid robotics. *Vaccine*, 31: 2772–2777.

Bhuyan, M. & Bardoloi, S. 2016. Nanobots: A panacea to HIV. *International Research Journal of Engineering and Technology*, 3: 2390–2395.

Bickmore, T. 2003. *Relational Agents: Effecting Change Through Human-Computer Relationships*. PhD Thesis, Massachusetts Institute of Technology, United States of America.

Bickmore, T., Silliman, R.A., Nelson, K., Cheng, D.M., Winter, M., Henault, L. & Paasche-Orlow, M.K. 2013. A randomized controlled trial of an automated exercise coach for older adults. *Journal of the Geriatrics Society*, 61(10): 1676–1683.

Broadbent, E., Garrett, J., Jepsen, N., Ogilvie, V.L., Ahn, H.S., Robinson, H. et al. 2018. Using robots at home to support patients with chronic obstructive pulmonary disease: Pilot randomized controlled trial. *Journal of Medical Internet Research*, 20(2): e45.

Brooks, R.A. 1990. Elephants don't play chess. *Robotics and Autonomous Systems*, 6(1–2): 139–159.

Davenport, T. & Kalakota, R. 2019. The potential for artificial intelligence in healthcare. *Future Journal Healthcare*, 6(2): 94–98.

Edelman, B.J., Meng, J., Suma, D., Zurn, C., Nagarajan, E., Baxter, B.S., et al. 2019. Noninvasive neuroimaging enhances continuous neural tracking for robotic device control. *Science Robotics*, 4(31): eaaw6844.

Fitzpatrick, K.K., Darcy, A. & Vierhile, M. 2017. Delivering cognitive behavior therapy to young adults with symptoms of depression and anxiety using a fully automated conversational agent (Woebot): A randomized controlled trial. *JMIR Mental Health*, 4(2): e19.

Fulmer, R., Joerin, A., Gentile, B., Lakerink, L. & Rauws, M. 2018. Using psychological artificial intelligence (tess) to relieve symptoms of depression and anxiety: Randomized controlled trial. *JMIR Mental Health*, 5(4): e64.

Golas, S.B., Shibahara, T., Agboola, S., Otaki, H., Sato, J., Nakae, T. et al. 2018. A machine learning model to predict the risk of 30-day readmissions in patients with heart failure: A retrospective analysis of electronic medical records data. *BMC Medical Informatics and Decision Making*, 18(1): 44.

Grand View Research. 2019. *Artificial Intelligence in Healthcare Market Size, Share, & Trends Analysis By Component, By Application, By Region, Competitive Insights, and Segment Forecasts, 2019–2025.* San Franscisco: Grand View Research.

Hamlet, P. & Tremblay, J. 2017. Artificial intelligence in medicine. *Metabolism*, 69S: S36–S40.

Hockstein, N.G., Gourin, C.G., Faust, R.A. & Terris, D.J. 2007. A history of robots: From science fiction to surgical robotics. *Journal of Robotic Surgery*, 1(2): 113–118.

Hu, W., Lum, G., Mastrangeli, M., et al. 2018. Small-scale soft-bodied robot with multimodal locomotion. *Nature*, 554: 81–85.

Jiang, F., Jiang, Y., Zhi, H., Dong, Y., Li, H., Ma, S., et al. 2017. Artificial intelligence in healthcare: Past, present and future. *Stroke and Vascular Neurology*, 2(4): 230–243.

Jin, C.Y. 2019. A review of AI technologies for wearable devices. *IOP Conference Series: Materials Science and Engineering*, 688: 1–6.

Kvedar, J., Coye, M.J. & Everett, W. 2014. Connected health: A review of technologies and strategies to improve patient care with telemedicine and telehealth. *Health Affairs*, 33(2): 194–199.

Law, M., Ahn, H., MacDonald, B., Vasjakovic, D., Lim, J., Lee, M., et al. 2019. User testing of cognitive training games for people with mild cognitive impairment: Design implications. In: M. Salichs et al. (eds.) *Social Robotics. ICSR 2019. Lecture Notes in Computer Science*, vol. 11876. Cham: Springer.

Li, Z. & Chiu, P.W. 2018. Robotic endoscopy. *Visceral Medicine*, 34(1): 45–51.

Liu, Y., Gadepalli, K., Norouzi, M., Dahl, G.E., Kohlberger, T., Boyko, A. et al. 2017. Detecting cancer metastases on gigapixel pathology images. *arXiv*, 1703: 1–13.

Loh, E. 2018. Medicine and the rise of the robots: A qualitative review of recent advances of artificial intelligence in health. *BMJ Leader*, 2: 59–63.

London, S. 1998. DXplain: A web-based diagnostic decision support system for medical students. *Medical Reference Services Quarterly*, 17: 17–28.

Mathotaarachchi, S., Pacoal, T.A., Shin, M., Benedet, A.L., Kang, M.S., Beaudry, T. et al. 2017. Identifying incipient dementia individuals using machine learning and amyloid imaging. *Neurobiology of Aging*, 59: 80–90.

McConnell, A., Moioli, R.C., Brasil, F.L., Vallejo, M., Corne, D.W., Vargas, P.A., et al. 2017. Robotic devices and brain-machine interfaces for hand rehabilitation post-stroke. *Journal of Rehabilitation Medicine*, 49: 449–460.

McCulloch, W.S. & Pitts, W. 1943. A logical calculus of the ideas immanent in nervous activity. *Bulletin of Mathematical Biophysics*, 5: 115–133.

Medina-Sánchez, M., Schwarz, L., Meyer, A.K., Hebenstreit, F. & Schmidt, O.G. 2016. Cellular cargo delivery: Toward assisted fertilization by sperm-carrying micromotors. *Nano Letters*, 16(1): 555–561.

Mintz, Y. & Brodie, R. 2019. Introduction to artificial intelligence in medicine. *Minimally Invasive Therapy & Allied Technologies*, 28: 73–81.

Mois, G. & Beer, J.M. 2020. The role of healthcare robotics in providing support to older adults: A socio-ecological perspective. *Current Geriatrics Reports*, 1–8.

Moyle, W., Jones, C.J., Murfield, J.E., Thalib, L., Beattie, E.R.A., Shum, D.K.H., et al. 2017. Use of a robotic seal as a therapeutic tool to improve dementia symptoms: A cluster-randomized controlled trial. *Journal of the American Medical Directors Association*, 18(9): 766–773.

Okun, S. & Wicks, P. 2018. DigitalMe: A journey towards personalized health and thriving. *BioMedical Engineering Online*, 17: 199.

Pentland, A. 2004. Healthwear: Medical technology becomes wearable. *Computer*, 37(5): 42–49.

Picard, R.W. 1997. *Affective Computing*. Cambridge, MA: MIT Press.

Pohl, J. 2015. Artificial superintelligence: Extinction or Nirvana? *International Conference on Systems Research, Informatics and Cybernetics*, Baden-Baden, Germany.

Rifat, T., Hossain, M.S., Alam, M.M. & Rouf, A.S. 2019. A review on applications of nanobots in combating complex diseases. *Bangladesh Pharmaceutical Journal*, 22(1): 99–108.

Robinson, H., MacDonald, B. & Broadbent, E. 2013. Physiological effects of a companion robot on blood pressure of older people in residential care facility: A pilot study. *Australian Journal on Ageing*, 34(1): 27–32.

Robinson, H., MacDonald, B. & Broadbent, E. 2014. The role of healthcare robots for older people at home: A review. *International Journal of Social Robotics*, 6(4): 575–591.

Sagar, M., & Broadbent, E. 2016. Participatory medicine: Model based tools for engaging and empowering the individual. *Interface Focus*, 6, 20150092. http://dx.doi.org/10.1098/rsfs.2015.0092

Schranz, M., Umlauft, M., Sende, M. & Elmenreich, W. 2020. Swarm robotic behaviors and current applications. *Frontiers in Robotics and AI*, 7(36): 1–20.

Schroeter, C., Mueller, S., Volkhardt, M., Einhorn, E., Huijnen, C., van den Heuvel, H., et al. 2013. Realization and user evaluation of a companion robot for people with mild cognitive impairments. *The IEEE International Conference on Robotics and Automation*, Karlsruhe, Germany.

Schwartz, W.B. 1970. Medicine and the computer: The promise and problems of change. *The New England Journal of Medicine*, 283: 1257–1264.

Shibata, T. & Tanie, K. 2001. Physical and affective interaction between human and mental commit robot. *Proceedings of the IEEE International Conference on Robotics and Automation*, Seoul, Korea.

Sivasankar, M. & Durairaj, R. 2012. Brief review on nano robots in bio medical applications. *Advances in Robotics and Automation*, 1: 2–5.

Soul Machines. 2020. Available at soulmachines.com

Sposaro, F., Danielson, J. & Tyson, G. 2010. iWander: An android application for dementia patients. *The 2010 Annual Conference of the IEEE, Engineering in Medicine and Biology Society*, Buenos Aires, Argentina.

Taylor, A.G., Mielke, C. & Mongan, J. 2018. Automated detection of moderate and large pneumothorax on frontal chest X-rays using deep convolutional neural networks: A retrospective study. *PLOS Medicine*, 15(11): e1002697.

Topol, E.J. 2019. A decade of digital medicine innovation. *Science Translational Medicine*, 11(498): 1–4.

Turkle, S. 2011. *Alone Together: Why We Expect More from Technology and Less from Each Other*. New York: Basic Books.

Weizenbaum, J. 1966. ELIZA- a computer program for the study of natural language communication between man and machine. *Communications of the ACM*, 9(1): 36.

Wrzeszczynski, K.O., Frank, M.O., Koyama, T., Rhrissorrakrai, K., Robine, N., Utro, F., et al. 2017. Comparing sequencing assays and human–machine analyses in actionable genomics for glioblastoma. *Neurology Genetics*, 3: e164.

21
AI, smart borders and migration[1]

Louis Everuss

Introduction

Through the early 21st century digital technologies have been increasingly integrated into the processes of daily life. This has meant that social interactions that were once based on physical information have become reliant on digitally stored and transmitted data. In this chapter I focus on this technological/social transition, referred to as digitisation, in the context of migration and the crossing of significant jurisdictional borders, namely those that exist between sovereign states. In synthesising extant scholarly work on this subject, I examine how digital technologies, including those capable of artificial intelligence, are being impregnated into the processes of migration and bordering, and the social outcomes that this is causing. As I will show, digitisation is not only changing the dynamics and experience of border crossing, it is changing the very nature of sovereign borders themselves.

While research has been conducted on AI, smart borders and migration from a wide range of disciplines, it is the social scientific examination of this subject that is the focus of this chapter. This work has studied the social implications of the digitisation of bordering and migration, including how it has impacted the institutions of nation-states (Jones et al., 2017), patterns of human mobility (Dekker, Engbersen, Klaver, & Vonk, 2018) and individual perceptions of selfhood (Elliott & Urry, 2010). Indeed, new subfields have developed around these topics, including 'digital migration studies' (Gough & Gough, 2019). This chapter focusses on five key features of the digitisation of borders and migration that have regularly come under social scientific examination. These are, one, that the digitisation of borders is causing their fracturing and disarticulation from space as they become embedded within flows of information in virtual networks and attached to the bodies of travellers biometrically tied to sovereign spaces and their outside (Broeders, 2007; Jones et al., 2017; Vukov & Sheller, 2013). Two, the technologies of modern borders produce generic digital subjects that are used to judge travellers in terms of their normativity (Haggerty & Ericson, 2000; Kafer, 2019). Three, the agencies that are exercised at the border are increasingly spread across human–machine and machine-machine interactions (Allen & Vollmer, 2018; Schindel, 2016). Four, migrations are themselves being facilitated by the digital technologies utilised by migrants (Dekker et al., 2018; Reichenberger, 2018). And finally, five, the experience of crossing borders is changing as it is becoming mediated by digital technologies that displace bordering labour onto travellers (Vukov & Sheller, 2013), embody borders in peoples' physical and mental being (Gough & Gough, 2019) and extend the activity of border crossing beyond sites of entry and exit leaving it forever in progress (Amoore, 2006).

In examining these topics, I will raise key issues that require additional study by scholars. For example, the emphasis on generic digital profiles in bordering processes is excluding people who are not able to fit within scales of normativity (Bigo, 2014, p. 219). Further work is required to identify the impact that this is having on minorities and vulnerable mobile populations, particularly given official insistences of the objectivity of digital bordering mechanisms (Lisle & Bourne, 2019, p. 683; Schindel, 2016). Additionally, the digitisation of borders is a process implemented by actors that exist across jurisdictions and within both government and private sectors (Csernatoni, 2018, p. 177; Molnar, 2019, p. 306). Research needs to probe the jurisdictional issues this causes in terms of how digital borders can receive appropriate levels of oversight in order to protect both travellers and border guards. In contrast to these lines of critique, this chapter also identifies positive potentialities of the digitisation of migration and bordering that are worthy of further examination. These include the ability of digital technologies to vastly increase the efficiency of border policing, and also to diminish the isolation experienced by migrants by keeping them constantly connected to home, destination, diaspora and other mobile communities (Gough & Gough, 2019; Zijlstra & Liempt, 2017). What is clear from this chapter is that in-depth and ongoing social scientific analysis of the digitisation of borders and migration – a process that is certain to continue over the coming decades – is required to understand how this contemporary alteration of a foundational political activity impacts populations.

The digitisation of borders and migration

While a complex web of different borders permeates life and social interaction, the borders primarily studied in this chapter are those that exist between nation-states. These sovereign borders are mythically tied to the modernisation of humanity beginning with the 1648 Peace of Westphalia, the political philosophies of the enlightenment and the late 18th century French and American revolutions. While the historical accuracy and teleological assumptions of stories framing global political history as a linear progression towards establishing 'natural' container societies held within sovereign states has been strongly criticised (Agnew, 2017; Everuss, 2020b), sovereign nation-states play a leading role in defining political communities and establishing the borders that migrants must cross in order to travel globally (Everuss, 2020a, 2020c; O'Dowd, 2010). Thus, this chapter is most concerned with how state borders, and the movements that cross them, are being digitised.

The digitisation of state borders is clearly visible in the enshrinement of new technologies in the apparatuses of borders themselves. Through the 21st century there has been an incredible push towards the digitisation of borders by wealthy and democratic states and regions, such as the European Union (EU) and United States (US) who are respectively spending billions of dollars on IT systems to support the digital management of migration (Trauttmansdorff, 2017, p. 108). What is of special interest to this chapter is the qualitative change occurring at the border when traditional state boundaries are digitised. This involves the creation of what are described as 'smart borders' or 'i-borders', which deploy the technological processes of biometrics, dataveillance and automation in tandem (Pötzsch, 2015). Biometrics are 'measurements of behavioral and physical characteristics, including facial expressions, gait, galvanic skin response, palm or iris patterns, and many others' (Crampton, 2019, p. 55). Significantly the physical features that can form the basis for biometrics are not always sedentary and include personal mobilities (Adey, 2009). From the way people walk to the micro shifts in their facial expressions, biometrics turns human bodies and movements into processable information (Amoore, 2006; Pötzsch, 2015, p. 106).

On a basic level, biometric information is used to link peoples' physical characteristics to their travel documentation. A primary example of this is the EU's Eurodac database, which became operational in 2003 and contains the fingerprints of asylum seekers along with details about their asylum applications including the place and time they were made (Trauttmansdorff, 2017, p. 113). Eurodac supports the implementation of the EU's Dublin Convention by making it possible to determine where initial claims for asylum are made and thus the member state responsible for processing them. On a more complex level, biometrics are used to categorise and judge the behaviour of travellers by coding and decoding bodies and their movements – including those that are unconscious outcomes of emotion and affect – as signs of mobile normality or deviance. Therefore, biometrics allow bordering systems and personnel to:

> draw actionable inferences about [a traveller's] personality, intent, emotional state, social conformity, sexual orientation, and many other formerly private attributes, positing that they manifest bodily.
>
> *(Crampton, 2019, p. 55)*

It is this step, beyond simple recognition of what features someone has to being able to make inferences about who they are, that gives modern biometric platforms substantial power (Crampton, 2019, p. 55). However, this process cannot be achieved by analysing an individual in isolation, because it involves comparing people to 'data doubles', digital identities that inform the functioning of borders in terms of how travellers are to be treated (Pötzsch, 2015, p. 106).

The biometric information used to construct data doubles is captured by the technological process of dataveillance: the mining and algorithmic analysis of everyday user data (Pötzsch, 2015, pp. 106–107). The objective of dataveillance is not to monitor specific individuals but to monitor everyone to create profiles that can be used to assess the threat posed by people. David Lyon (2014, p. 2) describes this as a shift in surveillance practices 'from targeted scrutiny of "populations" and individuals to mass monitoring'. Dataveillance consequently occurs not just at the border but across societies in which the public and private actions of people are observed (Kafer, 2019). Key government bodies involved in dataveillance include the US National Security Agency (NSA), the British Government Communications Headquarters (GCHQ), and the Australian Signals Directorate (ASD). These organisations share parts of their biometric data through the '5-Eyes' network that also includes agencies from Canada and New Zealand.

Dataveillance is also undertaken by private corporations such as social media and telecommunication companies, which manage key digital frameworks and online spaces (Lyon, 2014, p. 2; Pötzsch, 2015, p. 107). Dataveillance began as a by-product of the user services provided by these businesses but it has become a lucrative revenue stream with personal data used to direct marketing and sales. While private companies often claim that the data they collect is kept anonymous, there are documented cases of governments accessing it, such as in the NSA's PRISM program, which 'seemed to give the NSA direct access to the servers of some of the biggest technology companies, including Apple, Facebook, Google, Microsoft, Skype, Yahoo, and YouTube' (Lyon, 2014, p. 2). There are also an increasing number of private contractors who specialise in dataveillance and who are hired by governments to capture, store and analyse the big data required for the mass digital monitoring of populations (Gradecki & Curry, 2017). In 2007, Louise Amoore described the implementation of dataveillance by an assemblage of private and public actors in the Department of Homeland Security's US VISIT programme. US

VISIT determined the risk posed by travellers listed on plane passenger manifests. At the time of her article over 20 databases were being used by US VISIT, including:

> IDENT, a biometric database that stores and identifies electronic fingerprints on all foreign visitors, immigrants and asylum seekers; ADIS, storing travellers entry and exit data; APIS, containing passenger manifest information; SEVIS, containing data on all foreign and exchange students in the United States; IBIS, a 'lookout' watch list interfaced with Interpol and national crime data; CLAIMS3, holding information on foreign nationals claiming benefits; and an array of links to finance and banking, education, and health databases.
>
> *(Amoore, 2006, p. 340)*

The third feature, automation – commonly referred to as part of contemporary smart borders – is necessary to use biometrics and conduct dataveillance. This is because the amount of data and the levels of processing required to undertake biometric and dataveillance processes 'necessitates algorithm-driven forms of analysis' (Pötzsch, 2015, p. 108). However, automation is also a key part of how border systems respond to biometrics. This is one of the more novel facets of contemporary digital borders, because as Jose Sanchez del Rio, Moctezuma, Conde, de Diego, and Cabello (2016, p. 50) point out, biometrics in terms of passport photos have informed borders for more than 100 years, but the automation of the identification of travellers in line with passports only occurred when the technology became available in the 1990s.

Currently the most visible form of border automation is Automated Border Control (ABC) systems: fully automated mechanisms that perform traveller checks of varying degrees of complexity. A common ABC system is the use of e-gates, whereby travellers scan their own passports and are forced to have their photo taken, following which computer programs check they are the rightful owner of their travel documentation and assess whether they are a threat (del Rio et al., 2016, p. 50). ABC systems are not purely virtual because they require physical infrastructure to function, including passport scanners and cameras, automated gates, instruction signs and other barriers. However, while ABC systems require visible things to work, other automated border systems are more hidden. For example, the European Border and Coast Guard Agency (formerly FRONTEX) utilises a range of covert automated bordering technologies to enforce the external boundaries of Europe, including surveillance drones with 'considerable flight autonomy, and impressive data-processing capacity' (Csernatoni, 2018, p. 176). Raluca Csernatoni (2018, pp. 177–178) states that these drones 'construct high-tech "virtual walls" via augmented and highly technologised bordering and surveillance strategies to protect against risks associated with irregular migration'.

Another futuristic example of border automation can be seen in the testing of the iBorderCtrl system in the EU, in which an on-screen AI-driven avatar interviews travellers and assesses whether they are lying based on their facial micro expressions (Crampton, 2019, p. 54). The avatar's voice and demeanor becomes sterner if the system suspects a traveller of lying, which may also lead to the avatar referring the traveller to human border guards. Supporting iBorderCtrl is an Automated Deception Detection System (ADDS) developed at Manchester Metropolitan University, which draws on psychological theory to categorise biometrics in line with micro expressions deemed to be 'biomarkers of deceit' (Crampton, 2019, p. 54). Regardless of whether the iBorderCtrl system – which has been trialled at borders in Hungary, Latvia and Greece – is ever implemented in a large-scale fashion, it clearly demonstrates the potentialities of border automation in Europe. It fits within what Lucy Suchman, Follis, and Weber (2017, p. 985) describe as a 'shift of security regimes from a reactive to a proactive mode [that] is at the heart of contemporary state-based logics focusing on technological superiority and persistent surveillance'.

Alongside digitally enhanced borders, migrations are also becoming embedded with digital technologies. There is no greater example of this than the use of smart phones by migrants in order to navigate their passage across borders (Dekker et al., 2018; Mezzadra, 2017). Research has found that smart phones and other digital technologies connect migrants within more tightly bound diasporas and other mobile communities. As outlined by Sandro Mezzadra (2017, p. 2), migrants undertake both digital and geographical mobility, which 'intersect to foster the "collective power" of migrants and refugees'. This leaves migrants less isolated and makes migration a group project achieved by virtually connected communities, some of whom are normally positioned in receiving countries. However, smart phones are not just a medium for communication and sharing community information, they provide invaluable on-the-ground migration tools including access to maps, compasses and GPS systems (Dekker et al., 2018, p. 2). Research shows that such services have in many circumstances empowered migrants, making them less reliant on organised covert mobility services including what is commonly labelled people smuggling (Dekker et al., 2018, p. 6).

However, unlike research on the digitisation of borders, scholars examining the digitisation of migration have not identified a widespread displacement of migrant agency across digital infrastructures and systems. For the most part, new technologies are treated as tools used by and empowering migrants (Gough & Gough, 2019, p. 90), which do not automate aspects of the migration process in the same way that drone surveillance or virtual lie detectors automate the role of border guards. However, what is common to both the digitisation of borders and migration is that local acts of movement and their control rely on information technology networks that extend across the globe, fundamentally altering the spatiality and nature of borders and travel.

The movement, fracturing and disarticulation of digital borders

Borders, particularly those surrounding sovereign nation-states, are traditionally framed as geographically defined and static (Everuss, 2020b). While the historical accuracy of this statement is debated, it is now evident that what stability and spatial fixity sovereign borders have is being reshaped by their digitisation (Broeders, 2007; Jones et al., 2017; Trauttmansdorff, 2017; Vukov & Sheller, 2013). For example, the infrastructure that creates digital border walls, such as ABC e-gates, are not wholly located at the boundaries of sovereign states or their ports and places of entry/exit. They include servers, computer systems, cables, satellites and other material enablers of data transfer that are scattered across state territories. Indeed, in describing the various parts of smart borders, from the systems of dataveillance that monitor people to the analysis of biometrics and the computational power that underpins the automated screening of populations, very little infrastructure is located at what is traditionally conceived of as the border (Trauttmansdorff, 2017, p. 109). However, the shift that has taken place is more complex than a simple movement of bordering mechanisms away from the periphery of states, because digital borders are not defined by the computers that run them, but by the flows of information that those computers enable (Jones et al., 2017, p. 5).

Border digitisation also promotes the strategic shifting of state borders by governments seeking to increase their regions of influence and diminish their areas of rights. This process occurs independently of online digital technologies, such as through the creation of detention centres in external regions and the legal excision of populations (Everuss, 2020a, 2020b). However, the mobility of borders is enhanced by digital technologies that can target regions on either side of state boundaries, which occurs for example when the EU uses drones to monitor external regions (Csernatoni, 2018), and, 'computerized information systems for internal surveillance' (Broeders, 2007, p. 87). The digital extension of state power and reduction of state rights has been highlighted in leaks and scandals involving the mass surveillance of domestic populations, such as the Snowden Affair. In this instance Edward Snowden, an employee and subcontractor at the US Central Intelligence Agency (CIA) turned whistle-blower, revealed that national intelligence agencies in the US and UK were engaging in large-scale monitoring of their domestic populations, such as by accessing phone records and intercepting internet traffic in real time (Lyon, 2014, p. 2). The government action outlined by Snowden illustrates that state bordering occurs across the entirety of the state's territory through surveillance that can result in any member of society suddenly being treated as outside the normal boundaries of the polity. This is why Dennis Broeders (2007, p. 73) suggests that electronic databases have 'develop[ed] into the new digital borders of Europe'.

The increasing fluidity and ephemerality of digitised borders has led scholars to argue that they are disarticulated from geographical space (Trauttmansdorff, 2017, p. 115). For instance, digital borders have been described as having a portal-like logic because they fold distant locations into one another (Jones et al., 2017, p. 4). Such spatial transformations produce zones that are 'no longer strictly defined by the state's territory' (Trauttmansdorff, 2017, p. 115). However, digital borders function alongside and co-construct material and legal borders that are more linear in nature and tied more closely to traditional state boundaries (Jones et al., 2017, p. 4). Indeed, Jones et al. (2017, p. 4) argue that the two work in tandem as digital borders can remain porous, allowing economically necessary flows of capital and information, while geographically based sovereign boundaries can provide material closure, especially to human mobilities. However, as seen in the technological examples mentioned earlier, even the most material, linear and geographical of state boundaries is to some extent being digitised. Lilie Chouliaraki and Myria Georgiou (2019, pp. 600–601) make this point by illustrating the complex interactions between the symbolic borders developed in virtual spaces, such as social media and online news web pages, and digitally enhanced territorial borders. Chouliaraki and Georgiou (2019, pp. 600–601) state that 'The territorial border, for instance, is remediated in the [online] mass media . . . thereby intersecting with the symbolic border and its imaginaries of security, humanitarianism and migration'.

While digitised territorial borders are commonly represented by state governments as infallible (Amoore, 2006, p. 342), they are subject to rupture and subversion. For example, in examining the dataveillance systems that inform smart borders, Jennifer Gradecki and Derek Curry (2017, p. 1) found that systems often misinterpret language such as by coding sarcasm and jokes as actual threats of violence. Thus, Pötzsch (2015, p. 113) suggests that there is a 'gap between rhetorics of effective ubiquitous surveillance and control on the one hand, and limited technological capabilities, errors, and effective countermeasures on the other'. Bordering failures are often caused by the actions of travellers seeking to traverse them, which highlights that borders do not exist in isolation, and indeed in a Foucauldian sense, they are an expression of state power that is co-constructed by the resistance of travellers and migrants. Therefore, the agencies and actions of migrants should not be ignored or elided by discussions premised around border control. Paul Trauttmansdorff (2017, p. 110) illustrates this in relation to the EU's digitised Schengen border management system, which he describes as constantly 'challenged and contested by migratory action and struggle'.

However, to position migrants and governments on equal footing in relation to digital borders is a mistake. Indeed, an inherent feature of digital borders is that they are underpinned by big data to which there is unequal access (Gradecki & Curry, 2017, p. 2). For example, Jennifer Gradecki and Derek Curry (2017, p. 2) demonstrate that the wealth of information generated by Twitter is unequally available to people and organisations. They state that Twitter:

> only offers a limited amount of its datastream to the public and academic researchers through its Application Program Interface (API). However, the full "firehose" is available to companies (including government contractors) who have the ability to pay for and process it.
>
> *(Gradecki & Curry, 2017, p. 2)*

The power imbalances created by borders is also evident in the ways that they attach to, and follow, bodies (Pötzsch, 2015, p. 111). This involves the separation of different groups of people as opposed to different territorial spaces, which makes the site of the state and its external regions the bodies of those who are considered 'insiders' and 'outsiders' (Everuss, 2020a). The digitisation of borders promotes this process as biometrics make bodies codable and subsequently turns them into signifiers of 'acceptable' and 'unacceptable' mobility. For example, the US's VISIT program draws on biometrics to code the bodies of incoming migrants with risk profiles, which determines the likelihood that they will be excluded at the border (Amoore, 2006, p. 340). In the EU, the coding process extends sovereign state borders towards and beyond the outer edges of Europe. For example, for many migrants trying to reach Germany, the border they are seeking to cross spreads to meet them and begins to exclude them before they have reached Germany's geographical edge as their bodily data is recorded in European databases used by Germany when they enter Greece (Jones et al., 2017, p. 5). Thus, 'the body, in effect, becomes the carrier of the border as it is inscribed with multiple encoded boundaries of access' (Amoore, 2006, pp. 347–348).

The production of digital subjects

The attachment of digitised borders to individual bodies is underpinned by ideal virtual profiles or identities, which are produced from population level data sets and used to predict patterns of behaviour (Pötzsch, 2015, p. 105). This process was described back in 2000 by Kevin Haggerty and Richard Ericson (2000, p. 606), as:

> abstracting human bodies from their territorial settings and separating them into a series of discrete flows. These flows are then reassembled into distinct "data doubles" which can be scrutinized and targeted for intervention.

Digital subjects, or 'data doubles', are shaped by three factors: 1) the population data that is available and can be used for their construction; 2) the biometrics codable at the border and which can be used to connect individuals to data doubles and 3) cultural conventions regarding how normal subjects look, move and behave. Thus, digital subjects are not natural categories that pre-exist digitised borders but are instead produced by digitised borders that draw on social conventions to 'map and codify different flows of mobility through digitalization, categorizing and sorting subjects into various types, for which inclusion and/or exclusion is facilitated' (Trauttmansdorff, 2017, p. 115).

A concerning outcome of this process is the unfair targeting of non-normative people (Suchman et al., 2017). Systems of bordering and surveillance, which use big data based on the biometrics of populations to establish normality, inherently target minorities (Kafer, 2019, p. 24). This is because big data does not assess the threat posed by individuals, but instead their membership of certain classes, which are treated as proxies for their threat level. Gary Kafer (2019, p. 24) states that because these 'proxies (like zip code or consumer preferences) encode categories of social difference, people of colour, migrants, sexual minorities, the poor and other oppressed populations are overwhelmingly more likely to bear the burden of population-based classification'. This is why Bigo (2014, p. 219) argues that people who do not fit within normal categories of personhood become 'prisoners of data-double associations and virtual anticipations'.

Kafer (2019) demonstrates the targeting of non-normative people in an analysis of the 'Secure Flight' program in the US, an automated screening system that identifies high-risk passengers using the 'no fly list', which bans listed people from flying, and the 'selectee list', which requires listed people to undergo additional security checks. These lists are managed by the Terrorist Screening Centre and are provided to the Transportation Security Administration. Kafer (2019, p. 34) finds that inherent racial prejudices exist in the way the lists function, including in that they are calibrated on Western English naming conventions and Latin script, making names outside of these parameters inherently more likely to be coded as abnormal and subsequently suspicious (Kafer, 2019, p. 35). A similar conclusion was reached by Sanjay Sharma and Jasbinder Nijjar (2018, p. 73) in relation to the UK's 'Prevent program', a multi-agency strategy that monitors the apparent threat of Islamic extremism. Sharma and Nijjar (2018) found that 'Prevent's' official datamining characterised Muslims entering and residing in the UK as threatening, while failing to actually identify terrorist threats.

The creation of digital subjects described in this chapter is a new variant of an established myth production process, whereby composite identities – intertextual stereotypes produced from the combination of partial readings of stories and statistics (Kroll-Smith, 2000) – are given the appearance of objective truth. However, mythical digital subjects become self-fulfilling prophecies because they produce their Frankenstein identities, which are constructed from the bits and bobs of biometric big data. They do this by reducing travellers to examples of their categories, which is a radicalisation of the process by which borders produce the identities that they separate (Zureik & Salter, 2013, p. 2). While Muslim people are no more likely to be a terrorist threat than other religious/racial groups, the inclusion of Muslimness into the apparently 'objective' data-driven profile of a terrorist threat means that the bodies and religious beliefs of Muslim peoples become signs for terrorism and consequently evidence of the existence of the terrorist category (Sharma & Nijjar, 2018, pp. 78–79).

The tendency of digital subjects to exclude non-normative populations is a serious limitation of smart borders, but it is not beyond mitigation. For example, digital subjects can be made less biased if they are based on databases that include more diverse biometric categories. Extending the basis of digital subjects to include multinational populations, for example, makes them less likely to induce coding of national minorities as threatening. Additionally, the digital technologies available at the border can be turned to focus on assessing the material threat of individual travellers or objects, as opposed to whether they fit within predetermined categories that are believed to be threatening. This already occurs in the advanced digital systems that scan luggage and people for explosives. Further developments to such systems include the automated computer scanning of live videos for unattended and potentially dangerous bags in airports (Szwoch, 2016). In 2020, in response to the COVID-19 global outbreak, such digital systems were also implemented in airports, including the integration of thermal cameras into ABC systems to automatically detect people with a temperature who may be a potential COVID-19 spreading risk (Pitofsky, 2020). Such systems are not problem free, but their conclusions are less influenced by social and political bias and more based on actual real-world threats.

Non-human bordering agencies

The feature that makes digitised borders novel, and indeed 'smart', is automation. It is automation that turns biometrics from being a tool used to link people to travel documentation into the basis of bordering decisions and actions. To some extent automation necessarily occurs as algorithmic processing replaces human interpretation, which is required to analyse the large amounts of data informing modern border decisions. However, the processing in question includes judgements, notably decisions as to who should be targeted for border scrutiny, exclusion, violence, or in the extreme case of automated weapons systems, death (Suchman et al., 2017; Suchman & Weber, 2016). This occurs when 'the objects arrayed within, at, and around borders – gates, passports, computer chips – interact with processes of decision-making to produce "datafied" encounters with security' (Allen & Vollmer, 2018, p. 26). It happens for instance when databases and digital systems automatically flag people as being unable to fly, when they direct officials to detain or scrutinise certain travellers, or, when they make in/out border decisions in real time (Lisle & Bourne, 2019). It occurs in the more extreme examples of the extension of the US border into Pakistan and Yemen via targeted assassination programs where drones kill based on AI identified 'patterns of life' (Suchman et al., 2017, p. 984).

In such circumstances, not only is the position and functioning of borders spread across digital flows and systems, but the agencies of borders are, too (Allen & Vollmer, 2018; Schindel, 2016). Proponents of border automation highlight the accuracy, objectivity and instantaneousness of automated border decisions, which is said to allow the speedy transition of travellers through border sites while identifying and blocking anyone who poses a threat (Lisle & Bourne, 2019, p. 683; Schindel, 2016). However, critics of smart borders point out that 'what is presented as a smooth process of selection and management of human mobility, in reality has unbearable human costs, produces stranded populations, and harshly targets and punishes any form of "unruly" mobility' (Mezzadra, 2017, p. 2). In some instances, these negative outcomes are produced because the automated technologies are not sufficiently sophisticated to manage the agencies that they are expected to administer. For example, in 2012 two British students were sequestered and not allowed to enter the US because a joke made on Twitter by one of the students about '"diggin" Marilyn Monroe up', which was quoted from the TV show *Family Guy*, was coded as threatening and 'prompted authorities to search the couple's luggage for shovels' (Gradecki & Curry, 2017, p. 4).

However, the expression of bordering agency is not a one-way process because it involves the agencies of those who are being bordered. Through resistance, either to challenge state apparatus or merely in order to travel efficiently, migrants interact and push against the highly automated bordering systems that try to coerce, cordon and order them (Trauttmansdorff, 2017). Thus, the agencies of migrants, as well as those of automated systems, feed into the modern assemblage of digitised borders. This is the type of assemblage outlined in Bruno Latour's (2005) actor-network theory in which agency is spread across the assemblage's interactions, and the powers of humans and things co-constitute one another. The form of agency expressed by machines in such networks is based on the situational ability to impact humans and other entities, and does not strictly involve intentionality (Hsu, 2017). The novel agencies of contemporary digitised borders are not produced by atomised and intentional robotic or human actors, but by dynamic human–machine, human-human and machine-machine interactions (Chouliaraki & Georgiou, 2019; Suchman & Weber, 2016). Additionally, each of these interactions are socially situated and subsequently impacted by their political and cultural context (Allen & Vollmer, 2018). Border guards draw on local systems of meaning and understanding to judge international travellers and digital systems are designed to achieve political ends of state governments.

The increasing power of complex socio-technical assemblages in state bordering raises pressing questions about responsibility at the border. For example, who is to be held accountable when errors are made by automated border systems? Paul Virilio (2009) posed similar questions in relation to military technologies, notably rockets, with which there is very little time lag between attack, destruction and counter-attack. The instantaneousness of this chain of actions and events transfers human error from the 'action stage' to the 'conception stage' of technology (Virilio, 2009, p. 50). Virilio (2009, p. 54) describes this feature of modern warfare as 'tantamount to setting in place a series of automations . . . from which all political choice is absent'. Such an account of modern bordering/surveillance/military action is supported by Suchman et al. (2017, p. 985) who state that the design of technologies that automatically target people is the first act of violence, which means that greater accountability and scrutiny needs to occur at the design and implementation stages of bordering systems.

However, complicating the attribution of design responsibility is the wide spread of border design and management across different jurisdictions and public/private sectors (Csernatoni, 2018, p. 177; Molnar, 2019, p. 306). This is partly a side effect of incorporating cutting edge technologies into the management of migration, which requires the involvement of private sector actors who develop such technologies. Consequently, hand-in-hand with the digitisation of borders is a stretching of bordering responsibility beyond standard government agents. Molnar (2019) suggests that it is also an official tactic to spread and reduce the responsibility attached to the implementation of digital borders and migration control, so as to allow a degree of official experimentation in the management of populations. Molnar (2019, p. 306) states that:

> Through agency laundering, States are able to distance themselves from suspect actions on complex and difficult decisions by outsourcing responsibility for technological innovation to the private sector, complicating the public–private accountability divide.

Whether by design or necessity, the digitisation of borders forces travellers into relationships with agents who exercise authority over them but are not bound by the same social contracts and limitations as government officials. Developing methods to align bordering responsibilities alongside bordering agencies is key to ensuring that the digitisation of borders does not exclude people and places from the legal and ethical frameworks of democratic states.

Digitally enhanced migrations

As with official border tactics, migrant actions are digitised in that they increasingly rely on digital technologies and the transmission of digital data (Dekker et al., 2018). In Europe for instance, 'refugees have relied to an unprecedented degree on digital technologies such as GPS and social media in order to successfully navigate a maze of European borders' (Jones et al., 2017, p. 5). This form of migration digitisation is commonly framed in social scientific analysis as a new type of tool use that helps migrants to achieve their migration project (Dekker et al., 2018; Mezzadra, 2017). Gough and Gough (2019, p. 90), for instance, show how mobile phones have become a significant part of '"migration infrastructure", both in facilitating access to the migration industry and shaping migrants' journeys'. Likewise, Rianne Dekker et al. (2018, p. 2) describe mobile phones as 'information and communication resources that enable [migrants] to develop "smart" strategies'. These accounts of migrant mobile phone reliance are illustrated in statistics such as that in 2015, 95 percent of the Syrian and Iraqi refugees who entered Europe relied on a mobile phone at some point during their journey (Gough & Gough, 2019, p. 90).

One outcome of the digitisation of migration is that forced migrants are becoming more self-sufficient. Judith Zijlstra and Ilse van Liempt (2017, p. 178) demonstrate this by showing that digital technologies reduce the reliance that asylum seekers have on 'people smugglers' as they are able to plan and organise their, often prohibited, journeys themselves. Access to social media and up-to-date digital information helps migrants to improvise their plans and journeys in response to their current situation (Dekker et al., 2018, p. 1). Migrants also require less help to integrate and survive within host communities as they can search and access digital information about their new context (Gough & Gough, 2019, p. 90). For example, smart phones help migrants orientate themselves, translate both the foreign language and social environments in which they are located and access key services and the job market (Gough & Gough, 2019, pp. 95–96). Other types of travellers are also empowered by the digitisation of their migration streams. Business travellers and tourists for instance are increasingly able to manage their journeys and accommodations using flexible online platforms, such as Airbnb and Skyscanner, making them less reliant on travel agents.

The power that engagement with digital technologies provides travellers does however reinforce the digital divide between those with and without access to the relevant technologies and the knowledge required to utilise them. For example, Syrian asylum seekers are far more likely to be able to attain mobile phones than asylum seekers from Afghanistan, which increases the likelihood that Syrian asylum seekers will complete their forced migration journeys (Zijlstra & Liempt, 2017, p. 178). Among wealthy travellers from democratic countries, those that are younger and have greater digital competencies are more able to use digital technologies to flexibly combine work and travel than their older compatriots. This has led to the phenomenon of 'digital nomads', 'young professionals working solely in an online environment while leading a location independent and often travel reliant lifestyle where the boundaries between work, leisure and travel appear blurred' (Reichenberger, 2018, p. 364). Such generational divides are part of a broader trend in digitised economies whereby younger people, sometimes described as 'digital natives', can access opportunities that are effectively closed to older people, referred to as 'digital immigrations' (Palfrey & Gasser, 2011).

However, the effects of digital technology usage are not always positive, which is overlooked when framing technology purely as a tool and its use as a form of capital. Indeed, smart phones and other personal digital technologies create new threats and risks for migrants. For instance, 'the digital traces that migrants leave make them vulnerable to surveillance' (Gough & Gough, 2019, p. 90). Additionally, through digital communications and misinformation, 'migrants are often manipulated by malevolent actors and their networks of disinformation that can put vulnerable lives at risk' (Chouliaraki & Georgiou, 2019, p. 598). Even when users are not directly seeking to harm migrants, social media posts regularly promote false rumours and prejudicial opinions that can jeopardise migrations. Migrants are not however 'cultural dopes', and as found by Dekker et al. (2018, p. 9), they implement 'strategies to maintain access to social media, to avoid government surveillance, and to validate social media information'.

Seeing traveller-use of digital technologies purely as a form of empowerment also ignores the technical and emotional reliance that many travellers develop on technologies, leaving them materially and emotionally vulnerable to technology breakdown. Additionally, it overlooks the varied non-migration project-based ways that travellers engage with their digital technologies, such as for entertainment purposes and to reduce boredom. This engagement illustrates that the relationship between migrants and their technologies is complex and cannot be understood within the binaries of positive/negative or helpful/unhelpful. Instead traveller-technology engagement creates, at the same time, complex and interconnected potentialities and risks.

A final example of this can be seen in the migrant use of digital technologies to engage in political battles over their own symbolic construction and the policies that produce their bordering. Governments and media companies publish online articles and use virtual spaces to frame migrants in accordance with political and ideological positions (Chouliaraki & Georgiou, 2019). However, digital technologies provide migrants with a means to influence how they are represented to different publics (Chouliaraki & Georgiou, 2019, p. 598). Migrants use digital technologies and websites to tell their stories, which can contradict official narratives in order to critique state practices and advocate on the behalf of their cohorts (Martin, 2019; Rae, Holman, & Nethery, 2018). Lupton and Michael (2017, p. 255), for example, identify how populations use technologies to record and watch official practices in what they describe as 'watching from below' or 'sousveillance', a 'type of dataveillance [that] is often voluntarily taken up by people to challenge powerful authorities and draw attention to their wrongdoing'. This has occurred often in Australia's offshore immigration detention centres in Papua New Guinea (PNG) and the Pacific Island Nation of Nauru where detainees have filmed their treatment, showing abuse by centre guards and poor living conditions, and recorded their pleas for assistance and hospitality (Martin, 2019; Rae et al., 2018). Indeed, in one exceptional use of digital technologies, Kurdish Iranian journalist Behrouz Boochani, who was being held in the Manus Island Detention Centre on PNG, wrote a book about his journey and treatment using a smuggled mobile phone and the messenger app, WhatsApp (Boochani & Tofighian, 2020). The book *No Friend but the Mountains*, which was published in 2018, became a bestseller in Australia and won numerous awards, including the Victorian Prize for Literature, Australia's richest literary award.

Novel migration experiences

As digitisation alters migration and bordering, it changes how people experience travel and borders. Some of these new experiences are caused by the increasing embodiment of borders, whereby borders shape, disturb and augment people. This process is promoted by a shift in state bordering logics from capturing spatial territory to capturing bodies (Everuss, 2020a), which is promoted by the digital power of governments to monitor migrant populations even after they have crossed state boundaries (Amoore, 2006; Broeders, 2007). Borders digitally attach to the bodies of travellers, rendering them 'inside' or 'outside' a state based on the bordering logics of that state, not its geographical position. In the words of Louise Amoore (2006, p. 338) 'the crossing of a physical territorial border is only one border crossing in a limitless series of journeys that traverse and inscribe the boundaries of safe/dangerous, civil/uncivil, legitimate traveller/illegal migrant'.

The movement of borders to digitally track and follow travellers induces affective and emotional responses. Migrants feel the pressure of being constantly under digital surveillance, always subject to exclusion and never finishing a migration. Travellers are also physically and emotionally impacted by the specific bordering technologies they encounter. In terms of contemporary experiences of digital technologies more broadly, Deborah Lupton (2014, p. 165) suggests the body is now a 'cyborg assemblage' because it is 'enhanced, augmented or in other ways configured by its use of digital technologies that are worn, carried upon or inserted into the body, continually interacting with these technologies in dynamic ways'. Lupton's vision is mainly considering those digital technologies that are freely interacted with, even if the outcomes of the interactions are not fully understood by users. People willingly entangle themselves with digital consumer electronics in ways that impact their bodies, such as through the physical transformations motivated by fitness trackers, the emotional responses caused by smart devices that are evident in the affection people develop for their consumer electronics, or the joy and trauma caused by constant engagement with social media platforms (Lupton, 2014, p. 165). Such physical and emotional connections result in people seeing digital technologies as part of themselves (Lupton, 2014, p. 168).

However, the digital technologies that become embodied at the border are less freely engaged with than consumer electronics and social media, and more forced upon the bodies of travellers, whether that be through persuasion, coercion or clandestine action. Biometric systems, for instance, are experienced and incorporated into bodies when they force individuals to move and behave in certain ways (Amoore, 2006, pp. 343–344), such as when e-gates make travellers stand still in specific locations, take off their glasses and form neutral facial expressions in order to be properly captured and coded.

In accordance with Lupton's analysis, elite travellers do embrace many of the digital technologies that allow them smoother and more efficient movement through airports and other transitory zones, as well as the ability to work while on the move and away from home (Costas, 2013). Travellers use microchip-imbedded frequent flyer cards to not only board planes and get into airport lounges but to purchase goods and services while away from home. They use smart bag tags to reduce the steps required to check-in luggage and to display colour-coded status symbols of frequent travel. They use a wide variety of smart phone apps to purchase tickets and acquire and monitor traveller points and programs, as well as traverse airports and other transitory spaces. Such personal and electronic devices are incorporated into the physical and emotional self of travellers and used to express cultural capital and manage identity. This is part of the process through which Anthony Elliott and John Urry (2010, p. 3) argue that, in our current mobile world, '[i]dentity becomes not merely "bent" towards novel forms of transportation and travel but fundamentally recast in terms of capacities for movement'. Largely as a result of the digitisation of borders and movement, people develop what Elliott and Urry (2010, pp. 3–4) describe as 'portable personhood', forms of identity and self that are constituted through experiences of movement and bordering.

The construction of mobile identities using the digital technologies of movement is not limited to the kinetic elite. Like business travellers and tourists, asylum seekers and other forced migrants use digital technologies to establish their own portable personhood. For instance, Hannah Gough and Katherine Gough (2019, p. 90) show that refugees utilise smart phones to navigate the constant disruptions they are faced with in order to not only complete migration processes, but to complete existential quests to 'become someone'. Gough and Gough's (2019) research demonstrates the meaningful connections migrants develop with their technologies that extend well beyond the simple use of a new tool. Drawing on Ghassan Hage's conception of existential movement, they argue that engagement with digital technologies allows migrants to imagine social progression within their environment, which is a form of existential mobility that stops them from needing to migrate further (Gough & Gough, 2019, pp. 90–91).

Another experience that is being promoted by the digitisation of migration and borders is the shifting of bordering responsibilities onto travellers. Like embodiment, this process, which is described using the term 'prosumption' (Ritzer & Jurgenson, 2010), is identified in the digitisation of a vast range of social, political and economic processes. Prosumption is a type of activity in which a consumer is also expected to contribute to the production of the thing or service that they are consuming (Vukov & Sheller, 2013). George Ritzer and Nathan Jurgenson (2010) suggest that while prosumption has formed part of earlier forms of capitalism, recent digital technologies have radically increased levels of prosumption. Ritzer and Jurgenson (2010, p. 18) point to both examples of existing economic practices – including 'serving as a bank teller at the ATM machine [and] working at the checkout counter at the supermarket by scanning one's own food, bagging it, and paying for it by credit card' – as well as new presumption-based economic activities, such as the explosion of online industry based around user-generated content.

The digitisation of borders promotes prosumption in existing activities and creates new prosumption-based activity. In airports for example, travellers act as security and airline carrier employees by scanning their own passports and tagging and loading their own luggage. They also work to ensure that the digital profiles of smart borders can be effectively applied to them by exposing their biometric data to smart border systems such as by walking in an appropriate way, scanning their fingerprints and ensuring that security cameras capture them (Morosan, 2018). Tamara Vukov and Mimi Sheller (2013, p. 226) make this point stating that smart borders 'depend on the labor of "data-ready" travelers who produce themselves at the border'.

The digital subjects used to categorise travellers are also the result of prosumption as they are produced from biometric big data that is consciously or unconsciously shared by populations. Just like digitised borders themselves, the prosumption of borders extends beyond public boundary sites, such as airports and checkpoints, and into the everyday digitised activities of citizens and travellers. Pötzsch (2015, p. 111) makes this point stating that i-borders:

> enlist individual subjects as both target and source in bordering processes that disperse locally as well as across transnational space. In these processes, individuals become objects of governance to be analyzed and assessed, but also serve as implicit contributors to the databases enabling algorithm-driven mappings of patterns of behaviour and association.

Thus, prosumption is involved in aspects of smart borders from dataveillance to automation, further stretching bordering processes beyond sites of international travel and into the daily lives of ordinary citizens, refugees, tourists and business travellers alike.

Conclusion: the future of digitised borders

This chapter has brought together the social scientific analysis on the digitisation of borders and migration. I have suggested that this research coalesces around several key topics, notably the changing position and nature of state borders, the production of digital subjects, the development of non-human bordering agencies, the digital enhancement of migration and new digitally enabled experiences of bordering. These subjects are not an exhaustive list of the topics examined by social scientists in relation to the increasing presence of digital technologies at the border. For example, while my discussion has necessarily been limited to borders that exist and move across geographical space, there has also been an explosion of virtual and imaginative mobilities – whereby people move and act in different spaces and sense and affect others without physically leaving their material location (Bissell, 2018) – as well as the virtual boundaries separating online and imaginative spaces.

The digitisation of borders and migration is a dynamic and unpredictable process that will lead to outcomes that are yet to be identified. What is certain, however, is that the issues surrounding the digitisation of borders and migration that this chapter has introduced will only become more important as the development and implementation of digitised borders creates what mobilities systems scholars describe as a 'path dependency' promoting further border and migration digitisation (Dennis & Urry, 2009). In this sense, just like systems of automobility, border digitisation is a self-producing assemblage encouraging its own expansion (Merriman, 2009). This is evident in the fact that unintentional or unwanted border movements are framed as system failures requiring more technology, more AI, more automation and always, more data (Csernatoni, 2018, p. 176; Suchman et al., 2017, p. 984).

For the most part, the research discussed in this chapter has taken a critical stance in relation to the digitisation of borders. This criticism is based on the current outcomes of digitised borders and on certain rationalities that are believed to be embedded into the technologies of digitised borders (Suchman et al., 2017). Csernatoni (2018, pp. 177–178) and Suchman et al. (2017, p. 985), for instance, argue that the technologies in question, including drones, have a bias towards military-style engagement hard-wired into them, which naturally causes the conflation of state border policing and military activities. There is also the well-documented concern that the digitisation of borders creates new rationales and opportunities to surveil populations leading to what is described by social scientists as 'function creep' or 'surveillance creep': the processual broadening of surveillance powers and scope incorporated into the data that informs digital borders (Broeders, 2007; Trauttmansdorff, 2017).

The ultimate contemporary example of the negative and violent impulses of digitised borders is China's 'social credit' system, which scores and ranks 'the character and "trustworthiness" of each citizen' (Shore & Wright, 2018, p. 28). Social credit scores take into account a person's spending habits, hobbies, daily activities and political opinions, as well as the activities and opinions of their friends and family. Behaviour and opinions considered responsible are rewarded while apparently irresponsible behaviour, including criticism of the government, is punished by the provision or denial of opportunities and services respectively (Shore & Wright, 2018, pp. 27–29). The social credit system impacts people's ability to travel, as for example, people with low scores can find it difficult to hire vehicles or leave the country (Shore & Wright, 2018, p. 28). In contrast, people with high scores can travel more easily such as by earning reduced travel permit waiting times for Singapore and 'fast-track treatment in processing a Pan-European Schengen visa' (Shore & Wright, 2018, p. 28). Thus, the Chinese state's bordering processes are being folded inwards onto the entire domestic population, who are digitally traced, coded and monitored, and subsequently brought further within or excluded by the state depending on the perceived normalness or deviancy of their everyday activities.

However, to see the Chinese system as an anomaly ignores similar trends occurring in the digitisation of borders across democratic and wealthy settings. Everywhere that borders are being digitised, movement is becoming easier for elite travellers whose position within social credit systems – from China's social score to international frequent flyer programs and points-based immigration systems – give them greater ease of movement. And while the digitisation of borders in the US, UK and Australia may not holistically target entire national populations, it does demonise and punish select and often vulnerable minority groups. Kafer (2019, p. 24) states that in these settings 'surveillance is not a totalising force suppressing the social body, but rather a variegated power matrix that is distributed along axes of social difference under signs of empire, settler colonialism and white supremacy'.

However, as Trauttmansdorff (2017) suggests, it is important to avoid technological determinist perspectives in assessing the outcomes of digitisation in any sector of society. Such perspectives promote dualist utopian/dystopian conceptualisations of the impacts that technologies of digitisation will have on society, which elide the true complexity and uncertainty of digitised futures (Boyd & Holton, 2018; Holton & Boyd, 2019). As identified in this chapter, border digitisation is influenced by those responsible for designing and enforcing borders as well as the travellers and migrants who traverse them. There is consequently scope for border digitisation to be implemented in ways that avoid many of the detrimental outcomes identified by social scientists, which are also resisted by travellers.

Additionally, it is important to acknowledge that pre-digitised borders do not inherently produce better outcomes for people and indeed the efficiency of border management that digitisation offers can reduce the harm suffered by many migrants. For example, 'increasing backlogs are preventing individual status determination systems from functioning, even in some of the most well developed asylum systems' (Kagan, 2017, p. 197). This leaves asylum seekers in the highly vulnerable position of not being able to be officially recognised as refugees, despite having potentially suffered persecution and torture. Digital systems have the potential to enhance the workflow and efficiency of status determination processes, reducing the wait-time for asylum seekers. Additionally, digitised borders offer benefits to state-based sovereign polities. For example, the use of drones to monitor borders allows for cheaper, safer and more encompassing border surveillance, which can reduce the energy consumption of bordering, create a safer environment for border agents and save the lives of those traversing dangerous regions (Marin, 2017). Consequently, social scientific analysis should not seek to hold back the tide of border and migration digitisation, but instead, to identify positive border digitisation futures that can guide on-the-ground technological developments.

Note

1 This chapter is developed from research supported by the European Union Erasmus+ Jean Monnet "Cooperative, Connected and Automated Mobility: EU and Australasian Innovations" Network Grant (599662-EPP-1–2018–1-AU-EPPJMO-NETWORK).

References

Adey, P. (2009). Facing airport security: Affect, biopolitics, and the preemptive securitisation of the mobile body. *Environment and Planning D: Society and Space, 27*(2), 274–295.

Agnew, J. (2017). *Globalization and sovereignty: Beyond the territorial trap*. Lanham, MD: Rowman & Littlefield.

Allen, W. L., & Vollmer, B. A. (2018). Clean skins: Making the e-border security assemblage. *Environment and Planning D: Society and Space, 36*(1), 23–39.

Amoore, L. (2006). Biometric borders: Governing mobilities in the war on terror. *Political Geography, 25*(3), 336–351. https://doi.org/10.1016/j.polgeo.2006.02.001

Bigo, D. (2014). The (in) securitization practices of the three universes of EU border control: Military/Navy – Border guards/police – Database analysts. *Security Dialogue, 45*(3), 209–225.

Bissell, D. (2018). Proximity from a distance. In O. B. Jensen, S. Kesselring & M. Sheller (Eds.), *Mobilities and complexities*. London: Routledge.

Boochani, B., & Tofighian, O. (2020). No friend but the mountains and manus prison theory: In conversation. *Borderlands, 19*(1), 8–26.

Boyd, R., & Holton, R. J. (2018). Technology, innovation, employment and power: Does robotics and artificial intelligence really mean social transformation? *Journal of Sociology, 54*(3), 331–345.

Broeders, D. (2007). The new digital borders of Europe: EU databases and the surveillance of irregular migrants. *International Sociology, 22*(1), 71–92.

Chouliaraki, L., & Georgiou, M. (2019). The digital border: Mobility beyond territorial and symbolic divides. *European Journal of Communication, 34*(6), 594–605.

Costas, J. (2013). Problematizing mobility: A metaphor of stickiness, non-places and the kinetic elite. *Organization Studies, 34*(10), 1467–1485.

Crampton, J. W. (2019). Platform biometrics. *Surveillance & Society, 17*(1/2), 54–62.

Csernatoni, R. (2018). Constructing the EU's high-tech borders: FRONTEX and dual-use drones for border management. *European Security, 27*(2), 175–200.

Dekker, R., Engbersen, G., Klaver, J., & Vonk, H. (2018). Smart refugees: How Syrian asylum migrants use social media information in migration decision-making. *Social Media+ Society, 4*(1). doi:10.1177/2056305118764439.

del Rio, J. S., Moctezuma, D., Conde, C., de Diego, I. M., & Cabello, E. (2016). Automated border control e-gates and facial recognition systems. *Computers & Security, 62*, 49–72.

Dennis, K., & Urry, J. (2009). Post-car mobilities. *Car Troubles. Critical Studies of Automobility and Auto-Mobility, Burlington: Ashgate*, 235–252.

Elliott, A., & Urry, J. (2010). *Mobile lives*. London: Routledge.

Everuss, L. (2020a). Mobile sovereignty: The case of 'boat people' in Australia. *Political Geography*, 79, 102162. https://doi.org/10.1016/j.polgeo.2020.102162

Everuss, L. (2020b). Westphalian sovereignty as a zombie category in Australia. *Borderlands*, 19(1), 115–146. doi:10.21307/borderlands-2020-006

Everuss, L. (2020c). The new mobilities paradigm and social theory. In A. Elliott (Ed.), *Routledge handbook of social and cultural theory* (2nd ed.). London and New York: Routledge.

Gough, H. A., & Gough, K. V. (2019). Disrupted becomings: The role of smartphones in Syrian refugees' physical and existential journeys. *Geoforum*, 105, 89–98.

Gradecki, J., & Curry, D. (2017). Crowd-sourced intelligence agency: Prototyping counterveillance. *Big Data & Society*, 4(1). doi:10.1177/2053951717693259.

Haggerty, K. D., & Ericson, R. V. (2000). The surveillant assemblage. *The British Journal of Sociology*, 51(4), 605–622. doi:10.1080/00071310020015280

Holton, R., & Boyd, R. (2019). 'Where are the people? What are they doing? Why are they doing it?'(Mindell) Situating artificial intelligence within a socio-technical framework. *Journal of Sociology*. doi:10.1177/1440783319873046

Hsu, E. L. (2017). The sociological significance of non-human sleep. *Sociology*, 51(4), 865–879.

Jones, R., Johnson, C., Brown, W., Popescu, G., Pallister-Wilkins, P., Mountz, A., & Gilbert, E. (2017). Interventions on the state of sovereignty at the border. *Political Geography*, 59, 1–10. https://doi.org/10.1016/j.polgeo.2017.02.006

Kafer, G. (2019). Big data biopolitics. *Digital Culture & Society*, 5(1), 23–42.

Kagan, M. (2017). (Avoiding) the end of refugee status determination. *Journal of Human Rights Practice*, 9(2), 197–202.

Kroll-Smith, S. (2000). The social production of the drowsy person. *Perspectives on Social Problems*, 12, 89–109.

Latour, B. (2005). *Reassembling the social: An introduction to actor-network-theory*. Oxford: Oxford University Press.

Lisle, D., & Bourne, M. (2019). The many lives of border automation: Turbulence, coordination and care. *Social Studies of Science*, 49(5), 682–706.

Lupton, D. (2014). *Digital sociology*. London: Routledge.

Lupton, D., & Michael, M. (2017). 'Depends on who's got the data': Public understandings of personal digital dataveillance. *Surveillance & Society*, 15(2), 254–268.

Lyon, D. (2014). Surveillance, Snowden, and big data: Capacities, consequences, critique. *Big Data & Society*, 1(2). doi:10.1177/2053951714541861

Marin, L. (2017). The 'metamorphosis' of the drone: The governance challenges of drone technology and border surveillance. In *Embedding new technologies into society* (pp. 299–333). Singapore: Jenny Stanford Publishing.

Martin, G. (2019). Turn the detention centre inside out: Challenging state secrecy in Australia's offshore processing of Asylum Seekers. In *Crimmigration in Australia* (pp. 327–352). Cham: Springer.

Merriman, P. (2009). Automobility and the geographies of the car. *Geography Compass*, 3(2), 586–599.

Mezzadra, S. (2017). Digital mobility, logistics, and the politics of migration. *Spheres: Journal for Digital Cultures*, 4, 1–4.

Molnar, P. (2019). Technology on the margins: AI and global migration management from a human rights perspective. *Cambridge International Law Journal*, 8(2), 305–330.

Morosan, C. (2018). Information disclosure to biometric e-gates: The roles of perceived security, benefits, and emotions. *Journal of Travel Research*, 57(5), 644–657.

O'Dowd, L. (2010). From a 'borderless world' to a 'world of borders': 'Bringing history back in'. *Environment and Planning D: Society and Space*, 28(6), 1031–1050.

Palfrey, J. G., & Gasser, U. (2011). *Born digital: Understanding the first generation of digital natives*. New York: Perseus.

Pitofsky, M. (2020, May 14). Airports test thermal cameras, sanitation booths and other technologies to mitigate coronavirus. *The Hill*. Retrieved from https://thehill.com/blogs/blog-briefing-room/news/497909-irports-test-thermal-cameras-sanitation-booths-other

Pötzsch, H. (2015). The emergence of iBorder: Bordering bodies, networks, and machines. *Environment and Planning D: Society and Space*, *33*(1), 101–118. doi:10.1068/d14050p

Rae, M., Holman, R., & Nethery, A. (2018). Self-represented witnessing: The use of social media by asylum seekers in Australia's offshore immigration detention centres. *Media, Culture & Society*, *40*(4), 479–495.

Reichenberger, I. (2018). Digital nomads – A quest for holistic freedom in work and leisure. *Annals of Leisure Research*, *21*(3), 364–380.

Ritzer, G., & Jurgenson, N. (2010). Production, consumption, prosumption: The nature of capitalism in the age of the digital 'prosumer'. *Journal of Consumer Culture*, *10*(1), 13–36.

Schindel, E. (2016). Bare life at the European borders. Entanglements of technology, society and nature. *Journal of Borderlands Studies*, *31*(2), 219–234.

Sharma, S., & Nijjar, J. (2018). The racialized surveillant assemblage: Islam and the fear of terrorism. *Popular Communication*, *16*(1), 72–85.

Shore, C., & Wright, S. (2018). Performance management and the audited self. In B. Ajana (Ed.), *Metric culture: Ontologies of self-tracking practices* (pp. 11–35). Bingley, UK: Emerald Publishing Limited.

Suchman, L., Follis, K., & Weber, J. (2017). *Tracking and targeting: Sociotechnologies of (in) security*. Los Angeles, CA: Sage Publications.

Suchman, L., & Weber, J. (2016). Human–machine autonomies. In *Autonomous weapons systems: Law, ethics, policy* (pp. 75–102). Cambridge: Cambridge University Press.

Szwoch, G. (2016). Extraction of stable foreground image regions for unattended luggage detection. *Multimedia Tools and Applications*, *75*(2), 761–786. doi:10.1007/s11042-014-2324-4

Trauttmansdorff, P. (2017). The politics of digital borders. In C. Günay & N. Witjes (Eds.), *Border politics: Defining spaces of governance and forms of transgressions* (pp. 107–126). Cham: Springer International Publishing.

Virilio, P. (2009). The state of emergency. *The Virilio Reader*, 46–57.

Vukov, T., & Sheller, M. (2013). Border work: Surveillant assemblages, virtual fences, and tactical countermedia. *Social Semiotics*, *23*(2), 225–241.

Zijlstra, J., & Liempt, I. V. (2017). Smart (phone) travelling: Understanding the use and impact of mobile technology on irregular migration journeys. *International Journal of Migration and Border Studies*, *3*(2–3), 174–191.

Zureik, E., & Salter, M. B. (2013). Global surveillance and policing: Borders, security, identity – Introduction. In *Global surveillance and policing* (pp. 13–22). Cullompton: Willan.

Index

Note: Numbers in **bold** indicate a table. Numbers in *italics* indicate a figure on the corresponding page.

AARON 303–304
ABC *see* automated border control (ABC)
ABC-group (Austria, Brazil, Chile) 246
Abe, N. 149
Abilify McCite 319
Acemoglu, D. 82, 84–85
accountability xvii, 124, 126, 328, 330, 348; big data and 288; political 232; of robots 133; of social media 159; *see also* ACM FAccT; FATE
accountability gap 241
ACM *see* Association for Computing Machinery (ACM)
Adam, A. 60–61
Adam (second) 162
Adam's Curse 78
ADIS 342
Adobe 302
Adorno, T. W. 297–300, 307, 310
Affectiva 318
affective computing 318–319
affordances 87, 140, 310
Aggogeri, F. 328
AI4EU project 127
AI companion tool 317
AI for Good 254
AI High-Level Expert Group on Artificial Intelligence (AI HLEG) 211
AIMBOT 317
Airbnb 85m 349
airports 9–10, 23, 346, 351–352
AI translators 167
Akrich, M. 272
Alač, M. 96
Alexa (Amazon) 6, 141, 202
Alexy, R. 199
Algorithmic Justice League (United States) 291
almost-human 307
Alphabet 125
AlphaGo 39, 48
AlphaZero 35–37, 40
Altmann, J. 241–242

Amazon 6, 125, 128, 219
Amoore, L. 13, 59, 286, 290, 341, 350
Amoroso, D. 242
Anderson, C. 64, 284
Anderson, K. 239
androids 34, 129, 141–142, 216, 253; *see also* cyborg; humanoids
animism 109, 116–118
anthropology and robotics 107–120; framework for 108–109
anthropomorphism in machines 93, 97, 109, 115, 238; of cars 180; of computers 147; of robots 117–119, 141–142, 145, 201, 275; *see also* androids; cyborg; humanoids
APIS 342
Apple 125, 341; App Store 11; *see also* Siri
Apple Music 310
Apple Pay 13
Aristotle 205
arms control 231, 237, 240; international 245; nuclear and conventional 243; treaty 246
arms race 231
Arkin, R. 239
art and simulation 112–114
artificial companionship 91–105; and social robotics 92–95
artificial general intelligence (AGI) 131
Artificial Intelligence (AI): affects after 91–105; ancestors 162–163; and anthropology 107–120; automated mobilities and 172–184; and borders and migration 339–354; connectionist 58–59; consciousness 211; and culture industries and entertainment 295–311; current critiques of 63–66; cybersecurity 222–233; data-driven 58–69; development of 35–36; early critiques of 60–62; and employment and unemployment 74–87; episteme-ontological foundations of 58–69; ethics of 122–134; four fallacies of law for 203; in geography 17–27; governance of 255–257; law and regulation for 199–212; living with 38–39; and management and

357

Index

organization 157–170; and medicine and health sciences 313–336; as objects 122–132; perceptual 168; and psychiatry 30–52; and robotics 107; sociopolitical context of 62–63; as subjects 122, 132–134; symbolic 58–59; trust and digital control 165–166; and worldviews 251–264
artificial lifeforms 109–112
artificial superintelligence 162, 200, 209, 332–334
Asaro, P. 241
Asia Pacific 331
"As if" issue 112–114
Asimo (robot) 201
Asimov, I. 30, 120; Three Laws of Robotics 36, 139, 204
Askt, D. 77
Association for Computing Machinery (ACM) 138, 290
Association for Computing Machinery Conference on Human Factors in Computing Systems (CHI) 290
Association for Computing Machinery Conference on Fairness, Accountability, and Transparency (ACM FAccT) 290–291
Aurigi, A. 194
Australia 4, 51, 80–81, 291, 331; borders, digitization of 353; RCT trials, adults with dementia 321; Western Australia 84
Australian Signals Directive (ASD) 341
Automated Border Control (ABC) 342–343, 346
Automated Deception Detection System (ADDS) 342
automated mobilities 172–184; *see also* automobiles
automation and work, concerns regarding: contemporary debate over 79–80; history of 75–79
automobiles 7, 19, 21, 172–173; Volkswagen Beetle 180; Model T 180
automobility 173, 177, 181–183; culture 21; system 19, 192–193, 352
automotive industry 175, 177–178, 180–184, 242
autonomous weapons 130, 230, 327; *see also* lethal autonomous weapons (LAWs)
autonomy and autonomous systems 129–131
Autor, D. 47, 81, 87
autopoiesis 110
Avdeef, M. 307

Babylon Health GP at Hand 323, *324*
Baby X 333
Bannon, S. 16n22
Bartneck, C. 147
Batson, C. 49
Baudrillard, J. 159, 163
Bauman, Z. 158, 160, 166
Beatles, the 307
Becker, A. 25

Becker, B. 60
Becker, H. 103
Beck, U. 87
Bedau, M. 110
Beer, D. 283
Beethoven, L. van 299–300
Beetle (Volkswagen) 180
Bell, A.G. 8
Bell, D. 178
Bell, G. 78, 87n2
Bem, D. 37
ben Bezalel, Judah Loew (Rabbi) 162
Benjamin, W. 297–300, 307, 310
Bentham, J. 11
Berger, P. 103
Berger, T. 75
Berlin, I. 51
Berman, M. 74
Berners-Lee, T. 9
Bessant, J. 306
bias and discrimination in AI 127–128, 287; and data quality 329
Bickmore, T. 318
Big Brother society 282
big data 281–292; surveillance 345; *see also* dataism; metadata
Bigo, D. 346
Bing 13, 287
biocybernetics 59–60
biomarkers 169, 323
biometrics 11, 229, 339–347, 351–352
Bissell, D. 276n7
black boxed systems 287–288
black letter law 199–200; paradox of irrelevant law 203–204
blackmail 229
Black Swan events 206, 212, 218n93, 221n143
blockchain 160, 308
Bloomberg News 307
Bloom, L. (fictional character) 77, 79
Bode, I. 245
Boden, M. 297, 310–311
Bohr, N. 24
Bomy (mobile service robot) 327
Boochani, B. 350
Bootle, R. 44
borders and migration 339–354
Bostrom, N. 131–132, 161, 169; "treacherous turn" 203, 207
Boulanin, V. 244
Bourdieu, P. 304
Bowker, G. 63–64
boyd, d. 282–284
Boyd, R. xviii, 87n2
Breazeal, C. 115, 141
Brewer, W. 46
Broeders, D. 344

Index

Broekens, J. 267
Brooks, R. A. 319
Brynjolfsson, E. 161
Burrell, J. 37
Burri, S. 51
Burrows, R. 281, 284

Calo, R. 206–207
Cambridge Analytica xvii, 75, 126; data harvesting by 12–13
Cameron, J. 164
Campaign to Stop Killer Robots 245
Campbell, D. 37, 41, 50
Canals, J. 162
Canzler, W. 193
Čapek, K. 77, 163, 216n62, 315
capital: cultural 351; digital data as form of 349; flows of 344; investment 123; and labour 75; organized 78; political 192; social 179; symbolic 67; venture 208
capitalism 62–63, 74, 287; decline of 160, 162; industrial 76, 296–297; post-77, 160; surveillance 125
carebots 268–270, 275; *see also* elderly
Carpenter, R. 245
Carre, B. 307
Carr, N. 310
cars *see* automobiles; self-driving cars
Caspar, F. 41
Castells, M. 9
Cavell, S. 255
CCW *see* Convention on Certain Conventional Weapons (CCW)
Chan, J. 207
Chaplin, C. 296
Chartier, G. 149
chatbot 4, 6; ELIZA 112, 315, 325, 329; as imitator robot 24; limitations of 330; mobile 11; TESS 325; for therapy or medical triaging 322–325
CHI *see* Association for Computing Machinery Conference on Human Factors in Computing Systems (CHI)
China 7, 126, 161, 190, 225; healthcare technologies 317, 331; rivalry with US and Russia 242; social credit system 353
Chinese room problem 112–113
Chomsky, N. 35
Chouliaraki, L. 344
Christian, B. 6, 33
chronic obstructive pulmonary disease (COPD) 325, *326*
Chui, M. 81
ClaimBuster 308
CLAIMS3 342
Coeckelbergh, M. 270
cognitive-behavioral therapy (CBT) 325

Cohen, H. 303
Collingridge paradox 207, 211–212
Collins, H. 46
Collins, R. 97
Colvin, G. 51
commodities 74, 127, 296; data as 308
commodity society 299–300
Compagni, A. 83
CompanionAble (servce robot) 327
compatibilization 183
complexity and AI 7–14
computer interfaces, interactive design 140
contactless technologies 10
contact tracing 22–23, 332
confidentiality 223, 328, 330
Convention on Certain Conventional Weapons (CCW) (United Nations) 238, 244–246
Cook, D. 189
Copenhagen interpretation 24
Cortana (softbot) 202
Corti, K. 34, 43, 50
Coté, M. 285
Cotton Gin Paradox 76
Couldry, N. 285
Coupaye, L. 111–112
COVID-19 pandemic 22–23; artificial intelligence (AI) applications regarding 331; management (work and employees) 158, 164; post-COVID economy 87; and robots and robotics 168, 317, 332; security measures and smart borders 346; and telehealth 317
Cox, C.M. 85
Crawford, K. 63, 282–284
creativity: and artificial intelligence (AI) 51, 295–296, 310; augmented 307; historical 308; as test of the human 300–304; *see also* Turing Test
Crootof, R. 243–244
crowdsourcing 19, 164, 305–306
Crypton 305
Csernatoni, R. 353
Cugurullo, F. 194
Cummings, M. 242, 246
Curry, D. 244
cybersecurity 83, 85, 222–233
cyber-threat 227–228, 232; actors 233; detection 225
cyber-weapons 224, 232
cyborg 62, 163–164, 350; *see also* Haraway, D.
Cyborg system 307

Daimler 191–193
DARPA *see* Defense Advanced Research Projects Agency (DARPA)
Das, S.K. 189
Data Power and Data Justice conference 291
data agency 288
data double 341, 345–346

359

Index

data ethics *see* ethics
dataism 283
data justice *see* justice
data mining 11–13, 65, 80, 84, 236; and national security 346; optimizing hybrid systems 120; privacy and 295; *see also* big data; dataveillance
data sensing 5
data studies 283
dataveillance 282–283, 286–287; and automation 340; objective of 341–344; presumption 352; sousveillance 12, 350
data walks 288
Datta, A. 192
Dautenhahn, K. 103–104
Davenport, T. 161
daVinci telerobotics 316–317, 322
deception and deceit: biomarkers of 342; by corporations 125–126; by and of militaries 241–242; "nudges" as form of 126; by robots 43, 93, 128–129, 150, 269–270, 330
Deep Blue 20; *see also* IBM
deepfake 229
Deep learning 160, 166, 168–169; algorithm 323; artificial neural networks 157; data analyzed by 168; data inputs required for 302, 305; and machine learning 5, 315; new reality of 251; reinforcement-based 36, 43; and virtual artificial intelligence 314
DeepMind 246
Defense Advanced Research Projects Agency (DARPA) 127, 225
Dekker, R. 348–349
Deleuze, G. 66–67
Deloitte report 166–167
del Rio, J.S. 342
Dencik, L. 288
Der Derian, J. 62
Descola, P. 118
DeWall, F. 33
Dick, P.K. 166
digital handshake 332
digital revolution *see* revolution
digital subject *see* data doubles
digital transformation 159–161
digitization 7–9, 161; of borders and migration 339–340, 343–345, 347–352
digitized dissection 13
digitized labour 23
digitized surveillance 11–12, 350; *see also* dataveillance; surveillance
D'Ignazio, C. 285
discrimination in AI *see* bias and discrimination in AI
Docherty, B. 241
double, the: data 341, 345–346; fear of 108; operational 163
Dragon Systems 20
DXplain 316

Easterbrook (judge) 204
echoborg 34, 43
e-commerce 39, 159–161
Edgerton, D. 79
Einstein, A. 24
Eisenhower, D. D. 62
Ekbia, H.R. 15n1
Ekelhof, M. 244
Ekman, P. 143
elder care centers 107, 141
elderly: and AI in warfare 22; automation and 178; carebots and 269–274; data underrepresentation of 63; health care for 94; mobility in 179; monitoring of 12; robotics and 93, 97, 267, 319, 325; and wearables 318
Elish, M.C. 86
ELIZA *see* chatbot
ELIZA effect 329
Elliott, A. 159–161, 351
emergent model of law 201–202
emotional attachments 91, 93–98, 104; to machines 149–150, 329; via technology 351; to objects 129
emotional intelligence 49, 91
emotionality 61, 94, 100
emotional work 64
empathy 49, 119, 128, 144, 180, 318
encryption 3, 125, 226
Engelbert, J. 193
Engels' pause 76
'environment' (in social science) 189–190
epistemic communities 245
epistemology 111, 132, 158, 176; of anthropology 119; of artificial intelligence 252–255, 257, 264; of big data 283–285; of law 258; modern 259; of reproducibility 298; of science 112
episteme-ontological foundations of artificial intelligence (AI) *see* artificial intelligence (AI)
Epstein, R.A. 219n118
Ericson, R. 345
ethics lobbying 204
ethical model of law 202–204; and failure of good intentions 204–205
ethical relativism 204
ethics 208, 282, 287; of aged care robots 269–270, 277n13; of artificial intelligence 14, 58, 67–68, 122–134; business 129; data 127, 251, 288; deontological 202; machine 122–123, 132–133; of robotics 122–124, 128, 132, 134; virtue 202; in warfare 22
European Border and Coast Guard Agency (formerly FRONTEX) 342
European Commission (EC) 166, 203
Eve, J. 76
Ex Machina (film) 30
experimental social psychology 41–42
explainable artificial intelligence (XAI) 36

Facebook 9, 12–13, 174, 281; and Cambridge Analytica 75, 126; data collection 125; marketing 85; Messenger 11; surveillance 287
Facial Action Coding Systems (FACS) 143
facial recognition *see* recognition systems
FACS *see* Facial Action Coding Systems (FACS)
fairness, accountability, transparency and ethics (FATE) 287
FATE *see* fairness, accountability, transparency and ethics (FATE)
fauxtomation 242
fear: of artificial intelligence (AI) 122, 180, 203, 295; of automation technology 181; of Golem 163; of robots and robotics 38, 93, 108, 129, 131, 328; of the singularity 132; of standardization 310
Fitzpatrick, K.K. 325
Flandorfer, P. 271
Fleming, P. 161
Flickr 9
Floridi, L. 262–263
Flynn effect 31
Ford car factory 158
Ford, H. 180
Ford, M. 161
Fordism 78
Forlizzi, J. 146, 271
Fortunati, L. 93, 98–99
Foucault, M. 11–12, 15n18, 67, 165, 262, 344
Frankenstein (Shelley) 30, 163–164, 346
freedom 13, 158; determination and 254–255, 264; of expression 159, 295; privacy and 292; unlimited 197; of users 167; violence and 261; from work 78, 87, 108
freeing up of time 319, 323
free labour and services 74, 125, 308
freelancing 311
free speech 14, 201
free will 133
Freud, S. 47, 115
Frey, C.B. 45, 75, 80–81
FRONTEX *see* European Border and Coast Guard Agency (formerly FRONTEX)
Fuchs, C. 15n18, 15n21
Fukushima nuclear disaster 205

Gadamer, H.-G. 254
Galison, P. 46, 69
Garcia, D. 245
Gartner consultancy 6, 281
Gatebox 150
GCHQ *see* Government Communications Headquarters (GCHQ)
GDPR *see* General Data Protection Regulation (GDPR) (EU)
Gemignani, M 207, 209–210
Geminoïd robot 115–116, 129, 141

General Data Protection Regulation (GDPR) (EU) 126–127, 259–261
General Motors (GM) 315
geography and artificial intelligence (AI) 17–27
Georgiou, M. 344
German Data Ethics Commission 203
Gibson, J. 140
Giddens, A. 158–159
Gillespie, A. 34, 43
Gitelman, L. 63, 284
Go board game 48
Godspeed Questionnaire Series (GQS) 145
Golas, S.B. 323
Goldstein, M. 147
Golem 19, 162–163
Gombrich, E. 114
Good, I. 131
Goodman, B. 260
Google 9, 18, 27, 85, 281, 341; Assistant 332; biases of 287; data collection by 125; DeepMind 246; drones, regulation of 219; Glass 318; Home 141; and language translation and image recognition 302, 321; Pentagon 62; Translate 6; Wallet 13
Gough, H. 348–349, 351
Gough, K. 348–349, 351
governance of AI *see* artificial intelligence (AI)
Government Communications Head- quarters (GCHQ) 13
GP at Hand *see* Babylon Health
Gradecki, J. 344
Graham, M. 24
Graham, S. 192
Gray, M. 86
Great Depression 78
'green' ethics 123
'green men' *see* little green men
Greenfield, A. 9
Grimaud, E. 115
Grusin, R. 67
Gubrud, M. 241, 243
Guga, J. 306

Hage, G. 351
Haggerty, K. 345
Hajer, M.H. 194
Hall, E. 143
Harari, Y. N. 125, 162
Haraway, D. 68, 60, 62, 64, 66, 68–69, 163
Harnad, S. 33
Hassabis, D. 169, 246
Hawking, S. 24, 246
Heaven, W. 169
Heidegger, M. 251
Heintz, B. 70n8
Helmreich, S. 109–111, 114–115
Heyns, C. 241

361

Index

Hine, L. 296
Hitzler, R. 102
HLEG see AI High-Level Expert Group on Artificial Intelligence (AI HLEG)
Hobsbawm, E. 120n1
Hollands, R. 192
Holmes (Justice) 206
Holton, R. 80–82
Horkheimer, M. 165, 297–298, 310
HRW see Human Rights Watch
Hsu, E.L. 272
Hull, C.L. 37
humanoids 60, 94, 123, 129, 142, 184, 318; Golem as 19; intervening 180–181; MEDi 317; social robots as 141–142; see also Geminoïds
Human Rights Watch (HRW) 241, 243, 245
human-computer interaction (HCI) 138–139, 145; see also human-robot interaction (HRI)
human-human interaction 91, 129, 150, 347
human–machine interaction 138–152; context of 147–148; limitations in 149–151; sociological perspectives in 148–149
human-robot interaction (HRI) 39–40, 42–44, 138–139; as academic field 128; collaborative robot studies in 149–150; human or user-centered approach to 145; interpersonal spaces and 143; mimicry and imitation in 142
human qualities, absence of 329
Hupfer, S. 167
Husserl, E. 189–190

Iansiti, M. 162
IBIS 342
IBM 27, 281; Deep Blue 20; DeepLocker 229; Project Debater 6; Watson 85, 219n102, 322
iBorderCtrl system 342
i-borders 340, 352
ICRC see International Committee of the Red Cross (ICRC)
IDENT 342
idiot, the 195
Ihde, D. 82, 190
imitation: in art 114; by automatons 110–111; Golum 163; of human body 119; in human-robot interaction (HRI) 142–143; mimicry and 143
"imitation game" 32
India 225, 331; deities of 117; smart city planning 190
Indigenous Data Sovereignty Networks 291
Industrial Revolution see revolution
Industrial Strategy White Paper (UK) 5
inequality 64, 66, 68; digital 194; economic 82; increases in 84; and the smart city 189, 193–194; social 160, 178–179, 266, 274, 291, 329; in the United States 87
information revolution see revolution
Ingold, T. 190
Instagram 9, 12–13, 174, 302

Intel 27, 305–306
interactive design 140, 144–146; see also human–machine interaction
interactive embodied machine 141–143
Intermediate Range Nuclear Forces Treaty (INF) 246
International Committee of the Red Cross (ICRC) 238–239, 241, 244–245
International Federation of Robotics 167
International Panel on the Regulation of Autonomous Weapons (iPRAW) 244
Internet of Healthy Things (IoHT) 318–319, 325
IoHT see Internet of Healthy Things (IoHT)
iPRAW see International Panel on the Regulation of Autonomous Weapons (iPRAW)
Iraqi refugees 348
iRobot 319
I, Robot (film) 295
iRobi (telehealth robot) 325, *326*
Ishiguro, H. 115–116, 129, 141
Ishiguro, N. 268, 271
Islamic extremism, fear of 346
Itoh, H. 305
iTunes 9
iWander app 327–328

Jacobs, J. 192–193
Japan 4, 7, 80, 115, 225, 297, 331; care work technologies 271–275; idols 305–306; National Institute of Advanced Industrial Science and Technology 141, 320; Ory Laboratory 151; seismic hazard 205; as super-aging society 267–268; Tokku zones system 211; see also Miku, H., Mori, M.; Nissan; Toyota
Jarke, J. 290
Jentsch, E. 115
Jibo 141, 150
Jobin, A. 124
Joint Comprehensive Plan of Action (JCPOA) 246
Joyce, J. 77
Juregenson, N. 351
justice: AI ethics and 202; criminal 67, 166; data 283, 288–289; inequality and 68; mobility 19, 21; social 67, 284, 287–288, 292

Kabbalah 162
Kafer, G. 346, 353
Kant, I. 202
Karvonen, A. 194
Kasparov, G. 35
Kay, J. 45
Keepon (robot) 142
Keller, R. 181
Kendon, A. 143
Kennedy, H. 288, 290
Kenny, M. 85
Kesselring, S. 198

Keyners, J.M. 77–78
Kinesics 142
King, M. 45
King's College London 169
King, S. 34
Kirste, T. 189
Kissinger, H. 127
Kitchin, R. 283–286, 289–290
Klein, K. 285
Knie, A. 173, 193
Knoblauch, H. 100
Kobayashi, H. 306
Koch, S. 51
Kogan, A. 13
Kovacic, M. 273
Kovacs, T. 59
Kozima, H. 142
Kranzberg, M. 210, 218n91
Krishnan, A. 240, 246
Kröger, F. 183
Kuri 150
Kurzweil, R. 132, 162, 169
Kvedar, J. 319

LAIC *see* Longevity AI Consortium (LAIC)
Langton, C. 110
Lanier, J. 308–310
Latour, B. 173, 347
Lee, K.-F. 161
Leeson, C. 275
Leong, T.W. 273
Lestel, D. 111
lethal autonomous weapons (LAWs) 203, 209–211; systems 237–246
Levesque, H. 50
Levin, D. 43
Levinas, E. 262
Lévi-Strauss, C. 24
Levy, D. 202
Levy, F. 47
lifeways 146
lifeworlds 146, 189–190, 195, 287, 296
Li, F.-F. 18
"likes" (social media) 147, 392
LinkedIn 9
little green men, metaphor 213n2, 214n15
Loh, E. 321
Lombardo, G. 300
London School of Economics 34
Longevity AI Consortium (LAIC) 169
Lorenz, K. 141
Luddism 120n1
Luckmann, T. 100, 103
Lupton, D. 285, 289, 350–351
Lyft 85
Lyon, D. 341
Lyon (France) 76

machine agents, four types of 133
machine ethics 122–123, 132–133
machine learning (ML) and AI 4, 5–6, 20, 315–318; automation and 44; bias in 128; capitalism and 297; creative and cultural work involving 302; destabilization caused by 162; medical uses of 322–324, 336; opacity and 127; post-analysis phase of 60; and quantum computing 25; and robotics 79; self-learning 61; supervised 310; techniques of 64–66, 166, 212n1; technology of 35–38; virtual and virtualization 168, 314; weapons and weaponization of 241' *see also* Osbourne, M. A.
Malabou, C. 31
malware 228–229
Mandell, G. 207
Manderscheid, K. 174
manipulation (of data) 126
Manovich, L. 281–282, 304–306, 310
Manyika, J. 81
Mapping for Change 288
Marcuse, H. 78
Markov Decision Processes (MDPs) 36
Marshall, A. 77
Martens Clause 241
Martindale, C. 51
Martin Programme *see* Oxford Martin Programme
Matrix, The (film) 164, 253
Marx, K. 75, 77, 296–297
Marxism 287
Massachusetts Institute of Technology (MIT) 205, 315, 319
mass culture 298–299
Massey, D. 26
Mateescu, A. 86
Mayer-Schönberger, V. 63
McAfee, A. 161
McArdle, G. 282–283
McCarthy, J. 31, 157, 315
McConnell, A. 328
McCulloch, W. 59, 69, 113, 314
McKinsey Global Institute 81
McLuhan, M. 311
MDPs *see* Markov Decision Processes (MDPs)
mechanical reproduction *see* Benjamin, W.
Mecucci, A. 8
MEDi humanoid *see* humanoids
media equation theory 147
MediaLab (MIT) 115
mediatization 100
Meehl, P. 47
Meister, M. 94, 96–97
Mele, V. 83–84
Mercer, R. 16n22
Meskó, B. 81
metadata 257, 281–283; video 305
Meyrink, G. 162

363

Index

Mezzadra, S. 343
microchip, microchipping 10, 351
micro expressions 342
micromobilities 177
micropolitics 233
microcrobotics 334–335
microsociology 149
Microsoft 125; Kinect 140; Research 282
microsurgery 12
micro-targeting xvii, 13
microwork 23
migrants and immigrants 339–340, 343–353; IDENT database 342; labour 76
migration *see* borders and migration
Miku, H. (virtual celebrity) 150, 305–306
MikuMiku dance 305
Milan, S. 285, 287, 289
Milgram experiment 147
Miller, G.A. 32
Miller, T. 38
Millibot 335
mimesis 108, 111; virtualization 168
mimicry 4–5, 142–143, 257; dynamic 100; learning (human) as process of 302; in robots 314, 319, 330; songs that practice 307
Mindell, D. 83–84
Minsky, M. 31, 59, 78, 157, 204
Miremadi, M. 81
Mitchell, W.J.T. 174
mobilities *see* automated mobilities; automobilities
mobility justice *see* justice
Modern Times (film) 296
Molnar, P. 348
Moon, Y. 147
Moore's Law 131
Moor, J. 133
moral agents, artificial 133–134
Moral Machine Experiment 205
Mori, M. 115, 152
Morozov, E. 65
Morrison, B.W. 44
Moses, L.B. 207
Moyes, R. 243–244
Musk, E. 207, 246
MYCIN 35, 315–316

nanobot 334, 335
nanotechnology 10, 79
Nardi, B.A. 148
Nass, C. 147
National Aeronautics and Space Administration (NASA) (United States)148–149
National Institute of Advanced Industrial Science and Technology (Japan) 141, 320
National Security Agency (NSA) (United States) 341
natural language processing (NLP) 6, 123
Navlab 20

Neckom Institute 301
Neumaier, C. 182
neural network 5
Neuromate 316
Netflix 304
Neven, L. 268, 272, 276
New Collar Job Act (2017) 85
NewSTART 246
Newtonian paradigm 24, 60, 65
New Zealand 291, 341; Health Information Privacy Code 1994 330
Nicholls, L. 274
Nietzsche, F. 163
Nissan (car manufacturer), **175**, 181
Nix, A. 16n23
non-human 26, 117, 160, 189; artefacts 38; animals as 37; human and 195, 204, 306; interiority of the 118; and selfhood 6; sense-making of 190
Norman, D. 140
Norvig, P. 69n2
nudge 13, 126

objectophilia 150
Offe, C. 75
O'Neil, C. 70n9, 127
O★NET *see* United States (US) O★NET
opacity 127
Open Skies Treaty 246
Orihime-D 151
Orne, M. 44
Osbourne, M. A. 80–81
Oxford Martin Programme 80

Pagallo, U. 260
Palca, J. 310
panopticon 11–12, 22, 158, 165–166, 282, 287
Panasonic **176**, 181
Papua New Guinea (PNG) 350
paradox 164–165: Collingridge 207; Cotton Gin 76; of irrelevant law 203–204; Jevons 76
Paro (companion robot) 103, 129, 141, 143, 149, 320–322
Pasquale, F. 287–288
Paré, Z. 115
Parliament (European) 134, 218n102
partially observable (PO) process 36
PatientsLikeMe 317
pattern recognition *see* recognition systems
PayPal 13
Peine, A. 268, 277n11
Pentland, A. ("Sandy") 318, 330–331
Perceptron 59
personhood 14 346; free will and 133; legal **200**, 201; portable 351; and privacy 124; responsibility and 129
Petterson, L. 83

phenomenology 134, 190
Picard, R.W. 318
Pickering, A. 60
Pitrou, P. 111–112
Pitts, W. 59, 113
Pitts/McCulloch approach 69
POMDPs 36
Porter hypothesis 208
Porter, M.E. 208
Pötzsch, H. 344, 352
Powell, A. 285, 288, 290
Pratt, G. 18
Prevent program (United Kingdom) 346
privacy 282, 288, 292; in Age of AI 165–166; carebots and 269; data 225; datamining and 295; ethical concerns over 328; as externality **210**; and healthcare 330–332; regulation 206, 211; security vs. 232; and surveillance 38, 124–126; threats to 13; violations of 162; *see also* freedom
PRISM *see* United States (US) PRISM program
Prometheus (film) 30
prosumption 351–352
proxies 144, 346
proxemics 142
Przegalińska, A. 168
Pygmalion myth 150, 216n62

Q sensor 318
Quai Branley Museum, Paris 118
quantum cognition 44, 50
quantum effects 24
quantum computing 3–4, 10, 19, 25–27, 44, 170, 226, 231
quantum geography 24–27

racism and stereotyping in AI 61, 67, 287, 329, 346; *see also* bias and discrimination in AI
radio 8, 299
radioactivity 205
radiologists 321
radio silence 239
Rahwan, I. 36
Rammert, W. 103
randomized controlled trial (RCT) with robots 319, 321, 215
Rasskin-Gutman, D. 36
Ravasi, D. 83
Ray, T. 110–111
recognition systems 34, 48, 140; auditory 140; facial 116, 125, **200**, 202–203, 229, 318, 330; of gesture 140; human emotion 143; image 302; pattern 64, 157; speech 5, 20, 80, 140; user 161; visual 82; voice 18, 229
Reeves, B. 147
regulation, knee-jerk 205–206
remote patient monitoring (RPM) 325, *326*, 332–333

Restrepo, P. 82, 84–85
retrogressive listening 299
revolution: bourgeois 74; cognitive 31–32, 36; digital 3, 14, 161–162, 196, 253–255; industrial 74, 76, 85, 160, 296; information 263; managerial 166; telehealth 319, 321, 334; warfare 237, 240, 242
Revolution, American and French 340
Ricardo, D. 77
Rifkin, J. 78, 162
Riskin, J. 108, 110, 114
risk model of law 203
Ritzer, G. 351
Robinson, H. 267, 325–326
robot culture 275
Robodoc 316
robotic moment 329
robotics 3–4, 7, 10; aged care 266, 268–269, 271–273, 274; and anthropology and artificial intelligence 107–120; autonomous behavior-based 319; behavior-based 59; biorobotics 61; "Cambrian explosion" in 18; civil law rules in 203; cognitive 213n8; computer science and 120; end-effector and exoskeleton 328; ethics 122–124, 128, 132, 134; "fourth law" of 36; humanoid 129; immunity legal regime for 206; industrial 84; industry 150, 168; infectious disease 332; International Federation of 167; and medicine 313–; military 240; open 208; origins of 157; service 92; social 61, 91–105; smart cities and 19; telerobotics 11; work and 74–75, 79, 87; *see also* microrobotics; Three Laws of Robotics
Robotic Surgical Simulator 316
robots 37; AI-enabled 24, 108; care 269–270; companions 98, 319–321; cuteness in 142; and deception 128–129; discrete 180; as friends or enemies 108, 120, 180, 317; home assistive 150; multipurpose 4; single-purpose 3; social 92–105, 150–151; surgical 83; *see also* androids; cyborg; humanoids; human-robot interaction (HRI); safety; uncanny valley
Rockmore, D. 301–302
Roff, H. 243–244
Roomba 141, 146, 319, 327
Rosenblatt, F. 59
Rosert, E. 245
RPM *see* remote patient monitoring (RPM)
Rubeis, G. 274
Rubinstein, Y. 307
Ruppert, E. 282–283, 285–287
Russia 9, 75, 242, 246

Šabanović, S. 273
sabotage 229
Sadler, M. 38
safety 84; impact of AI on public 201; of automated vehicles 133, 181–183, 191, 210;

365

Index

of robots 129, 145; of "verifiable AI" 130; of weapons and defense systems 243; *see also* cyber security
Salvini, P. 273
Sangiuliano, M. 193
Santoni de Sio, F. 244
Sarrica, M. 92
SARS-CoV-2 246, 317, 331; *see also* COVID-19 pandemic
Sauer, F. 241–242, 245
Savage, M. 284
scamming 229
Scharr, P. 239, 241–242
Schengen border 344
Schneier, B. 13–14
Scholtz, C. 101–102
Schranz, M. 335
Schulte-Mecklenbeck, M. 51
Schütz, A. 103
Schwab, K. 4, 162
Schwartz, W.B. 316, 323, 330
Searle, J. R. 112–113, 116, 131
Seaver, N. 37
Secure Flight program (United States) 346
Sejnowski, T. 35–36
self-awareness in AI 34, 44, 334
self-checkout systems 86
self-driving cars 4, 18, 20, 205–207, 210, 238, 242; *see also* automobiles
self-healing software 335–336
self-learning by AI 5, 61, 160, 191, 257
self-monitoring by machines 79
self-service machines 82, 86
self-tracking tools 10, 12, 318
SEVIS 342
Shakespeare, W. 33, 301
Shannon, C. 31
Sharkey, A. 268–269
Sharkey, N. 240, 242, 268–269
Sharma, S. 346
Sheller, M. 275, 352
Shelley, M. 30, 163, 216n62
Shelton, T. 194
Shibata, T. 320
Simonton, D. 51
simulacrum, simulacra 108, 114, 159, 163
simulation 34–35, 41, 108–113; of animal behavior 320; of a character 46; culture of 96; deception and 93; of emotions 61; of human capacities 45; of human intelligence 313; of human interaction 318; mechanical 108; medical 316; probabilistic prediction and 64; robot 37, 39, 50, 93, 119–120
simulation industry 62
Singapore 331–332, 353
singularity: creative 307; human 256
singularity, the 122, 131–132, 134, 162, 169, 295

Siri 6, 18, 202
Sirinho 17, 20, 22–23
Skinner, B.F. 32–33, 35
Skyscanner 349
Sloane, M. 67
smart city 191–192; experiments 192; inequality 193–194
smart environments 188–197
smartphone 8–11, 140, 317; AI-enabled 327; in healthcare 333; migrants, use by 343–344, 348–349
Smids, J. 87
Smith, T. S. J. 24, 26
smuggling 349–350
Smuha, N. 208
Snapchat 13, 174
Snow, C.P. 1
Snowden, E. 11, 281–283, 286, 344
social credit score (China) 353
social media xvii, 3, 8–9, 229, 281, 284; accountability of 159; algorithms 167; and decentralization 12; and digital Maoism 309; Miku and 306; and political propaganda 126; and social robotics 96; and surveillance economy 125
social robotics 61, 92–105; *see also* robotics
social theory and artificial intelligence (AI) 3–15
Society of Automotive Engineers 238
softbot 6, 202
software 8, 10, 237; artificial intelligence (AI) 308, 314; applications 61; datamining 11; deceit in 242; exploiting holes in 23; frameworks 226; medical 317; music 305–307; open source 85; photo-editing 302; robot 115, 123, 138; self-healing 336; smart cities and 191; speech recognition 20, 80, 140; Tierra 110; video teleconference 323; workplace introduction of 78
software-based interface 110–111
software engineering 133
Solum, L. 201
Sophia robot 128
Soul Machines 333
sousveillance 12, 350; *see also* dataveillance
South Korea 7, 305, 311, 331
Spada, H. 51
Spagnoletti, R. J. 206
Sparrow, L. 269–270
Sparrow, R. 240–241, 269–270
Spearman, C. 31
Special Interest Group on Computer-Human Interaction (SIGCHI) 138
speech-recognition software *see* software
Sperber, D. 117
spermbot 335
Spotify 9, 310
Squash video application 308
Stanford Report, The 201, 214n26

Stanford University 144; Artificial Intelligence Laboratory 18
Star, S. L. 63, 108
Stengers, I. 111, 195
Straub, I. 115
Steinmüller, K. 183
Stockholm International Peace Research Institute (SIPRI) 244
Suchman, L. 60, 109, 114–115, 146–147, 342, 348
Suleyman, M. 246
supercomputers 3, 9; Deep Blue 20
superintelligence, artificial *see* artificial superintelligence
Suri, S. 86
surveillance 8, 11–15, 23; big data 345; blanket 125; border 354; CIA 11; data 308; data-driven 287, 289; digital 11–12, 350; drones 342; ethics of 38; global 14; mass 13, 341, 344; military 246; National Security Agency (NSA) 11, 281; security 343; smart city 282, 286; state government 124, 295, 349; targeted 125, 341; *see also* dataveillance
surveillance creep 353
surveillance economy 125–126
Susskind, D. 80, 162
Susskind, R. 80, 162
swarm robots 335–336
synthetic media 229
Syrians 348–349

Taleb, N. 206
Talmud 162
taste (aesthetic) 99, 263, 299, 304
Taylor, A.G. 321
Taylorism 158
Taylor, L. 288
technogenarians 266–276
technoscience 58–69
Tegmark, M. 161, 246
telecommunications 11, 80, 159, 341
telegraphy 8
telehealth 317, 319, 321, 323–326, 332
telemedicine 12
telementoring 334
teleoperation 151, 314
telephone, telephony 8–9, 100, 126, 308; *see also* smartphone
telepresence 87, 115; robots 267, 269; surgery 317
telerobotics 314, 316
teletherapy 324
television 8, 147, 322
telework 164
Terminator, The 34, 164, 209, 237
Terrorist Screening Centre 346
Tetlock, P. 48, 51
Thatcher, J. 62, 287
Three Laws of Robotics 36, 139, 204

Thrift, N. 192
Tierra 110
Tokku zones system 211
Touraine, A. 78, 160
Townsend, A. 190–191
Toyota (car manufacturer) 178–179; Concept-i **176**, 181
Toyota Research Institute 18
TraceTogether 332
Tracey, T. 51
Transportation Security Administration (TSA) (United States) 346
Trauttmansdorff, P. 344, 353
Trump, D. 13, 16n22–23, 76
Tubaro, P. 23
Tufekci, Z. 13
Turing, A. 20, 31, 112, 314–315; theory of computation 69n3
Turing machines 60, 300–301
Turing Test 32–34, 38, 51, 302, 315
Turkle, S. 10, 61, 96–98, 100–101, 104, 329
Twitter 9, 12, **176**, 282, 284, 345, 347

Uber 9, 85
Uexküll, J. von 189–190
Umwelt 189–190
uncanny, the 109, 115
uncanny valley 34, 115, 307–309; theory 142
Unimate 315
United Kingdom (UK) Data Protection Act 2018 330
United Nations (UN) *see* Convention on Certain Conventional Weapons (CCW) (United Nations)
United States (US) Air Force 84
United States (US) Central Intelligence Agency (CIA) 343
United States (US) Department of Homeland Security 341
United States (US) Health Insurance Portability and Accountability Act (HIPAA) 330
United States (US) National Security Agency (NSA) 341
United States (US) O*NET 80
United States (US) PRISM program 13, 341
United States (US) VISIT programme 341–342
University of Massachusetts 316
Urry, J. 8, 196, 275, 351
user experience personalization 304
user experience questionnaire (UEQ) 145
UVD robots 317, 332

Valiant, L. 65
Vallor, S. 268–269
Vandemeuelebroucke, T. 270, 277n13
van Dijck, J. 282–284, 286
van Liempt, J. 349
van Oost, E. 97–98
van Wynsberghe, A. 129

Index

Vasari, G. 120n2
Vaucanson, J. 76
Verdiesen, I. 244
Verizon 13
Verne, J. 216n63
Vertesi, J. 148
Vesa, M. 162
Vidal, D. 109, 117–118
Vimeo 174
Viitanen, J. 191
Virilio, P. 348
virtual agora 65
virtual artificial intelligence (AI) 314
virtual assistants 4, 6, 18, 79, 125, 331–334
virtual characters 150; idols 305
virtual class 62
virtual healthcare 319, 321, 323–324
virtual reality (VR) 9, 44, 48–49; as simulacrum 163; simulation 316; technologies 84
virtual space 66, 110, 158–159, 344; politics of 286, 350, 352
virtual workplace 87, 164; buisnesses 168; teams 165
Vocaloid 305
Volkswagen Group **175**, 179–180, 193
Vollmer, S. 51
Von Neumann, J. 31
von Scheve, C. 95, 97
Vukov, T. 352

Wachowskis (directors) 164
Wajcman, J. 274
Walker, A. 301
Walsh, T. 5
Warner Bros. studio 305
Watson 85, 219n102, 322; *see also* IBM
Weak AI (Narrow AI) 169
weapons, biological 332
weapons systems *see* autonomous weapons; lethal autonomous weapons (LAWs)

wearables 8, 10, 313, 317–319; contract tracing via 332; critiques of 329; data privacy issues 330–331; health or fitness tracking 323–324, 328
Weber, J. 272, 342
Weber, M. 74, 95, 158
Weiner, N. 31
Weizenbaum, J. 112–113, 315
Weizmann Institute, Israel 163
Wheeler, M. 253
Whitney, E. 76
Wikipedia 9, 85, 306
Wiener, N. 163
Wiig, A. 194
Willcocks, L. 81, 83
Winner, L. 58
Winograd, T. 35
Wittgenstein, L. 214n31, 252, 255–256
Wizard of Oz technique 145–146
Woebot 322, 324–325
World Economic Forum 4
World War One 120
World War Two 78
World Wide Web 9
Wright, J. 274
Wylie, C. 13

X2A1 325
Xerox PARC 146

Yahoo 13, 341
Yeomans, M. 37, 43
YouTube 12, 174, **175–176**, 341; content creators 309; fandoms 306; "rabbit hole effect" of 304

Zeng, Z. 23
Zeus system 316–317
Zijlstra, J. 349
Zook, M. 194
Zuboff, S. 166
Zysman, J. 85

Printed in the United States
by Baker & Taylor Publisher Services